ENCOUNTERS

ENCOUNTERS

An Anthology from the First Ten Years
of *Encounter* Magazine

Editors:
STEPHEN SPENDER, IRVING KRISTOL,
MELVIN J. LASKY

Selected by
MELVIN J. LASKY

BASIC BOOKS, Inc., Publishers
NEW YORK

CONTENTS

CONTENTS

Acknowledgements

Editors' Note:

Editors' Note: grateful acknowledgement is made to all the writers, publishers, and literary agents who facilitated our requests for copyright clearances, and to Miss Bryan Healing of the *Encounter* staff who hacked her way through this jungle.

For permission to publish we are indebted to the following: Chatto and Windus, Ltd., and The Macmillan Company, N.Y. for Goronwy Rees's *Innocent in Prussia* from *A Bundle of Sensations;* Farrar, Straus and Cudahy, Inc., and William Heinemann, Ltd., for Mary McCarthy's *My Confession* from *On the Contrary*; Harper and Brothers, and Longmans, Green and Co., Ltd., for *Bull Fever (Madrid Interlude)* from the book *Bull Fever* (c) 1955 by Kenneth Peacock Tynan; Cassell and Co., Ltd., and International Authors N.V. for Robert Graves' *The Whitaker Negroes* and *The Second-Fated*; Chatto and Windus, Ltd., Penguin Books, Ltd., and Random House, Inc., for Wayland Young's *Sitting on a Fortune*; The Free Press of Glencoe, Illinois, for Daniel Bell's *American Dissent* from *The End of Ideology*; The Literary Executors of Robert Warshow for *The Gentleman with a Gun*, originally entitled *The Westerner* and first published in *Partisan Review*; Faber and Faber, Ltd., and Random House, Inc., for W. H. Auden's *The Fallen City*, reprinted in *The Dyer's Hand* as *The Prince's Dog*; Secker and Warburg, Ltd., and Beacon Press, Inc., for Lionel Trilling's *The Smile of Parmenides* from *A Gathering of Fugitives*; Rupert Hart-Davis, Ltd., for R. S. Thomas's *Lament for Prytherch* from *Song at the Year's Turning,* and for W. S. Merwin's *The Mountain* from *Green With Beasts*; André Deutsch, Ltd., for David Wright's *Monologue of a Deaf Man* from the book of the same name, for Elizabeth Jennings's *Mirrors* from *A Way of Looking*, and for Roy Fuller's *The Final Period* from *Brutus's Orchard*; Faber and Faber, Ltd., for W. S. Graham's *Blind Tide Emblazoning* from *The Night Fishing*, for Thom Gunn's *On the Move* from *The Sense of Movement,* and for Louis MacNeice's *Solitary Travel* from *Solstice*; The Dolmen Press for Richard Selig's *The Boyhood of Theseus* from *Poems*; David Higham Associates, Ltd. for Dylan Thomas's *Elegy* (c) for the Trustees for the copyrights of Dylan Thomas 1956; New Directions and Faber and Faber, Ltd., for Vernon Watkins's *Angel and Man* from *Cypress and Acacia*; Chatto and Windus, Ltd., and Oxford University Press, N.Y., for Richard Eberhart's *The Return* from *Collected Poems 1930–1960*; Jonathan Cape, Ltd., for William Plomer's *Ludwig the Second* from *The Collected Poems*; Faber and Faber, Ltd., and Harper and Brothers for Ted Hughes' *Thrushes* from *Lupercal*; Putnam and Co., Ltd.,

ACKNOWLEDGEMENTS

for Oliver Bernard's *Trees* from *Country Matters*; Faber and Faber, Ltd.,
and Grove Press for Edwin Muir's *The Day Before the Last Day* from
Collected Poems; Eyre and Spottiswoode Ltd., for Alan Ross's *Rock Paintings, Drakensberg Mountains* from *African Negatives*.

PREFACE

"...For how can we recapture, between the covers of a book, the tempo of a monthly review? Editing a magazine is a form of the good life; it is creating when the world is destroying, helping where it is hindering..."

CYRIL CONNOLLY

"To be learned and right is no doubt the first requisite—but to be ingenious and original and discursive is perhaps something more than the second in a publication which can only do good by remaining popular—and cannot be popular without other attractions than those of mere truth and correctness..."

FRANCIS JEFFREY (Editor, *Edinburgh Review*, 1806)

"A writer for magazines must above all be interesting, for there is not enough of him in any one issue to justify boring the reader. Similarly, he must extract from the conditions of his work—the hurried deadline, the last-minute change—the liveliness of time itself...A magazine is always a date, 'an issue', a moment; it is created out of an exacting sense of time and it is about time. The spirit of occasion, the tone of conversation, the modesty of the passing moment, are what most belong to it. Let the magazine writer be faithful to this spirit of gaiety..."

ALFRED KAZIN

LIKE EVERY OTHER anthologist, one must begin by making excuses. I was faced with a decade of *Encounter*, ten annual volumes of a thousand pages each, almost a million words. My first selection was carefree and comprehensive; it included everything that was good, representative, and worth preserving; and it constituted four books the size of this one. One had to select again, and to wrestle with the principles of pruning. Should one really omit everything that was once topical? Dare one take space to include famous *Encounter* essays which have already been collected? How could one ever face all the authors whose memorable little contributions did not in the end make the table of contents? No point in burdening the reader with private editorial woes. We cut with heavy heart: for what editor's joy is there like that of republishing an infatuating text which, once printed, was thought to be gone for ever? Here, then, is the final sampling, partial, prejudiced, but perhaps characteristic and expressive. For *Encounter* readers who are not inveterate back-number browsers there will be, one hopes, the pleasant shocks of reunion and recognition; for new readers, the intellectual charm and excitement which, I feel sure, these pieces of prose and poetry still communicate. Some of them—like Herbert Luethy's essay on Montaigne are from the year 1953 when the first number appeared (three years after the demise of Connolly's *Horizon*) under the editorship of Stephen Spender and Irving Kristol. Others—like James Agee's "A Mother's Tale" and Stuart Hampshire's essay on *Dr. Zhivago*—are from the year 1958 when I succeeded Mr. Kristol in London as the American co-editor. Only a few are from the more recent years when the *Guardian* on the occasion of the hundredth number of *Encounter* was prompted to observe, "When a British intellectual monthly sells close on thirty thousand copies something is happening which we thought had gone out with the decline of the great Victorian reviews . . ."

At the risk of making a vice out of what might otherwise appear to be a merely casual cosmopolitanism, I should like to register a systematic indebtedness to all our friends abroad who helped to turn ten years of editing into such an open-minded international adventure . . . to Michael Josselson, of the Congress for Cultural Freedom in Geneva; Irving Kristol, now our corresponding editor in New York; Dr. Hellmut Jaesrich, editor of *Der Monat* in Berlin; Friedrich Torberg, editor of *Forum* in Vienna; Messrs. Ignazio Silone and Nicola Chiaromonte, editors of *Tempo Presente* in Rome; and François Bondy, editor of *Preuves* in Paris. Perhaps a further word of acknowledgement is due to Mr. T. S. Eliot who, although he has no knowledge of it and certainly no responsibility, was the begetter of it all. We had, in the early post-war years, listened to his words recalling his own efforts in the 'twenties and 'thirties (as editor of *Criterion*) at "bringing together the best in new thinking and new writing in its time, from all the countries . . . that had anything to contribute to the common good".* From London he made contact with periodical editors in Paris, in Zürich, in Rome, Frankfurt and Madrid; and we heard him reiterating his faith that ". . . the existence of such a network of independent reviews, at least one in every capital of Europe, is necessary for the transmission of ideas—and to make possible the circulation of ideas while they are still fresh. The

* "The Unity of European Culture", first broadcast by the B.B.C. to Germany in the spring of 1946, reprinted in Mr. Eliot's *Notes Towards the Definition of Culture* (1948).

editors of such reviews, and if possible the more regular contributors, should be able to get to know each other personally, to visit each other, to entertain each other, and to exchange ideas in conversation. In any one such periodical, of course, there must be much that will be of interest only to readers of its own nation and language. But their co-operation should continually stimulate that circulation of influence, of thought and sensibility, between nation and nation in Europe, which fertilizes and renovates from abroad the literature of each one of them. And through such co-operation, and the friendships between men of letters which ensue from it, should emerge into public view those works of literature which are not only of local, but of European significance . . ." It is in something of this spirit that our own review has developed, but perhaps with the new and additional range which is characteristic of our own time : not merely international but intercontinental; not merely European but with a vital sense of the world-wide unities which embrace Europe, Africa, Asia and America.

Finally, if I were to attempt to express what it is we have been about in a few words, I would put it this way : a review is a way of looking at the world, a record of glimpses and perspectives, concerned with the colour of things and not only with their meaning, with the visible surface of life as well as its hidden patterns. A review is also a way of talking with the world, and, if worth listening to at all, alive with a sense of conversation, a feeling for the continuous dialogue which alone, in our days of agitated pictures and violent excitements, can sustain an imaginative interest in words and texts.

London, April 1963   *M.J.L.*

Part I

PERSONS & PLACES

LAURIE LEE

A Festive Occasion

I CAME DOWN TO Cannes in a four-berth couchette with a Parisian clerk, an Algerian widow, a club-footed grandma, and a dog. At some point during the night the clerk bit the widow, the dog bit the clerk, and the ancient club-booted me in the shins for trying to turn the light on. We entered the dawn in a state of watchfulness, while the clerk licked his wounds and muttered low: "What a pretty pet. What agreeable companions."

Two hours from Marseilles rose the Mediterranean Sea, as smoothly lecherous as ever, silkily tonguing its tiny red-rock coves. And again I was struck by the power of this water—oily with rainbows of morning sun—to shrive as always my nordic nerves and to say: "Forget: indulge!"

It was the opening day of the Festival of Film, and the gate at Cannes station was crowded. Crew-cut newsmen, with cameras charged, had gathered to meet the train. They were pale-drawn and petulant; they stamped up and down, and gazed glumly through all the barriers. "Who's coming, for goodness sake?" they asked. A Festival Officer fussed around them. "Well. For instance. Eddie is coming. Eddie Constantine is. For instance..." There were howls and groans and a spit on the floor. But not even he came. Nobody came. Save me, and the club-footed woman.

The Hall of Festival was facing the sea, shining, splendid and rich. Its façade was dressed in the flags of all nations that stirred to a north-east wind. Inside were pressmen of all the nations, dressed in American coloured shirts, stirring each other for stories. But we were all too early. No names had come. All was chaos and nothing was ready. The publicity booths were only half built; and even our press-cards were lost. A wet-faced woman, with white-cropped hair, met us with soothing moans. "Patience, messieurs. Your cards will soon come. Meanwhile Eddie Constantine is here..." More gloom and groans while we kicked our heels. Then we were shown to the press-room; and sure enough Eddie Constantine *was* there, in a yachting cap, lonely and worried. We ignored him, and smoked, and looked out at the sea—which was slicing up now into mint-green blocks well-sugared by whipping winds. Eddie C. was too early. We were all too early. There was nothing to do but wait.

Then I heard that someone was handing out tickets for the Gala Première that night: "Around the World in 80 Days", by bounty of Michael Todd. I went to the press-desk and stood in line very ready for anything free. But admission it seemed was by invitation only. "You are not on the list, monsieur." "Scandal!" I cried, without emotion, and wandered back to the press-room.

A flashing of cameras greeted me there. Eddie C. had been launched, on a flood of ennui. They had found him a girl—white-shorted, cream-haired—and posed her at one of the typewriters. He leaned on the desk and leered hysterically. The girl fluttered, typed, and looked into his face. Eddie looked into the cameras. The cameras looked into her blouse. There were professional cries of joy and encouragement. Someone undid some more buttons. The girl resettled her corn-brown legs, the star resettled his yachting cap, a few extra bulbs were sacrificed, and the party broke up well pleased.

But I was entranced by the ritual; and as the tiny starlet sidled away I watched her bare heels with interest. Plant-like, crisp, and exquisitely portable, she was the first of the crop I had seen. Who was she, I wondered? From what fresh field had she sprung? Her typewriter, deserted now, still held a piece of paper in it; inscribed no doubt with her secrets. Stealthily, then, I whipped it out; on the crumpled sheaf I read:

"Mi chiamo Grazia uf e sono a Cannes per fare un prov di v nostro f f a ho remi f chiamo Grazia e sof a Cann edmo koi s dmmila anos fr sino non . . ."

A cry of near-wordless ecstasy. Alas, I never saw her again.

In the afternoon I collected my press-card, together with publicity material weighing one and a half kilos. It was to be, it seemed, a very Olympiad of Films, with entries from thirty countries. The major powers had booths in the Festival Hall; the minor ones worked from the bars. Most of the iron-screened countries were represented, as were the obvious free States, and such unknown starters as Tunisia, Ceylon, and the Lebanon. There would be four films a day for the next two weeks. Meanwhile the curtain had not yet risen, and there was little to be witnessed save the pasting of posters that were going up all over the town.

These posters, bright as heraldic shields, seemed part of a private battle. Those of Britain, it's true, were remote and exclusive. They showed white waves breaking on rocky cliffs, or over the bows of destroyers, or against the stern British chin of Mr. Richard Todd. They properly told our rough island story and seemed to claim to have invented the sea. But the other big countries mixed the battle more closely. Hollywood led with a girl in black tights. Italy countered with a girl in brown tights; even younger, and with a doll. Japan from Italy reclaimed her rice-fields with a young girl knee-deep in a bog. And Russia, astonishingly, moved right in on Hollywood with two lovers embracing in water.

With a book of free tickets stuffed into my pocket, and no films to be seen till the morrow, I walked up the sunlit, windy front, thinking how lucky I was. A mile of white poles were set out like standards, each bearing its propaganda. And my country was not at all backward here, for every fourth pole bore a well-known likeness, each done in that malted-milk tradition so suggestive of homely night-caps. The cosy pantheon of Pinewood stars—brother, sister, scout-leader, and nurse—they gazed reassuringly down upon me alone in that sinful crowd.

Further up was the Carlton, sugar-white and beflagged, holding the Festival's flesh and blood. In the street outside a crowd of witnesses had gathered. Butter-faced schoolgirls with autograph books were waving at a porter in an attic window. The porter waved back—it was Eddie Constantine. I continued my walk and came back an hour later. The girls had all gone, but Eddie C. was still there, drumming his fingers on the window sill. The crowd had moved to stare at the beach, where a large gas-balloon was swelling. As the balloon inflated, so Eddie wilted, but bravely he stuck to his post. The air-bag was one of Mike Todd's devices and a squad of police were on guard. I approached one of these and showed him my card. "A quelle heure partir le ballon?" I asked. The official turned crimson and could not speak. But an older, more sober comrade answered: "It departs, monsieur, at eight o'clock—but only to fifteen metres."

I sat down at a beach-bar and ordered a drink. It was that lambent half-hour, before the setting of the sun, when the light of this coast works miracles with one's self-esteem. The wind had dropped and the world seemed transfigured. Never had mankind looked so well. A coral glow embossed the crowds with a rich and magnificent carnality. Old women passing looked flushed as flowers, old men as noble as Aztec gods; lovers went wrapped in immortal hues; and little pink girls ran over the sands with bare feet trailing pink powdery clouds. There were smells in the air of wine and pine, scorched leaves and sun-festering lilies. For a long, slow instant this minor Babylon hung up gardens of seven wonders. Then the sun sank at last, the cold wind rose, our cheeks turned grey; and the neon lights took over . . .

That opening night was America-Night, thanks to Todd and his Jules Verne Colossus. With a series of exclamation marks, nicely chosen, he dominated the town. First came the balloon, a corking stunt : precisely at eight, as the policeman said, it rose floodlit over the sea. And there it swung, at fifteen metres, like a tethered planet or lantern. Two gum-chewing boys, in Victorian dress, hung precarious in its basket. From time to time they doffed their toppers, released more sand, snatched wildly at ropes, looked sick, and cried out through their megaphones. An attempt by ruffians to cut them adrift was beaten off by the police.

Next came the showing of the film—a mink and tiara job. A magnificent squadron of mobile police—the Household Cavalry of Dough—in rampant uniform, with motor-bikes couchant, had been hired to line the approaches. A hundred more, armed with sticks and revolvers, hid in side-streets behind the Hall. Fish-finned cars slid up to the entrance dispensing blonde girls like eggs. Mr. Todd and his wife arrived at last—he biting his lip like a worried schoolboy, she moist as a bunch of violets. Up the carpeted steps he shielded her, scowling most stern and proud. Then the Hall of Festival shut firmly down for the three and a half hours of the film.

Later, at midnight, came the Casino Party, with champagne and caged lions and lobsters. The invitation list of course was limited; but such was Mike Todd's popularity that we all wished to do him honour. Two hundred cards, stolen beforehand, were sold in the streets and bars. Then as the guests arrived, their cards were collared and whipped back to the streets again. The whole of Cannes was at the party; it was the greatest party of all. Mr. Todd, with his missile in the sky; and Todd A-O, the ultimate detergent, had together captured the Festival.

I didn't see Todd's film that night; instead I went to a cinema in the town where an unofficial film was showing—"L'Empire du Soleil", a blazing trail of the Andes, made by the makers of "The Lost Continent". How contrived it is I cannot say, but I watched it with drunken pleasure. It is a visual bombardment by a world unknown: a vast cinescope of thunderous mountains; there are Peruvian Indians dressed like straw dolls of harvest; dances, festivals, work, and love. There is a woman in labour hanging from a tree; a vulture riding a fighting bull; clouds of black cormorants bombing the sea; surprise, amazement, and poetry...

Dazed by, and dreaming of, this film, I went next morning to see Mike Todd's—which was being shown again for the peasantry. Vigorously con-ceived, superbly made, and acted with immaculate polish, it sets a girdle round the earth in eighty clichés. (I know where I'm going, and I know what they'll show me...) France?—there was Paris and a postcard château. Spain had its bullfight and gipsy dance. ("For the bulls get the best, what's-his-name? Dominguin; for the gipsy that guy José Greco.") Then India, yes, a pretty big place. We'll have rope-tricks and elephants and sacred cows, sutte, a Princess, and General Blimp. Siam is easy; its the

King and I. For the old U.S.A., the old-time works : democratic elections, saloon-bar molls, a free-lunch counter, a Kentucky crook, the railroad spanning the Middle West, a Red Indian raid, and some buffaloes. England, of course, is club-life and cabs, a hint of Royalty, and incipient decline . . . It was jolly, bounding fun all round; but as globe-circling Fogg neared the shores of Britain (sailing mysteriously into a westering sun) I felt the merriment pale a little. It was like being dragged, at once, through a Bædeker dream-book and an international casting-directory (starred pages only). Nothing was spared to us except surprise.

From "Around the World" I came out to the sun, blinded as by a sea of milk. When my sight returned I looked about me. A noon-day party was in full-swing on the beach, watched by a solemn crowd. I flashed my card and joined the revellers and a drink was thrust into my hand. It was one of those gilded anonymous gatherings which seemed to spring up instantly whenever there was a patch of sun. Fat, busy film-men, their backs to the wind, sold projects one to another. Long-haired girls languored here and there in stately Borzoi silences. Cameramen clicked and crawled and hunted, selecting and rejecting the girls. They posed a red-head with a rubber horse; she flashed frantic smiles, they flashed their bulbs, and the glaring old sun was ignored. A toasty morsel in a raffia skirt watched glumly for a while. Presently the cameras turned upon her. She dilated, and stripped in the gritty wind, and took up a hundred postures. She writhed on the sands, nubile and shiny, knotting and unknotting her limbs. The cameras sought her, circling slowly. Their long phallic lenses pried and prodded; and she opened generously to them all, fondling with every gesture her idea of the knowledge they had of her.

The power of the levelled camera on a girl. A moment ago she was a dull-faced bun; now her flesh seemed to burn like an electric fire, and her long green eyes, turning restlessly upon us, sparked with voluptuous longings. I couldn't bear it a minute longer : with my small cheap camera swinging between my legs I waded into the fray.

"It's no good wearing *that*," said a voice. "These girls are experts; they demand *equipment*. Anything less than a Rolliflex and they'll book you for indecent exposure."

The sage who spoke, a pink, Sunday columnist, was squatting at ease on the sand.

"And it's no good looking at her either. That little number is fiendishly faithful. She's got eyes for no one but her girl-friend Lola. Why did you come? This place is a wash-out. There's no love, but *no love* at all. All the girls are on yachts, or are queer as nutmegs. And look at the weather—like a Trades Union Congress. I think I'll go back to Twickenham."

We lunched together in the strong east wind, with the table-cloth nailed to the table. Other gossip-men joined us, wailing, wailing. What are we going to send home? No personalities, no griff, no stories. Princess Grace won't play, I've tried her. Ex-King Peter? No good; only wants puffs for his book. Do you know Somerset Maugham? Well, I've got Dorothy Dandridge. How about getting them together? I'd pay you, you know. A pity. If only Eva Bartok would come . . .

We drank Calvados through the long afternoon, then drove to the hills for a party. It was given in a villa of rich Baroque icing, commanding a magnificent view. Our host was a painter whose pink-lipped nudes had made him a considerable fortune. There was champagne in the garden, and a swimming pool; the wind had turned soft, and the evening was the colour of peacocks. All the guests began to appear very familiar to me. There were the cameramen from the beach-party. And there were the girls from the beach-party. There were the two cropped boys from the balloon. And there was Mr. Eddie Constantine. When I left at last, the desperate newsmen were trying to get him to jump in the pool . . .

That night they were showing "Celui Qui Doit Mourir", Jules Dassin's long-looked-for adaptation of Nikos Kazantzakis' "Le Christ Recrucifié". Alas, I never got to see it. Instead, I ran full-tilt into an unexpected taboo. At least, it was a surprise to me.

Having arrived at the theatre and shown my card to the flunkey, he suddenly barred my path. "But monsieur is not wearing his 'smoking'," he said. "Then, alors, he cannot pass." I stood perplexed in the flower-banked foyer. "Who said anything about 'smoking'?" I asked. The big man shrugged. "For the evening, it is obliged," he said. I was cross : I said I had come a thousand miles; I said I had no "smoking"; I even said I was a poet. Streams of black ties were flowing past us. The doorman sent for his superior. "He says he's a poet and has no 'smoking'." "Throw him out," rapped the chief. So they did.

I went off to a café and worked up indignation. Capitalist dummies and dolls! Was I really going to stand for this? Would Stephen Spender stand for it? Very well, neither would I. I sat down at a table, called for paper and ink, and wrote off a note to Jean Cocteau.

"Cher Maître," I began (in so many words). "This night I was ejected from the Hall of Festival because I wore no 'smoking'. I have no smoking. I come from England to see the films of the world and not to attend a parade. May I, with all the admiration I cherish for you—you who have broken every rule to achieve the supreme law of your own genius—protest against this sartorial dictatorship?" The note had the right Gallic flourish, I thought. The next day, his reply : "You should make as I do," he wrote, in

French. "Go to bed at night—and so avoid the necessity of the 'smoking'. But failing this, I enclose a note to help you—though my wishes do not necessarily correspond with my authority." The note he enclosed was sharp as a lance. "To whom it may concern," it ran. "M. Laurie Lee has come to Cannes without his 'smoking'—*mais avec son cœur*! Please be kind enough to receive him *in the manner which he merits*. Signed: Jean Cocteau. President du Festival de Cannes."

Armed with this note I returned the next night. "But monsieur is without his 'smoking'," droned the flunkey. "He cannot pass." "But, look," I exclaimed, "regard this paper." Slowly, mumbling, he did so. "Please be kind enough to receive him in the manner which he merits," he read . . . So they threw me out again.

I stood in the street, dazed and nonplussed, as though a cheque had bounced hard in my face. Then I gathered myself and fought my way back. I found the superior and rubbed the note in his face. "Read it," I cried. "These are not idle words." He read it twice, and slumped, and bit his lip. "All right," he sighed wearily. "I suppose you must pass. But not till the lights go down."

In fact, from then on, I was admitted, *sans smoking*, to soirées of every description.

Cannes Film Festival is a great Spring Fair which caters for all lines of business. Nationalism offers its barking side-shows and distributes free dollops of snake-oil. Film-renters meet to buy and exchange—job-lots, shockers, new or old, a Sofia Loren for two Monroes—according to the state of the market. Famous screen shadows incarnate themselves, can be seen on the beaches and touched in the bars. Girls, with new lines in thighs or eyebrows, offer themselves here for discovery. Newspaper-gossips, their ears in the sand, hatch the rumours their readers know. Everyone lives on expenses and bluff, Cannes takes its cut; and the films themselves, chosen for showing, are inclined to come least on the list.

But the glue that binds this Fair together is mixed by the parties that everyone gives. According to the geography of our particular hosts, we lived in Canes on champagne and nuts, champagne and vodka, champagne and schnapps, champagne and saké, champagne and gin. Every morning we wore, like a national decoration, a different species of hangover. And although every party had a separate point of departure, each achieved common ground in the end.

I go to the Carlton, the Casino, the Martinez; I go to the Whisky à Gogo. The hosts that receive me are from all over the forest; the resulting scrum is the same. A fight at the bar formally opens the ball. Contemptuous waiters, stern and forbidding, ladle drinks like free soup for the poor. The champagne flows, or trickles, or dries, in controlled and strategic tides. I am rubbing elbows now with a lifetime of filmgoing. Little did I think, I say. Once cherished faces, the sex-symbols of my youth, swim fading before my eyes. Vivian Romance leans near and asks for a light (her shape on that Naples bed!). And there's Lilian Harvey—with whose image I once climbed a beech-tree ... Both comfy now, like my Auntie Alice. Maria Schell embraces me, smiling bright: "Dear poet," she sighs, "we must meet again." She turns to the arms of her co-star, Curt Jurgens. Photographers gather; lights flash; they cling together. But not for long, alas. A carbon-eyed girl slides into the picture, grabs Curt's other arm and stays put. "My very best husband," she breathes in his ear. Her cat-like body strokes him slowly, her inked face purrs and glows. Who is this? Eva Bartok! A happy sensation. Miss Maria Schell looks grave, Miss Bartok looks legal, Herr Jurgens a double-head winner.

So the parties sparkle, and spill, and flatten. There is Ram Gopal, in an astrakhan hat, leaning beautifully against a pillar. And a Russian star, with a water-scrubbed face—strict Baptist Chapel, she. The Japanese soirée meets all our wishes. Lanterns surround us. Little men bow. Their girls have piled hair, kimonos, and clogs, and pretty print parachutes at the rear. Recorded music comes out of the walls—drums and plucked strings and pipes. "What music is this?" I ask a small doll. She drops her slant-eyes, bobs her bobbin-filled hair: "It is very provincial," she says. "It does not signify." "Your kimono is beautiful." "It's the first time I wear one. I live in South Kensington, see." Rice-chicken and saké are served until two —then the lights are switched off like a pub.

But the party I remember best of all was the luncheon served up by the French. We were piled into coaches and driven from Cannes as though in full flight from the plague. At a handsome auberge, alone by the sea, the hors d'œuvres lasted two hours. Food, and flowers, and wine, and girls, entirely surround us there. And the girls, printed on my eyes by that hot afternoon sun, are those I remember now.

There was Jackie, a cool, blue, straw-hatted beauty who smiled blindly at the call of her name. There was a bare-footed Tahitian who sang love songs to a guitar, then covered her face in confusion. There was a young French actress, schooled at Gerrards Cross, who spoke fondly of hockey and rissoles. There was a tumbled, teen-age apparition, with wide, crushed, elderberry eyes set in a cream-white face, who looked vague, dreamy, and ever-ready for bed. And there was Eva Bartok. There she was with the long hair, and violet eyes, and tight check trousers buttoned down the back. And there was Eva Bartok. There was the kitten with fringe, exhausted childish face, and chemical yellow lips. And a tiny Italian scampi scampering among her lovers. And again there was Eva B ...

But such are the flesh of the cinema, the figured flames through which it projects itself. Britain, it's true, seems to get on pretty well without them, relying for the main burden of its message on the shutter-lipped hero and the family joke—with the girls, at most, their stooges and waiting wives. Hollywood has built up the lactic, ageless Mom, sterile by rule, but whose lovers become her sons. But here and there, on the fringes of France and Italy, the White Goddess of cinema is still a force. One saw her in Cannes again and again—live-blooded, hare-brained, earthy-beautiful—her very vagueness itself a vessel of truth, her figure a legend-bearer. Such girls, mysterious in origin, renew themselves each year, bringing skins of light and names of poetry—Nicole, Mylene, Ma-Ea-Fior. As they pass from darkness into darkness their motions, shapes, and unstoried faces are the camera's ideal reflectors. They are the divine animators of the cinema dream, and can endure in that priceless purpose. So long as they are loved, encouraged in mystery, kept womanly raw, and told nothing.

As for the films themselves : my stay was limited, I saw about half, but these included some of the most notorious. One could not believe that all were their country's best; their selection at times was inscrutably unexplained; pains had been taken that no one should be offended; but almost all of them shared one quality. Blatant or implied, according to origin, most films enshrined some large or tiny lie without which they would not have been made. The high cost and corporate talent involved in modern film-making depends for its existence on sponsorship. And every sponsor—be he political, moral, or plain money-grubbing—demands the transmission of some particular illusion. Even so, we had fun and saw much to arrest us; spotting the angle was part of the fun.

The Russian film, "Forty and One", was the greatest curio of them all. Slow, long, and exquisitely coloured, at first one just could not believe it. A girl partisan, and her White Russian prisoner, are cast on a desert island. She guards him with scorn and contempt to begin with, then radiantly falls in love. Sequences of extraordinary tenderness follow, but he's a White Russian after all. His companions come to rescue him, and she shoots him in the back. It seems you may love your enemy—if you kill him in the end.

Another that finally betrayed itself, though not before exploring some sharp, uneasy truths, was "The Bachelors' Party", made by the "Marty" team. Here is a film of smooth and cunning realism. It is the cry of the American male caught fast in the bogs of biology and business. Four clerks on a spree, depressed and hysterical, are seeking their lost stag-selves. All in a way are ham-strung by sweethearts and wives, and at last they decide to rebel. For an awful moment they reach a state of aching honesty with each other. Then the police-cars of conscience pick them up one by one, and family life is saved.

The other films, though wildly mixed in quality, all strained to sell something or other. The Polish "Kanal", a savage nightmare of the last days of the Warsaw Rising, seemed to me entirely pitiless. The doomed resisters, in their battlefield of sewers, are slowly and bestially slaughtered. All is useless sacrifice, filth, and nihilism. So perish all heroes, everywhere, who rise without Soviet sanction. The Lebanon's "Destination Unknown" is a slow, amateurish parable designed to discourage emigration. "Earth", from Bulgaria, is a tale of greed, demonstrating how the personal land-hunger of a selfish young man can lead him in turn to betray his sweetheart, marry a hunch-back, murder his brother, lose all his friends, and die in the snow from d.t.'s. There was also Yugoslavia's "Valley of Peace", a moving allegory in which two young children, and a Negro G.I., search for a world without war. A wild white horse, the burial of a doll, and a motionless mill-wheel are typical of its symbolism.

But the "House of the Angel", from the Argentine, was for me the best of them all. This is a stifling study of Catholic claustrophobia, a tragedy of manners. A fourteen-year-old girl imprisoned by the brooding proprieties of her class, feels the first fevers of sexual desire. Her sleep-walking body becomes the centre of storm. Thunder-cloud images pile up around her —bedrooms, shutters, trees, faces, the black crêpe of her mother, stilted walks in the park. Even her nightly bath, in a nun-like shift, brings its touch of strangling horror. Then a friend of her father's, on the eve of a duel, comes to spend the night in the house. Convinced he will die, she is drawn to his room. The storm hangs between them, then savagely breaks. In a silent lashing of limbs and hair, the man subdues and rapes her. She returns to her room and waits for his death. But he survives the duel to haunt her. In a trance of shame she lives out her life. Each week her ravisher dines at her house; bound to him now in her disgust, withered and dumb by that strike of lightning, she still waits for his death, or for hers.

After the showing of this film, its director, Leopoldo Torre Nilsson, made an anti-Peron speech and praised the new Argentine government. But his remarks seemed irrelevant to his achievement. For of all the films I saw at the Festival this one seemed to possess the least strings. In its power of mood and flow of image, in the startled handwriting of its personal style, it was a perfect gem of cinema. Shuffled off-handedly into a morning double-feature, it was loudly acclaimed by the critics. But as far as I know it got not official recognition. Nor did the remarkable "Kanal", for all its brutal cynicism. Nor did any of the other bold ones. The Golden Palm went to "Friendly Persuasion"—Wyler's whimsey in Quaker Corn.

The Festival was already half-way through when my time for departure arrived. Cruel winds whipped the sea and chilled all spirits. The U.S. 6th Fleet was away off Jordan. H.M.S. *Birmingham* arrived to see Todd down the Yangtse. Pressmen packed up and pursued scandals to Rome. Most stars had long fled—even Eddie Constantine was gone.

So I looked my last at carnal Cannes, and drank milky-Pastis and studied the crowds. The locals already seemed back to normal. Moneyed widows with huskies swept by in flash cars. Old ladies tottered off to the Tables. There was a beach-girl in briefs parading around with a trade-name lipsticked on her bottom. And every so often a honey-locked boy, handsome, tight-trousered, with matted chest, walked up and down, and up and down —a dream of hairy with the light brown jeans.

Hazily I tried to sum up the films I had seen while television in the bar behind me snared the old fishermen's eyes. My mind clicked with images and I started a poem. But for whom? The printed word was out of date, old and gone as the clay tablets of Ur. Instruction now was for medieval peasants, a shade on a wall, and a preaching voice. "One picture," they say, "is worth a thousand words; and a moving picture a library." I wrote no more, but watched the sun go down. Then I looked through a telescope at the crisp half-moon and at Jupiter spinning its balls.

Finally, I took the night train to Paris, and slept, and had a dream. I dreamed I walked with the Queen of Festival, a pocket-sized beauty in white. Her Grecian dress was too big for her. So I gathered it up and fastened it with a brooch, which I'd swiped from a suicide's body. "You're the prettiest desiccated man I know; the fastest one without feet," she said. We walked hand in hand through the crowded town. Nobody saw or cheered.

JULY 1957

13

GORONWY REES

Innocent in Prussia

IT IS HARD now, twenty-five years later, to explain even to myself the kind of attraction which Germany exerted on young men of my generation at Oxford. The image of Germany which we found so seductive has been irretrievably shattered by the events of the last twenty-five years; at the most a few scattered splinters are left, like the shards and fragments from which an archæologist tries to reconstruct a lost civilization. To try and recover the original image of Weimar Germany by which I, and so many others, were attracted is like trying to restore some lost masterpiece which has been painted over by a succession of brutal and clumsy artists; and in this case the task is all the harder because the masterpiece never really existed and the Germany of Weimar in which we believed was really only a country of the imagination.

First of all, one would have to reconstruct the illusions under which we suffered at that time; the illusion, for instance, that in the war of 1914–18 there was no distinction of guilt between the Allies and the Central Powers, and that both sides were equally responsible for that appalling catastrophe; to which we added the emotional and irrational corollary that somehow or other the defeated were less responsible than the victors. In this illusion we were happily confirmed by reading Brandenburg, Lowes Dickinson, and Bernard Fay. It followed, for us, that the terms of the Versailles Treaty, which was then hardly older than the Potsdam agreement is now, were manifestly unjust, a pure assertion of the rights of the strong over the weak and of the victor over the vanquished; and for this reason it was clear that Germany deserved our sympathy and our understanding more than any other country, including our own. It must be remembered that we were very young men, who will always respond to ideas of this kind. The young dislike power, because they do not share it; the middle-aged adore it, because it gives them some assurance that the world will continue to be as they have known it.

We were all agreed, therefore, that the terms of the Treaty were unjust; it was equally obvious that they were futile. This illusion was firmly rounded on Maynard Keynes's *Economic Consequences of the Peace*. Thus the Treaty was evidence not only of the brutality of the Allies, but of their stupidity. By contrast, Germany, still suffering under the injustices of the Treaty and without power to redress her wrongs, appeared as an innocent victim calculated to appeal to all our liberal and progressive instincts.

To those who said that, whether the Treaty was just or unjust, Germany might one day try to redress her defeat by force of arms, we replied scornfully that such fears ignored all the realities of the international situation; for we set great store by realities. For did not the League of Nations, supported by all the power of the Allies, exist to prevent the recurrence of war? We could not refrain from adding that even to question the power and intention of the League only threw further suspicion on the post-war policies of the Allies. But even if the League, as an instrument of Anglo-French capitalism, could not be trusted, was it not clear that there was an even stronger foundation for our belief in the maintenance of perpetual peace between nations? For the real bulwark of peace was not the League but the international working-class movement, and was not Germany, with its massive trade union and social democratic organizations, the strongest representative of that movement?

In saying this, of course, we were expressing our feelings just as much about our own country as about her defeated enemy. To sympathize with Germany was a mark of our violent revulsion against the Great War and its consequences, and against the generation which had helped to make it and to conduct it to victory. Germany was for us at the opposite extreme from everything we disliked in the land of our fathers; Germany, indeed, had done her best to kill our fathers, and we were not ungrateful to her for her efforts and sympathized with her failure, and to adhere to her cause and her culture was for many of us the most effective and the easiest protest we could make against the England of Mr. Stanley Baldwin, Lord Birkenhead, and Sir William Joynson-Hicks.

For politics were only a part of our infatuation with Germany. Weimar also represented to us all those experiments, in literature, in the theatre, in music, in education, and not least in sexual morals, which we would have liked to attempt in our own country but were so patently impossible in face of the massive and infuriating stupidity of the British middle classes. Was it not typical that our own *Beggar's Opera,* which as produced by Sir Nigel Playfair and Lovat Fraser was nothing more than a pretty and insipid *operetta,* should under German skies become the cynical and subversive farce of Brecht's *Dreigroschenoper?*

We received reports of these experiments, not only through the press, through German films, through books, but by word of mouth. Ever since the inflation young Englishmen had visited Germany in greater and greater numbers, and they returned to us in Oxford with wonderful travellers' tales of this land of freedom and, even better, licence; where one could be on the right side, the proletarian side, in politics, and at the same time take advantage of the fact that social disapproval had ceased to exist; where morals had been discarded as a bourgeois prejudice; where sex was permitted, indeed encouraged, to take any form it chose, however eccentric; where night-club tables were decorated with phalli made of marzipan; where Mr. Issyvoo was having a perfectly delightful time living in a slum in the Hallesches Tor; what more could a young man need to satisfy his heart's desire?

II

It may well seem to others, in the light of what happened later, that only a lunatic could have been quite so foolish as I was in those days; yet what I have written is by no means an exaggerated account of what I thought and felt about Germany at that time. I was very much a creature of fashion; I found the attraction of Germany irresistible; and so, in my first year at Oxford, I determined that in the summer vacation I too must make the pilgrimage to Weimar and to Wedding, see the whores and the queens and the Lesbians on the Kurfürstendamm, observe the violence and confusion of German politics at first hand, so that I might have at least some idea of what politics might be like if they were properly conducted; I too must tramp in the Black Forest with the *Wandervögel*, and breathe the inexpressibly sweet air of a society in decay. And indeed I succeeded in my objective of going to Germany; I should have felt terribly ashamed of myself if I hadn't; but somehow, as so often happened to me in those days, things turned out entirely differently from what I had intended.

Perhaps the reason was that I, unlike most of my friends, had no money for foreign travel; I used to wonder bitterly why I could not win scholarships to maintain myself in some *Nachtlokal* in Berlin instead of in the Wykehamist respectability of New College. How much more I should learn, I used to sigh. If I was to reach Germany in the summer I had to have a job, and so I answered an advertisement circulated by some student organization for a tutor to teach a German boy who wished to learn English. The advertisement gave no name or address but simply invited applications and for a few weeks after I had replied I wondered happily what my destination would be if I were lucky enough to get the job. Would it be Berlin? I thought. Would I meet Mr. Issyvoo and savour the delights of Hallesches Tor? Or Hamburg, which was highly recommended by the more extreme hedonists among my friends? And whom would I live with? Social-Democrats? Communists? poets, musicians, sculptors, painters? It seemed to me at that time that the entire population of Germany consisted of left-wing politicians or artists of some kind.

The reply to my application put an end to all these speculations. I had indeed been successful; somehow I had never doubted it; for how else could I get to Germany that summer? But somehow my pupil's address had never figured in any of my day-dreams; there was something about it which even to me, infatuated though I was, looked somewhat barbarous and repellent: *Boguslavitz, bei Breslau, Schlesien.*

This was not at all what I had anticipated; and the name of my employer was equally disconcerting: Herr Baron Franz von Reichendorf. It seemed to me impossible that out of the eighty million people in Germany I should have picked on a Silesian Baron to spend my long vacation with. The name itself had sinister overtones. I had associated war, for the Germans, with a desperate struggle against odds which in the end proved overwhelming, with defeat, disaster, starvation and revolution; and somehow this had made the Germans sympathetic. The name Reichendorf had none of these associations; the only holder of it of whom I knew had indeed been killed, but he had been killed in his glory as a famous German air-ace in the Great War. He had been a part of everything in Germany against which Weimar was a protest. He had been Germany's greatest flying ace, a Junker of the Junkers; there was nothing about him which was either pitiful or defeated; his name had the sound of something formidable, a *nasty* ring, almost, of heroism. I hardly dared say it to myself as I set out for Germany, but I had a horrid feeling within me that once again I was going to find myself, as so often before and after, *in the wrong set.*

III

These feelings did not become quite clear to me until I found myself in the train from Berlin to Breslau. Until then my preconceived picture of Germany had not been seriously damaged. Cologne especially, with its great clean glass-vaulted station, had delighted me; here was *Modernismus,* here was *Baukunst,* here was Social Democracy at work! I thought with contempt, mingled with pity, of poor dingy old Liverpool Street, from which I had set off to Harwich the day before. From Cologne to Berlin the train had been crowded, and from the carriage window I caught sight of new buildings, factories, offices, villas, in steel and glass and concrete; I had an impression of a universal coming-and-going, of large numbers of people catching and leaving trains on purposes which, I was sure, were connected with politics, art, or literature. After all, what else was Weimar for?

In Berlin, I only had time to cross to the *Ostbahnhof*; with a pang of the heart, I had to leave Wedding, Alexanderplatz, the Kurfürstendamm unvisited. It was like passing through Rome without seeing the Sistine Chapel. And as the train left the *Ostbahnhof* I became aware that a strange, almost sinister emptiness had descended upon it. There were no more comings and goings on urgent and exciting business; I sat alone in my compartment and when I walked up and down the corridor I saw that the other compartments were deserted also. And as the train rolled through the dusk, across a plain which seemed as sombre, monotonous, and featureless as the dusk itself, it suddenly seemed to me that I had still as far to go as when I had landed at The Hook that morning. I felt as if I had already crossed Germany once that day; could it be that there was another Germany to cross before I reached my journey's end? As darkness fell, I stared out of the carriage windows and on the bare platforms of deserted stations I saw strange incomprehensible names that seemed more Slav than German. I felt suddenly and acutely that if this were indeed still Germany, it had nothing to do with anything I had known or thought about Germany until now.

Journeys make us abnormally sensitive to impressions; landscapes acquire a significance which they do not usually have; we find hidden meanings everywhere. When night finally blotted out the views from the carriage window, it seemed to me that the train racing into the darkness had no reason to stop or even falter until it reached the shores of Asia. What occasion could there ever be to halt in that everlasting plain which repeated itself for mile after mile like a sad, meaningless refrain. I felt slightly frightened, perhaps because I was tired at the end of the long day; but also because, alone in my brightly lit compartment, I felt as if I were travelling through some immense solitude. I told myself that such feelings were absurd; after all, Breslau was not Kamchatka, and thousands of very ordinary travellers must take precisely that same route from Berlin to Breslau every day. It was only, I said, that I was rather cold, that I had been travelling for a long time, that I was tired; that, after all, I *was* a very long way from Oxford and even further from my home in Wales. It was no good; whatever I said I could not shake off my impression of a landscape that stretched around me for thousands of miles, flat, grey and mournful, of the darkness outside that was not the familiar comforting darkness of home but was foreign, alien, and somehow hostile. It even *smelled* different.

To restore my spirits I went to the restaurant car where I ate a large and heavy German dinner, and treated myself to a bottle of wine and drank too much German brandy. I said to myself that here I was, at eleven o'clock at night, in a Mitropa car, alone, in the middle of Europe;

that if I wanted to I could go on as far as Warsaw, or even further, that there was no one who could prevent me from doing exactly what I liked, and that therefore I ought to be very happy; but I could not reassure myself, my melancholy only deepened. When I returned to my compartment I fell asleep, and when I awoke at Breslau I was still so dazed with sleep and drink that I hardly had sense enough to get out. When I did so, I stood for a few moments alone on the platform until a man in a peaked cap and a leather coat came up to me and said that the Herr Baron was waiting for me at the hotel and he was to take me to him.

He took my bags and led me to the car, an ancient open Adler, and drove me through the empty streets to the hotel. There, waiting for me, were Herr Baron and his son Fritz, who bowed and spoke to me in very broken English to which I replied in even more broken German, and they said that I must be very tired after my long journey, and that they hoped I would be very happy at Boguslavitz, and that Fritz had a horse for me to ride; I suddenly felt that these were very kind people, and they insisted on my drinking some coffee and a great deal of brandy. It seemed to me that they said they were hoping to shoot some wild cats on the way home, but I felt that this was too improbable to be true and that I must have misunderstood them.

I was really too tired to take in much of what they said or where I was. In that room, in that hotel, five years later, Heines, Gauleiter of Silesia, sprawled back in his chair and took pot-shots with his revolver at the portrait of the Führer hanging on the wall; but when I read about this in the newspapers I could remember nothing about the room or the hotel. I could only remember kind voices and the smell of cigars and brandy. When finally we went to the car I fell asleep immediately, and when I awoke we were driving slowly through a dark forest. The rough track in front of us was brilliantly lit by the Adler's headlamps. The Baron was standing in the front of the car beside the chauffeur, silhouetted against the light like a cardboard figure. He had a gun in his hand. As I watched, a large black cat leaped out of the forest across the track. The Baron raised his gun and fired down the track. The cat gave one convulsive jump and then seemed to disintegrate completely. I could not be quite sure whether I was awake or still dreaming, and in a moment I had fallen asleep again.

IV

When I awoke the next morning I saw something I had never seen before in my life. It moved me as the first sight of the sea must move those who have never seen it before. I had slept in a plainly furnished room above the stables; it was probably meant for a groom or a stable-boy, and

19

it was as bright and polished as a horse's harness. A wooden veranda ran round the stables at the level of my room, and I stepped out on to it through the french windows. As I stood there in my pyjamas, to north and south and east I could see nothing but mile after mile of golden corn that stretched away to the horizon as far as the eye could see; only in the very farthest south, hardly to be seen, there was a faint blue shadow of mountains.

At first sight, I could hardly credit the reality of this great golden ocean of corn that lapped me round on every side. It seemed so vast, boundless, drawing the eye on and on as if there was no limit at which it could stop. I suddenly remembered, and for the first time understood, a statement I had read somewhere; Germany has no frontiers. And later, when the first shock of surprise was over and I became accustomed to the presence of this single immense cornfield that filled the world to its farthest horizons, I began to feel for the landscape an emotion that seemed as vast and boundless as itself. When I stood on my veranda and looked out, like the captain of a ship from his bridge, I felt as if I were cradled and rocked on the great golden bosom of the corn, as if I floated in some element that would both cherish and feed me. And sometimes, as if in response, the surface of the corn would move, and the corn stalks gently incline their heads, as the clouds passing over cast a shifting shadow upon them; in the brazen heat a little breeze sprang up and rippled the heads of the corn for mile after mile until the impulse seemed to expend itself at last on some far off and invisible shore.

Fritz and I would get up every morning before dawn, while it was still cold and dark, and ride to the racecourse outside Breslau, five miles away. He had a powerful bay mare which he was preparing for the races at Halle later in the summer; I rode beside him on a little cossack pony that was convinced it could do everything, whether jump or gallop, at least as well as the mare could do. In the hour before dawn, the cornfields were duncoloured and sighed softly as the dawn wind passed over them; and as we rode, and as his English and my German began to improve, Fritz and I discussed the matters which filled his head and his heart and which to me seemed strange beyond belief.

He was seventeen, with a lean sunburned horseman's face and thick blond hair that perpetually fell in a heavy lock across his cheek; and I was twenty and therefore looked down on him from the heights of an intellectual superiority which made me dismiss his ideas as childish imaginings. All the more so, because I quickly found that they were in all respects at variance with mine, and indeed seemed to reflect a world which bore no relation to any I had ever known.

Fritz thought a great deal about the Great War, but in a way which was quite alien to me, who shared the fashionable view among my contemporaries that the war had been a culpable aberration of our fathers, which had best be forgotten as soon as possible. For Fritz the war, or rather its result, was a personal affront, and he fought all its battles over again in his mind as if by thinking he could change Germany's defeat into victory. One day he puzzled me considerably by talking about Germany's naval victory at Skagerrak, and it took me a long time before I could identify this as the Battle of Jutland, which I (and I had assumed everyone else) knew to have been won by the Royal Navy. But when I tried to explain his error to him, as kindly as I could, I found to my distress that he knew so much about the battle, its strategy and tactics, the weight of guns employed, the details of ships sunk, that I was in no kind of position to refute him.

I found also that in discussion with Fritz it was difficult to preserve my feelings of sympathy with the defeated Germans. His attitude was quite simply that the Germans had not been defeated at all; they had won the war, but somehow the result had been wrongly recorded. He was like a boxer who knows that he knocked out his opponent in the third round but finds to his amazement and indignation that the verdict has been given against him on points. His conviction that the German army had won the war brought an added element of confusion into my ideas about Germany, which were already confused enough.

It is quite easy, and does not require any large degree of imagination, to sympathize with an enemy who has been totally defeated and disarmed. It is much less easy when the enemy regards himself as the rightful victor, who has been cheated of the spoils of his victory by some monstrous perversion of history. And it is even less easy when the enemy thinks, as Fritz did, that his first duty in life is to ensure that the error should be corrected at the first possible moment.

Fritz's passionate belief that, in the name of historical justice, there must be a radical revision of Germany's status in the world was all the more confusing because it was enriched by literary and romantic associations which at that time conveyed little or nothing to me. It was strange to find a boy, whom I found extremely likeable and attractive, in love with ideas which seemed to me harsh and repellent and, very often, ugly. At Oxford I had been brought up to admire Proust and James Joyce and Virginia Woolf and Lytton Strachey; we went in for a combination of cynicism in regard to the feelings of those who did not agree with us, and extreme sensitiveness in regard to our own. *Only connect* we said in Mr. Forster's famous words, but we were very careful and exclusive about whom we connected with. Now Fritz introduced me to writers whose names even, in some cases, were utterly strange to me and whose ideas were even stranger. Some of these writers, like Nietzsche, of whom then I knew nothing, carried with them an air of faded nineteenth-century romanticism; how was I to know that this was also the air of a world which was yet to come? And what was I to make of the great English writer, Houston Stewart Chamberlain? Fritz was profoundly shocked by my ignorance when I had to confess that I had never even heard of him, but forgave it as a typical example of British philistinism, and kindly gave me a copy of *Der Mythos des neunzehnten Jahrhunderts* to read. And novel and disconcerting as these writers were, they were all the more so because, for Fritz, they spoke with a voice that was also the voice of Hölderlin, and Stefan George, and Rilke—and also of Moeller van den Bruck and Josef Göbbels. For me these writers, as I came to know them, seemed so disparate, both in content and in quality, that it was impossible to accept that they were part of a single literary tradition; the ideas of some of them, certainly, seemed to reach such a pitch of lunacy and brutality that it was impossible to take them seriously. But for Fritz they were all profoundly and equally serious; to him they all spoke a secret wisdom which provided him with an answer to life. And through him, indeed, I came to admire and love Hölderlin and Nietzsche, George and Rilke, but I could never understand how it was that to him they could mean such utterly different things from what they meant to me.

Fritz was a charming companion and friend, and I was puzzled that I should find him none the less so even though most of his ideas and beliefs were to me both fantastic and repellent. I solved this contradiction for myself by dismissing them as the imaginings of a half-educated schoolboy, and for this reason I never came to suspect that, in various forms, they were shared by thousands of young men and women all over Germany. It seemed to me that no one could seriously believe in such a farrago of nonsense, and what is more, such brutal and barbarous nonsense; coming from Oxford, I was firmly convinced that the irrational is the unreal. And so I did not take Fritz's ideas about politics and literature seriously; any more, for instance, than I took him seriously when he talked to me with rapture about his hero, the ex-Crown Prince Wilhelm, and more particularly about the beauty of his Hohenzollern profile, in which one could see, said Fritz, all the courage and virtue of his race.

Riding along beside him, on the dusty Silesian roads, I dismissed this as yet another of Fritz's absurd fantasies; and indeed it was no odder than many of the ideas which formed the staple of our conversation at Boguslavitz. When we reached home, the rest of the family would be having breakfast on the veranda which ran across the plain stone front of the house. On the table were bowls of boiled eggs, a crock of fresh butter, black bread, smoked ham, and innumerable varieties of cold sausage. The sun was already hot overhead, and the long grass of the overgrown lawn looked cool and green in the shade of the pine-trees surrounding the tennis court. The Baron was finishing his enormous breakfast and threw scraps of sausage to the dachshunds; under the admiring eyes of his two plump and sturdy daughters, and of his wife, who was small and gentle and came from the Rhineland and was half French, he discoursed eloquently and violently on the political events of the day.

V

The Baron was *Reichstagsabgeordneter* for Lower Silesia. He was a devoted and conscientious member of the German Nationalist party, though he never ceased complaining because his parliamentary duties took him away to Berlin from the affairs of his estate. During the first few days of my stay at Boguslavitz I seized eagerly upon the opportunity of discussing German politics with him, but I soon came to realize that, however hard we tried to understand one another, we were divided by an abyss which no amount of effort could bridge, so profound indeed that the words of our discussions seemed to reverberate meaninglessly in its depths.

I had felt in honour bound to explain to the Baron, at the start of our acquaintance, that I was a socialist, and it was quite obviously completely incredible to the Baron that any Englishman could hold such political views. *Kommt nicht in Frage,* he would say curtly, and proceed with the discussion on his unshakeable assumption that, like himself, I was an old-fashioned country gentleman. It did not help when I explained that I was not an Englishman but a Welshman; that was all the same to the Baron. No one could have been more acutely sensitive to racial, and social differences, between his own countrymen, but the British Isles he regarded as inhabited by one single homogeneous race whose individual members were all without exception, gentlemen, and being gentlemen could not possibly be socialists. It followed for the Baron that when I said I was a socialist either I could not be telling the truth or I did not know the meaning of the word. On the whole, I think, he favoured the latter solution, but in any case I soon realized that he regarded my political ideas in exactly the same light as I regarded Fritz's, that is to say, as childish fantasies which no one could possibly take seriously. This solved the matter very satisfactorily for the Baron, who was very fond of me, and having dismissed my politics as a form of infantile disease he proceeded to lavish upon me all the affection which he invariably showed to children and to animals.

His kindness indeed went so far that he tried to explain to me what kind of people socialists really were and why therefore I could not possibly be one. In the first place, they were all Jews, and there were no Jews in

England, or at least English Jews were not really Jews at all; the only real Jews came from over there, he said, waving his hand vaguely in the direction of Poland and the Ukraine. Moreover, socialists were men who were ready at any moment to betray their country. Indeed, they had betrayed Germany, the German army, and the Kaiser. Further, their sexual habits were disgusting and obscene, they did not love God or their country, and they knew nothing about agriculture. And as his catalogue of sins continued, his bright little eyes would shine affectionately at me and he laid his hands upon my shoulder as if to say that I must now surely see how impossible it was for me to believe I was a socialist.

In the early days of my stay at Boguslavitz, I used to reply to this kind of appeal by reaffirming my socialist beliefs and by trying to expose the absurdity of the Baron's own views. In particular, I used to attack the Baron's own party, the *Deutschnationalen,* and its leader Hugenberg, the Beaverbrook of Germany, as the representatives of aggressive German capitalism and nationalism. But it had no effect; Fritz, the Baron and I were caught up in a kind of chain reaction of misunderstanding. The Baron regarded me as a child, and I regarded Fritz as a child, and both Fritz and I, in our different ways, regarded the Baron as a child, a kind of foundling left on our doorstep from an age which had entirely vanished. Our misunderstandings, indeed, were so comic that for the first time an element of scepticism began to creep into my dogmatic political outlook. I began to wonder whether perhaps all political conflicts were not based upon similar misunderstandings and a universal inability to take any point of view seriously except one's own. But comic as the situation was, it was also, in a sense, tragic. Because in misunderstanding Fritz and the Baron I was in fact misunderstanding all the ideas which later were to coalesce and provoke the most profoundly revolutionary movement of the twentieth century.

In any case, it was futile for me to discuss politics with the Baron because he obstinately refused to accommodate himself to my preconceived political categories. When I denounced Hugenberg, the Baron heartily agreed with me and broke out into far more violent denunciations. For the Baron, I discovered, belonged to a faction of the party which had followed Graf Westarp, "a good old man" said the Baron, when he had been driven out of the leadership by Hugenberg; and if my attacks on Hugenberg were violent in the sense that they abounded in the stereotyped terms of abuse which in those days the Left used against the Right, the Baron's were far more impressive and effective because expressed in good earthy obscenities, straight from the sty and the stall. Even so, they did not exhaust his indignation. They left him red-faced and furious, yet somehow still smiling, as if pleased because our common hatred of Hugenberg showed that in the end our ideas and feelings were the same. "We must put an end to all that," he said, pointing in the direction of Berlin, as if he and I together were entrusted with the historic task of cleaning out the Augean stables of German parliamentary democracy.

I was even more surprised by the Baron's reaction to my attacks on the senile President of the Reich, Field-Marshal von Hindenburg. For after all, I thought, to whom could the Baron give his loyalty and admiration if not to the Field-Marshal and ex-Supreme Commander of the German armies which the Baron, like Fritz, believed to have never been defeated. The Baron totally ignored any reasons I had for criticizing the Reichs-president, but he warmly welcomed any condemnation of him. "What a man!" he cried. "What a President! A traitor to his country! A Field-Marshal who broke his oath and drove out his Kaiser. What a difference from that poor Ludendorff! You don't have men like that in England." Tears came into his eyes at the thought of the Kaiser. He seized my hand and shook it warmly, and so once again, to my intense irritation, I found myself drawn into the Baron's political embrace. Indeed on this occasion he was so moved that before the loving eyes of his family he flung his arms around me and from that day on had no shadow of doubt but that we were the firmest of political allies.

VI

Because of this, but also because the Baron was a man of warm and impulsive affections, he insisted thenceforth on making me share all his pursuits and pleasures. Most of Fritz's time was taken up with his horses; his thin figure, in very elegant white breeches and black riding-boots, was always to be seen in the stables, where he spent hours with his groom endlessly discussing his chances of winning in the races at Halle. At first he had tried to involve me in these discussions; but the groom was a wizened little old Englishman from Swindon, who in spite of forty years spent in Germany promptly recognized me for what I was, a would-be intellectual from Oxford, and refused to speak a word about such mysteries in my presence. As for my duties as a tutor, one hour's English lesson a day on the veranda after breakfast seemed to be all that was expected of me; for the rest of the time I was at the Baron's disposal.

Boguslavitz was one of the largest estates in Silesia; it was also one of the most modern and the most highly mechanized, for however reactionary his political views, the Baron's farming methods were extremely advanced. Each day the Baron inspected some part of his estate, or one of his enter-prises, taking me with him. With a patience, an absorbing interest, a quite inexhaustible and insatiable curiosity, which sometimes wearied me to the point of exhaustion, he examined crops, farms, machinery, houses, schools, accounts, woodlands, new-born babies, newly married wives, horses, pigs, granaries and, most frequently of all, his estate railway that carried his crops down to the junction on the boundary of the estate. We talked to managers, bailiffs, tenants, labourers, engineers, tractor men, gamekeepers, carpenters, schoolmasters, children, and to each as if our lives depended on obtaining the last and minutest detail of their activities. But when at last the end of the day came, and the heat of the sun began to die, and as it seemed to me we had inspected every particular ear of corn on all the Baron's thousands of acres, a happy smile would come across his face, he would take my arm and lead me to the decrepit Adler, and we would drive at an appalling speed to one of his forests to shoot deer.

In the cool of the evening, with the same endless patience and cunning which he showed in administering his estates, the Baron stalked the deer for hours, and I clumsily tried to follow his movements. And once again the Baron should have been disappointed in me, or at least should have begun to revise his idea of the British people as a race composed exclusively of sporting gentlemen. For I am, and always have been, violently gun-shy and have a profound repugnance to shooting anything, even human beings. But after my first stalk with the Baron, I realized there was no need for me to be nervous. After hours of patient pursuit, while the forest green grew darker and darker, and in the cool damp undergrowth each fern seemed to have its own sweet particular scent, the Baron at last had the stag's head between his sights; for a moment they stared at each other across them, and then the Baron lowered his rifle and, his eyes misty, muttered apologetically : *Die sind aber so schön.* Then we walked together through the forest to his forester's little hut where he and I and the forester drank beer in great quantities, and he and the forester, who had been his batman during the war, talked of Langemarck and Verdun, and with great gusto and pleasure of their bloodthirsty experiences as *Ostkämpfer* in the Balticum after the war and in the Polish insurrection in Upper Silesia in 1921. And it was there in the hut that I first heard the names, until then unknown to me, of Maercker, and Schlageter, and Salomon, of Erhardt, *der Kapitän*, and Kern and Fischer and von Pfeffer, who to the Baron were heroes, saints, and martyrs, though in fact they were the most depraved, because the most idealistic, of assassins and murderers.

In such strange pursuits I spent most of my time at Boguslavitz. They were only interrupted when the Baron had to leave for Berlin to attend the Reichstag, and from these visits he would return in a fury of rage and disgust with all politicians. In his absence I rode with Fritz, I played tennis with his sisters, we paid visits to the Reichswehr garrison in Breslau, where Prittwitzes and Nostitzes, Schwerins and Moltkes and Haases flirted in an extraordinarily stiff and old-fashioned way with the Richthofen girls, and where one night Fritz and I became outrageously drunk under the portrait of Frederick the Great which hung on the wall of their mess.

And now the end of my visit began to approach. Fritz's training schedule was almost complete, and soon the entire family were to move to Halle in order to watch him ride his race. The Baron, however, was very anxious that, during their absence, I should spend a few weeks with a friend of theirs who had a large estate on the Baltic and who, he said, would be delighted to have me to stay and tutor his grandchildren. This was an East Prussian gentleman named Oldenburg-Januschau and I had what I thought at the time the extreme good sense to refuse. For one thing, even the name of Oldenburg-Januschau frightened me; and moreover, if the Baron and his family could quite reasonably be regarded as somewhat conservative in their outlook and habits, even by their own description it seemed as if Herr von Oldenburg-Januschau's way of life had as yet hardly advanced as far as the feudal stage of civilization. But I had already begun to feel that from any serious point of view I had completely wasted my time in Germany. I had seen none of all the many things I wanted to see; of all the progressive, revolutionary, subversive movements I had hoped to study I had found not a trace; for all I had learned of Marxism and Social Democracy in action I might just as well have been at the court of the Great Elector as at Boguslavitz. I felt that to visit Herr Oldenburg-Januschau on the Cimmerian shores of East Prussia, among his lakes and forests, his wolves and bears and wild cats, would take me even further than I was already from the realities of modern Germany; and after all, what had I come to Germany for, except to study reality?

So I refused the invitation which the Baron extended to me on his friend's behalf, even though I could hardly resist the simplicity and sincerity of his assurance : "Oldenburg-Januschau is a real Prussian. There aren't many like him left. You would like him." I told the Baron that it was really time for me to return home and devote myself to my vacation reading, of Bradley and G. E. Moore, of Hume, Locke, and Berkeley, whose ideas seemed somehow strangely thin and insubstantial in the great corn-laden immensities of the Silesian plain. It seemed to me then that, for once, I had made a serious and responsible decision; but like all the serious and responsible decisions I ever came to in my youth, I greatly regret it. If I had gone to Herr Oldenburg-Januschau's I might have made a little further progress in my peculiar and unwilling initiation into German life and politics. Indeed, if I had eyes to see, which seems improbable, I might have learned a great deal about some of the most practical realities of German political life. For Herr Oldenburg-Januschau had some very business-like views about the duties which the state owes to its patrons. He was a great friend of Oskar von Hindenburg, the President's son, and together they had promoted the purchase of the estate which had been presented to the President by his admirers. And I suppose it was at just about the time of my proposed visit to him that he was engaged in the wholesale plundering of the *Osthilfe* funds which he regarded as a reasonable *quid pro quo,* which helped to destroy the government of Herr Brüning, and thus to inaugurate the triumph of the National Socialists. Today I would give much to know what kind of conversation went on in Herr Oldenburg-Januschau's house that summer.

My refusal of his suggestion depressed the Baron; he had hoped that after visiting Herr Oldenburg-Januschau I would rejoin them at Boguslavitz. He seemed genuinely upset at the idea that I must leave, but he recovered his spirits when he came to the conclusion that, since I would not change my mind, some very special farewell party must be arranged for me. For a few days he was unable to decide what form it should take; his sunburned forehead, above the straight fine Prussian nose, was furrowed with his effort to devise something that would really be good enough for me. Then one morning he cried out happily : "We'll go to see Felix!", and I could see from the faces of the family that at last the Baron had found the perfect solution to his problem. *"Grossartig!"* cried Fritz; the others smiled with delight at the mere idea of the pleasure the Baron was going to procure for me.

Felix it appeared was the Baron's cousin, Graf Felix Waldstein, who owned an estate some distance away from Boguslavitz. He was, the Baron assured me, a perfectly delightful person, though recently he had become somewhat of a recluse because of the disasters and evils which had come upon Germany as the result of her defeat. He had handed over the management of his estate to a bailiff, and lived alone as an *Einsiedler,* or pioneer, in a cabin he had built for himself in one of his own forests, where he devoted himself to ornithology and botany and only at rare intervals encountered any of his fellow-men. But in the depths of his retirement he retained one distinction which seemed to me quite fabulously improbable; he held the European record for duck-shooting. And in spite of having abjured a world in which a German Kaiser had been forced to abdicate, it appeared that Graf Felix still occasionally welcomed a visit from relatives and friends. "He will like to see you," the Baron said confidently, as if his description of his cousin showed quite clearly how much we had in common.

Sofort anrufen! shouted the Baron to Fritz. He was so struck by the brilliance of his idea that he was in a fever to leave at once. It was typical of him that he should have chosen this expedition as his last particular parting gift to me. Though he knew how incompetent I was with a gun, how badly I rode, he could not disabuse himself of the idea that somewhere inside me was concealed an English country gentleman, who spent his days in hunting, shooting, and fishing and in the evenings retired to his library to drink port and read Houston Stewart Chamberlain.

But the Baron had to restrain his impatience. It appeared that Graf Felix, in his wilderness, was engaged in writing a philosophical treatise on the psyche of flowers, birds, and plants, and that his train of thought was so absorbing at the moment that it could not be interrupted; he would welcome a visit, in particular because of *the Englishman*, but he would not be free to receive us until the very day before I was due to leave for England. This information, reported by Fritz after a telephone conversation with Graf Felix, provoked a flood of speculation among the ladies of Boguslavitz; they could not quite believe that it was philosophy which was occupying him in the depths of his forest. "If only he would marry," they sighed; "he is so handsome." But the Baron swept all this aside as womanly chatter. It seemed to him quite natural that the holder of the European record for duck-shooting should be preoccupied with philosophy, and he ordained that we should leave Boguslavitz on the appointed day, taking my luggage with us, and that after visiting Felix we should drive direct to the station at Breslau in time to catch my train.

VII

So early one morning the Baron, Fritz and I set out in the Adler and drove wildly and dangerously to Graf Felix's estate about a hundred miles away. The Baron and Fritz stood up as we drove, their guns at the ready to annihilate any cats that crossed our path. I forget what our bag was that day, but they shot several. I was fascinated by the way in which the animals seemed to disintegrate completely on the impact of the shot. At one moment the dark sleek body of the cat filled a given area of space; at the next, there was nothing there. But these isolated acts of slaughter were as nothing compared with the holocaust of game that took place on our arrival. Graf Felix had so far transcended his misanthropy, and surmounted his philosophical difficulties, that he had invited a few other friends to join us. They seemed to have driven immense distances in order to enjoy the privilege and the pleasure of meeting Graf Felix, but once having arrived they seemed intent on blazing away with their guns until every form of animal life in Silesia had been destroyed.

The sound of their guns deafened and confused me. I have a memory now only of a group of tall, slender men, long-headed, long-nosed, who all seemed to be of the same physical type, dressed in belted jackets with fur collars and in heavy boots, which seemed somehow to emphasize the military air with which they carried themselves. They moved stiffly, like soldiers. They spoke in hard, clipped Prussian accents, and their very sentences seemed to aim at the same ideal of style as Stendhal's, a style that should be *soldatesque*. Their long, narrow heads, with the prominent bones, suggested some fine animal which is both finely bred and savage and for once I almost began to understand Fritz's extravagant rhapsodies about what he called "the Hohenzollern type". They were immensely polite to me and I had the distinct sensation that on the slightest provocation they would have cut my throat or shot me in the back.

I remember also how damp and quiet it was in the forest and on the fringe of the marshes in the evening, and again in the dawn, with the cold mist circling round our ankles and in the east the first flush of dawn beginning to climb into the sky. Waiting there, among the reeds on the edge of the marsh, for the guns to fire and momentarily destroy the silence until it as suddenly returned again, I watched the slender figures of my companions and had an acute melancholy sense of the vast monotonous distances surrounding us and the huge sky which overreached us. I say melancholy, not only because of the mysterious silence of the forest, the cold, bleak breeze that blew across the marsh, but because I and my companions seemed pitifully small and impotent amid their immensities. I felt as if I were in the company of the disinherited, of men who had lost everything and would waste their own lives and the lives of a million others in the attempt to recover what had never really belonged to them.

In part this feeling may have been an effect of the conversation in Graf Felix's cabin the previous night. When night had fallen, we had eaten a vast cold supper washed down with wine and beer and schnapps; I received the impression that Graf Felix's solitude was not quite as complete as it seemed. His cabin was built of logs, on a pattern familiar to Germans from the novels of Karl May; it had one long room which served as sitting-room and dining-room, a study filled with his specimens and books, and two small bedrooms. After supper we sat in his study and drank huge quantities of brandy and schnapps. The room filled with cigar smoke. I was tired after the long day in the open air, drowsy with food and drink, indeed I suppose half tipsy. I sank into a kind of torpor in which I was only half conscious of the conversation that went on around me until late into the night, indeed it was almost dawn, and time to take to the fields and the forest once again.

I heard the Baron repeat his denunciations of the politicians in Berlin, and his familiar refrain : *we must put an end to all that*. I heard Graf Felix, melancholy and yet passionate, deliver a long soliloquy, which I only half understood, on the necessity for Germany to return to a more simple and primitive way of life, to live as the plants and animals do, by nature and by instinct, which apparently implied that the working classes should recognize a hierarchical order and a principle of authority in the organization of society. Apparently, also, the secret and mysterious life of nature, to which Germany should revert, required a periodical blood-letting in the state.

Such thoughts were too deep for me, especially because, for the others, who enthusiastically agreed with them, they seemed to lead to extremely practical conclusions; as for instance, that the salvation of Germany was dependent upon a thorough liquidation of all the existing political parties and a restoration of the Prussian virtues of probity, self-sacrifice, and military efficiency. The programme they proclaimed seemed to me both confused and impractical; certainly it never occurred to me that one day it would be put into practice, though with a brutality which I am sure my companions of that evening would have found distasteful.

As the evening wore on, politics gave way to reminiscences, of the war, of the *Stosstrupps* and the Argonne, of the *Freikorps* and the Balticum, episodes in history that had played no part in our Oxford studies of the war and its aftermath; but to these men they represented some ideal of soldierly violence which had been betrayed and degraded by Weimar. And from this they went on to telling soldiers' stories and singing soldiers' songs, tears in their eyes as they recalled one act of violence after another; until in my eyes, tired and confused as I was, they began to take on the air of drunken conspirators, plotting some revenge of unimaginable savagery which would satisfy all their feelings of hatred, bitterness, and humiliation. But by now their faces seemed so blurred and vague, their voices so distant, the cigar smoke hung so heavily in the cramped book-lined little room, the words they uttered seemed so improbably sinister, that I felt as if I had entered a world of fantasy and dream, that nothing I heard that evening could possibly have any relevance to the world to which I would wake in the morning. I seemed to be in one of those nightmares which never reach the ultimate revelation of evil because even as one horror opens on to another one can still say to oneself reassuringly : "It's all right; it's only a dream."

And indeed when I awoke in the morning, and as we walked the forest, and as we drove back to Breslau, I could not believe that my memories of the previous night were anything but the products of an over-excited imagination, that the improbable scraps of conversation which recurred to me, the sudden glimpse of a violent gesture seen through a haze of cigar smoke, had any basis in fact. I must have been drunk, I thought, I must have fallen asleep, I must have been dreaming; they could not really have said such things. So that when at last, on Breslau station, the Baron finally embraced me with tears in his eyes and I boarded the train for Berlin, my most vivid memory of my visit to Silesia was of something which, as it seemed to me, had never really happened at all.

VIII

How could I have known that I would never see any of them again? that their dreams of revenge would be realized in a form that exceeded their most violent imaginings, and that in the realization they would suffer even worse humiliations than those on which they brooded so intensely? In today's paper I read that the large estates in Silesia, having been broken up after the war, then communized, are now being broken up again, because the peasants are refusing to work the land; it gives me a shock to think that one of these estates is Boguslavitz, and I wonder what has happened to the Baron's estate railway, of which he was so proud, and whether the corn still stretches away as far as the eye can see. In the same way it gives me a shock to look beside me at the photograph of the Baron which I still possess, at the short straight nose and high cheekbones and the firm and smiling mouth under the little grey moustache; and I wonder at precisely what moment, and under what circumstances, he and his family succumbed to the disaster which overcame them. I only know that under the National Socialists, the Baron, still clinging to the principles of that "good old gentleman" Graf Westarp, was confined to his estate; but though he survived the displeasure of the National Socialists, he did not survive their defeat. And I wonder if he was fortunate enough to die or be killed, or whether in some Asiatic prison-camp he still lives to discourse on the virtues of being a Prussian.

I never went back to Boguslavitz. And when I returned to Oxford in the autumn for the Michaelmas term I did not boast about my experiences in Germany. My friends who also returned from Germany after the vacation came back with far more interesting stories. They had been to the Rhineland and to Munich and to Hamburg and Berlin and Bayreuth; they had been to the theatre, had met artists and writers, had had love affairs and attended political demonstrations; and all they had seen and done had given them an even greater enthusiasm for the progress of social democracy and for the free air and freer culture of Germany. Who could doubt, on such evidence, that Germany was approaching a crisis in her affairs that would gloriously inaugurate the revolution? All this seems difficult to believe now. To us it seemed obvious; and under such conditions what possible importance or significance could I or anyone else attach to Boguslavitz, or to the Reichendorfs, who seemed in retrospect both dull and slightly absurd? How could anyone believe that those ridiculous political fantasies, compounded of Nietzsche and Houston Stewart

Chamberlain, were to have far more effect on the future of Germany than the complicated and refined theoretical structure elaborated by Marxists and Socialists?

I certainly did not believe it; I gladly and passionately believed the opposite. Like many others whose education had been almost exclusively literary, I had a wonderful faculty for ignoring what lay under my nose and clinging to purely verbal constructions for which I possessed no empirical evidence whatever. I lived in a glorious state of euphoria in which facts were only valuable when they proved what one wanted to believe. It never occurred to me that at Boguslavitz, in the Baron and in Fritz, in Graf Felix and his friends, I had been introduced to a type of political thinking which was going to determine my own life as well as theirs, that the conspiracy which had seemed so dreamlike and unreal in Graf Felix's log cabin was in fact a real conspiracy which had its roots throughout Germany; that it was Weimar which was the dream. It was only later, when Weimar had been liquidated in shameful defeat and disaster, that I began to think again about my visit to Boguslavitz and wonder whether there I had not stumbled across a secret which might help to explain some of the events which followed Weimar's collapse.

APRIL 1956

33

MARY McCARTHY

My Confession

EVERY AGE HAS a keyhole to which its eye is pasted. Spicy court-memoirs, the lives of gallant ladies, recollections of an ex-nun, a monk's confession, an atheist's repentance, true-to-life accounts of prostitution and bastardy gave our ancestors a penny peep into the forbidden room. In our own day, this type of sensational fact-fiction is being produced largely by ex-Communists. Public curiosity shows an almost prurient avidity for the details of political defloration, and the memoirs of ex-Communists have an odd resemblance to the confessions of a white slave. Two shuddering climaxes, two rendezvous with destiny, form the poles between which these narratives vibrate : the first describes the occasion when the subject was seduced by Communism; the second shows him wrestling himself from the demon embrace. Variations on the form are possible. Senator McCarthy, for example, in his book, *McCarthyism, the Fight for America*, uses a tense series of flashbacks to dramatize his encounter with Communism : the country lies passive in Communism's clasp; he is given a tryst with destiny in the lonely Arizona hills, where, surrounded by "real Americans without any synthetic sheen", he attains the decision that will send him down the long marble corridors to the Senate Caucus Room to bare the shameful commerce.

The diapason of choice plays, like movie music, round today's apostle to the Gentiles : Whittaker Chambers on a bench and, in a reprise, awake all night, at a dark window, facing the void. These people, unlike ordinary beings, are shown the true course during a lightning storm of revelation, on the road to Damascus. And their decisions are lonely decisions, silhouetted against a background of public incomprehension and hostility.

I object. I have read the reminiscences of Mr. Chambers and Miss Bentley. I too have had a share in the political movements of our day, and my experience cries out against their experience. It is not the facts I balk at—I have never been an espionage agent—but the studio atmosphere of sublimity and purpose that enfolds the facts and the chief actor. When Whittaker Chambers is mounted on his tractor, or Elizabeth Bentley, alone, is meditating her decision in a white New England Church, I have the sense that they are on location and that, at any moment, the director will call "Cut". It has never been like that for me; events have never waited, like extras, while I toiled to make up my mind between good and evil. In fact, I have never known these mental convulsions, which appear quite strange to me when I read about them, even when I do not question the author's sincerity.

Is it really so difficult to tell a good action from a bad one? I think one usually knows right away or a moment afterwards, in a horrid flash of regret. And when one genuinely hesitates—or at least it is so in my case— it is never about anything of importance, but about perplexing trivial things, such as whether to have fish or meat for dinner, or whether to take the bus or subway to reach a certain destination, or whether to wear the beige or the green. The "great" decisions—those I can look back on pensively and say, "That was a turning-point"—have been made without my awareness. Too late to do anything about it, I discover that I have chosen. And this is particularly striking when the choice has been political or historic. For me, in fact, the mark of the historic is the nonchalance with which it picks up an individual and deposits him in a trend, like a house playfully moved by a tornado. My own experience with Communism prompts me to relate it, just because it had this inadvertence that seems to me lacking in the true confessions of reformed Communists. Like Stendhal's hero, who took part in something confused and disarrayed and insignificant that he later learned was the Battle of Waterloo, I joined the anti-Communist movement without meaning to and only found out afterwards, through others, the meaning or "name" assigned to what I had done. This occurred in the late fall of 1936.

Three years before, I had graduated from college—Vassar, the same college Elizabeth Bentley had gone to—without having suffered any fracture of my political beliefs or moral frame. All through college, my official political philosophy was royalism; though I was not much interested in politics, it irritated me to be told that "you could not turn the clock back". But I did not see much prospect for kingship in the United States (unless you imported one, like the Swedes), and, *faute de mieux,* I awarded my sympathies to the Democratic Party, which I tried to look on as the party of the Southern patriciate. At the same time, I had an aversion to Republicans—an instinctive feeling that had been with me since I was a child of eight pedalling my wagon up and down our cement driveway and howling, "Hurray for Cox", at the Republican neighbours who passed by. I disliked business men and business attitudes partly, I think, because I came from a professional (though Republican) family and had picked up a disdain for business men as being beneath us, in education and general culture. And the anti-Catholic prejudice against Al Smith during the 1928 election, the tinkling amusement at Mrs. Smith's vulgarity, democratized me a little in spite of myself : I was won by Smith's plebeian charm, the big coarse nose, and rubbery politician's smile.

But this same distrust of uniformity made me shrink, in 1932, from the sloppily dressed socialist girls at college who paraded for Norman Thomas and tirelessly argued over "cokes"; their eager fellowship and scrawled placards and heavy personalities bored me—there was something, to my mind, deeply athletic about this socialism. It was a kind of political hockey played by big, gaunt, dyspeptic girls in pants. It startled me a little, there-fore, to learn that in an election poll taken of the faculty, several of my favourite teachers had voted for Thomas; in them, the socialist faith appeared rather charming, I decided—a gracious and attractive oddity, like the English Ovals they gave you when you came for tea. That was the winter Hitler was coming to power and, hearing of the anti-Jewish atroci-ties, I had a flurry of political indignation. I wrote a prose-poem that dealt, in a mixed-up way, with the Polish Corridor and the Jews. This poem was so unlike me that I did not know whether to be proud of it or ashamed of it when I saw it in a college magazine. At this period, we were interested in surrealism and automatic writing, and the poem had a certain renown because it had come out of my interior without much sense or order, just the way automatic writing was supposed to do. But there my political development stopped.

The depression was closer to home; in New York I used to see apple-sellers on the street corners, and, now and then, a bread-line, but I had a very thin awareness of mass poverty. The depression was too close to home to awaken anything but curiosity and wonder— the feelings of a child con-fronted with a death in the family. I was conscious of the suicides of stock-brokers and business men, and of the fact that some of my friends had to go on scholarships and had their dress allowances curtailed, while their mothers gaily turned to doing their own cooking. To most of us at Vassar, I think, the depression was chiefly an upper-class phenomenon.

My real interests were literary. In a paper for my English Renaissance seminar, I noted a resemblance between the Elizabethan puritan pundits and the school of Marxist criticism that was beginning to pontificate about proletarian literature in the *New Masses*. I disliked the modern fanatics, cold, envious little clerics, equally with the insufferable and ridiculous Gabriel Harvey—Cambridge pedant and friend of Spenser—who tried to introduce the rules of Latin quantity into English verse and vilified a true poet who had died young, in squalor and misery. I really hated absolutism and officiousness of any kind (I preferred my kings martyred) and was pleased to be able to recognize a Zeal-of-the-Land-Busy in proletarian dress. And it was through a novel that I first learned, in my senior year, about the Sacco-Vanzetti case. The discovery that two innocent men had been executed only a few years back while I, oblivious, was in boarding school, gave me a disturbing shock. The case was still so near that I was tantalized by a feeling that it was not too late to do something—try still another avenue, if Governor Fuller and the Supreme Court obdurately would not be moved. An unrectified case of injustice has a terrible way of lingering, restlessly, in the social atmosphere like an unfinished equation. I went on to the Mooney case, which vexed not only my sense of equity but my sense of plausibility—how was it possible for the prosecution to lie so, in broad daylight, with the whole world watching?

When in May, 1933, however, before graduation, I went down to apply for a job at the old *New Republic* offices, I was not drawn there by the magazine's editorial policy—I hardly knew what it was—but because the book-review section seemed to me to possess a certain elegance and independence of thought that would be hospitable to a critical spirit like me. And I was badly taken aback when the book-review editor, to whom I had been shunted—there was no job—puffed his pipe and remarked that he would give me a review if I could show him that I was either a genius or starving. "I'm not starving," I said quickly; I knew I was not a genius and I was not pleased by the suggestion that I would be taking bread from other people's mouths. I did not think this a fair criterion and in a moment I said so. In reply, he put down his pipe, shrugged, reached out for the material I had brought with me, and half-promised, after an assaying glance, to send me a book. My notice finally appeared; it was not very good, but I did not know that and was elated. Soon I was reviewing novels and biographies for both the *New Republic* and the *Nation* and preening myself on the connection. Yet, whenever I entered the *New Republic*'s waiting-room, I was seized with a feeling of nervous guilt towards the shirt-sleeved editors upstairs and their busy social conscience, and, above all, towards the shabby young men who were waiting too and who had, my bones told me, a better claim than I to the book I hoped to take away with me. They looked poor, pinched, scholarly, and supercilious, and I did not know which of these qualities made me, with my clicking high heels and fall "ensemble", seem more out of place.

I cannot remember the moment when I ceased to air my old royalist convictions and stuffed them away in an inner closet as you do a dress or an ornament that you perceive strikes the wrong note. It was probably at the time when I first became aware of Communists as a distinct entity. I had known about them, certainly, in college, but it was not until I came to

New York that I began to have certain people, celebrities, pointed out to me as Communists and to turn my head to look at them, wonderingly. I had no wish to be one of them, but the fact that they were there—an un-reckoned factor—made my own political opinions take on a protective coloration. This process was accelerated by my marriage—a week after graduation—to an actor and playwright who was in some ways very much like me. He was the son of a Minnesota normal school administrator who had been the scapegoat in an academic scandal that had turned him out of his job and reduced him, for a time, when my husband was nine or ten, to selling artificial limbs and encyclopædia sets from door to door. My husband still brooded over his father's misfortune, like Hamlet or a charac-ter in Ibsen, and this had given his nature a sardonic twist that inclined him to behave like a paradox—to follow the mode and despise it, live in a Beekman Place apartment while lacking the money to buy groceries, play bridge with society couples and poker with the stage electricians, dress in the English style and carry a walking-stick while wearing a red necktie.

He was an odd-looking man, prematurely bald, with a tense, arresting figure, a broken nose, a Standard English accent, and wry, circumflexed eyebrows. There was something about him both baleful and quizzical; whenever he stepped on to the stage he had the ironic air of a symbol. This curious appearance of his disqualified him for most Broadway roles; he was too young for character parts and too bald for juveniles. Yet just this disturbing ambiguity—a Communist painter friend did a drawing of him that brought out a resemblance to Lenin—suited the portentous and equivocal atmosphere of left-wing drama. He smiled dryly at Marxist terminology, but there was social anger in him. During the years we were married, the only work he found was in productions of "social" signifi-cance. He played for the Theatre Union in *The Sailors of Cattaro,* about a mutiny in the Austrian fleet, and in *Black Pit*, about coal-miners; the following year, he was in *Winterset* and Archibald MacLeish's *Panic*—the part of a blind man in both cases. He wrote revue sketches and unproduced plays, in a mocking, despairing, but none the less radical vein; he directed the book of a musical called *Americana* that featured the song, "Brother, Can You Spare a Dime?" I suppose there was something in him of both the victim and the leader, an undertone of totalitarianism; he was very much interested in the mythic qualities of leadership and talked briskly about a Farmer-Labour party in his stage English accent. Notions of the superman and the genius flickered across his thoughts. But this led him, as it happened, away from politics, into sheer personal vitalism, and it was only in plays that he entered "at the head of a mob". In personal life he was very winning, but that is beside the point here.

The point is that we both, through our professional connections, began to take part in a left-wing life, to which we felt superior, which we laughed at, but which nevertheless was influencing us without our being aware of it. If the composition of the body changes every seven years, the composition of our minds during the seven years of our engagement and marriage had slowly changed, so that though our thoughts looked the same to us, inside we had been altered, like an old car which has had part after part replaced in it under the hood.

We wore our rue with a difference; we should never have considered joining the Communist Party. We were not even fellow-travellers; we did not sign petitions or join "front" groups. We were not fools, after all, and were no more deceived by the League against War and Fascism, say, than by a Chinatown bus with a carload of shills aboard. It was part of our metropolitan sophistication to know the truth about Communist fronts. We accepted the need for social reform, but we declined to draw the "logical" inference that the Communists wanted us to draw from this. We argued with the comrades backstage in the dressing-rooms and at literary cocktail parties; I was attacked by a writer in the *New Masses*. We knew about Lovestoneites and Trotskyites, even while we were ignorant of the labour theory of value, the law of uneven development, the theory of permanent revolution *v.* socialism in one country, and so on. "Lovestone is a Lovestoneite!" John wrote in wax on his dressing-room mirror, and on his door in the old Civic Repertory he put up a sign: "Through these portals pass some of the most beautiful tractors in the Ukraine."

The comrades shrugged and laughed, a little unwillingly. They knew we were not hostile but merely unserious, politically. The comrades who knew us best used to assure us that our sophistication was just an armour; underneath, we must care for the same things they did. They were mistaken, I am afraid. Speaking for myself, I cannot remember a single broad altruistic emotion visiting me during that period—the kind of emotion the simpler comrades, with their shining eyes and exalted faces, seemed to have in copious secretion. And yet it was true: we were not hostile. We marched in May Day parades, just for the fun of it, and sang, "Hold the Fort, for We are Coming", and *"Bandiera Rossa"*, and "The Internationale", though we always bellowed "The *Socialist* International shall be the human race," instead of "The International Soviet", to pique the Communists in our squad. We took part in evening clothes in a consumers' walkout at the Waldorf to support a waiters' strike; the Communists had nothing to do with this and we grew very excited (we did have negative feelings) when another young literary independent was arrested and booked. During a strike at a department store, John joined the sympathetic picketing and saw two of his fellow-actors carried off in the Black Maria; they missed a matinée and set off a controversy about what was the *first* responsibility of a Communist playing in a proletarian drama. We went once or twice to a class for actors in Marxism, just to see what was up; we went to a debate on Freud and/or Marx, to a debate on the execution of the hundred and four White Guards following Kirov's assassination.

Most ex-Communists nowadays, when they write their autobiographies or testify before congressional committees, are at pains to point out that their actions were very, very bad and their motives very, very good. I would say the reverse of myself, though without the intensives. I see no reason to disavow my actions, which were perfectly all right, but my motives give me a little embarrassment, and just because I cannot disavow them : that fevered, contentious, trivial show-off in the May Day parade is still recognizably me.

We went to dances at Webster Hall and took our uptown friends. We went to parties to raise money for the sharecroppers, for the Theatre Union, for the *New Masses*. These parties generally took place in a borrowed apartment, often a sculptor's or commercial artist's studio; you paid for your drinks, which were dispensed at a long, wet table; the liquor was dreadful; the glasses were small, and there was never enough ice. Long-haired men in turtle-necked sweaters marched into the room in processions and threw their overcoats on the floor, against the wall, and sat on them; they were only artists and bit-actors, but they gave these affairs a look of gangsterish menace, as if the room were guarded by the goons of the future. On couches with wrinkled slipcovers, little spiky-haired girls, like spiders, dressed in peasant blouses and carapaced with Mexican jewellery, made voracious passes at baby-faced juveniles; it was said that they "did it for the Party", as a recruiting effort. Vague, soft-faced old women with dust mops of whitish hair wandered benevolently about seeking a listener; on a sofa against a wall, like a deity, sat a bearded scion of an old Boston family, stiff as a post. All of us, generally, became very drunk; the atmosphere was horribly sordid, with cigarette burns on tables, spilled drinks, ashes everywhere, people passed out on the bed with the coats or necking, you could not be sure which. Nobody cared what happened because there was no host or hostess. The fact that a moneyed person had been simple enough to lend the apartment seemed to make the guests want to desecrate it, to show that they were exercising not a privilege but a right.

Obviously, I must have hated these parties, but I went to them, partly because I was ashamed of my own squeamishness, and partly because I had a curiosity about the Communist men I used to see there, not the actors or writers, but the higher-ups, impresarios and theoreticians—dark, smooth-haired owls with large white lugubrious faces and glasses. These

were the spiritual directors of the Communist cultural celebrities and they
moved about at these parties like so many monks or abbés in a worldly
salon. I had always liked to argue with the clergy, and I used to argue with
these men, who always had the air, as they stood with folded arms, of
listening not to a disagreement but to a confession. Whenever I became
tight, I would bring up (oh, *vino veritas*) the Tsar and his family. I did not
see why they all had had to be killed—the Tsar himself, yes, perhaps, and
the Tsarina, but not the young girls and the children. I knew the answer,
of course (the young Tsarevitch or one of his sisters might have served as
a rallying point for the counter-revolutionary forces), but still I gazed hopefully into these docents' faces, seeking a trace of scruple or compassion. But
I saw only a marmoreal astuteness. The question was of bourgeois origin,
they said with finality.

The next morning I was always bitterly ashamed. I had let these omniscient men see the real me underneath, and the other me squirmed and
gritted her teeth and muttered, Never, never, *never* again. And yet they
had not convinced me—there was the paradox. The superiority I felt to the
Communists I knew had, for me at any rate, good grounding; it was based
on their lack of humour, their fanaticism, and the slow drip of cant that
thickened their utterance like a nasal catarrh. *And yet* I was tremendously
impressed by them. They made me feel pretty shallow; they had, shall I
say, a daily ugliness in their life that made my pretty life tawdry. I think
all of us who moved in that ambience must have felt something of the
kind, even while we laughed at them. When John and I, for instance,
would say of a certain actor, "He is a Party member," our voices always
contained a note of respect. This respect might be mixed with pity, as
when we saw some blue-eyed young profile, fresh from his fraternity
and his C average, join up because a sleazy girl had persuaded him. The
literary Communists I sincerely despised because I was able to judge the
quality of the work they published and see their dishonesty and contradictions; even so, when I beheld them in person, at a Webster Hall dance, I
was troubled and felt perhaps I had wronged them—perhaps there was
something in them that my vision could not perceive, as some eyes cannot
perceive colour.

People sometimes say that they envied the Communists because they were
so "sure". In my case, this was not exactly it; I was sure, too, intellectually
speaking, as far as I went. That is, I had a clear mind and was reasonably
honest, while many of the Communists I knew were pathetically fogged
up. In any case, my soul was not particularly hot for certainties.

And yet in another way I did envy the Communists, or, to be more
accurate, wonder whether I ought to envy them. I could not, I saw, be

a Communist because I was not "made that way". Hence, to be a Communist was to possess a sort of privilege. And this privilege, like all privileges, appeared to be a sort of power. Any form of idiocy or aberration can confer this distinction on its owner, at least in our age, which aspires to a "total" experience; in the thirties it was the Communists who seemed fearsomely to be the happy few, not because they had peace or certitude but because they were a mutation—a mutation that threatened, in the words of their own anthem, to become the human race.

There was something arcane in every Communist, and the larger this area was the more we respected him. That was why the literary Communists, who operated in the open, doing the hatchet work on artists' reputations, were held in such relatively low esteem. An underground worker rated highest with us; next were the theoreticians and oracles; next were the activists, who mostly worked, we heard, on the waterfront. Last came the rank and file, whose work consisted of making speeches, distributing leaflets, attending party and fraction meetings, joining front organizations, marching in parades and demonstrations. These people we dismissed as uninteresting not so much because their work was routine but because the greater part of it was visible. In the same way, among individual comrades, we looked up to those who were close-lipped and stern about their beliefs and we disparaged the more voluble members—the forensic little actors who tried to harangue us in the dressing-rooms. The idea of a double life was what impressed us : the more talkative comrades seemed to have only one life, like us; but even they, we had to remind ourselves, had a secret annex to their personality, which was signified by their Party name. It is hard not to respect somebody who has an alias.

Of fellow-travellers, we had a very low opinion. People who were not willing to "go the whole way" filled us with impatient disdain. The only fellow-travellers who merited our notice were those of whom it was said : the Party prefers that they remain on the outside. I think some fellow-travellers circulated such stories about themselves deliberately, in order to appear more interesting. There was another type of fellow-traveller who let it be known that they stayed out of the Party because of some tiny doctrinal difference with Marxism. This tiny difference magnified them enormously in their own eyes and allowed them to bear gladly the accusation of cowardice. I knew one such person very well—a spruce, ingratiating swain, the heir to a large fortune—and I think it was not cowardice but a kind of pietistic vanity. He felt he cut more of a figure if he seemed to be doing the Party's dirty work gratuitously, without compulsion, like an oblate.

In making these distinctions (which were the very distinctions the Party made), I had no idea, of course, that I was allowing myself to be influenced by the Party in the field where I was most open to suspicion—the field of social snobbery. Yet in fact I was being deterred from forming any political opinions of my own, lest I find I was that despised article, a "mere" socialist or watery liberal, in the same way that a young snob coming to college and seeing who the "right" people are will strive to make no friends rather than be caught with the wrong ones.

For me, the Communist Party was *the* party, and even though I did not join it, I prided myself on knowing that it was the pinnacle. It is only now that I see the social component in my attitude. At the time, I simply supposed that I was being clear-sighted and logical. I used to do research and typing for a disgruntled middle-aged man who was a freak for that day—an anti-Communist Marxist—and I was bewildered by his anti-Party bias. While we were drinking hot tea, Russian style, from glasses during the intervals of our work, I would try to show him his mistake. "Don't you think it's rather futile," I expostulated, "to criticize the Party the way you do, from the outside? After all, it's the *only* working-class Party, and if *I* were a Marxist I would join it and try to reform it." Snorting, he would raise his small deep-set blue eyes and stare at me and then try patiently to show me that there was no democracy in the Party. I listened disbelievingly. It seemed to me that it would just be a question of converting first one comrade and then another to your point of view till gradually you had achieved a majority. And when my employer assured me that they would throw you out if you tried that, my twenty-three-year-old wisdom cocked an eyebrow. I thought I knew what was the trouble: he was a pathologically lazy man and his growling criticisms of the Party were simply a form of malingering, like the aches and pains he used to manufacture to avoid working on an article. A real revolutionary who was not afraid of exertion would get into the Party and fight.

The curious idea that being critical of the Party was a compelling reason for joining it must have been in the air, for the same argument was brought to bear on me in the summer of 1936—the summer my husband and I separated and that I came closest to the gravitational pull of the Communist world. Just before I went off to Reno, there was a week in June when I stayed in Southampton with the young man I was planning to marry and a little Communist organizer in an old summer house furnished with rattan and wicker and Chinese matting and mother-of-pearl and paper fans. We had come there for a purpose. The little organizer had just been assigned a car—a battered old Ford roadster that had been turned over to the Party for the use of some poor organizer; it may have been the very car that figured in the Hiss case. My fiancé, who had known him for years, perhaps from the peace movement, was going to teach him to drive. We were all at a pause in our lives. The following week our friend was supposed to take the car to California and do propaganda work among the migrant fruit-pickers; I was to go to Reno; my fiancé, a vivacious young bachelor, was to conquer his habits of idleness and buckle down to a serious job. Those seven days, therefore, had a special, still quality, like the days of a novena you make in your childhood; a part of each of them was set aside for the Party's task. It was early in June; the musty house that belonged to my fiancé's parents still had the winter-smell of mice and old wood and rust and mildew. The summer colony had not yet arrived; the red flag, meaning that it was dangerous to swim, flew daily on the beach; the roads were nearly empty. Every afternoon we would take the old car, canvas flapping, to a deserted stretch of straight road in the dunes, where the neophyte could take the wheel.

He was a large-browed, dwarfish man in his late thirties, with a deep widow's peak, a bristly short moustache, and a furry western accent—rather simple, open-natured, and cheerful, the sort of person who might have been a small-town salesman or itinerant newspaperman. There was an energetic, hopeful innocence about him that was not confined to his political convictions—he could *not* learn to drive. Every day the same thing happened; he would settle his frail yet stocky figure trustingly in the driver's seat, grip the wheel, step on the starter, and lose control of the car, which would shoot ahead in first or backward in reverse for a few perilous feet till my fiancé turned off the ignition; Ansel always mistook the gas for the brake and forgot to steer while he was shifting gears.

It was clear that he would never be able to pass the driver's test at the county seat. In the evenings, to make up to him for his oncoming disappointment (we smiled when he said he could start without a licence), we encouraged him to talk about the Party and tried to take an intelligent interest. We would sit by the lamp and drink and ask questions, while he smoked his short pipe and from time to time took a long draught from his highball, like a man alone musing in a chair.

And finally one night, in the semi-dark, he knocked out his pipe and said to me : "You're very critical of the Party. Why don't you join it?" A thrill went through me, but I laughed, as when somebody has proposed to you and you are not sure whether they are serious. "I don't think I'd make very good material." "You're wrong," he said gravely. "You're just the kind of person the Party needs. You're young and idealistic and independent." I broke in : "I thought independence was just what the Party didn't want." "The Party needs criticism," he said. "But it needs it from the inside. If people like you who agree with its main objectives would come in and criticize, we wouldn't be so narrow and sectarian." "You admit the Party is narrow?" exclaimed my fiancé. "Sure, I admit it," said Ansel, grinning. "But it's partly the fault of people like Mary who won't come in and broaden us." And he confided that he himself made many of the same criticisms I did, but he made them from within the Party, and so could get himself listened to. "The big problem of the American Party," said Ansel, puffing at his pipe, "is the smallness of the membership. People say we're ruled from Moscow; I've never seen any sign of it. But let's suppose it's true, for the sake of argument. This just means that the American Party isn't big enough yet to stand on its own feet. A big, indigenous party couldn't be ruled from Moscow. The will of the members would have to rule it, just as their dues and contributions would support it." "That's where I come in, I suppose?" I said, teasing. "That's where you come in," he calmly agreed. He turned to my fiancé. "Not you," he said. "You won't have the time to give to it. But for Mary I think it would be an interesting experiment."

An interesting experiment . . . I let the thought wander through my mind. The subject recurred several times, by the lamplight, though with no particular urgency. Ansel, I thought (and still think), was speaking sincerely and partly in my own interest, almost as a spectator, as if he would be diverted to see how I worked out in the Party. All this gave me quite a new sense of Communism and of myself too; I had never looked upon my character in such a favourable light. And as a beneficiary of Ansel's charity, I felt somewhat ashamed of the very doubt it raised : the suspicion that he might be blind to the real facts of inner Party life. I could admire where I could not follow, and, studying Ansel, I decided that I admired the Communists and would probably be one, if I were the person he thought me. Which I was afraid I was not. For me, such a wry conclusion is always uplifting, and I had the feeling that I mounted in understanding when Sunday morning came and I watched Ansel pack his sturdy suitcase and his briefcase full of leaflets into the old roadster. He had never yet driven more than a few yards by himself, and we stood on the front steps to await what was going to happen : he would not be able to get out of the driveway, and we would have to put him on the train and return the car to the Party when we came back to New York. As we watched, the car began to move; it picked up speed and grated into second, holding to the middle of the road as it turned out of the driveway. It hesitated and went into third : Ansel was driving! Through the back window we saw his figure hunched over the wheel; the road dipped and he vanished. We had witnessed a miracle, and we turned back into the house, frightened. All day we sat waiting for the call that would tell us there had been an accident, but the day passed without a sound, and by nightfall we accepted the phenomenon and pictured the little car on the highway, travelling steadily west in one indefatigable thrust, not daring to stop for petrol or refreshment, lest the will of the driver falter.

This parting glimpse of Ansel through the car's back window was, as it turned out, ultimate. Politically speaking, we reached a watershed that summer. The first Moscow trial took place in August. I knew nothing of this event because I was in Reno and did not see the New York papers. Nor did I know that the Party line had veered to the right and that all the fellow-travellers would be voting, not for Browder as I was now prepared to do (if only I remembered to register), but for Roosevelt. Isolated from these developments in the mountain altitudes, I was blossoming, like a lone winter rose overlooked by the frost, into a revolutionary thinker of the pure, uncompromising strain. The detached particles of the past three years' experience suddenly "made sense", and I saw myself as a radical.

"Book Bites Mary," wrote back a surprised literary editor when I sent him, from Reno, a radiant review of a novel about the Paris Commune that ended with the heroine sitting down to read the Communist Manifesto. In Seattle, when I came to stay with my grandparents, I found a strike on and instantly wired the *Nation* to ask if I could cover it. Every night I was off to the Labor Temple or a longshoreman's hall while my grandparents took comfort from the fact that I seemed to be against Roosevelt, the Democrats, and the tsars of the A. F. of L.—they did not quite grasp my explanation, that I was criticizing "from the left".

Right here, I come up against a puzzle : why didn't I take the *next step*? But it is only a puzzle if one thinks of me not as a concrete entity but as a term in a logical operation : you agree with the Communist Party; *ergo*, you join it. I reasoned that way but I did not behave so. There was something in me that capriciously resisted being a term in logic, and the very fact that I cannot elicit any specific reason why I did not join the Party shows that I was never really contemplating it, though I can still hear my own voice, raised very authoritatively at a cafeteria-table at the Central Park Zoo, pointing out to a group of young intellectuals that if we were serious we would join the Communists.

This was in September and I was back in New York. The Spanish Civil War had begun. The pay-as-you-go parties were now all for the Loyalists, and young men were volunteering to go and fight in Spain. I read the paper every morning with tears of exaltation in my eyes, and my sympathies rained equally on Communists, Socialists, Anarchists, and the brave Catholic Basques. My heart was tense and swollen with Popular Front solidarity. I applauded the Lincoln Battalion, protested non-intervention, hurried into Wanamaker's to look for cotton-lace stockings : I was boycotting silk on account of Japan in China. I was careful to smoke only union-made cigarettes; the white package with Sir Walter Raleigh's portrait came proudly out of my pocketbook to rebuke Chesterfields and Luckies.

It was a period of intense happiness; the news from the battlefront was often encouraging and the practice of virtue was surprisingly easy. I moved into a one-room apartment on a crooked street in Greenwich Village and exulted in being poor and alone. I had a part-time job and read manuscripts for a publisher; the very riskiness of my situation was zestful—I had decided not to get married. The first month or so was scarifyingly lonely, but I survived this, and, starting early in November, I began to feel the first stirrings of popularity. A new set of people, rather smart and moneyed, young Communists with a little "name", progressive hosts and modernist hostesses, had discovered me. The fact that I was poor and lived in such a funny little apartment increased the interest felt: I was passed from hand to hand, as a novelty, like Gulliver among the Brobdingnagians. During those first days in November, I was chiefly conscious of what a wonderful time I was starting to have. All this while, I had remained ignorant of the fissure that was opening. Nobody had told me of the trial of Zinoviev and Kamnev—the trial of the sixteen—or of the new trial that was being prepared in Moscow, the trial of Pyatakov and Radek.

Then, one afternoon in November, I was taken to a cocktail party, in honour of Art Young, the old *Masses* cartoonist, whose book, *The Best of Art Young*, was being published that day. It was the first publisher's party I had ever been to, and my immediate sensation was one of disappointment: nearly all these people were strangers and, to me, quite unattractive. Art Young, a white-haired little kewpie, sitting in a corner, was pointed out to me, and I turned a respectful gaze on him, though I had no clear idea who he was or how he had distinguished himself. I presumed he was a veteran Communist, like a number of the stalwarts in the room, survivors of the old *Masses* and the *Liberator*. Their names were whispered to me and I nodded; this seemed to be a commemorative occasion, and the young men hovered in groups around the old men, as if to catch a word for posterity. On the outskirts of certain groups I noticed a few poorly dressed young men, bolder spirits, nervously flexing their lips, framing sentences that would propel them into the conversational centre, like actors with a single line to speak.

The solemnity of these proceedings made me feel terribly ill-at-ease. It was some time before I became aware that it was not just me who was nervous: the whole room was under a constraint. Some groups were avoiding other groups, and now and then an arrow of sarcasm would wing like a sniper's bullet from one conversation to another.

I was standing, rather bleakly, by the refreshment table, when a question was thrust at me: Did I think Trotsky was entitled to a hearing? It was a novelist friend of mine, dimple-faced, shaggy-headed, earnest, with a whole train of people, like a deputation, behind him. Trotsky? I glanced for help at a sour little man I had been talking with, but he merely shrugged. My friend made a beckoning gesture and a circle closed in. What had Trotsky done? Alas, I had to ask. A tumult of voices proffered explanations. My friend raised a hand for silence. Leaning on the table, he supplied the background, speaking very slowly, in his dragging, disconsolate voice, like a school-teacher wearied of his subject. Trotsky, it appeared, had been accused of fostering a counter-revolutionary plot in the Soviet Union—organizing terrorist centres and conspiring with the Gestapo to murder the Soviet leaders. Sixteen old Bolsheviks had confessed and implicated him. It had been in the press since August.

I blushed; everybody seemed to be looking at me strangely. "Where has she *been*?" said a voice. I made a violent effort to take in what had been said. The enormity of the charge dazed me, and I supposed that some sort of poll was being taken and that I was being asked to pronounce on whether Trotsky was guilty or innocent. I could tell from my friend's low, even, melancholy tone that he regarded the charges as derisory. "What do you want me to say?" I protested. "I don't know anything about it." "Trotsky denies the charges," patiently intoned my friend. "He declares it's a GPU fabrication. Do you think he's entitled to a hearing?" My mind cleared. "Why, of course." I laughed—were there people who would say that Trotsky was *not* entitled to a hearing? But my friend's voice tolled a rebuke to this levity. "She says Trotsky is entitled to his day in court."

The sour little man beside me made a peculiar sucking noise. "You disagree?" I demanded, wonderingly. "I'm smart," he retorted. "I don't let anybody ask me. You notice, he doesn't ask me?" "Shut up, George," said my novelist friend impatiently. "I'm asking *her*. One thing more, Mary," he continued gravely. "Do you believe that Trotsky should have the right of asylum?" The right of asylum! I looked for someone to share my amusement—were we in ancient Greece or the Middle Ages? I was sure the U.S. Government would be delighted to harbour such a distinguished foreigner. But nobody smiled back. Everybody watched dispassionately, as for form's sake I assented to the phrasing: yes, Trotsky, in my opinion, was entitled to the right of asylum.

I went home with the serene feeling that all these people were slightly crazy. *Right of asylum, his day in court!*—in a few hours I had forgotten the whole thing.

Four days later I tore open an envelope addressed to me by something that called itself "Committee for the Defence of Leon Trotsky", and idly scanned the contents. "We demand for Leon Trotsky the right of a fair hearing and the right of asylum." Who were these demanders, I wondered, and, glancing down the letterhead, I discovered my own name. I sat down on my unmade studio couch, shaking. How dared they help themselves to my signature? This was the kind of thing the Communists were always being accused of pulling; apparently, Trotsky's admirers had gone to the same school. I had paid so little heed to the incident at the party that a connection was slow to establish itself. Reading over the list of signers, I recognized "names" that had been present there and remembered my novelist-friend going from person to person, methodically polling ...

How were they feeling, I wondered, when they opened their mail this morning? My own feelings were crisp. In two minutes I had decided to withdraw my name and write a note of protest. Trotsky had a right to a hearing, but I had a right to my signature. For even if there had been a legitimate misunderstanding (it occurred to me that perhaps I had been the only person there not to see the import of my answers), nothing I had said committed me to Trotsky's *defence*.

The "decision" was made, but according to my habit I procrastinated. The severe letter I proposed to write got put off till the next day and then the next. Probably I was not eager to offend somebody who had been a good friend to me. Nevertheless, the letter would undoubtedly have been written, had I been left to myself. But within the next forty-eight hours the phone calls began. People whom I had not seen for months or whom I knew very slightly telephoned to advise me to get off the newly formed Committee. These calls were not precisely threatening. Indeed, the caller often sounded terribly weak and awkward, as if he did not like the mission he had been assigned. But they were peculiar. For one thing, they always came after nightfall and sometimes quite late, when I was already in bed. Another thing, there was no real effort at persuasion : the caller stated his purpose in standardized phrases, usually plaintive in tone (the Committee was the tool of reaction, and all liberal people should dissociate themselves from its activities, which were an unwarranted intervention in the domestic affairs of the Soviet Union), and then hung up, almost immediately, before I had a proper chance to answer. Odd too— the voices were not those of my Communist friends but of virtual strangers. These people who admonished me to "think about it" were not people whose individual opinions could have had any weight with me. And when I did think about it, this very fact took on an ominous character : I was not being appealed to personally but impersonally warned.

Behind these phone calls there was a sense of massed power, as if all over the city the Party were wheeling its forces into disciplined formations, like a fleet or an army manœuvring. This, I later found, was true : a systematic telephone campaign was going on to dislodge members from the

Committee. The phone calls generally came after dark and sometimes (especially when the recipient was elderly) in the small hours of the morning. The more prominent signers got anonymous messages and threats.

And in the morning papers and the columns of the liberal magazines I saw the results. During the first week, name after name fell off the Committee's letterhead. Prominent liberals and literary figures issued statements deploring their mistake. And a number of people protested that their names had been used without permission.

There, but for the grace of God, went I, I whispered, awestruck, to myself, hugging my guilty knowledge. Only Heaven—I plainly saw—by making me dilatory had preserved me from joining this sorry band. Here was the occasion when I should have been wrestling with my conscience or standing, floodlit, at the crossroads of choice. But in fact I was only aware that I had had a providential escape. I had been saved from having to decide about the Committee; *I* did not decide it—the Communists with their pressure tactics took the matter out of my hands. We all have an instinct that makes us side with the weak, if we do not stop to reason about it, the instinct that makes a householder shield a wounded fugitive without first conducting an inquiry into the rights and wrongs of his case. Such "decisions" are simple reflexes; they do not require courage; if they did, there would be fewer of them. When I saw what was happening, I rebounded to the defence of the Committee without a single hesitation —it was nobody's business, I felt, how I happened to be on it, and if anybody had asked me, I should have lied without a scruple.

Of course, I did not foresee the far-reaching consequences of my act— how it would change my life. I had no notion that I was now an anti-Communist, where before I had been either indifferent or pro-Communist. I did, however, soon recognize that I was in a rather awkward predicament —not a moral quandary but a social one. I knew nothing about the cause I had espoused; I had never read a word of Lenin or Trotsky, nothing of Marx but the Communist Manifesto, nothing of Soviet history; the very names of the old Bolsheviks who had confessed were strange and almost barbarous in my ears. As for Trotsky, the only thing that made me think that he might be innocent was the odd behaviour of the Communists and the fellow-travelling liberals, who seemed to be infuriated at the idea of a free inquiry. All around me, in the fashionable Stalinist circles I was now frequenting, I began to meet with suppressed excitement and just-withheld disapproval. Jewelled lady-authors turned white and shook their bracelets angrily when I came into a soirée; rising young men in publishing or advertising tightened their neckties dubiously when I urged them to examine the case for themselves; out dancing in a night-club, tall, collegiate young Party members would press me to their shirt-bosoms and tell me not to be silly, honey.

And since I seemed to meet more Stalinists every day, I saw that I was going to have to get some arguments with which to defend myself. It was not enough, apparently, to say you were for a fair hearing; you had to rebut the entire case of the prosecution to get anybody to incline an ear in your direction. I began to read, headlong, the literature on the case—the pamphlets issued by Trotsky's adherents, the Verbatim Report of the second trial published by the Soviet Union, the "bourgeois" press, the Communist press, the radical press. To my astonishment (for I had scarcely dared think it), the trials did indeed seem to be a monstrous frame-up. The defendant, Pyatakov, flew to Oslo to "conspire" with Trotsky during a winter when, according to the authorities, no planes landed at the Oslo airfield; the defendant, Holtzmann, met Trotsky's son, Sedov, in 1936, at the Hotel Bristol in Copenhagen, which had burned down in 1912; the witness, Romm, met Trotsky in Paris at a time when numerous depositions testified that he had been in Royan, among clouds of witnesses, or on the way there from the south of France.

These were only the most glaring discrepancies—the ones that got in the newspapers. Everywhere you touched the case something crumbled. The carelessness of the case's manufacture was to me its most terrifying aspect; the slovenly disregard for credibility defied the credence, in its turn. How did they dare? I think I was more shaken by finding that I was on the right side than I would have been the other way round. And yet, except for a very few people, nobody seemed to mind whether the Hotel Bristol had burned down or not, whether a real plane had landed, whether Trotsky's life and writings were congruent with the picture given of him in the trials. When confronted with the facts of the case, people's minds sheered off from it like jelly from a spoon.

Anybody who has ever tried to rectify an injustice or set a record straight comes to feel that he is going mad. And from a social point of view, he *is* crazy, for he is trying to undo something that is finished, to unravel the social fabric. That is why my liberal friends looked so grave and solemn when I would press them to come along to a meeting and listen to a presentation of the facts—for them this was a Decision, too awful to be considered lightly. The Moscow trials were an historical fact and those of us who tried to undo them were uneasily felt to be crackpots, who were trying to turn the clock back. And of course the less we were listened to, the more insistent and earnest we became, even while we realized we were doing our cause harm. It is impossible to take a moderate tone under such conditions. If I admitted, though, to being a little bit hipped on the subject of Trotsky, I could sometimes gain an indulgent if flickering attention—the kind of attention that stipulates, "She's a bit off but let's hear her story." And now and then, by sheer chance, one of my hearers would be arrested by some stray point in my narrative; the disparaging smile would slowly fade from his features, leaving a look of blank consternation. He would go off and investigate for himself, and in a few days, when we met again, he would be a crackpot too.

Most of us who became anti-Communists at the time of the trials were drawn in, like me, by accident and almost unwillingly. Looking back, as on a love-affair, a man could say that if he had not had lunch in a certain restaurant on a certain day, he might not have been led to ponder the facts of the Moscow trials. Or not then at any rate. And had he pondered them at a later date, other considerations would have entered and his conversations would have had a different style. On the whole, those of us who became anti-Communists during that year, 1936–7, have remained liberals—a thing that is less true of people of our generation who were converted earlier or later. A certain doubt of orthodoxy and independence of mass opinion was riveted into our anti-Communism by the heat of that period. As soon as I make this statement, exceptions leap into my mind, but I think as a generalization it will stand. Those who became anti-Communist earlier fell into two classes : the experts and those to whom any socialist ideal was repugnant. Those whose eyes were opened later, by the Nazi-Soviet pact, or still later, by God knows what, were left bruised and full of self-hatred or self-commiseration, because they had palliated so much and truckled to a power-centre; to them, Communism's chief sin seems to be that it deceived *them,* and their public atonement takes on both a vindicating and a vindicative character.

We were luckier. Our anti-Communism came to us neither as the fruit of a special wisdom nor as a humiliating awakening from a prolonged deception, but as a natural event, the product of chance and propinquity. One thing followed another, and the will had little to say about it. For my part, during that year, I realized, with a certain wistfulness, that it was too late for me to become any kind of Marxist. Marxism, I saw, from the learned young man I listened to at Committee meetings, was something you had to take up young, like ballet dancing.

So, I did not try to be a Marxist or a Trotskyite, though for the first time I read a little in the Marxist canon. But I got the name of being a Trotskyite, which meant, in the end, that I saw less of the conventional Stalinists I had been mingling with and less of conventional people generally. (My definition of a conventional person was quite broad : it included anyone who could hear of the Moscow trials and maintain an

unruffled serenity.) This, then, was a break or a rupture, not very noticeable at first, that gradually widened and widened, without any conscious
effort on my part, sometimes to my regret. This estrangement was not
marked by any definite stages; it was a matter of tiny choices. Shortly
after the Moscow trials, for instance, I changed from the *Herald-Tribune*
to the *Times*; soon I had stopped doing crossword puzzles, playing bridge,
reading detective stories and popular novels. I did not "give up" these
things, they departed from me, as it were, on tiptoe, seeing that my
thoughts were elsewhere.

To change from the *Herald-Tribune* to the *Times*, is not, I am aware,
as serious a step as breaking with international Communism when you
have been its agent; and it occurs to me that Mr. Chambers and Miss
Bentley might well protest the comparison, pointing out that they were
profoundly dedicated people, while I was a mere trifler, that their decisions
partook of the sublime, where mine descended to the ridiculous—as Mr.
Chambers says, he was ready to give his life for his beliefs. Fortunately
(though I could argue the point, for we all give our lives for our beliefs,
piecemeal or whole), I have a surprise witness to call for my side, who did
literally die for his political views.

I am referring to Trotsky, the small, frail, pertinacious old man who
wore whiskers, wrinkles, glasses, shock of grizzled hair, like a gleeful
disguise for the erect young student, the dangerous revolutionary within
him. Nothing could be more alien to the convulsed and tormented moon-
scapes of the true confessions of ex-Communists than Trotsky's populous,
matter-of-fact recollections set out in *My Life*. I have just been re-reading
this volume, and though I no longer subscribe to its views, which have
certainly an authoritarian and doctrinaire cast that troubles me today,
nevertheless, I experience a sense of recognition here that I cannot find in
the pages of our own repentant "revolutionaries". The old man remained
unregenerate; he never admitted that he had sinned. That is probably why
nobody seems to care for, or feel apologetic too, his memory. It is an
interesting point—and relevant, I think, to my story—that many people
today actually have the impression that Trotsky died a natural death.

In a certain sense, this is perfectly true. I do not mean that he lived
by violence and therefore might reasonably be expected to die by violence.
He was a man of words primarily, a pamphleteer and orator. He was
armed, as he said, with a pen and peppered his enemies with a fusillade
of articles. Hear the concluding passages of his autobiography. "Since my
exile, I have more than once read musings in the newspapers on the
subject of the 'tragedy' that has befallen me. I know no *personal* tragedy.
I know the change of two chapters of revolution. One American paper
which published an article of mine accompanied it with a profound note to

the effect that in spite of the blows the author had suffered, he had, as evidenced by his article, preserved his clarity of reason. I can only express my astonishment at the philistine attempt to establish a connection between the power of reasoning and a government post, between mental balance and the present situation. I do not know, and I never have known, of any such connection. In prison, with a book or pen in my hand, I experienced the same sense of deep satisfaction that I did at mass-meetings of the revolution. I felt the mechanics of power as an inescapable burden, rather than as a spiritual satisfaction."

This was not a man of violence. Nevertheless, one can say that he died a natural death—a death that was in keeping with the open manner of his life. There was nothing arcane in Trotsky; that was his charm. Like an ordinary person, he was hospitably open to hazard and accident. In his autobiography, he cannot date the moment when he became a socialist.

One factor in his losing out in the power-struggle at the time of Lenin's death was his delay in getting the telegram that should have called him home from the Caucasus, where he was convalescing, to appear at Lenin's funeral—*had* he got the telegram, perhaps the outcome would have been different. Or again, perhaps not. It may be that the whims of chance are really the importunities of design. But if there is a Design, it aims, in real lives, like the reader's or mine or Trotsky's, to look natural and fortuitous; that is how it gets us into its web.

Trotsky himself, looking at his life in retrospect, was struck, as most of us are on such occasions, by the role chance had played in it. He tells how one day, during Lenin's last illness, he went duck-shooting with an old hunter in a canoe on the River Dubna, walked through a bog in felt boots—only a hundred steps—and contracted influenza. This was the reason he was ordered to Sukhu for the cure, missed Lenin's funeral, and had to stay in bed during the struggle for primacy that raged that autumn and winter. "I cannot help noting," he says, "how obligingly the accidental helps the historical law. Broadly speaking, the entire historical process is a refraction of historical law through the accidental. In the language of biology, one might say that the historical law is realized through the natural selection of accidents." And with a faint touch of quizzical gaiety he sums up the problem as a Marxian : "One can foresee the consequences of a revolution or a war, but it is impossible to foresee the consequences of an autumn shooting-trip for wild ducks." This shrug before the unforeseen implies an acceptance of consequences that is a far cry from penance and prophecy. Such, it concedes, is life. *Bravo*, old sport, I say, even though the hall is empty.

FEBRUARY 1954

KENNETH TYNAN

Bull Fever

ONE GOES TO Madrid not to look but to listen; the eye, once pacified by the Prado, can rest without loss behind sunglasses. The modern part of the city, which is most of it, acts as a mart rather than a Mecca for tourism; here you bathe and shave, make reservations, buy clothes for the south, eat lavishly, and call for the English-speaking doctor, who restores intestinal friction with a dark, gritty porridge. Madrid is a city perpetually under construction, where housing developments refuse to develop and planning schemes plot their own frustration; from the amount of scaffolding, and the number of deserted cement-mixers and piles of abandoned bricks, you would think its suburbs were peripatetic, their destinies in the hands of men paid to keep them, stone by stone, in motion. At head-height all is clean, bright plateau air, but dust ambles around the ankles. Busy, official, social, and sensual, Madrid has never had time to become a showplace. Instead, it is a sounding-board for the noisy, fatiguing variety of Spanish conversation, which devotes itself to what William Styron, the American novelist, has described as the writer's five main preoccupations: Love Requited, Love Unrequited, Death, Insult, and Hilarity.

I had a week to spare before the Valencian fair began, and two novilladas to see, one in the Madrid ring of Las Ventas, and the other sixty miles away at Segovia, where the cartel was to include Pedrés and Jumillano, the young lions of the season. Meanwhile I eavesdropped, most fruitfully, on the foreign aficionados in the bar of the Palace Hotel. Multilingual bull-talk may be heard here any time from March to September, but the climax is reached in May, when Madrid celebrates the *feria* of San Isidro. Then, alive with an almost proprietary zeal, the French contingent arrives, sallow and learned, taking its tauromachy very seriously and insisting on the use of classical bullfight terminology in all discussions. The corrida has, after all, penetrated as far north as Bordeaux; it is gaining ground all the time, and French bullfight critics, secure in the terrible finality of utterance to which their tongue lends itself, write with a frankness seldom achieved by their more partial Spanish colleagues. Occasionally an English aficionado breaks through the currency barrier and goes to the fights, wrestling spasmodically with his sense of shame and his love of horses, items of psychological luggage which seem overwhelmingly important after a bad corrida, and irrelevant after a good one. But for every Englishman there are fifty Americans with bull fever; it is too often our habit, as it is rarely theirs, to condemn things unseen. A visit to a bullfight is an emotional experiment which the English fear to risk. The Americans, surprised legatees of that store of energy and elasticity which has been moving mysteriously westward ever since the heyday of Greek civilization, have no such qualms. They accept and embrace the bullfight, some for the right reasons, others because it can all too easily be absorbed, along with big-game hunting and whaling, into the curious religion of toughness, and others again because it is expensive and spectacular to photograph.

There are the rich and retired, with a metabolism attuned to manzanilla and elaborate mid-Atlantic accents ("Litri's a *tarny* little chap, practically a midget, but such artistry! If he were British you'd have *narded* him by now!"); there are college girls on the Grand Tour who saw one bullfight in France and cancelled their reservations in Rome in order to follow the bulls south; there are picturesque vagabonds spending dollars which they earned on the construction of airfields in North Africa; and there are employees of the predominantly bull-mad United States consulates. All are enthusiasts, exhausting themselves by the effort of wanting the fights to be good : "I saw Vázquez last month, and, my God, you talk about guts? Here's what I say to anybody who tries to tell me it's cruel. Just get in there with those bulls, if you love them so damn much. Just get in there. And *brother . . .*"

A common tableau is that in which a young, crew-cut novice tries out his aficion on an older expatriate, whose smudged-ochre eyeballs and rusty complexion tell of long addiction to the Spanish way of life. The acolyte has been explaining, with broad gestures and head-shakes expressive of rueful wonder, his admiration for the valour of Pedrés—"And then he got it, right in the gut, and so help me he got right back on his feet and went through with the kill——" The older man nods wisely :

"Yeah, I heard he was good that afternoon. Trouble with that boy, he'll never learn how to coast. Just won't take it easy. I've told him a million times. 'Relax, baby, relax' : but no, he's got this Spanish pride and he stays as tensed-up as a watch-spring."

"You know him, huh?"

"Know him?" A huge commiserating grin. "Why, we've broken bread with the guy, haven't we, Daisy?"

Daisy is his wife, startlingly pretty with dark hair in a bun. Looking nervously up from the Paris *Herald Tribune,* she supports the half-truth :

"Sure—sure we have!"

After all, they arrived at the party only a matter of seconds after Pedrés left.

"Pedrés," continues her husband, with pedagogic emphasis on the second syllable, "P'drace is my boy, kind of a protégé of mine. Carlos Arruza and I went up to a *tienta* in Salamanca two winters ago, and there was this skinny little kid, shaking in his shoes and looking like a breath of wind'd knock him over. Well, I took one good look at him and I said to Carlos, 'I know what you're thinking, but you're wrong. The kid's got what it takes.' Well, Carlos kidded me for a while—Carlos is a great kidder —but sure enough when P'drace got out there with the muleta, that crowd simply went crazy."

"I saw Arruza in Mexico," says crew-cut. "You known him long?"

"Honey, Arruza"—pronounced Arootza— "Arootza and me are like that. Carlos would cut his right arm for me. And as for Daisy—why, the guy is just wild about her, do anything for her, isn't that so, Daisy?"

And Daisy, remembering a polite handshake in an airport waiting-room, wishfully agrees.

Snobbism of this sort is the occupational disease of the foreign aficionado. Not to have attended a *tienta,* the trial of young fighting cows which takes place on the ranches during the winter and early spring, is a fearful stigma, almost as bad as not having run before the bulls at Pamplona. Since the death of Manolete at Linares in 1947, there is little point in claiming to have known him; everybody does it, from Orson Welles (who actually did know him) to the cloakroom attendant at any Madrid café. A sciolistic acquaintance with a few great nineteenth-century names—Mazzantini, Lagartijo, Frascuelo—is *de rigueur*; and to have known someone who was in the Madrid arena when Granero was mortally gored in 1922 is practically compulsory. Of matadors living but retired, some degree of familiarity with Belmonte and Rafael El Gallo is essential, and it is advisable to refer to Belmonte by his nickname "Terremoto", which means earthquake. It is no longer fashionable to describe the bullfight as "basically a sacrificial rite", the preferred phrase is "a kind of balletic hunt". One should also observe from time to time that the *fiesta brava* is in decay, that Manolete ruined it, and that nobody has killed *recibiendo* since 1925. The aficionado's preparation, *mutatis mutandis,* is curiously similar to that of the dramatic critic.

The study of bullfighting is all niceties, fine technical points which the English language must struggle to convey, and the number of English-speaking authorities is necessarily small. Hemingway, in spite of an absence from Spain which lasted from the civil war to the summer of 1953, thereby denying him access to the thrones of Manolete and Luis Miguel

Dominguín, is among the few who combine passion with genuine knowledge; a tauriform titan with a schoolboy's enthusiasms, a prefect's pre-
judices, and a games master's geniality. Another real devotee is John
Marks, the author of that fine handbook *To The Bullfight,* whose appearance, pouchy and reposeful, puts one in mind of the Rembrandt self-
portrait in the Prado with the whiskers shaved off. Crustily holding court
at a café on the Gran Via, Marks hits the manner of Spanish bull-critics off
to perfection, speaking of contemporary toreros as of a gang of unruly
children whose caprices may be tolerated and condoned but never mistaken
for absolute virtues. It is Marks's misfortune to have acquired an un-
challengeable expertise on a subject about which his compatriots are profoundly incurious. But neither he nor Hemingway can compete in length
of service with an indomitable and (I swear) non-fictional Englishwoman
whom I call Lady Black.

Lady Black saw her first bullfight shortly after the armistice of 1918, and
aficion instantly took possession of her soul. No woman for half-measures,
she determined to spread the word abroad and, backing up her imperfect
Spanish with all the tenacious optimism of Pont Street, assembled three
inexpensive matadors, their protesting cuadrillas, and a small herd of
groggy bulls. These she transported, with a display of organizing ability
which would have done credit to Hannibal, across the south of France into
Italy, where they arrived by train in the summer of 1923. Overwhelming
the authorities with her title, her rhetoric, and her refusal to be discouraged,
she succeeded in presenting twenty-seven slightly ragged bullfights in the
velodromes of Turin, Milan, Bologna, and Naples. Understandably elated,
she laid plans to repeat the expedition a year later, only to be foiled by
unyielding opposition from the Roman Catholic Church, which, though
it expressed no objection to the impaling of bulls, took the view that fighting
them was tantamount to committing suicide and ought therefore to be
prohibited. This attitude must have worried some of the troupe, fearful for
their souls, but it had no effect whatever on Lady Black, whose Empire-
building forebears had taught her to display nothing but amused indifference when faced with hostile tribal taboos. Her caravan was already
approaching the Italian frontier when the velodrome proprietors cancelled
their contracts. Rather than retreat, she continued defiantly eastwards,
passing with her bulls, horses, and men straight through northern Italy
to the Balkans. The men, whose morale she describes as splendid, were
nevertheless becoming difficult to discipline; some of them, in spite of her
expostulations, firmly regarded the entire safari as an elaborate game in
which no holds were barred, and every time the train pulled into a station
there were playful attempts to disgorge a bull or two into the midst of the
crowds on the platform. By keeping her wits about her and bringing the

mutineers with money and wine, Lady Black managed to escort her party as far as Budapest, where it disembarked, blind drunk, in the early autumn of 1924. Sensing that no time was to be lost if the boys were to be dissuaded from running amuck, she at once took a short lease on an athletics stadium just outside the city. Here, magnificently, she held six formal corridas of bulls, over which she presided, a Junoesque Madam Chairman with a fan rendered prettily redundant by the icy east wind. The Hungarian audiences, she says, took to bullfighting "like ducks to water", and the fits of mystified acclamation with which they greeted each pass ring still in her ears. Her mission accomplished, she received from the mayor what may have been either a decoration or a small fingerbowl, and returned to England for the grouse season. She left the railway tickets for her band of tourist executioners in the care of the senior matador, but it was many weeks before they made use of them. Some, indeed, never came back to Spain; the hospitality of Hungarian hostesses is a byword in the Balkans, and to Lady Black, contentedly banging away in her shooting-box, there filtered through disquieting rumours about chandeliers smashed, duels fought, and homes wrecked by her impetuous troupe. Swallowing her qualms, she sent kind messages of disbelief to her informants, begging them not to repeat idle gossip. The experience, however, must have shaken her, for she has revisited Hungary never, and Spain seldom. Since the civil war she has banished herself from the bulls completely, but her aficion still burns. You may still meet her at small parties in Kensington, to which, on occasion, she brings her guitar; and, with any luck, as the night wears on, nostalgia will sweep over her and she will sing, in an ululation throaty but sweet, as much as she can remember of the flamenco chants which beguiled that terrible train journey thirty years ago. The idea of a bullfight on ice, which I once propounded to her, did not strike her as in the least bizarre. She is a marvellous woman.

The Madrid novillada was held on Thursday, which thus took on the familiar shape of a bullfight day—a slow, tedious parabola mounting to the fight, and a precipitate slump after it. Abstract thought is an impossibility on bullfight days: two questions rap hard on the mind: whether the rain will hold off, and whether the wind will drop. At five, restlessly, one joins the honking queue of cars lining the Calle de Alcalá, which leads out to the bullring; the pavements are already full of fast-walking crowds, the men predominantly in blue, that bilious shade which is the trade-mark of cheap Spanish tailoring, and the women pouter-pigeoned in black and crested with mantillas. Though the air is electric, the streets are not as jammed as they would be for a football match. Spanish *futbolistas* easily outnumber the aficionados; the two largest bullrings in

Spain, that of Las Ventas in Madrid and the Monumental in Barcelona, hold respectively 23,000 and 20,000 spectators, who would look like gnat-rain on a wedding-cake if spread out on the stands of an international football stadium.

The seats at Las Ventas rise steeply from the sand, giving to the place an intent, focused look which is somehow reflected in the audience. This is the Cathedral of Tauromachy, the end of the pilgrimage; here the matador's visa to glory must finally be stamped; and there is none of Pamplona's tipsiness or Valencia's partisanship. The fight I saw, a minor affair, was none the less conducted in a spectral, concentrated hush. A special pathos attaches to the effort of novilleros to prove themselves; I remembered the agony of José Gutiérrez Somoza, who, in April 1947, made his début in a fight at Zamora, displaying such terror and incompetence that he was taken to prison and fined 3,000 pesetas for cheating the public. After a disaster like that, unless one is gifted with the unearthly aplomb of a Cagancho or a Luis Procuna, one cannot live easily. Cagancho and Procuna brush off their disgraces with a shrug, but Gutiérrez Somoza, having once been seen naked and shaking, concluded that he did not wish to be seen anywhere again, and on June 26th of the same year committed suicide.

None of the three novilleros cut an ear, but none of them disgraced himself; the fight was taut and exciting, largely because of the contrast between Navarrito, a Sevillian boy with the sober style of Ronda, and Joselito Torres, a Venezuelan with all the venturesome lightness of Seville. It is, of course, an anachronism to speak of Seville and Ronda as "schools" of bullfighting; Ronda has not produced a torero of much quality since Niño de la Palma, and today there are more madrileño bullfighters than sevillanos. Even so, the terms have their uses, as convenient abbreviations, and that is why they persist. The third fighter was Fernando Jiménez, Manolo González's younger brother, moderately brave, but irremediably clumsy with the muleta; and the Yagüe bulls had, as one journalist wrote afterwards, *"poca casta y no mucha carne"*—little breeding and not much meat. What gave the afternoon its dignity was the spectacle of Navarrito and Torres controlling their nerves, steadying their bodies to let opposed traditions speak through their youth. The line of his limbs and the strength of his wrist are all a matador has with which to set a signature on his work; and the signature must not offend decorum with its flamboyancy. As Orson Welles puts it, each passing of the bull must announce "not *who I am*, but *what we are*".

Navarrito, wearing a black arm-band in memory of his father, who had died a few days before, was tall and possessed drooping, waxen eyelids like those of a saint in effigy. With his first bull, a cowardly and short-winded little brute, he declared himself: a poker-faced but passionate dominator.

His opening veronicas were admonitions to the bull's vivacity, school-master's passes, and when Torres danced in with some cheeky chicuelinas during the picking, it was as if a child had thumbed his nose while the teacher's back was turned. Navarrito scowled loftily, and the scowl deepened when he saw that the bull was cheating him of his faena by refusing to take the picks. Nor would more than two of the banderillas stay in place : had the creature rubber withers? Navarrito, giving nothing away of his rage, unfurled the muleta and began with four slow, perfect naturals which must have astonished the bull; in the same mood of entranced lethargy he shifted to the right hand, patiently instructing the volatile animal to stay on course. After repeating both series of passes he seemed certain of an ear, but ruined his chances with a bad, nervous kill. His second bull was a menace, an irrational, high-chopping pick-hater which his technique was not good enough to master; imagine Clyde Beatty given ten minutes to teach a man-eating tiger to jump through hoops, and you have some idea of Navarrito's problem. His peons loyally mimed extreme fright, vaulting in and out of the ring at the least provocation to indicate to the crowd how anxious they were for their employer's safety, but it was no use : Navarrito was baffled. Nothing beautiful could be done with the creature : this was bullfighting as an English audience might enjoy it, an approximately equal contest in which man and bull looked equally stupid, and I hated it as much as Navarrito did. He killed, furiously and in great peril, at the second thrust.

Little Torres likewise lost heart with his second bull, a vague perambulator; he yelled shrilly at it like a man hailing a passing cab, but failed to attract and hold its attention. Embellishment, not domination, is his forte, as he had already shown in his first bull, by far the best of the afternoon; a ready charger of which he took advantage to the extent of six impudent veronicas and a sweeping farol, threatening to submerge himself in the folds of the cape like a Boy Scout beneath a collapsed tent in a storm. The picadors and banderilleros did their work admirably, and for a moment Torres stood in their shadow, Gulliver in Brobdingnag; then, jauntily, he sprang out with the muleta and easily roused the olés. Bullfighting achieves its proper beauty only when the rhythm of the contest transcends its danger, when you are lulled by the fighter's skill into forgetfulness of the risks he is taking. Of this beauty Torres was not old enough to be capable : a swift, agile stylist, he is effective in fragments but worlds away from Navarrito's sinister, compelling sloth. Citing the bull square-shouldered, he gave us naturals and then passes *en redondo*, followed by high *derechazos* and a couple of ill-timed *desplantes*; the whole faena being chancy, disorganized, and much applauded. "*Il ne leur importe*," said Samuel Sorbière, a French visitor to London in 1667, of English theatregoers, "*que ce soit un pot-*

pourri, parce qu'ils, n'en regardent disent-ils, qu'une partie après l'autre, sans se soucier du total." This is equally true of modern bullfight audiences, and it is getting truer every season; the longest cheers go to the pot-pourri experts, such as Pedrés or Chicuelo II, who specialize in disconnected bursts of emotion, rather than to the patient, progressive craftsmen who match their methods to the bull and, working within a strictly limited area, impose on the faena a total shape which stays in the mind after individual passes have faded. Yet Torres's whirlwind improvisations were what the public wanted, and had he not bungled the kill the award of an ear would have been inevitable. This kind of modern bullfighting—which is four-fifths of it—might be described as classical bullfighting reflected in a smashed mirror. It would not be too much to say that the ideal bull-fighter is one who puts into practice the Stoic tenet of *apatheia* as Lionel Trilling defines it: "The principled refusal to experience more emotion than is forced upon one, the rejection of sensibility as a danger to the integrity of the self." In the persistence of their appeal to and dependence of sensibility, toreros of Pedrés's sort become the sentimentalists of the bullring. Intent on fraying our nerves, they debauch our vision. A perfect faena imprints on the consciousness a pattern almost abstract, the pattern of Senecan Stoicism as one finds it in the last act of a tragedy, when the hero stares death in the eyes, and conquers it through indifference. Your Stoic *in extremis* does not exclaim: "See how terribly I am threatened! See what risks I am running! It will be a miracle if I survive!" He says, in effect: "There is no terror. I run no risk that is not of my choosing. I shall survive." This is the statement made by a good bullfighter on his best days, the affirmation that one goes to the bullring to hear.

After a corrida, as Jimmy Durante says in another context, food becomes secondary. It was half-past midnight, late even for Spain, before I dined, my companion being an American script-writer who revealed that he shared my own bewitched admiration for the English menus so thought-fully provided by many Spanish restaurants. He cited a wine-list in Barcelona which offered "Xeres from Sherry of the Frontier". I replied with a *trouvaille* from San Sebastian. It had begun, quietly enough, with "Several Kinds of Shells" and "Calamary in his Own Ink"—*calamares en su tinta*. Then, suddenly, the mystery sprang upon one: "Anahogs in a Seamanlike Manner." I never discovered what these were, and did not dare to ask, lest they should be brought (or led) snarling and clanking and hornpiping to the table. I carry at the back of my mind an image of an anahog, feral and shipshape, which comes saluting into my dreams, dis-rupting every banquet my subconscious prepares for me. Perhaps this was a vestigial anahog, a corruption of an earlier "anchovy" which the scribe, in his ignorance, had confused : I do not know, and it would take a textual critic to find out. At all events, the San Sebastian translator kept up a high standard throughout, ending with a notable flourish on :

FRUITS OF THE SEASON
TART OF THE HOUSE

I am not sure, though, that I do not prefer the *carte* gleaned by my friend in Santander, which included a frugal "Ham with Pea", some pleasantly homely "Cow-Chops", and the macabre recommendation, as *spécialité de la maison*, of "Toadstool Omelette".

We discussed the novillada at length, went on to the style of the Sevillian fantastiks in general, and then by what seemed a natural progression, found ourselves talking about Chaplin. I had noticed this happening before, in many other conversations; there is an undoubted kinship between the tidy skippings of the fastidious little tramp, his alertness in avoiding disaster by ducking under a beefy arm or sliding down a drain-pipe, and the equally slick manœuvres of Sevillian toreros eluding the horns. What W. C. Fields said of Chaplin has been echoed by many American aficionados speaking of Manolo Vázquez : "The guy's a goddamn ballet-dancer." In both cases the man exposes himself, in a spirited, volatile, balletic manner, to all kinds of danger, and emerges unhurt. The quiet, withdrawn Ronda style has nothing of this : there is philosophy in it, something more august and profoundly moral than the practical, life-loving shrug of the Sevillians. With the *rondeño* fighter the bull takes on a majesty it seldom achieves with a Sevillian, to whom it is merely a threat to be skirted as glibly and neatly as human reflexes will permit. Hence tragedy belongs to Ronda, because tragedy is not, as a rule, animated or vivacious but still and reflective. Ronda is imaginative and classical; Seville is fanciful and baroque. The distinction is much the same as that which can be drawn between *cante hondo,* the pure form of Andalusian song, and *cante flamenco*, its more popular derivative. The Sevillian (not Hemingway's horse) is the true comedian of the bullfight; his pre-eminent quality is not so much courage as pluck; he charms rather than binds a spell.

He reminds one, not too distantly, of the clown-bullfighters who somersault baggy-trousered over the horns of yearling calves in the arc-lit circus spectacles which invade many bullrings during fiesta weeks, offering a nocturnal parody of the afternoon's serious business. And here we are back once more to Chaplin, for comic bullfights, known as *charlotadas*, were invented in direct imitation of Chaplin's early one-reelers. The first and greatest of the Chaplinesque toreros was Carmelo Tusquellas "Charlot", who made his début as a burlesque matador, complete with bowler, cane, moustache, and high-buttoned frock-coat, in Barcelona on May 8th, 1916; his success was immediate and the local impresario, Eduardo Pagés, at once formed a full comic cuadrilla. In addition to Charlot, he engaged Rafael Dutrus "Llapisera", already well known as a taurine *farceur*. Llapisera's trick was to enter the ring clad in flawless evening dress with what Cossío, the historian of bullfighting, describes as "all the seriousness of an English humorist". The combination of Llapisera and Charlot (who must have resembled Keaton and Chaplin) was irresistible, and the team was and is widely mimicked. So that in linking Chaplin with bullfighting I am merely repeating what Pagés intuitively spotted nearly forty years ago. In his celerity, his serio-comic delicacy when matched with a mighty Mephistophelean bruiser, Chaplin behaves much as a *torero sevillano* behaves in the presence of a bull. We laugh at Chaplin because the peril is artificial; the bullfighter, on the other hand, may be killed before our eyes. Though one smiles at Sevillian antics, one is always conscious that one's amusement is a form of *Galgenhumor*.

It is appropriate that Chaplin's most celebrated party-turn, never seen on the screen, should be an impersonation of a nervy matador. And it is equally revealing when a recent biographer, Robert Payne, quotes him as saying of the tramp-character he originated: "I am always aware that Charlie is playing with death. He plays with it, mocks it, thumbs his nose at it, but it is always there. He is aware of death at every moment of his existence; and he is terribly aware of being alive."

Another actor who uses a Sevillian approach to drama is Jean-Louis Barrault, a brilliant mime, tumbler, talker, and thinker whose stage presence is nevertheless without real weight. He and Chaplin have much more in common with each other and the bullfight than they have with, say, Olivier in the great days of his *Oedipus Rex*. For a hint of the ideal *rondeño* actor, one must go to John Gielgud, whose style is surgical in its detachment, nobly removed from the tumult; like Manolete, he has a way of sadly averting his head, as if something malodorous offended him, whenever the character he is playing is beset by danger, blood, death, or the loss of a job. And though he lacks Manolete's baleful compassion, he shares with him the knowledge that he is a cynosure on whom the impressionable will model their ideals of human dignity. Gielgud's remoteness, his commanding poise are the marks of the swordsmen of Ronda. Their pride, the pride of men able to dominate through the mind rather than the muscles, informs and vivifies all he does.

Toughness, it should by now be clear, is no part of a bullfighter's equipment; many of the best have been tubercular or syphilitic. No aggressively masculine skills are required for the job; indeed, if a torero's work announces too blatantly his gender, it often militates against the best of which he is capable, as if a painter were to assert that he was a man first, and an artist second. This is not to say that there are more effeminates in bullfighting than in any other profession involving self-exhibition. It is simply to suggest that interpretative art, particularly in such a stylized form as the bullfight, does not depend on the projection of the executant's sex. Universality is aided by ambiguity. We laugh at a comedian when he exposes the feminine traits which lie beneath the masculine appearance; when Bob Hope, having bragged of his fearlessness, screams at the sight of a mouse; when Jack Benny broods about crows-feet and thinning hair; or when Sid Field dons his velvet coat and transforms himself into a fairy-legged photographer. Chaplin, especially in his early films, is the arch-effeminate of comedy: observe the bashful hunching of the shoulders and the girlish grin with which he accepts an unexpected compliment, and notice how, in *The Cure*, he squirms with coyness when constrained to undress in the men's changing room. In all acting where finesse is uppermost, there is a female spring in the mechanism, and this is true of the bullfight since Belmonte developed it from a hunt into a form of self-expression.

Anyone whose business is the study of human behaviour in a crisis—and this of course includes actors—can learn a great deal from the corrida. Ristori once nettled Coquelin by declaring that to simulate an emotion it was necessary for an actor to have experienced it; to which Coquelin replied: "Yes, madame—but I have often seen you die!", thus ending the dispute. Myself, I think Ristori was in error, for I have seen too many actors "feeling" an emotion so intensely that they were quite unable to communicate it; but I believe she might have answered Coquelin's point if she had remembered the bullfight. At the climax of a good faena, you know precisely how a man looks and behaves and, with cognate clarity, something of what he feels and thinks in the presence of death. An actor might play Cyrano better for having seen Cagancho in the ring, alternating the high jinks of comedy with tragic pride; and anyone contemplating Mio in Maxwell Anderson's *Winterset* and wondering how to cope with the death-shrouded last act would be well advised to watch Litri facing a Murube bull. When you have seen that, you know a little about dying.

A deep mistrust of rubble-spattered Spanish roads and wine-flown English drivers moved me to take the train to Segovia. Half-way there, a sudden hailstorm sent knobs of ice as big as knuckles clattering down on to the starved Castilian plain, and I had a twinge of aficionado *Angst*: a black cloud on bullfight day is as bad as a burst blood-vessel. But the sky was soon wiped blue, and I spent the rest of the trip quarrelling with an English-speaking Spaniard, who maintained that the bullfight was barbarous, though he had seen only one, and that a good one, in which eight ears were cut. Though I protested, I could not help seeing his point, against which there is no fool-proof argument. There will always be those to whom the thought of a bullfight is *per se* repellent, like an unopened book whose contents are reputed to be pornographic. No matter how hard such people try to keep their eyes impartial, prejudice betrays them; the obscenity leaps out from the page, vile and glaring, and even if their deeper judgement pronounces it not obscenity at all but an essential detail of a great design, they will ever afterwards think of the volume as a dirty book, and themselves as slightly contaminated by contact with it. The censor in one's mind is as capricious and twice as inconsistent as the Lord Chamberlain, and his power is absolute.

All the same, I should quake to see him evicted, and the bullfight held to be a pansy pursuit, which is what Nero or Caligula would have thought it. Reading Suetonius's gossip about the midnight games in which Nero, dressed in a lionskin, would roar through the arena savaging the flesh of tethered slaves, I try to isolate the qualities which make this revolting and the bullfight acceptable. Both involve bloodshed; both are intended to enliven an audience; and both are exhibitions of fundamentally needless cruelty. In both cases, pain is publicly inflicted, and no apologist for the bullfight, however strong his convictions, could reasonably offer as a moral justification the excuse that animals feel pain less intensely than human beings. I have no respect for the aficionado who fails to argue the matter out with himself, though I have to admit I do not know the solution. Must one go to the awful length of saying that, in the case of the bullfight, the end justifies the means? Which implies agreement with the view of Ximenes, that the unification of Spanish worship justified the Inquisition : a hard doctrine for most of us. When all the debating points have been made, I am still unable to reconcile the logical reasons for loathing the corrida, which are as logical as the reasons for loathing horror-camps or the building of the Pyramids, with my own obstinate awareness that it represents for me a summit of human aspiration.

On two questions, however, the dispute on the train helped me to make up my mind. My opponent scoffed at the notion that bullfighting was an art; and at bottom, though I offered a token shriek of scorn, I found myself of his opinion. It is not an art in itself, but the cause that art is in other men —poets, for example, painters, sculptors, and musicians. The matador is not, by any definition that pretends to strictness, an artist any more than Beowulf or Odysseus were artists : like them he is an epic adventurer in whose deeds there is enormous incidental beauty, whose life is the raw material for an unwritten narrative poem, a *Belmontiad* or *Litriad* in embryo.

Shifting his fire, the Spaniard next insinuated that there was a strong element of overt sexuality in bullfighting, a line of argument so naïve that I almost asked him how much overt sexuality he thought there was in the annual championships at Bisley. Nobody denies that Nero's cannibal frolicking had a specific sexual purpose; and it is certainly possible to read sexual symbolism into the events of a bullfight—I know a girl whose psychiatrist told her that the bull represented her mother and the matador her father, adding that she herself was the horse. But it is nonsense to hold that algolagnia, sexual pleasure in the infliction of pain, plays any part in the ritual; the corrida is never, in the ordinary sense, sadistic.

On the other hand, in another, more precise sense of the word, it is sub-limely, even exultantly sadistic. Mr. Geoffrey Gorer has defined de Sade's general philosophy as one of "pleasure in the ego's modification of the external world". This pleasure can—and in de Sade's case did—lead to indulgence in pyromania and kindred fantasies: but it is present, less aggressively, in most of us. And nothing satisfies it better than the sight of a man demonstrating his mastery over a force as objective and uncom-promising as a fighting bull. Some of us, finding nobility in the spectacle, can accordingly cite as our text: "The admiration of the noble draws us upwards." Others, finding nothing there but self-indulgence, turn away in horror and all efforts to convert them are wasted. The question of bull-fighting probes spots so sore that for the aficionado Jowett's advice is perhaps the best. Never apologize, never explain.

APRIL 1955

MELVIN J. LASKY

An Indian Notebook

RECEPTION

OUT OF GREECE, where Parthenon and Piraeus were drearily shrouded in the grey wetness of a European spring, and on to hot and humid Bombay Island. At the white-marbled airport I note the weather report which coolly lists the day's temperature as "38 degrees C., 101 degrees F., humidity 89 p.c., normal . . ." The overnight plunge into the tropics has given me a chill. I confine myself to my hotel room under a slow-moving fan.

Bombay friends come to call on me. They comfort me by telling me how badly I look. One reminds me considerately that Alexander had also come from Greece, and he had died of an Indian fever. It is a bewildering, dispiriting reception. Later I am told that to say "You do not look well" is the most polite, friendly, and solicitous remark that can be made on meeting an acquaintance, and one which should be appreciated by the person addressed with almost a lump in his throat. Choked up with gratitude, I thank my informant and register the first confusing lesson of the journey.

FAIR BRIDES

Miss Ghose is kind enough to invite me to a wedding. It is, alas, not her own, but the seventh in four days (and nights) of one of her friends or relatives. Apparently all the auspices are propitious. The "beneficent planets", among which are Mercury, Jupiter, Venus, and the Moon, seem to be in unusually happy combination. Miss Ghose assures me that no family would risk the fate and fortune of their children without a most exact calculation of the Zodiac.

I am left with a Mr. Backliwal as Miss Ghose joins all the other brilliantly *sari*-ed women under the traditional four-posted garden tent, positively gleaming in the spectrum of Indian silks. He promises to explain all. The ceremony proceeds according to Sikh rites, although neither of the families is of the Sikh faith; it is the nostalgia of urbanized Hindus for ancient ways, and when the old white-bearded priest appears they put a shiny silver microphone before him, and it whistles and hums chaotically like loudspeaker systems the world over. The *tabla* drum, the *vamsi* flute, and the

68

dvitara two-stringed lute, the glories of Indian quarter-tone music, begin their booming and twanging rhythms. The guests stand up uncertainly, and are motioned down again by an assistant priest. I whisper to Mr. B., a prosperous local merchant, asking whether his own marriage had been similarly arranged. It had. All the planets had been propitious? They were. No interference from an ascendant Saturn? "None that could be discerned," he said, "but to make sure our astrologer advised a wedding immediately after midnight. Thus I was married shortly before three o'clock in the morning . . ." Everything, I presumed, has since been going well. "Well, yes, very well . . . But in these modern days among our young people, I sometimes suspect that the astrologers are being bribed. Or the heavens are not so beneficent as they were . . ."

The young groom was of a golden-brown complexion, the girl at his side, by contrast, could almost pass for a light European beauty. These are, evidently, factors of the utmost importance. Colour, I was confounded to learn, is a constant chronic concern of Indian social (and sexual) life. The "fair bride" is the only true prize to be won. Strangely enough, the most striking specimens of Indian womanhood I meet and talk with are mostly from the South, dark-skinned creatures of uncommon beauty, grace, and intelligence. But, says Miss B., under some pressure, and with a tone of bitterness, "we just have to be more witty, more charming . . ." By and large, barring huge dowries or other ingenious family arrangements, they would seem to be the undesirables of the marriage market. When I press Miss M. as to her real motives for wanting so much to go northwards to Europe, she admits, hesitantly, embarrassedly, that she hopes, that she is sure, her skin "would become lighter . . ."

Am I bewildered? I am. The Indian is outraged by colour-discrimination in Mississippi. The Indian Republic, which historically is a kind of "melting-pot" of Moslems and Persians from the West, Malays from the East, "Indo-Aryans" from the North, and dark Dravidians in the South, stood in Bandung with brown, black, and yellow brethren for progressive racial equality. But orthodox Hindu society itself had been organized around a principle of *Varna* or colour, and its scriptures condemned *Varna-sankara,* the mixing of colours.

The real tragic difficulty would seem to be that these peoples do not feel well or at ease in their own skin. I am shown matrimonial advertisements which call for "fair brides", and even one asking for a bride of "Jewish complexion". (Wasn't it Herodotus who wrote of some Indians being "white like the Egyptians"?) A Bengali tells me that until recently it was not uncommon to rub apparently fair-looking girls with a wet towel to find out whether their complexion was natural; and some harassed fathers have even tried to give guarantees that their daughters would become "fifty per cent fairer" within three months of marriage.

WORSE THAN MURDER

Like a mad dog or an Englishman, into the noon-day sun, and then back to the hotel and into the bar. Never was so small a drink needed so much. But hope was brief and cruelly deceptive. I was never served nor even allowed to remain and stare. Prohibition. This was the "Permit Room", and I had no permit. Tomorrow, I promised desperately, I would stand in a long exhausting queue before some steaming government building and obtain the legal concession extended to pleasure-loving foreigners. Then until tomorrow, said the bartender relentlessly. Not another minute in this one available oasis. Parched, pained, unpacified, I turned and left, without even so much as a last backward glance.

"Illegal?" explained Vivek to me at our dry and hopeless dinner. "Worse than that. It is sinful. Or so at least do the present rulers of our land read the injunctions of religion . . ." Nobody offered consolation, only sober little facts.

"Sinful?" said Nirid. "Worse than that. In Hindu sacred laws the drinking of alcohol is one of the five major sins."

"Murder . . ." I murmured.

"Worse than that," Nirid pursued implacably. "Among our major sins, murder as such, unless it is the murder of a Brahmin, is not one, whereas even association with a man who drinks is!"

In inexpressible discomfort, now tempered at least by a vague sense of virtue and a high-minded satisfaction that the laws of the land were being properly observed, I listened on with dehydrated curiosity. But no. Apparently there was neither virtue nor law. True, the Supreme Court of India had confirmed the constitutionality of the Prohibition Acts of Bombay and Madras and elsewhere. Thereupon the prices doubled, even of the local pseudo-methylated *arrack*, and poor and rich alike were more intemperate than ever.

"More people drink now," Vivek reports, "and they drink more. A new class has grown up—illicit distillers, profiteers, black-marketeers. Should we not have learned from the boot-legging epoch of America that Prohibition is unenforceable? We did not. Wherever it has been tried it has failed. Of all religions the one that condemns liquor categorically, regarding it like so many of our ministers as the origin of all evil, is Islam—yet even the zeal of the devout Muslims has not led them to such unwisdom . . ."

"Drinkers have always been foreigners," explains Nirid. "Our urban ways have always come from the outside, from the Middle East, from the Mediterranean. Our rural traditions are more truly Aryan, and therefore more in accord with Brahmanic principles. The old Brahmanic sanctions were directed against hateful enemy habits. Against the hated and despised aboriginals and outcasts. Against Muslim and then British conquerors ... Today the enemy is within. Who have the privileged positions? An Anglicized administrative class. Who runs the country?"

WITCHES

The spectacle of Mardivala, returning for lunch after the morning session of the High Court, drenched and heat-sick in his formal black coat and black tie and stiff, white collar, quite convinces me that civilization is a form of masochism : it is the price that comfort pays to culture. Naked are the natives, and justice must be wool-clad.

He tells me—as we sit in front of his home-made air-conditioner, a contraption called the "desert-cooler", which is an old-fashioned fan married to a huge cake of ice in a vented tin box—of the case which the judges had just closed with a decision. Six persons, "Adivasi women" belonging to the Warli tribe and dressed in their traditional way, had been charged with the murder of a man, with cooking his flesh in a magical fire and eating it after sharing it with the victim's 16-year-old daughter. M., as a lawyer, was a bit sceptical of the charges, but as the State prosecution had it, the six accused were initiating Navshi and Patteri (two minor girls) in the art of witchcraft. Navshi was commanded to offer her father as a sacrifice to please the demoniac deity. On the appointed day (and I summarize from the account of the court record) all the accused and the two girls discarded their clothes; four of the accused, through their magical powers, became pigmies and mounted two canine steeds and went to the place where Navshi's father was sleeping. He was awakened and told that he was to be offered as a sacrifice; as a result of the magic of one of the accused, the victim followed silently. After taking him to a nearby jungle, all the accused women killed the victim, named Vajya, cut him to pieces with scythes and put the flesh into two metal pots. One of the accused waved a magic wand, and fire came out of a fissure in the earth. Vajya's flesh was cooked and devoured, and they all drank liquor.

The key prosecution witnesses were the two girls, Navshi, aged 16, and Patteri, 9, who gave the court the details of the witchcraft ritual. The wife of the victim knew only that her husband had disappeared after having gone to cut grass in a nearby village. The court doctor testified, after examining the bones in the pot, that only the skull and mandible could have been those of a human being. Villagers reported that the six women had long been held to be witches, and that all local deaths due to illness had been attributed to them.

The judge, a Mr. D. G. Gatne, found it all "highly incredible". He dismissed the case, and acquitted the accused. The six women rose, folded their hands, and thanked and blessed the court.

THE CHINESE SHADOW

It is some five years since I visited Eric da Costa in New Delhi at *The Eastern Economist*; I remember his buoyant confidence in the future of the country, darkened only by his preoccupation with the "challenge of China". His thesis was (and remains) that an Asia at the cross-roads could take either of two paths—the Indian or the Chinese, a "middle way" of freedom and social reconstruction, an extreme way of total regimentation. I was elated to find him still so dedicated, still so assured; I was pained to tell him that I thought he must be about the only man in the land who so felt.

"If India falls," Gandhi once said, "Asia dies." But India appears to be afraid of this warning today : it fills her with too much self-consciousness, it gives her too burdensome a sense of historic mission. That she should point the way for a whole continent full of struggling peoples? An exaggeration. The challenge of China? Better not talk about that.

So Da Costa alone has this vision of these two slumbering giants, awakening to a modern competition—two ancient but still dynamic civilizations, both of which have in the past given profound original life to philosophical and artistic systems, one in the valley of the Yellow River, the other on the Gangetic Plain. But to whomever else one talks in Nehru's India, the response is only an uncertain laugh ("how romantic you Westerners are about such matters!") or a changing of the subject. I suspect it is not merely due to natural modesty and a weak sense of national adventure; it is, of course, in good part that the contemporary Indian mind, troubled and unsure of itself among the strange new problems of progress, lacks a feeling for its own destiny. The Gandhian mission, supported by an unforgettable generation of passionate spirits, has been fulfilled : India is independent and free. In the Nehru epoch she has continued to remain so, heightened only by a general awareness of modernizing change and a very vague impression of self-importance in world-political affairs. Deep conviction, and any large, clear, inspiring vision of the future, is missing. This is also due, I think, to the way in which Pandit Nehru has tried to orient India in international relations. In the atmosphere of a foreign policy which prefers to find in totalitarian neighbours friends of peace and progress, it is very difficult for an Indian to see his way through to the uniqueness and importance of his own democratic experiment. Liberty thrives on the pride in what it uniquely is. To accept "the challenge of China" would be to stress differences and contrasts; this, obviously, would be a gesture of unfriendliness. Neutrality, which is not infrequently a useful instrument of diplomatic machinery, thus becomes a mental and moral outlook, and the very assertion of what one is, and what one can be, is taken to be a dangerous and disagreeable posture.

So it is that my friend Da Costa stands almost alone, and in his isolation has turned to the spinning of fine political myths to make up in personal hope what is lacking on the national scene.

"We in India," he says, with slightly frenetic patriotism, "have always been a tolerant, liberty-loving, and non-violent people."

"And the Chinese?" I ask, half-afraid of what is coming.

"Well, haven't they always been militant, intolerant, authoritarian, regimented by centralizing Cæsars, excelling in the arts of mass extermination? Think of our whole Indian tradition from Asoka the Great to Mohandas Karamchand Gandhi—in essence, it is God-fearing, liberal, and non-violent; politically, decentralized; individually, democratic. And then think of the Chinese tradition, from Shih Huang-ti, the founder of the Chinese Empire, through the last of the Manchus down to Chairman Mao. I find there atrocities and massacres, monolithic patterns, burnings of books. With a single order an Emperor sweeps away regional languages and unifies the writing of the country—and orders all road axles for carts to be of the same size. How true to tradition the Communist revolution in China has run!"

We argue a bit. Certainly India needs the support of a usable past, but not at the price of depriving China of her own. History should be "past politics", not present polemics. It reminds me just a bit too acridly of the hard-hearted readings of the German past in order to strike a blow against Hitler, and even the stone-faced interpretations of Russian history to lengthen the shadow of Stalin through all Slav time. Had Communism come to power on the Gangetic Plain and a free and open society established itself along the Yellow River, we might be hearing lurid tales of Indian cynical violence from Kautilya* to Aurangzeb,† and the civilizing mildness of Confucian wisdom.

* *Kautilya* is a fourth-century (B.C.) Indian contemporary of Aristotle, and if Aristotle was the political adviser to Alexander, Kautilya was the chief theoretician of the Mauryan Empire and prime minister to Chandragupta. Had Alexander's campaign gone further into India, two great theories of politics and power might have had an historic collision. I spent some time hunting down an edition of Kautilya's *Arthasatra,* the ancient manuscript of which was only found in our day; both J. J. Meyer (Leipzig, 1925) and R. Shamasastry (Bangalore, 1915) have made valuable translations from the Sanskrit. In form and in general atmosphere it is strikingly akin to Machiavelli's *Prince,* full of shrewd, cynical, and systematic advice on how to exercise power and maintain an empire. But how utterly cold and cruel it is! It has neither the humanist irony of the great Florentine, nor, of course, the Athenian's classic sense of individual liberty.

† *Aurangzeb* (1659–1707), whose grave I visited in Daulatabad and whose

AJANTA

En route to the caves we stop off in the old town which lies about five miles to the south. It is, so says the guide-book, "surrounded by a strong wall and a deep moat..." The wall, dusty and crumbling in the hot sun, looks as if it would be blown away by a mild summer breeze; and the moat is deep, but empty and dry.

On the inside of the old wall, among the open halls of what must once have been a caravanserai, I find a school. There are hundreds of small boys, but only a very few girls. The villagers, I am told, are still very much against co-education. In one hallway there is a small exhibition of children's drawings and paintings, full of perfectly enchanting motifs from the fresco and Mogul styles. In another there is a biology class (or is it only hygiene?), and on the wall there is a painted skeleton, absolutely frightening (to me) in its black-and-white coloration and curious distortions. In foreshortening, perspective, and other artistic techniques there is a primitivism everywhere which is less amusing than inexcusable; in a nearby town (and, as a matter of fact, in many large cities) there is a statue of Mahatma Gandhi in a public square which must have been, I was sure, smaller than life-size! ... I also peek into the language-class, and there on the walls in nicely-printed Latin letters (there are tiny Hindi translations below) hang the maxims of their life and their new world—"Knowledge Is Power", "Health Is Wealth", "No Exercise, No Food". But in one corner I also read: "Might Is Right". Somebody must have got his Sanskrit signals crossed.

Along the crescent of the Ajanta caves, excavated in rock on the scarped side of a deep ravine, I look for the stream, and the seven waterfalls, and the picturesque greenery. "Come after the monsoon," Ram advises me, "then it is all there ... for the tourists."

In Cave 9, as we paused to examine the little cup-like dugouts in the stone floor (which served the Ajanta artists as palettes), we were joined by a villager. An old man, bare-footed, loin-clad, carelessly turbanned; and

---

run-down imitation of the Taj Mahal can be seen in Aurangabad (as poetic justice would have it, neither of there is registered in any of my guide-books), was the last of the great Moghuls. He was the descendant of both Timur (Tamerlane) and Genghiz Khan. Fanatical, bigoted, and corrupt, he imprisoned his own father, demolished temples, banned music, and by means of war and hatred destroyed the empire which Babur had founded and Akhbar the Great had so firmly established. Dr. Pannikkar, with the pious generosity of all national-minded historians, writes of Aurangzeb: "He died a broken and defeated man, but he died for an ideal—the unification of India ..." I prefer the bizarre but not unintelligent interpretation of a self-educated village chronicler who explained to me that "Aurangzeb is the burnt-ash of the dynasty. He has the madness of decadence. He is Hitler ..."

none of the attendants bothered to put on any lights for him. He squinted into the darkness, and we went on. In the twenty-sixth and final cave, we found each other again. He was standing, wide-eyed and entranced, in front of the left wall, before the colossal image of the dead Buddha about to enter Nirvana. This, apparently, was what he had come for. His name is Rup Chand, and he walked twenty miles that day from one of the nearby villages. Did he know anything of the Ajanta caves or of Buddha? He knew nothing. He was a bricklayer. Many of his friends in the village had for years been telling him stories. What kind of stories? The story of a great and powerful man. A giant, in size and in strength. Who might that be? "Bhima," the old man says, "Bhima." This, suggests Ram, is the Hercules-figure of ancient Indian mythology. "A man so large," adds Rup Chand, "that if I were to stand at one end I could not see the other . . ."

Or so he had been told. Now he was seeing with his own eyes, but sceptically. He moved backwards against the right wall and took in the full view of the reclining Buddha. Then he moved forward again, and with the practical sense of the artisan began to remove his turban in order to measure the true proportions of his not quite so endless Bhima. He counted out in folded lengths the size of the grey tattered cloth he had been wearing around his head. I held one end at Bhima's toes, and Rup Chand stretched his turban out till it reached the giant's navel. Then I stood at the navel with my end, and the measurement was done. Bhima was finite, a little more than two full lengths of the turban. We measured it again, this time going the other way. Rup Chand was almost satisfied. He walked back and forth, and I trotted along with him. Colossal, it was, he said. The largest thing he had ever seen in his life. (My own calculations put it at about twenty-seven feet.) A giant, truly. Bhima himself. But his village friends had not quite told him the truth. From either end, he had reassured himself, he could see the whole.

REAL DESIRES

Before taking leave of Ram this afternoon I mustered enough courage to attack his gentle reserve with a number of personal, and hence exceedingly embarrassing questions. What a charming companion he has been, and how touching a guide. In Ajanta he would say, "Don't you think these are as important as the frescoes of Assisi, Siena, and Florence?" (and he has never been to Italy, or even, I suspect, seen good photographs). In Ellora he would remark, "And doesn't this remind you of Canova?" (and it didn't, not even remotely). But the "real Ram Krishna", aged 19, born in Secunderabad, salary 60 rupees a month, was a creature very far removed from a brief training in cosmopolitan æsthetic chatter and a short-lived accommodation to gadabout Western curiosity.

75

He lived in a little room by himself, in a suburb not very far from here, paid 7 rupees rent, managed to cook for himself on a food budget of 15 rupees (goat-meat three times a week), and sent his savings home to his parents. His father was a "butler" in a local hotel, that is to say, one of the "Harijans" (children of God, as Gandhi decided to call the untouchables). Ram's ambition, if one could designate his very tepid life-passion with that burning word, was to go into government service, and he was actually waiting for his appointment to the railways. "Will it be a good job, Ram?" I ask solicitously. It is a wrong question. "How do you mean?" he replies. "That depends entirely on me. Whatever it is I will try to be satisfied. That makes all work easy and satisfactory. I will do my allotted duties." "But it will, after all, give you a little more money." "Oh, yes, I will then have 120 rupees each month." "And that, perhaps, will give you a chance to live a little better—to have a bit of social life . . . to go out with a few girls— possibly to get married some day soon?" "Oh, no," he corrected me, with quiet tolerance. "Oh, no, that will all be done according to Hindu traditions." "But are you that traditional, working and living here all by yourself, away from your family, meeting and talking with foreigners, reading all kinds of strange translated books?" "Well, in some ways I suppose I have changed. I do not subscribe to the Hindu pantheism. I do believe in one god, even if he is invisible. But the girl I will marry will be decided by my parents. They will select a bride for me." "What of their selection? Could you possibly suggest to them a preference?" "How do you mean?" "A girl that you know or have seen and whom you like?" "Oh, I couldn't do that. My parents love me very dearly. More than I deserve." "And when their choice is made, is it possible that you might be happier—or disappointed?" "Oh, I cannot really concern myself with such things."

"And what about those books you were telling me about, all those novels —you certainly have heard about love, and read about it—in those European novels?"

"Oh, I have stayed away from the bad life. Many of my friends in school have turned to the romantic ways. But without me. I have studied."

My discomfort (and perplexity) mounted as my interrogation went awry; but Ram bore with me as with a summer storm. "You see, in my life I have no desires. My parents—I am to serve them. I have no other real wishes."

"But then," I ventured, with inexcusable brashness, "unreal wishes?"

"With a little more money I could buy another white shirt, another pair of white slacks, and keep myself a little cleaner. I would look to my dress."

"And to nothing else? A radio for your little room?" "No." "A bicycle to ride into town?" "No." "A small library of your own?" "No," he said again, with no impatient finality, but only that look of sadness and forgiveness, which was in part politeness and in part humility.

"And your son, Ram, your first son—what future for him? Would you wish for him a better life than your own?"

"But how could we tell that? How could we control that? The nature of the boy will determine, whatever our efforts, whether he will be better, in some ways, than I, or worse, in other ways. Is that not a principle of life?"

UNREAL DESIRES

Back from the villages, cramped and medieval, into the bustling metropolis of Bombay, with the endless lights of the Marine Road Drive glittering along the bay. The transition is violent and puzzling. Mohan picks me up to take me to a "typical party", typical that is for India's unique cosmopolitan centre. It is a *chic* affair, and for a moment I felt myself in Paris or New York, except for the fact that the women were more beautiful, the men wittier, the whole atmosphere gayer and more informal. The host is a wealthy Sikh who publishes *avant-garde* literature. Jim B. is a filmmaker who has just won a national prize for a Burmah-Shell documentary. K. is a pilot with Air-India. Mrs. P. is a divorcée who now works in an advertising agency and dreams of going to America. Mulk Raj Anand is the distinguished novelist, wears achkan and jodhpurs, and longs for the youth years when everybody ("even your European friends", he says to me sharply) was loyal to pure revolutionary ideals. K.K.T. is a Parsi merchant who has just returned from North German ports where he has bought two freight-ships. Good London gin (bought on the anti-prohibitionist black-market) flows too easily. I remember now only sitting in the corner with Moti Lal, my hastily appointed *guru* for the evening, pressing for information and enlightenment. I look at Mrs. P., so darkly beautiful in a charcoal-brown sari, who seems so flirtatious. "To yield to spontaneous emotion," I hear Moti Lal saying, "or to sensual appetite is felt to be wrong." Here too? I asked, here too? "This is especially the case with sexual satisfaction. Somehow it is always felt to be illicit and somehow impious." My confusion is only matched by my disappointment. But Moti Lal is relentless. "And the most scandalous conduct of all would be for a man and a woman to exchange smiling glances in public." I turn away from further enlightenment, avoid the path of the lovely Mrs. P., and become very depressed when Ranjee announces, in a drunken drawl, that the black-market gin is all gone.

ONE IN SEVEN

Modern demographers, like the demoniac witch-doctors of old, speak a curse. At the end of the second Five-Year Plan alone (1961) there will be 25 million more to provide for; by 1976 at least 100 million more. Is the problem being faced? (But then : are problems anywhere ever really faced?) In some of the book-stores I see old copies of Marie Stopes prominently displayed. In many of the villages there are odd tales of the coming of contraception. Among a few experts there is talk of the legalization of abortion. Meanwhile, according to something called "a pilot research monograph in family planning", I learn that in the Lucknow area "total fertility comes to 6·015 children per mother, with a gross reproduction rate of 2·379". Among the other indelicate conclusions : (1) unless fertility is so reduced as to limit the average number of children to three, the present rate of population growth cannot be stemmed; (2) only one in six of the mothers of child-bearing age are responding positively to "family planning"; (3) no suitable method is yet available that "may generally be accepted and be easily adopted by the women".

But in this morning's newspaper I read that Mr. V. K. Krishna Menon, the new Defence Minister, with the sensitivity which all army leaders have for raw material, says that "the people is our country's greatest wealth", and that "India is the second greatest country in the world because she has the second largest population in the world".

Size continues to exert a peculiar fascination in Indian minds. Even Minoo Masani, that cool, calculating intelligence, writes in the very opening lines of his *Our India* (a best-selling book for the young, which I pinched from his library last night)—"One man in every seven is an Indian. The other six are, let's say, an American, a European, a Negro, an Arab, a Russian, and a Chinese . . . Doesn't that make you feel very important?"

I asked A. D. Gorwala—who has written so bitterly on "the disease of surplus population" and other problems that hardly a publication in the country dares print him any more—for some guidance in the moral and medical complexities. The religious Hindu believes that continence and abstinence are the only tolerable approaches. The socialist is convinced that population control is only a capitalist fetish; and in as much as full employ-ment will guarantee work and livelihood for all, the more the merrier. The statistician comforts himself with the fact that India's rate of increase is lower than that of Japan or the United States or Canada, and far lower than that of South American countries. The patriot, distressed at the lack of Indian achievement in so many spheres, finds consolation in the thought of the enormous population. The traditionalist would leave the problem to the usual checks : pestilence, war, and famine.

So, says Gorwala, "our life will generally continue to be, if not short, still nasty and brutish—unless we recognize that biology is our priority. It is the key to India's economic welfare and to our political stability. What we need is a vigorous, large-scale, country-wide propaganda and action programme. The birth-rate can and must be brought down . . ."

Gorwala's eloquence is convincing. But when he begins to go into the surgical details of his plan for the sterilization of men with three children or more, I find myself making a move to change the subject.

KRISHNA MENON

What manner of man is V. K. Krishna Menon? Last week he was asked for his opinion on India's thorny language question, and he replied testily that he had none, for "I speak no Indian language". An irascibly gauche reply in public for a man whose political ambition has carried him into the cabinet and into Nehru's favoured circle. Yesterday in Travancore he was pressed with the issue of the mounting opposition to the Communist government in Kerala—and he answered by saying that it would be "beneath the dignity" of the Congress party to ally itself with the other dissidents (and this at a moment when the Communists maintain a majority by only one seat!). What is he up to? Purshottom, relentless pessimist that he is, thinks only the worst. "The die is cast. Menon will succeed Nehru. And that is the end of our free India." Almost everybody sees him as the witch-doctor, the dark medicine-man of Indian politics. He is respected with reluctance, and feared irrationally. "You will never understand his power," says Shankar, "unless you understand his relationship with Panditji, and that I am afraid is lost in the thousand-year-old loving-hating tensions between fair North-Indian Brahmins and black South-Indian warrior castes . . . " Everybody has a different theory.

So the speculations of the day went. I asked A. R., the *New York Times* correspondent, and he too psychologized. "With Menon," he says, "there is always a strange drive to get the insult in first. I have often wondered where it comes from. Perhaps from his colour sensitivity. Or his loneliness. Or his poverty, or his insecurity . . ." Frank Moraes suggests that "he combines a masculine mind with a feminine spirit, much given to tantrums and exhibitions of pique, verbal volubility and the tired airs and graces of a peevish prima donna . . ." "You know," he adds, "like John Foster Dulles, Menon delights in playing the combined rôles of matador and bull. When in America I was asked my opinion of the man I always used to say placidly, 'Krishna Menon is *our* Mr. Dulles.' "

Ushered into his Ministry of Defence office this afternoon, I paused under a huge portrait of Gandhi as three colonels were escorted out. Menon was polite, patient, and cool. (This evening I happened to learn at dinner from a woman who had lunch with him that he had been plying her with questions as to "who" I was, and I shudder to think of the astrological coincidence of my puzzling over his inmost soul while he was sketching a psychograph of me, probably based, alas, on the evening paper's interview which listed me most strangely as "a Berliner who edits a German magazine, sports a French beard, and speaks fluent English but with a strong American accent".

"You must understand the tragic complication of our Indian task. You in the West first had your industrial revolution, and then came modern politics. Here we first had to have our political revolution, and now comes modern economics. You first had wealth, then power. We have power, and have to create wealth ... And how full of ironies and surprises it all is! I flew recently along our North-Eastern frontier areas. There I landed to visit one of the local tribes. This was a people who had never seen a wheel until my plane rolled to a stop on one of their fields."

We chatted, not unamiably, for half an hour, and the difficult issues were sedulously avoided. His was a brief performance, a one-acter intended only to exhibit a bit of charm, wit, and intelligence. "After all, you are seeing the Prime Minister tomorrow, aren't you? ... Oh, he's a pregnant thinker! He is the real man of thought ... I? Oh, I'm not an intellectual, I'm not a thinker. Or even an educated person. I don't read any books. I'm just a——" And here he made an elegantly nervous gesture with his hand and angular fingers, not without some of the South Indian grace which Kathakali dancers have made famous.

In jesting clumsy imitation I waved my own hand and begged him to say exactly what that might be ...

"Oh," he said, "just an ... aimless ... flutterer ..."

Then I left, and this time there were two generals standing under the oil of Gandhi as I was escorted out.

FACELESS MODERN

New offices, new apartments, new ministries—"faceless modern" is the way we build. Is the world becoming like every place? It is. Certainly the furious despair of the Indian architects I meet is familiar. "What is all this going up?" Rajendra fumes, flailing his arms as if to sweep away all the scaffolding on the horizon. "An indigenous modern architecture? Nothing but empty-minded translations of jazz. Everywhere just another mass of brick and concrete, with holes punctured to breathe in and out. Doesn't anybody realize what horrors we are going to leave behind as the land-marks of our times? Aren't these the slums of our soul?"

Mansinh Rana complains—for me, not quite convincingly—against the middle way, with a bit of "old sentimental remembrances" and a bit of the new "international style of living" in boxes-on-stilts. Some of the new structures I see seem to me a happier departure from the Gropius norm than the timid heresies which Western architects are uncertainly allowing themselves these days. Still, no one anywhere appears to know what modern truly is, and how, if at all, the sentimental glories of the past should fit into a present full of continuous cantilevers and reinforced concrete. In Athens I found an absurd taste for brand new Corinthian columns, and here, in New Delhi, there is likely to be a mindless return to the ornamental roundness of Indo-Saracen epochs.

I have yet to hear a good word spoken for even a scrap of marble or red sandstone going up. The capital full of bureaucrats and bo-trees is contemptuously dismissed as "Washington (or Bonn) in the Punjab", in the style of (according to one disagreeable local wag) "Victorian-Wrighteousness". As for Le Corbusier's Chandigarh, a hundred miles or so north of here—this is Vighneswara's report:

"What is it other than miles of asphalted road dumped on the flat, arid country? Can anything grow there? I saw an avenue of our *kalyana-murungai,* and they were putting up a brave fight against the pitiless sun. Didn't M. Le Corbusier know that these are extremely fragile trees? . . . And that new city. Everything is meticulously numbered. All the public buildings have enigmatic exteriors. And the long ribbons of elongated flats were for me a nightmare of asymmetrical geometry. In the High Court there are Picassoesque interiors which I presume are supposed to strike terror into the hearts of malefactors. I felt only claustrophobia, without a single ray of natural light."

I concede the grotesquerie, but stubbornly insist on a sign that we know not merely what we are against, but what we are for.

"The idea of conjuring up a whole city out of the void is impious!" Apparently it trespasses on "Brahma's exclusive right", but where would Brahma build today, and how?

"Our cities were always built, or rather imperceptibly grew, from a central nucleus, a temple or a palace." It seemed hardly likely that the Planning Commission would provide such convenient new points of urban departure.

We finally compromise on an agreement that it was folly to spend millions for Le Corbusier's Chandigarh when hardly 40 miles away there was Patiala, admirably suited for development.

"I tell you, such a folly would be inconceivable anywhere except in the snob's paradise which is modern India!"

I let that pass, without sad Western qualifications. I was afraid we might have to have another drink (read: lemon squash) in the enormous and empty halls, bars, and lobbies of the new Asoka Hotel, a shiny, massive, frightening void, India's very own contribution to the architectural disease of white elephantiasis . . .

M.P.S AND COOLIES

I spend the morning in the *Lok Sabha*; until recently it was still known as "The House of the People" and it still looks, as an Indian Parliament inevitably must, like a vaguely Saracen version of Westminster. But the chamber is quite peaceful. Pandit-ji, as Nehru is called with some affection, is seated in the first seat, first row, to the left of the speaker, and he wears, as do a hundred other followers (curiously, even indoors), the little white cap which Gandhi-ji made famous. There is an attractive sprinkling of women M.P.s. When Nehru rises to speak there appears to be no sudden sense of excitement; in addition to being Prime Minister he is also Director of Planning and Minister of Atomic Energy and it is only another departmental report that has to be given. A not-very-bright back-bencher interrupts to put a foolish and interminably eloquent question about isotopes. The Prime Minister, with a weariness which seeps through his formal cloak of parliamentary patience, replies with the necessary facts and figures about the construction of piles and reactors ... All in all, a dull, routine, and hence, as democracies go these days, not unimpressive session.

In the afternoon, I wandered through the halls of the government buildings, and was embarrassed to cause so much unrest, for at each turn a host of squatters rises and remains standing until one passes. These are supposed to be known by their new official appellation, namely, "Grade IV Employees", but everywhere when some small thing is needed the cry goes up, as in the days of the British Raj, for *"Bearer"*. Strange. I would have supposed that these words of humiliation, these vestiges of "imperialist command" and native indignity, would have been mouth-washed out of the language in the new India. But they seem to be on more lips than ever before. In the railway station, as the train comes in and porters are in demand, I hear the shouting on all sides for *"Coolie!"*

A MIXED MARRIAGE

Abdul K. M. was a foreign medical student at the university when I knew him twenty years ago; he has since become a brilliant young Muslim surgeon in Agra. He still appears to be something of a stranger in his own country, and it is with the warmhearted, unnatural frankness of two strangers that we come to speak of personal things.

He tells me of his friendship with a young assistant in the hospital. She is the daughter of one of India's most distinguished doctors, a Hindu. For six years they were in love, but dared not to marry. ("Mixed marriages", as everybody has been politely telling me, are more frequent these days.) Two years ago they decided to make their own arrangements. Since then his wife has been cut off from her family: her father never speaks of her, her mother obediently refrains from writing. They both have lost all contact with their old circle of friends. His own appointment to a university was cancelled; his contract with his clinic was not renewed. "Oh, there was nothing personal in all this," he explains, "it was simply the formal proper sign of respect to my distinguished father-in-law, a fine and honourable man whom nobody wanted to hurt further . . . But I did receive one personal congratulation. How elated we were! A famous colleague went out of his way to befriend us. But then I learned that he was a lower-caste man . . . The difference? The difference is that he had become eminent through achievement, and he knew the pain of being an outsider. His gesture, you see, was a private, a personal matter. It was pity, and self-pity. It was not a matter of principle . . ."

So there they were again in their utter loneliness which I, even more of an outsider, even more irrelevantly personal, was quite helpless to relieve.

ON TIME

I only noticed this morning, with an accidental passing glance at the little note from the Prime Minister's Secretariat, that what I took to be the official correspondence number—*Chaitra 19, 1880*—was something quite different. On today's copy of the "Amrita Bazar Patrika" I am struck, too, that next to the usual newspaper dateline (April 13, 1958) there is also the following: *Chaitra 30, 1364 B.C.* (*Chaitra 23, 1880 Sakabda*). The calendar? Then never was a subscriber so reassured that the copy in his hand was the very latest.

Apparently, as Colonel S. says, with that weary resignation which I often confound with the heritage of British understatement, "there is a great deal of confusion at present prevailing in regard to the calendar." For some seven centuries under Muslim rule India had used the lunar Hejira calendar—except for the brief period when Emperor Akbar had insisted on the Tarikh Ilahi, the Iranian solar calendar. When the British came (1757), the Gregorian calendar was introduced. That, according to my calculations, should make three—but no, there are, with the usual Indian talent for proliferation, at least thirty. I am shown a bewildering variety of *panchangs,* and in each of these almanacs the holidays and religious festivals are differently listed, some differing between Bengal and Orissa by as much as a month. Which is, I suppose, only normal, considering that the calculations were made by indigenous astronomers who did their moon-gazing with the naked eye. Nor did the local scribes fail to introduce deviations of their own. Colonel S. does some rapid researches on the date 21 March, 1957. In Bengal this is Chaitra 7, in Orissa Chaitra 8, and in the South (where everything is always different) Panguni (Phalguna) 8. Small wonder that some of our friends have reputations for coming, not minutes or hours but days and even weeks late for appointments!

How can all this confusion be resolved? By committee, obviously. But the governmental committee must limit itself only to "secular" reforms, which would leave the chaos of religious holidays intact. This is a little embarrassing, for even the Catholics on detecting that the Julian calendar was miscalculating the equinoxes, corrected it in the year 1582, on the advice of Pope Gregory XIII. India kept on losing as much as 23 minutes a year for some 14 centuries. The accumulated error makes March 21, or the vernal equinox, fall on April 13 or 14.

From the name of the astrologer caste, the Sakadvipi Brahmins, comes the chosen "Saka era", which still runs some 78 years behind the Christian era. The day, so the committee has ruled, should be reckoned from midnight to midnight—except, of course, for religious purposes, and there the local sunrise systems may be followed. The All-India Radio now opens each broadcast with both the Gregorian and the new Indian dates.

Colonel S. tells me that Nehru, too, had once asked about the Saka calendar. "He didn't understand it either."

NEHRU

My plans for Agra and Fatehpur Sikri are upset by the news that Pandit Nehru would see me that evening, and I rush about foolishly, taking a frantic quick glance at everything and, of course, a snap-shot of the Taj Mahal. The plane brought me back in time for tea at the Prime Minister's residence.

He asked me whether I had seen the *Moti Masjid* in the Red Fort of Agra, but I am afraid I hadn't. Or the inscription, attributed to Jesus, on the *Buland Darwaza* in Fatehpur Sikri—"The world is a bridge, Pass over it, But build no house upon it, The world endures but an hour..."—but I must have passed it by with so many other Sanskrit carvings. But one thing I had seen, I said (with a shade too much enthusiasm, as if to cover up my tourist shame and embarrassment), a house worth building, a unique and enduring thing of the human spirit. I meant the *Diwan-i-Khas* (and it had, in fact, preoccupied me in the royal, long-deserted city of the Great Moghuls). He did not seem to recall it. This was, I reminded him, "the hall of the private audience". It is centred remarkably on a single pillar, half of which is carved in Hindu and the other half in Moslem designs. Crowning the pillar was the Emperor Akhbar's seat, and radiating out were four causeways to the four corners of the gallery, and there sat each of the ministers. So, apparently, did Akhbar engage in disputations. Here, I thought, caught in curved and cornered sandstone, was the perfect image of political power in the context of a free dialogue. Whereupon he did me one better (and how easily, and with what appeared to be genuine scholarship), and told me of the rock-engraved proclamations of the Emperor

Asoka which are still being discovered by the archæologists. Asoka had been stricken with remorse (two thousand years ago, but not irrelevant) at the useless carnage of his victorious wars against enemies, and announced his repentance in a series of pronouncements. From the various Rock Edicts now dug up there still breathes, Nehru felt, the spirit of peace, goodwill, and compassion in the world...

Which brought us to the frontiers of the Cold War. When I gave him a copy of my book on the Hungarian revolution, he seemed to strike an apologetic note about India's slow and inaccurate comprehension of events (it took a month to reverse Menon's, and his own, wild misreading of Budapest). He asked about the apparently conciliatory Soviet moves on the questions of European disengagement and atomic bombs. I could only tell him what I had from two former Ambassadors in Moscow, namely, that they (Messrs. Kennan and Bohlen) waited expressly for years for one small, serious, substantial sign that the Bolsheviks wanted to settle some open problem with the Americans—in vain. For my own part, no creditable Soviet initiative could be expected from May Day speeches or slogans on the front page of *Pravda*. "But then," he countered, "is Mr. Dulles the model of diplomacy by 'small signs'? ... I know there are times when even the men in Moscow look out towards the West for a signal which could break the deadlock. Khrushchev himself spoke of this with me, even asked me to help. I reminded him that so much of what he has been saying would only serve to reinforce the recalcitrance of the other side ... But the hardness and blindness is, I am afraid, mutual. Abuse and recrimination is the meaning of the Cold War."

I was eager to talk about Indian affairs, and he was relaxed enough to take a thoughtful backward glance at the path the nation had taken in ten years. The deal with the Maharajahs to establish national unity still seemed to him a defensible expedient, although, as he added, "sometimes I think we were much too generous" (for the compensations to the princes were often almost as fabulous as the bejewelled empires surrendered). The killings of the Pakistan Partition period were "awful" and still horrified and shamed him. He felt pleased about the break-through in India of new science and technology. He felt happy about the new type of "community villages" being fostered throughout the countryside. He thought that the several general elections the new Indian democracy had experienced were surprising achievements. He remained amazed at how the "Personal Law" which he had helped to draft had actually revolutionized the status of women (how it had made divorce possible, given them property titles and right of inheritance, etc.).

And what, in the present, filled him "with despair"? Here he began to speak with a frown, nervously, and even the fading rose on his jacket suddenly looked utterly wilted. Issues become smaller and spirits become weaker. He deplored "the new provincialism" in the land, especially the controversy (and occasional violent outbursts) over the linguistic issue. He was saddened by the return of the caste problem, "which has been going out socially, but is now coming back politically" (for all parties manœuvre cynically for the caste-man's vote). His explanation was that "in the absence of external danger a people always multiplies the divisions within itself . . ."

"Does Pandit-ji really look so tired, so weary?" How can one tell across a tea-table? A night's sleep, or a fortnight's holiday, might restore a bit of bounce. Would it touch the deeper fatigue? When I spoke of Berlin, Nehru recalled that he had been there twice, once in the twenties, but before that in the pre-World War I period with vivid memories of the Kaiser's pageantry, Wilhelm's moustaches, and all that; I was forcibly reminded that he quite possibly belonged to that aged generation whose last political adventure always seems these days to be retirement.

In the evening, in exchange for odd scraps of the above, A.R., of the *Times* offers me his theory of Nehru's celebrated fatigue. "This man is the leader of the government," he says, "the leader of the majority party, the one force in Parliament, the chief economic planner, the chief social-reformer, the leading military thinker, the foreign affairs analyst, the man who decides everything." More than that : "He is everywhere . . . Here he is scolding the police, ridiculing superstition, censoring movies, inspecting schools, peering down construction shafts. He once told me that to him India was a crowd, that in the past nine years he had never visited a shop in New Delhi, taken a quiet walk in the streets, ridden in a taxi. The weariness is the burden of devotion . . ."

"That is too physiological," comments P., "and not ideological enough. Pandit-ji is faced with the most disagreeable, the most unattractive political battle of his life—fighting the Communists. This is the campaign which will make or break Indian democracy. He knows it. He will even acknow-ledge it privately. He may conscript himself for the battle, but he will never enjoy it. Weariness is often only a symptom of spiritual reluctance."

My own suggestion was less inspired, more bureaucratic. These days have been full of governmental appointments. I have gone in and out of ministries and secretariats. The men around Nehru? Think of the men around Gandhi! The Mahatma was able to develop and to hold strong and keen-witted personalities around him. There was the intellectual fox-like Rajagopolachari (whose daughter married Gandhi's son), the modernist like Nehru (who confessed, "I loved the old man but never understood him"), the ascetic like Vinoba Bhave (who inherited his loin-cloth), the political revolutionary like Jayaprakash Narayan . . . What a galaxy to carry on!

And around Nehru today? There seems to be no one. And, after Nehru goes, to carry on? There seems to be nobody.

Weariness is often just another word for loneliness.

CHOLERA IN CALCUTTA

Today remains the seventh and worst day of Calcutta's cholera epidemic. Thousands are ill, hundreds have died. On the streets, once or twice, I had a sickening glimpse of the symptoms, and on Brabourne Road, near the Portuguese Church, stinking garbage has been lying for days uncleared. The hospitals are already bulging, and where there is a clinic with a spare corner and some extra straw-matting there are no vehicles to transport the stricken. There are only 22 ambulances, and five have broken down, eight are still being tinkered with by mechanics, and two or three others just won't move.

I sipped tea with my friends uncomfortably, reassuring myself all the time that it was in fact boiling hot. They had, of course, been inoculated? Oh, no. Why not? No good reason. Didn't they believe the reports in the papers? To be sure. And the health of their children——? Resignation. I took a last sip of the tea and found it alarmingly luke-warm . . .

In the evening, with Mazumdar, and in inflexible antiseptic calculation, we drink only Chinese whisky. He tells me that the health authorities of the city administration have promised "to investigate the causes of the epidemic", and "to take appropriate action". I storm. The causes have been known for a century. And the appropriate action lies at the tip-end of a hypodermic needle! and in cleaning the garbage off the streets! and in digging sanitary wells! and boiling the water! and in getting ambulances that run! When there was so-called "germ warfare" on a Korean frontier thousands of miles away, there were Indian demonstrations and protests, and no one in Calcutta knew for certain whether there were any casualties or even a single real germ. Now it is all real, at home, and fatal; and nobody utters a peep. "Cholera may be curable," says Mazumdar, "but what seems incurable is our attitude that life is expendable." Still, he promises to write an editorial note about it (and does). "Good to be alive," he toasts, and we all gulp hard.

My frients have just telephoned. They apologize for the lateness of the hour, but they want to please me with the information that they all had just gone to the doctor's to receive their vaccine—more out of conciliatory politeness, I suspect, than out of a sense of urgent necessity. That would bring the city's total for inoculations up to about a million. Only a few more million to go.

THE LANGUAGE PROBLEM

When people have not been fighting over frontiers or precious treasure, then they have been quarrelling over the colour of skins—and the colour of words. In Bombay the supporters of the Gujerati language (especially well-to-do merchants) and the Maharashtrans (whose lower-class elements have been agitated by the Communists) have rioted—and murdered—in the city streets. In Ceylon the Tamil minority, outraged by the letter "*sri*" on the new licence plates, have been overturning—and burning—buses, trams, and automobiles. Somewhere in the Indian countryside (I have been searching for him, but in vain) there is Dr. Ram Manohar Lohia, the brilliant and unpredictable Berlin-educated socialist leader, in the midst of proclaiming an "*Angrezi Hatao*" or "Banish English" week; and he has been marching with volunteer bands, roving from street to street, tearing down signboards, erasing English names.

In November 1949, the Constituent Assembly, although sharply divided (the debates, of course, were in the mother tongue of the British Raj), approved by a majority of one vote the decision to make Hindi the official language of India. The strange paradox of this question of the English language would seem to be that those who speak English have opposed it, and those who have always resented it have suddenly become the champions of "the language of Shakespeare and modern scientific truth".

"I was a sentimentalist, too," Rajogopolachari confessed one evening in Madras to me. "I was, after all, the last Governor-General of India, and I could not help feeling—then—that the continuance of a foreign language would be derogatory to our national prestige. English was the speech of the conquerors whom we allowed to take possession of our country. We disliked them. But now that Englishmen are gone, anger has gone. We have become calmer, quieter. And what the Englishman has left behind is no longer his property. Why should we throw it away? Have we thrown away his railways and telegraph wires? We have not even sent back the statues still standing in our parks. The decision was an erroneous step taken when thought was not ripe. It should be suspended. I have said so publicly and Nehru has accused me of 'waging a cold war' against him. But Hindi is simply not rich enough and good enough for all our purposes. We need English for science, for intellectual life, for international affairs. At home our people should continue to speak their mother-tongues, in my own case Tamil."

But not all the new defenders of English against "Hindi imperialism" are friends of the other thirteen national languages. (It is probably fourteen official competitors now, for in Delhi I heard a clever editor put on a show of dialectics in a press conference with Nehru—"if our Anglo-Indian community shares equal rights in Indian democracy, is then their language,

English, also not a national tongue of our people?"—whereupon he got what he wanted, namely, a weary concession from the Prime Minister, "I suppose so . . .")

"Beware of all of our eloquence on the linguistic issue," Purshottam warned, "beware of all of our *bunk*! Most of the languages which are with us today have been preserved only by illiteracy! They would have passed away generations ago if people could read and write something else. What was the Gujerati I learned as a boy? Nothing but a miserable dialect. And today I never use it. My wife is from the South, but I know no Malayalam. So we have always spoken to each other in English. And every now and then, in some outburst of infantile romanticism, we might quote some of our own tender love poetry to each other. But what are these verses really— nothing more than a few flowery phrases, and these are passed off nowadays as the richness of regional cultural traditions."

Yet, in Calcutta, they would not love English so much had they not loved Bengali more. This is the land of Rabindranath Tagore, and even the most solicitous of guides would have dragged me off to Shanti Niketan, a hundred blistering miles away, to see his Bengali manuscripts and his Bengali landscapes. Ayyub hand-winds his old victrola to play Tagore songs for me. Buddhadeva Bose reads rapturously a single line of his Bengali poetry.

Nishidin bharsha rākhish, oré mon habei habé

which, in its "utter untranslatability", comes out only as "Have hope, O my heart, hope day and night, for it will be . . ."

There is here a literary pride of fierce intensity. And what a brilliant campaign has this shrewd and effective intelligentsia conducted on the Indian political scene! Seen from here, Hindi seems almost to be a lost cause.

S. K. CHATTERJI : "Is it true that the Hindi-speaking minority in India amounts to 42 per cent of our population? It is not. This figure has been inflated by improperly combining the figures for Rajasthani, Kosali, Bhojpuri, Urdu Punjabi, and Maithili, some of which are totally distinct . . . We are faced by a very serious menace to Indian unity in this linguistic chauvinism. Some have even started a slogan, '*Hindi, Hindu, Hindi,* these three are one!' "

BUDDHADEVA BOSE : "Nor is it a fact that Hindi, which is our official language and is soon to be our national language, is 'spoken and understood in practically every part of the country'. You have probably listened to *bazaar*-Hindi in our railway stations. But this is not a language known to god or man! It is only a collection of corrupt words devoid of grammar or syntax, in which the crudest communication is just barely possible. What is it good for? For haggling! But this peculiar form of oriental activity can be conducted in signs and gestures, as you no doubt have discovered, without benefit of any language at all ..."

AMLAN DATTA: "This whole misfortune in India has been based only on a misreading of the nineteenth century in Europe. Scraps of Herder have led to absurd notions of the relations between nationality and language. As if Belgium didn't have two languages, and Switzerland three, as if the future united Europe would not have a dozen! If no other country in history has ever adopted a 'foreign' language for official use, then let India be the first."

ABU SAYEED AYYUB : "Our country 'unified and integrated' by a common shared tongue—this is a wish. And wishes are good horses to ride. But India, you see, has never had *one* national language. In ancient times Sanskrit was the language of a strictly limited *élite* (and only of men). In Moghul times Persian was exclusively the language of the court. Now it is true that in addition to *bazaar*-Hindi, with its makeshift vocabulary of a few hundred words, there is the prosy 'Khariboli' Hindi, a fine and difficult tongue. But it scarcely existed a century ago. It has neither ancient richness nor modern usefulness. Brahmin pandits will have to create a dictionary full of new words and phrases! Let us not search for simple or heroic solutions. We believe and take pride in the fact that India's chief contribution to the progress of civilization is a spirit of synthesis which reconciles differences without obliterating them, which welcomes diversity of culture and tradition, of race and religion. Should we now therefore be ready to recognize and proclaim to the world that India has not one but a dozen national languages, just as it has not one but half a dozen national religions?"

Still : if not all champions of English are supporters of the traditional languages, not all spokesmen for the regional cultures command fluency in the beloved mother tongues. Even in Bengal one writer told me that he still has "difficulties", for he had lived too long in the Indian west. And in the south one impassioned young man insisted that "a people should have the language in which it dreams!"—but then admitted that his own Telegu, alas, was not good enough for dreaming.

RAJAJI

"Never will there be an evening like this even if we have seven rebirths!" whispered the young man to me, as old Rajagopolachari hobbled away from our garden circle. It had been something of a rare occasion for the worshippers of Rajaji (in fact for us all) to be in the presence of this wizened, aged man, said by so many to be the wisest and most fearless in the land. He alone, of all the former close associates of Gandhi, has remained politically independent, without official position, a gadfly of the State. How weird are all the local loving appellations for this man who has never been outside of India—a "modern Socrates", an "Asian Savonarola", a "brahmanized Gladstonian liberal".

He sat with us for hours, talking, listening, and I was magnetized by this most impressive and unforgettable personality I had met in India. He reminded me, as we sat there, of what the Mahatma must have been like— hunched and shrunken together, and behind the soft voice and smile, a piercing, subtle, understanding intelligence.

"Gandhi?" says Prabhakar later, in our last argument. "Oh, no. Gandhi-ji has the wisdom and the cleverness—and the face!—of a child. Rajaji has the wisdom and the foxiness—and the face!—of an old woman." But perhaps this was only because Rajaji had prevented Prabhakar, with a small, stern, non-violent gesture of his hand, from copying wicked little quotations into his notebook.

I now regret that Prabhakar did not get away with his secret jottings. Rajaji said many extraordinary things, some gently, some savagely, but above all he prodded and parried in the most spectacular way. He disdains the mantle of "minor saintlessness", and spurns popular messages of hope. He did not mind being taken for a whining old man longing for the past. He was sad, but not sentimentally so, rather out of the sense of loss which civilizations in decay inevitably impart. Yet if he prefers no record, let us say that all the details were lost in the luminous enchantment of the evening.

TAKING OFF

In the last minutes of a journey one finally learns how to ask the questions with which one should have begun. I sit fastened on to my plane seat, and search through my pockets and papers for scraps of notes, backs of envelopes, calling cards, loose clippings, and hotel messages. It comes to an untidy but reassuring pile. All the answers, surely, must be in there, somewhere. Odds-and-ends begin to slip away from me, and I ask the Air-India stewardess (in *sari*) for a bag or a piece of string. (She is dark-skinned and well-educated—but what Indian language does she speak? does she adore Nehru? is she happier in a machine than her mother in the village? will she have difficulties getting married?) I get a single piece of matted hair from a jute bag in the back, and the whole plunder is safely secured. I fondle it playfully, but with increasing uneasiness. Had I found everything, and had I gotten it all right? An old familiar uncertainty begins to upset me. I recall the night when work, at last, was finished on my book on the Hungarian revolution and I felt, nightmarishly, a hand on my shoulder drawing me away pitilessly from the litter on my desk, and a voice said, "In the first place, it was not a revolution but an earthquake, in the second place it was Bulgaria not Rumania, and in the third place..."

SEPTEMBER 1958

ROBERT GRAVES

The Whitaker Negroes

HAUNTINGS, WHETHER IN waking life or dream, are emotionally so powerful, yet can be so seldom ascribed to any exterior agency, that they are now by common consent allotted to the morbid pathologist for investigation—not, at once, to the priest or augur. A number of hauntings "yield to treatment", as the saying is. The great Dr. Henry Head told me once about a patient of his who was haunted by a tall dark man, always standing on the bedside mat. Head diagnosed a trauma in the patient's brain, of which the tall dark man was a projection, and proved his case by moving the bed slowly around; the tall dark man swung with it in a semicircle until he ended on a veranda just outside the french window. An operation removed him altogether. And I read in an American medical paper the other day of a man who, as a result of advanced syphilis, was haunted by thousands of women every night; after he had been given extract of snake-root they were reduced to the manageable number of one only.

There are also occasional hauntings which most psychologists would tend to dismiss as fantasies, or as symbols of some inner conflict; but which, however grotesque, deserve to be accepted at their face value and placed in the correct historical context. Let me describe a persistent haunting from my own case-history. I am glad to say that it did not originate in a ghost-ridden childhood and is therefore easier to assess, though I cannot claim to have been in good mental or physical health at the time; on the contrary, I was suffering from vivid nightmares and hallucinations of the First World War, in which I had just fought. Shells used to burst on my bed at night, by day I would throw myself flat on my face if a car backfired, and every rose garden smelt terrifyingly of phosgene gas. However, I felt a good deal better now that the War seemed to be over : an armistice had been signed, and the Germans were not expected to renew the struggle.

January 1919 found me back with the Royal Welch Fusilier reserve battalion at Limerick; where twenty years before my grandfather had been the last Bishop of the Established Protestant Church of Ireland. Limerick was a firm stronghold of Sinn Fein, King George Street had become O'Connell Street, and when our soldiers took a stroll out of barracks they never went singly and were recommended to carry entrenching-tool handles in answer to the local shillelaghs. This return as a foreign enemy to the city with which my family had been connected for over 200 years would have been far more painful but for old Reilly, an antique dealer, who lived near the newly-renamed Sarsfield Bridge. Reilly remembered my father and three of my uncles, and gave me fine oratorical accounts of my Aunt Augusta Caroline's prowess in the hunting field, and of the tremendous scenes at my grandfather's wake—at which his colleague, the Catholic Bishop, had made attendance compulsory in tribute to his eminence as a Gaelic scholar and archæologist. I brought several things from Reilly : Irish silver, prints, and a century-old pair of white, elbow-length Limerick gloves, left by the last of the Misses Rafferty and so finely made (from chicken-skin, he told me) that they folded into a brass-hinged walnut shell.

The shop smelt of dry rot and mice, but I would have gone there to chat more often, had it not been for a nightmarish picture hanging in the shop entrance; a male portrait brightly painted on glass. The sitter's age was indeterminate, his skin glossy-white, his eyes Mongolian, their look imbecile; he had two crooked dog-teeth, a narrow chin, and a billycock hat squashed low over his forehead. To add to the horror, some humorist had provided the creature with a duddeen pipe, painted on the front of the glass, from which a wisp of smoke was curling. Reilly said that the picture had come from the heirs of a potato-famine emigrant, returned at last with a bag of dollars to die comfortably of drink in his native city. Why this face haunted and frightened me so much I could not explain; but it used to recur in my imagination for years, especially when I had fever. I told myself that if I ever saw a midnight ghost—as opposed to midday ghosts, which had been common enough phenomena during the later, neurasthenic stages of the War, and less frightening than pathetic—it would look exactly like that.

In the spring of 1951, when Reilly had lain thirty years in his grave, Julia Fiennes visited me in Majorca. She was an American : Irish Italian on her father's side, New Orleans French on her mother's; a textile designer by profession; young, tall, good-looking, reckless and romantic. She had come "to take a look at Europe before it blows up". When we first met, a shock passed between her and me of the sort usually explained in pseudo-philosophic terms as "We must have met in a previous incarnation." Psychologists postulate "compatible emotion-groups". I am content to call it "Snap!" Indeed, as it proved, Julia and I could converse in a joking verbal shorthand, which meant little to anyone else, but for us expressed a range of experience so complex that we could never have translated it into everyday language. An embarrassing, if exhilarating discovery, because this rapport between us, strong as it was, proved inappropriate both to her course of life and mine. We wanted nothing from each other except a humorously affectionate acknowledgement of the strength of the link; thirty-three years separated us; we belonged to different civilizations; I was perfectly happy in my own life, and she was set on going on and on until she came to a comfortable stop in either contentment or exhaustion; which she has since done.

With Beryl, to whom I am married, I enjoy the less spectacular but more relevant rapport which comes from having all friends in common, four children, and no secrets from each other. The only eccentric form which our rapport takes is that sometimes, if I am working on some teasing historical problem and go to bed before I reach a solution, its elements may intrude not into my dream but into hers. The classic instance was when she woke up one morning, thoroughly annoyed by the absurdity of her nightmare : "A crowd of hags were swinging from the branches of a large tree in our olive grove and chopping off the ends with kitchen knives. And a horde of filthy gipsy children were waiting below to catch them . . ." I apologized to Beryl. I had been working on textual problems in the New Testament, and establishing the relation between Matthew xviii, 20 and Isaiah xvii, 6 which ran : "As the gleaning of an olive-tree : two or three berries at the top of the topmost branch"; and of this with Deuteronomy xxiv, 20 : "When thou beatest thine olive-trees thou shalt not go over the boughs again : the gleanings shall be for the stranger, the fatherless and the widow." I went to bed wondering idly how the fatherless and the widow managed to glean those inaccessible olives, if no able-bodied stranger happened to be about.

"Well, now you know!" Beryl answered crossly.

Once when Julia and I were taking a walk down a dark road not far from the sea, and exchanging our usual nonsense, I suddenly asked her to tell me something really frightening. She checked her pace, clutched my arm and said : "I ought to have told you, Robert, days ago. It happened when I was staying with my grandmother in New Orleans, the one who had the topaz locket and eyes like yours. I guess I must have been twelve years old, and used to ride to school on my bicycle about half-a-mile away. One summer evening I thought I'd come home by a different route, through a complicated criss of cross-streets. I'd never tried it before. Soon I lost my way and found myself in a dead-end, with a square patio behind a rusty iron gate, belonging to an old French mansion overgrown with creepers. The shutters were green too. It was a beautifully cool, damp place in that heat. And as I stood with my hand on the latch, I looked up, and there at an attic window I saw a man's face. He grinned and rapped on the glass with leprous fingers and beckoned to me . . ."

By Julia's description it was the identical face that had been painted on glass in Mr. Reilly's shop. When I told her about it, we broke into a run of perfect terror, hurrying towards the nearest bright light.

I thought it over afterwards. Perhaps Julia had become aware of my long-buried fear, which then became confused in her imagination with child-hood memories of New Orleans; and it stood out so vividly that she really believed that she had seen the face grinning at her. She mentioned no pipe; but then the pipe could be discounted as extraneous.

After supper, an American called Hank, a New York banker's son, burst into the house, in a state of semi-collapse. Since he came of age, Hank had fallen down on every job found for him by his father, and now drifted about Europe as a remittance-man. He wanted to write, though without an inkling of how to begin, and was more than a bore about his problems. Hank told me once: "The night before I sailed, my father said a very cruel thing to me. He said: 'Hank, you're a good watch, but there's a part missing somewhere.'" As a regular time-piece Hank was certainly a dead loss; and the place of the missing part had been filled by an erratic ancillary movement which by-passed time altogether. For instance, a few days before this, Hank had begun to jabber hysterically about a terrifying earthquake, and wondered whether the world were coming to an end. Next morning the papers mentioned a very limited earthquake in Southern Spain, which had swung pictures on walls, dislodged cornices from half a dozen buildings in a small town, and made several telephone operators faint for terror. Now, Hank could hardly have felt the distant shock, although Majorca is said to form part of a range, mostly submerged, which continues south-west-ward to the mainland; but he had certainly caught the emotion of the frightened telephone girls.

"What's new, Hank?" I asked coldly.

"I've had a most horrible experience," he gasped. "Give me a drink, will you? I took a car to Soller this afternoon. The heel had come off my walk-ing-shoe and I wanted to get it fixed. You know Bennasar the shoemaker, off the market square? I was just about to go in when I looked through the window..."

Julie and I glanced at each other. We both knew what Hank was going to say. And he said it: "I saw a frightful face..."

That made us feel more scared than ever.

Soon afterwards Julia went off on a rambling-tour through France, Austria, and Italy, and next year revisited Majorca with her mother. That was September 1952. She found me collaborating in a film-script with Will Price. Will comes from Mississippi; but New Orleans is one of his family's stamping grounds, so he and Mrs. Fiennes were soon discussing third and fourth cousins. One day as we all sat outside a café, Julia happened to mention Hank. "Who's Hank?" the others wanted to know. We explained, and Julia repeated the story of the New Orleans face. Her mother gasped and shook her roughly: "Darling, why in Heaven's name didn't you tell me about it at the time?"

"I was terrified."

"I believe you're making it up from something I told you, sweetie. I saw the same face myself before you were born—*and* the rusty iron gate—*and* the creepers and the shutters."

"You never told me anything of the sort. Besides, I saw it myself. I don't have other people's visions. You mustn't confuse me with Hank."

It occurred to me: "Probably her mother had the vision, or whatever it was, first. And then Julia as a child must have heard her telling the story to somebody, and incorporated it in her own private nightmare world."

But Will eased back in his chair and, turning to Mrs. Fiennes, asked in the playful Southern accent that they were using: "Honey, did you ever hear them up there in the old attic, sloshing water all over the place?"

None of us understood what he meant.

That night when we were sitting about, drinking coñac, Will raised his voice: "Ladies and gentlemen, may I have your permission to spin a yarn?"

"Why, of course."

Will started: "A good many years ago my father's law firm, Price and Price, acted for the mortgagees of a bankrupt property in Mississippi. Money was not forthcoming, so my father consented to take his fees in real estate—about eighty acres of almost worthless land at Pond near Fort Adams. Fort Adams was once a prosperous river port for the cotton country east of the River; the town itself was perched on the high bluffs which overhang the water hereabouts. But the River suddenly chose to change course five miles to the west and left Fort Adams with a wide frontage of swamp, so that all trade moved along to Natchez and Baton Rouge, which were still ports. These bluffs form the edge of a three-hundred-mile line of hills raised, they say, by prehistoric dust-storms blowing in from the Great Plains, and cut up by streams and swamps. There used to be dozens of rich plantations in the hills, but when the River deserted Fort Adams they were abandoned and allowed to revert to jungle.

"A victim of this catastrophe was Pond, a village that got its name from the cattle-pond which its leading citizen, old man Lemnowitz, dug and surrounded with two-storey framestores and warehouses. It used to be a tough job to fetch cotton over the hills from the plantations in the interior. The bales were loaded on enormous, sixteen-wheeled wagons drawn by from six to ten yoke of oxen. Teamsters and planters would camp at Pond before making the final drive uphill to Fort Adams. Old man Lemnowitz hired them extra oxen for the effort, and carried on a thriving trade in supplies of all sorts which he had hauled up from the River in the off-season.

"There were still traces of ancient wealth near Pond when I visited it —ruins of the antebellum mansions and slave-quarters, with huge, twisted vines writhing up through the floors—and at Pond itself Lemnowitz's warehouse, formerly a sort of Macy's, was still in business under the same name. But only one corner was now occupied : by a small, not very elegant, store that sold tobacco, notions, staples, and calico. It also called itself the Pond Post Office.

"The rest of Pond was jungle. My mother had come down there to see whether Price and Price owned any camellias; because sometimes these old planters collected rare flowers, and camellias could still be found grow-ing wild in their deserted gardens. No! No orchids in that area, but camellias had been imported from all over the world, including even the Chinese mountains where they originally belonged. I was there to keep my mother company and check the land lines. Well, I went to buy a packet of cigarettes in the Lemnowitz store, and before I could get my change, a Thing walked in.

"It was undoubtedly human, in a weird way—walked upright and had the correct number of limbs. It even strode up to the counter and held out a dime for a can of snuff. But for the rest . . . The face was a glazed greenish white, with four fangs that crossed over the lips, and a protruding under-lip. It had dark-brown hair, dripping with wet, under a black felt hat— the sort that gave the po' white trash from Georgia their nickname of 'wool-hats'. Long arms ending in gauntlets—the local work-gloves of canvas and leather with stiff cuffs—which hung below its knees as it walked. Muddy 'overhawls', leather brogans called 'clod-hoppers', and a stink as if fifty cess-pools had been opened simultaneously. I said nothing, except perhaps 'Oh!' What would any of you have said in the circumstances? Imagine the dark cavern of a mouldering warehouse behind you, with acres of empty shelves lost in the gloom, and then in It comes through the door with the blazing sun behind It. When It vanished again, I ran to the window to make sure that my mother had not fainted, and then tip-toed back to the counter. '*What was that?*' 'Why, that was only a Whitaker Negro,' Mr. Lemnowitz said casually. 'Never seen one before?' He seemed to be enjoy-ing the situation."

As Will told the story my old terrors came alive again. "Well, what was it really?" I croaked.

"I guess it was just a Whitaker Negro," said Will. "Later, I decided to check up on my sanity. Mr. Lemnowitz told me that for a couple of nickels

Boy Whitaker, who was only a half-Whitaker, would guide me to where his folk lived. And he did. There are, or were, several families of Whitaker Negroes near Pond, tucked away in the jungle swamps where nobody ever ventured, not even the Sanitary Inspector. You have to understand the geography of these hills and reckon with their amazing verdancy and complete lack of vistas. One can march in a straight line up and down hills and over swamps for scores of miles without seeing a self-respecting horizon. The jungle is so thick in places that whole families have grown up and died within a mile of neighbours whose existence they didn't even suspect; and we Mississippians are noted for our gregariousness. I don't know how I ever reached the place myself, because I was working to windward and the stench spread for a half a mile around the place. I nearly threw up even before I arrived. They live tax-free and aren't mentioned in the census, and don't of course have to send their kids to school, still less get drafted for military service. The kids live in wallows under their huts, which are built on piles; apparently they don't come out much until they're fourteen years old or so—can't stand the sun. A good documentary sequence could be taken of a sow and her litter wallowing in the slime with a bunch of young Whitaker monsters : you could title it *Symbiosis*—which is what we call a 'fo'bit' word.

"The adults make a sort of living by raising hogs and chickens : enough to keep them in snuff and brogans and gauntlets and other necessities. The 'hair' proved to be mostly spanish-moss clapped wet on the head to keep it cool—it comes grey-green and goes dark when you soak it; but their real hair is also long, brown and wavy, not kinky in the usual negroid style. The brogans and gauntlets were filled with water. You see, they have no sweat-glands—that's their trouble. It's a hereditary condition and their skin needs to be kept wet all the while, or they die. They're Negroes; but said to be mixed with Choctaw Indian, also perhaps a strain of Chickasaw and Natchez."

Someone asked : "Didn't the snuff get a bit *damp,* Will?"

Will answered blandly : "No, sir, it did not! Snuff is 'dipped', not sniffed, in those parts. It comes in cans about an inch and a half high. The lid of the can is used to dip a little snuff into the buccal pouch—which is another 'fo'bit' word meaning the hollow under your nether lip, excuse me for showing off."

Most of the coñac-drinkers grinned incredulously, but Will turned to me : "Did you ever hear of Turtle Folk? That's what they call whites afflicted by the same disease. There are quite a few cases up and down the Mississippi—Natchez, Vicksburg, Yazoo City, Baton Rouge—kept a close secret, though. Once I was in a house at Natchez where they kept a turtle-man in the attic, and I heard him sloshing water about overhead. That was what Julia must have seen in New Orleans, and Mrs. Fiennes before her. And I guess what you saw in Limerick was a portrait of a turtle-man brought back from the South as a curiosity."

We asked Will : "How did they get there? And why are they called 'Whitaker Negroes'?"

He answered : "I was coming to that. Around 1810, or so the story goes, a big planter named George Whitaker grew disgusted with his labour problems. He was an intelligent, wide-eyed, gullible New Englander, with Christian leanings, who wanted to reform the South and incidentally get even richer than he already was. He disliked the business of buying slaves and breeding them like cattle—with the result, he said, that they had no traditions, no morals, and no discipline but what could be instilled into them by fear. Ideally, he thought, a planter should be able to take a long vacation, like a European landlord, and come back to find work proceeding smoothly under Coloured overseers—only petty crimes to punish, and the crops properly harvested. He argued that if the early slave-traders had kept families and clans together under their African chiefs, the labour problem would not have existed. Then it occurred to him : Why not experiment? And he went down to New Orleans, where he interviewed the famous pirate Jean Lafitte. 'Sir,' he said, 'I wish you to visit Africa on my behalf and bring me back a whole tribe of Negroes. Two hundred is the figure I aim at, but a hundred would do. I'll pay you two hundred dollars a head : men, women, and children. But mind, it must be a whole tribe, not samples from a score of them, or I don't buy.'

"George was a serious man, and Jean Lafitte decided to close with him. He sailed to the Gold Coast with his brother Pierre on the next tide and there, almost at once as luck would have it, surprised a whole tribe on the march. The Negroes had been expelled from somewhere in the interior and, being in a pretty poor way, offered no resistance. The Lafittes got two hundred of them aboard, made ingenious arrangements for their welfare on the voyage, and brought across alive one hundred and fifty— smuggled them through Fort Adam and the Bayou St. John until Pond came in sight. This constituted, you see, fraudulent evasion of the 1808 Federal embargo on the importation of slaves; so two hundred dollars a head was not an unreasonable price, considering the risk. But think of it in terms of money! Well, Mr. Lemnowitz told me, at Pond, that when George Whitaker saw the livestock that the Lafittes had brought back from Africa, and realized they were now his responsibility—though because of their constitution, of no more use as field workers than the bayou alligators —he turned deathly white. He paid Jean Lafitte without a word; then he went home, made out his will, bequeathing the bulk of his land to the then

99

'Territory of Mississippi'—after which he and his young wife jumped into the River, hand in hand, and were not seen again.

"Someone took over the plantation, but allowed the Whitakers to remain in a swamp and make out as best they could. And they hung on there long after the Whitaker mansion was swallowed up by the jungle. Their 'forty' is tax-free and inviolable because the original deed of gift represented taxes paid in perpetuity. About fifteen years ago a Whitaker went crazy—they are none of them very bright—and hit the trail for he didn't know where. He travelled from swamp to swamp, living off the land, and eventually reached the town of Woodville which is not very far away as the crow flies, but a thousand miles as the jungle grows. The good people of Woodville, who normally publish an extra of their local paper only when a war is declared or a President assassinated, hurried one through the press with the banner headline: 'MAN FROM MARS!', because the poor wretch was half-dead and couldn't explain himself, and all the horses in the town were bolting, and the women screaming their heads off."

"And the Choctaw blood?"

"The Choctaws and Chickasaws were the local Indians, who obligingly moved away from the neighbourhood to make room for cotton. I was told that a few rogue males stayed behind in the swamps, mostly pox-cases, and intermarried with the Whitaker Negroes for want of other women."

"Did your mother find any camellias?"

Will, detecting a hint of irony in the innocent question, answered: "Thank you, ma'am. She got a lapful."

Later, my friend Tom Matthews, then managing editor of *Time,* sent me the medical column of December 14th, 1931 :

TURTLE FOLK

At Houston, Miss., a Mrs. C. keeps a tub of water in her back yard for an extraordinary purpose. It is a ducking tub for her five-year-old son. Every time he feels uncomfortable he jumps in, clothes and all. Mrs. C. does not scold. For that is the only way the boy can keep comfortable. He lacks sweat glands, which in normal people dissipate two to three quarts of cooling perspiration every day.

Mrs. C. has another son, an infant, who likewise lacks sweat glands. He is too young to go ducking himself. So she dowses him from time to time with scuppers of water. Neither child can sleep unless his night clothes and mattress are wet. They take daytime naps in their damp cellar, with moist sacks for pillows.

Nearby at Vardaman, Miss., are two farmer brothers similarly afflicted. They have a sweatless neighbour woman who must also wet herself for comfort. At Vicksburg, Miss., there is a seventh of these folk who, like turtles, must periodically submerge themselves. He is a 12-year-old boy.

Dr. Ralph Bowen of Memphis has made a medical report on the phenomenon. The seven suffer from "hereditary ectodermal dysplasia of the anhydrotic type". That is, they lack sweat glands, and the lack is hereditary. However, the seven Mississippi cases are related only as indicated above. This suggests that the failing is not so uncommon as heretofore believed. Along with the lack of sweat glands goes a lack of teeth. None of the seven Mississippi cases has more than two teeth.

Tom also sent me a typescript from *Time*'s research files :

From ANDREWS' DISEASES OF THE SKIN
Hereditary ectodermal dysplasia

There are numerous anomalies of the epidermis and appendages due to faulty evolution of the epiblastic layer of the blastoderm. Atrichosis congenitalis with or without deformities of the nails and teeth is common, and is accompanied at times by nevi and other congenital anomalies. Congenital absence or malformation of the nails and teeth is also of frequent occurrence, and in circumscribed areas it is not out of the ordinary to find that the sebaceous and sweat glands are absent or impaired. In restricted areas there may be a complete absence of the epidermis and appendages at birth . . . The appearance of these patients is typical and conspicuous, as they have a facies that is suggestive of congenital syphilis. The skin is hairless, dry, white, smooth, and glossy. The teeth are entirely absent or there may be a few present, but the development is always defective.

There are dystrophic disturbances in the nails. The scalp hair is sparse and of a fine soft texture. The cheek bones are high and wide, whereas the lower half of the face is narrow. The supra-orbital ridges are prominent; the nasal bridge is depressed, forming a "saddle-back nose". The tip of the nose is small and upturned, while the nostrils are large and conspicuous. The eyebrows are scanty, none being present on the outer two-thirds. The eyes slant upwards, producing a Mongolian facies. At the buccal commissures radiating furrows, "pseudo-rhagades", are present . . . The lips are thickened, the upper one being particularly protrusive. The patient studied by Dr. Mackee and myself never sweated.

The affection is familial, generally affecting males, and seems to be due to an injury during the third month of uterine life. Some of these patients are mentally deficient, but the majority of them have normal mentality because the anlage of the nervous system is distinct from the cutaneous ectoderm long before the injury occurs ...

I was now in a position to review the story from the beginning. In 1919, I had been neurotic, as a result of having spent thirteen months in the trenches under continuous bombardment, and had begun to "see things" in France even before a fragment of eight-inch shell went clean through my right lung and knocked me out. Limerick was a dead-alive city haunted by family ghosts, and the glass picture focused my morbid fears of the past and future—yes, it must have been the portrait of a turtle-man brought back to Ireland from the Southern States.

Julia and I: because of the unusually close rapport between us, partly explained by her Irish blood, it was not surprising that we should be scared by the same sort of face. Will had testified that the original was highly terrifying to any but a physician who could look coldly at it and characterize it as a *facies*. And why should Julia's mother not have stumbled across the same old house in New Orleans, and seen the same turtle-man peering through the attic window twelve years previously?

Hank: no natural sympathy existed between him and me, or between him and Julia. But he did have a remarkable receptivity for the emotions of people at a distance, and the trick of converting them into waking visions of his own. Clearly, he had subjectivized the fright which Julia and I conveyed to each other into something horrible that he had himself seen.

Will Price: he had a keen dramatic sense, but I found him far more accurate than most of my friends about names, dates, and facts, and could not disbelieve his story. That is to say, I could accept what he saw with his own eyes. And what Mr. Lemnowitz told him about George Whitaker and the Lafitte brothers was, Will himself confessed, "shrouded in local myth". On principle I suspect any legend about the Lafittes, as I do any legend about Paul Revere, Paul Jones, or Paul Bunyan. Besides, what connection could there be between the Whitaker Negroes and the White Turtle Folk who occur spasmodically on the Lower Mississippi? Nobody has suggested that sophisticated white women of Natchez, Vicksburg, Vardaman, Baton Rouge, Yazoo City, and New Orleans ever paid clan-destine visits to Pond in search of a new sexual *frisson*. It therefore seems probable that if the Lafittes did indeed smuggle a shipload of Negroes to Pond, these were healthy enough when they arrived, but proved suscep-tible to the turtle-disease, which is endemic to the Mississippi; and because of inbreeding it became hereditary among them. The families affected were disowned by their masters but permitted to camp on the swampy fringes of the Whitaker estate, after George dragged his wife with him into the River—which he probably did, if at all, for some simple domestic reason.

And because high cheek-bones and a weak growth of hair are characteristics of the turtle-folk *facies*—which resembles that of the congenital syphilitic —there seems to be no reason for bringing the pox-ridden Choctaws and Chickasaws into the story either.

This is not yet all. In 1954, I broadcast a short summary of the foregoing story for the BBC. As a result, a letter came to me from Mrs. Otto Lobstein, an Englishwoman who was going off some months later with her husband for a tour of the Southern States, and proposed to check up on the Whitaker Negroes. I provided the necessary map references, and in due process of time she sent me a letter and photograph. The photograph showed a Mississippi finger-post pointing south to Woodville, north to Pickneyville, east to Pond and Fort Adams; and the fine condition of the three roads suggested that prosperity had returned to the neighbourhood since Will Price's visit there more than twenty years previously. This was the letter.

New Orleans,
Feb. 1st, 1955

Dear Robert Graves,

We spent an interesting day tracking down the Whitaker Negroes, after camping for a night in the Mississippi woods—a wretched night because this was the hardest frost of the winter. But the early morning sun was startlingly warm and the fields beautiful; no wind blew and thin, erect strings of smoke came from the small shacks along the road.

Pond is not on the map, so we took the road to Fort Adams until we came to a very lovely old plantation home, where one Rip White directed us to the Whitaker plantation . . . When we reached the plantation, we met Mr. Whitaker, the owner, who was going somewhere in a hurry, but told us that the old mansion some way back in the fields had been demolished a few years before. (Its place was now taken by a large, hard-looking, unromantic modern bungalow.) He also told us that the land had been split up at the same time between the various Whitaker sons— which didn't seem to coincide with Will Price's story that the land had been deeded to the State, unless perhaps a brother of the man who committed suicide had contested the deed of gift and won it back. Anyhow, Mr. Whitaker advised us to ask Mrs. Ray about the story; she had raised all the Whitaker whites for two or three generations.

Dear old Mrs. Ray gave us interesting recollections of what her mother and father had told her as a child : how, when the overseer had whipped a slave over a log for not picking enough cotton, the rest would creep out of the plantation after dark and go into a "holler"—bending their heads low down so as not to be heard, they would sing and pray for freedom. But she had no stories about Whitaker Negroes.

At Woodville, a small town on the way to Pond, we visited the Court House to look for records of the original George Whitaker. There we found an intelligent official, Mr. Leek, who had actually met some of the Whitaker Negroes, when he helped them to fill up questionnaires during the Second World War. He told us that they were dying out fast. In winter, he said, they wore ordinary clothes; in summer, heavy underclothes soaked in water. The Court House records, however, did not show that any Whitaker land had been deeded to the State since 1804, when they began. Mr. Leek's explanation of why the Whitaker Negroes were so called was that the first sufferer had "Whitaker" as his Christian name.

At last we reached Pond. Pond Post Office is a big, barn-like structure which, as in the days of trading-posts, carries everything and deals in sacks of flour and rolls of cotton; the large, serene pond mentioned by Will Price lay at the foot of the hill. Mr. Carroll Smith, the post-master in succession to Mr. Lemnowitz, sold us some safety-pins. He was small and silver-haired, with sensitive brown eyes. At first he showed a certain reticence when we questioned him, but gradually shed it. He confirmed that very few Whitaker Negroes are left, and said that they lived on the plantations, not in the swamps. Nowadays, only one member of a family of five or six children would inherit the disease. Occasionally a Whitaker Negro visited the store, which was always an unpleasant experience, because the glandular excretions emitted through his mouth conveyed an appalling odour of decay. Mr. Smith had never heard the story of George Whitaker's suicide and believed, with Mr. Leek, that the original sufferer was an immigrant Negro from Virginia. He suggested that we should visit a Mr. McGeehee in Pickneyville, the nearest village, who had a couple of Whitaker Negroes working for him. He would say no more on the subject, though we talked for some time about sharecropping. So we drove on.

Mr. McGeehee's plantation was very English, with a tree-lined driveway running through park-like meadows (where Herefords and Red Devons grazed) to a big, unpretentious house. Mr. McGeehee himself was most hospitable; so was his mother, a gentle little old lady, looking like a pressed flower. We chatted politely in the spacious drawing-room about farming and children and plantation houses; but both the Mc-Geehees remained emphatic that we must not meet the two Whitaker Negroes working for them. Mr. McGeehee, very rightly, felt responsible for his employees, and said that too many sightseers had come to stare at the pair recently, which made them sensitive. So my husband

and I did not press the point; and in any case, we felt the point slipping away from us. A group of people with a strange history, living in odd conditions and with a bizarre inherited disease, are one thing, and a few sick individuals who happen to have been born into normal families are quite another . . .

Yours sincerely,
ANNA LOBSTEIN

This calm and practical travelogue has dispelled my haunting nightmare for ever. Terror gives way to pity; the pirates Jean and Pierre Lafitte, together with the rogue Choctaws and Chickasaws, are banished to the realms of macabre legend. Only the hospitable Mr. McGeehee and his gentle old mother, who resembles a pressed flower, are left on the stage, in charge of two sensitive sufferers from hereditary ectodermal dysplasia of the anhydrotic type, whose principal purpose in life is to herd silky-grey Brahmini cattle in lush parkland—a far more agreeable example of *symbiosis* than the one reported by Will Price.

JULY 1955

WAYLAND YOUNG

Sitting on a Fortune

"I'd been working in that factory five years before I realized I was sitting on a fortune all the time."

A PROSTITUTE

THIS ARTICLE is not about what ought to be done about prostitution, but about what it is. There are two good recent books about it: *Women of the Streets* (1955), written by Rosalind Wilkinson and edited by C. H. Rolph, and *Cast the First Stone* (published in London in 1958) written by Judge John M. Murtagh and Sara Harris. The first is a sociological study conducted by Mrs. Wilkinson among prostitutes she engaged in conversation as they came out of the London Magistrates' Courts, and kept in touch with later. It is a sober and balanced job, excellent within its limits, which are that it includes no call-girls and hardly touches on the prostitutes' sex-lives. The second consists mainly of a few life stories written up with unabashed sensationalism but great intelligence and feeling. Judge Murtagh sees prostitutes day in day out at the principal court in New York City where they are dealt with. My own small experience confirms all that they say, and in what follows I rely on them to a certain extent. (But the best piece of writing about prostitutes and their clients, indeed the only one I know which goes straight to the heart of the thing in one intuitive leap, is Jean Genet's play, *Le Balcon*.)

Who can know a prostitute? Not her client; his relation with her is hopelessly charged with his need, his guilt, his money, and his natural tendency to believe that she rather enjoys him. He goes to her for illusion and gets it; he cannot know her. A magistrate cannot know her; he sees her day after day in an endless parade : guilty, fine; guilty, fine; guilty, fine. She is no more than a raw material in the processing-plant of justice. A probation officer can know her a little, but only in a special way. The probation officer sees her when things are bad, when she is unhappy, when she wants to get off the game. She also sees the very young ones. She does not see the adult prostitute as a going concern, in her natural surroundings. A reporter looking for a routine story on vice or the organization of vice cannot know her. He gets a stereotyped response: Yes, there is vice. Yes, there is even a little organization of vice. Five pounds, thank you. The Wolfenden Committee did not see a single prostitute. Her own friends and associates, her ponce, the other girls on her street, they can know her all right; but they are themselves part of the underworld, a very real thing, and they cannot see how it fits in with the rest of society. They are inside the tank looking out. The rest of us are outside the tank looking in.

What follows is the result of a handful of short-lived friendships, which I built up with prostitutes, both street-girls and call-girls. This isn't easy. I asked the advice of the first I got to know on how to approach others.

Well, you'll find it very difficult. I'll tell you the best way for a street-girl. Put a bottle of gin in your pocket and go up to her and settle the price. Then go back to where she works, to her gaff, and pay up as soon as you're inside the door. She'll say: "Do you want to see some pictures?" You say: "No thanks, I only want to talk. I've got a train to catch in half an hour." Or: "My wife's left me and I'm lonely." Then she'll open up; you'll be money for jam. You say: "Nice place you've got here," whether she has or not. "Thanks," she says. "Cost you a lot, I suppose?" you say. She says: "Mind your own flipping business," or else: "Yes, would you believe it; I pay twenty-five quid a week for it," which isn't true. "That's a lot," you say, and then she tells you what a mean bastard the landlord is, which isn't true either. She's got a ruddy great Alsatian, and you say does she like animals? And she says: "Oh yes, I love them," which isn't true because it's there for protection. Then you say: "Generally people who like animals are fond of children," and she says of course she is, she has a little girl of eight who's away at school in the country. Then she brings out a snapshot of someone else's little girl. Or else she's doing it for her old mum.

So I didn't try this, but always managed to get some sort of introduction. Even so, it took time and effort to get past the natural initial belief that I was a perverse client looking for kicks through conversation, or an agent of the police, or a reporter from one of the Sunday hypocriticals. Next there was a stage of absolute amazement at anybody simply wanting to know them for their own sakes and lastly, even more naturally, a relaxation, a holiday feeling, a flood of reminiscence, of comment, and of questions about how the other half lives, about my own marriage and sex-life.

But first I'm in a difficulty about language. The language of prostitutes is the language of love-making, and we all make love. But when we come to write about love, or to talk about it with people we don't know very well, we use a different language, one compounded of heavy latinisms and coy periphrases. We say *penis* and *intercourse* as though we were so many specimens in a botanist's collection instead of men and women made of flesh and spirit. Or we say *having a good time*, as though we were children at a party, or *making time* with someone, as though we were trains running late. But as soon as we get into bed we begin to talk English like people.

A lawyer who represented a prostitute in a divorce case told me the following story. He said to her during the conference while he was preparing her case: "And did you go to bed with this man?" "No," she said, "certainly not." A day or two later he found out, only just in time for the case, that to her "going to bed with" someone meant spending the whole night with them. They were not speaking the same language and, if it had not been for a chance clarification, that lawyer would have based his whole case on something other than the truth. The moral of the story is that when it comes to something important, in other words when you are dealing with reality, as you must in a law-court and should in literature, there is no substitute for English. In every sphere of life except sex it is taken for granted that the best language is the clearest language.

So, too, in the history of English poetry, each successive revolution in poetic diction, approved, welcomed, and taught in the schools, is based on a rectification of the tendency to slide away into remote and artificial language. The preface to *Lyrical Ballads* with its insistence on the short, the household, the immediate and earthy in diction, is the usual starting point for literary criticism in our schools. The pattern recurred most recently a quarter of a century ago with the poetic revolution carried through particularly by Auden and Spender, the revolution one could call "low-falutin".

In sexual matters as much as any other, unreal and remote language is a bar to understanding and consequently favours error. In this article I have tried to use a language which is as short, clear, human, and ordinary as is compatible with the remaining taboos on certain words and uses of words.

A whore is a woman who goes through the motions of love for money. If you pay her enough she pretends to come.

There's some of them lies still as stones, they think it's more ladylike or something; but I say they don't know which side their bread's buttered. Listen; if you lie still the bloke may spend half the night sweating away. But if you bash it about a bit he'll come all the quicker and get out and leave you in peace. Stupid to spin it out longer than you need, isn't it? I learned that from Margaret. Wonderful actress, that girl. I learned from her in exhibitions when I was first on the game. She wasn't the first girl I did an exhibition with; that was a coloured girl who used to pitch near

me. I was dead scared of any of that at first; I can't bear a woman near me.
I go all rigid; as a matter of fact the man sometimes thinks I'm loving it.
Well, anyhow, one night this coloured girl comes across to me and says:
"Bloke here wants an exhibition; three pounds each. Will you help me out?"
I was scared, but she said do it just to help her, so I said: "Do we have to go
turn and turn about?" But she said she'd lead all the time. Was I grateful!
Anyhow, like I said, this Margaret and I used to do exhibitions after that.
Wonderful actress. Of course you know they're all faked, exhibitions are.
It's quite easy to hide what's really going on. It was from her I learned to
grunt and groan.

And then, you know, there are all sorts of little gentle things you can do
to a client so that with a bit of luck they come before they even get into
me. When they do I look ever so loving and gentle and say: "Traitor."
Well, I'm not paid just to be a bag, am I? I'm paid to make them feel good.
It's easy for me, so why not? That's how I see it.

Mark that she learned to "grunt and groan" not from herself, not from
any man, but from another whore. And that one word "Traitor!" sums up
the whole structure of pretence which is whoring.

The pictures on the wall? I cut them out of a German pornographic
book. No, I don't use photos much. There's some likes them, and occasion-
ally it helps to get a bashful client started. I did a day's photographic work
yesterday, as a matter of fact, but that wasn't pornographic. I've been
asked to, though. Bloke rang up once and offered me fifty pounds for an
afternoon's work. Said he'd find the male model. Said he'd take my head
out too and put someone else's in. But I didn't believe him. And anyhow,
I don't do that.

The photographs are sold, quarterplate size, in most of the shops in Soho
which have girlie mags on show above the counter. They come in cello-
phane packets of five; ten shillings for breasts being kneaded by a pair of
man's hands, a pound for "attitudes", and twenty-five shillings "when you
get some action". Also "kinky" (perverse) and lesbian scenes and trios for
twenty or twenty-five shillings. Nobody looks happy in them.

What is the whore's own sex-life? Here are several glimpses from
different girls. What is common to them all is the feeling of discrepancy,
of abnormality, of "I'm different", "I can't", or "Let me explain".

Have you ever come yourself?
Yes, I think so; twice. Twice in my life I've thought to myself—now
maybe this is what they talk about. That was before I was on the game.
And didn't you want to keep that man?

Keep him? No! I couldn't bear the sight of him afterwards. He couldn't get out quick enough for me.

I get my kicks from dancing, Latin American dancing mostly. I don't know, there's something about the movements. My first man was after a dance; I didn't know where I was. And the father of my child was after a dance too. It's always dancing with me.

I'm rather abnormally built. You see, my clitoris is very high—I'm not embarrassing you by talking like this? I guess everything's a bit far apart with me. I can only come if a man realizes this; but I can't ask them, can I? They're not there for my pleasure; I'm there for theirs. That's how the game is. I tell you, it's not all ninepins.

I don't know why I like girls. It feels safer, somehow. And I'm not talking about pregnancy. I think everybody agrees now—take Kinsey—that the clitoris is where women get their pleasure.

The man in the boat's my mascot. As a matter of fact it's every woman's mascot, though there's not many men'll recognize it.

You know, the young men seem to be getting bigger and bigger. It must be the Welfare State. I hate it though; it splits me.

Sandra would be no good on the game. She likes men and she enjoys sex.

As to how they get on to the game. Mrs. Wilkinson in her book lays stress on a preliminary period of vague, floating promiscuity, of what she calls elsewhere "increasing irrelation to society". This is something different from maladjustment, which she sees as a deformed relationship, a warped and impracticable relationship, but one which may be as strong as any other. "Irrelation" is an absence of all relationship. The girl comes to London—most London whores come from provincial industrial towns—and bums around living with this man and that, perhaps frequenting the Stepney cafés which the Government is now going to have watched. Or perhaps as a hostess in a night-club; there are one or two night-clubs which seem to be simply highroads into the game. This intermediate phase is the one when the girl is called a *mystery*; is she going to take to the game or not? Generally speaking, nobody pushes her. This is an important point; the popular conception of well-organized recruiting agencies is a mistaken one. The motive for entertaining the illusion is fairly clear: the more a "respectable" man idealizes women, and the higher the value he sets on the merits of conventional society, the less will he believe any girl capable of abandoning it except under pressure or devious corruption. To such a man, all whores will be "poor unfortunate girls", and his mind will people Soho and Stepney with drug-peddlers, razor-slashers, and so forth.

I have heard two stories about young men, operating alone and by kindness, who attach newcomers to themselves, lay them, gradually get them used to the bright lights and the pretty things, and then gently ease them out on to the street. But both these stories came from girls who believed that they had themselves only just found out in time and escaped, so they would have every reason to play the thing up. Both very much regretted having to break with such smashing young men and looked back on that time with nostalgia. That's all.

One way on to the game is even before they come to London. A girl who has been easy at school—not generally because she likes sex but because she wants to find out if it isn't possible to like it more—takes work as a waitress or chambermaid at a provincial hotel. She sleeps with the odd commercial traveller, and then one day one of them gives her a pair of nylons. The next one gives her a pound to buy her own, and the penny drops. She has been paid for it. Next stop London, and the big money.

Perhaps the commonest way in of all is by the urging of an older friend or elder sister.

Wake up, girl; how much longer are you going to exist *on seven pounds a week? Come on out and* live. *You leave it to me and you'll be earning a hundred a week before you've even noticed.*

For instance, Dorothy, a three-pound street-walker. A pound more for stripping, but she'll do it all the same if the client can't raise the extra. Hates kissing. Undertakes most kinks if she's feeling like it, but no buggery which is grounds for money back and throw them out. She was illegitimate, and brought up without a father. When she came home after school she would find her mother smooching away with some man. When she was eleven and twelve the neighbourhood kids used to ask her : "Had your R.C. yet?" She did not know what it meant, but shook her head, and they said : "All right, you can stay with us." R.C. meant "red change", or first period. She had her R.C. one day during an exam at school. She fainted, and the invigilator carried her to the headmistress who said : "Are you ill?" "I don't think so." "I mean, er, have you eaten anything?" Yes, she had steadied her nerves by guzzling Rowntree's clear gums, and to this day feels sick at the sight of them. So much for sex education.

At sixteen she had her first man, and at nineteen bore a child to an

American soldier. While she was carrying the child she took up with a medical student.

He taught me hygiene, too. And I may say most of the girls don't know a thing about it. They just put some soap on their fingers and tickle themselves a bit. But he taught me to use a douche, and not more than once a week, otherwise it hurts your insides. He told me masturbation gives you a bellyache, too.

When her mother asked her who the child's father was, she said she really didn't know. She had passed out at a party and didn't know what had happened to her. Her mother legally adopted the child, a girl, and Dorothy never sees either of them. She blames her mother for her own upbringing and fears she may bring up her grandchild in the same way, but it's nothing to do with her. It's miles away now.

After the birth of the child she came to London and took work as a barmaid. She went concurrently with the manager of the hotel in the afternoons and a well-off married man every third Sunday. One night in a clip-joint she got drunk and started telling the manager of this joint what was wrong with the place; the wallpaper was all wrong, the place was dirty, the girls were badly dressed. He took her on the spot as his mistress and co-manager, and she lived with him for four years. Then it broke up, and she was underfed and began hitting the bottle. (This was the "period of increasing irrelation".) She had a taste for "pretty things" and bright lights, as well as for drink; one night she got drunk at a party and the next morning found she'd been paid. (It wasn't till the day after she told me this that I realized it was the same story she'd told her mother about the baby.) So there she was, a whore. She began walking the street, though she didn't stand yet.

Standing is the end of irrelation; you are accepted into the underworld. Some older whore invites the walker to pitch beside her; if the street is full, a new pitch is carved out, but usually there's plenty of room. There may be a lesbian arrangement, and there will probably be something of a team about it. "With your looks and youth, you could earn well; that is, if you consent to profit by my experience." Perhaps they will do exhibitions together. The older woman may get a rake-off in return for her patronage. The arrangement will be a fleeting one, like everything in the underworld.

Here is another life story, one from the other end of the social scale; prostitution, like everything else in England, is shot through with class values. Mary is now a successful call-girl, and occasionally reaches the maximum possible earnings, up to fifty pounds for an all-night fix. When she was twelve she was "the only girl without a title" at a snob boarding school run by nuns. Her parents were cold, but not cruel. The father was blind and the mother, having had a total hysterectomy, cut out love not only from her bed but also from her whole life. Then, within a year, three things happened to Mary. She found papers on her mother's desk which taught her that she was the illegitimate daughter of a housemaid. Her true mother had put her in an orphanage when she was three years old, and she had been adopted by the people she thought were her parents on medical advice to compensate them for the death of their own son. She had her first period at school, didn't know what was happening, feared disease, and was told to take an aspirin. And thirdly, perhaps not surprisingly, she created a scandal at school by refusing to believe in the Virgin Birth. Her adoptive parents were sent for, and she was told to have faith.

At seventeen she wanted to go to a university, but was taken abroad instead by a relative of her adoptive parents. She was not allowed to learn the language of the country, or to take a job there. She quarrelled, came back to London, and took work as a hotel receptionist. Her adoptive parents died, and she set to work to trace her true family. She found her grandmother first, herself the illegitimate daughter of an illegitimate woman; there hadn't been a marriage in the family for generations. The grandmother was not interested. Later she found her mother, and this last door slammed in her face with a peculiarly horrible twist when she learned that her mother had put her away when she was three because she was pregnant again. She had preferred the unborn child to the child of three, and had in fact brought the second child up.

A sitter? Nobody with that childhood could not have turned round and got their own back on society? The axe of bad circumstance may hack terribly at the tree of individual nature, and some will stand and some will not. There's no knowing.

A staple of conversation among prostitutes is the kinkies. You can see the ads in Soho shop windows: *Miss du Sade, Miss du Cane, Miss de Belting* (flagellation). Lady's black mackintosh for sale. Boots, high-heeled shoes, plastic raincoats for sale, all with the girl inside them, of course. Miss *Kiki* This or *Kiki* That (anything). *Fifi*, or *Froufou*, gives French lessons, recently back from France, French and English conversation . . . When the "normal citizen" reads or hears kink stories (or goes to Genet's plays) he is tempted to consider them as myths. Or, he will think it all old hat; it is all in Krafft-Ebing, and that is where it ought to stay. But it is absolutely central to the prostitute's life that she is engaged day after day in realizing the myths, in enacting the hopeless, silly dream. These are not amazing, disgusting, or funny stories to her; they are her work, her day-by-day tangible work, as dressing wounds is to a hospital nurse, for which she is paid.

Well, as for kinkies, it depends how I'm feeling. If I'm feeling cheeky, all right and good luck to them. But you can't do it every day. Client came to me one night and offered me three quid for three. Fine, said I. So he got into the drag; had it with him in a suitcase, and for me too. Black nylons, high wedge shoes and all. He said he was a servant girl called Millie and I was his mistress. They often want that, you know. I had to say: "Where were you last night, Millie?" And he said he'd been out with a boy. And I had to say: "Now it was clearly understood between us when you came to work for me that you were to be a good girl, Millie, and there was to be none of that." He was licking my shoes all the time. "And I think you deserve a beating, don't you, Millie?" "Oh yes, Madam, I do, I do!" So then I gave him the three he'd paid for. But I don't know what it was; I was just feeling like it, I suppose, but I suddenly lost my temper, oh, not only with him, with everything and everybody. So I gave him four more and took another four pounds off him and chucked him out. I really lit into him. He loved it. And yet people ask me why I like cats.

I heard kink stories of such majestic oddness that it was hard to believe in their actual truth, although circumstantial details sometimes force one to.

A client took me back to his place, and as soon as I got in the door there was a dirty great coffin standing open. He put me in a white nightie with a rosary in one hand and a Bible in the other and a wreath of roses on my head. Then I had to lie down in the coffin. I thought: "Is this a gag to get my money?" But no, I had my bag in with me. Then he started nailing the lid down, and all the time he was shouting out: "You're dead now, God damn you to hell!" He'd told me his wife had died. He'd given me a big spanner to knock the lid up again, but I tell you I was wondering if I'd ever get out. I did, though, and when I looked round the place, he'd gone.

Most kinkies are over forty, and the girls incline to a theory of association in seeking to explain how they get like that.

＊

As I said, there are social gradations in the game. Two pounds down the Bayswater Road, three in Park Lane, four in Bond Street, three again in Shepherd Market and Stafford Street. Better in Wardour Street than in Lisle Street or Compton Street. Low again in the Commercial Road, Cable

Street, and Cannon Street Row, down in Stepney. Low round Waterloo, Victoria down to Pimlico, Paddington, Euston, King's Cross. No fixed traditions round the suburban commons (Clapham, Putney Heath, Finsbury Park) or in the incipient trade along the arterial roads in the outer suburbs, like the A40 at Hillingdon. In the outlying places it is often West End girls having a change.

But once off the street and among the call-girls, you are in a different world. Take the word *whore*. The street-girls use it quite naturally; it is the simplest and the obvious word for what they are. The phrase, almost a signature tune, "Whoring it along the 'Dilly", has a fine generous ring to it. An occasional highbrow tart who quotes Auden and keeps up with the sexual oddities of the eminent will use the word about herself with a conscious, open-eyed feeling, in the same way that Bernard Shaw used to call himself "an old entertainer". But the average call-girl uses it to imply all that she is not. She uses it as synonymous with *slack*, which is the call-girls' word for a street-girl.

I don't look like one, do I? You wouldn't ever know, would you? Not ever? Would you? Would you?

The call-girl is tremendously nice. Her flat where she lives and her gaff where she works, if she has a separate place, are spotless; dusted, loved, every ornament balanced by eye against the others; shiny, warm, welcoming. The taste will be contemporary, very much aware of fashion, but not necessarily intelligent.

The first thing you must realize is that I'm not a whore. I have my friends, but I don't take anybody. Like for instance if a man rings up and says he's been given my number by so-and-so, I don't just leave it at that. I put him through it. When did you last see so-and-so? How was he? Where did you meet? Has he shaved his beard off? He said he was going to. Oh, there are all sorts of ways to find out if they're on the square. All right, then he comes round. Maybe I don't like the look of him. "Ooooh, I'm sorry; it's really too bad. She's just gone out. Would you believe it; isn't that just too bad." And even afterwards, after we've been to bed, if I haven't liked him I tell him I'm going off the game, or I'm going away on holiday. He'd better not come again.

You know, half my work's what we call social work. That is, say some friend of mine has someone come to London to visit his firm, and he gives him my number. I have connections with a lot of good firms; advertising businesses most of them. All right, he takes me out; dinner, a show, perhaps a party. Often a party, really, because then I go down on the expense account as prestige or promotion or whatever it is. It may lead to sex, it may not. Often it doesn't. I don't mind. In fact I'm glad.

Again :

It's a hell of a life. You know, I imagine the slack is afraid of disease, and afraid of the sex maniac who thinks it'd be fun to strangle her. Well, that's not what we're afraid of. The trouble in this game is when you're afraid of slipping. Some days you sit and sit by the telephone, smoking and smoking, and nobody rings, and you think—Look out, kid, you're slipping. What have I done? WHAT HAVE I DONE? *Are they telling each other I'm no good?*

A London prostitute in the prime of life, then, is something like this. Of course she comes in all colours and shapes of temperament, but there is enough in common to make it worth saying something about the not so obvious ways in which she differs from other women. She has no sense of time, because her life is without routine. Time is divided into day and night, and that's all. She has a sense of obligation, but it is shakier than other people's. It works in an immediate way, because she is used to payment on the spot. If she says she will meet you somewhere in half an hour, she will. Tomorrow, or next Tuesday, is another matter. If you take her to a public place, say a restaurant, she is a little awkward and embarrassed, or by contraries flamboyant, going in and out; everybody is looking at her, but can they tell? Once settled, she relaxes at once. She is an excellent listener; interested, amused, sympathetic. Listening, next only to sex, is what she does most of in her work. Her own favourite topics are the wealth and eminence of her clients, the sexual hypocrisy of our culture, kink stories, money, clothes, interior decoration, bars, coffee-bars, night-clubs. She prefers the pageant of life to vicarious involvement through the arts, but she is blind to politics and the organization of society in general. She notices and comments on the women round her more than the men, partly out of straight lesbian interest, and partly because she is comparing herself to this mysterious competitor, the Wife. She is probably a fairly heavy drinker. When she is watching her words and thinking what to say next she will tell you she went on the game with a conscious decision, "for the pelt". She saw a way of multiplying her earnings tenfold, made up her mind, and did so. She continues on it because it's interesting, and she's used to it. I never heard one say it was satisfying. When she is quite relaxed, and talking without care or discretion, the picture changes. She drifted into the game; very often she will make out that she hardly noticed how or when. This may be perfectly true, or it may be that she noticed all too well and is denying and suppressing the memory.

Here is a story I heard from a man:

I met this girl at a party one night; she'd been sleeping around for some time with all sorts of men. I gave her a lift home afterwards, and as she was getting out of the car I asked her to have dinner with me a day or two later. She kind of paused, and then she said: "Look, that dinner's going to cost you about three pounds. Why don't you just give me the three pounds and come along in and do me now?" So I did.

In that story you can hear the penny dropping with a clear chink.

To revert; she is afraid, as all outlaws are. She is afraid of disease, more so perhaps than is any longer justified since penicillin, but there is still the fear of infecting a client's wife, or even her unborn child, a running fear which can never be either confirmed or laid. She is afraid of the sex maniac who may want to kill her—there were two murders like this while I was working on this article—and it is for this reason that she may keep a dog, or, if she can afford it, a maid. If she has no ponce,* she may take care to live in a house where the neighbours will accept her and her occupation, so that she can shout for them in an emergency. If she is a street-girl, she is afraid of being nicked; however often it happens—and Mrs. Wilkinson mentions a Belgian woman who was arrested 219 times—the appearance at Marlborough Street is always a humiliation. Now, since the Government announced the new Bill, she is afraid of prison. Whether she will be so much afraid that she will leave the streets and become a call-girl remains to be seen. I believe she will.

Above all, whether she walks the streets or answers the telephone, she is afraid of old age. It is when you approach this topic of *getting out* that your heart really sinks. It is almost impossible. The older whore will say quite simply: "There is no way out." The younger ones will keep their chins up and pretend to themselves that they're not like the rest. Nobody ever went into the game for keeps.

Of course, I'm only in it for five years.
For a few years.
Until I've something put by.
Until I'm bored with it.

* In current English usage (as opposed to American), a *ponce* is a man who lives on a prostitute's earnings; he is the French *souteneur* or *mec*. A *pimp*, on the other hand, is a prostitute's procurer. "You want a nice girl?" There are plenty of ponces in London now, but hardly any who make a living by pimping.

For five years.
For five years. I've got it all worked out. Then I'll . . .
Buy a shop.
Go into partnership with a friend who has a garage.
Buy house property and let rooms.
Buy a coffee-bar.
Buy a restaurant.
Club together with one or two other girls and buy a hotel.
Get some old sucker to marry me.
Put my savings into . . . Put my savings into . . . Put my savings into . . .

It makes you weep, because not one in a hundred can save. The ability to save goes only with the retentive personality, with foresight, caution, affective momentum, deep and even narrow feelings. The whore is all on the surface; mercurial, short-sighted, chaotic, clitoral, or even wholly frigid.

What usually happens is that they go on and on, into their fifties and even sixties. They pass downward into a class called *four-to-sixers*, who go on the streets before dawn when the clients are too drunk to notice their age. Some become maids to younger women, which is perhaps the happiest conclusion. Then there is a saying: "End up drinking red biddy in the docks."

The elderly whore, the old-timer, often has delusions of social grandeur. She has missed the few possible escape lines, and gets attached in the half-light of unreality to the idea of what she might have been. She cannot deny what she is, so she may sideslip into denying that she is something else which she is. If she is Jewish, she may take pleasure in proving that she is not, and looking down on the Jewish client. If she is poor she may try to prove that she is rich, if Irish, English, and over and over again if she is dark, she will pretend to be fair. Conversely, she may try to prove that the innocent little woman in the flat upstairs is a whore.

One of these old-timers asked me to tea the other day. I went along, and there was just her and me. She poured out the tea with her little finger crooked and told me how she'd been invited to Buckingham Palace. Afterwards she entertained me by playing Gounod's Ave Maria *on the piano.*

The fascination that crime in general and prostitution in particular have for certain highly educated young people with plenty of money is perhaps partly to be explained by the "lady" wishing to be a whore just as the whore may wish to be a "lady". Some will go so far as to do it. But it is also to be explained by the uncertain aim of impatient generosity which may rush not so much to rescue the victim of oppression as to fraternize with the merely unfamiliar. Then, too, there is the "mystery of the inferior" (for an analysis of which see Simone de Beauvoir, *Le Deuxième Sexe,* and Gunnar Myrdal, *An American Dilemma*).

Some whores do get married, or set up what is meant to be a permanent liaison with a man. He may be a former customer or not. If he does not even know what his wife has been, the situation is of course emotionally hopeless. If he does, it may last, conceivably. But it's difficult. If a woman is capable of sustaining a regular relationship, why didn't she do it at first instead of going on the game? They usually come back, the ones who marry, not because of the attractions of whoring, but because the marriages don't work. When they do come back, they are welcomed with open arms; their return justifies all the others.

I know one girl who has got out. She has done it in the most favourable circumstances; she is young and intelligent, she loves her husband, and he loves her. He knows what she was. But, even so, it is little less than a heroic enterprise. Wherever they go together, street, pub, parties, job-hunting, home-hunting, the slightest flicker of attention, of interest, from some man will bring back that which has to be trodden underfoot. The man may simply be thinking: "Now where have I seen that girl before?" It may even have been in a cinema queue. But she knows that her husband will not know where it was . . . If anything goes wrong—some people who were coming to dinner cry off at the last minute, a job falls through—have they found out? There is no defence against the suspicion. Laughter at one's own groundless suspicions is about the most mirthless kind there is.

That is what the woman who gets out has to face with other people. What she has to face in bed with her husband is easily enough imagined. It can be done, and it is done; but it's no wonder that it is not often done.

The way off the street is feet first.

In the Parliamentary debate on the Wolfenden Report, Mr. Butler promised stiffer penalties against living on immoral earnings as a "consolation". It was not clear what for. Mr. Edwards, the Member for Stepney, a prostitute area, described ponces as: "the dirtiest, filthiest lot in creation". Dr. Reginald Bennett spoke of "monarchs of the industry". Until 1948, convicted ponces could be flogged, and the criminal law still discriminates against them in two quite exceptional ways. It denies them the right to trial by jury; the magistrate can send them up, and the prosecution can ask that they be sent up, but the defence cannot (1898). It also places the onus of proof on them; if a man is proved to be "habitually in the company of a known prostitute", then it is up to him to prove that he is not living on her earnings (1912). How often in the recent discussions has one not seen someone writing to the papers saying this or that about the prostitutes themselves and ending up : "... and reserve the really heavy penalties for the ruffians who batten on these unfortunate girls".

The very word *ponce* suggests *pounce*; fifty years ago ponces were called *bullies,* which sounds even fiercer. Assuming that you come new to this topic, try consulting your own feelings about the ponce. There he is, this unspeakably debased male, lurking in the shadows of doorways and pouncing on his unsuspecting (or at best hypnotized) prey, tearing her hard-earned three pounds out of her pathetic clutch, and roaring away in his Ford Zodiac to the next girl, whom he threatens with a razor. He spends the night going round twenty or thirty of his hundred and fifty girls, or perhaps his section of the big syndicate administered by his super-boss, slashing his rivals, doling out shots to the junkies, coshing a client or two, and squaring four or five detective inspectors. Towards dawn he goes, surrounded by henchmen, to the girl he has chosen for himself that night and, little recking that her flaccid flesh is still reeking from the forty or fifty slavering lechers who have been before him, enjoys her.

None of the girls I met had ever had a proper ponce, though some had tried a candidate for a few days and then chucked him out. They regretted this, and wished they could be lucky enough to find a good one. One, rather drunk, even thought it would be a good plan if I took this on in my spare time. She needed someone to kick her out on the street when it was time, to make sure she had the rent ready on rent day, to keep her off the bottle, to tell her what clothes she looked nice in, and, perhaps most important of all, to help her see if she couldn't have some sort of a sex-life of her own. She thought that with a "sixty minute man" things might happen.

The ponce—in London today : always with that reservation—is neither more nor less than the whore's husband. He provides stability for her, a bit of discipline, someone to listen to her adventures. He makes love to her as much for her sake as for his own, and takes trouble over it. He is also a gauge of her prestige. If she keeps him well in hand-made shoes and black silk shirts, then her credit goes up among the whores, and his among the ponces.

Mine's a good earner. Just look at this shirt.

Economically, he corresponds to the wife of the normal citizen. But the fact that he is living on her earnings and not she on his is only of secondary importance to either of them. It may arise like this. A man is earning twelve pounds a week, and he takes up with a girl who is earning a hundred. His self-respect may lead him to keep his own job on for a bit but then one day she is ill, or her child is ill, or perhaps she is picked up and he wants to go to court with her. He stays off work and loses his job.

Their earnings drop from a hundred and twelve a week to a hundred. So what the hell? He's a ponce; all right, so he's a ponce. There are plenty of others.

Mrs. Wilkinson published figures showing that about forty per cent of those *convicted* of poncing have also been convicted of other crimes. It cannot, of course, be known what proportion of ponces are never convicted either of poncing or of anything else. But the street-girl is herself technically a criminal—we make her one with our laws—and she develops a modified form of the criminal personality. It is not surprising that she takes up with criminals for company. Moreover, minorities against whom the majority discriminates will also seek each other out, and this is the main reason for the disproportionate number of Negroes among the ponces, which is a certain fact in New York and is widely believed to be a fact here too.

I used to live in Knightsbridge when I first went on the game. It was horrible. I didn't seem to be real; it was as if no one could see me. But since I moved over here among the coloured people I'm—well, you know— I feel kind of at home. I don't have to pretend any more.

Some whores share a ponce with another, or even with two others. This arrangement, which is the rule in New York, is the exception in London. It does not arise because the ponce is able to subject two or three silly but reluctant women for his own gain. It arises because in the world of prostitution—as in all other minority worlds which are at once defined and discriminated against by the majority world, like the criminal world proper, the Negro world, the world of the arts, and, in former days, the worse-off working class—in such worlds monogamy is not the rule. Add to this that in the world of prostitution chastity is by definition something which does not come in, and that many whores are at least a bit lesbian, and the multiple ponce becomes comprehensible.

Then there are the call-house madams or switchbawds. These are women with a two- or three-bedroom flat and a list of twenty or thirty telephone numbers. The client rings and gives his order; she calls the most suitable girl, and he meets her at the flat. He pays the madam, and the madam passes on a proportion to the girl, always alleged by the girl to be too small. Or the madam allows the client to go to the girl's flat, and the girl passes on the rake-off. The call-house madam is just as criminal as the male ponce, but society is not somehow so angry with her. After all, she's a woman, she's probably a superannuated whore herself, and women are never so frightening anyhow.

A full-scale racket for the exploitation of prostitution is a rare event in twentieth-century London, but it does sometimes happen. When it does, it may go like this. The organizer may buy the best girls out of the legal brothels of France, Belgium, and Italy (which are for the most part now closed) and bring them to London. This is of course a white slave traffic, and sounds terrible; but for the girls themselves it has been, at certain times, a merciful deliverance. In the licensed houses of the Continent they would have been taking up to fifty men a day and getting anything down to a shilling a go for it. How they got there is another matter, but once they were there, anyone who was prepared to get them out again would look more like a St. George than a Bluebeard. To come to London was every girl's dream. In London they would perhaps be set up two by two in shared flats and provided with gaffs elsewhere to work in. They might even be run on service lines, and pay over their entire earnings each week, receiving only spending money. What was left after the organization rake-off would be banked for them in deposit accounts. They would be supplied with an issue of the most destructible clothing, nylons and so on, and with food, and a bottle of wine a day would be sent to their living flats. The organizer or one of his agents would inspect the pitches nightly to see that standards of dress and deportment were satisfactory. Other girls would be allowed to pitch there too, provided they reached these standards; if they did not, they would be hustled off by the organization girls themselves. If any girl earned outstandingly well, she might be given a bonus in kind, typically a mink coat. Free weekly medical examination, free hospital treatment, a free return ticket home each year. In a very tight organization of this sort, it would be most unlikely that any of the whores' savings would be released to them until they were judged unemployable. When they were, however, the savings would probably be honestly handed over.

This sort of organization flourished only among imported foreign whores, and the English whores tended to look at it all between envy and contempt; envy for the safety and regularity, and contempt for the discipline and spoonfeeding. This is the same mixture of feelings that the English whore has always had for the idea of licensed brothels, and the appearance of large-scale organizations in London may in one sense be regarded as an alien tissue-graft on our culture. It does not commonly prove viable.

Apart from these rare occurrences of an alien pattern, allegations that so-and-so is "running a string of girls" generally turn out to mean only that he is giving them a cut-rate on his string of taxis, or that he lets rooms to them, but in no sense controls them. The Wolfenden Report recognized this.

So why are we so hot against the ponce? Partly for historical reasons. In the nineteenth century the "white slave traffic" was still a reality in London, and the brutal exploitation of under-educated and underfed girls was still possible. I have noticed that the attitude of respectable women to the ponce depends on their ages; the older women were brought up by mothers who in *their* youth really did have to watch their step when a handsome stranger offered to help them cross the road. But to get nearer the heart of our aversion to the ponce we must first ask ourselves what we feel about the whore herself. We are all in touch with her, or in touch with her image in our minds. She has been around for millennia. Every man has thought of going to her, even if he hasn't been. Every woman has thought of her husband or son going to her. It is enough to ask yourself, if you are a man, or your closest man if you are a woman, under what circumstances you would go to her. You go to her when you want a woman. But if there was a woman by you who loved you, why should you go to a whore? Even if there was a woman by you who did not love you but was sexually synchronous, why should you go? Even if she were a complete stranger, at a party, say, and you did not know whether it was going to be good or not, you would still probably not prefer a whore, because if you did you would be paying for the certainty of pretence instead of taking the chance of reality free. By now we are pretty low down on the scale, if a complete stranger at a party is preferable; we are pretty far away from love. I think the only circumstances in which a man who has experienced love, even casually and generously in friendship, could go to a whore would be if he was completely alone in a foreign city and had the most terrible stone-ache. (Either that, or else if he just *liked* pretence.)

But age? What about the old man, not handsome, got a pot, and his wife's dead, or past it. He may have experienced love in the greatest fullness, and yet turn to a whore now. The present study which Dr. Gibbens is making of clients may show that this happens, or it may show that such elderly men have in fact gone to whores all their lives.

So, who does go? "Kinkies", first. Men who are only pleased if they're allowed to dress up as this or that, or use the cat, or throw cream buns about; men who have associated the experience of orgasm with something which most people find quite irrelevant to it.

Then the physically deformed; not directly because they are deformed, but because the shyness born of deformity may have prevented them ever learning the experience of love. If the whore has a useful social function, as many people say she has, it is with the kinkies and the deformed.

Then there are the men who want to avoid trouble and complication, who simply want the "sneeze in the loins" without responsibility, emotional contact, give and take, or indeed any involvement whatever; the duckers.

They know I'm *not going to ring up and tell them I'm lonely, or write them long letters, or go whining to them with this or that.*

Lastly, there are all the men, all the millions of men in England, who believe, who feel, that sex is something apart from society they live in. They may be simply burning to do this or that and daren't ask their wives. They may be unmarried, and terrified at the thought of having a mistress. They may quite simply never have found out that women are capable of orgasm too. All these will fetch up with the whores, because they have been twisted out of sight of their own natures by the puritan society they grew up in. If once you get to believe that sex is something separable, and even more if you believe it's degrading, regrettable, un-mentionable, something you wish to spare a refined woman, then there's not much reason why you shouldn't buy it. And if you've never found out that women come too, you may find the whore's pretence quite irresistible, and it may make you feel a hell of a fellow. She hopes it will.

And so back to the ponce. The whore has done her little turn and she has been paid for it. It doesn't cross the client's mind that he could have something more exciting and satisfying with a real girl if he got up and took it, so he doesn't worry much about the money. But the thought that the first thing the whore does when his back's turned is to hand that money over to someone else, and that someone a man, and that man having her for free, and for all you know sneering with her at your peculiarities—why, it's absolutely revolting. It makes you bust with rage. If ever you laid hands on such a man, you'd beat the life out of him—because he is living proof that what you've had was counterfeit. He is your disillusionment. Into prison with him, and let the illusions flourish. And if two years isn't enough, let him have five, and that will be some consolation to us all.

In (unpublished) evidence for the Wolfenden Committee Mrs. Wilkin-son wrote (and kindly allows me to quote):

The society formed by prostitutes and their associates, though not heredi-tary, is continuous; it has a fairly permanent structure and composition; its stability depends on its nature as a counter-society. It exists because it absorbs a-social or anti-social personalities; it is economically dependent on the expression of an anti-social tendency in members of ordinary society. Its cohesion is strengthened by the attitudes of the general public towards the prostitute, her guilt feelings which prevent her return to ordinary life by causing her to exaggerate and anticipate critical attitudes towards her, and by attitudes within the society itself towards its members who try to break away.

I don't think this could be improved on. The whore world is like a little gearwheel engaged with a big one; it goes round faster, and in the opposite direction. You can see the gears engaging on the pavements of Piccadilly; the whores stand still and the men pour past, looking, considering, pausing to haggle, passing on to the next. The counter-society or underworld is, like the society or overworld which has expressed it from its own body, class-ridden, intolerant, but free from oppression. As to the rest of us, we cherish and pay it with one hand and belabour it with the other. That's how it gets like it is. The overworld sees the whore as a social problem or a social service, according to the amount of use it makes of her. The whore judges the overworld by what she sees. First, she sees the client, whom she holds in contempt for his gullibility and in respect for his purse. Through him she sees his wife who, he inevitably tells her, is cold. To the English whore, England is a country of women as frigid as she is, or frigider, but who don't even try to pretend.

Ask me, the only difference between me and some of these wives is that they don't keep the bargain and I do.

Once when a call-girl was splashing scent about behind her ears, I said : "That's nice." "Want some?" she said, and sprayed my mouth with it. The point was *on the kisser*. This was the mark of the underworld which I was to take back to my presumably frigid wife.

If you read Judge Murtagh's account of the medical examination to which New York whores are subjected when they are sent to prison, you get an impression of a ritual rape of the whore by society, a symbolic indignity to which she is subjected when she falls into the power of the big wheel.

And here in London you see the two wheels engaged above all in the Magistrates' Courts at the regular conviction for soliciting. This conviction is popularly supposed to be fortnightly, but is not necessarily so; I met street-girls who had not been arrested for more than a year. The fortnight is a minimum gap; the police act on a tacit understanding that more than once a fortnight is too often. When the conviction does come round, its forms are those of the criminal law, but its effect is fiscal. Two pounds down, and out you go till next payment day. If a whore is arrested with no money on her, it is well understood by the police that, after she has been charged, she must be let go to earn the money for next day's fine. There is, of course, no medical examination. The thing is a tax collected at random.

Though the whore-world is "continuous", as Mrs. Wilkinson says, it is not exactly the same as it always was.

Aren't any of you girls ambitious for anything beyond money?
Like what, for instance?
Like power? Politics?
Oh gosh, no! Look what happened to that Nitribitt girl in Germany.

She was murdered.

The courtesan, the *alta cortigiana,* is as far as I can discover completely lacking from the scene. When a floozy gets into the upper reaches of society she almost always marries her men one after the other. This is no good in politics, because one divorce is about all a politician can permit his wife to have behind her at the moment. The floozy is consequently back-tracked into the world of the gossip-columns, which is without power.

There are also now several smaller worlds which mitigate the former raw dependency of the majority society on prostitution, one could think of the relationship as a ball-bearing. For instance, there are "the scrubbers"; very young girls who follow jazz bands round the country on their tours.

She's scrubbing with the Piddle Valley Stompers now, isn't she?

These girls ought to be studied soon by some social anthropologist. They compete for the favours of the musicians, and when they get a good scalp they chalk it up with a lipstick circle on their breasts. Predatory ritual. What happens to them later?

There are the girls I call the bums-with-clean-faces. They frequent pubs in the Fulham Road and King's Road, and correspond in the middle class to the Stepney café-floaters. Go anywhere, do anything sexually or touristically interesting. County Dublin, Positano, Ibiza, Tangier.

There are the telly aspirants, the advertising executive aspirants, the promotional expense-account aspirants, the screen and stage aspirants, all of whom overlap with the call-girls on the one hand and the bums-with-clean-faces on the other. There will soon be the scandal-mag stool-pigeons, as in America; girls who get in the way of the newsworthy personality, get laid, and then report back to the editor. There are even still some of the detective agency girls, who will go to Brighton or Paris with a man who wants to give his wife grounds for divorce, and then get discovered in moderately *flagrante delicto* by the detective, perhaps their uncle.

Husband seeking divorce: "Aren't you warm in here, my dear? Wouldn't you like to take your coat off?"
Detective agency girl: "Oh, I can't; I've got no dress on. You see, we have to be ready to get caught at a moment's notice."

And on the game itself, the specialist varieties are endless. There are motherly whores with glasses, nymphet whores, pregnant whores, Negro whores, Indian and Arab, Chinese and other East Asian whores; fat, thin; rowdy, prim; mannish, dowdy, brilliant. Judge Murtagh tells of a New York whore who underwent a sterilization operation—it cost her seven hundred dollars—because like that she wouldn't ever have to bother with contraceptives and so could pretend to be seduced every time against her will, and thus build up the egos of clients who were escaping from their dominating wives. All these meet the demand of some man whose need has been conditioned into this or that idiosyncrasy by his experience in the majority society, in the overworld.

Well, that's prostitution, known to the whores as The Game. It is a game, too; it is a market in illusion, a shop window like the ones in Holborn where you can buy bits of rubber that looks like poached eggs. It's a market where you can buy grunts and groans that are supposed to sound like love. That's all. In the last resort, the client is having his own money.

We in England can do what we like about it in the way of raising or lowering penalties for soliciting and poncing; we can sweep it under the carpet, or up the chimney if we like; it will certainly continue in some form or other. Before we can hope to understand the causes, we must learn to treat that pleasant, beautiful, interesting and useful faculty all men and women have for sex in the same way that we treat our other important faculties, like learning, work, and prayer; by welcoming it, enjoying it, studying it, and talking about it without constraint, without "reverence", without botanizing, and in English. To do otherwise, as we do now, is to deny our own origins, and thus to deny ourselves. The silences and cir-cumlocutions of denial do not go unheard—nothing ever does—and each child which doubts its own origin and the pleasure and beauty which was in its origin doubts also its own humanity. From this deep doubt to the shallow counter-affirmation of whoring is not far.

I shall take for colophon something said to me by a girl of twenty who was brought up in a part of London where whoring is part of the everyday scene. Her friends who are whores and ponces are often on at her to go on the game; so this was not something she learned at her mother's knee but something she had to find out for herself against constant pressure the other way.

I don't see how you can, do you? Not if you know what love is.

MAY 1959

Part II
PROBLEMS & POLEMICS

H. R. TREVOR-ROPER

Arnold Toynbee's Millennium

ARNOLD TOYNBEE'S BIBLE—for so one can reasonably describe his ten-volume *Study of History*—has not been well received by the professional historians. I agree with them in regarding it as untrue, illogical and dogmatic. But in this essay I do not intend to argue its historical truth or falsehood, its logical coherence or incoherence, its empirical validity or invalidity. I intend to consider its significance as a document of our time. For true or false, logical or illogical, empirical or abstract, this book has excited a great deal of attention. Although every chapter of it has been shot to pieces by the experts, and although it is written in a style compared with which that of Hitler or Rosenberg is of Gibbonian lucidity, it has been hailed by the unprofessional public, at least in America, as "an immortal masterpiece", "the greatest work of our time", "probably the greatest historical work ever written". As a dollar-earner, we are told, it ranks second only to whisky. Its success has carried its already much-travelled author round and round the globe, lecturing, flower-crowned, from China to Peru. Surely this phenomenon requires some explanation. It is not enough to say that the work is intellectually erroneous. We must ask why such error has such a vogue. What is the meaning of Toynbee's message in the context of our time? To answer this question we must look at Toynbee's message in a different spirit from that in which most of his critics have regarded it. They were primarily concerned with its truth. They tested the validity of his arguments. I am now concerned with his meaning. What kind of future does Toynbee (rightly or wrongly) envisage? What part, in the unfolding of history, does he invite us to play?

To understand Toynbee's message, it is important to remember the stages in which it was delivered and the events which were happening in the world at that time. For Toynbee's Bible was not delivered to the world all at once. It consists of two Testaments, separated from each other by some fifteen years—fifteen years which included the war of 1939–45. The Old Testament, which comprises volumes 1–6, appeared between 1932 and 1939. The New Testament, which comprises volumes 7–10, was published in 1954. Moreover, the New Testament ends with a remarkable volume, which sheds a great deal of light on the purpose and character of the whole work, volume 10 or the Book of Revelation. If we are to understand the message of Toynbee fully, we must examine his Bible in the order in which it was written, beginning with Genesis and ending with Revelation.

Now Toynbee's general message, the message of his Old Testament, is simple and reasonably clear. His Book of Genesis is the story of the Fall of Civilizations. All civilizations, according to Toynbee, are comparable; all pass through similar stages; all flourish and decay according to the same general laws, the same general time-scale of growth and change; all ultimately die. There may be different forms of death. Some civilizations die sudden, violent deaths without living out their time; others may seem to linger on, but in reality they are dead, mere fossils of themselves. For there is no exemption from the law of mortality. Always there is an end, and our own Western Civilization, which we once thought unique and immortal, is in fact no different from the others. It too must die. As a matter of fact, it must die very soon. Has it not already shown all the signs of senility, as diagnosed by the scientific doctor of civilizations? Did it not reach its peak 400 years ago? Are not 400 years the time invariably allotted, by the mystical mathematics of History, to the "Time of Troubles" which precedes the death of a civilization? Is not our civilization already visible in dissolution? Surely its end is near.

Such is Toynbee's general message. It is a determinist message. But it has another characteristic too. It is also a fundamentally obscurantist message. For although Toynbee, in analysing civilizations, claims to be dispassionate and scientific, in fact his whole analysis is governed by strong emotional prejudice. In spite of its Hellenic training, his mind is fundamentally anti-rational and illiberal. Everything which suggests the freedom of the human reason, the human spirit, is to him odious. This illiberalism again and again distorts his own logic. Terms which, for his "scientific" purpose, should be neutral, like "decline" or "decay", are by him given a moral significance and arbitrarily equated with the processes which he happens to dislike—i.e. the growth of liberalism or rationalism. So, in his Book of Genesis, the Fall of our Civilization is dated from the time when our ancestors ate the fruit of the Tree of Knowledge and sought to be like gods, knowing good and evil—the time of the Renaissance. To Toynbee the Renaissance was the begining of the irreversible decline of the West, and every further manifestation of human reason is to him yet another milestone on the road to ruin. Europe's greatest centuries, the centuries of the Reformation, the New Philosophy of the seventeenth century, the Enlightenment, the gradual conquest of disease and famine, are to him its darkest ages. The European Enlightenment of the eighteenth century, that incomparable period of human emancipation, the age of Bach and Mozart, Gibbon and Voltaire, is to him merely "a spell of low ideological temperature", a weary lull in the otherwise fatal course of Europe's disintegration and decay, a brief respite between "a first and a second paroxysm of its deadly seizures". The seizure, we may note in passing, was already deadly even before the lull. Europe's death was already decreed, not when industrialism or communism or the hydrogen bomb arose to threaten it, but when the Renaissance, that great spiritual disaster, descended like a fatal curse upon us. It was then that disintegration set in, then that sentence of death was passed which is now, after the preordained term of 400 years, about to be executed upon us.

Is there then no hope? Can nothing stay our doom? No, says Toynbee, nothing. The best we can do is to find our way back into that Paradise of medieval innocence from which, by our fatal presumption, we have been expelled. Since it was the Renaissance and the Reformation which, by opening the eyes and the mind of man, set us on the 400-year slope leading to destruction, let us now seek to go back behind those fatal episodes, deny them and their consequences, pretend that they have never been. Let us confess that, for the last four centuries, we have all been miserable sinners. We have broken the holy eggshell of Catholic unity in which we had been happily and innocently enclosed, insulted the primitive taboos which before had kept us there, and crept out into the fresh, clear light of day. But now, thanks to the inspired "science" of the Prophet Toynbee, we have discovered that the daylight is misleading, the open air cold. Let us then, with devout hands, piece together the festering relics of that cosy shell and creep back again into its warm darkness. Who knows but that holy old hen, Mother Rome, though understandably somewhat stand-offish after such long insubordination, may consent to sit again upon her naughty but now penitent brood? We shall not reverse the iron laws of History, but perhaps we shall mitigate our doom. By sin came death. We cannot now escape the decree of death; but at least let us repent of our sin.

Such in general, was the message of Toynbee's Old Testament. It is worth while to consider briefly its pedigree and its application to current affairs. For there is nothing very original about it, except the monstrous systemization to which everything is subjected. The "decline of the West" is, relatively at least, an obvious fact—though with certain limitations to which Toynbee pays little attention. That is to say, the technical conquest and organization of great land-masses by railways, motor power, and air transport has deprived the small maritime powers of Europe of one of their advantages and has mobilized instead the naturally far greater resources of huge, but previously unorganized, countries like America and Russia. But this shift in the balance of power has, of course, nothing whatever to do with the mere flow of time, the "ageing" of cultures, or the corroding effects of the Renaissance. It was remarked by geographers like Sir Halford Mackinder before Toynbee seized upon the same fact and, separating it from its real causes, ascribed it instead to the cosmic processes which he assumed. These cosmic processes have in turn another pedigree.

It is a German pedigree. The theory that all history is predetermined and that the stages between one predetermined phase and another are marked by catastrophic convulsions seems to be a peculiar product of the German mind. It was advanced by Hegel, by Marx, by Nietzsche; and in the twentieth century, when great catastrophes seemed to be descending with particular force on Germany, it became, in varying ways, the orthodoxy of various German schools. For after the defeat of the First World War, in the aftermath of that exhausting struggle, surrounded by the *débris* of ancient empires, and faced with terrible social problems, it was easy and even natural for Germans to draw on these native ideas and imagine a universal catastrophe. So the Marxists, hating the "capitalist" West, announced with glee that a whole age was over. The West, with its culture, was finished, and must be transformed by conquest : conquest which must come from the new, non-Western power that had accepted the German doctrine of Marxism, Soviet Russia. Theirs was a confident message, because they hoped to be the heirs of the West, the beneficiaries and rulers of the new age. On the other hand conservative German intellectuals, drawing on the same tradition, accepted the same conclusions with much less glee. It was with wailing and gnashing of teeth that Oswald Spengler declared that the turn of the West had come : that "civilizations" were comparable and all mortal; and that the hour of dissolution for our civilization was at hand.

It was at this point that Toynbee came in. An English amateur, tagging somewhat incongruously along behind these German professionals, he repeated Spengler's general theory. He was also a conservative, and as a classical scholar he loved the past : it was therefore with some sorrow that he envisaged the crumbling of an ancient order. On the other hand, as an obscurantist, moved by a detestation of human reason and its works, he clearly enjoyed a certain Germanic *Schadenfreude* in equating the decline of the West with the rise of rationality. This equation, one may add, was not new : it was a favourite equation of the obscurantist school of writers —Belloc, Chesterton, T. E. Hulme. Incidentally it is also inconsistent with Toynbee's general theory. For since Toynbee ascribes an equal time-span to all civilizations, regardless of their relative rationality, it is clear that decay, to him, is a function of age, not of reason. Still, it pleased Toynbee to make this equation : it enabled him to wring his hands with more prophetic gusto if he could say to a dying civilization not only, "You are old, you have one foot in the grave, you shall surely die", but also, "You have sinned, your sins have found you out, you deserve to die! I told you so! Repent."

Thus Toynbee's Old Testament, like the ponderous vaticinations of Spengler, can be seen as the obverse of Germanic radicalism, as the despairing wail of conservative defeatism. "The old order is perishing," cried the radicals, "it is doomed to perish. Let us give it one more knock, and it will be finished. Then the reign of the new ruling class will begin." Such has been the cry of radical revolutionaries at all times. It was the cry of the Anabaptists of Münster in the sixteenth century, of the English Saints in the seventeenth century. However, society is a good deal tougher than radicals suppose, as the Anabaptists and the Saints quickly found. When radicals scream that victory is indubitably theirs, sensible conservatives knock them on the nose. It is only very feeble conservatives who take such words as true and run round crying for the last sacraments.

For these reasons Toynbee's Old Testament was not taken very seriously in England. It was still only in Germany that such catastrophic views enjoyed any currency. And indeed in Germany they soon achieved a new lease of life. For although the Marxists proved unable to realize their dream of conquering Germany, another anti-Western radical party, which had stolen the Marxist thunder, was soon able to exploit the theory of "the Decline of the West". Adolf Hitler, like Spengler and Toynbee, was a student of history. Like them he ranged over the centuries and crammed such facts as he found it convenient to select into a monstrous system. The true facts of geography joined the rubbish of the philosophers in his head, and he saw himself as the Phœnix of centuries, the Messiah who would roll up one age of history and open out a new. The West, he said, was finished; but Germany was not, or at least need not be—if only it would repudiate the West. He would revive Germany by detaching it from the embraces of a dying civilization. He would breathe into it a primitive, barbarian, irrational spirit. He would wrest from Marxist Russia the leadership of the new, non-Western, non-capitalist, non-rational age and establish a new empire over the ruins of the West. To demoralize his intended victims he assured them that the iron laws of "historical necessity" were on his side; and having demoralized as many as were frightened by such words, he gathered up his forces and, in 1939, he struck.

When the German legions marched over Europe, trampling on its liberties, it must have seemed to many that Toynbee's dismal prophecies were coming true. Surely this was the end of the West. Was it not written in the Holy Writ? Then if defeat was certain, was it not most sensible to accept it in its least painful form, by prompt surrender? So everywhere in

Europe a class of men appeared who were not Nazis, or pro-Nazis, who did not relish the prospect before them, who were in fact conservatives, but who accepted as inevitable "the New Order" that was threatened from Berlin. The West, they said, was finished : why should it not surrender in the hope of saving at least those elements of Western Civilization which were worth preserving? Freedom of all kinds could be sacrificed, provided the essentials of civilization—the social hierarchy and the Church—were saved. We have sinned, such men cried, we have eaten the forbidden fruit; let us repent and retire out of history, leaving the future to the Nazi Millennium. In future let us be good and let who will be clever; we shall not try to think, but only to pray. The patron saint of such men throughout Europe was Marshal Pétain. He was the patron of all those whose will had been sapped by the messianic claims of Hitler and the dismal certitudes of Toynbee. For Toynbee, in so far as he had any influence, was the unconscious intellectual ally of Hitler in the non-Nazi world, the true prophet of European Pétainism.

I say "unconscious" because in fairness to Toynbee we must admit that he has no particular preference for a German conquest of Europe. He seems not to care who destroys the West, so long as the West is destroyed and thus vindicates his theory. Nor has he ever prophesied who will be its destroyer. Certainly he never foresaw that it might be Hitler. In 1936, after a long interview with Hitler, Toynbee declared himself "convinced of his sincerity in desiring peace in Europe". Even in 1939 he was blind, or indifferent, to the particular threat of Nazi Germany. For civilizations, he maintains, always succumb to internal age, not external blows; or at least external blows are only the occasion, not the cause of their dissolution. Even the Incas were not really destroyed by the Spaniards but because their civilization had reached its logical term when the Spaniards arrived. The apparent destroyer is in fact not a destroyer but merely a demonstrator of internal rottenness. Still, by 1940, Hitler had proved himself a demonstrator of some capacity. If the West was really so rotten that it was about to crumble through natural decay, it was reasonable to expect that the first external knock would complete the process. This is what the Pétainists believed. It was naturally mortifying to them when, in spite of all the blows which it received, in spite of historical necessity, and in spite of the combined eloquence of Hitler and themselves, the West did not merely not crumble : it resisted; it was victorious; it survives.

What was Toynbee to do when faced with this unexpected survival of the civilization whose doom he had so confidently pronounced? Change his views? That is too much to expect of any prophet. A slight re-interpretation is the most we can reasonably require. And sure enough, this is what we get. In 1954, after fifteen years of silence, Toynbee published his New

Testament, and, in publishing it, admitted not indeed error—he has never admitted to any error—but a certain development in his views. In the past fifteen years, he writes, "my inner world had been undergoing changes which, on the miniature scale of an individual life, were for me of proportionate magnitude" to the vast changes which the great war of 1939–45 had caused in the world without.

What were these inner changes? Something of them had already been revealed, obliquely, in a public discussion which Toynbee had held in 1948 with the most formidable of his critics, the distinguished Dutch historian Professor Geyl. In this discussion Geyl had described Toynbee, on the basis of his Old Testament, as a determinist. To his surprise, he found that Toynbee now indignantly repudiated the charge. "With the awful warning of Spengler's dogmatic determinism before my eyes," Toynbee declared, "I always have been and shall be mighty careful, for my part, to treat the future of our civilization as an open question." It was in vain that Geyl protested that this suspension of judgement simply does not exist in Toynbee's book: indeed "as regards the future, in one place in your book you are very near to drawing, as you put it, 'the horoscope of our civilization' from the fate of other civilizations, and you suggest repeatedly that we have got into the disintegration stage which you picture to us so elaborately in your book as leading inevitably to catastrophe". Toynbee simply refused to admit this conclusion. All his arguments might lead thither, but now, suddenly, he refused to pronounce the final doom. He did not give any reason for this refusal to accept the only conclusion to which all his "laws" seem infallibly to lead. All he would say was that although he had established the laws under which all other civilizations have perished, and although he had shown that our civilization too is subject to those laws and has now reached the stage at which death can hardly be postponed, nevertheless—who knows? Something may yet turn up. What? we ask. But we receive no answer. All we are told is that Toynbee is not a determinist. And he adds (somewhat testily we are told), "I suppose I must be the last judge of what my own beliefs are." To which one can only answer, "No doubt: but not of the rationality or consistency of those beliefs."

What was the escape-clause which Toynbee, by 1948, had discovered in his own determinist system? For answer, we look to his New Testament, which he was meditating at that time in the light of those profound inner changes caused by the war, and which, six years later, was to be published to the world as volumes 7–10 of his *Study of History*. These volumes do indeed add a very significant message to the message of the Old Testament: a message not this time of despair but of hope—of a kind.

It is not that Toynbee sees any prospect of the survival of Western Civilization as we understand it. On that point his message is unchanged. Not even the events of 1939–45 can change his eagerness to see "the West" destroyed, and indeed he seems at times positively impatient with those events for their obstinate non-conformity with his theory. Why, he seems to overhear us asking, did the West not crumble finally before the might of Hitler? Poof! he answers. Hitler was no threat at all—how could he have been if even the rotten West did not crumble at his touch? Hitler's armies were phantom armies only : it was only the decadent pacifism of Europe which made him appear formidable. He had not made Germany a military power, he had merely "coaxed, duped, and flogged" it "into being one degree less unwarlike than its neighbours". "In the realm of the blind the one-eyed man is king." Nor does Toynbee allow the war of 1939–45 to be a real war—had he not already committed himself to the assertion that the war of 1914–18 was the last major war of which enfeebled Europe, according to the Toynbeean Tables, was capable? So Hitler's war is dismissed as a mere "supplementary war", beneath the notice of the historical scientist, and therefore unable to disturb the perfect symmetry of those Tables. And finally, if the feeble Hitler let the Professor down by failing to establish universal domination over the ruins of Europe, let us not suppose that that was due to any resistance by the still feeble Europe. No. That was due to "a chapter of lucky accidents" such as no historian could or indeed should be expected to prophesy, and such—Toynbee adds with relish—as cannot conceivably occur again. Thus Hitler's war, which Toynbee had not predicted in 1939, was written off, after it was over, as an irrelevant "secondary war", a mere airshot which does not in the least invalidate the general theory that the West is ripe for conquest. It is inconceivable, we are assured, that our next assailant will repeat the "accidental combination of incidental errors" which led to Hitler's failure. Therefore let us not lose faith—faith in the gospel of our own inevitable defeat.

Where then, we may ask, is the novelty of Toynbee's New Testament? Where is that escape-clause at which he had hinted in his discussion, in 1948, with Professor Geyl? The answer is that the glad tidings of great joy which Toynbee now offers is not that Western civilization as we know it can be saved. It is that something far more important than our rotten civilization can be born out of its ruin. In the 1930s Townbee had lamented the impending death of our civilization because then, along with much that was rational and therefore bad, the good, irrational elements must also perish. He had therefore hoped against hope that by some modification, some deliberate weakening of the rational and strengthening of the irrational elements, the structure might be preserved. But now Toynbee had admitted the fragility, the logical weakness of any such hope. He has yielded at last to the pressure of his own determinist system. But he has been able to do so without reluctance because he has discovered a new, a very important and—to him—a consoling truth.

The truth which dawned on Toynbee in the years of Hitler's war, the years between the Old Testament and the New, is basically very simple. It is that human civilizations are not, after all, organic wholes. Their elements are detachable and can survive, as vital and vivifying parts, in other civilizations, in the "universal states" which shall succeed them. Why then, he asks, should we not separate the essential from the inessential elements, the good from the bad, and, having done that,

> *let determin'd things to Destiny*
> *Hold unbewail'd their way?*

Why should not our Western Civilization go to its doom, the sooner the better, carrying with it the rubbish with which human reason has by now fatally deformed it, provided that the valuable parts of it, its primitive pre-Reformation faith, can be preserved as one of the vitalizing ingredients of the new "universal state"? Surely this is a more logical, more positive, and (to some) more cheering conclusion than that desperate, defeatist proposal so feebly tackled on to Toynbee's Old Testament. Now there is no question of mere reaction. Now salvation will come not by forlorn retreat into the shrivelled womb of Mother Church, but by moving onwards on our predetermined path, which proves not to be so fatal after all. Our civilization shall indeed perish; but what, after all, is civilization? "Civilizations," we are now told, "have forfeited their historical significance except in so far as they minister to the progress of religion." Therefore, what does it matter how soon or by whom Western humanity is decimated, Western justice mocked, Western art and letters snuffed out, Western freedom abolished? Our religion—or rather, one strand of it: for Toynbee still seems to reject Protestantism—shall survive, not indeed alone or exclusive, but as part of a higher religion, the religion of a universal state.

Such is Toynbee's new Dispensation. It is, of course, not entirely new; for Toynbee's whole system is by definition repetitive. Therefore this new Dispensation too has a historical precedent. The precedent is taken, as always, from Græco-Roman civilization. For although Toynbee claims to base his system on a number of past civilizations, in fact, as the critics have often pointed out, it is based on Græco-Roman civilization only—the only civilization which Toynbee has really studied and to whose pattern, as he interprets it, all other civilizations are now arbitrarily told to conform. So now the decline of the West must be made to resemble the decline of Greece and Rome, and the new universal Church, of which Toynbee is the prophet, must resemble the old Christian Church, in the days when it was new. The wheel of history has once again come full circle. The future is once again made clear by the past.

For did not the ancient pagan civilization of the Hellenic world, obedient to the Toynbeean Laws, duly decompose? Were not its political forms—the independent Greek cities, the Hellenistic monarchies, the Roman republic itself—utterly extinguished? Did not the memory of its poets and philosophers happily fade away, burnt out of human recollection by the purifying fires of clerical bigotry, until the rot of the Renaissance allowed them to return? But did not the more essential parts of that civilization, its mysteries and mummeries, its sacraments and sacrifices, Isis and Adonis and Mithras, happily survive, gathered up and preserved in that new syncretist religion, "that quaint Alexandrian *tutti-frutti*", as Norman Douglas once described it, Christianity? Even so, Toynbee tells us, our Western civilization is now fast decomposing. We shall be conquered, destroyed, absorbed. Our political forms, our liberties, our culture shall be crushed out. But what of that? For our religious beliefs, which alone matter, will be preserved, pickled as one of the ingredients of a new syncretist religion, a new *tutti-frutti*, "a mish-mash", as one commentator has described it, "of the Virgin Mary and Mother Isis, of St. Michael and Mithras, of St. Peter and Muhammad, of St. Augustine and Jalalad-Din Mawlana". Such, we are now assured, is to be the new "universal religion" which will render political conquest a positive boon and will replace for all mankind the use of human reason and the remembrance of its great landmarks, the Renaissance, the Reformation, the New Philosophy, the Enlightenment.

But how is this new Dispensation to come in? Will our conquerors themselves bring it in? Certainly not. The Roman Emperors did not invent Christianity, they merely created a political system within which it was able to spread. The beginning of the new religion was quite separate. At a certain point in time during the decomposition of Hellenic society there arose a Messiah. The Messiah preached a Word, a Message, which altered the immutable sentence of the Book of Genesis and gave to mankind, predetermined to physical death, a new hope of spiritual life. Around this Message the disciples of the Messiah afterwards assembled and crystallized the miscellaneous mythology of other religions. Even so today the necessity of a new religion requires the appearance of a new Messiah : a new Messiah who, incidentally, has certain advantages over the old. For the old Messiah acted naïvely : he uttered his message, and his disciples slowly did the rest of the work, so that the new religion grew up, as it seemed, spontaneously, over centuries, obedient to impersonal laws. But the new Messiah can do better than that. Knowing the laws, he can himself operate them, or at least further their operation, much more expeditiously. He knows in advance what the final form of the new religion must be. He can foreshorten the centuries of change and preach the new religion, the new *tutti-frutti*, "the Mish-Mash of the Virgin Mary and Mother Isis" all at once.

And who is to be this new Messiah? It surprises me that among so many commentators of Toynbee's work, none (so far as I know) has publicly posed or answered this question. And yet the answer seems to emerge clearly—only too clearly—from the text. It is true the Messiah is never explicitly named; even on this point the Prophet does not deviate into clarity; but discreetly and repeatedly, as the great work nears its end, he is identified until finally, there can be no mistake. In the tenth volume of his work, the last book of his Bible, his Book of Revelation, the secret is laid bare: the Messiah steps forth: he is Toynbee himself.

I know that this statement will seem outrageous to some. It will be said that Toynbee is personally a modest and humble man and that this is to ascribe to him *hybris* and blasphemy. I do not wish to ascribe anything to him which does not seem to me to emerge inescapably from his published work. I shall therefore try to document the conclusion I have expressed.

First of all I should say that I am not impressed by Toynbee's alleged "humility". It is perfectly true that he himself often praises this virtue. "Spiritual humility", he says, is one of the distinctive signs of the great historian, and he congratulates himself on being free from that "blight of egocentricity" which has prevented other historians from seeing as far as he has done. This "contrite humility, the first of Christian virtues", has, he says, fortified him throughout his superhuman task, and it has also guided his hand in everything he has written; for "in the writing of a book, as in every other human endeavour, the worst of all vices is the *hybris* that is the nemesis of self-conceit. An author is convicting himself of being past praying for if ever he allows the Old Adam in him to close his mind to a suggestion for some modification of his first draft by answering, What I have written I have written".

Now this is all very well, but when we look further into Toynbee's work we find it very difficult to discover this "humility" of which he so regularly boasts. For instance, when has Toynbee ever modified his text in answer to criticism? Some very formidable criticisms were made of some of the arguments used in his early volumes. Has Toynbee ever paid the slightest attention to them or made the slightest modification of those arguments or their conclusions? His only reply has been to include, in his later volumes, a chapter of abuse against those purblind modern historians who, enslaved by a barren devotion to the minutiæ of their technique, have had the *"hybris"*, the "sin", not to admit the validity of his historical laws. As

for his claim to be free from "the blight of egocentricity", it is instructive
to look at his last volume of all. There, in the index, it will be found that
whereas the entry "History", which is, after all, the subject of the whole
work, occupies only five column-inches, the entry "Toynbee, Arnold
Joseph" occupies twelve column-inches, and there are separate entries for
twelve other members of the Toynbee family who owe this distinction
entirely to their relationship with the Professor. The "Acknowledgements
and Thanks", too, which cover thirty pages, are awarded not only to the
usual suppliers of information, correctors of proofs, and benevolent publishers, but to all who, since the beginning of History, have deserved
immortality by contributing, each according to his capacity, to that ultimate
creation of the ages, the mind of Toynbee. Æschylus, Pindar, Aristotle are
there; the Bible, St. Augustine, Fra Angelico have done their bit; thanks
are conveyed to "the glory of God" and, on either side of it, to the also
beneficent city of York and uncle William Toynbee. Plato is thanked for
teaching the Professor "when, in a mental voyage, I found myself at the
upper limit of the atmosphere accessible to Reason, not to hesitate to let my
imagination carry me up into the stratosphere on the wings of a myth".
William of Wykeham is thanked for having founded Winchester College
and having thoughtfully "made this provision for me 507 years before I was
elected a scholar of his college". It is clear, from such evidence, that Toynbee regards himself as a portent no less significant than his work. All creation has been groaning and travailing to produce him; Winchester College
has at last, in him, achieved its purpose; the ultimate bounds of human
reason have at last, by him, been pierced.

All this being so, I do not think we are obliged to ascribe to Toynbee that
almost unnatural humility which he so often goes out of his way to claim.
Or, at least, his humility must be relative : his own greatness must seem
to him so clearly superhuman that it shows remarkable condescension in
him to claim, in public, no more than unique mortal genius. As for the
humility which he preaches as a necessary virtue of the historian, we are
forced to conclude that he is not really thinking of himself at all : he is thinking of his critics. If only *they* were more humble, how much better it would
be! Then they would not presume to criticize one who had so splendidly
outsoared the shadow of their night.

Thus I do not consider it *a priori* inconceivable that Toynbee should
regard himself as the Messiah. And in fact, if we examine the autobiographical part of his work in a little more detail, we can hardly help
observing the repeated evidence that this is how he does regard himself. In
fact we shall discover that Toynbee, unlike previous Messiahs who were
lamentably careless in this respect, has made scrupulous provision for his
future devotees. Having himself (since History—as he has shown—repeats

itself) tasted almost all the experiences of his prototype, he has contrived so to record these experiences, their dates and places, that there will be no danger of heresy or error in such important matters. Tucked away in the corners of his New Testament, we can find the authentic record of everything that matters in his Life : the minor prophets who dimly heralded his coming; the Holy Family; the precocious Infancy; the youthful Temptations; the missionary Journeys; the Miracles; the Revelations; the Agony. Moreover, looking forward as well as back, he has, by considerately recording the places he has visited and the objects he has touched, made provision for a constant traffic in those pilgrimages and relics upon which the religion of the Mish-Mash, like all true religion, must depend.

Am I serious? Alas, I am. Toynbee's truly monstrous self-adulation, combined with his fundamental obscurantism, do indeed emotionally repel me. But let us not give out all the heat we may feel. Perhaps the subject is best treated with detachment, even if it requires an artificial detachment. So let us interpose the cooling concept of an imaginary century. Let us transport ourselves, in imagination, a century or so onward in time, so that we can look back calmly upon the phenomenon before us. Let us suppose that all has worked according to plan. The Time of Troubles is over. Western Civilization, long declining, has now at last (thank God) foundered, and all that is good in it, and in other civilizations, has been preserved and pickled in the universal world-state with its universal world-religion of Mish-Mash. From this vantage post I invite my readers to look coolly back at the figure of Toynbee as it will then emerge from his own New Testament and from the glosses with which his disciples, in the course of a century, will naturally have enriched it.

It is noon. The drowsy doggerel of the Founder's Litany "Mother Mary, Mother Isis, Mother Cybele, Mother Ishtar, Mother Kwanyin, have compassion on us . . ." is rhythmically sounding in all the Churches of Mish-Mash. We know the history of this Litany of course : how the Disciples asked the Master to teach them to pray, and how in "London, at 6.25 p.m. on 15th June 1951, after looking once more, this afternoon, at Fra Angelico's picture of the Beatific Vision", the Master obliged by uttering this formula (Vol. X, p. 143). As the unintelligible sounds issue mechanically from his lips, the worshipper will, of course, allow his eyes to stray. Perhaps they will light on a stained-glass window, illuminated from without by the rational daylight. What will it represent? That, of course, will vary with the locality. At Abersoch, in Wales, for instance, a richly painted window will naturally illustrate the great local miracle of the Epiphany: how the Founder, at the age of two, already driven forward by intellectual curiosity and a philosophy of action, "took and carried out a decision to run into the sea in order to find out what would happen", and was hauled back by an anxious nurse who, though she sprained her ankle in the act, has since been amply compensated by her official beatification. The church at Abersoch is now rich, thanks to the resort of pilgrims eager to baptize their children in those now curative seawaves, so the window is a fine one, and the artist has not failed to point the moral of the incident. How could he, when the Master has himself so clearly emphasized it : "There was no benevolently officious nurse to pull him back from the intellectual plunge that he made, six years later, into the Ocean of History" (X. 19).

"Six years later," the inattentive worshipper may well muse, "that means that our Founder took his first decisive intellectual plunge at the age of eight. When? Where? In what parish church or rural shrine is this great event worthily commemorated?" On this point, unfortunately, the Scriptures are ambiguous. For the Founder himself tells us (X. 218) that he was only seven when he read, in the Book of Genesis, about Noah's three sons and thence precociously took note of "the differentation of the Human Race into divers groups and sub-groups and the historical problems raised by the question how these groups are related to one another"; and again (X. 235) that he was not yet eight when he read *Paradise Lost* in three days and imbibed from it "the idea of a theodicy"; and it was at the age of seven, too, he tells us, that he received from his mother the inscribed copy of her *True Stories from Scottish History* "which stands behind his shoulder in his study at No. 45 Pembroke Square, London", and which he has "just now" taken down (X. 18) . . .

How thoughtful, incidentally, of the Founder always to identify the placing of his books! These helpful details have made it possible to reconstitute his study exactly as he kept it, even down to that translation by Gilbert Murray which he took out of the row on May 11th, 1951 (X. 217); and Aunt Gertrude Toynbee's copy of Mommsen which he received from her in September 1906, which he read in the summer of "A.D. 1907" (now A.T. 18) and which was "here on my desk in May 1951" (X. 229); and the four volumes of *The Story of the Nations*, with the bookplate of Grandmother (now the Blessed) Harriet Toynbee in them, which were "all four of them on my table on this 21st day of February 1951" (X. 219); and the map of Greece which he used on April 26th, 1912, and is still "lying at his elbow at this moment" on September 23rd, 1952; and the forty-two sheets of an early MS. by himself which, "as he wrote these words, he took out of a drawer in a bookcase given him by his mother in his study at 45 Pembroke Square, Kensington, London" (X. 22). The study, of course, is now no longer in Pembroke Square. Like the Virgin's House at Bethlehem, which miraculously migrated to Loreto in Italy, it has now been removed intact to the great Toynbeeum in California, and a mere replica has replaced it in

Kensington. But London is not entirely without original relics. The three volumes of Grote's work on Plato, for instance, which the Founder "took down from the shelf in the Athenæum Club" are now preserved in the club in a jewelled reliquary and exposed for the worship of members on the anniversary of the day, April 23rd, 1951 (formerly St. George's Day), on which the Founder records that he touched them (X. 20).

Meanwhile, in other churches throughout the world, similar thoughts must be occurring to other worshippers. At Dunwich, Suffolk, a statue of Mother and Child naturally commemorates the Founder's Mother giving him, when he was five years old, that sagacious tip ("the Wisdom of Dunwich") which enabled him, five years later, to write a better essay than the other boys in his school (X. 41). At the school itself, Wootton Court near Canterbury (now a training college for the Mish-Mash clergy), a splendid church is of course dedicated to the Confounding of the Elders in the matter of the Parthian Cataphracts (X. 224). Further afield, in Osaka, Japan, a rich temple marks the spot where the Founder, in November 1929, was inspired by a puppet-show to entertain profound thoughts about determinism and free-will (X. 231). In Greece, in the wild country between Káto Vezáni and Gythion, a rural shrine marks the spot where, on April 26th, 1912, the Founder drank dysentery from an infected stream and thus escaped the dangers of military service. (The lucky stream now cures the disease it then inflicted.) At 12 Westbourne Terrace, London, a fine wall-painting depicts the Founder there listening to his great-uncle Captain (now St.) Henry Toynbee discoursing on the rig of sailing ships (X. 213); and at Arezzo the old daubs by Piero della Francesca have been painted over with more truly devotional frescoes representing the Founder fruit-fully questioning the rector of the church on "the affinities of certain forms of headgear" (X. 239). The spot where the Founder swam the Euphrates (IX. 38) is of course a great place of pilgrimage, pickpockets, and baksheesh. In Yorkshire, the less ambitious tourist will find, on Slingsby Moor, the barrow where the Messiah was able to catch "still unspent reverberations of waves of psychic events" since unrecorded time; and, at Ampleforth Abbey, a noble altar-piece commemorating the Founder's famous Dream in "A.D. 1936" (A.T. 47) of clinging to the Crucifix: the premonition of his later Passion (IX. 634).

Of these lesser shrines there is no end. For the Founder not only excelled St. Paul and St. Francis Xavier in his travels, he was also considerate enough to supply the faithful with a very detailed record of them. The mere list of places visited by him fills, in his index, three and a half column-inches. But some reference must be made to the seven great centres of the new religion, the Seven Stations as they are now called, where the

Founder had his seven direct historical revelations—such an improvement on "the sole flash of inspiration with which Gibbon was ever visited" (X. 103)—when he was "rapt into a momentary communion" with incidents in the distant past. The first Station was at Oxford (now Arnoldopolis) in "A.D. 1911" (A.T. 22). Others were on a peak of Pharsalus on January 10th, 1912 (conducted tours on the anniversary); at Monemvasía on April 23rd, 1912, where "the quietly browsing goats" (X. 136) are now stylized figures in local art, like the ox and the ass of Bethlehem in Italian painting; and on a peninsula in the Gulf of Chihli on November 24th, 1929, where, in spite of this important event, the ungrateful natives are unhappily not yet settled in the new faith. But the great revelation is the seventh, which took place near Victoria (now "the Seventh") Station in London. On that occasion the Master "found himself in communion not just with this or that episode in History, but with all that had been, and was, and was to come. In that instant he was directly aware of the passage of History gently flowing through him in a mighty current and of his own life welling like a wave in the flow of this vast tide" (X.139). How unfortunate that the Founder "failed to record the exact date" of this experience. In the absence of evidence the Church has had to name a conventional date for its annual commemoration : the Day of Toynbee's Transfiguration is now kept on December 25th (formerly Christmas).

Of course the Founder's life was not without its frustrations. In his early days there was the Temptation in Buckinghamshire when the Devil, in the form of Uncle Paget Toynbee ("*vivebat* A.D. 1855–1932"—for the Founder always gives these useful biographical data about the Holy Family) and Aunt Helen Toynbee ("*née* Helen Wrigley, of Bury, Lancs.") sought to divert him at age of seventeen into "a wrong intellectual turning". "Your Aunt Nellie and I," said this plausible old uncle, "have come to the conclusion that you have been dispersing your interests too widely, and our advice to you is to make your choice of some single subject and to concentrate hereafter on that." Fortunately the young Messiah had an "instantaneous conviction that this advice was bad". He put Satan firmly behind him, and continued to pursue the superficial omniscience which he afterwards so triumphantly attained. Then there was the sad case of the Betrayal, when the Master was "wholesomely shocked" by the defection of his supposed disciple G. L. Iscariot Cheesman. Cheesman, we are told, so far yielded to "the dismal orthodox cult of specialization" that he insisted on learning thoroughly the subject which he was employed to teach. Fortunately the Master survived all the dangers, and now his "narrow escape from intellectual perdition" (X. 35) is the theme of many a vivid fresco (and many a dull sermon) in the new age. During the years of his mission he was of course past the danger of temptation, although he was never free from carping critics whom, by one of his happy historical parallels, he would designate as "Scribes and Pharisees". This, however, was to be expected. Even in his schooldays he had premonitions of his future Agony, "though I had not yet tasted the cup for myself" (X. 235); nor had he yet—as he was afterwards, like St. Francis of Assisi, to do— received "Christ's stigmata" (IX. 644).

However, all that is now over. The words, the very names of the critics are now extinct, except in so far as the Master has deigned to take note of them . . . And here, no doubt, our worshipper's mind will again digress to commend the providence of the Founder who salvaged so much of past literature (in so far as he approved of it) from the wholesome conflagration of the pre-Mish-Mash culture. Readers of Toynbee today sometimes object to his numerous and (to a superficial view) irrelevant quotations from ancient and modern literature. And why, they ask, all these careful references : may one not remark that human projects sometimes "gang agley" without appending a footnote reference to "Burns, Robert: to a Mouse, stanza 7"? May not one use the phrase "eyes that see not" without giving chapter and verse for the nine passages of the (Christian) Bible in which it occurs? A moment's thought should silence these impertinent questioners. Do they not realize that the Master is not writing for us but for our descendants in the Half-Baked Millennium of which he is the Prophet? By then all previous "pagan" literature will of course have been destroyed, so that only those passages which are, as it were, pickled in the new Bible can participate in its immortality; just as fragments of Hebrew secular literature survive embalmed in the Christian Scriptures. Naturally such detached gobbets from the lost literature of the past will need an explanatory apparatus which to us, who still know the originals, may well seem otiose. Instead of cavilling at the overcrowded pages, we should express our gratitude to Toynbee for allowing so much of pre-Toynbeean literature to enter, in these stormy times, into the Noah's Ark of his Holy Writ.

I have said enough. The temptation of fantasy is irresistible when dealing with this huge, presumptuous, and utterly humourless work, and perhaps I have gone a little further than the orthodox Toynbeean priesthood may go. But the quotations I have given are really enough to prove my point. Has any other writer, however apocalyptic his message, taken such pains to acquaint the public with the trivial details of his own life, the successive signs of his Election, or to represent himself personally as the culminating end-product of one civilization, the herald, law-giver, and prophet of another? Has any other Christian scholar thus applied to himself the successive incidents of the Christian myth? If the conclusions were stated without the evidence, they would be rejected as incredible. Such egotism leaves the claim of Mohammed, to be the unique prophet of God, nowhere. But then Mohammed, as Toynbee says, was "a conspicuously unsuccessful prophet". He only spread his message from China to Nigeria, from Indonesia to Spain. Toynbee, it is clear, is the Messiah of a much wider world.

But let us forget these details. It is not the content of Toynbee's work that interests me. To me it is a matter of indifference whether he read some unimportant book in the library of the Athenæum Club or in No. 45 Pembroke Square, in the summer of 1907 or in September 1952. I am interested in the character, not the content of his work; and I am interested in it because, fundamentally, I find it not merely erroneous—that is not a matter for emotion—but hateful. For Toynbee does not only utter false arguments and dogmatic statements, calling them "scientific" and "empirical"; he does not only preach a gospel of deliberate obscurantism; he seems to undermine our will, welcome our defeat, gloat over the extinction of our civilization, not because he supports the form of civilization which threatens us, but because he is animated by what we can only call a masochistic desire to be conquered. If Hitler and Stalin rejoiced in the prospect of destroying the West, theirs at least was a crude, intelligible rejoicing. They smacked their lips because they looked for plunder. Toynbee has no such clear interests in supporting a conqueror. He hungers spiritually not for this or that conquest, but for our defeat.

Defeat by whom? Toynbee does not care. To him it does not matter whether it is Hitler's New Order or World Communism which provides the irrelevant secular structure for the religion of Mish-Mash. And so there have been various claimants. For instance, in 1947–51, the American ex-Marxist James Burnham, having swallowed Toynbee's Old Testament whole, declared that "Western civilization has reached the stage in its development that calls for the creation of its Universal Empire" and urged the American government to seize its chance by rising and destroying the Russian government, "if necessary by total war". This ambition was not very different from that of Hitler. Indeed, if we look closer at Mr. Burnham's policy, we find that it is very like that of Hitler: for he declared that the value of European allies was to be measured not by their attachment to any liberal values, but solely by their hatred of communism. Consequently he rejected all other national leaders except General Franco, General Chiang Kai-shek, General de Gaulle, and the Pope. If this is the measure of virtue, it seems a pity that Hitler had not been left in peace. He was, after all, incontestably anti-communist; and he might have been necessary to reinforce Mr. Burnham's seedy army of crusaders. As it is, it seems unlikely that these three generals and the Pope would make much of a showing against the Red Army, and therefore it is a Russian conquest of Europe that Toynbee must envisage. He envisages it without apparent dismay. The essential thing to him is that a world empire should be established. The secular details are irrelevant. Christianity needed the secular framework of the Roman Empire : what did it matter whether the emperor was Augustus or Nero, Elagabalus or Diocletian? Perhaps in the end, after three centuries, there will even be a Constantine.

Thus Toynbee is still the philosophic ally of any conqueror who will destroy the West. And this, I think, is the explanation of a paradox which certain critics have noted in his work. For although Toynbee always presents himself as a "gentle" figure, a "pilgrim" humbly seeking universal understanding, in fact his history is primarily concerned with dynasties and conquests. He is uninterested in the arts and sciences, in trade and industry, in administration and finance. His mind prefers to dwell among the horrors of war, the march of armies, the seizure of empires, the founding of tyrant houses. "Such preoccupation with violence," says one critic, "might seem puzzling in so pronounced a pacifist and humanitarian if Freud had not taught us the meaning of ambivalence." In fact, I fear, the explanation is simple. Like many intellectuals, Toynbee seems fascinated by brute power and longs to surrender to it. And since he identifies himself with the History of the world which he has felt "gently flowing through him like a mighty current", he wants the whole world to surrender to it too.

Such, I believe, is Toynbee's philosophy. It is a doctrine of messianic defeatism. Toynbee detests Western civilization because it is basically liberal and rational. Detesting it, he wishes to see it destroyed, and he does not care who destroys it. On its ruins he envisages a new society, or rather, the religion only of a new society. The new society itself, as far as he is concerned, can be the nightmare society of 1984, provided that the religion is the religion of Mish-Mash, of which he is the prophet and Messiah. And this he calls a great hope for the West! Is it any wonder that the greatest of his critics has called it "a blasphemy against the West"?

For in fact there is no reason to fold our hands and resign ourselves to the inevitable death of Western civilization. There is, of course, a relative decline in the power of Western Europe : a decline due to the technical achievements of Western Europe in mobilizing the resources of the much greater areas which now overshadow it. It is not now conceivable that Western Europe—that is, Britain, France, the Low Countries, and Italy—should dominate the world to the extent that they have done in the past. But who regards "domination" as an essential mark of civilization? And anyway this real decline is relative not absolute : it is quite improper to

149

ascribe a "disease" to a man who, while as healthy as ever, has been out-grown by a giant. Moreover, if we compare Western Europe today with Western Europe in the 1930s, we find that in some respects it is positively healthier today. In the 1930s Germany and Italy were lost to the West. Today all Italy and half Germany are firmly recovered. In the 1930s the social situation throughout Western Europe was rendered precarious by "the contradictions of capitalism" which both Hitler and Stalin sought to exploit. Today those contradictions have been so largely resolved that no Western country seriously fears revolution. Indeed, the boot is on the other leg. It is in the communist countries of Eastern Europe that the contradic-tions of communism are now threatening revolution, and the intellectuals of Poland, Hungary, and Russia itself look to Western "social capitalism" as the answer. In such circumstances to talk of the West as if it were not merely reduced in relative power but a diseased civilization is not only incorrect: it is absurd.

Those who look to history for lessons should look to both sides of it. They will then find that the West has "declined" before now. For instance, in the early sixteenth century, Christendom saw itself reduced to frontiers almost as narrow as any it had known since the fall of the Western Roman Empire. The once Christian cities of Asia and North Africa had long been lost; now the Turks had advanced into the heart of Europe. The long Christian islands of the Mediterranean, the Christian cities of Belgrade and Budapest were all lost. When, men asked, would the remorseless con-quest be stayed? Europe only survived, they said, thanks to the Sophy of Persia, who distracted the Turks in Asia. And then, on top of these disasters, came the great schism of the Protestant Reformation. What wonder that the Toynbee of those days, Pope Clement VII, believed that the Last Days predetermined in the Apocalypse were about to come and, in this mood, commissioned Michelangelo to paint, on the wall of the Sistine Chapel, the Last Judgment? And yet, looking back, it is not this aspect of the sixteenth century which seems to us significant. The sixteenth century, to us, is the beginning of the greatness of the West. Even to Toynbee, who regards the greatness of the West as its decay, the sixteenth century is the beginning, not the end, of the process.

A similar point could be made about the early seventeenth century. Then, too, certain sad spirits supposed that the world was coming to an end. Nature, they said, was in decay, and while enthusiasts looked eagerly for the Millennium, defeatist spirits, repeating, like Sir Thomas Browne, that " 'tis too late to be ambitious, the great mutations of the world are over", resigned themselves to the impending doom. And yet this was the age of Bacon and Descartes, the beginning of those scientific discoveries which had enriched and alleviated the life of man!

Therefore, let us hear no more of the Decline of the West. Speaking absolutely, not relatively, the phrase has no meaning. The Toynbeean tables are about as relevant to modern historical knowledge as the chronology of Archbishop Ussher. And as for the Messiah and the Millennium, if we think of them at all, let it be only as a bogey. If the politics of 1984 and the religion of the Mish-Mash are all that our new prophet can offer us as the reward of acquiescence in the "inevitable" ruin which he "scientifically" predicts, that at least should spur us to throw this Jonah overboard and resist. After all, as some sage philosopher once observed, the irresistible is very often merely that which has not been resisted.

JUNE 1957

GEOFFREY GORER

The Pornography of Death

"Birth, and copulation, and death.
That's all the facts when you come to brass tacks;
Birth, and copulation, and death."
T. S. Eliot. SWEENEY AGONISTES (1932)

PORNOGRAPHY IS, no doubt, the opposite face, the shadow of prudery, whereas obscenity is an aspect of seemliness. No society has been recorded which has not its rules of seemliness, of words or actions which arouse discomfort and embarrassment in some contexts, though they are essential in others. The people before whom one must maintain a watchful seemliness vary from society to society: all people of the opposite sex, or all juniors, or all elders, or one's parents-in-law, or one's social superiors or inferiors, or one's grandchildren have been selected in different societies as groups in whose presence the employment of certain words or the performance of certain actions would be considered offensive; and then these words or actions become charged with effect. There is a tendency for these words and actions to be related to sex and excretion, but this is neither necessary nor universal; according to Malinowski, the Trobrianders surround eating with as much shame as excretion; and in other societies personal names or aspects of ritual come under the same taboos.

Rules of seemliness are apparently universal; and the non-observance of these rules, or anecdotes which involve the breaking of the rules, provoke that particular type of laughter which seems identical the world over; however little one may know about a strange society, however little one may know about the functions of laughter in that scociety (and these can be very various) one can immediately tell when people are laughing at an obscene joke. The topper of the joke may be "And then he ate the whole meal in front of them!" or "She used her husband's name in the presence of his mother!" but the laughter is the same; the taboos of seemliness have been broken and the result is hilarious. Typically, such laughter is confined to one-sex groups and is more general with the young, just entering into the complexities of adult life.

Obscenity then is a universal, an aspect of man and woman living in society; everywhere and at all times there are words and actions which, when misplaced, can produce shock, social embarrassment, and laughter. Pornography on the other hand, the description of tabooed activities to produce hallucination or delusion, seems to be a very much rarer phenomenon. It probably can only arise in literate societies, and we certainly have no records of it for non-literate ones; for whereas the enjoyment of obsenity is predominantly social, the enjoyment of pornography is predominantly private. The fantasies from which pornography derives could of course be generated in any society; but it seems doubtful whether they would ever be communicated without the intermediary of literacy.

The one possible exception to this generalization is the use of the plastic arts without any letterpress. I have never felt quite certain that the three-dimensional *poses plastiques* on so many Hindu temples (notably the "Black Pagoda" at Konarak) have really the high-falutin Worship of the Life Force or Glorification of the Creative Aspect of Sex which their apologists claim for them; many of them seem to me very like "feelthy" pictures, despite the skill with which they are executed. There are too the erotic woodcuts of Japan; but quite a lot of evidence suggests that these are thought of as laughter-provoking (i.e. obscene) by the Japanese themselves. We have no knowledge of the functions of the Peruvian pottery.

As far as my knowledge goes, the only Asiatic society which has a long-standing tradition of pornographic literature is China; and, it would appear, social life under the Manchus was surrounded by much the same haze of prudery as distinguished the nineteenth century in much of Europe and the Americas, even though the emphasis fell rather differently; women's deformed feet seem to have been the greatest focus of peeking and sniggering, rather than their ankles or the cleft between their breasts; but by and large life in Manchu China seems to have been nearly as full of "unmentionables" as life in Victoria's heyday.

Pornography would appear to be a concomitant of prudery, and usually the periods of the greatest production of pornography have also been the periods of the most rampant prudery. In contrast to obscenity, which is chiefly defined by situation, prudery is defined by subject; some aspect of human experience is treated as inherently shameful or abhorrent, so that it can never be discussed or referred to openly, and experience of it tends to be clandestine and accompanied by feelings of guilt and unworthiness. The unmentionable aspect of experience then tends to become a subject for much private fantasy, more or less realistic, fantasy charged with pleasurable guilt or guilty pleasure; and those whose power of fantasy is weak, or whose demand is insatiable, constitute a market for the printed fantasies of the pornographer.

Traditionally, and in the lexicographic meaning of the term, pornography has been concerned with sexuality. For the greater part of the last two hundred years copulation and (at least in the mid-Victorian decades) birth were the "unmentionables" of the triad of basic human experiences which "are all the facts when you come to brass tacks", around which so much private fantasy and semi-clandestine pornography were erected. During most of this period death was no mystery, except in the sense that death is always a mystery. Children were encouraged to think about death, their own deaths and the edifying or cautionary death-beds of others. It can have been a rare individual who, in the nineteenth century with its high mortality, had not witnessed at least one actual dying, as well as paying their respect to "beautiful corpses"; funerals were the occasion of the greatest display for working class, middle class, and aristocrat. The cemetery was the centre of every old-established village, and they were prominent in most towns. It was fairly late in the nineteenth century when the execution of criminals ceased to be a public holiday as well as a public warning. Mr. Fairchild had no difficulty in finding a suitably garnished gibbet for his moral lesson.

In the twentieth century, however, there seems to have been an unremarked shift in prudery; whereas copulation has become more and more "mentionable", particularly in the Anglo-Saxon societies, death has become more and more "unmentionable" *as a natural process*. I cannot recollect a novel or play of the last twenty years or so which has a "death-bed scene" in it, describing in any detail the death "from natural causes" of a major character; this topic was a set piece for most of the eminent Victorian and Edwardian writers, evoking their finest prose and their most elaborate technical effects to produce the greatest amount of pathos or edification.

One of the reasons, I imagine, for this plethora of death-bed scenes—apart from their intrinsic emotional and religious content—was that it was one of the relatively few experiences that an author could be fairly sure would have been shared by the vast majority of his readers. Questioning my old acquaintances, I cannot find one over the age of sixty who did not witness the agony of at least one near relative; I do not think I know a single person under the age of thirty who has had a similar experience. Of course my acquaintance is neither very extensive nor particularly representative; but in this instance I do think it is typical of the change of attitude and "exposure".

The natural processes of corruption and decay have become disgusting, as disgusting as the natural processes of birth and copulation were a century ago; preoccupation about such processes is (or was) morbid and unhealthy, to be discouraged in all and punished in the young. Our great-grandparents were told that babies were found under gooseberry bushes or cabbages; our children are likely to be told that those who have passed on (fie! on the gross Anglo-Saxon monosyllable) are changed into flowers, or lie at rest in lovely gardens. The ugly facts are relentlessly hidden; the art of the embalmers is an art of complete denial.

It seems possible to trace a connection between the shift of taboos and the shift in religious beliefs. In the nineteenth century most of the inhabitants of Protestant countries seem to have subscribed to the Pauline beliefs in the sinfulness of the body and the certainty of the after-life. "So also is the resurrection of the dead. It is sown in corruption; it is raised in incorruption : it is sown in dishonour; it is raised in glory." It was possible to insist on the corruption of the dead body, and the dishonour of its begetting, while there was a living belief in the incorruption and the glory of the immortal part. But in England, at any rate, belief in the future life as taught in Christian doctrine is very uncommon today even in the minority who make church-going or prayer a consistent part of their lives; and without some such belief natural death and physical decomposition have become too horrible to contemplate or to discuss. It seems symptomatic that the contemporary sect of Christian Science should deny the fact of physical death, even to the extent (so it is said) of refusing to allow the word to be printed in the *Christian Science Monitor*.

During the last half-century public health measures and improved preventive medicine have made natural death among the younger members of the population much more uncommon than it had been in earlier periods, so that a death in the family, save in the fullness of time, became a relatively uncommon incident in home life; and, simultaneously, violent death increased in a manner unparalleled in human history. Wars and revolutions, concentration camps and gang feuds were the most publicized of the causes for these violent deaths; but the diffusion of the automobile, with its constant and unnoticed toll of fatal accidents, may well have been most influential in bringing the possibility of violent death into the expectations of law-abiding people in time of peace. While natural death became more and more smothered in prudery, violent death has played an ever-growing part in the fantasies offered to mass audiences—detective stories, thrillers, Westerns, war stories, spy stories, science fiction, and eventually horror comics.

There seem to be a number of parallels between the fantasies which titillate our curiosity about the mystery of sex, and those which titillate our curiosity about the mystery of death. In both types of fantasy, the emotions

155

which are typically concomitant of the acts—love or grief—are paid little or no attention, while the sensations are enhanced as much as a customary poverty of language permits. If marital intercourse be considered the natural expression of sex for most of humanity most of the time, then "natural sex" plays as little rôle as "natural death" (the ham-fisted attempts of D. H. Lawrence and Jules Romains to describe "natural sex" realistically but high-mindedly prove the rule). Neither type of fantasy can have any real development, for once the protagonist has done something, he or she must proceed to do something else, with or to somebody else, more refined, more complicated, or more sensational than what had occurred before. This somebody else is not a person; it is either a set of genitals, with or without secondary sexual characteristics, or a body, perhaps capable of suffering pain as well as death. Since most languages are relatively poor in words or constructions to express intense pleasure or intense pain, the written portions of both types of fantasy abound in onomatopæic conglomerations of letters meant to evoke the sighs, gasps, groans, screams, and rattles concomitant to the described actions. Both types of fantasy rely heavily on adjective and simile. Both types of fantasy are completely unrealistic, since they ignore all physical, social, or legal limitations, and both types have complete hallucination of the reader or viewer as their object.

There seems little question that the instinct of those censorious busybodies preoccupied with other people's morals was correct when they linked the pornography of death with the pornography of sex. This, however, seems to be the only thing which has been correct in their deductions or attempted actions. There is no valid evidence to suppose that either type of pornography is an incitement to action; rather are they substitute gratifications. The belief that such hallucinatory works would incite their readers to copy the actions depicted would seem to be indirect homage to the late Oscar Wilde, who described such a process in *The Portrait of Dorian Gray*; I know of no authenticated parallels in real life, though investigators and magistrates with bees in their bonnets can usually persuade juvenile delinquents to admit to exposure to whatever medium of mass communication they are choosing to make a scapegoat.

Despite some gifted precursors, such as Andréa de Nerciat or Edgar Allen Poe, most works in both pornographies are æsthetically objectionable; but it is questionable whether, from the purely æsthetic point of view, there is much more to be said for the greater part of the more anodyne fare provided by contemporary mass media of communication. Psychological Utopians tend to condemn substitute gratifications as such, at least where copulation is involved; they have so far been chary in dealing with death.

Nevertheless, people have to come to terms with the basic facts of birth, copulation, and death, and somehow accept their implications; if social prudery prevents this being done in an open and dignified fashion, then it will be done surreptitiously. If we dislike the modern pornography of death, then we must give back to death—natural death—its parade and publicity, re-admit grief and mourning. If we make death unmentionable in polite society—"not before the children"—we almost ensure the continuation of the "horror comic". No censorship has ever been really effective.

OCTOBER 1955

NANCY MITFORD

The English Aristocracy

THE ENGLISH ARISTOCRACY may seem to be on the verge of decadence, but it is the only real aristocracy left in the world today. It has real political power through the House of Lords and a real social position through the Queen. An aristocracy in a republic is like a chicken whose head has been cut off: it may run about in a lively way, but in fact it is dead. There is nothing to stop a Frenchman, German, or Italian from calling himself the Duke of Carabosse if he wants to, and in fact the Continent abounds with invented titles. But in England the Queen is the fountain of honours and when she bestows a peerage upon a subject she bestows something real and unique.

The great distinction between the English aristocracy and any other has always been that, whereas abroad every other member of a noble family is noble, in England none are noble except the head of the family. In spite of the fact that they enjoy courtesy titles, the sons and daughters of lords are commoners—though not so common as baronets and their wives who take precedence after honourables. (So, of course, do all knights, except Knights of the Garter who come after the eldest sons and the daughters of barons, but before the younger sons.) The descendants of younger sons, who, on the Continent would all be counts or barons, in England have no titles and sit even below knights. Furthermore, the younger sons and daughters of the very richest lords receive, by English custom, but little money from their families, barely enough to live on. The sons are given the same education as their eldest brother and then turned out, as soon as they are grown up, to fend for themselves; the daughters are given no education at all, the general idea being that they must find some man to keep them—which, in fact, they usually do. The rule of primogeniture has kept together the huge fortunes of English lords; it has also formed our class system.

But there is in England no aristocratic class that forms a caste. We have about 950 peers, not all of whom, incidentally, sit in the House of Lords. Irish peers have no seats, though some Irish peers have a subsidiary U.K. peerage giving a seat; Scottish peers elect sixteen representatives from among themselves. Peeresses in their own right are not, as yet, admitted.

Most of the peers share the education, usage, and point of view of a vast upper middle class, but the upper middle class does not, in its turn, merge imperceptibly into the middle class. There is a very definite border line, easily recognizable by hundreds of small but significant landmarks.

When I speak of these matters I am always accused of being a snob, so, to illustrate my point, I propose to quote from Professor Alan Ross of Birmingham University. Professor Ross has written a paper, printed in Helsinki in 1954, for the *Bulletin de la Société Neo-philologique de Helsinki*, on "Upper Class English Usage". Nobody is likely to accuse either this learned man or his Finnish readers of undue snobbishness. The Professor, pointing out that it is solely by their language that the upper classes nowadays are distinguished (since they are neither cleaner, richer, nor better-educated than anybody else) has invented a useful formula : U (for upper class) -speaker versus non-U-speaker. Such exaggeratedly non-U usage as "serviette" for "napkin" he calls non-U indicators. Since "a piece of mathematics or a novel written by a member of the upper class is not likely to differ in any way from one written by a member of another class ... in writing it is in fact only modes of address, postal addresses and habits of beginning and ending letters that serve to demarcate the class" ... The names of many houses are themselves non-U; the ideal U-address is PQR where P is a place name, Q a describer, and R the name of a county, as "Shirwell Hall, Salop." (Here I find myself in disagreement with Professor Ross—in my view abbreviations such as Salop, Herts, or Glos, are decidedly non-U. Any sign of undue haste, in fact, is apt to be non-U, and I go so far as preferring, except for business letters, not to use air mail.) "But," adds Professor Ross, "today few gentlemen can maintain this standard and they often live in houses with non-U names such as Fairmeads or El Nido." Alas!

He speaks of the U-habit of silence, and perhaps does not make as much of it as he might. Silence is the only possible U-response to many embarrassing modern situations : the ejaculation of "cheers" before drinking, for example, or "it was so nice seeing you", after saying good-bye. In silence, too, one must endure the use of the Christian name by comparative strangers and the horror of being introduced by Christian and surname without any prefix. This unspeakable usage sometimes occurs in letters —Dear XX—which, in silence, are quickly torn up, by me.

After discoursing at some length on pronunciation, the professor goes on to vocabulary and gives various examples of U and non-U usage.
Cycle is non-U against U *bike*.
Dinner: U-speakers eat *luncheon* in the middle of the day and *dinner* in

the evening. Non-U-speakers (also U-children and U-dogs) have their *dinner* in the middle of the day.

Greens is non-U for U *vegetables.*

Home: non-U—"they have a lovely *home*"; U—"they've a very nice house."

Ill: "I was *ill* on the boat" is non-U against U *sick.*

Mental: non-U for U *mad.*

Note paper: non-U for U *writing paper.*

Toilet paper: non-U for U *lavatory paper.*

Wealthy: non-U for U *rich.*

To these I would add :

Sweet: non-U for U *pudding.*

Dentures: non-U for U *false teeth.* This, and *glasses* for *spectacles,* almost amount to non-U indicators.

Wire: non-U for U *telegram.*

Phone: a non-U indicator.

(One must add that the issue is sometimes confused by U-speakers using non-U indicators as a joke. Thus Uncle Matthew in *The Pursuit of Love* speaks of his *dentures.*)

Finally Professor Ross poses the question : Can a non-U-speaker become a U-speaker? His conclusion is that an adult can never achieve complete success "because one word or phrase will suffice to brand an apparent U-speaker as originally non-U (for U-speakers themselves never make mistakes)." I am not quite sure about this. Usage changes very quickly and I even know undisputed U-speakers who pronounce girl "gurl", which twenty years ago would have been unthinkable. All the same, it is true that one U-speaker recognizes another U-speaker almost as soon as he opens his mouth, though U-speaker A may deplore certain lapses in the conversation of U-speaker B.

From these U-speakers spring the sensible men of ample means who generally seem to rule our land. When the means of these sensible men become sufficiently ample they can very easily be ennobled, should they wish it, and join the House of Lords. It might therefore be supposed that there is no aristocracy at all in England, merely an upper middle class, some of whom are lords; but, oddly enough, this is not so. A lord does not have to be born to his position and, indeed, can acquire it through political activities, or the sale of such unaristocratic merchandise as beer, but though he may not be a U-speaker he becomes an aristocrat as soon as he receives his title. The Queen turns him from socialist leader, or middle-class businessman, into a nobleman, and his outlook from now on will be the outlook of an aristocrat.

Ancestry has never counted much in England. The English lord knows himself to be such a very genuine article that, when looking for a wife, he can rise above such baubles as seize quartiers. Kind hearts, in his view, are more than coronets, and large tracts of town property more than Norman blood. He marries for love, and is rather inclined to love where money is; he rarely marries in order to improve his coat of arms. (Heiresses have caused the extinction as well as the enrichment of many an English family, since the heiress, who must be an only child if she is to be really rich, often comes of barren or enfeebled stock.) This unconcern for pedigree leads people to suppose that the English lords are a jumped-up lot, and that their families are very seldom "genuine" and "old". One often hears it said, "No Englishman alive today would be eligible to drive in the carriage of a King of France." "Nobody really has Norman blood." "The true aristocracy of England was wiped out in the Wars of the Roses." And so on.

There is some truth in all these statements, but it is not the whole truth. Many of our oldest families have never been ennobled. Some no longer hold peerages. The ancient Scrope family has, in its time, held the baronies of Scrope of Marsham and Scrope of Bolton, the earldoms of Wiltshire and of Sunderland, the sovereignty of the Isle of Man, but the head of the family is now Mr. Scrope. If he should be offered a peerage he would no doubt proudly refuse. The only existing families known to descend from knights who came over with William the Conqueror in time to fight at Hastings, the Malets, the Giffards, and the Gresleys, are another case in point. Of the Norman knights who came during William's reign or later, some were never anything but country gentlemen, but some are the direct ancestors of modern peers : St. John, Talbot, West, Curzon, Clinton, Grey, Seymour, St. Aubyn, Sinclair, Haig, and Hay, for instance. There are 100 peers of England from before the Union (including Prince Charles, as Duke of Cornwall). All of them are descended in the female line from King Edward III, except possibly Lord Byron, though a little research would probably find him an Edward III descent. All peers, except barons, are officially styled "Cousin" by the Queen; as regards most dukes and earls this is not so much fiction as a distant truth. Only 26 earls have been created in this century and they have all been great men like Lloyd George and Haig. (The Haigs have borne arms and lived at Bemersyde since the twelfth century but had never previously been ennobled.)

The dukes are rather new creations. When James I came to the throne there were no dukes at all, the high traitors Norfolk and Somerset having had their dukedoms attainted. They were both restored in 1660. Between 1660 and 1760, 18 dukedoms were created. On the whole, Englishmen are made dukes as a reward for being rich or royal (4 descend from bastards of

Charles II), though dukedoms have sometimes been bestowed for merit. The oldest title is that of Earl. Several medieval earldoms still exist. Sixty-five barons hold titles from before 1711. Three hundred and twenty-seven of the present-day peerages were created before 1800, 382 belong to families which have borne arms in the direct male line since before 1485 and which are therefore eligible, as far as birth is concerned, to be Knights of Malta.

But whether their families are "old" or "new" is of small account—the lords all have one thing in common : they share an aristocratic attitude to life. What is this attitude? The purpose of the aristocrat is to lead, therefore his functions are military and political. There can be no doubt of the military excellence of our noblemen. Two hundred and fourteen peers alive today have been decorated in battle or mentioned in despatches. The families of the premier duke and the premier earl of England hold the George Cross. In politics, including the unglamorous and often boring local politics, they have worked hard for no reward and done their best according to their lights.

The purpose of the aristocrat is most emphatically not to work for money. His ancestors may have worked in order to amass the fortune which he enjoys, though on the whole the vast riches of the English lords come from sources unconnected with honest toil; but he will seldom do the same. His mind is not occupied with money, it turns upon other matters. When money is there he spends it on maintaining himself in his station. When it is no longer there he ceases to spend, he draws in his horns. Even the younger sons of lords seem, in all ages, to have been infected with this point of view : there is nothing so rare as for the scion of a noble house to make a fortune by his own efforts. In the old days they went into professions —the Army, the Navy, diplomacy, and the Church—in which it is impossible to earn more than a living. Those who went to the colonies were administrators, they rarely feathered their nests—the great nabobs were essentially middle class. Nowadays younger sons go into the City, but I have yet to hear of one making a large fortune; more often they lose in unwise speculations what little capital they happen to own.

All this should not be taken as a sign that our lords are lazy or unenterprising. The point is that, in their view, effort is unrelated to money. Now this view has, to a large extent, communicated itself to the English race and nation with the result that our outlook is totally different from that of our American cousins, who have never had an aristocracy. Americans relate all effort, all work, and all of life itself to the dollar. Their talk is of nothing but dollars. The English seldom sit happily chatting for hours on end about pounds. In England, public business is its own reward, nobody would go into Parliament in order to become rich, neither do riches bring public

appointments. Our ambassadors to foreign states are experienced diploma-
tists, not socially ambitious millionairesses.

This idiosyncratic view of money has its good side and its bad. Let us
glance at the case history of Lord Fortinbras. Fortinbras is ruined—we
are now in the 1930s. (All English noblemen, according to themselves, are
ruined, a fantasy I shall deal with later, but Fortinbras really is.) He is not
ruined because of death duties, since his father died when he was a child,
before they became so heavy, but because he and his forebears have always
regarded their estates with the eyes of sportsmen rather than of cultivators.
It is useless for him to plead that the policy of cheap corn has been his down-
fall; an intelligent landowner has always been able to make money with
prize cattle, racehorses, market gardens, timber, and so on. But Fortinbras's woods have been looked after by gamekeepers and not by woodmen,
his farms have been let to tenants chosen for their tenderness towards foxes
and partridges rather than for their agricultural efficiency. His land is
undercapitalized, his cottagers live in conditions no better than those of
their Saxon forebears, water and electric light are laid on in his stables but
not in the dwellings of his tenantry. He has made various unwise speculations and lost a "packet" on the Turf. In short, he deserves to be ruined
and he is ruined.

Now what does he do? He is young, healthy, and not stupid; his wife,
the daughter of another peer, is handsome, bossy, and energetic. She is the
kind of woman who, in America, would be running something with
enormous efficiency and earning thousands. They have two babies,
Dominick and Caroline, and a Nanny. Does it occur to either Lord or
Lady Fortinbras to get a job and retrieve the family fortunes? It does not.
First of all they sell everything that is not entailed, thus staving off actual
want. They shut up most of the rooms in their house, send away the
servants (except, of course, Nanny) and get the Dowager Lady Fortinbras
and her sister to come and cook, clean, dust, and take trays upstairs to the
nursery. Old Lady Fortinbras is quite useful, and Lady Enid is a treasure.
The Fortinbrases realize that they are very lucky, and if at heart they wish
there were a mother's hall for the two ladies to sit in of an evening, they
never say so, even to each other. Fortinbras chops the wood, stokes the
boiler, brings in the coal, washes the Morris Cowley, and drives off in it to
attend the County Council and sit on the Bench. Lady Fortinbras helps in
the house, digs in the border, exercises the Border terriers, and also does
a great deal of committee work. They are both on the go from morning
to night, but it is a go that does not bring in one penny. Their friends and
neighbours all say, "Aren't the Fortinbrases wonderful?"
Comes the war. They clear the decks by sending Nanny and the children

to an American couple, the Karamazovs, whom they once met at St. Moritz and who have sent them Christmas cards ever since. Fortinbras goes off with his territorials and Lady Fortinbras joins the A.T.S. Their war records are brilliant in the extreme, their energy, courage, and instinct for leadership have at last found an outlet, and in no time at all they both become generals. After the war they are not surprised to find themselves more ruined than ever. The Karamazovs, whose lives for several years have been made purgatory by Dominick, Caroline, and Nanny, especially Nanny, send in a modest bill for the schooling of the young people which Fortinbras has no intention of settling. It would seem unreasonable to pay for one's children to be taught to murder the English language and taught, apparently, nothing else whatever. Dominick, failing to get into Eton, has had to be sent to some dreadful school in Scotland. Besides, what did the Karamazovs do in the war? Nothing, according to Nanny, but flop in and out of a swimming pool. The Karamazovs come to England expecting to be thanked, fêted, and paid, only to find that their friends have left for the Northern Capitals.

Now the Fortinbrases are getting on, over fifty. Dominick having come of age, they have broken the entail and sold everything, very badly, as the house is full of dry rot and the farms are let to tenants who cannot be dislodged. However, a little money does result from the sale. They arrange a mews flat behind Harrods where, generals once again, they will continue to cook and wash up for the rest of their days. They both still sit on endless committees, Fortinbras goes to the House of Lords, they kill themselves with overwork, and have never, except for their Army pay, earned one single penny. "Aren't the Fortinbrases wonderful?" Well yes, in a way they are.

Now, while the Fortinbrases have the typical aristocratic outlook on money, the state of their finances is by no means typical. Most people, nowadays, take it for granted that the aristocracy is utterly impoverished, a view carefully fostered by the lords themselves. It takes a shooting affray, letting police and reporters into a country house, to remind the ordinary citizen that establishments exist where several men-servants wait on one young woman at dinner. There are still many enormous fortunes in the English aristocracy, into which income tax and death duties have made no appreciable inroads. Arundel, Petworth, Hatfield, Woburn, Hardwicke, Blenheim, Haddon, Drumlanrig, Alnwick, Stratfield Saye, Harewood, Knole, Knowsley, Wilton, Holkham, Glamis, Cullen, Cliveden, Highclere, Althorp, Mentmore—all vast houses—are still inhabited by lords who have inherited them, and this little list is a mere fraction of the whole. The treasures such houses contain are stupendous. When the Duke of Buccleuch came to visit the Louvre, the curator, who had been to England and seen the Duke's collection of French furniture, greeted him with the words : "I apologize for the furniture of the Louvre, M. le Duc."

Another English duke owns a collection of *incunabula* second only to that formerly in the possession of the Kings of Spain, and more Groslier bindings than the Bibliothèque Nationale. A jeweller told me that out of the one hundred finest diamonds in the world, sixty are in English families. One could go on citing such instances indefinitely.

The English, so censorious of those foreigners (the French peasantry for instance) who do not pay their taxes as they should, have themselves brought tax evasion within legal limits to a fine art. Death duties can be avoided altogether if the owner of an estate gives it to his heir and then lives another five years. One agreeable result of this rule is that old lords are cherished as never before. Their heirs, so far from longing to step into their shoes, will do anything to keep them alive. Doctors and blood donors hover near them, they are not allowed to make the smallest effort, or to be worried or upset, and are encouraged to live in soft climates and salubrious spots.

The crippling effects of supertax also can be overcome in various ways by those who own large capital sums. The aristocrat can augment his fortune in many a curious manner, since he is impervious to a sense of shame (all aristocrats are : shame is a bourgeois notion). The lowest peasant of the Danube would stick at letting strangers into his home for 2s. 6d., but our dukes, marquesses, earls, viscounts, and barons not only do this almost incredible thing, they glory in it, they throw themselves into the sad commerce with rapture, and compete as to who among them can draw the greatest crowds. It is the first topic of conversation in noble circles today, the tourists being referred to in terms of sport rather than of cash—a sweepstake on the day's run, or the bag counted after the shoot.

"I get twice as many as Reggie, but Bert does better than me."

The baiting of the trap is lovingly considered.

"Mummy dresses up in her Coronation robes, they can't resist it."

"I say, old boy, look out—you don't want to pay entertainment tax."

"No, no—I've taken counsel's opinion."

"We've started a pet's cemetery—a quid for a grave, three quid for a stone, and a fiver if Daphne writes a poem for it."

Of course the fellow countrymen of people who will descend to such methods of raising cash imagine that they must be driven to it by direst need. The fact is they thoroughly enjoy it. Also it has become a matter of policy to appear very poor. The lords are retrenching visibly, and are especially careful to avoid any form of ostentation : for instance, only five of them saw fit to attend the last coronation in their family coaches. Coronets on luggage, motor-cars, and so on, are much less used than formerly. Aristocrats no longer keep up any state in London, where family houses hardly exist now. Here many of them have shown a sad lack of civic responsibility, as we can see by looking at poor London today. At the beginning of this century practically all the residential part of the West End belonged to noblemen and the Crown. A more charming, elegant capital city would have been far to seek. To the Crown—more specifically, I believe to King George V in person—and to two Dukes, Westminster and Bedford, we owe the fact that London is not yet exactly like Moscow, a conglomeration of dwellings. Other owners cheerfully sold their houses and "developed" their property without a thought for the visible result. Park Lane, most of Mayfair, the Adelphi, and so on, bear witness to a barbarity which I, for one, cannot forgive.

The lords have never cared very much for London, and are, in this respect, the exact opposite of their French counterparts who loathe the country. But even where his country house is concerned, the English nobleman, whose forebears were such lovers of beauty, seems to have lost all æsthetic sense, and it is sad to see the havoc he often brings to his abode, both inside and out. His ancestors spent months abroad, buying pictures and statues, which he cheerfully sells in order to spend months abroad. Should one of his guests perceive that a blackened square of canvas in a spare bedroom is a genuine Caravaggio, that picture will appear at Christie's before you can say Jack Robinson, though there is no necessity whatever for such a sale. The Caravaggio buyer planted his estate with avenues and coppices and clumps of cedar trees. The Caravaggio seller fiddles about with herbaceous borders, one of the most hideous conceptions known to man. He never seems to plant anything larger than a flowering prunus, never builds ornamental bridges, or digs lakes, or adds wings to his house. The last nobleman to build a folly on his estate must have been Lord Berners and he was regarded as foolish indeed to do such a thing. The noble eccentric, alas, seems to be dying out. Lord Berners was one, another was the late Duke of Bedford, pacifist, zoologist, and a good man. One of the chapters of his autobiography, I seem to remember, was headed "Spiders I have Known", and he tells of one spider he knew whose favourite food was roast beef and Yorkshire pudding. The great days of patronage, too, are over, though there are country houses which still shelter some mild literary figure as librarian. The modern nobleman cannot, however, be blamed for no longer patronizing art, music, and letters. Artists, musicians, and writers are today among the very richest members of the community and even an English aristocrat could hardly afford to maintain Mr.

Somerset Maugham, M. Stravinsky, or M. Picasso as part of his establishment.

Voltaire very truly said that those who own are those who wish to own : this wish seems to have left the English lords. Divest, divest, is the order of the day. The nobleman used to study a map of his estate to see how it could be enlarged, filling out a corner here, extending a horizon there. Nowadays he has no such ambitions; he would much rather sell than buy. The family is not considered as it used to be; the ancestors are no longer revered, indeed they are wilfully forgotten, partly perhaps from a feeling of guilt when all that they so carefully amassed is being so carelessly scattered. The dead are hardly mourned. "Far the best for him", the children say, cheerfully (so long, of course, as he has lived the requisite five years). Nobody wears black any more. The younger generation is no longer planned for, and there is a general feeling of *"après nous le déluge"*.

The instinct of the lords to divest themselves of age-long influence and rights extends to their influence and rights in the Church. Most of them are members of the Church of England; though there are forty-seven Roman Catholics with seats in the House of Lords. On the whole, the lords, in common with most of their fellow countrymen, have always regarded religious observance as a sort of patriotic duty. The Church is the Church of England and must be supported to show that we are not as foreigners are. A friend of mine voiced this attitude during the war : "Well, you know, I don't do fire-watching or Home Guard and I feel one must do something to help the war, so I always go to Church on Sunday." I am sure he did not imagine that his prayers would drive back the German hordes; he went as a gesture of social solidarity. Hitherto, the livings of our Church have been the gift of landowners, who have generally chosen downright, muscular Christians of low Church leanings. "Don't want lace and smells in my Church." Zeal has always been frowned upon. As it is impossible to remove a parson once he is installed in his living, some of the most ringing rows of all time have been between the Manor and the Vicarage. Now, however, faithful to the spirit of divest, divest, the temporal lords are busily putting their livings at the disposal of their spiritual colleagues, the Bishops. Many people think that this will lead to more lace, more smells, and more un-English zeal in the Church, and indeed greatly alter its character. Incidentally, the marriage customs of the peerage have lately become very lax. One peer in eight has divested himself of his wife, and foreigners notice that there are rather more duchesses than dukes in London society today.

As for the House of Lords which gives the English aristocrat his unique position, Lord Hailsham, himself an unwilling member, says that the majority of peers are voting for its abolition "with their feet", by simply neglecting their hereditary duties. It must be said that the number of regular attendants has never been very large, and the august chamber has always been characterized by an atmosphere of the dormitory if not of the morgue. This is distressing to an active young fellow like Lord Hailsham but it is nothing new. One of the merits of the Upper House has been to consist of a hard core of politicians reinforced now and then by experts, and only flooded out in times of crisis by all its members. These have hitherto proved not unrepresentative of public opinion. Now, however, it seems that it is hardly possible to get through the work, so small is the attendance.

Does this apparent abdication of the lords in so many different directions mean that the English aristocracy is in full decadence and will soon exist only like the appendix in the human body, a useless and sometimes harmful relic of the past? It would not be safe to assume so. The English lord has been nurtured on the land and is conversant with the cunning ways of the animal kingdom. He has often seen the grouse settle into the heather to rise and be shot at no more. He has noticed that enormous riches are not well looked on in the modern world and that in most countries his genius is extinct. It may be that he who, for a thousand years has weathered so many a storm, religious, dynastic, and political, is taking cover in order to weather yet one more. It may be that he will succeed. He must, of course, be careful not to overdo the protective colouring. An aristocracy cannot exist as a secret society. Nor must he overdo an appearance of destitution. There is the sad precedent of George Neville who was deprived of his dukedom (Bedford) by Act of Parliament because "as is openly known he hath not, nor by inheritance may have, any livelihood to support the name, estate and dignity . . ."

But the English lord is a wily old bird who seldom overdoes anything. It is his enormous strength.

SEPTEMBER 1955

An open letter to the
Hon. Mrs. Peter Rodd (Nancy Mitford)
on A VERY SERIOUS SUBJECT
from Evelyn Waugh

DEAREST NANCY,

Were you surprised that your article on the English aristocracy caused such a to-do? I was not. I have long revered you as an agitator—agitatrix, *agitateuse*?— of genius. You have only to publish a few cool reflections on eighteenth-century furniture to set gangs on the prowl through the Faubourg St. Germain splashing the walls with "Nancy, go home". Class distinctions in England have always been the matter for higher feeling than national honour, the matter of feverish but very private debate. So, when you brought them into the open, of course everyone talked, of course the columnists quoted you and corrected you. Letters poured in to the various editors, many of them, I am told, unprintably violent. You were the subject of a literary competition (which produced very sad entries) and now here am I, late but implacable, chipping in too.

Should delicacy have restrained you? your friends anxiously ask. There are subjects too intimate for print. Surely class is one? The vast and elaborate structure grew up almost in secret. Now it shows alarming signs of dilapidation. Is this the moment to throw it open to the heavy-footed public? Yes, I think it is, and particularly, as you have done, to the literary public. My reproach is that, in doing so, you have in your skittish way bamboozled a great number of needy young persons. Have you ever heard of the "Butler Education Act"? I suppose not, although it happened in the days when you still lived among us. It was one of the things that politicians did when no one was looking, towards the end of the war. It has nothing at all to do with training male indoor-servants nor with instructing the designer of the "Unknown Political Prisoner" in the intricacies of his craft. The name derives from the Mr. Butler who at the time of writing has just knocked something off the price of my clothes. Clearly he is a generous fellow. In his Education Act he provided for the free distribution of university degrees to the deserving poor. Very handy for splitting atoms and that kind of thing, you will say. But quite a lot of Mr. Butler's protégés choose, or are directed into, "Literature". I could make your flesh creep by telling you about the new wave of philistinism with which we are threatened by these grim young people who are coming off the assembly lines in their hundreds every year and finding employment as critics, even as poets and novelists. L'Ecole de Butler are the primal man and woman of the classless society. Their novelists seem to be aware of the existence of a rather more expressive world than their own—bars in which spirits are regularly drunk in preference to beer, loose women who take taxis, crooks in silk shirts—but of the ramifications of the social order which have obsessed some of the acutest minds of the last 150 years, they know less than of the castes of India. What can their critics hope to make of the undertones and innuendoes, the evocative, reminiscent epithets of, say, Tony Powell or Leslie Hartley?

It was a worthy project to take them through a rudimentary course of social map-reading and no one should have been better qualified for the task than you with your host of friends in every class.

Nor was L'Ecole de Butler your only source of pupils. Consider the cinema trade, the immigrant producers from God knows where who perhaps have never set foot in a private house in the kingdom. Their solecisms glare at us in blazing colour and shriek at us from amplifiers. And the BBC and, for all we know, the Television. A huge mission field was white for your sickle. Eager, appealing eyes were turned to you through the cigarette smoke. Was it kind, dear Nancy, to pull their legs?

II

You very properly steer clear of the royal family and start your exposition with the peerage. You remark, correctly, that a title in England has a precise legal significance as it has scarcely anywhere else, and that, partly from our system of primogeniture, titled people do not constitute a separate caste. But you go on to say that a man "becomes an aristocrat as soon as he receives a title"; " . . . his outlook from now on will be the outlook of an aristocrat". You know jolly well that that isn't true.

The relationship between aristocracy and nobility in England is certainly baffling. I do not suppose you could find any two people in complete agreement about it. My own estimate would be that about half the nobility are aristocrats and about two-thirds of the aristocracy are noble (in which catalogue I loosely include baronets and people descended in the male line from peers, whether or no they are themselves titled). The official order of precedence is, of course, quite irrelevant in determining true social position. By no means all earls are the superiors of all barons or of baronets or even of plain gentlemen. Nor is there any greater degree of equality in the

Upper House of Parliament than in the Commons. Ancestry, possessions, even intelligence and good looks, have their part in deciding real precedence. You say: "Ancestry has never counted much in England." As a guide to human character, pedigrees are, I suppose, about as valuable as horoscopes. Well, some of the world's greatest men have resorted to astrologers and millions of subtle Asiatics direct their lives by them today. Learned opinion may change. It may be decided that there was something in the stars after all. My own scepticism is based on the impossibility of identifying the real fathers in the ages when adultery was very common and divorce very rare. Whenever there is a scandal elderly persons will remark, "Ah, that is the Fortinbras blood coming out," and explain that all their mother's generation were irregularly conceived. But undoubtedly most of our fellow-countrymen attach great importance to ancestry. Take a look at the shelves marked "Genealogy" in any large secondhand bookshop. You will find displayed at modest prices hundreds of volumes expensively produced, mostly during the last hundred years, for the sole purpose of exalting their authors' families. Genealogy is still as thriving a trade as it was in the days of Elizabeth I, when the Officers of Arms began fabricating the great pedigrees that link the despoilers of the Church with the age of chivalry. People in the last century have been caught filling their parish churches with bogus tombs. Scholars such as Round and Baron spent their lives in exposing fraudulent pedigrees and many who are not scholars, but who, like myself, cherish the delusion that we possess a "historical sense", have felt the fascination of this sonorous and decorative pursuit.

However, you give us some genealogical figures. Are you sure you have got them right? I know you went to high authority for them, but I can't help wondering how much the present Officers of Arms regard themselves as bound in honour to support the decisions of their less scrupulous predecessors. You say that 382 peers have arms granted before 1485 *and have inherited them in the male line*. My italics, as they say; for the statement staggers me. Neither of us is an expert. We can only look about us and go by rough personal impressions. It seems to me that a large number of our ancient families have the entry "assumed by royal licence the name and arms" somewhere in their pedigrees. Look at the Fortinbrases. Sly Ned Fartingbrass who got the estate at the Dissolution was known to all. It was for his grandson that the Heralds invented a link with the extinct crusaders, Fortinbras. The peerage was granted by Charles I and failed in the male line in 1722 when Mr. Binks married the heiress and sat in the Commons as Mr. Fortinbras-Binks, exercising the full political influence of his wife's family. His son, who called himself Mr. Binks-Fortinbras, married well, could return two members; he was rewarded by a peerage, Fortinbras, in the second creation. From that time Binks was dropped and the stolen coat of Fortinbras moved across, with the connivance of the College of Heralds, to the first quarter.

You say that 65 existing baronies were created before 1711. Do you include the quaint house of Strabolgi?

Noble families die out almost as fast as new ones are created. I have just taken a sample from Burke's *Peerage and Baronetage 1949* and compared it with the issue for 1885. The volumes fall open, need I say it? at Redesdale. Of the succeeding dozen names only one (and that, incidentally, a family of foreign origin) is to be found in the earlier edition; and of the twelve families who followed Redesdale in 1885, six are already extinct. That is a big turnover in two generations. Perhaps you will argue that it is the new families who die out, since only direct heirs of the original grantee can succeed, and that the older the family the further you can cast back for an heir. Well, looking round, the feudal overlords in the district I inhabit were the Berkeleys. That earldom has just become extinct. And their next-door neighbours, who bear a medieval name and arms, have borne and changed no less than five surnames in the last eight generations as the property devolved on female heirs. I think you should have questioned your pursuivant more closely before accepting his figures.

III

The Fortinbrases are a delicious vignette, typical of your fictions. I find one fault only. Surely they should have more children? Impotence and sodomy are socially O.K. but birth control is flagrantly middle-class. But you invented them, I know, to illustrate your theme that aristocrats can't or won't make money. I could remind you of half a dozen prosperous and industrious City men of impeccable origins but I should have to admit that they have not worn well. The acceptance of high living and leisure as part of the natural order is a prerequisite of the aristocratic qualities and achievements. The debonair duke living by his wits, so popular on the stage, soon grows to resemble the plebeian crook. His brother who goes into business and sticks to it and makes good, is soon indistinguishable from his neighbours in Sunningdale. You should have said, not that aristocrats can't make money in commerce, but that when they do, they become middle-class.

It is here that we reach the topic that has caused the pother—the supposed gulf between what you inelegantly describe as "U and non-U". This gulf exists in every English mind. What has shocked your critics is that you fix it where you do, definitely, arbitrarily, and, some would say, capriciously. There is an unwholesome contemporary appetite—the product, perhaps, of psychiatry and the civil service—for categories of all kinds. People seem to be comforted instead of outraged when they are told that their eccentricities entitle them to membership in a class of "psychological types". They are inured to filling in forms which require a "description" of themselves and their houses. So they have fastened with avidity on the section of your comprehensive essay which pretends to provide the mechanism for grading themselves and their friends.

Everything turns on "the grand old name of gentleman". We have no equivalent phrase in English to *"noblesse oblige"*. All precepts of manners and morals define the proper conduct of "gentlemen". Lord Curzon, a paragon of aristocratic usage, when, as Chancellor of Oxford University, he was shown the menu of a proposed entertainment of the King at Balliol, remarked succinctly : "No gentleman has soup at luncheon"; he did not say : "No monarch . . ." or "No marquis . . ." He appealed above the standards of court or castle to the most elusive standard in the world.

When I was last in Palestine I asked a Zionist how he defined a Jew. Immigrants from every climate from China to Peru were jostling round us. There were atheist Slavs and negroes from the Upper Nile who are reputed to eat snakes. It seemed a pertinent question. He answered : "Everyone who thinks he is a Jew, is one."

In the same way, the basic principle of English social life is that *everyone* (everyone, that is to say, who comes to the front door) *thinks he is a gentleman*. There is a second principle of almost equal importance : *everyone draws the line of demarcation immediately below his own heels*. The professions rule out the trades; dentists, vets; doctors, dentists; the Services, the professions; the Household Brigade, the line regiments; squires, squireens; landed families who had London houses ruled out those who spent all the year at home; and so on, in an infinite number of degrees and in secret, the line is, or was, drawn. It is essentially a process of ruling *out*. If you examine the accumulated code of precepts which define "the gentleman" you will find that almost all are negative.

Few people are aware, still less observant, of more than a small fraction of this code. Most people have a handful of taboos, acquired quite at random. Usually at an impressionable age someone has delivered a judgement which has lodged in the memory. The lack of reason in these dooms makes them the more memorable, and no subsequent experience mitigates their authority.

For example, there is a cousin of yours, a jolly baron, who affects a nautical nonchalance in dress. He and I were talking one day when there passed an acquaintance, a grandee, a member of the Jockey Club, your cousin's superior and *a fortiori* mine. Your cousin, not a very serious man normally, regarded this sleek, susset figure with aversion and said, with deep seriousness : "My father told me that no gentleman ever wore a brown suit."

Another cousin of yours, of ducal family, is a man notorious for the grossness of his vocabulary. He has only to hear a piece of *argot* from the Bowery to adopt it as his own. But once, in early youth, he was sharply corrected for calling a kinsman his "relative" or "relation". He cannot remember which, but both words have become anathema. Of all the sage advice poured out on him by schoolmasters and clergymen and dons and commanding officers, that alone remains, and if either word is used in his hearing, he starts as though stung and, being what he is, he rounds on the speaker with abuse.

All nannies and many governesses, when pouring out tea, put the milk in first. (It is said by tea fanciers to produce a richer mixture.) Sharp children notice that this is not normally done in the drawing-room. To some this revelation becomes symbolic. We know a woman, far from conventional in other ways, who makes it her touchstone. "Rather m.i.f., darling," she says to convey inferior social station.

I could multiply examples almost without end. There is practically no human activity or form of expression which at one time or another, in one place or another, I have not heard confidently condemned as plebeian, for generations of English have used the epithets "common" and "middle-class" as general pejoratives to describe anything which gets on their nerves.

It is natural to the literary mind to be unduly observant of the choice of words. Logan Pearsall Smith was the classical case. I met him once only. He did not speak to me until we stood on the doorstep leaving. He then said : "Tell me, how would you describe the garment you are wearing? A greatcoat? An overcoat? A top-coat?" I replied : "Overcoat." "Ah, would you? Yes. Most interesting. And, tell me, would that also be the usage of an armigerous admiral?"

That way lay madness and I fear that if you are taken too seriously you and Professor Ross may well drive your readers into the bin. When in your novel you made "Uncle Matthew" utter his catalogue of irrational prohibitions, you were accurately recording a typical conversational extravagance. When you emerge *in propria persona* as the guide to Doric youth, you are more mischievous. Of course, it is broadly true that the phrases you dub "U" come more naturally to most ladies and gentlemen, but every family and set develops its private vocabulary and syntax and everyone regards every usage but his own as either pedantically affected or as barbarous. I know of a family whose epithet of condemnation is quite simply "NLU" (not like us). Phrases that were originally adopted facetiously, in inverted commas as it were, pass into habitual use; the chic jargon of one decade— Philip Sassoon's "I couldn't like it more", for instance—becomes the vulgarism of the next; words once abhorred, like "week-end", become polite. If Professor Ross's Finns or your literary critics wander out into the English world armed with your lexicon, seeking to identify the classes they encounter, they will drop many bricks.

For there are no classes in England; there is only precedence. A professor likes to mark anything α β γ. The socialist likes to speak of "capitalists, bourgeois, intellectuals, and workers". In England these easy categories do not apply. There is a single line extending from Windsor to Wormwood Scrubs, of individuals all justly and precisely graded (no one knows this order of precedence : it is a Platonic idea), and the organization of English society has never been, as I understand it is in many other countries, a system of horizontal strata. You do not find a dozen viscountesses sitting together in a drawing-room while twenty-two baronets play cricket in the park. The grandees met occasionally on state occasions or on the racecourse, but they kept away from one another's houses. English society was a complex of tribes, each with its chiefs, witch-doctors, elders, and braves, each with its own dialect and deity, each strongly xenophobic.

IV

It is when we come to the last part of your article, much the most important part, which has nevertheless attracted least notice, that my amusement at your prank becomes a little strained.

"The English lord is a wily old bird" you take as your text, and your theme is that he is enormously rich. He pays neither taxes nor death duties. He "glories" in turning his house into a public museum. He has given up London simply because he is not witty enough to keep a salon. He sells his pictures because he does not appreciate them. He prefers herbaceous borders and flowering shrubs to formal parterres, which require two dozen gardeners. His reduced circumstances are all a hoax. He is biding his time until the present craze for equality has passed, when he will re-emerge in all his finery to claim all his privileges, to ravish peasant brides and transport poachers to Botany Bay.

Can you really believe any of this, even living, as you do, so remote from the scene you describe? Not long ago an American cutie, married to a Labour politician, published a book propounding the same argument. Everyone tolerantly asked : "What can an American cutie married to a Labour politician hope to know of such things? Ask her to dinner and let her see for herself." But what are we to say now when Nancy, Queen of the Hons, comes out with the same malicious errors? The English, you should remember, have a way of making jokes about their disasters, but you would find, if you lived here, that the loudest jokes about opening Stately Homes are made by the wives who have recent and perhaps direful associations with them, rather than by the husbands. The state-rooms of Bowood, you should know, are being demolished because their owner prefers privacy. I am not familiar with the household accounts of the few magnates who still preserve a recognizable ghost of their former establishments, but I am pretty sure something has to be sold every year to keep going. But instead of expostulating with you, let me turn to your dupes and tell them two facts, which you have never attempted to hide, bless you, but which are not well known.

The first is rather endearing. You were at the vital age of twelve when your father succeeded to his peerage, and until less than a year before there was little likelihood of his ever succeeding. It was a great day for "Hons" when you and your merry sisters acquired that prefix of nobility. Hitherto it had been the most shadowy of titles, never spoken, and rarely written. You brought it to light, emphasized and aspirated, and made a glory of it. And with that magic vocable came (very briefly it is true) a sensational change of fortune. If your uncle had not been killed in action, if your posthumous cousin had been a boy, all you enchanting children would have been whisked away to a ranch in Canada or a sheep-run in New Zealand. It is fascinating to speculate what your careers would then have been. Anyway, at that impressionable age an indelible impression was made; Hons were unique and lords are rich.

The other fact is not nice. You are a socialist every bit as staunch as the American cutie. What is more, as you mention in your article, you regard Lloyd George as a great man (and, we must suppose, as a great aristocrat, too, in his last days). Did you, perhaps, once, to tease your father, learn the Limehouse speech by heart? Your incitement to class-war reads like it.

"You think the upper-classes are down and out, do you? Don't you believe it, comrades. They despise you. They spend their time sneering at the way you talk. They are a fascist underground. Smash 'em, comrades, *now*."

Is that what you are really saying, Nancy? I hope you are just teasing, as I am. I hope. I wonder.

Fondest love,
EVELYN

DECEMBER 1955

EDWARD SHILS

British Intellectuals

BLIMPS AND DISSIDENTS

When Basil Seal joined the Commandos, Sir Joseph Mainwaring, an old Blimp, said, "There is a new spirit abroad. I see it on every side," and Evelyn Waugh, who was himself invaded by the new spirit, closed the book with the words : "And poor booby, he was bang right."

He was bang right. It was the end of two decades of rebellion against society, against the middle classes, against capitalism, against British institutions and manners. Even as the period came to an end, one of England's most brilliant poets, perhaps the leading figure of his generation, renounced his country and took up residence in America. There went with him one of the more talented writers of the period. Earlier, two of the most esteemed writers of the twenties, Aldous Huxley and D. H. Lawrence, had already expatriated themselves, one to California, the other wandering restlessly until his death. Other eminent British writers, e.g. Norman Douglas, Richard Aldington, Robert Graves, *et al.*, found life at home unsatisfactory and preferred to live abroad. English writers were on the move : travel books became a category of literature with a new intellectual significance. Who had a good word to say then for Britain among the intellectuals? Who had a good word then to say for British towns, where "every street (was) a blow, every corner a stab"; or for the British countryside and for English village life—those scenes of harsh inequality, of social snobbery and death-bringing gossip? "England's Green and Pleasant Land" was the façade of iniquity, and the British past was an elaborate pretence.

T. S. Eliot was still the poet of those who felt contemporary England to be a waste land. Graham Greene, whose specifically political interests had died very soon after their birth, portrayed a seedy, peeling, sinister, violent and treacherous England, an England without faith and without order, while Evelyn Waugh's England was a contemptibly irresponsible, frivolous land in which silliness ruled. E. M. Forster was not much of a revolutionary but his three cheers for friendship and his devotion to "love, the Beloved Republic" took their place—a more refined place, to be sure—in the general alienation from institutions and traditions.

The capitals of the intellectuals' ideal commonwealths varied. For some it was Moscow, which held the hearts of more than members of the Communist Party; for others, it was Baghdad, or Paris, or Berlin, or Los Angeles—it was in any case not London. It was certainly not Manchester or Bristol or Liverpool or Glasgow. It might be in some other period or it might be in the realm of the imagination; it was certainly not in twentieth-century Britain. A dreary country, ruled by an "old gang", by philistines and middlebrows, where the muse lay dying or in chains—who could give his heart to it?

The thirties was the time of the Left Book Club, whose authors seized any stick with which to beat the British dog, and every pretext to announce its death; it was the time of *In Letters of Red*, of *Fact*, of *The Coming Struggle for Power* and *Forward from Liberalism* and of the powerful movement of Marxism in British science. The London School of Economics was at the height of its reputation as a fountain of radical criticism of British life and institutions, as well as a mine of scholarship. The hatred of British society was not a matter simply of the fervent revolt of adolescence and youth, nor was it just a criticism of particular aspects of British life while leaving the whole untouched.

Indeed, even when he loved his cottage, or his Regency house, or some little spot of English soil, the intellectual's love of Britain was overshadowed by a feeling of repugnance for its dreary, unjust, and uncultured society, with its impotent ruling classes and its dull and puritanical middle classes. It was not particular institutions or attitudes that were repellent but the whole notion of Britain or of England. This was not just the view of the Communists or the æsthetes. It was the view of nearly everyone who in the 1920s and 1930s was considered worthy of mention in intellectual circles in Great Britain.

The pattern of alienation by no means covered all parts of the intellectual class—nor were the alienated uniformly and equally alienated. The Civil Service was not swept off its feet nor the whole of the journalistic world, nor every one in the universities, new and old. Nonetheless, the prevailing attitude, in quantity and emphasis, was one of alienation. Divergence from this view was a sort of disqualification for being taken seriously. *The Times* and *The Times Literary Supplement* were the stuffy representatives of a deadening official culture, a writer like Arnold Bennett was as contemptible as a businessman. Those who were still proud of their country or who invoked its history and traditions were dismissed as Blimps.*

* The chief admirers of British institutions during most of this period were the Germans, who found in England the ideal of the Christian gentleman and an austerely responsible aristocratic governing class.

REDISCOVERING THE OLD SCHOOL TIE

Look at the British intellectuals now. Could anything be less like what I have just described? How rare has become the deeply critical voice. Not long ago I heard an eminent man of the Left say, in utter seriousness, at a University dinner, that the British Constitution was "as nearly perfect as any human institution could be", and no one even thought it amusing. Who criticizes Britain now in any fundamental sense, except for a few Communists and a few Bevanite irreconcilables? There are complaints here and there and on many specific issues, but—in the main—scarcely anyone in Great Britain seems any longer to feel that there is anything fundamentally wrong. On the contrary, Great Britain on the whole, and especially in comparison with other countries, seems to the British intellectual of the mid-1950s to be fundamentally all right and even much more than that. Never has an intellectual class found its society and its culture so much to its satisfaction. Is it conceivable that any British literary periodical—of the few that now survive—would have the audacity to publish, as *Horizon* did about ten years ago, a series on "Where Should John Go?" in which the young Briton, bored and fed up with his country, had surveyed for him the wide range of possible places to which he could emigrate? (But even at that moment Mr. Connolly was already out of touch with the times—has not Mr. V. S. Pritchett recently attributed to him a mid-nineteenth-century Bohemianism?)

The post-war years, it is true, tarnished the patriotic enthusiasm of 1944 and 1945 for the new Britain. Socialism turned out to be less than some had hoped it would be, others found it more than they cared for. The merciless appetite of the Inland Revenue is complained about on all sides but it is not accused of injustice, and the public and the welfare services which impel its action are not assailed in principle, even by their severest critics. The arbitrary and inflexible rulings of bureaucracy have given rise to a little restiveness and the unforthcomingness of many of the beneficiaries of the bounties of the Labour Government has caused sardonic disgruntlement and crankiness. But criticism of the comprehensive schools from one side, of the American alliance in foreign policy from the other, and of many more details, from all sides, never gives the impression of a deeply penetrating cleavage or withdrawal. Fundamental criticism of the trend of British society has become rare. Whereas in the inter-war period, Wyndham Lewis was distinguished only by his talent and his violence of expression and not by his fundamental negation of society, now he is a rare bird.

The British intellectual has come to feel proud of the moral stature of a country with so much solidarity and so little acrimony between classes.

The disapproval of public school culture—long a stock in trade—still crops up from time to time, but it is no longer of serious concern to either side. The public schools have stealthily crept back into the hearts of the intellectuals where they repose more securely and more vitally than ever before. To cite only one of many examples, not Long ago the *New Statesman and Nation*, in response to a recommendation by one of the younger M.P.s for the abolition of the Public Schools by legislative action, replied that they represented quality and not just privilege. It was not even embarrassed to say that "even the conscientious socialist with a little money is forced to send his child to a private school or to face the self-criticism that he has sacrificed his chances in life to a political prejudice." The "old school tie" has ceased to be an accusation of British injustice; it is now taken as evidence of British quality.

Even India, that ancient sore on the conscience of the forward-looking, has become in retrospect a credit to Britain. Philip Woodruff's work on *The Men Who Ruled India* is everywhere and rightly acclaimed, but one is struck by the reviewer's tone of national self-congratulation for having produced such a class of men capable of ruling with such justice and humanity. Practically everyone agrees that it was proper to have withdrawn from India; at the same time, there seems to be no question at all that the British Raj itself was something very great indeed—the very extreme opposite of that cause for shame which it was once alleged to be by the liberal intellectuals.

When, in 1942, the late George Orwell rehabilitated Kipling against the unjust denigration of "pansy-left circles" and praised him in particular for his identification with the official classes and for his sense of responsibility for the maintenance of an orderly society, it was clear that one of the extreme positions was being evacuated. Another had been evacuated from the other side in the previous year, when the poet of *The Waste Land* took on himself the task of reasserting the merits of that same "vulgar apologist" of imperialism.

While the welfare state has raised the floor of British society, the symbols of hierarchy and authority have found increasing acceptance. Do the fifties have anything to match the refusal of a peerage by one of the greatest intellectuals of the twenties and thirties, reported in Dr. Thomas Jones's correspondence? On the contrary, it can show an avowed anarchist and an ardent exponent of the *avant garde* in art and literature accepting a knighthood.

What has brought the intellectuals back to the nation? What has made them with all their complaints and grievances, conscious and proud of being British? What has put them at ease with the symbols of sovereign authority? Why have they come once more to appreciate British institutions? What has produced this extraordinary state of collective self-satisfaction?

II

As Sir Joseph Mainwaring sensed, it was with the war that the new spirit began. It was, however, really not a beginning. It was rather a renewal. The cranky antinomianism of the twenty years between the wars was more like a digression from the main course of the British intellectual class in its relations with British institutions. The intellectuals in the first half of the nineteenth century had never been as revolutionary, as æsthetic, as anti-bourgeois, as anti-political, as hostile to the symbols of authority as their opposite numbers on the Continent. There had been lots of criticism and disagreement in the second half of the century, but the union of the intellectuals with the Civil Service, the Church, the Houses of Parliament, the Press, and the leadership of the political parties, through the ancient universities primarily, but also through kinship and through the social and convivial life of London upper-class society, constituted a bond from which few could escape and which no other country could then or has since matched. Neither socialism nor the æsthetic revolt of the turn of the century ever bred a doctrine or practice of complete alienation. Many of the major figures in the twin, sometimes separate, sometimes joint, revolts of art and justice, were outsiders—Irishmen mainly. The British intellectuals might have appeared dull to the Continental firebrands and gipsies but they were dutiful and loyal.

This residual loyalty which had been beaten down by the rancour of rebelliousness, this civility which had been suppressed by æsthetic disdain, had been lying in wait all through the inter-war period to be summoned back to ascendancy. It was embarrassing at first for many to perceive within themselves the stirring of national sentiments against which they had earlier set their faces and the denial of which had indeed been central to their outlook. Richard Hillary was one of the first to record his return to the bosom of the nation. He was not describing himself alone when he told of how anomalously uneasy he felt to act in the service of the symbols of a society which he had rejected and to which, despite his conscious rejection, he became aware of a genuine attachment below the surface.

Unlike the First World War of 1914–18, there was no butchery from thoughtlessness in the Second; there was boredom but there was little waste of human life in aimless large-scale military operations. Two of the most eminent British generals of the 1939–45 war were renowned for their humane concern for their troops. The purblind unimaginativeness which sacrificed so many young men's lives in the First World War, and which contributed so mightily to the greatest alienation of the British intellectuals from civil society in the entire history of Great Britain, was absent in the Second World War.

Furthermore, the war against Nazism and Fascism made a little more sense to the newly-ideological intellectuals, who were thus enabled more easily to disregard the suspect influence on their conduct of considerations of national interest and national loyalty. The alienation of the twenties and thirties was an alienation from the primordial institutions. It was an alienation from kinship, from tradition of tribe and land, from the established church and the civil state—all in the name of life in accordance with principles freely chosen. It was a smoother passage to return to the objects of primordial attachments through what seemed to be a war for principles.

Then, too, the war gave much more for intellectuals to do as intellectuals. Not only the scientists but the historians, economists, linguists, the philosophers, and other scholars, found hospitality in official circles, in the Cabinet Offices, in the Ministry of Information, in the Political Warfare Executive, in the BBC, in Military Intelligence, in the War Office Selection Boards, etc. These and others provided an appreciative audience for the intellectuals in their intellectual capacities—and it contrasted very sharply with the intellectual's image of official anti-intellectualism of the period between the wars. British society too seemed to become more cultivated during the war. The Committee for the Encouragement of Music and Arts—the parent of the Arts Council—the concerts in the National Gallery, the increase in the sale of books and some corresponding increase in their reading, the flowering of discussion circles even under official auspices, as in ABCA and the National Fire Service, facilitated the growth among the intellectuals of the idea that the country was not hostile to them.

THE BLURRING OF IDEOLOGIES

Of at least equal importance was the fact that the Government during the war, despite inefficiencies and errors, gave the appearance of being just.

The WOSB was a direct refutation of the old complaint by outsiders and rebels that the Public School system, in the words of Captain Grimes, "never lets one down". It disregarded breeding, accent, and background and concentrated on what was necessary for the effective performance of the duties of the officer. Rumours, true or untrue, that Lord So and So's nephew or Sir This and That's son had been unable to meet the requirements of the Selection Board contributed to the impression that considerations of inefficiency and justice had penetrated into a sphere which had hitherto been reserved for the Old Guard. The system of officer selection in the Second World War helped to dissolve some of the rancour against antebellum Britain.

No one seemed to be getting rich out of the war, and the nearly universal discomfort, squalor and poor food were equated with virtue. There were black marketeers, but they were not seen as products of the moral deficiencies of the ruling class, and society was not to be blamed for them. Many thought they were foreigners.

The magnanimous wartime figure of Mr. Churchill, above parties and especially above the old gang of vulgar businessmen, bloated Tories, and exploiting imperialists, was a reassurance that bourgeois Britain would not come back into the saddle after the war. The victory of the Labour Party at the polls in 1945 was a further reassurance that intellectuals could continue to regard Britain as their own country, where, in union with civil servants, they could either rule or feel themselves intimately affiliated with those who ruled. Mr. Attlee, with his background in a professional family, his Oxford education, his respectable military record, and his almost exaggerated restraint in speech and attitude, kept the conservative intelligentsia from alienation, however much they disliked the expected consequences of some of the policies of his government. On the other hand, the mere incumbency of the Labour Party in the seats of authority reconciled many of its intellectual members, who were disgruntled on specific issues, to the society against which their doctrine and principles logically aligned them.

Responsibility, through their party, for the fortunes of the country curbed the oppositional mentality. Such responsibility at a time when the country seemed to be declining in power in the world, and to be in great economic trouble as well, reinforced the curb. The latent patriotism which had been partially suppressed when the country appeared safe and powerful came back to the surface of consciousness when the country was threatened. Those who had ridiculed and abhorred patriotism began to find themselves patriots. The emancipation of India, Burma, and Ceylon, which politically-minded Leftist intellectuals had sought so long, had many repercussions. The feeling of being without an empire, a feeling of being bereft of something, a feeling of loss, enhanced the sense of national identity. Also, the nation seemed to be cleaner and more worthy of being embraced when it was divested of its immoral imperial appurtenances. Little Englanders could feel more comfortable in such a country and could love it more easily, and they could embrace its past without feeling that its present disgraced them.

Then, too, there was America. From a harmless, amiable, good natured, powerful, ridiculous, loyal ally—a sort of loutish and helpful nephew—it suddenly seemed to develop into a huge challenging empire, wilful, disregarding Britain, criticizing Britain, lording it over Britain, and claiming to lord it over everyone everywhere. Loyal British backs were arched at this peril, and the terrible economic crises of the second half of the forties accentuated impatience with America. Patriotism in this atmosphere was nurtured by anti-Americanism.

Animosity against naïve, boorish, and successful America heightens the gratification which British intellectuals derive from their national self-contemplation.

On the Continent, in the years after the war, France went without governments, and Italy and Germany were in ruins, the rich ate well, the poor rummaged in dustbins—and that too enhanced British self-esteem. Whereas in the great days of the Empire, imperialistic Britons thought Britain should be tutor to the world by active teaching, and the intellectuals denounced such arrogance, now former anti-imperialists began to think of Britain as a model commonwealth, a paragon of how to do things without corruption, with public spirit, with a sense of responsibility, with respect for the past and an openness towards the future, free from ideological fanaticism, and without ambitions of self-aggrandizement. This imaginative self-transformation into an ideal commonwealth was fed by and made for patriotism.

There is another factor too in this process. Although the war, for the previously alienated intellectuals, had been a war of principle, the war itself, and the course of events in Britain and in the world at large since then, marked a downward path for ideology. As I have just said, the rediscovery of national sentiments in the wartime experience, and partly the state of siege in which Britain lived during most of the post-war decade, focused attention and feeling on the symbols of the nation. Symbols of party and class lost some of their power. Abroad and at home, meanwhile, an almost complete evaporation of the basis for a doctrinal socialism was occurring.

British socialism has never been doctrinaire—except for inconsequential corners—and the vicissitudes of governing and the achievement of many of their most tangible goals had made it even less so. The practical conversation by the Conservative Government of most of Labour's innovations has helped to blur the edges of the socialist ideology. The extremes of planning or of *laissez-faire* are not espoused in Britain today by very many intellectuals. There are still a few extremists who would underscore the differences, but for the most part there is not a wide difference between the intellectual proponents of liberalism and socialism. The differences are, moreover, not made into differences in fundamentals, in *Weltanschauung*, and a consensus of matter-of-factness has settled over most discussions of economic policy. The main direction of present-day British political philosophy is to emphasize the inarticulate and inarticulatable wisdom of institutions and traditions, and to delimit the power of man to control events through the strength of his reason and the power of his organizations.

As a result of this evaporation of ideology, and of socialist ideology in particular, the range of dispersion of the British intellectuals has been much narrowed. Without a doctrine which they can espouse, the handful of extremists are forced to confine their extremism to mood and disposition and to express it *ad hoc*. They can scarcely form a sect on such a basis.

One more factor may be mentioned—the fostering of cultural institution by public authority. How can a society which maintains the Third Programme, the Arts Council, the British Council, etc., with their numerous opportunities for the employment of intellectuals, be regarded as lacking in sympathy for intellectual things? On the contrary, such a society arouses the intellectual's appreciation as well as giving him a sense of responsibility for its support.

III

There is, however, something deeper than this. It is the vindication of the culture associated with the aristocracy and gentry, and its restoration to pre-eminence among the guiding stars of the intellectuals. It is a change which is not confined to the intellectuals. All English society has undergone this process of submission to the moral and cultural—but not the political or economic—ascendancy of the aristocracy and gentry.

For nearly a century, the culture of the aristocracy and gentry was in retreat. When their political power and their privileges were increasingly restricted and their economic strength damaged by American and Australian agriculture and the legislation of pre-1914 Liberalism, their cultural power too seemed to be broken. It had been subjected to fierce criticism by the intellectuals. Nineteenth-century radicalism, the æstheticism of the end of the century and after, the diversified and penetrating denunciation of H. G. Wells, John Galsworthy, D. H. Lawrence, and G. B. Shaw made people distrustful of class privilege, of snobbery, of elaborate etiquette, of the display of power.

In contrast, bourgeois culture—the culture of the business classes—seemed slowly and steadily on the upgrade in the nineteenth century, both in London and the provinces—especially in the provinces. As long as Dissent lived in inner exile, excluded from the ancient universities, and excluded therefore from the opportunities to which those universities gave access, as long as it was shunned by the gentry and nobility because it was "in trade" or manufacture, its culture maintained a high intensity in both its religious and secular forms. After or alongside of money-making it made the improvement of civic life its concern; it founded literary and philosophical societies, libraries, and above all, through its own benefactions and through the local government which it controlled, it raised its chief monuments, the modern universities—to show that it too, even though excluded and thought barbarous, could pursue truth and glorify the dingy cities in which its money was made. Living to itself, puritanical, pharasaical, proud, and excessively sensitive to the slights and denials of the traditional society, the bourgeoisie of the big provincial towns, partly from local patriotism, partly from resentment, partly from a love of learning, created, before their submission, a genuine civilization—earnest, searching, and profound. Matthew Arnold, Ruskin, Carlyle, and the other great critics of the Victorian bourgeoisie which was dissenting and provincial, did less than justice to their victims.

However that may be, the businessman's Dissenting culture of the nineteenth and early twentieth centuries—the culture which founded the modern universities, the musical and literary institutions of the provinces —has now been routed. Sons sent to Oxford or Cambridge, or into the Army as professional officers, themselves removed southward and Londonward, the Chapel renounced for the Church—these are the signs of the surrender of the British bourgeoisie to its upper-class antagonists.

THE LONDON—OXFORD—CAMBRIDGE AXIS

The movement towards London in the twenties and thirties was not merely a demographic fact. It was associated with the assertion of the cultural supremacy of London society—and with it, of Oxford and Cambridge—over the provincial centres.

The aristocratic-gentry culture has now come back into the saddle, and with little to dispute its dominion. The twenties and thirties which did it so much damage, did even more damage to the provincial bourgeois culture. The rebellion of the intellectuals was rather against bourgeois culture than against the aristocratic-gentry culture. The latter never abdicated. Some of its offspring might revolt against it, but they could not find anything to substitute for it except Bohemianism and an utterly spurious proletarianism, both completely unviable. Bourgeois culture on the other hand, as soon as it came freely into contact with aristocratic-gentry culture, lost its self-esteem and its spiritual autonomy. It could not win the youth, even those brought up in its own atmosphere. It seemed paltry and mean alongside aristocratic-gentry culture.

This is not relevant solely to the description of the class structure of contemporary Britain. It has the most significant consequences for the development of the British intellectuals because the change in the status and self-esteem of the classes was paralleled by changes in the status and self-esteem of the cultural institutions patronized by the classes. I shall illustrate with reference to the relations between the ancient and the modern universities.

The modern British universities, which in scholarship and science take second place to none in the world, have—despite efforts of the University

Grants Committee and many worthy men who have loved them—been belittled in their own eyes. They have never had a place in that image of the right life which has evolved from the aristocratic, squirearchal, and higher official culture. To those who accept this image, modern universities are facts but not realities. They would not deny that Manchester, Liverpool, Birmingham, and the other urban universities actually exist and yet they do not easily admit them to their minds. Oxford and Cambridge are thought of spontaneously when universities are mentioned. If a young man, talking to an educated stranger, refers to his university studies, he is asked "Oxford or Cambridge?" And if he says Aberystwyth or Nottingham, there is disappointment on the one side and embarrassment on the other. It has always been that way.

True, very many more persons are now factually aware of the modern universities than, say, thirty years ago. They have established themselves as bulwarks of research in science and scholarship, and without them Great Britain would be poorer in every respect. Nonetheless, fundamentally, the situation has scarcely improved. It has perhaps become even worse. The deterioration is revealed in the diminution in self-esteem which these universities have undergone among their own staff, graduates, and patrons.

The modern universities have by no means declined in relative intellectual stature. On the contrary, in some subjects the modern universities now take the lead. The differences in prestige, however, have probably been accentuated. There is less contentment now in being in a modern university than there used to be. It is becoming more difficult to get first class younger men to leave Oxford and Cambridge—and London—for professorships in the provincial universities, however superior the traditions of the chair to be filled. It is more difficult to keep young men in the provinces; they are less contented with the prospect of a career in one of the great provincial universities, and look on them instead as jumping-off places, as places where they can keep alive and wait until something better comes along. They are moreover even quite open in disclosing their motives, as if that were and always had been quite the normal thing. And the writers of the present day who are setting out to show the humanity and vitality of provincial life—particularly Mr. William Cooper, Mr. Kingsley Amis, and Mr. John Wain—do not their heroes, on their different levels of talent, find their appropriate salvation in Oxford and London? Does not Dr. C. P. Snow's chronicle of the world of Lewis Eliot move southward and reach its plateau in the professional class in London and Cambridge, where over sunlit polished tables on which stand old silver milk jugs, few appear to do any hard work and all live graciously and spaciously?

IV

The internal unity of the British *élite* has often been remarked. The re-establishment of amicable and harmonious relations between the intellectuals and British society has really been the unification of the intellectuals with the other groups of the ruling *élite*; it has been a resumption of friendly relations with the Government, with the Houses of Parliament and the Civil Service, and with the complex of institutions around the central institutions of authority, the Law Courts and the Inns of Court, the Church of England, the ancient Universities, etc.

The culture which has now regained moral ascendancy is not an aristocratic culture in the sense that it is the present culture of an active aristocracy, nor is it the actual culture of the gentry. It is the culture traditionally inspired by those classes, the culture appropriate to certain institutions allied to these classes. Many of the aristocracy and gentry are quite ignorant and boorish but when they become cultivated, their culture takes that tone : moderate, unspecialized and unobsessed, civil, restrained, diversified, and personally refined.

It is a pluralistic culture within itself : it has room for politicians, for sportsmen, for travellers, for civil servants and judges and barristers and journalists, for artists and writers of different persuasions. It is an unbourgeois culture, even though members of the bourgeoisie and their offspring people it most densely. It is an exclusive culture into which the rest of the society is rarely admitted except on the terms of the host. The "insideness" of the British *élite* is part of a great social machine for creating "outsiders". Its internal unity is intimately related to the tangibility of its external boundaries.

Their conquest, like all conquests, is incomplete. It has left under the surface of the conquered a mass of sentiments and loyalties and suspicions which are far from dissolved. For years, the division of British society—on the one side, the society of aristocracy and gentry and their allied institutions, and, on the other the Dissenting bourgeois with their provincial, modern society—rendered possible and even easy the public expression of the cultural aspirations and social and æsthetic sensitivity of "the other nation". The reconquest by aristocratic-gentry culture has rendered this expression more difficult, just as it has obscured the persistent and effective division of the nation and given a spurious impression of unity. Among the British intellectuals there are thickly scattered Judes and Leonard Basts and Bruce Truscotts, experiencing with distress, while hating to acknowledge, the line which separates them from the inside, from the charmed circle of cultivation, affluence, worldliness, and ease.

Earlier there was rivalry and even antagonism between the two nations of British culture but there was little emulation. The bourgeoisie was too concerned with the intrinsic importance of its own cultural and philanthropic works, and too apprehensive of rebuff to worry itself profoundly about its conformity with the standards of the aristocracy and gentry. Indeed, the mere notion that the aristocracy and gentry prized one way of doing things led the business classes to follow another path. The small class of clerks, shop assistants, and self-educated workmen were not sufficiently in contact with, or near to, the uppermost classes in the social hierarchy to be substantially affected by their standards. When they studied at night it was from sheer love of learning or to advance themselves in the knowledge required for progress in their own occupations.

The intellectual's desire to move in the aura of the aristocratic-gentry culture is only about half a century old—its first distinguished representative in the twentieth century was Leonard Bast and only in the 1930s did such young people become noticeable in large numbers. The two wars with the opportunities which they afforded for great numbers of young men to be schooled as officers and gentlemen, the increase in the demand for professional and clerical skills, the increase in grammar school and university attendance between the wars and their tremendous increase after the Second World War, have all created a public zealous for the culture of the refined classes.

Continental holidays, the connoisseurship of wine and food, the knowledge of wild flowers and birds, acquaintance with the writings of Jane Austen, a knowing indulgence for the worthies of the English past, an appreciation of "more leisurely epochs", doing one's job dutifully and reliably, the cultivation of personal relations—these are the elements in the ethos of the newly emerging British intellectual class. It is around an ethos of this sort that nowadays the new attachment to Great Britain is formed. It is in its attachment to symbols of a culture which have always been associated with a "stake in the country" that the British intellectual has been finding its way home. It is through the limited range of sympathy characteristic of that culture, elegant and admirable though it is, that the present-day British intellectual restricts his attachments to British society, and it is around that ethos that the misery and uneasiness of the incompletely assimilated are focused.

INSIDERS AND OUTSIDERS

The triumph of the contemporary version of the aristocratic-gentry culture has not resulted in the complete assimilation of the intellectuals to the nation and its institutions. It has only meant a reattachment to a sector of the upper classes. The aristocratic-gentry culture assumes and implicitly praises a considerable stratification of the British society; it makes clear the inferiority of the business world, of the mere technician, of the practical man, and of the enthusiast, moral, religious, and political. It praises the authority which rests ultimately on the Crown and on the land, and it derogates authority which is unconnected with those two sources. It measures its praise in accordance with the proximity of a person to those sources or to the institutions associated with them. The acceptance of this ideal by the intellectuals, then, cannot be without serious consequences for a society which is still a largely bourgeois society in its economic organization and which still possesses much more than traces of cultures other than the aristocratic-gentry one.

The reconquest has created the problems which are characteristic of situations in which a superior culture is superimposed on more backward cultures. There is a tendency towards "over-assimilation"—becoming more genteel than gentility requires—on the part of marginal persons, and there is also much resentment generated within the minds of those who "over-assimilate". At the same time, on the top, there is a tendency for the beneficiaries of the superior culture to confine themselves to their own culture and its realm and to close themselves off from the rest.

Let us deal first with the latter consequence—the narrowness of the range of sympathy and curiosity of the British intelligentsia within its own society. Many students of English literature over the past half century have remarked on the limited scope of its subject-matter. Novels of working-class life are certainly extremely rare, both in general and among the writers who succeed in being taken up by the arbiters of taste in the literary reviews, on the BBC, etc. If one surveys the works of the chief writers of the present day, what does one find? In the writings, for example, of Anthony Powell, Julia Strachey, William Cooper, William Plomer,* Elizabeth Bowen, Elizabeth Lake, Antonia White, et al., we do not find the working classes treated at all. Do we find shopkeepers, clerks, small business? There is a little more openness there. William Sansom treats Suburbia because its dull placidity is an excellent foil for diabolism; V. S. Pritchett comes closer to a sympathetic depiction but nonetheless It May Never Happen, effectively, and Mr. Beluncle, ineffectively, use a petit-bourgeois atmosphere to uncover amusing eccentricities, minor and fairly amiable madnesses. Businessmen do very poorly. The old-fashioned business brute whom Mr. Pritchett kills off in Nothing Like Leather, the cultured Northern business family so fascinating to the narrating outsider and so sympathetically described by Mr. Priestley in Bright Day, are as close as the present-day British intellectual comes to intimacy with the world of commerce and industry. Mr. J. D. Scott contrasts the business twisters—significantly enough, of

* William Plomer's The Invaders is an exception which argues that an effort to enter into contact with the lower classes will be hopelessly frustrated.

the film world which apparently represents the world of business at large —with the educated, dutiful, and virtuous Civil Servant and the glamorous film creator; Mr. Geoffrey Cottrell contrasts the business scoundrels, to whom the climber from the lower middle classes has gained connections by marriage, with his old friends who have virtuously gone ahead in Labour politics.

This is not intended as criticism of the contemporary English novel, but only as an indication of the spontaneous inclinations and the objects of aversion of the intellectuals. It reveals the very special area of attachment of the intellectuals to British society. Their very attachment, and the patriotism associated with it, blinds them to British society in its wider reaches. It does not, to be sure, breed hostility or bitterness or contempt towards the other classes in society; and the attachment to this culture makes for a greater homogeneity within the class itself. While this is, morally and politically, an advantage, it is intellectually a disadvantage. It makes them less good as intellectuals, among whose tasks—there are many others—is the truthful interpretation of their national society and its culture to their own countrymen and the world.

There is another consequence of this specialized affection of the intellectuals for British society. This is the invisible but painfully tangible ring *within* the intellectual class which shuts off those inside the charmed circle from the fellow travellers and aspirants—which separates those who are thought to live fully in the culture of the aristocracy and gentry from those who admire them for doing so, and who would do so themselves if they could.

It is manifested in many ways. Recently we have heard again the charges that there is a literary clique, an organized body of friends, which dominates British literary life. This is an extreme manifestation, it is true, of that eternal affliction of the "outsider" in every society—namely, the belief that at the centre of the magic circle a closed group schemes and rules to the deliberate disadvantage of the excluded. For years Dr. Leavis has assailed the wickedness of Bloomsbury, its coterie culture, its meretricious standards and its improper influence *via* the BBC, the British Council, and other official organs, and his lament sounds once more as an overtone in the skirmishes of the new provincialism against the Oxford–Cambridge–London triangle. This preoccupation with an inner circle, is very evident in the modern universities where Oxford and Cambridge—and London, as far as the provinces are concerned—are invisible presences; in the Common Rooms, appointments and disappointments at Oxford and Cambridge are as real and immediate as if they were happening right there. Questions about students in the modern universities are very often met with a bitter complaint that the students at the local university are poor—with the addition that the good ones go to Oxford or Cambridge, and sometimes London is added in a sober afterthought. The desire to be at the institution as little as possible, and away as much as possible, is part of the injury done to corporate and individual self-esteem by the vestigial but persisting traces of the barrier between the Two Nations within the intellectual class—the Nation of London, Cambridge, Oxford, of the higher Civil Service, of the genteel and sophisticated; and the Nation of the provinces, of petit-bourgeois and upper working-class origin, of bourgeois environment, studious, diligent, and specialized.

THE UNSOLVED PROBLEM

The assimilation of the new intellectuals into the ideal pattern of the old intellectual class is a terribly difficult task which still remains to be solved. On the surface, it appears to go on merrily and cheerfully; the new intellectual rejoices in every new cultural acquisition which brings him nearer the old—like the brilliant young university lecturer who, a few years ago, could not tell grape juice from wine except by the after-effects and who now takes such pleasure in sparing no one from his knowledge of vintages and vintners, and who even can tell the difference between the wines produced on two neighbouring California hillsides.

Underneath the surface, however, all does not go so well. At the very top of the profession, a man who has talent, genius, or good fortune, finds acceptance by his peers and admission to their society. The strain of being an outsider is more painfully experienced in the young and in those who do not quite reach the pinnacle of achievement. The insecurity is not, by any means, just a matter of personal achievement; it is also affected by the status of school and university through which this man has passed as a student, and of the institution of which he is a member. It is also in part a matter of his social or family origin although that is less important than the other factors mentioned. The man doomed to live at a provincial university feels it—he feels it if he is a graduate of a provincial university and he feels it worse if he is a graduate of an ancient university. Injured sentiments, memories of slights and rejections accumulate, and fantasy accentuates it all. Mostly, however, the sense of being in the outer circle is expressed in faint sniffs of distaste for students, in mockery and irony. It affects the young more than it does their elders and students more than staff.

Nor is it entirely a matter of the subjective creation of a barrier by those who feel themselves to be outsiders. Part of the exclusiveness of the aristocratic-gentry higher civil service culture arises, not from the organization of a coterie, but from the fact that it is a humanistic culture, hostile to unbalanced specialization and hostile therefore to those professions, the practice and traditions of which necessitate the preoccupations of specialization, and in which the modern universities are so strong. We see it in the ambivalence towards post-graduate research at Oxford and Cambridge and in a more trivial way we see it in the attitude towards the academic titles of address of Professor and Doctor in those universities. Much more importantly we see it in the long-drawn-out and unsatisfactory discussion about the development of institutions of higher technological studies. The training of technologists on this level is repugnant to the ancient universities and their proponents who feel perhaps rightly that such studies are too practical and too "unhumane" to be admitted to their universities; at the same time, they also do not like the idea of independent specialized institutions of University rank where technological research and studies can be carried on, as if they were on the same dignity as traditional university studies.*

Finally a word may be said on the influence of the coterie itself. It seems to be no more important in England than in any other centralized country where the leading men in each field of intellectual activity come to know one another personally, either because they happen to have been at school together or because their eminence at the peak of their profession has brought them together. On the whole, although there occasionally seem to be some odd goings-on made possible by anonymous reviewing, British intellectual life does not seem to be regulated internally by personal attachments to a much greater extent than in other countries. To a very considerable degree it seems to be governed by impersonal standards that are in part standards which have been associated with certain restricted classes and institutions, themselves the objects of strong, if ambivalent, sentiment.

Those who have grown up inside the culture of these classes and institutions feel very much at home in them nowadays. But those who have not are powerfully attracted by them and are yet put off by the implication of their unworthiness for not having been so born. It is not an accident that the *New Statesman and Nation* with its wide circulation should present an apparently contradictory table of contents: cranky radicalism in its

* It has sometimes been said that the reason why scientists, especially in Great Britain, have been inclined towards political radicalism lies in the nature of the subject, which requires the use of reason unaided by tradition and which involves the manipulation of material things in accordance with rational principles. Quite apart from the dubious picture of scientific work which this explanation adduces, it seems to suffer from disregard of some simple facts: namely, that in Great Britain, science which is less than pure science is *infra dig*, and that a disproportionately large amount of the best scientific work of Great Britain, pure as well as applied, is carried on in the modern universities which can confer on their numbers little prestige beyond what they can achieve by their work. Scientists, even pure scientists, and certainly applied scientists in Great Britain, live and work in an atmosphere which makes at least some of them regard themselves as outsiders.

political pages and genteel culture in its literary and cultural sections; or that it should combine Bevanism in politics with a special wine supplement.

V

The New Elizabethans who were conjured up in aspiration two years ago as the carriers of British tradition have petered out into thin air. The culture of this age is nothing like the old Elizabethan culture. The new Elizabethan age is an age of very notable talent but it is a talent of fine lineaments, of delicate but not deep voice, of restraint which binds no passion, of subtlety without grandeur. Outside the China of the Mandarins, no great society has ever had a body of intellectuals so integrated with, and so congenial to, its ruling class, and so combining civility and refinement. The consensus thus achieved is remarkable. What are the costs?

Just as in the nineteenth century the public schools and the universities had the task of assimilating into the ruling classes the heirs and descendants of wealthy businessmen who had made the necessary concessions to the spiritual *ancien régime*, so present-day Britain has the equally important task of assimilating into its great traditions the new aspirants to the ruling classes, broadly conceived, who come from the lower-middle and upper-working classes. It was easier to assimilate newcomers when they were only a trickle and when the institutions of assimilation were thoroughly governed by the older culture. It is more difficult now, when the numbers are greater and when many of the institutions themselves have only an ambivalent and uncertain hold on the older culture. The success of the present process of assimilation and refinement is being achieved at the cost of a narrowing of sensibility and imagination, and of a hard, conflict-engendering pressure on those who crowd the periphery.

APRIL 1955

DANIEL BELL

American Dissent

DISSENT IS ONE of the few cultural periodicals in the United States avowedly socialist in politics and radical in its criticism of contemporary culture. It is, like *Universities and Left Review* in England and *Arguments* in France, at odds with the doctrinaire interpretation of orthodox Marxism, and at one with the widening search for a new basis for a socialist humanism. But in important respects, *Dissent*'s difference from these European journals is greater than its similarity. *Universities and Left Review* arose out of the ferment in the Communist world following the Khrushchev admissions that the Stalin régime had criminally murdered thousands of innocent Communists and cruelly masked this terrorism with judicial frame-ups. *Arguments* (in both a French and an Italian edition) came into being after the events in Poland and Hungary, and in its intensely philosophical preoccupation reflects the revisionist discussions which have been taking place in Eastern Europe. Both are part of the post-Stalinist phenomenon. *Dissent*, five years older than the other two, was founded largely by individuals who had left the Trotskyite movement (the "class of 1950"), and who were already well-schooled in the doctrinal debates of Marxist exegetics.

The difference in origin accounts for the differences in tone and content. The first two are products of the fifties, cut off from the past by the war and the tales of their elders; the latter is an echo of the thirties, repeating, in mournful anger, the obsessions and debates of the past. *Universities and Left Review* and *Arguments* represent a new political generation, with all the appeal of the tyro, and the bitter-sweet disillusionment of first love. *Dissent* is a magazine of the epigone, the jejune and weary. *Universities and Left Review* and *Arguments* are intense, phrenetic, naïve, and bursting with a new sense of auto-didactic wonder about theoretical issues that had been wrangled over by the Left twenty years before; *Dissent* is querulous, scornful, magisterial, sectarian, but infinitely more sophisticated about political issues.

These differences in style caricature, as extreme statements tend to do, the opposition between European and American radicalism. It is not only that America has become an affluent society, offering place (in the universities and the publishing houses) and prestige (if not in society as a whole, certainly in the universities and the publishing houses) to the one-time radicals—and it is interesting to note that the two chief editors of *Dissent*, Irving Howe and Lewis Coser, are university professors, as are most of their luminaries, like C. Wright Mills, whose books, in paper-back editions, circulate in some 50,000 copies—but American radicalism had, intellectually, long ago disposed of the questions that until recently had racked the serious European Left. It is this point—as well as the fact that American society, through the modifications introduced by Roosevelt and Truman, has belied the orthodox Marxist predictions of "fascism and collapse"— which explains many of the disparities in intellectual atmosphere between the two continents.

This is a seeming paradox. Europe, in legend, has always been the home of subtle philosophical discussion; America was the grub land of pragmatism. Questions laid to rest in Europe had their reincarnation (as an old quip put it) twenty years later in the United States. Whatever truth this remark may once have had, the reverse is true today. The questions which in the last five years preoccupied Sartre and Camus in France, Wolfgang Harich in East Germany, Kolakowski in Poland—those of ends and means, class truth, the validity of dialectic materialism as a scientific construct, the definition of a workers' state, party democracy, the nature of bureaucracy, the relationship to literature of propaganda, the mixed economy—were thrashed out more than twenty years ago by Sidney Hook, Ernest Nagel, Lewis Corey, Edmund Wilson, Philip Rahv, John Dewey, and dozens of others in the pages of *Partisan Review*, *The New International*, and *The New Leader*. It is not that these men had greater theoretical acumen than European Marxists, many of whom, invidually (most notably Ignazio Silone, in *Bread and Wine*), had explored the same problems. But while in Europe only a small number of intellectuals left the Communist orbit before the war, in the United States almost the entire group of serious intellectuals who had been attracted to Marxism had broken with the Communist Party by 1940. Thus, as an intellectual problem, Bolshevism disappeared from the American scene almost twenty years ago.

The sociological reasons for these differences in atmosphere and response are varied. Being 3,000 miles from Europe the American radicals were not caught up in the immediate political struggles of fascism—or faced with the possibility of becoming refugees. There was thus far less reason to suppress political doubts fired by the Moscow Trials and the Nazi-Soviet Pact. In America, moreover, the Communist Party never had a large following in the labour movement, so there was no strong emotional force the party could use to hold the intellectuals. And, being free-floating intellectuals rather than functionaries or officials who had to swing a large political movement with them, political discussion was more "irresponsible", yet by the same token freer and more intense.

As a result of such free-spiritedness, the basic political drift of the former Left intelligentsia in the United States in the forties and fifties has been anti-ideological—that is to say, sceptical of the old rationalist claims that socialism by eliminating the economic basis of exploitation, would solve all social problems, and sceptical, in fact, of any ideological formulas for social change. To a great extent this scepticism of rationalism is the source of the American intellectuals' devotion to Freudianism and neo-orthodox theology (as expounded by Reinhold Niebuhr and Paul Tillich). In addition to this change in intellectual temper, the old Left began discovering new virtues in the United States because of its pluralism, its acceptance of the Welfare State, the spread of education, and the expanding opportunities for intellectual employment. And, in the cold war, they accepted the fact that Soviet Russia was the principal threat to freedom in the world today. These political attitudes were reflected primarily in the pages of *Partisan Review*, *Commentary*, and *The New Leader*, the three magazines, along with the writers grouped around them, who in large part became the core of the American Committee for Cultural Freedom.

On the academic level, these re-evaluations called into question the accepted idea of populist basis of American radicalism and argued that the political conflicts of the fifties, like McCarthyism, were more fruitfully explained by sociological concepts such as "status anxiety" than by the more conventional notions of class or interest group conflicts. These significant changes in intellectual temper can be seen in Lionel Trilling's *The Liberal Imagination*, Richard Hofstadter's *The Age of Reform*, Edward Shils's *The Torment of Secrecy*, and the various essays on "McCarthyism" in *The New American Right*.

It was in this context of the break-up of the old Left, and as reaction to these re-evaluations, that *Dissent* came into being. While it talked of the conformism of American society, its real concern was to defend the shards of Marxism against those who were calling the entire range of radical ideas —not just Bolshevism—into question. And the "internal" debate was carried on, as is usually the case in the United States, in that large, exotic cauldron, the New York intellectual world. Little of this, unfortunately, is reflected in the recently published volume, *Voices of Dissent* (Grove Press in America; John Calder Ltd., in England), a selection of articles from the twenty or so issues brought out in the magazine's five-year history. The editors may have thought that book publication might attract a more general audience; hence, the more parochial—and more interesting—aspects of the magazine were muted.

To take *Voices of Dissent* on its own terms: we find some fairly commonplace reportage about America, some thoughtful discussion of the errors of Marxism, some reflective essays about estrangement in contemporary society—the best of these, by Silone, Chiaromonte, Milosz, and Richard Lowenthal, were published first in other magazines in fact, those sponsored by the Congress for Cultural Freedom—but there are few pathbreaking thoughts about radicalism. "What Shall We Do?" asks one of the editors, Lewis Coser, in the one programmatic essay in the anthology. "Above all, it would seem to me," says Coser after a long wind-up, that the radical "must be concerned with maintaining, encouraging, fostering the growth of the species 'radical'. If it becomes extinct, our culture will inevitably ossify from want of challenge."

But challenge to what? Radical about what? *Dissent* attacked *Partisan Review* and *Commentary* for not being radical. But, beyond attacking these magazines, there was scarcely anything in *Dissent* that was anything more than hortatory. It never explained what it meant by radicalism; and it has not been able, especially in the area of politics, to propose anything new. For *Dissent* has been hoist, as has been the "Left" as a whole, on the very meaninglessness of the term "radicalism". In the past, radicalism had vitality because it was a form of *apocalyptic* thought—it wanted to wash away an entire society in one tidal wave. ("I went to Cuba," writes Livio Stecchini in a recent issue of *Dissent*, in an article which characteristically expresses in extraordinary fashion the romantic pathos of the magazine, "because over the years I have become disappointed with revolutionary ideas and experience. Selfishly I wanted to share the exhilaration that comes from living by hope and desire *before the dawn of reality*.") But where the problems are today, as Karl Popper put it, those of "piecemeal technology", the prosaic, yet necessary, questions of school costs, municipal services, urban sprawl, and the like, bravura radicalism becomes simply a hollow shell.

If *Dissent* has had little new to say about politics, it has been in an even greater quandary, on the question of radical expression in the arts. In the United States today, whatever calls itself *avant-garde*, be it abstract expressionism or beatnik poetry, is quickly acclaimed and enthroned. In part this is due to the familiar desire of Americans for novelty and sensation. But on a more serious level the arbiters of taste are sensitive to the criticism of the past, and many of the cultural arbiters (Clement Greenberg and Harold Rosenberg in painting, Lionel Trilling and Alfred Kazin in literature) are part of the *ancien* Left. This acceptance of the *avant-garde* has become so vexing that Hilton Kramer (an editor of *Arts*, writing in *Dissent*) was moved to say—I quote him exactly: "The fact of the matter is that since 1945 bourgeois society has tightened its grip on all the arts by allowing them a freer rein."

If *Dissent* has had a single unifying idea—and this is what gives any radical magazine character—it is its concept of America as a *mass society*, and its attack on the grotesque elements of such a society. And it is here that *Dissent* begins to have a tone identical with the *Universities and Left Review*, and with the other new voices of the Left which attack modern society.

The concept of the *mass society*, however, is peculiarly amorphous. Those who used the older vocabulary of radicalism could attack "the capitalists" or even "the bourgeoisie", but when talking about *mass society* one simply flails out against "the culture", and it is hard to discover who, or what, is the enemy. This is not true of the older group of writers who first employed the idea of the mass society, principally Ortega y Gasset, Joseph Pieper, Karl Jaspers, and T. S. Eliot. They were men with an aristocratic, or Catholic, or *élite* conception of culture and for them the standards of taste and excellence set by the educated and the cultivated have been torn down by the mass. They stand against egalitarianism and industrial society. But it is difficult for the young radicals to take this aristocratic stance. Nor can they absorb intellectually the pastoral image (deriving from German sociology) that the communal roots of the old nourishing *gemeinschaft* have been torn up by the soulless, impersonal, mechanized society. This cry has always been the protest of rural society against the anonymity (which is also privacy and freedom!) of the city; and the young radicals are not "rural idiots".

The question of the *mass society* is complex, and not easily summarized within the boundaries of a note. The meaning of a *mass* society is that for the first time the mass has been brought into *society*, and are no longer excluded from the political rights and cultural heritage which previously only a few had claimed. I find the image of the mass society, as used by *Dissent* and *Universities and Left Review*, to be quite wrong, for I believe that modern society is, for the mass, more differentiated, variegated, and life-enhancing, in its cultural aspects, than traditional society. The bringing of the "mass" *into* society is a process which began only in the last twenty-five years, and as Edward Shils has shown, it is a difficult one. Obviously it is not just the spread of mass media but the raising of wages and reduction of hours and the consequent gain in leisure, and the spread of higher education that shapes the problem of how standards of quality can be maintained.

In the United States, one minor but positive consideration, about the new mass society, can be noted. The cultural *élite*, to the extent that there is one (and I believe there is), is primarily an academic *élite*—the culture of

Harvard, Columbia, Berkeley, and other large centres—and, in contrast to what was true fifty years ago, it is a "liberal" culture, receptive to ideas, critical in its outlook, and encouraging to dissent. To that extent—and this is the final paradox—even *Dissent* is an accredited member of the culture, and a welcome one.

SEPTEMBER 1959

ARTHUR KOESTLER

The Trail of the Dinosaur

LET US IMAGINE a kind of temperature chart on which the growing power of *homo sapiens* over his environment is represented by a curve. For something of the order of half a million years, from Java man to about 5000 B.C., the curve would remain nearly static, represented by a roughly horizontal line. With the invention of the pulley, the lever, and a few simple mechanical devices, the muscular strength of man would appear amplified, say, five-fold; and after that, the curve would again remain nearly horizontal for the next five or six thousand years.

But, in the course of the last three hundred years, the curve would, for the first time in the history of the species, rise steeply in leaps and bounds, until it pointed almost vertically upward. To draw this chart true to scale, we would have to use graph paper several miles long; even so we would only have an inch or less of the paper left to plot the sudden, dramatic lifting of the curve's head—like a cobra stabbing upward.

Another more specific chart, representing the destructive potentialities of the growth of power, would look even more dramatic—one merely has to remember that after the First World War, only forty years ago, statisticians reckoned that on the average ten thousand rifle bullets or ten artillery shells were needed to kill one enemy soldier.

Now let us contrast these two charts with a third one, on which we plot the progress of the species man in moral philosophy, in cosmic awareness and spiritual clarity. This curve will show a slow rise during the prehistoric miles of nearly-flat stretch; then, when the power-curve (P) starts rising, the spiritual curve (S) will begin to undulate with indecisive ups and downs; finally, on the last, dramatic one-millionth part of the chart, where the P-curve shoots skyward with insane acceleration, the S-curve goes into a steep decline. The spiritual void at the end of the chart is less obvious than the accumulation of power; I shall come back to the "S-curve" later on.

The point of these imaginary charts is that they show a very unusual type of curve, a geometrical freak which forces us to measure time at first in units of hundred thousands, then of thousands of years, then in centuries and decades, until, towards the end, a single year weighs more than ten thousand years did before. A process which, once past a critical limit, shows this type of catastrophic acceleration is called in physics an explosion. A dispassionate observer from another world, to whom centuries are as seconds, able to survey the whole curve in one sweep, would have to come to the conclusion that our civilization is either on the verge of, or in the process of, exploding.

I would like to labour the geometrical aspect of human evolution a little further by suggesting two more curves, the first representing progress in communication (C), the second progress in understanding (U). The C-curve, which would comprise travel and communication by visual and acoustic means, would again remain nearly flat for æons; then, with the invention of the printing press, the steamship, railway, motor-car, gramophone, telephone, cinema, aeroplane, radio, video, radar, and jukebox (all, except for the printing press, crowded into a single century) the curve would rise steeply to near-saturation—the point where the whole surface of the planet is visually and acoustically interconnected. One should have expected that this shrinking of the terrestrial surface in terms of communication would lead to a proportionate increase in its intellectual cohesion, but this did not happen. The shrinking of the distance between nations did not bring them "nearer" to each other; three-dimensional travel did not abolish Chinese Walls and Iron Curtains, but merely extended them into atmospheric space; the unifying medium of the ether was split up by censorship and jamming. Even between such close neighbours and allies as the people of England and France, mutual comprehension and human sympathy is not markedly greater now than at a time when they were days, instead of hours, apart.

Nor did the extension of the range of the sense-organs through radio and television increase the intellectual range of the human mind, its powers of abstraction and synthesis. It seems rather that the reverse is true : that the stupendous amplification of vision and hearing caused a rapid deterioration of the intellectual and moral content of communication. In the new generation born into the age of television, not only the habit of reading, but the faculty of thinking in abstract, conceptual terms seems to be weakened by the child's conditioning to easier and more primitive forms of visual perception. The dangers of this regression from the conceptual to the perceptual, from abstract language to picture-strip language, are less obvious and immediate, but in the long run no less grave, than the spectacular increase in destructive power.

To sum up, our diagrams would show an unprecedented increase in the range and power of the species' sensory and motor organs coincident with a marked deterioration of the integrative functions which determine spiritual maturity and social ethics. There are frequent instances in history of moral slumps followed by a new upward trend; the alarming thing is the coincidence of a period of unprecedented spiritual decline with an equally unprecedented increase of power. The Promethean myth seems to be coming true with a horrible twist : the giant reaching out to steal the lightning from the Gods is morally insane. Hence the difficulty, as Bertrand Russell wrote a few years ago, "to persuade mankind to acquiesce in its own survival".

Any attempt at such persuasion must take both the short-term and the long-term aspects of the situation into account. The first is political, the second transcendental in nature; and the two interact more directly than we realize. The politician unaware of the transcendental background of the crisis can only offer makeshift measures; and the saint who remains aloof in an emergency sins by omission.

On the level of practical policy, it is essential to distinguish between the desirable and the possible. We know by now that atomic war would be tantamount to a collective suicide of the species. To abolish the threat of atomic war is certainly desirable, but not in the realm of the possible. Interdiction of atomic weapons can only be effective if both parties agree to international supervision under conditions which include permanent inspection—the throwing open of the locked doors of secret laboratories, factories, plants, mines, and military installations. But such a policy runs counter to the tradition of secrecy and distrust which Russia and the Asian nations have practised for centuries past; and it also runs counter to the basic principles and political structure of all dictatorial régimes, Communist or other. A dictatorship that accepted democratic controls, internally or internationally, would cease to be a dictatorship. The Chinese Wall and the Iron Curtain are not accidents of history, but massive symbols of national traditions and social régimes whose existence depends on their ability to block the movement of people and ideas.

Even if the present rulers of Russia desired to submit to genuine international control and inspection, they could not afford to do so any more than they could afford to abolish censorship, the one-party system, the political police, and other essential requisites of dictatorship. Whether the dictatorship is good or bad, whether it is a dictatorship of the workers, peasants or dentists, of a bureaucracy or a theocracy, is irrelevant in this context.

It is equally irrelevant under what pretexts the Soviet government evades the issue of genuine inspection and control—whether by procedural subterfuges, or by rejecting "infringements of national sovereignty", or by spurious peace campaigns and the demand for a platonic ban on atomic weapons which would work against the side that manufactures and tests its bombs openly, and which would set a premium on secrecy. Oak Ridge, Harwell, Bikini, are widely discussed subjects in the West, while the corresponding places and events in the East are shrouded in complete secrecy.

I repeat: the abolition of atomic weapons under effective international control is entirely desirable, and by the nature of things just as impossible as it proved impossible to enforce disarmament in the defunct League of Nations' days. From this realistic starting-point, three courses are open to the West: to continue developing nuclear weapons in full awareness of the danger to the human species; or to renounce nuclear weapons one-sidedly, in full awareness of the decisive advantage thereby accorded to the opponent; or, finally, to start a "preventive" war (which is of course a contradiction in terms), based on the assumption that the West still possesses a decisive superiority in atomic weapons, that this advantage is being lost, and that war at the present level of atomic developments would be less devastating than war in five or ten years' time and would impose a lasting peace on a unified world.

The third possibility we must reject out of hand, on the grounds that it is based on the old Ends and Means fallacy. All social progress, all human justice, requires a certain amount of ruthlessness; all surgical cures, the infliction of a certain amount of pain. But this justification of the means by the end is confined to very narrow limits, to situations where all the factors are of manageable order and the results predictable with reasonable certainty—otherwise, the surgeon's lancet turns into the butcher's hatchet. With regard to preventive war, none of the above conditions is present. The amount of damage that would be inflicted on humanity is incalculable, the factors in the equation are unmanageable, and the results unpredictable. Even on the inadmissible premiss that morality should be sacrificed to expediency and the present generation sacrificed in the interest of future ones —even on these premisses preventive war must be ruled out on the grounds that the magnitude and complexity of factors are beyond the computing capacity of the human brain.

Unfortunately, the premisses that we reject are not rejected by the philosophy of dialectical materialism which is the credo of our opponents; and our scepticism regarding the limits of man's ability as a computing machine is not shared by them. Thus the possibility that our opponents may start "preventive" war at a moment which they judge "historically favourable", and under any convenient pretext, cannot be ruled out.

I would like to make this point clearer. In the previous paragraph I was not concerned with the question whether certain members of the Politburo think it practicable to start a war in six months or six years, or whether they think that the inevitable Communist world state can be realized without war. My point is that their philosophical approach to, and their terms of reference regarding the problem of, war are different from ours. The West has no unified philosophy, but it has a long and continuous ethical tradition which more or less articulately, more or less consciously, permeates the thinking of both leaders and people and limits the former's freedom of action. The leaders of the other side are not subject to such limitations either by the philosophy to which they adhere or by the machinery of democratic control. It is an unequal contest where one side believes in its historic mission which justifies all means including war, whereas the other does not; where one party is bound by certain rules of the game, the other party is not.

This difference ought to be constantly present in the minds of all responsible politicians, Left or Right, and guide their decisions, large and small. But psychologically, this is a rather difficult thing to ask for, because the tactical oscillations of Soviet policy, the occasional easing of surface tensions, and the frequent unmannerliness of American politicians tend to obscure and blur the basic difference in philosophy. Wishful thinking, infatuation with pious platitudes, and the tempting road of least resistance are constantly lessening the West's chances of survival.

Marxist theory teaches that the proletariat must exploit to the full the constitutional freedoms which bourgeois democracy is obliged to grant (for the bourgeoisie is bound to be "its own gravedigger"), until an "objectively revolutionary situation" occurs. At that moment the proletariat will rise and inter its opponents in their self-prepared grave. *Mutatis mutandis* the same theory applies to the international scene, where the notion of the "objectively revolutionary situation" is replaced by the "historically favourable situation" for adding another vassal nation to the existing ones. One-sided atomic disarmament would automatically create a "historically favourable situation" for Russia's bid to unify the world after its own fashion in the interests of mankind.

There is nothing new about the argument that the only deterrent against atomic aggression is an atomic stockpile. But there is a new development regarding the value of an atomic stockpile against non-atomic, local aggression. The theory that the atomic superiority of the West could prevent local aggression by the threat of massive retaliation has become obsolete for two reasons: first, Western atomic superiority is on the wane; secondly, the destructive power of the new weapons is now so monstrous that the punishment of limited and camouflaged aggression by the unleashing of open atomic war has become politically and morally impossible. A policeman, armed with an atom bomb and nothing else, could not prevent the escape of a couple of housebreakers without blowing the whole town to glory, himself included. We are faced with a new paradox : the superior power of a weapon may reduce its bearer to helplessness.

The policeman's part is made even more difficult by the fact that political crimes are easier to camouflage than common burglaries. Russia has conquered one half of Europe and a large portion of Asia through acts of aggression in varying disguises of varying plausibility, none of which presented a clear-cut *casus belli*. The possibilities of veiled aggression are inexhaustible; and it is unrealistic to believe that we can stop it by the threat of "massive retaliation"—which, if taken seriously, would mean that we ought to have reacted to the defenestration of Masaryk, or ought to react to the next "People's Rising" in Afghanistan, by unleashing the nuclear nightmare.

The upshot of this argument is that policing the world and guaranteeing collective security never was and never will be possible through reliance on the West's industrial superiority and dreams of push-button retaliation. To put it into a nutshell : atomic weapons are necessary as a deterrent against atomic aggression, but ineffective as a deterrent against local and camouflaged aggression. The security of our streets cannot be guaranteed by tanks, only by police constables in sufficient numbers, armed with conventional weapons to cope with conventional crimes. The practical conclusions are distressingly simple. The most conventional of all weapons, and the one which no nation can dispense with, is a people determined to fight on the beaches and to fight in the streets in defence of their freedom. However brave they are, they will never be able to stand up against an aggressor using the methods of total war. But if they are strong enough and brave enough, they will survive because of the aggressor's reluctance to engage in total war. The oft-heard argument "what is the good of arming a few more divisions when we know that in the case of a showdown Europe cannot be defended anyway" is both cowardly and false. Any European defence community can never aim at more than to make Europe unconquerable *short of total war*. But it can never aim at less than this. If, in the early post-war period, Czechoslovakia and Poland had been equipped with the number of divisions and the unbroken spirit of Finland in 1939, the Russians could not have deposed the Polish Government, nor pulled their Prague coup. They would have been forced to show their hand and engage in open warfare—and the odds are that they would not have dared to take the risk. It is indeed distressingly simple : free men must be prepared to defend their freedom or lose it.*

* The re-arming of Western Germany is a side-issue which may be settled by the time this essay appears in print; but the passions raised by it will persist for some time and be exploited by the conscious and unconscious enemies of

At the beginning of this essay, I made a distinction between the short-term and long-term aspects of the present crisis. All that I have said so far refers to the short-term aspect and to short-term measures. The best we can hope to achieve by these measures is to gain time. Even if courage and reason prevail to a much greater extent than in recent years, the result cannot be more than a strategic and economic patchwork on a divided planet.

And yet by gaining time, by prolonging this misery of co-existence, mankind may hope for a reprieve. The nature of this tenuous hope is based on the possibility of some unexpected mutation in man's dominating passions and interests. Whenever history became polarized between two competing power-centres, roughly one of two things happened. Either one of the contestants was subjugated (the Rome versus Carthage pattern); or a stalemate was reached (the Christianity versus Islam pattern). Such stalemates have always started as unstable and precarious forms of "co-existence", spotted with local outbreaks which threatened to grow into a total conflict. But under certain favourable conditions the stalemate became a permanent one, co-existence gradually changed into collaboration, and the crisis was over.

The conditions for this to happen are partly of a physical, partly of a psychological nature. The physical basis of the stalemate is balance of power, both "central" and "peripheral". By "central" power I mean the total strength which each side would be capable of throwing into a total showdown, and which acts as a mutual deterrent from risking such a showdown. By "peripheral" strength I mean the physical and moral capacity of exposed outposts and conclaves to defend themselves and hold out, if only for a limited time. This "peripheral" strength is essential to the balance, because it makes the potential aggressor realize that he cannot have his way in a swift and discreet manner, and thus multiplies the risks attached to aggression. The Christian enclaves in Jaffa and Acre during the Crusades, the Protestant enclaves in Catholic countries, and vice versa after the Thirty Years War, seem to prove that a stalemate may extend to the oddest geographical patchwork if the above-mentioned conditions are ful-

---

Western survival. The emotional resistance of the former victims of German militarism is understandable, but unfortunately beside the point; without German divisions Europe cannot be defended. The fear that the re-arming of Western Germany may lead to a repetition of 1914 and 1939 reflects a humiliating inferiority complex, and implies that Europe and the United States will repeat the mistakes which made German aggression possible. If the Atlantic Community cannot trust itself to keep under control a limited number of German divisions under unified command, then it has no chance to survive.

filled. The Night of the Long Knives carries such vivid memories because it was an exception, and not the rule. On the other hand, the fate of the Jewish minorities in Europe, and of the Armenian enclaves in Turkey was a kind of St. Bartholomew in permanence, because there was neither a "central" power nor any peripheral strength to defend them.

However, a stalemate based on the balance of physical power is in itself not enough to prevent an ultimate showdown. The second condition is a change of the spiritual climate, a spontaneous mutation of interest, which blunts the horns of the dilemma. While the process of polarization is at its height, it looks as if the whole world must either go Moslem or Christian, either Catholic or Protestant, either Monarchist or Republican, either Socialist or Capitalist. But if the deadlock lasts long enough, an unexpected mutation of the mass-mind may occur, the inevitable choice no longer appears inevitable, passion drains away and people simply become interested in something else. Religious consciousness yields to national consciousness, the fight for space to the fight for markets, the struggle between "Left" and "Right" to the struggle between East and West. The word "heretic" has now gone into metaphorical use, though once it meant torture and the stake; and whether we live under a King or a President is the least of our worries. Over and again it happened in history that the dynamo which generates the light and the sparks was switched off just before the fuses blew. But in order that this may happen, some new dynamo must enter into action producing a different type of current, a shift of interest to a different set of values, conflicts, and predicaments.

Every branch of human activity—literature, the arts, philosophy, even medicine—seems to be subject to these unpredictable periodic mutations; see the sudden shifts of emphasis in painting from narrative to composition, from contour to surface, from the sculptural to the dynamic, from representational to geometrical. It is not fashion that changes but the focus of the eye and the mind, concentrating its attention on different aspects, in due turn, of the complex entity, man—religious man, economic man, *homo politicus, homo faber, homo liber.*

One of these changes of spiritual climate, which is of particular relevance to us, seems to have occurred somewhere half-way through the Thirty Years War. I am quoting from Miss Wedgwood's classic work on the subject, *The Thirty Years War*:

> Never have the Churches seemed stronger than in the opening decades of the seventeenth century. Yet a single generation was to witness their deposition from political dominance. The tragic results of applied religion had discredited the Churches as the directors of the State. A new emotional urge had to be found to fill the place of

spiritual conviction; national feeling welled up to fill the gap. The terms Protestant and Catholic gradually lose their vigour, the terms German, Frenchman, Swede, assume a gathering menace. A new standard of right and wrong came into the political world. Insensibly and rapidly after that, The Cross gave place to the flag, and the "Sancta Maria" cry of the White Hill to the "Viva España" of Nördlingen.

Admittedly, by the time this great change came into the world, the war had run half its course and taken its toll of death and devastation; and it took another thirteen years to end. But perhaps the Russian conquest of Eastern Europe and the wars in Greece, China, Korea and Indo-China constitute the first half of our thirty years' war; and perhaps the second half need not be repeated—at least it may be argued that the conflict between Bourbon and Hapsburg had little relation to the original religious issue.

The age of religious conflict was superseded in the course of the seventeenth century by the emergence of two apparently unrelated factors : the rise of national consciousness, and the rise of a new philosophy. The latter, based on the discoveries of Copernicus, Galileo, and Kepler, was gradually penetrating wider and wider strata of the public mind. If the earth no longer stood firmly planted by God in the centre of His universe, and was merely a small planet hurtling through space, then, though religious belief did survive, it could no longer command the exclusive interest of man. The sky around him had remained the same, but the focus of his eyes had radically changed since he had learnt that the fixed stars of the firmament did not dance attendance to him, and were blinking down with detached irony at the tiny creature on his spinning cannon ball. Within a century, more or less, the mind of European man had undergone a mutation more radical and fraught with consequences than if he had acquired a third eye or additional limb.

It was a historic turning-point—the point where religion and science, religion and art, logics and ethics, began to part company and go their own separate ways. From the beginnings of civilized life, man's fate had been determined, and his conscience guided, by some superhuman agency; from now on this function was taken over by sub-human agencies. The deities of the past may have been coarse or sublime, scandalous Olympians, or a pure God of love; yet they were wiser, more powerful, on a higher plane of existence than man himself. The new determinants of man's fate—mechanical laws, atoms, glands, genes—which gradually took over, were of a lower order than man himself; they defined his condition, but could provide no guidance whatsoever for his conscience.

The consequences of this shift of "destiny from above" to "destiny from below" became only gradually apparent. Before the shift, the various religions had provided man with explanations of a kind which gave to everything that happened to him meaning in the wider sense of a transcendental causality and a transcendental justice. But the explanations of the new philosophy were devoid of meaning in this wider sense. The answers of the past had been varied, contradictory, primitive, superstitious or whatever one likes to call them, but they had been firm, definite, imperative. They satisfied, at least for a given time and culture, man's need for reassurance and protection in an unfathomably cruel world, for some guidance in his perplexities. The new answers, to quote William James, "made it impossible to find in the driftings of the cosmic atoms, whether they work on the universal or on the particular scale, anything but a kind of aimless weather, doing and undoing, achieving no proper history, and leaving no result". In a word, the old explanations, with all their arbitrariness and patchiness, answered the questions after "the meaning of life", whereas the new explanations, with all their precision, made the question of meaning itself meaningless.

Our thinking habits are so entirely conditioned by post-Copernican developments that we automatically assume thinking always to have followed the same method. We take the ethical neutrality of our "natural laws", the split between "religious" and "scientific" truth so much for granted that we assume they must have always existed. It requires a great imaginative effort to realize the full significance of the "shift of destiny" of three hundred years ago, and that it constitutes a new departure, a break in the curve of man's spiritual evolution as unprecedented and unique as the sudden vertiginous rise of his physical power. We don't know how many tens of thousand years ago man for the first time asked the question about the meaning of life; but we do know at what point, so close to us in time, he lost the answer to it.

For a long time the majority of mankind remained unaware of the implications of the new philosophy. Its pioneers talked in a timid and tentative voice, without quite realizing what they were saying and doing to the mind of man, and often frightened of facing the consequences of their own theories. There were exceptions, men far-sighted enough to realize that the twilight of the gods was at hand, and foolish enough to shout it from the tree-tops—like that *enfant terrible*, Giordano Bruno, the Bertrand Russell of his age, who was burned alive. But when Copernicus set the earth spinning, he did so with a timid and apologetic gesture; Kepler saved his faith by declaring that God was a mathematician by profession; Galileo's career was a life-long walk on a tightrope; Newton wrote a treatise on the locations of Paradise and Hell; and at the end of the long chain Professor

Townbee claimed that the Catholic Church, possessing the ultimate truth, was quasi exempt from the laws of history.*

Thus the new philosophy, with the exception of some of its more brutal propounders in the eighteenth and nineteenth centuries, made no frontal attack on religious beliefs; but it gradually undermined their foundations, on which all previous civilizations had been based. In the old days, man hoped to influence the superior powers which decided his fate through magic and prayer; now he could manipulate the mechanical components of his destiny, glands and humours, atoms and genes, and determine his own determinants. Prayer did not fall into disuse but its function, the influencing of fate, was taken over by the laboratories. Slowly but inevitably, divine providence was replaced by the drift of cosmic weather, ethical guidance by the ethical neutrality of science, humility before the supernatural by a feeling of arrogant, unlimited power.

Religion did not die, nor was it driven underground by the new philosophy—it was merely relegated to an airtight compartment of the mind and sealed off from contact with logical reasoning. The incompatibility between the two halves of the split mind was smoothed over by the churches' diplomatic appeasement of science, and by the believers' psychological resistance against admitting the split. Yet in spite of these mental shock-absorbers, religion gradually lost its power, became brittle and fragmentary; once the controlling force of daily life, it became a spiritual luxury. The "oceanic feeling" could no longer fill man's horizon; it was preserved in a neat reservoir whose level kept steadily falling through drainage, leaks and evaporation.

Life was so exciting during these hectic, unprecedented centuries, that man did not realize what was happening to him. The navel cord through which he received his spiritual nourishment was shrivelling up, but there were plastic substitutes for it, and various forms of artificial nourishment. For a while the words *Liberté, Egalité, Fraternité*, produced a new magic, a seemingly apt substitute for the Holy Trinity. There were breathtaking attempts to create a Humanist creed, and attempts to worship the Goddess of Reason; political movements and secular religions succeeded each other, exerting their immensely dynamic, but short-lived appeal. The vertiginous rise of the power-curve was accompanied by mass-upheavals, ideological crusades, and fanatical pursuits of Utopian mirages. Each of them promised a secular millennium, a Thousand Years' Reich of a Classless Society, born out of a revolutionary apocalypse. Yet all the time, throughout these toxic excesses and spurious illuminations, there was a muffled feeling of uneasiness, of growing frustration, of spiritual desiccation. The explanations of

* *Civilization on Trial*, London, 1948, pp. 238 ff. More recently Professor Toynbee seems to have changed his view on this point.

science became more and more formal, non-committal and meaningless as answers to man's eternal question. As his science grew more abstract, his art became more esoteric and his pleasures more chemical. In the end he was left with nothing but "an abstract heaven over a naked rock".

With the beginning of the twentieth century, signs appeared which seemed to indicate an impending turn of the tide. The descendants of Galileo and Newton found that they had been too optimistic in believing that the universe could be reduced to a mechanical model. The perfected measuring instruments signalled the presence of quantities and processes which not only eluded measurement, but by their very nature would always elude it. At nearly the same time, similar crises broke out in the other sciences: cosmology, biology, genetics, psychology. Physical determinism was shaken, rigid causality yielded to the elastic laws of probability; science had to admit that it can never predict, only guess, what will happen next. The living whole asserted its primacy over the measurable aspects of the parts; medicine had to lay increasing stress on the power of mind over matter. The most fashionable school of psychotherapy reverted to the Jamesian view that a transcendental faith was a biological necessity for man and that "the total absence of it leads to collapse"—the dark, feverish night of the soul.

Slowly, hesitatingly, the pendulum seemed to start swinging back. Man seemed to be getting ready for a new shift of focus, a new mutation. But so far this has failed to materialize; and all attempts at a spiritual revival within the framework of the established churches proved artificial and abortive. History may move in a spiral, but it never moves in circles, never returns to a previous point of departure. The physicist who has witnessed the collapse of his mechanical model of the universe has become a humbler and wiser man, but he cannot be expected to return to Aristotle's four elements and to Ptolemy's sky rotating on hollow crystal spheres; nor will the physician, who has learnt to accept his limitations as a healer, revert to a pre-Harveyan view of the body. Yet the established churches demand from all of us who shiver in the darkness precisely that kind of intellectual suicide and surrender of the critical faculties. To ask twentieth-century man to believe in a loving god who condemns half his children to eternal damnation without hope of an amnesty is really a bit thick. The reassuring statements of some modern theologians that Hell does exist but is empty, or that it merely means exclusion from grace without overheating, are hardly on a more adult level; and Mr. Greene's defence of the bodily ascent of the Virgin in the pages of *Life* magazine would embarrass even a saint. John Donne's "with a great, sober thirst my soule attends" was the statement of a perennial faith in the language of his time; "The Cocktail Party" and "The Living Room" is a parody of it.

Perhaps if Luther had been born after Copernicus and Newton, the gulf between faith and reason would be less disastrous. As it is, the established churches are venerable anachronisms. They are capable of giving a limited number of individuals a limited reassurance and a limited, sporadic uplift; but the Sunday driver does not answer the need for public transportation, and a Sunday faith is no answer to the peril threatening our race. We may postpone the atomic Sodom for a few years; but we cannot indefinitely prevent it.

Unfortunately, changes of this kind, the next mutation, the next jump ahead, are not only unpredictable but beyond the power of imagination. The causes which lead to these extraordinary transformations of the global mood—the springtide of Christianity, the ground-swell of the Renaissance, the hurricane age of Science—are equally obscure, even in retrospect. Hegel's dialectic, Spengler's cycles, Toynbee's challenge-and-response patterns are beautiful prophecies in reverse—and as doubtful as all prophecies are, though they merely predict the past. The more we realize the infinite complexity of historic causation, the Nostradamus-in-reverse character of all philosophies of History, the more helpless we feel in trying to predict the next mutation. We can point to certain analogies, abstract certain patterns from the Persian carpet, isolate certain trends and chart their curves; the rest is guesswork, hope and prayer.

My own guess and hope, which I have indicated before, is the spontaneous emergence of a new type of faith which satisfies the "great sober thirst" of man's spirit without asking him to split his brain into halves; which restores the navel cord through which he receives the saps of cosmic awareness without reducing him to mental infancy; which relegates reason to its proper humble place yet without contradicting it. It all sounds very vague and irreverent, partly because we can imagine the machines, but not the beliefs of the future, and partly because we have become so accustomed to religion occupying one half of the split mind, that the idea of restoring its unity appears blasphemous.

Is it really too much to ask and hope for a religion whose content is perennial but not archaic, which provides ethical guidance, teaches the lost art of contemplation, and restores contact with the supernatural without demanding reason to abdicate?

Clearly, the devout will regard this question as presumptuous and as betraying a lack of comprehension for the revealed, or symbolic, or mystic essence of faith, according to his notion of it. "After all," he will say with indignation, or contempt, or pity, "you cannot expect a religion made to measure like a suit to satisfy your specific requirements." The answer, I submit in all humility, is that the indignation of one's Catholic, Protestant, Jewish, and Moslem friends mutually cancel out; and secondly, that the objection is historically untrue. For every culture and every age did have its faith "cut to measure", and did re-state the perennial content of all religions on its own level and in its own language and symbols. It is neither an irreverent, nor an impossible hope that this will happen again in the future. But it *is* impossible to turn back to the language and symbols of a past epoch, of a mental climate which is no longer ours.

My starting-point was an imaginary chart, which showed a vertiginous rise of the power-curve coinciding with an equally unprecedented decline of the spiritual curve of living faith. It is this coincidence of the two curves which makes the present crisis so grave, which makes us feel that we are travelling at breakneck speed through the night with the throttle open at full and the steering broken down.

The decline of the spiritual curve remained for a long time hidden or obscured by more dramatic events; and its consequences have only become fully apparent in our day. When, a century and a half ago, the sailors at Spithead and the Nore started their famous mutiny, they took pains to assert their loyalty to the King, and to point out that they were merely rebelling against certain Admiralty rules. They continued to take the supreme authority for granted and regarded themselves as His Majesty's loyal rebels. In a similar manner the founders of new, and reformers of old religions always took the existence of God for granted; they all were the Lord's loyal heretics. This seems to hold true for any period of human culture as far back as the beam of history is able to penetrate into the dark, and as far up towards the present as the beginning of the eighteenth century. At this point, the unique break occurs. God is dethroned and although the incognisant masses are tardy in realizing the event, they feel the icy draught caused by that vacancy. Man enters upon a spiritual ice age; the established churches can no longer provide more than Eskimo huts where their shivering flock huddles together, while the camp-fires of rival ideologies draw the masses in wild stampedes across the ice. Yet even this desolate state of affairs is preferable to the threat of the medicine men to remedy the climate by turning the frozen waste into a blazing furnace.

The horror of it is that they have the power to do it. If only half the official statements about the new nuclear and bacteriological weapons are true, then the next few decades, or the next half century at the utmost, will decide whether *homo sapiens* will go the way of the dinosaur, or mutate towards a stabler future.

We shall either destroy ourselves or take off to the stars. Perhaps the conquest of interplanetary space will cause a Copernican revolution in reverse, the emergence of a new type of cosmic consciousness. Perhaps the creation of artificial moons and similar toys will prove such an absorbing diversion that the old passions are deflated and their causes forgotten. Perhaps some unexpected discovery in the field of extra-sensory perception will provide us with a new spiritual insight, a new basis for our metaphysical beliefs, a new intuition for our ultimate responsibilities.

All this is vague and wild speculation, yet less wild and fantastic than what will happen to man if the near-miracle fails to materialize and the giant mushrooms start sprouting into his sky and lungs. The trouble with all near-miracles, such as our ancestors' rising on their hind legs, or the rise of the new star over Bethlehem, or Galileo's climbing the tower of Pisa, is the unpredictability of their timing. Once we hoped for Utopia; now, in a chastened mood, we can at best hope for a reprieve; pray for time and play for time. For had the dinosaur learnt the art of prayer, the only sensible petition for him would have been to go down on his scaly knees and beg, "Lord, give me another chance."

MAY 1955

C. P. SNOW

Afterthoughts on the "Two Cultures" Controversy

WHEN I GAVE THE Rede Lecture last May [1959; published in *Encounter*, June and July 1959] I intended it as a call to action. Action, to begin with, of a humdrum kind, such as seeing English and American children get a reasonable education : then action on a major scale, but still immediately practicable, in helping to industrialize the East. I wasn't over-hopeful that I should produce any effect. I said in the lecture, "I don't know how we can do what we need to do, or whether we shall do anything at all." I still don't know. It is too early to say whether there will be any result on the plane of action. If there is no result, then the lecture is a failure. It is either a first stirring of activity, or it is nothing. Those who have understood most exactly what I was trying to do (Walter Allen, *New Statesman*, May 29th; Bertrand Russell, David Riesman, John Cockcroft, A. C. B. Lovell, all in *Encounter*, August; John Sharp, *Listener*, September 10th) understand that also. We may all sink back into combination-room cosiness. If we do, I shall have wasted everyone else's time, and my own.

Meanwhile, there have been some consequences which I confess I did not bargain for. Almost everyone I have met since May wishes to argue on the subject. I have found myself in the middle of a complex and proliferating debate. Comments come in from all over the place, not only from Europe and the U.S., but from the Soviet Union and the East. In October, in the United States, the arguments were going on round me. All this is no thanks to me. It means simply that, almost entirely by chance, a nerve has been plucked. This nerve exists not only in Western society, but, much more than I realized, in the Communist society too. When it is plucked, one gets a sense of the reserves of creative and moral energy latent in the world. But to release that energy needs, of course, much more than the plucking of a nerve. Until the energy is released, we shall not begin to solve the problem I tried to set out. At present, I repeat, we are all playing at it, and we must not let ourselves think that anything at all has been achieved.

216

The debate has, however, thrown up a good many points of interest. First, I think it is fair to say that the concept of "the two cultures" has been generally accepted. Accepted, that is, within the modest limits I defined in the lecture—"something a little more than a dashing metaphor, a good deal less than a cultural map". Almost no one has quarrelled with me about that. Professor T. B. L. Cottrell has told me that he would be happier if the term "cultures" was restricted to creative persons on both sides of the divide; in conversation at Harvard, Archibald MacLeish said something much the same. Julian Symons (*Encounter*, September) is, as far as I know, alone in believing that one ought not to speak of a scientific culture. Does this need establishing at the present point of time? I should have thought not. Culture, in the intellectual sense, means the development of the mind : does anyone really imagine that in Rutherford's Cambridge, Franck's Goettingen, Bohr's Copenhagen, Landau's Moscow, Cockcroft's Harwell, the fortunate inhabitants weren't individually and collectively developing theirs? Culture also means the development of the moral and æsthetic senses : does anyone imagine, after Hardy's *A Mathematician's Apology* and Bronowski's *Science and Human Values,* that these are not inherent in the pursuit of science itself? Culture is not necessarily tied to the past, though some parts of it may be : where do you think an artist of the High Renaissance, say Verrocchio or Mantegna, would be most at home—in our artistic culture, or in the Princeton Institute? Mr. Michael Ayrton (*Encounter*, August) has answered that question once for all.

Just as the concept of "the two cultures" has been accepted, so has the existence of a gulf between them. I said that this gulf, in its present gaping *Apology* and Brownski's *Science and Human Values*, that these are not been seriously challenged. Lord Russell gave, from his own experience, examples of nineteenth-century connection between the cultures. American scholars have reminded me of the links between literature and physics during the Enlightenment (Michael Polanyi made the same point, *Encounter*, September). The only apparent dissentient has been J. H. Plumb (*Encounter*, August), with a baffling piece of what American friends call "psychologizing". He remarked that people have always had different temperaments and different temperamental needs. That is true enough, but not surprising. He then said that William Shakespeare and William Perkins would have had as much difficulty understanding each other as Rutherford and Virginia Woolf. That is a curious red herring. No one but an ass expects that all people are going to understand each other at all levels. *Of course* people have different gifts, different needs, and will live different lives. The most one can hope for—and this is the bone of my case—is that, *on the level of intellect,* they should reach, in Comenius's term, the first stage of understanding. That is, they should be able to say "I see" across the gulf. In those terms, it is nonsense to suggest that Shakespeare and Perkins could not say "I see" to each other.

Perkins was not, as one might think from the context, an Elizabethan scientist. He was the most eloquent preacher of the 1590s in Cambridge, with a command of beautiful, forthright, Authorized Version prose; he was, as it were, the public relations officer for the Puritan wing of the Church of England and one of the spiritual fathers of Massachusetts Bay. How in the world can Plumb come to believe that he and Shakespeare would have found each other intellectually unintelligible? They would have had a similar school education. Perkins devoted most of his sermons—and splendid sermons they are—to the central tenets of Calvinist theology, Predestination and Justification by Grace. In Stratford, which was a Calvinist town, Shakespeare must have heard those arguments time and time again. And though Calvinist theology is pretty subtle, it isn't all that incomprehensible. The comparatively simple people to whom Perkins preached, one supposed, grasped some of it. Dr. Plumb and I can do so, three hundred and fifty years later : why ever shouldn't Shakespeare?

Plumb's second point, though it has some poetic force, doesn't seem to me much more precise or valid. It is that the gulf in the cultures has occurred because of the supersession of the "old possessing class". Some of the climate of the traditional culture has had that feel, I agree; but the trouble is, one gets the same gulf in societies where both the history and the contemporary structure are unlike ours. In the United States, for example, the gulf exists to an extent not very different from ours—some of my informants think it is about the same; Edmund Wilson thinks it is significantly less; but all agree that the gulf exists. What is more revealing, there is a good deal of evidence that it also exists in the Soviet Union.

Some of my Soviet friends have made no bones about it. I think I should have guessed it anyway, after studying the new curricula for Soviet high schools. These are part of the educational reforms carried out in Khrushchev's name. The policy of full-time high-school education for everyone up to seventeen-plus has been abandoned, and a large slice of the population are now taking courses from fifteen-plus, which are very like our craft and student apprenticeships, though with much more training in arts subjects. For the academically clever children, the school education continues to seventeen-plus, as before, with mathematics, experimental science, and arts subjects in *everyone's* course; but there are two differences. The proportion of time spent on arts subjects has been slightly increased : and now every—I repeat, everyone—not has to do some workshop training, if possible in a factory.

This is, of course, a conscious attempt to make sure that the entire intellectual class, whether they finish up as managers or writers or professors of archæology, know at first-hand something about the industrial life. It is also, one guesses, an attempt to keep common ground between the non-scientific and scientific cultures—and also between the pure and applied halves of the scientific culture, since, perhaps because of their rigorous mathematical training, Russian pure scientists are always liable to become more remote than ours. No one has any idea how this plan is going to work out, but I believe that in principle it is well-judged and wise. The fact that it is necessary, however, leads one to the suspicion that the division between the cultures is inherent in an advanced industrial society. The difference between the Russians and the West is that they are trying to minimize it, and we are not.

As soon as I mention advanced industrial society, or indeed society at all, I am likely to give pain. For a good many people whom I respect, this part of the lecture was the edge which worried them. Some of that I could not avoid. No one, certainly no one I respect, would wish me to make false compromises. But some I both could and should have avoided. When I read the sensitive and sympathetic comments of Mr. John Beer (*Cambridge Review*, November 7th), Mr. G. H. Bantock (*Listener*, September 17th), Mr. E. D. Mackerness (private communication), I wished I had made some qualifications. May I say here and now that I am sorry I didn't? I should have made it clear that, when I spoke of the illiberal influence of twentieth-century literature culture, I was thinking only of the major creative artists. As Lionel Trilling wrote in *The Liberal Imagination* :

> For it is in general true that the modern European literature to which we can have an active, reciprocal relationship, which is the right relationship to have, has been written by men who are indifferent to, or even hostile to, the traditional of democratic liberalism as we know it. Yeats and Eliot, Proust and Joyce, Lawrence and Gide—these men do not seem to confirm us in the social and political ideas which we hold.

I stick to that. In fact, when I take a crude quantitative test, and ask about the literary theses written last year at U.S. universities, I estimate that not one in ten of the modern writers studied—which means the modern writers influential upon the intelligent young—could, even in the wildest and most romantic use of the term, be considered in any conceivable sense liberal. That was what I intended when I made my categories. But let me say now what I should have said before, that many other writers, though they have not dominated literary sensibility so heavily, have been as concerned about man's social hopes as anyone could be; and that is at least as true, and perhaps more true, of other members of the literary culture, scholars, writers, and connoisseurs.

As a matter of fact, during this controversy, I have often thought that critics like Mr. Bantock have much more goodwill than I have. When they are affected by a writer of genius, they are affected totally : themselves wishing good to all men, they cannot credit that the writer of genius does not wish the same. This is a generous attitude, but it has its dangers. It leads to explaining away what ought not to be explained away. In the last extremity (not that Mr. Bantock would go so far) it leads to the Court Jester view of art—"poor old Ezra, poor old Wyndham Lewis, they don't really mean what they say". Myself, I am less charitable and more sceptical, and I have my own kind of unsinkable belief in art and its responsibilities. I can credit that these distinguished men mean what they say. I am sure that, to take them seriously, we are bound to do so. I can even credit that a much greater man, such as Dostoievsky, meant what he said; so it doesn't surprise me that Russian critics, from his own time to ours, have always had reserves about him, muffled here.

In the same way, I can credit what writers have had to say against the scientific-industrial revolution, and here I cannot compromise. In my view, they have shown a lack—understandable if you like, but in effect serious— of the extended imagination. They have been so aware of the existential horror that they haven't been able to stretch, either in time or space. At this existent moment, none of us has the imagination to grasp the simple brutal truth of Brecht's maxim, *"Erst kommt das Fressen, dann kommt die Moral."* Yet that, as I have tried to explain, obviously without much force, is the compelling truth for more than half our fellow human beings. Until we know it, we can't even begin to talk to them. We have grown too far away.

In that brutal sense, as I said before, industrialization is the only hope of the poor. Of course, industrialization brings with it losses in the quality of life : but they are not the losses which writers have denounced it for. In the lecture, I drew a careful distinction between the individual condition and the social condition. There is much in the individual condition which is irremediable. About the social condition I said, and continue to say, the exact opposite. By the social condition I mean the condition of each of us in society, our relations with others as we work, the nature of our practical lives, and I exclude from it the condition of man-alone and the deepest part of those personal relations which (though they are affected by society, as indeed is the solitary life) are nearest to individual experience.

Judged by those criteria I should have no doubt that the social condition in advanced industrial society is out of comparison better than any the human race has managed up to now. I mean by that, that the factory workers in, say, Schenectady or Stafford, are not only better-fed and longer-lived than any mass population in the history of the world; not only have they better education, and enormously more leisure; but also their personal relations in their working lives are less humiliating, freer from what Lawrence called the "assertive will" than in any less articulated society. The assertive will is necessary to us collectively. It is necessary to an artist (Proust, Joyce, Lawrence himself would have been submerged without it), but we all know that it is intolerable between man and man. Highly organized society is the only way we have yet found of diluting the assertive will. We do not understand this kind of society very well yet, but at least we are beginning to avoid the worst insults to men's dignity.

What have writers said about this? Mr. Bantock quotes Lawrence against me. I don't particularly relish this. Lawrence was a man of genius, and if I am going to match quotation with quotation, I shall have to show him at his least inviting. But the ground is not of my choosing. Mr. Bantock used the well-known passage in *Women in Love* about Gerald Crich:

> "He had a fight to fight with Matter, with the earth and the coal it enclosed. This was the sole idea, to turn upon the inanimate matter of the underground, and reduce it to his will. And for this fight with matter, one must have perfect instruments in perfect organization, a mechanism so subtle and harmonious in its workings that it represents the single mind of man, and by its relentless repetition of given movement, will accomplish a purpose irresistibly, inhumanly. It was this inhuman principle in the mechanism he wanted to construct that inspired Gerald with an almost religious exaltation."

One might observe that coal-mining fifty years ago was a most primitive industry. But that's by the way. Is this insight any more valuable than the one into Birkin, earlier in the same book?

> "But I [Birkin] abhor humanity, I wish I was swept away. It could go, and there would be no *absolute loss*, it every human being perished tomorrow. The reality would be untouched. Nay, it would be better. The real tree of life would then be rid of the most ghastly, heavy crop of Dead Sea fruit, the intolerable burden of myriad simulacra of people, an infinite weight of mortal lives."

Would it be so exaggerated to call that a "scream of horror"? If not, what is? And what about this, for another insight into the social condition?

It is a great mistake to abolish the death penalty. If I were a dictator, I should order the old one to be hanged at once. I should have judges with sensitive, living hearts; not abstract intellectuals. And because the instinctive heart recognized a man as evil, I would have that man destroyed. Quickly. Because good, warm life is now in danger. (*Sea and Sardinia*.)

There are lessons to be drawn from those quotations, as we try to make the social condition better. The chief one is, of course, that we all feel sometimes as Lawrence felt on those occasions—and, if human life is to be endurable at all, or indeed to survive, we have to set up checks against those feelings, checks imposed against the Rousseauian optimism—which believes that, if each man acts according to his feelings, we shall have a good world. No one ever acted more truly according to his "instinctive heart" than Adolf Hitler, and we very nearly didn't have a world at all.

There is, however, deep conviction behind Mr. Bantock's and Mr. Beer's criticism of the industrial society. They speak often as though there had been a much better society, somewhere, or at some time. Mr. Bantock talks of the loss of "sensuous awareness" and of "the old intuitive life"; Mr. Beer, in a review from which I learned a lot, of the loss of "individual differences".

The point about sensuous awareness—which of course Mr. Bantock attributes to Lawrence, who had as much of the quality as any man who ever lived—is a difficult one. It has roused the irritation of Professor C. H. Waddington, who is a connoisseur of the graphic arts as well as an eminent geneticist. "Sensuous awareness!" he says. "What makes writers think they are competent to talk about this? They've heard about the necessity of it from Lawrence. But how dare they talk about it to experimental scientists, who *live* just by that gift itself?" Professor Waddington might have added that Donald Bradman, Denis Compton, thousands of games players, pilots, and so on, live by sensuous awareness too; and there is a faintly Max Beerbohm-like flavour about the picture of any literary intellectual lecturing them. But Mr. Bantock is not, I am sure, using "sensuous awareness" in the straightforward physical sense. Any more, I am also sure, than he and Mr. Beer are implying historicity when they talk about "loss" of it, or "loss" of individuality. If they were implying genuine historicity, then one would be compelled to say—"Look! We now know a good deal about pre-industrial societies. Plenty of them are still existing on earth. Most of the evidence suggests that people in such societies are less individualized, not more, so far as those words mean anything at all. The distribution of sensuous gifts is very much scattered. There is no evidence that it is either impaired or improved by advanced society. Tell us. In what place, or in what time, did men have these benefits which we have lost? Where and when was this Eden?''

There is one real loss, in the historic sense. It is what I believe Mr. Bantock is hinting at with the phrase "the old intuitive life", or Mr. Beer with his "reserves of health which depend on the instincts or emotions", though it is not precisely either. It is the loss of significance in commonplace acts. Thus, in some pre-industrial societies, not in all, if you walk, say, a hundred yards north at sunset, this act is significant. It means something to the other people in the society. It is, like a whole set of your other commonplace acts, not private but part of the social condition. This we have lost. And the loss, which begins to occur at the earliest stages of industrialization, is linked perversely not with a decrease of individuality but an increase of it. The loss of significance, together with the increase of individuality, means that men have lost a support. The industrial workers of Schenectady are probably more individual than members of any pre-industrial community : they have far more free choices; but the binding forces of sacred custom have left them, and they are more alone.

This loss we may eventually replace, but I shouldn't be too hopeful about that. There were probably, as I mentioned in a footnote to the lecture, losses as grave in the other great change in social evolution, when men changed from hunting and food-gathering to agriculture. I don't think it is seriously arguable, at least by anyone with reverence for the human life, that both prices were not worth paying. But I recognize that a sense of our more recent loss may hang over much of the artistic feeling of the age, and may partially explain—only partially and perhaps only indirectly—its looking-backward to the primitive. In a comment which I found most moving, Mr. Michael Ayrton (*Encounter*, August) talked of the primitiveness and mindlessness of the twentieth-century graphic arts. What can a clever man do, he said in effect, when before practising them, his first requirement is to take off his head? In a couple of articles which, though only tangentially related to the original debate, have an important bearing upon it, Professor Frank Kermode (*Spectator*, September 11th; *Encounter*, November) has examined the roots of myth-seeking, primitivism, anti-intellectualism in contemporary literature. Professor Kermode admires the products of this kind of literature rather more than I do; but (I hope I am not misrepresenting him) he would be as concerned as I should if, in any advanced society, this was the only way which literature could go.

Well, it may be so. The forces driving the cultures apart are very strong. If they are too strong, then art and primitivism will become one and the same thing. But if that happens, other and even graver consequences will happen too. There seem to me good chances that we (and here I mean the whole intellectual world, in Communist countries as well as the West) shall be able to prevent them.

It is worth remembering that in the intellectual climate, particularly in the artistic climate, the present moment always seems more durable than it is. Professor Kermode, Mr. Beer, Mr. Bantock, Mr. Ayrton, and all of us are living, more totally immersed than we realize, in the climate of the 1950s. Let us notice that in 1882, Ibsen, on January 3rd, wrote to George Brandes : "*I hold that that man is in the right who is most closely in league with the future.*"

That would have been the view of Tolstoy, Chekov, even Dostoievsky, nearly all the great nineteenth-century masters. It may again be the view of Russian, American, English masters at the end of the twentieth century. Whether that happens or not, is not inevitable. That may be the direction of Time's Arrow. Alternatively, the sliding-out of art into primitivism may be. It depends upon how much we can bind the cultures together now.

That is as much as I want to add to the theoretical discussion at this minute. The danger of this kind of debate is that one falls into the eristic temptation. Up to now, nearly all those who differ from me have set a good example, which I am trying to follow.

I haven't so much as mentioned a number of contributions of great interest. Michael Polanyi's (*Encounter*, September) I can't begin to touch within the scope of this article. He is arguing, as it were, at right-angles to my original line. I have had a great, though somewhat mystified, regard for him, as he knows, for years : but I feel about his attack on scientific rationalism as I feel about Arthur Koestler's in *The Sleepwalkers*, that there is no answer in intellectual or moral terms, but only in religious. And one cannot *invent* a religion. People secure in their religion, like some of my Benedictine friends, Dom Illtyd Trethowan, Dom Mark Pontifex, Dom Sebastian Moore, seem to find my argument acceptable in its own order.

Final round-up. *1.* There are three verbal mistakes in the lecture, which will be put right. *2.* Dr. Charles Singer has ingeniously suggested that the differences between the English patent law and the patent law of the German States account for the German technical invasion of England in the mid-nineteenth century. *3.* Mr. W. J. Walls suggests that lawyers, even more than literary intellectuals, best represent the anti-scientific pole. *4.* Sir Christopher Cox has protested about the use of "scientific revolution" in at least three different contexts, e.g. A. R. Hall uses it for the period 1500–1700, and I of the controlled use of science, exemplified by the date of sub-atomic particles in industry, which we might date from 1906. Cox is quite right. Perhaps we ought to have a terminological conference. I am ready to admit that my phrase ought to be "Scientific-Revolution-in-Industry", which is rather a mouthful.

Last of all, I want to finish as I began. The test of all this is in action.

FEBRUARY 1960

Part III

ARTS & LETTERS

ROBERT WARSHOW

The Gentleman with a Gun

They that have power to hurt and will do none,
That do not do the thing they most do show,
Who, moving others, are themselves as stone,
Unmoved, cold and to temptation slow;
They rightly do inherit heaven's graces,
And husband nature's riches from expense;
They are the lords and owners of their faces,
Others but stewards of their excellence.

THE TWO MOST successful creations of American movies are the gangster and the Westerner : men with guns. Guns as phsical objects, and the postures associated with their use, form the visual and emotional centre of both types of films. I suppose this reflects the importance of guns in the fantasy life of Americans; but that is a less illuminating point than it appears to be.

The gangster movie, which no longer exists in its "classical" form, is a story of enterprise and success ending in precipitate failure. Success is conceived as an increasing power to work injury, it belongs to the city, and it is, of course, a form of evil (though the gangster's death, presented usually as "punishment", is perceived simply as defeat). The peculiarity of the gangster is his unceasing nervous activity. The exact nature of his enterprises may remain vague, but his commitment to enterprise is always clear, and all the more clear because he operates outside the field of utility. He is without culture, without manners, without leisure, or at any rate his leisure is likely to be spent in debauchery so compulsively aggressive as to seem only another aspect of his "work". But he is graceful, moving like a dancer among the crowded dangers of the city.

The gangster is lonely and melancholy, and can give the impression of a profound worldly wisdom. He is the "No" to that great American "Yes" which is stamped so big over the official culture and yet has so little to do with the way we Americans really feel about our lives. But the gangster's loneliness and melancholy are not "authentic"; like everything else that belongs to him, they are not honestly come by : he is lonely and melancholy not because life ultimately demands such feelings but because he has put himself in a position where everybody wants to kill him, and eventually somebody will. He is wide open and defenceless, incomplete because unable to accept any limits or come to terms with his own nature, fearful, loveless. And the story of his career is a nightmare inversion of the values of ambition and opportunity. From the window of Scarface's bullet-proof apartment can be seen an electric sign proclaiming : "The World is Yours", and, if I remember rightly, this sign is the last thing we see after Scarface lies dead in the street. In the end it is the gangster's weakness as much as his power and freedom that appeals to us; the world is not ours, but it is not his either, and in his death he "pays" for our fantasies, releasing us momentarily both from the concept of success, which he denies by caricaturing it, and from the need to succeed, which he shows to be dangerous.

The Western hero, by contrast, is a figure of repose. He resembles the gangster in being lonely and to some degree melancholy. But his melancholy comes from the "simple" recognition that life is unavoidably serious, not from the disproportions of his own temperament. And his loneliness is organic, not imposed on him by his situation but belonging to him intimately and testifying to his completeness. The gangster must reject others violently or draw them violently to him. The Westerner is not thus compelled to seek love; he is prepared to accept it, perhaps, but he never asks of it more than it can give, and we see him constantly in situations where love is at best an irrelevance. If there is a woman he loves, she is usually unable to understand his motives; she is against killing and being killed, and he finds it impossible to explain to her that there is no point in being "against" these things : they belong to his world. Very often this woman is from the East and her failure to understand represents a clash of cultures. In the American mind, refinement, virtue, civilization, Christianity itself, are seen as feminine, and therefore women are often portrayed as possessing some kind of deeper wisdom, while the men, for all their apparent self-assurance, are fundamentally childish. But the West, lacking the graces of civilization, is the place "where men are men"; in Western movies, men have the deeper wisdom and the women are children. Those women in the Western movies who share the hero's understanding of life are prostitutes (or, as they are usually presented, bar-room entertainers)—women, that is, who have come to understand in the most practical way how love can be an irrelevance, and are therefore "fallen" women.

The Westerner is *par excellence* a man of leisure. Even when he wears the badge of a marshal or, more rarely, owns a ranch, he appears to be unemployed. We see him standing at a bar, or playing poker—a game which expresses perfectly his talent for remaining relaxed in the midst of tension —or perhaps camping out on the plains on some extraordinary errand. If he does own a ranch, it is in the background; we are not actually aware that he owns anything except his horse, his guns, and the one worn suit of clothing which is likely to remain unchanged all through the movie. It comes as a surprise to see him take money from his pocket or an extra shirt from his saddle-bags. Yet it never occurs to us that he is a poor man; there is no poverty in Western movies, and really no wealth either: those great cattle domains and shipments of gold which figure so largely in the plots are moral and not material quantities, not the objects of contention but only its occasion. Possessions too are irrelevant.

Employment of some kind—usually unproductive—is always open to the Westerner, but when he accepts it, it is not because he needs to make a living, much less from any idea of "getting ahead". Where could he want to "get ahead" to? By the time we see him, he is already "there": he can ride a horse faultlessly, keep his countenance in the face of death, and draw his gun a little faster and shoot it a little straighter than anyone he is likely to meet. These are sharply defined acquirements, giving to the figure of the Westerner an apparent moral clarity which corresponds to the clarity of his physical image against his bare landscape; initially, at any rate, the Western movie presents itself as being without mystery, its whole "universe" comprehended in what we see on the screen.

Much of this apparent simplicity arises directly from those "cinematic" elements which have long been understood to give the Western theme its special appropriateness for the movies: the wide expanses of bare land, the free movement of men on horses. As guns constitute the visible moral centre of the Western movie, suggesting continually the possibility of violence, so land and horses represent the movie's material basis, its sphere of action. But the land and the horses have also a moral significance: the physical freedom they represent belongs to the moral "openness" of the West—corresponding to the fact that guns are carried where they can be seen. (And, as we shall see, the character of land and horses changes as the Western film becomes more complex.)

The gangster's world is less open and his arts not so easily identifiable as the Westerner's. Perhaps he too can keep his countenance, but the mask he wears is really no mask: its purpose is precisely to make evident the fact that he desperately wants to "get ahead" and will stop at nothing. "Do it first," says Scarface, expounding his mode of operation, "and keep on doing it!" With the Westerner, it is a crucial point of honour not to "do it first"; his gun remains in its holster until the moment of combat. There is no suggestion, however, that he draws the gun reluctantly. The Westerner could not fulfil himself if the moment did not finally come when he can shoot his enemy down. But because that moment is so thoroughly the expression of his being, it must be kept pure. He will not violate the accepted forms of combat though by doing so he could save a city. And he can wait. "When you call me that—smile!"—the villain smiles weakly, soon he is laughing with horrible joviality, and the crisis is past. But it is allowed to pass because it must come again : sooner or later Trampas will "make his play", and the Virginian will be ready for him.

What does the Westerner fight for? We know he is on the side of justice and order, and, of course, it can be said he fights for these things. But such broad aims never correspond exactly to his real motives; they only offer him his opportunity. The Westerner himself, when an explanation is asked of him (usually by a woman), is likely to say that he does what he "has to do". If justice and order did not continually demand his protection, he would be without a calling. Indeed, we come upon him often in just that situation, as the reign of law settles over the West and he is forced to understand that his day is over; those are the pictures which end with his death or with his departure for some more remote frontier. What he defends, at bottom, is the purity of his own image—in fact his honour. He fights not for advantage and not for the right, but to state what he is, and he must live in a world which permits that statement. The Westerner is the last gentleman, and the movies which over and over again tell his story are probably the last art form in which the concept of honour retains its strength.

Of course, I do not mean to say that ideas of virtue and justice and courage have gone out of culture. Honour is more than these things : it is a style, concerned with harmonious appearances as much as with desirable consequences, and tending therefore towards the denial of life in favour of art. "Who hath it? he that died o' Wednesday." On the whole, a world that leans to Falstaff's view is a more civilized and even, finally, a more graceful world. It is just the march of civilization that forces the Westerner to move on; and if we actually had to confront the question it might turn out that the woman who refuses to understand him is right as often as she is wrong. But we do not confront the question. Where the Westerner lives it is always about 1870—not the real 1870, either, or the real West—and he is killed or goes away when his position becomes problematical. The fact that he continues to hold our attention is evidence enough that, in his proper frame, he presents an image of personal nobility that is still real for us.

Clearly this image easily becomes ridiculous : we need only look at William S. Hart or Tom Mix who, in the wooden absoluteness of their virtue, represented little that an adult could take seriously. Some film enthusiasts claim to find in the early unsophisticated Westerns a "cinematic purity" that has since been lost; this idea is as valid, and finally as misleading, as T. S. Eliot's statement that *Everyman* is the only play in English that stays within the limitations of art. The truth is that the Westerner comes into the field of serious art only when his moral code, without ceasing to be compelling, is seen also to be imperfect. The Westerner at his best exhibits a moral ambiguity which darkens his image and saves him from absurdity; this ambiguity arises from the fact that, whatever his justifications, he is a killer of men.

In *The Virginian*, which is an archetypal Western movie as *Scarface* or *Little Cæsar* are archetypal gangster movies, there is a lynching in which the hero (Gary Cooper), as leader of a posse, must supervise the hanging of his best friend for stealing cattle. He is thus in a tragic dilemma where one moral absolute conflicts with another and the choice of either must leave a moral stain. If he had chosen to save his friend, he would have violated the image of himself that he had made essential to his existence, and the movie would have had to end with his death, for only by his death could the image have been restored. Having chosen instead to sacrifice his friend to the higher demands of the "code"—the only choice worthy of him, as even the friend understands—he is none the less stained by the killing, but what is needed now to set accounts straight is not his death but the death of the villain Trampas, the leader of the cattle thieves, who had escaped the posse and abandoned the Virginian's friend to his fate. Here the woman intervenes: Why must there be *more* killing? What good will it be if Trampas should kill him? But the Virginian does once more what he "has to do", and in avenging his friend's death wipes out the stain on his own honour. Yet his victory cannot be complete: no death can be paid for and no stain truly wiped out; the movie is still a tragedy, for though the hero escapes with his life, he has been forced to confront the ultimate limits of his moral conceptions.

This mature sense of limitation and unavoidable guilt is what gives the Westerner a "right" to his melancholy. It is true that the gangster's story is also a tragedy—in certain formal ways more clearly a tragedy than the Westerner's—but it is a romantic tragedy, based on a hero whose defeat springs with almost mechanical inevitability from the outrageous presumption of his demands. The Westerner is a more classical figure, self-contained and limited to begin with, seeking not to extend his dominion but only to assert his personal value, and his tragedy lies in the fact that even this circumscribed demand cannot be fully realized. Since the Westerner is not a murderer but (most of the time) a man of virtue, and since he is always prepared for defeat, his story need not end with his death (and usually does not); but what we finally respond to is not his victory but his defeat.

Up to a point it is plain that the deeper seriousness of the good Western films comes from the introduction of a realism, both physical and psychological, that was missing with Tom Mix and William S. Hart. As lines of age have come into Gary Cooper's face since the time of *The Virginian* so the outlines of the Western movie in general have become less smooth, its background more drab. The sun still beats upon the town, but the camera is likely now to take advantage of this illumination to seek out more closely the shabbiness of buildings and furniture, the loose, worn hang of clothing, the wrinkles and dirt of the faces. Once it has been discovered that the true theme of the Western movie is not the freedom and expansiveness of frontier life, but its limitations, its material bareness, the pressures of obligation, then even the landscape itself ceases to be quite the arena of free movement it once was but becomes instead a great empty waste, cutting down more often than it exaggerates the stature of the horseman who rides across it; we are more likely now to see the Westerner struggling against the obstacles of the physical world than carelessly surmounting them. Even the horses, no longer the "friends" of man or the inspired chargers of knight-errantry, have lost much of the moral significance that once seemed to belong to them in their careering across the screen. It seems to me the horses grow tired and stumble more often than they did, and that we see them less frequently at the gallop.

In *The Gunfighter*, a remarkable film of a couple of years ago, the landscape has virtually disappeared. Most of the action takes place indoors, in a cheerless saloon where a tired "bad man" (Gregory Peck) contemplates the waste of his life, to be senselessly killed at the end by a vicious youngster setting off on the same futile path. The movie is done in cold, quiet tones of grey, and every object in it is given an air of uncompromising authenticity, suggesting those dim photographs of the nineteenth-century West in which Wyatt Earp, say, turns out to be a blank, untidy figure posing awkwardly before some uninteresting building. This "authenticity", to be sure, is only æsthetic; the chief fact about nineteenth-century photographs, to my eyes at any rate, is how stonily they refuse to yield up the truth. But that limitation is just what is needed: by preserving some hint of the rigidity of archaic photography (only in tone and décor, never in composition), *The Gunfighter* can permit us to feel that we are looking at a more "real" West than the one the movies have accustomed us to—harder, duller, less "romantic"—and yet without forcing us outside the boundaries which give the Western movie its validity.

We come upon the hero of *The Gunfighter* at the end of a career in which he has never upheld justice and order, and has been at times, apparently, an actual criminal; in this case it is clear that the hero has been wrong and the woman who has rejected his way of life has been right. He is thus without any of the larger justifications, and knows himself a ruined man. Indeed, if we were once allowed to see him in the days of his "success", he might become a figure like the gangster, for his career has been aggressively "anti-social" and the practical problem he faces is the gangster's problem : there will always be somebody trying to kill him. Yet it is obviously absurd to speak of him as "anti-social", not only because we do not see him acting as a criminal but, more fundamentally, because we do not see his milieu as a society. Of course it has its "social problems" and a kind of static history : civilization is always just at the point of driving out the old freedom; there are women and children to represent the possibility of a settled life; and there is the marshal, a bad man turned good, determined to keep at least his area of jurisdiction at peace. But these elements are not, in fact, a part of the film's "realism", even though they come out of the real history of the West; they belong to the conventions of the form, to that accepted framework which makes the film possible in the first place. The true "civilization" of the Western movie is always embodied in an individual, good or bad is more a matter of personal bearing than of social consequences, and the conflict of good and bad is a duel between two men. Deeply troubled and obviously doomed, the gunfighter is the Western hero still, perhaps all the more because his value must express itself entirely in his own being—in his presence, the way he holds our eyes—and in contradiction to the facts. No matter what he has done, he *looks* right, and he remains invulnerable because, without acknowledging anyone else's right to judge him, he has judged his own failure and has already assimilated it, understanding that he can do nothing but play out the drama of the gunfight again and again until the time comes when it will be he who gets killed. What "redeems" him is that he no longer believes in this drama and nevertheless will continue to play his rôle perfectly : the pattern is all.

The proper function of realism in the Western movie can only be to deepen the lines of that pattern. It is an art form for connoisseurs, where the spectator derives his pleasure from the appreciation of minor variations within the working out of a pre-established order. If the hero can be shown to be troubled, complex, fallible, even eccentric, or the villain given some psychological taint or, better, some evocative physical mannerism, to shade the colours of his villainy, that is all to the good. Indeed, that kind of variation is absolutely necessary to keep the type from becoming sterile; we do not want to see the same movie over and over again, only the same form. But when the impulse towards realism is extended into a "re-interpretation" of the West as a developed society, drawing our eyes away from the hero, if only to the extent of showing him as the one dominant figure in a complex social order, then the pattern is broken and the West itself begins to be uninteresting. If the "social problems" of the frontier are to be the movie's chief concern, there is no longer any point in re-examining these problems twenty times a year; they have been solved, and the people for whom they once were real are dead. Moreover, the hero himself, still the film's central figure, now tends to become its one unassimilable element, since he is the most archetypal and "unreal".

The most striking example of the confusion created by a too conscientious "social" realism is in the celebrated *High Noon*. Here we find Gary Cooper, still the upholder of order that he was in *The Virginian* but twenty-four years older, stooped, slower moving, awkward, his face lined, the flesh sagging, a less beautiful and weaker figure, but with the suggestion of greater depth that belongs almost automatically to age. Like the hero of *The Gunfighter*, he no longer has to assert his character and is no longer interested in the drama of combat; it is hard to imagine that he might once have been so youthful as to say, "When you call me that—smile!" In fact, when we come upon him, he is hanging up his guns and his marshal's badge in order to begin a new, peaceful life with his bride, who is a Quaker. But then the news comes that a man he had sent to prison has been pardoned and will get to town on the noon train; three friends of this man have come to wait for him at the station, and when the freed convict arrives the four of them will come to kill the marshal. He is thus trapped; the bride will object, the hero himself will waver much more than he would have done twenty-four years ago, but in the end he will play out the drama because it is what he "has to do". All this belongs to the established form (there is even the "fallen woman" who understands the marshal's position as his wife does not). Leaving aside the crudity of building up suspense by means of the clock, the actual Western drama of *High Noon* is well handled and forms a good companion-piece to *The Virginian*, showing in both conception and technique the ways in which the Western movie has naturally developed.

But there is a second drama intertwined with the first. As the marshal sets out to find deputies to help him deal with four gunmen, we are taken through the various social strata of the town, each group in turn refusing its assistance out of cowardice, malice, irresponsibility, or venality. With this we are in the field of "social drama"—of a very low order, incidentally, altogether unconvincing and displaying a vulgar anti-populism that has marred some other movies of Stanley Kramer's. But the falsity of the "social drama" is less important than the fact that it does not belong in the movie to begin with. The technical problem was to make it necessary for the marshal to face his enemies alone; to explain *why* the other towns-people are not at his side is to raise a question which does not exist in the proper framework of the Western movie, where the hero is "naturally" alone. In addition, though the hero of *High Noon* proves himself a better man than all around him, the actual effect of this contrast is to lessen his stature: he becomes only a rejected man of virtue. In our final glimpse of him, as he rides away through the town where he has spent most of his life without really imposing himself on it, he is a pathetic rather than a tragic figure. And his departure has another meaning as well; the "social drama" has no place for him.

But there is also a different way of violating the Western form. This is to yield entirely to its static quality as legend and to the "cinematic" temptations of its landscape, the horses, the quiet men. John Ford's famous *Stagecoach* (1938) had much of this unhappy preoccupation with style, and the same director's *My Darling Clementine* (1946), a soft and beautiful movie about Wyatt Earp, goes further along the same path. The highest expression of this æstheticizing tendency, however, is in George Stevens's *Shane*, where the legend of the West is virtually reduced to its essentials and then fixed in the dreamy clarity of a fairy tale. The mere physical progress of the film is so deliberately graceful that everything seems to be happening at the bottom of a clear lake. The hero (Alan Ladd) is hardly a man at all, but something like the Spirit of the West, beautiful in fringed buckskins, who emerges mysteriously from the limitless plain, breathing sweetness and a melancholy which is no longer simply the Westerner's natural response to experience but has taken on spirituality. The choice of Alan Ladd to play the leading rôle is alone an indication of this film's tendency. Actors like Gary Cooper or Gregory Peck are in themselves, as material objects, "realistic", seeming to bear in their bodies and their faces mortality, limitation, the knowledge of good and evil. Ladd is a more "æsthetic" object, with some of the "universality" of a piece of sculpture; his special quality is in his physical smoothness and serenity, unworldly and yet not innocent, but suggesting that no experience can really touch him. Stevens has tried to freeze the Western myth once and for all in the immobility of Alan Ladd's countenance. If *Shane* were "right", and fully successful, it might be possible to say there was no point in making any more Western movies; once the hero is apotheosized, variation and development are closed off.

Shane is not "right", but it is still true that the possibilities of fruitful variation in the Western movie are limited. The form can keep its freshness through endless repetitions only because of the special character of the film medium, where the physical difference between one object and another—above all, between one actor and another—is of such enormous importance, serving the function that is served by the variety of language in the perpetuation of literary types. In this sense, the "vocabulary" of films is much larger than that of literature and falls more readily into pleasing and significant arrangements. (That may explain why the middle levels of excellence are more easily reached in the movies than in literary forms, and perhaps also why the status of the movies as art is constantly being called into question.) But the advantage of this almost automatic particularity belongs to all films alike. Why does the Western movie especially have such a hold on our imagination?

Chiefly, I think, because it offers a serious orientation to the problem of violence such as can be found almost nowhere else in our culture. One of the well-known peculiarities of modern civilized opinion is its refusal to acknowledge the value of violence. This refusal is a virtue, but like many virtues it involves a certain wilful blindness and it encourages hypocrisy. We train ourselves to be shocked or bored by cultural images of violence, and our very concept of heroism tends to be a passive one : we are less drawn to the brave young men who kill large numbers of our enemies than to the heroic prisoners who endure torture without capitulating. In art, though we may still be able to understand and participate in the values of the *Iliad*, a modern writer like Ernest Hemingway we find somewhat embarrassing : there is no doubt that he stirs us, but we cannot help recognizing also that he is a little childish. And in the criticism of popular culture, the presence of images of violence is often assumed to be in itself a sufficient ground for condemnation.

These attitudes, however, have not reduced the element of violence in our culture but, if anything, have helped to free it from moral control by letting it take on the aura of "emancipation". The celebration of acts of violence is left more and more to the irresponsible : on the higher cultural levels to writers like Céline, and lower down to Mickey Spillane or Horace McCoy, or to the comic books, television, and the movies. The gangster movie with its numerous variations, belongs to this cultural "underground" which sets forth the attractions of violence in the face of all our higher social attitudes. It is a more "modern" genre than the Western movie, perhaps even more profound, because it confronts industrial society on its own ground—the city—and because, like much of our advanced art, it gains its effects by a gross insistence on its own narrow logic. But it is antisocial, resting on fantasies of irresponsible freedom. If we are brought finally to acquiesce in the denial of these fantasies, it is only because they have been shown to be dangerous, not because they have given way to a higher vision of behaviour.

In war movies, to be sure, it is possible to present the uses of violence within a framework of responsibility. But there is the disadvantage that modern war is a co-operative enterprise in which violence is largely impersonal and heroism belongs to the group more than to the individual. The hero of a war movie is most often simply a leader, and his superiority is likely to be expressed in a denial of the heroic; you are not supposed to be brave, you are supposed to get the job done and stay alive (this too, of course, is a kind of heroic posture, but a new—and "practical"—one). At its best, the war movie may represent a more civilized point of view than the Western, and if it were not continually marred by ideological sentimentality we might hope to find it developing into a higher form of drama. But it cannot supply the values we seek in the Western.

These values are in the image of a single man who wears a gun on his thigh. The gun tells us that he lives in a world of violence, and even that he "believes in violence". But the drama is one of self-restraint: the moment of violence must come in its own time and according to its special laws, or else it is valueless. There is little cruelty in Western movies, and little sentimentality; our eyes are not focused on the sufferings of the defeated but on the deportment of the hero. Really, it is not violence at all which is the "point" of the Western movie, but a certain image of man, a style, which expresses itself most clearly in violence. Watch a child with his toy guns and you will see: what most interests him is not (as we so much fear) the fantasy of hurting others, but to work out how a man might look when he shoots or is shot. A hero is one who looks like a hero.

Whatever the limitations of such an idea in experience, it has always been valid in art, and has a special validity in an art like the movies, where appearances are everything. The Western hero is necessarily an archaic figure; we do not really believe in him and would not have him step out of his rigidly conventionalized background. But his archaicism does not take away from his power; on the contrary, it adds to it by keeping him just a little beyond the reach both of commonsense and of absolutized emotion, the two usual impulses of our art. And he has, after all, his own kind of relevance. He is there to remind us of the possibility of style in an age which has put on itself the burden of pretending that style has no meaning, and, in the midst of our anxieties over the problem of violence, to suggest that even in killing or being killed we are not freed from the necessity of establishing satisfactory modes of behaviour. Above all, the movies in which the Westerner plays out his rôle preserve for us the pleasures of a complete and self-contained drama—and one which still effortlessly crosses the internal boundaries which divide our culture—in a time when other more consciously serious art forms are increasingly complex, uncertain, and ill-defined.

MARCH 1954

STEPHEN SPENDER

European Notebook

PRISONERS

Tosca, Aïda, Fidelio—how many operas are about prisoners. The prisoner is above all a nineteenth-century concept of the early Romantic Movement, which began when the ideals of nationalism were fused with those of the French Revolution. Thus Byron's *Prisoner of Chillon* echoes in many European poems. The prisoner becomes the symbol of enslaved nationalism inspired by social justice and burning with hope and the sense of wrongs. The prisoner, being entirely involved in the public ideal, is purged of personal wrong-doing. He is not tragic, because he lives in a tragedy for which History has promised a happy ending. One might even say that the Prisoner is a tragic hero in reverse, living in a tragedy which begins with entombment and will end with the opening up of tombs. In *Fidelio*, all the prisoners are set free in the third act.

When the prisoner has passed the test which proves that, although virile and capable of manly love, his private life is no blot on his symbolic one, then he becomes in secret truth not the prisoner at all but the hidden enclosed judge of the rest of society. It is assumed that, when released, he will invent a society in which there are no prisoners like him. The prisoners will have become the just rulers.

Thus an argument of moral force in politics is that which attempts to show that the "other side" has prisoners—i.e. has locked up the true judges. Since, in fact, during this century, there have been a great many prisoners, governments have gone to extraordinary lengths in order to effect the moral condemnation of these. Techniques which are even more secret than those for making atomic weapons have been evolved to make prisoners condemn themselves out of their own mouths. The point is not so much to incriminate the prisoner (this is perhaps impossible) as to show that in the modern world innocence has no force. The confession does not prove that the Prisoner is guilty, but that he can, in all and any circumstances, be made to confess. He is made to condone the system which belies his truth. Instead of proving to us that we can identify ourselves with his heroic truth, he shows that there is no heroic truth which cannot be annihilated

240

by a lie. If the concept of the prisoner who is free in his soul and who condemns his judges is destroyed, then the idea of freedom is also destroyed and *there is no escape for those outside prison*.

When gaolers are condemned there is always a phase of hope. No doubt another gaoler could take the place of a Beria or a Perón; but meanwhile all the prisoners whom he condemned out of their own mouths are morally acquitted. All the same, a grave doubt still exists in this century as to whether the man in the darkest dungeon is free.

NOVEMBER 1955

POST-WAR GERMANIES

After the First World War, Germany was spiritually and economically wasted, but not physically a ruin. The result : a desire to invent new forms.

After this war, the cities lay in ruins. The result : desire for restoration, much as when someone loses all his teeth he would like a false set the replica of those he lost. Hamburg, for instance, I saw in 1929, then a ruin in 1945, and now in 1955 as like what it was in 1929 as the jack of a jack-in-the-box.

Western Germany today is the glittering promenade : the Kurfürstendamm shining with show windows past which people walk up and down all day and most of the night, looking from one another to brand-new goods displayed, and thinking : "We have got all this back, better and brighter than before." Kiel has two great, lit promenades, with all traffic shut out, laid down like tracks of Success driving through the middle of the town.

These two Germanies of the twenties and fifties are laboratory demonstrations of the effects of history. In 1920, the desire for imaginative, individual self-expression to fill the void : today, simply for filling the gap of loss.

In East Berlin one sees another demonstration : the Soviet Embassy and the Stalinallee. The Soviet Embassy is of that phase of recent Russian history which so strangely recalls Queen Victoria. Put it down in Exhibition Road, it would pass unnoticed among the museums, the colleges, and the technical institutes.

The Stalinallee, without being "modern architecture", is formidably of this time. Built on either side of an avenue so wide that it depresses like a parade ground, the two masses of tenements, offices, shops, deploying at curves, halting at cross roads, and then continuing in exactly the same formation beyond them, suggest an army—each block a company or division under the eyes of a frowning commander. These windows are not

241

even cells of a hive : they are squares on the sheet of an immense graph in which a human dweller would vainly seek not merely his name but even his number.

*

MODERN ARCHITECTURE THIRTY YEARS AFTER

After thirty years of modern building, two paradoxical features of functional architecture are surely evident. One : that the bare economic style is only overwhelmingly effective when it looks extremely new and extremely expensive—only a millionaire or a community can afford to build a functional building. The other is that modern architecture, invented by nordics in nordic climates, looks best in the southern hemisphere. It is buildings like the immense Ministry of Education at Rio de Janeiro (a cloud of glass and concrete upraised on columns above the street) that astonish with their fantastic evocation of new forms and opaque colours on flat surfaces. But these need hard sharp shadows, hard fields of light. They are like magnificent dry tropical cacti. A grey sky, or stains of damp or discoloration, and they look spongeous and squalid.

DECEMBER 1955

FOR 1956

An obvious New Year resolution : not to discuss what is U and Non-U. Yet there are two points which have not been brought out, and which lead to other things. One : a confused, obscure but genuine question : whether, after all, the aristocracy does at times defend certain usages from vulgarization. The other : whether one class is today less vulgar than another.

The only real defence that can be made of upper-class usage is that the upper class is a carrier of certain unvulgarized values. Yet I doubt whether this is so. Itself it is made vulgar, partly by members of that class themselves, partly by interlopers.

Nevertheless, in maintaining that one should say "false teeth" rather than "dentures", one catches the gleam of an authentic local god haunting a wood where the trees are called trees, and spades aspire to be known by their real name. After that glimpse, one plunges into absurdity. False teeth are themselves a mechanically realized euphemism : so it might be better to have gaping gums than not to have authentic teeth.

*

THE OPPOSITE OF VULGAR

The truth is that today no class has a monopoly of usage which is "authentic", because none has a monopoly of not being vulgar, and nothing shows more clearly that we are all vulgar than an examination of the words and idioms we use.

There ought to be a word to express a quality, once common to the aristocrat and the peasant, setting them apart in their expressions from any intermediate class. It would mean whatever is the opposite of vulgarity. It is not quite the same as "aristocratic".

Lacking such a word, one can only talk about unvulgarity. This is a very negative way of expressing a very positive idea. Unvulgar are those who contemplate and name any and every aspect of the human condition without evasions, euphemisms, or false shame. To be unvulgar means to have a mind that converses equally with birth, copulation, and death. An aristocratic or upper-class tradition remains unvulgar so long as it also remains part peasant, part priestly tradition. An absentee aristocracy, coining chic idioms which are really an apology for evasion, is vulgar.

*

REFRIGERATED CORPSES

Towns are great vulgarizers because they enable those who can so afford, to ignore or gloss over or distort and vitiate the basic realities of birth, life, and death. Industrialism produces a machinery to fabricate false living.

At Cincinnati, I noticed hanging outside a shop which was a Funeral Parlour a neon sign surely directly inspired by the Muse of Vulgarity. It read:

FROZEN CASKETS TO SPARE YOUR LOVED ONES INHUMAN EMBALMING

The vulgar have their own idea of what is and what is not vulgar : that complicates discussions about usage. In general, the vulgar think that topics unsuitable for a hypothetical polite conversation on an ideally correct social occasion are unsuitable on any other occasion. Respectability cuts across classes.

But the struggle against vulgarity is part of the larger struggle for honesty. If the respectable had ever completely won out, there would have been painted no nudes, and no study of anatomy in medicine could have been completed. D. H. Lawrence's struggle against the censorship was the major battle of the unvulgar in our time.

*

ANNIVERSARY
Dylan Thomas died in New York
Having written these words I went to bed and dreamed about Dylan

Thomas. It was in a large and beautiful chapel, like King's, where the choir was singing a requiem in his memory. The chorale was modern and yet like something of Monteverdi, though not pastiche. Dylan was lying down on the floor beside the place where I was standing, rather pale, but still transparently alive.

I woke up thinking there was something I now knew: death was an absurd pretence invented by the living that the dead were not here—whereas, in reality, they were alive and omnipresent. As I realized, waking, that my sense of Dylan's physical presence was fading, I was still hammered on, as it were from *inside* my head, by this realization of how alive the dead are. I felt tired of their always forcing themselves on to us with that persuasion and wholeness which the living lack.

M—— (aged 8), who was sleeping in my room during my wife's absence, had woken me, as usual, with the dawn. We heard a drumming of hooves in the road outside. It was the cavalry on parade from the barracks nearby. M—— slipped out of bed, drew back the curtains of the window, and kneeled on the floor. "Look! Look! Their heels are on fire!" he said. I explained: "They always do that." I realized this was the first time he had ever seen so much iron strike sparks from stone. As I knelt beside him, I suddenly saw the hooves agitating through the darkness against the road surface and breaking into small white flowers of sparks, and the shadowy horses moving through the milky darkness, just as M—— saw them—for the first time. This first-time-ness also woke me to a sense of how Dylan saw them and how he would describe them, entering into the reality of the scene and singing from core and centre of its being. At the same time, I realized that I myself see things clearly but from the outside, at a distance, through the instrument of what I am—small and clear and upside-down, as on a camera's ground-glass screen.

JANUARY 1956

INVITATION TO WARSAW

The President and the Secretary of the Warsaw Branch of Writers' Union, both wrote inviting me for a week to Warsaw to attend the *soirée* com-memorating the centenary of the national poet of Poland, Adam Mickiewicz. Not knowing what kind of myth I might be approving, I answered that I would gladly attend if I were allowed to speak for a few minutes on a topic: *The Uses to which we should put the Reputations of the Dead.*

"My theme," I wrote, "would be that if we use the dead to illustrate the ideology of the living, we turn our contemporary existence into nothing but a prison of our own contemporary ideas : a prison on the walls of which the pictures of the dead are posters projecting the propaganda of our own ideologies . . . We should regard the dead as points from which to criticize our own contemporary existence."

The secretary of the society, Anton Slonimsky, telephoned from Warsaw that the *soirée* would not be an occasion for a controversial address.

While awaiting this answer, I consulted refugees in London and Paris, and found them fairly equally divided about the usefulness of such visits. If one accepts, who uses whom, they asked? The visitor to a country behind the Iron Curtain may be a participant in struggles he is unaware of—for instance, propaganda to persuade refugees to return to their country of origin. When Graham Greene went to Poland, refugees in Paris and London might—it was argued—be more easily persuaded that in returning to their own country they would not be cut off from all contacts with the West.

On the other hand, many refugees felt that the advantages of such visits outweigh their disadvantages. To my mind, the essential thing has always seemed that there should be open and free discussion between hosts and guests. I declined to go just to attend a celebration, but telegraphed that I would be glad to do so if and when such discussion could be arranged. But I was delighted to hear that Laurie Lee, who has no political commitments, was going.

*

WE LOVE THE DEAD

Czeslaw Milosz wrote some brilliant reflections on the Mickiewicz celebrations, opening with the exclamation : "We love the dead!" He raised the important question whether in our time such centennial festivities should not be abolished altogether.

Can we today be sure that when we invite the dead to be the objects of celebrations they are not guests in the same sense as other deceived travellers who go to countries in the grip of ideologies?

Two questions ought to be asked. (1) Do we select from the past in order to find figures there which illustrate the ideological theses of the present? or (2) do we study the past with the will to discover situations and lives in past history from whose viewpoint we can judge and criticize our contemporary situation?

If we do (i) then such anniversaries are ways of using the past in order to illustrate contemporary aims. If we do (ii) then we may discover through the past ways of escape from that bondage within the ideas of our own time which is characteristic of us all, on whichever side of the Iron Curtain.

FEBRUARY 1956

AN INQUIRY INTO BEAUTY?

Beauty is a word that has largely dropped out of use. It is employed today as knowing clannish jargon, in the way technicians talk: "a beautiful job": picture, poem, or jet turbine engine that is "a beauty".

Although fortunes have been spent inquiring into people's sexual habits, how they spend their money, whom they vote for, what they think about their leaders, etc., no one seems to know whether they require beauty in their surroundings nor what enhancing or depressing rôle the beautiful and the ugly play in their lives.

The fact that little seems to be known about all this, makes every endeavour to construct beautiful cities seem a theoretical or dogmatic attempt on the part of people who care, to impose their tastes on those who don't care. When planners and—even—politicians talk about the beauty of new cities, one feels that they may have æsthetic values of their own but they never seem to be addressing themselves to known human needs. All discussions today about rebuilding London seem to fall between fanatical purists, well-intentioned philistines, and senile academic hypocrites. The one thing no one seems convinced of today is that beauty is *necessary*. And since we live in the age of necessity in public affairs, beauty, as a public cause, might as well be abandoned. Perhaps that is why we are ashamed to speak of it.

Yet I am convinced that to write of people being starved of beauty is not just a figure of speech. I think it could be proved that they are starved. The reason why it might even be a worthwhile subject of inquiry is that until this is demonstrated no one will believe it.

*

ARCHITECTURE IS LANDSCAPE

Here, by beauty, I do not mean conscious appreciation of the arts but an immediate enhancement of being which people may or may not get (I think they do sometimes get it) from living in beautiful surroundings.

The difference between conscious æsthetic awareness and such immediate satisfaction of an appetite can be indicated like this. A man who goes into a gallery and looks at a picture—say the *Tempesta* of Giorgione —of another man who is living in very beautiful surroundings, is still outside the world conveyed in the picture. A man who lives in a beautiful city or landscape is a man inside a beautiful picture. This is both æsthetic and a natural state in which to be. The difference between architecture and the other arts is that architecture is, after all, a form of landscape gardening, and to live in a garden is a different thing from either going to a public art gallery or living in a back yard. Architecture, however rococo, remains the most innocent of the arts, always creating a natural surrounding for its inhabitants. Myths, from the Garden of Eden to that of the late eighteenth century of the innocent savage, recognize that to live amidst beauty (as apart from going to look at art) is a primary instinctual satisfaction. Without this satisfaction, we are maimed.

Most people agree that blindness is almost the greatest misfortune that can befall anyone. The strongest argument for thinking so is that it cuts him off from the beauty of the visible world. When one thinks about the blind one does not wonder how they get about but what visual compensations they develop.

If we live in irremediably ugly surroundings we are living in what is a mockery of vision, a kind of enforced parody of blindness. That this is so, seems acknowledged by the passion of modern town-dwellers to get away from their towns. Tourism is not just "modern restlessness". It is the result of a very understandable wish to satisfy a visual instinct that has been repressed. We are told that French and Italians who live in beautiful cities are not great travellers. Whether this is true or not, we readily believe it. There would be no passionate need to move if we were not starved of things to enjoy with our eyes.

THE APPETITE FOR BEAUTY

In the mouth of an æsthete, the phrase "I simply live for beauty" sounds insincere, though it may be truer than he himself realizes. The fact surely is that a great many people do live more for beauty than for "personal relations" or for anything else. My statistical inquirers here would try to find out how many people think all the year round of their Italian holiday and what proportion of their savings they spend on this.

For such people, beauty must be the one entirely reliable source of pleasure in their lives which does not let them down or betray them, which, if they are able to experience and then memorize it, is a treasure no government, husband, wife, or tax-collector can take away.

For Italians who live in a beautiful city (I have noticed in Verona) the fact that the city stays there, is outside them, is not subject to their whims, cannot be disregarded—and yet can be entered into, can receive them into its outsideness, thus enhancing their inner life with *its* outer life—all this provides them with an increasing satisfaction. All other satisfactions are spasmodic, and often disappointing. Beauty is the only appetite that can be permanently satisfied.

When we cover the countryside with hundreds of thousands of houses which offer no satisfaction to this instinct, we are producing a repression which is similar to that of the sexual instinct. It is inevitable that people living in the "subtopias" should want television sets that show them somewhere else, automobiles that get them away from the streets in which they live, more and more holidays. But these things are only added frustrations, because they are of their nature so fleeting. Nothing really makes up for the satisfaction which is cut off at the root of life by hideous surroundings.

So the prevalent idea that in building our cities, there are "needs" which have to be satisfied (which may, after other things have been dealt with, include "culture" piped down from "specialized agencies") is as repressive to an instinctive natural condition as the Victorian attitude towards sex.

＊

A VISIT TO JAMINI ROY AT CALCUTTA

His whole house is a shrine devoted to his paintings. The paintings are not hung, they are placed, on the floor, and on shelves. The walls are completely white, and the furniture consists of rectangular box-shaped seats.

Each room represents a different phase of his work. In the earlier rooms, there are some conventional studies, and even exercises in the manner of the French impressionists. But the European manner is alien to him. Instead, he has tried to assimilate Christian symbolism into Hindu mythology, in a style based on village art. The most recent paintings, in very broken colours, are of a goddess, and of a crucifixion, painted in earth colours, on palm-leaf matting.

Jamini Roy is 66, with white hair, a rather pale complexion, a lined, yet almost boyish, acolyte's face. Here he is amongst his "things" which he shows you joyously. His English is monosyllabic but it conveys subtleties, as well as essentials. All his life he has been painting the metamorphosis of myth into myth. With his brush he has gently tried to develop the Christian myth (there are here the Last Supper and the Flight into Egypt as well as the Crucifixion) towards Eastern ones.

I noticed a recent painting of a man in a loin-cloth seated cross-legged on the ground. "Is that Gandhi?" I asked. He smiled: "It might become that." I said: "If it were not for photographs which have fixed too much the literal appearance of Gandhi in our minds, he would perhaps be your painting." "I try to paint the essentials, and naturalism has nothing to do with these.

"Living in this time, I disagree." Several times he repeated the phrase, "I disagree." He disagreed most of all with the tendencies of other Indian painters. Showing me some recent paintings of a horse, cows, and calves, a cat with a lobster in its mouth, he said: "Now that I am an old man, and because I disagree, I go back to painting like a child. I have learned to paint again from my five-year-old grandson." He showed me a very Indian-looking study of Shiva by his grandson. "I am very alone," he said. "Other painters want to introduce European ideas into their painting. I want to paint India."

MARCH 1956

THE QUESTION OF HAPPINESS

Happiness is really a question and not a problem. In this, it resembles poetry, every observation concerning which is accompanied by a What-is-poetry? like an outrider. And as with poetry, the question seems only answered when it is not asked—*kommt nicht im Frage*. It does not arise when time seems endless. Thus animals must doubtless at times know happiness, and so do children, to whom time, though not endless, seems immensely long and none of their business, because it is controlled by the adults. But "pursuit of happiness" is an illusion, because one can only pursue things along lines. What one can pursue is pleasure, which is much realer than virtuous people suppose. In fact the religious are right to say that only the simple and the saintly can forget time, and therefore be happy, but are wrong, surely, to be supercilious about pleasure. Unhappiness is not the opposite of happiness. Thinking it is so makes many people imagine that because they know they are not happy, they must be unhappy. Actually unhappiness is a positive condition of awareness of loss, like bereavement. Animals can be unhappy because though unaware of death, they can be aware of loss. Unhappiness is conscious of a gap which cannot be filled. Ivan Ilych, going about with his approaching death like a hole in his side, was unhappy. Rimbaud cultivated unhappiness like a drug which scoriates the sensibility. Most people live in a stupor of contentment alternating with a stupor of discontentment.

JULY 1956

DESERT ISLANDS

Recently the head of a famous art school told me of his bewilderment at the activities of some of his students on their vacations. Leaving their suburban homes, they entrain for Italy where, influenced by Guttuso, they paint pictures supposed to represent miserable villages, starving peasants. Their lack of curiosity about the real condition of the workers at Fiat's factory outside Turin, or Pirelli at Milan, is total. Nor for that matter have they ever asked themselves what subject matter they would be confronted with if they went not to the wretchedest villages they can find in the South of Italy but to the main streets of Budapest or Prague.

And yet this concentration on a subject matter which, if it is supposed to represent the condition of contemporary Europe, describes a fictitious poverty, has fervour and passion, and is the most interesting work being done. To question its authenticity is perhaps to make the mistake of thinking its subject matter the same as that which after all formed the realistic background of the thirties—unemployment, terrible slums, the dole, etc. Of course, these evils still exist, but perhaps today the young who paint or describe them are really describing themselves. The "squalid" imagery of the thirties which was derived from photographed horrors of war and unemployment today provides symbols for the young artist's own life. What he is portraying is not "the workers" but the complete isolation, in a world of collectivized reconstruction, of the individualist faith and way of life of Bohemians. At the same time perhaps this symbolism—which is of his own predicament—also describes a spiritual impoverishment which reaches further than his attic. Perhaps what used to be physical unemployment has now shifted to another plane. As in the nineteenth century it is the upholders of *other values* who are unemployed.

*

ANGRY YOUNG MAN

Some such impression was made on me by John Osborne's play *Look Back in Anger* at the Court Theatre. At first sight this play seems a Hard Luck story of Social Comment of a kind (Frozen to Death Shovelling Snow, Killed Under a Heap of Coal) made familiar by *New Writing* before the war. The scene is a garret, and as one watches Mr. Osborne's two young men lean back and unfold their newspapers, one automatically assumes them to be victims of the economic situation. Then one realizes that the curtain only goes up on their Sundays. The rest of the week they are selling sweets at a stall. Their apparent poverty, in a world where the consumption of sweets is probably only equalled by that of petroleum, must be a *tour de force* of the Bohemian life, or perhaps of their being spiritual neighbours of Mr. Wyndham Lewis who seems to have cast a kind of spell over a part of London that strongly resembles their Midlands, turning the whole neighbourhood into houses consisting of nothing but cellars and garrets.

This play, with its beautiful rhetoric, is the nearest thing to true poetic drama we have had on the stage for many years. If one feels the anger is misdirected, to some extent incomprehensible, it is of the nature of anger to be confused. One might also think that the anger was about the fact that there is nothing in the particular situation of the play to be angry about. The characters are only poor because they are young. Directly the hero has written the flame and fury of a contemplated work he mentions in the course of his diatribes, he will be elevated to the "posh" Sunday newspapers or the weeklies, with other members of his generation who have puffed down their straw or red-brick hovels to find themselves instantly transported to the highly-taxed luxury prison of a successful literary career.

Of course, there are things to be angry about : the incommensurability of our poetic aspirations with our world set headlong on the straight broad path of material Progress. In the latter half of this century we may find ourselves in the Uranium Rush that corresponds to the Gold Rush, and with the artists woebegone prophets like Ruskin and Carlyle, foretelling catastrophes postponed until the twenty-first century. And after all, the catastrophe may happen quite soon in our world of two futures—one future of everything for all, the other of total nothing.

●

ON BEING A WRITER
Young writers can be greatly helped by the situation into which they are born, or—perhaps I should say—by their ability to dramatize their rôle in history. In this century, Pound and Eliot could see themselves as upholders of civilized values in the declining West. Yeats in his *Autobiographies* describes the pagan or esoteric or depraved behaviour which were the Masks of the poets of his time. In the 1930s there was the rôle of the artistic conscience become aware of its humanity to respond to the needs of the victims of that time. It is certainly difficult to see what kind of Mask could be twisted from a subtopian setting.

AUGUST 1956

MEETING WITH RAKOSI
In the second summer after the war, I went to Budapest to give some talks for the British Council. Those seem very far off days now. Although Communists were in the government, Rakosi being deputy prime minister, the Communist coup was by no means completed. I stayed in Budapest with Count Michael Karolyi, who had returned to Hungary in 1946, after his exile which began in 1919 (his memoirs, published by Cape earlier this year, make fascinating reading today). Karolyi at this time performed the functions of a kind of roving Foreign Minister. He favoured the idea of a Danubian Federation, which would form a buffer between East and West, and I remember him telling me at the time that the Communist leader whom he found most sympathetic to his ideas, and most intelligent as a personality, was Tito.

One evening Countess Karolyi invited Rakosi to dinner. It was a small party consisting of the Karolyis, Rakosi, a lady who was writing about Hungary for the *New Statesman,* and myself. Rakosi arrived in a large American car with two guards who remained posted outside the house.

He was thick-set and tough-looking. As soon as we had been introduced, he said to me (in English, I think, but perhaps he spoke French): "You are English, huh? You come from that Fascist country?" This was at the time of the Labour Government. I asked him why we were a Fascist country. "For two reasons. One, the Labour Party has not filled the British Army with socialist generals. Two, the Labour Party has not taken over Scotland Yard." This seemed a Through-the-Looking-Glass definition of a Fascist country, so I said: "But look what we have done for India." At this, the *New Statesman* lady contradicted me, taking Rakosi's side and pointing to our "Fascist" behaviour in various parts of the world.

The party was enlivened by Rakosi's accounts of his life in various prisons under various governments. Altogether, he said, he had spent sixteen years in prison, eleven of them in solitary confinement. (From what he told me, one cannot really blame him if he thought that the difference between being a government and being governed was that between being out of and inside prison.) He said that all the Party members of his government had been educated by him in prisons to which they had been sent. "A political prisoner becomes a virtuoso of his imprisonment," he said. And he illustrated this by a description of his time during the war.

Hitler sent the Horthy government his own special plans for ideal cells for the most dangerous prisoners. In Hungary, these consisted of three metal cells at the top of a flight of stairs, separate from the rest of the prison; here there were kept the most dangerous political prisoners. "We were in contact with the outside world throughout the whole war," said Rakosi. "In fact, we saw all the instructions sent to the prison governor before he himself did. What they had overlooked was that the warder who was responsible for us was himself a Communist."

In his cell, there was, for some reason, a map of Europe on the wall. Rakosi, getting all the governor's information every day before he did, used to follow the progress of the war on this. However, he knew better than to mark the map, or even touch it. One day—it was the day of the fall of Belleville before the German invasion of France—the prison governor came into the cell. Rakosi saw him looking sideways at the map to see whether the shining surface had been fingermarked at Belleville. After a few moments, he left the cell, clanging the door. Rakosi lifted his arms and expelled a gasp of relief. At that moment the door opened quickly, the governor popped his head in and said: "Ah, you *are* in touch with the outside world!"

Stories like this perhaps throw light on Rakosi, though I did not discover in them what Karolyi calls in his memoirs Rakosi's "notorious charm".

JANUARY 1957

THE PUPPETS AND THEIR AIDES

In Japan, the theatre that puzzled me most was the puppet performance at Osaka. In a Japanese puppet play, the puppet actors and actresses on the stage are accompanied by two masked men, and one unmasked, who is the master operator. These three figures stand behind the puppet, plunging their hands into its insides, to manipulate its face and limbs. Two of them assistants, and the third with a serious attentive expression, they look like a surgeon and his aides who galvanize a lifeless body into movement. When the play demands ten or more puppet actors there are thirty or more of these intent manipulators on the stage all performing their operations at once.

The audience apparently manages to discount the attendants and to concentrate on the puppets as though they were unaccompanied. Myself, I found I was fascinated by the black-hooded assistants and the master-surgeons, and took little notice of the puppets. Since my return home, the image of the puppets with their triple aides has gradually suggested to me the following thought : that everyone who acts out his or her drama absorbs into it at least two people who are completely occupied, and one other whose gestures are counterpart to his or her own, acting out the story and at the same time making it happen. I doubt whether this has any connection with the symbolism of the Japanese puppet theatre, which deliberately imposes on the audience the artificiality of the mechanical medium. But perhaps it does show how one can be haunted by a metaphor which goes through one's mind until it finds an object of experience to which it can attach itself, like one of Pirandello's *Six Characters in Search of an Author*. I doubt whether I shall ever come to appreciate the puppet performances for what they really signify, but they have added to my store of mental images for describing a phenomenon which I had scarcely observed (that whoever acts out a drama has silent assistants) until I saw a stage crowded with thirty figures manipulating ten dolls.

JANUARY 1958

HERE AND THERE

There are signs perhaps that we are living in a period in which there could be a literature expressing, within the context of a particular place, a world situation. Political barriers have frustrated that development of the consciousness of all humanity which Goethe envisaged as the world literature of a future that lay just beyond his time.

The division of the world into political camps, more or less completely shut off from each other, frustrates our consciousness that in the modern world people are involved in one another's civilization and values as never before in history, and because of the frustration leads to a peculiar kind of contemporary uneasiness and sense of inadequacy. Different values, different experiences, different standards of living *over there*, undermine the realities and values *over here*. Thus from one point of view the immense proliferation of American literature in this century is a triumph of the values of individualist freedom : but, from another, judged by the experiences, the standards of living, the involvement in social environment of nine-tenths of the world, the epics of American neuroses are an immense fuss about nothing.

Yet when Western writers try to emphasize their social awareness by drawing attention to their own victims—John Osborne's soldier killed at Suez, John Berger (in *A Painter of Our Time*) describing a meeting with a Cypriot woman in Soho—behind these isolated examples there lie the victims of Hungary, and (a little further back in time) those of Auschwitz and Buchenwald, the forced labour camps of Siberia and the Arctic Circle. Hence, then, those frantic efforts to grip at the larger realities by equating them with the smaller ones, "Cyprus is just as bad as Hungary", "We have our economic slavery", "What we do is exactly as bad in its way as what they have done". Hence even the feeling that our freedom is a delusion since, in enabling us to express ourselves freely, it imprisons us in our individuality, and cuts us off from the social context which provides the basis of contemporary reality.

Yet *over there* surely the converse of all this is felt. There Western freedom is apprehended as forbidden fruit leading to terrible truth and knowledge. Its very existence in the world undermines and falsifies the values of the conformist society run by and for man, the social unit. There, without Western freedom, the most "progressive" societies are accompanied by the strange contradiction of the most reactionary arts. Hence behind the shrieks and lamentations *over there* about *Dr. Zhivago*, walk surely ghosts of unwritten masterpieces (masterpieces by Western standards)—books which the other Soviet writers resisted the temptation of writing, because the values of independent witness would have undermined the Soviet view of reality. Pasternak has surely excited *over there* feelings not just of hostility, but of anguish.

Poland left me feeling that for the Polish intellectuals, at any rate, consciousness is all they can cling to in a situation where they are free to speak freely, but to write much less freely. And the consciousness they need is not only their own self-consciousness in a political vacuum. They need us to have a consciousness which includes awareness of them as they are, in their situation, and which is not just the parlour game of identifying what happens here with what happens there. One writer quoted to me the lines of a Polish poem, which he freely rendered—"If we have to die, O God, let the people be aware of how we die."

DECEMBER 1958

W. H. AUDEN

The Fallen City

SOME REFLECTIONS ON SHAKESPEARE'S *Henry IV*

IT HAS BEEN OBSERVED that critics who write about Shakespeare reveal more about themselves than about Shakespeare, but perhaps that is the great value of drama of the Shakespearian kind, namely, that whatever he may see taking place on stage, its final effect upon each spectator is a self-revelation.

Shakespeare holds the position in our literature of Top Bard, but this deserved priority has one unfortunate consequence; we generally make our first acquaintance with his plays, not in the theatre, but in the classroom or study, so that, when we do attend a performance, we have lost that naïve openness to surprise which is the proper frame of mind in which to witness any drama. The experience of reading a play and the experience of watching it performed are never identical, but in the case of *Henry IV* the difference between the two is particularly great.

At a performance, my immediate reaction is to wonder what Falstaff is doing in this play at all. At the end of *Richard II*, we were told that the Heir Apparent has taken up with a dissolute crew of "unrestrained loose companions". What sort of bad company would one expect to find Prince Hal keeping when the curtain rises on *Henry IV*? Surely, one would expect to see him surrounded by daring, rather sinister, juvenile delinquents and beautiful gold-digging whores. But whom do we meet in the Boar's Head? A fat, cowardly tosspot, old enough to be his father, two down-at-heel hangers-on, a slatternly Hostess and only one whore, who is not in her earliest youth either; all of them seedy, and, by any worldly standards, including those of the criminal classes, all of them *failures*. Surely, one thinks, an Heir Apparent, sowing his wild oats, could have picked himself a more exciting crew than that. As the play proceeds, our surprise is replaced by another kind of puzzle, for the better we come to know Falstaff, the clearer it becomes that the world of historical reality which a Chronicle Play claims to imitate is not a world which he can inhabit.

If it really was Queen Elizabeth who demanded to see Falstaff in a comedy, then she showed herself a very perceptive critic. But even in *The Merry Wives of Windsor*, Falstaff has not and could not have found his true home because Shakespeare was only a poet. For that he was to wait nearly two hundred years till Verdi wrote his last opera. Falstaff is not the only case of a character whose true home is the world of music; others are Tristan, Isolde, and Don Giovanni.*

Though they each call for a different kind of music, Tristan, Don Giovanni, and Falstaff have certain traits in common. They do not belong to the temporal world of change. One cannot imagine any of them as babies, for a Tristan who is not in love, a Don Giovanni who has no name on his list, a Falstaff who is not old and fat, are inconceivable. When Falstaff says, "When I was about thy years, Hal, I was not an eagle's talent in the waist; I could have crept into an alderman's thumb-ring"—we take it as a typical Falstaffian fib, but we believe him when he says, "I was born about three in the afternoon, with a white head and something of a round belly."

Time, for Tristan, is a single moment stretched out tighter and tighter until it snaps. Time, for Don Giovanni, is an infinite arithmetical series of unrelated moments which has no beginning and would have no end if Heaven did not intervene and cut it short. For Falstaff, time does not exist, since he belongs to the *opera buffa* world of play and mock-action governed not by will or desire, but by innocent wish, a world where no one can suffer because everything they say and do is only a pretence.

Thus, while we must see Tristan die in Isolde's arms and we must see Don Giovanni sink into the earth, because being doomed to die and to go to hell are essential to their being, we cannot see Falstaff die on stage because, if we did, we should not believe it; we should know that, as at the battle of Shrewsbury, he was only shamming. I am not even quite sure that we believe it when we are told of his death in *Henry V*; I think we accept it, as we accept the death of Sherlock Holmes, as his creator's way of saying, "I am getting tired of this character"; we feel sure that, if the public pleads with him strongly enough, Shakespeare will find some way to bring him to life again. The only kind of funeral music we can associate with him is the mock-requiem in the last act of Verdi's opera.

> *Domine fallo casto.*
> > *Ma salvaggi l'addomine*
> *Domine fallo guasto.*
> > *Ma salvaggi l'addomine.*

---

* If Verdi's *Macbetto* fails to come off, the main reason is that the proper world for Macbeth is poetry not song; he won't go into notes.

There are at least two places in the play where the incongruity of the *opera buffa* world with the historical world is too much, even for Shakespeare, and a patently false note is struck. The first occurs when, on the battlefield of Shrewsbury, Falstaff thrusts his sword into Hotspur's corpse. Within his own world, Falstaff could stab a corpse because, there, all battles are mock battles, all corpses straw dummies; but we, the audience, are too conscious that this battle has been a real battle and that this corpse is the real body of a brave and noble young man. Pistol could do it, because Pistol is a contemptible character, but Falstaff cannot; that is to say, there is no way in which an actor can play the scene convincingly. So, too, with the surrender of Colevile to Falstaff in the Second Part. In his conversation, first with Colevile and then with Prince John, Falstaff talks exactly as we expect—to him, the whole business is a huge joke. But then he is present during a scene when we are shown that it is no joke at all. How is any actor to behave and speak his lines during the following?

LANCASTER—*Is thy name Colevile?*
COLEVILE—*It is, my lord.*
LANCASTER—*A famous rebel art thou, Colevile?*
FALSTAFF—*And a famous true subject took him.*
COLEVILLE—*I am, my lord, but as my betters are,*
   That led me hither. Had they been ruled by me,
   You would have won them dearer than you have.
FALSTAFF—*I know not how they sold themselves: but thou, kind fellow,*
   gavest thyself away gratis, and I thank thee, for thee.
LANCASTER—*Now have you left pursuit?*
WESTMORELAND—*Retreat is made and execution stay'd.*
LANCASTER—*Send Colevile, with his confederates,*
   To York, to present execution.

The Falstaffian frivolity and the headsman's axe cannot so directly confront each **other.**

Reading *Henry IV*, we can easily give our full attention to the historical political scenes, but, when watching a performance, attention is distracted by our eagerness to see Falstaff re-appear. Short of cutting him out of the play altogether, no producer can prevent him stealing the show. From an actor's point of view, the rôle of Falstaff has the enormous advantage that he has only to think of one thing—playing to an audience. Since he lives in an eternal present and the historical world does not exist for him, there is no difference for Falstaff between those on stage and those out front, and if the actor were to appear in one scene in Elizabethan costume and in the next in top-hat and morning-coat, no one would be bewildered. The speech of all the other characters is, like our own, conditioned by two factors, the external situation with its questions, answers, and commands, and the inner need of each character to disclose himself to others. But Falstaff's speech has only one cause, his absolute insistence, at every moment and at all costs, upon disclosing himself. Half his lines could be moved from one speech to another without our noticing, for nearly everything he says is a variant upon one theme—"I am that I am".

Moreover, Shakespeare has so written his part that it cannot be played unsympathetically. A good actor can make us admire Prince Hal, but he cannot hope to make us like him as much as even a second-rate actor will make us like Falstaff. Sober reflection in the study may tell us that Falstaff is not, after all, a very admirable person, but Falstaff on the stage gives us no time for sober reflection. When Hal or the Chief Justice or anybody else indicate that they are not bewitched by Falstaff, reason might tell us that they are in the right, but we ourselves are already bewitched, so that their disenchantment seems out of place, like the presence of teetotallers at a drunken party.

Suppose, then, that a producer were to cut the Falstaff scenes altogether, what would *Henry IV* become? The middle section of a political trilogy which could be entitled *Looking for the Doctor*.

The body politic of England catches an infection from its family physician. An able but unqualified practitioner throws him out of the sick-room and takes over. The patient's temperature continues to rise. But then, to everybody's amazement, the son of the unqualified practitioner whom, though he has taken his degree, everyone has hitherto believed to be a hopeless invalid, effects a cure. Not only is the patient restored to health but also, at the doctor's orders, takes another body politic, France, to wife.

The theme of this trilogy is, that is to say, the question : What combination of qualities is needed in the Ruler whose function is the establishment and maintenance of Temporal Justice? According to Shakespeare, the Ideal Ruler must satisfy five conditions. (1) He must know what is just and what is unjust. (2) He must himself be just. (3) He must be strong enough to compel those who would like to be unjust to behave justly. (4) He must have the capacity both by nature and by art of making others loyal to his person. (5) He must be the legitimate ruler, by whatever standard legitimacy is determined in the society to which he belongs.

Richard II fails to satisfy the first four of these. He does not know what Justice is, for he follows the advice of foolish flatterers. He is himself unjust, for he spends the money he obtains by taxing the Commons and fining the Nobility, not on defending England against her foes, but upon maintaining a lavish and frivolous court, so that, when he really does need money for a patriotic purpose, the war with Ireland, his Exchequer is empty and

in desperation he commits a gross act of injustice by confiscating Bolingbroke's estates.

It would seem that at one time he had been popular but he has now lost
his popularity, partly on account of his actions, but also because he lacks the
art of winning hearts. According to his successor, he had made the mistake
of being over-familiar—the ruler should not let himself be seen too often as
"human"—and in addition, he is not by nature the athletic, physically
brave warrior who is the type most admired by the feudal society he is
called upon to rule.

In consequence, Richard II is a weak ruler who cannot keep the great
nobles in order or even command the loyalty of his soldiers, and weakness
in a ruler is the worst defect of all. A cruel, even an unjust king, who is
strong, is preferable to the most saintly weakling because most men will
behave unjustly if they discover that they can with impunity; tyranny, the
injustice of one, is less unjust than anarchy, the injustice of many.

But there remains the fifth condition : whatever his defects, Richard II
is the legitimate King of England. Since all men are mortal, and many men
are ambitious, unless there is some impersonal principle by which, when
the present ruler dies, the choice of his successor can be decided, there will
be a risk of civil war in every generation. It is better to endure the injustice
of the legitimate ruler, who will die anyway sooner or later, than allow a
usurper to take his place by force.

As a potential ruler, Bolingbroke possesses many of the right qualities. He
is a strong man, he knows how to make himself popular, and he would
like to be just. We never hear, even from the rebels, of any specific actions
of Henry IV which are unjust, only of suspicions which may be just or
unjust. But in yielding to the temptation, when the opportunity unexpectedly offers itself, of deposing his lawful sovereign, he commits an act of
injustice for which he and his kingdom have to pay a heavy price. Because
of it, though he is strong enough to crush rebellion, he is not strong or
popular enough to prevent rebellion breaking out.

Once Richard has been murdered, however, the rule of Henry IV is
better than any alternative. Though, legally, Mortimer may have a good or
better right to the throne, the scene at Bangor between Hotspur, Worcester,
Mortimer, and Glendower convinces us that Henry's victory is a victory
for justice since we learn that the rebels have no concern for the interests of
the Kingdom, only for their own. Their plan, if they succeed, is to carve up
England into three petty states. Henry may wish that Hotspur, not Hal,
were his heir, because Hotspur is a brave warrior ready to risk his life in
battle against England's foes, while Hal appears to be dissipated and
frivolous, but we know better. Hotspur is indeed brave, but that is all. A
man who can say

> *I'll give thrice so much land*
> *To any well-deserving friend;*
> *But in the way of bargain, mark ye me,*
> *I'll cavil on the ninth part of a hair*

is clearly unfitted to be a ruler because his actions are based, not on justice but on personal whim. Moreover, he is not interested in political power; all he desires is military glory.

Thirdly, there is Prince Hal, Henry V to be. To everyone except himself, he seems at first to be another Richard, unjust, lacking in self-control but, unfortunately, the legitimate heir. By the time the curtain falls on *Henry V*, however, he is recognized by all to be the Ideal Ruler. Like his father in his youth, he is brave and personable. In addition, he is a much cleverer politician. While his father was an improviser, he is a master of the art of timing. His first soliloquy reveals him as a person who always sees several steps ahead and has the patience to wait, even though waiting means temporary misunderstanding and unpopularity, until the right moment for action comes; he will never, if he can help it, leave anything to chance. Last but not least, he is blessed by luck. His father had foreseen that internal dissension could only be cured if some common cause could be found which would unite all parties but he was too old and ill, the internal quarrels too violent. But when Hal succeeds as Henry V, most of his enemies are dead or powerless—Cambridge and Scroop have no armies at their back—and his possible right to the throne of France provides the common cause required to unite both the nobles and the commons, and gives him the opportunity, at Agincourt, to show his true mettle.

One of Falstaff's dramatic functions is to be the means by which Hal is revealed to be the Just Ruler, not the dissolute and frivolous young man everybody has thought him; but, so far as the audience is concerned, Falstaff has fulfilled this function by Act III, scene 2 of the First Part, when the King entrusts Hal with a military command. Up to this point the Falstaff scenes have kept us in suspense. In Act I, scene 2, we hear Hal promise

> *I'll so offend to make offence a skill,*
> *Redeeming time when men least think I will.*

But then we watch the rebellion being prepared while he does nothing but amuse himself with Falstaff, so that we are left wondering whether he meant what he said or was only play-acting. But from the moment he engages in the political action of the play, we have no doubts whatsoever as to his ambition, capacity, and ultimate triumph for, however often henceforward we may see him with Falstaff, it is never at a time when his advice and arms are needed by the State; he visits the Boar's Head in leisure hours when there is nothing serious for him to do.

For those in the play, the decisive moment of revelation is, of course, his first public act as Henry V, his rejection of Falstaff and company. For his subjects who have not, as we have, watched him with Falstaff, it is necessary to allay their fears that, though they already know him to be brave and capable, he may still be unjust and put his personal friendships before the impartial justice which it is his duty as king to maintain. But we, who have watched his private life, have no such fears. We have long known that his first soliloquy meant what it said, that he has never been under any illusions about Falstaff or anyone else and that when the right moment comes to reject Falstaff, that is to say, when such a rejection will make the maximum political effect, he will do so without hesitation. Even the magnanimity he shows in granting his old companion a life competence, which so impresses those about him, cannot impress us because, knowing Falstaff as they do not, we know what the effect on him of such a rejection must be, that his heart will be "fracted and corroborate" and no life competence can mend that. It is Hal's company he wants, not a pension from the Civil List.

The essential Falstaff is the Falstaff of *The Merry Wives* and Verdi's opera, the comic hero of the world of play, the unkillable self-sufficient immortal whose verdict on existence is

> *Tutto nel mondo è burla . . .*
> *Tutti gabbàti. Irridè*
> *L'un l'altro ogni mortal.*
> *Ma ride ben chi ride*
> *La risata final.*

In *Henry IV*, however, something has happened to this immortal which draws him out of his proper world into the historical world of suffering and death. He has become capable of serious emotion. He continues to employ the speech of his comic world :

> I have forsworn his company hourly any time this two-and-twenty years, and yet I am bewitched with the rogue's company. If the rascal have not given me medicines to make me love him, I'll be hanged. It could not be else. I have drunk medicines.

But the emotion so flippantly expressed could equally well be expressed thus :

If my dear love were but the child of state,
It might for Fortune's bastard be unfathered,
As subject to Time's love or to Time's hate,
Weeds among weeds, or flowers with flowers
*   gathered.*
No, it was builded far from accident;
It suffers not in smiling pomp, nor falls
Under the blow of thralled discontent,
Whereto th'inviting time and fashion calls.
It fears not Policy, that heretic
Which works on leases of short numbered hours,
But all alone stands hugely politic.

As the play proceeds, we become aware, behind all the fun, of something tragic. Falstaff loves Hal with an absolute devotion. "The lovely bully" is the son he has never had, the youth predestined to the success and worldly glory which he will never enjoy. He believes that his love is returned, that the Prince is indeed his other self, so he is happy, despite old age and poverty. We, however, can see that he is living in a fool's paradise, for the Prince cares no more for him as a person than he would care for the King's Jester. He finds Falstaff amusing but no more. If we could warn Falstaff of what he is too blind to see, we might well say : Beware, before it is too late, of becoming involved with one of those mortals

> *That do not do the thing they most do show,*
> *Who, moving others, are themselves as stone . . .*

Falstaff's story, in fact, is not unlike one of those folk tales in which a mermaid falls in love with a mortal prince : the price she pays for her infatuation is the loss of her immortality without the compensation of temporal happiness.

Let us now suppose, not only that Falstaff takes no part in the play, but is also allowed to sit in the audience as a spectator. How much will he understand of what he sees going on?

He will see a number of Englishmen divided into two parties who finally come to blows. That they should come to blows will in itself be no proof to him that they are enemies because they might, like boxers, have agreed to fight for fun. In Falstaff's world there are two causes of friendship and enmity. My friend may be someone whose appearance and manner I like at this moment, my enemy someone whose appearance and manners I dislike. Thus, he will understand Hotspur's objection to Bolinbroke perfectly well.

Why, what a candy deal of courtesy
This fawning greyhound then did proffer me.
Look, when his infant fortune came of age,
And "gentle Harry Percy" and "kind cousin".
O the devil take such cozeners.

To Falstaff, "my friend" can also mean he whose wish at this moment coincides with mine, "my enemy" he whose wish contradicts mine. He will see the civil war, therefore, as a clash between Henry and Mortimer who both wish to wear the crown. What will perplex him is any argument as to who has the better right to wear it.

Anger and fear he can understand, because they are immediate emotions, but not nursing a grievance or planning revenge or apprehension, for these presuppose that the future inherits from the past. He will not, therefore, be able to make head or tail of Warwick's speech "There is a history in all men's lives..." nor any reasons the rebels give for the actions which are based upon anything Bolingbroke did before he became king, nor the reason given by Worcester for concealing the king's peace offer from Hotspur.

It is impossible, it cannot be
The King should keep his word in loving us.
He will suspect us still and find a time
To punish this offence in other faults.

To *keep his word* is a phrase outside Falstaff's comprehension, for a promise means that at some future moment I might have to refuse to do what I wish, and, in Falstaff's world to wish and to do are synonymous. For the same reason, when, by promising them redress, Prince John tricks the rebels into disbanding their armies and then arrests them, Falstaff will not understand why they and all the audience except himself are shocked.

The first words Shakespeare puts into Falstaff's mouth are "Now Hal, what time of day is it, lad?" to which the Prince quite rightly replies, "What the devil hast thou to do with the time of day?" In Falstaff's world, every moment is one of infinite possibility when anything can be wished. As a spectator, he will keep hearing the characters use the words *time* and *occasion* in a sense which will stump him.

What I know
Is ruminated, plotted, and set down
And only stays but to behold the face
Of that occasion that shall bring it on.

The purpose you undertake is dangerous, the time
itself unsorted ...

... I will resolve to Scotland. There am I
Till time and vantage crave my company.

Of all the characters in the play, the one he will think he understands best is the least Falstaff-like of them all, Hotspur, for Hotspur, like himself, appears to obey the impulse of the moment and say exactly what he thinks without prudent calculation. Both conceal nothing from others, Falstaff because he has no mask to put on, Hotspur because he has so become his mask that he has no face beneath it. Falstaff says, as it were, "I am I. Whatever I do, however outrageous, is of infinite importance because I do it." Hotspur says: "I am Hotspur, the fearless, the honest, plain-spoken warrior. If I should ever show fear or tell lies, even white ones, I should cease to exist." If Falstaff belonged to the same world as Hotspur, one could call him a liar, but, in his own eyes, he is perfectly truthful, for, to him, fact is subjective fact, "what I am actually feeling and thinking at this moment". To call him a liar is as ridiculous as if, in a play, a character should say "I am Napoleon", and a member of the audience should cry, "You're not. You're Sir John Gielgud."

In Ibsen's *Peer Gynt*, there is a remarkable scene in which Peer visits the Troll King. At the entertainment given in his honour, animals dance to hideous noises, but Peer behaves to them with perfect manners as if they were beautiful girls and the music ravishing. After it is over, the Troll King asks him: "Now, frankly, tell me what you saw." Peer replies: "What I saw was impossibly ugly"—and then describes the scene as the audience has seen it. The Troll King who has taken a fancy to him, suggests that Peer would be happier as a troll. All that is needed is a little eye-operation, after which he will really see a cow as a beautiful girl. Peer indignantly refuses. He is perfectly willing, he says, to swear that a cow is a girl, but to surrender his humanity so that he can no longer lie, because he cannot distinguish between fact and fiction, that he will never do. By this criterion, neither Falstaff nor Hotspur is quite human, Falstaff because he is a pure troll, Hotspur because he is so lacking in imagination that the troll kingdom is invisible to him.

At first, then, Falstaff will believe that Hotspur is one of his own kind, who like himself enjoys putting on an act, but then he will hear Hotspur say words which he cannot comprehend.

... time serves wherein you may redeem
Your banished honours and restore yourselves
Into the good thoughts of the world again.

In Falstaff's world, the only value standard is importance, that is to say, all he demands from others is attention, all he fears is being ignored. Whether others applaud or hiss does not matter; what matters is the volume of the hissing or the applause.

Hence, in his soliloquy about honour, his reasoning runs something like this: if the consequences of demanding moral approval from others is dying, it is better to win their disapproval; a dead man has no audience.

Since the Prince is a personal friend, Falstaff is, of course, a King's man who thinks it a shame to be on any side but one, but his loyalty is like that of those who, out of local pride, support one football team rather than another. As a member of the audience, his final comment upon the political action of the play will be the same as he makes from behind the footlights.

> Well, God be thanked for these rebels: they offend none but the virtuous. A young knave and begging. Is there not employment? Doth not the King lack subjects? Do not the rebels need soldiers?

Once upon a time we were all Falstaffs: then we became social beings with super-egos. Most of us learn to accept this, but there are some in whom the nostalgia for the state of innocent self-importance is so strong that they refuse to accept adult life and responsibilities and seek some means to become again the Falstaffs they once were. The commonest technique adopted is the bottle and, curiously enough, the male drinker reveals his intention by developing a drinker's belly.

If one visits a bathing beach, one can observe that men and women grow fat in different ways. A fat woman exaggerates her femininity; her breasts and buttocks enlarge till she comes to look like the Venus of Wilmersdorf. A fat man, on the other hand, looks like a cross between a very young child and a pregnant mother. There have been cultures in which obesity in women was considered the ideal of sexual attraction, but in no culture, so far as I know, has a fat man been considered more attractive than a thin one. If my own weight and experience gives me any authority, I would say that fatness in the male is the physical expression of a psychological wish to withdraw from sexual competition and, by combining mother and child in his own person, to become emotionally self-sufficient. The Greeks thought of Narcissus as a slender youth but I think they were wrong. I see him as a middle-aged man with a corporation, for, however ashamed he may be of displaying it in public, in private a man with a belly loves it dearly: it may be an unprepossessing child to look at, but he has borne it all by himself.

> I do walk here before thee like a sow that hath overwhelmed all her litter but one...

I have a whole school of tongues in this belly of mine, and not a tongue of them all speaks any other word but my name. My womb, my womb undoes me.

Not all fat men are heavy drinkers, but all males who drink heavily become fat.* At the same time, the more they drink, the less they eat. "O monstrous! But one halfpenny worth of bread to this intolerable deal of sack!" exclaims Hal on looking at Falstaff's bill, but he cannot have expected anything else. Drunkards die, not from the liquid alcohol they take so much of, but from their refusal to eat solid food, and anyone who has had to look after a drunkard knows that the only way to get enough nourishment into him is to give him liquid or mashed-up foods, for he will reject any dish that needs chewing. Solid food is to the drunkard a symbolic reminder of the loss of the mother's breast and his ejection from Eden.

A plague on sighing and grief. It blows a man up like a bladder . . .

So Falstaff, and popular idiom identifies the kind of griefs which have this fattening effect—eating humble pie, swallowing insults, etc.

In a recent number of *The Paris Review*, Mr. Nicholas Tucci writes:

The death song of the drunkard—it may go on for thirty years—goes more or less like this. "I who was born a god, with the whole world in reach of my hands, lie now defeated in the gutter. Come and listen: hear what the world has done to me."

In Vino Veritas is an old saying that has nothing to do with the drunkard's own truth. He has no secrets—that is true—but it is not true that his truth may be found under the skin of his moral reserve or of his sober lies, so that the moment he begins to cross his eyes and pour out his heart, anyone may come in and get his fill of truth. What happens is exactly the opposite. When the drunkard confesses, he makes a careful choice of his pet sins: and these are non-existent. He may be unable to distinguish a person from a chair, but never an unprofitable lie from a profitable one. How could he see himself as a very insignificant entity in a huge world of others, when he sees nothing but himself spread over the whole universe. "I am alone" is indeed a true cry, but it should not be taken literally.

The drunk is unlovely to look at, intolerable to listen to, and his self-pity is contemptible. Nevertheless, as not merely a worldly failure but also a wilful failure, he is a disturbing image for the sober citizen. His refusal to

*All the women I have met who drank heavily were lighter and thinner than average.

accept the realities of this world, babyish as it may be, compels us to take another look at this world and reflect upon our motives for accepting it. The drunkard's suffering may be self-inflicted, but it is real suffering and reminds us of all the suffering in this world which we prefer not to think about because, from the moment we accepted this world, we acquired our share of responsibility for everything that happens in it.

When we see Falstaff's gross paunch and red face, we are reminded that the body politic of England is not so healthy either.

> *The Commonwealth is sick of its own choice.*
> *Their over-greedy love hath surfeited . . .*
> *Thou (beastly feeder) are so full of him*
> *That thou provokest thyself to cast him up.*
> *So, so, thou common dog, didst thou disgorge*
> *Thy glutton bosom of the royal Richard . . .*
>
> *Then you perceive the body of our kingdom,*
> *How foul it is: what rank diseases grow,*
> *And with what danger near the heart of it.*

It might be expected that we would be revolted at the sight and turn our eyes with relief and admiration to the Hero Prince. But in fact we aren't and we don't. Whenever Falstaff is on stage, we have no eyes for Hal. If Shakespeare did originally write a part for Falstaff in *Henry V*, it would not have taken pressure from the Cobhams to make him cut it out; his own dramatic instinct would have told him that, if Henry was to be shown in his full glory, the presence of Falstaff would diminish it.

Seeking for an explanation of why Falstaff affects us as he does, I find myself compelled to see *Henry IV* as possessing, in addition to its overt meaning, a parabolic significance. Overtly, Falstaff is a Lord of Misrule; parabolically, he is a comic symbol for the supernatural order of charity as contrasted with the temporal order of Justice symbolized by Henry of Monmouth.

Such readings are only possible with drama which, like Shakespeare's, is secular, concerned directly, not with the relation of man and God, but with the relations between men. Greek tragedy, at least before Euripides, is directly religious, concerned with what the gods do to men rather than with what men do to each other : it presents a picture of human events, the causes of which are divine actions. In consequence a Greek tragedy does not demand that we "read" it in the sense that we speak of "reading" a face. The ways of the gods may be mysterious to human beings but they are not ambiguous.

There can be no secular drama of any depth or importance except in a culture which recognizes that man has an internal history as well as an external; that his actions are partly in response to an objective situation created by his past acts and the acts of others, and partly initiated by his subjective need to re-create, re-define, and re-choose himself. Surprise and revelation are the essence of drama. In Greek tragedy these are supplied by the gods; no mortal can foresee how and when they will act. But the conduct of men has no element of surprise, that is to say, the way in which they react to the surprising events which befall them is exactly what one would expect.

A secular drama presupposes that in all which men say and do there is a gratuitous element which makes their conduct ambiguous and unpredictable. Secular drama, therefore, demands a much more active rôle from its audience than a Greek tragedy. The audience has to be at one and the same time a witness to what is occurring on stage and a subjective participant who interprets what he sees and hears. And a secular dramatist like Shakespeare who attempts to project the inner history of human beings into objective stage action is faced with problems which Aeschylus and Sophocles were spared, for there are aspects of this inner history which resist and sometimes defy manifestation.

> Humility is represented with difficulty—when it is shown in its ideal moment, the beholder senses the lack of something because he feels that its true ideality does not consist in the fact that it is ideal in the moment but that it is constant. Romantic love can very well be represented in the moment, but conjugal love cannot, because an ideal husband is not one who is such once in his life but one who every day is such. Courage can very well be concentrated in the moment, but not patience, precisely for the reason that patience strives with time. A king who conquers kingdoms can be represented in the moment, but a cross-bearer who every day takes up his cross cannot be represented in art because the point is that he does it every day.
>
> *(Kierkegaard)*

Let us suppose, then, that a dramatist wishes to show a character acting out of the spirit of charity or *agape*. At first this looks easy. *Agape* requires that we love our enemies, do good to those that hate us and forgive those who injure us, and this command is unconditional. Surely, all a dramatist has to do is to show one human being forgiving an enemy.

In *Measure for Measure*, Angelo has wronged Isabella and Mariana, and the facts of the wrong become public. Angelo repents and demands that the just sentence of death be passed on him by the Duke. Isabella and

Mariana implore the Duke to show mercy. The Duke yields to their prayers and all ends happily. I agree with Professor Coghill's interpretation of *Measure for Measure* as a parable in which Isabella is an image for the redeemed Christian Soul, perfectly chaste and loving, whose reward is to become the bride of God; but, to my mind, the parable does not quite work because it is impossible to distinguish in dramatic action between the spirit of forgiveness and the act of pardon.

The command to forgive is unconditional: whether my enemy harden his heart or repent and beg forgiveness is irrelevant. If he hardens his heart, he does not care whether I forgive him or not and it would be impertinent of me to say "I forgive you". If he repents and asks, "Will you forgive me?" the answer "Yes" should not express a decision on my part but describe a state of feeling which has always existed. On the stage, however, it is impossible to show one person forgiving another, unless the wrongdoer ask for forgiveness, because silence and inaction are undramatic. The Isabella we are shown in earlier scenes of *Measure for Measure* is certainly not in a forgiving spirit—she is in a passion of rage and despair at Angelo's injustice—and dramatically she could not be otherwise, for then there would be no play. Again, on the stage, forgiveness requires manifestation in action, that is to say, the one who forgives must be in a position to do something for the other which, if he were not forgiving, he would not do. This means that my enemy must be at my mercy; but, to the spirit of charity, it is irrelevant whether I am at my enemy's mercy or he at mine. So long as he is at my mercy, forgiveness is indistinguishable from judicial pardon.

The law cannot forgive, for the law has not been wronged, only broken; only persons can be wronged. The law can pardon, but it can only pardon what it has the power to punish. If the law-breaker is stronger than the legal authorities, they are powerless to do either. The decision to grant or refuse pardon must be governed by prudent calculation—if the wrongdoer is pardoned, he will behave better in the future than if he were punished, etc. But charity is forbidden to calculate in this way: I am required to forgive my enemy whatever the effect on him may be.

One may say that Isabella forgives Angelo and the Duke pardons him. But, on the stage, this distinction is invisible because, there, power, justice, and love are all on the same side. Justice is able to pardon what love is commanded to forgive. But to love, it is an accident that the power of temporal justice should be on its side; indeed, the Gospels assure us that, sooner or later, they will find themselves in opposition and that love must suffer at the hands of justice.

In *King Lear*, Shakespeare attempts to show absolute love and goodness, in the person of Cordelia, destroyed by the powers of this world, but the price he pays is that Cordelia, as a dramatic character, is a bore.

If she is not to be a fake, what she says cannot be poetically very impressive nor what she does dramatically very exciting.

> *What shall Cordelia speak? Love and be silent.*

In a play with twenty-six scenes, Shakespeare allows her to appear in only four, and from a total of over three thousand three hundred lines, he allots to her less than ninety.

Temporal Justice demands the use of power to quell the unjust; it demands prudence, a practical reckoning with time and place; and it demands publicity for its laws and its penalties. But Charity forbids all three —we are not to resist evil, if a man demand our coat we are to give him our cloak also, we are to take no thought for the morrow and, while secretly fasting and giving alms, we are to appear in public as persons who do neither.

A direct manifestation of charity in secular terms is, therefore, impossible. One form of indirect manifestation employed by religious teachers has been through parables in which actions which are ethically immoral are made to stand as a sign for that which transcends ethics. The Gospel parable of the Unjust Steward is one example. These words by a Hassidic Rabbi are another :

> I cannot teach you the ten principles of service but a little child and a thief can show you what they are. From the child you can learn three things :
>
> He is merry for no particular reason.
> Never for a moment is he idle.
> When he wants something, he demands it vigorously.
>
> The thief can instruct you in many things :
>
> He does his service by night.
> If he does not finish what he has set out to do in one night, he devotes the next night to it.
> He and all those who work for him, love one another.
> He risks his life for slight gains.
> What he takes has so little value for him that he gives up for a very small coin.
> He endures blows and hardships and it matters nothing to him.
> He likes his trade and would not exchange it for any other.

If a parable of this kind is dramatized, the action must be comic, that is to say, the apparently immoral actions of the hero must not inflict, as in the actual world they would, real suffering upon others.

Thus, Falstaff speaks of himself as if he were always robbing travellers. We see him do this once—incidentally, it is not Falstaff but the Prince who is the instigator—and the sight convinces us that he never has been and never could be a successful highwayman. The money is re-stolen from him and returned to its proper owners; the only sufferer is Falstaff himself who has been made a fool of. He lives shamelessly on credit, but none of his creditors seems to be in serious trouble as a result. The Hostess may swear that if he does not pay his bill, she will have to pawn her plate and tapestries, but that is shown to be the kind of exaggeration habitual to land-ladies, for in the next scene they are still there. What, overtly, is dishonesty becomes, parabolically, a sign for a lack of pride, humility which acknowledges its unimportance and dependence upon others.

Then he rejoices in his reputation as a fornicator with whom no woman is safe alone, but the Falstaff on stage is too old to fornicate, and it is impossible to imagine him younger. All we see him do is defend a whore against a bully, set her on his knee and make her cry out of affection and pity. What in the real world is promiscuous lust, the treatment of other persons as objects of sexual greed, becomes in the comic world of play a symbol for the charity that loves all neighbours without distinction.

Living off other people's money and indiscriminate fornication are acts of injustice towards private individuals; Falstaff is also guilty of injustice to others in their public character as citizens. In any war it is not the justice or injustice of either side that decides who is to be the victor but the power each can command. It is therefore the duty of all who believe in the justice of the King's side to supply him with the best soldiers possible. Falstaff makes no attempt to fulfil this duty. Before the battle of Shrewsbury, he first conscripts those who have most money and least will to fight and then allows them to buy their way out, so that he is finally left with a sorry regiment of "discarded unjust serving men, younger sons to younger brothers, revolted tapsters and ostlers trade fallen . . ." Before the battle of Gaultree Forest, the two most sturdy young men, Mouldy and Bullcalf, offer him money and are let off, and the weakest, Shadow, Feeble, and Wart, taken.

From the point of view of society this is unjust, but if the villagers who are subject to conscription were to be asked, as private individuals, whether they would rather be treated justly or as Falstaff treats them, there is no doubt as to their answer. What their betters call just and unjust means nothing to them; all they know is that conscription will tear them away from their homes and livelihoods with a good chance of getting killed or returning maimed "to beg at the town's end". Those whom Falstaff selects are those with least to lose, derelicts without home or livelihood to whom soldiering at least offers a chance of loot. Bullcalf wants to stay with his friends, Mouldy has an old mother to look after, but Feeble is quite ready to go if his friend Wart can go with him.

Falstaff's neglect of the public interest in favour of private concerns is an image for the justice of charity which treats each person, not as a cypher, but as a unique person. The Prince may justly complain:

> I never did see such pitiful rascals.

but Falstaff's retort speaks for all the insulted and injured of this world:

> Tut tut—good enough to toss, food for powder,
>   food for powder.
> They'll fill a pit as well as better. Tush, man,
>   mortal men, mortal men . . .

These are Falstaff's only acts: for the rest, he fritters away his time, swigging at the bottle and taking no thought for the morrow. As parable, both the idleness and the drinking, the surrender to immediacy and the refusal to accept reality, become signs for the Unworldly Man as contrasted with Prince Hal who represents worldliness at its best.

At his best, the worldly man is one who dedicates his life to some public end, politics, science, industry, art, etc. The end is outside himself, but the choice of end is determined by the particular talents with which nature has endowed him, and the proof that he has chosen rightly is worldly success. To dedicate one's life to an end for which one is not endowed is madness, the madness of Don Quixote. Strictly speaking, he does not desire fame for himself, but to achieve something which merits fame. Because his end is worldly, that is, in the public domain—to marry the girl of one's choice, or to become a good parent, are private, not worldly, ends—the personal life and its satisfactions are, for the worldly man, of secondary importance, and should they ever conflict with his vocation, must be sacrificed. The worldly man at his best knows that other persons exist and desires that they should—a statesman has no wish to establish justice among tables and chairs—but if it is necessary to the achievement of his end to treat certain persons as if they were things, then, callously or regretfully, he will. What distinguishes him from the ordinary criminal is that the criminal lacks the imagination to conceive of others as being persons like himself; when he sacrifices others, he feels no guilt because, to the criminal, he is the only person in a world of things. What distinguishes both the worldly man and the criminal from the wicked man is their lack of malice. The wicked man is not worldly but anti-worldly. His conscious end is nothing less than the destruction of others. He is obsessed by hatred at his knowledge that other persons exist beside himself and cannot rest until he has reduced them all to the status of things.

But it is not always easy to distinguish the worldly man from the criminal or the wicked man by observing their behaviour and its results. It can happen, for instance, that, despite his intention, a wicked man does good. Don John in *Much Ado About Nothing* certainly means nothing but harm to Claudio and Hero, yet it is thanks to him that Claudio obtains insight into his own shortcomings and becomes, what previously he was not, a fit husband for Hero. To the outward eye, however different their subjective intentions, both Harry of Monmouth and Iago deceive and destroy. Even in their speech one cannot help noticing a certain resemblance between

> *So when this loose behaviour I throw off*
> *And pay the debt I never promised,*
> *By how much better than my word I am.*
> *I'll so offend to make offence a skill*
> *Redeeming time when men least think I will.*

and:

> *For when my outward action doth demonstrate*
> *The native act and figure of my heart*
> *In compliment extern, 'tis not long after*
> *But I will wear my heart upon my sleeve*
> *For daws to peck at. I am not what I am . . .*

and the contrast of both to Sonnet 121:

> *No, I am that I am and those that level*
> *At my abuses reckon up their own.*
> *I may be straight though they themselves are*
> *   bevel.*

Falstaff is perfectly willing to tell the world: "I am that I am, a drunken old failure." Hal cannot jeopardize his career by such careless disclosure but must always assume whatever manner is politic at the moment. To the degree that we have worldly ambitions, Falstaff's verdict on the Prince strikes home.

> *Thou art essentially mad without seeming so.*

Falstaff never really does anything, but he never stops talking, so that the impression he makes on the audience is not of idleness but of infinite energy. He is never tired, never bored, and until he is rejected he radiates happiness as Hal radiates power, and this happiness without apparent cause, this untiring devotion to making others laugh becomes a comic image for a love which is absolutely self-giving.

Laughing and loving have certain properties in common. Laughter is contagious but not, like physical force, irresistible. A man in a passion of any kind cannot be made to laugh; if he laughs, it is a proof that he has already mastered his passion. Laughter is an action only in a special sense. Many kinds of action can cause laughter, but the only kind of action that laughter causes is more laughter; while we laugh, time stops and no other kind of action can be contemplated. In rage or hysteria people sometimes are said to "laugh" but no one can confuse the noises they make with the sound of real laughter. Real laughter is absolutely unaggressive; we cannot wish people or things we find amusing to be other than they are; we do not desire to change them, far less hurt or destroy them. An angry and dangerous mob is rendered harmless by the orator who can succeed in making it laugh. Real laughter is always, as we say, "disarming".

Falstaff makes the same impression on us that the Sinner of Lublin made upon his rabbi.

In Lublin lived a great sinner. Whenever he went to talk to the rabbi, the rabbi readily consented and conversed with him as if he were a man of integrity and one who was a close friend. Many of the hassidim were annoyed at this and one said to the other: "Is it possible that our rabbi who has only to look once into a man's face to know his life from first to last, to know the very origin of his soul, does not see that this fellow is a sinner? And if he does see it, that he considers him worthy to speak to and associate with?" Finally they summoned up courage to go to the rabbi himself with their question. He answered them: "I know all about him as well as you. But you know how I love gaiety and hate dejection. And this man is so great a sinner. Others repent the moment they have sinned, are sorry for a moment, and then return to their folly. But he knows no regrets and no doldrums, and lives in his happiness as in a tower. And it is the radiance of his happiness that overwhelms my heart."

Falstaff's happiness is almost an impregnable tower, but not quite. "I am that I am" is not a complete self-description; he must also add—"The young prince hath misled me. I am the fellow with the great belly, and he is my dog."

The Christian God is not a self-sufficient being like Aristotle's First Cause, but a God who creates a world which he continues to love although it refuses to love him in return. He appears in this world, not as Apollo or Aphrodite might appear, disguised as a man so that no mortal should recognize his divinity, but as a real man who openly claims to be God And the consequence is inevitable. The highest religious and temporal authorities condemn Him as a blasphemer and a Lord of Misrule, as a Bad Companion for mankind. Inevitable because, as Richelieu said, "the salvation of States is in this world", and history has not as yet provided us with any evidence that the Prince of this world has changed his character.

NOVEMBER 1959

KATHERINE ANNE PORTER

A Wreath for the Gamekeeper

THE DUBIOUS CRUSADE is over, anybody can buy the book now in hardback or paper-cover, expurgated or unexpurgated, in drug-stores and railway stations as well as in the bookshops, and 'twas a famous victory for something or other, let's wait and see. Let us remark as we enter the next phase that we may hope this episode in the history of our system of literary censorship will mark the end of one of our most curious native customs—calling upon the police and the post office officials to act as literary critics in addition to all their other heavy duties. It is not right nor humane and I hope this is the end of it; it is enough to drive good men out of those services altogether.

When I first read *Lady Chatterley's Lover*, thirty years ago, I thought it a dreary, sad performance with some passages of unintentional hilarious low comedy, one scene at least simply beyond belief in a book written with such inflamed apostolic solemnity, which I shall return to later; and I wondered then at all the huzza and hullabaloo about suppressing it. I realize now there were at least two reasons for it—first, Lawrence himself, who possessed to the last degree the quality of high visibility; and second, the rise to power of a demagoguery of political and social censorship by unparalleled ignoramuses in all things, including the arts, which they regarded as the expression of peculiarly dangerous forms of immorality. These people founded organizations for the suppression of Vice, and to them nearly everything *was* Vice, and other societies for the promotion of Virtue, some of them very dubious, and their enthusiasms took some weird and dangerous directions. Prohibition was their major triumph, with its main result of helping organized crime to become big business; but the arts, and especially literature, became the object of a morbid purblind interest to those strange beings who knew nothing about any art, but knew well what they feared and hated.

It is time to take another look at this question of censorship and protest which has been debated intermittently ever since I can remember. Being a child of my time, naturally I was to be found protesting : I was all for freedom of speech, of action, of belief, of choice, in every department of human life; and for authors all this was to be comprehended in the single perfect right to express their thoughts without reserve, write anything they chose, with publishers to publish and booksellers to sell it, and the vast public gloriously at liberty to buy and read it by the tens of thousands.

It was a noble experiment, no doubt, an attempt to bring a root idea of liberty to flower; but in practice it soon showed serious defects and abuses, for the same reason that prohibition of alcohol could not be made to work : gangsters and crooks took over the business of supplying the human demand for intoxication and obscenity, which hitherto had been in the hands of respectable elements, who regulated it and kept it more or less in its place; but it still is a market that never fails no matter who runs it. (I have often wondered what were the feelings of the old-line pious prohibitionists when they discovered that their most powerful allies in the fight to maintain prohibition were the bootleggers.)

Publishers were certainly as quick to take advantage of the golden moment as the gangsters, and it did not take many of them very long to discover that the one best way to sell a book with "daring" passages was to get it banned in Boston, or excluded from the United States mails. Certain authors, not far behind the publishers, discovered that if they could write books the publisher could advertise as in peril from the censor, all the better. Sure enough, the censor would rise to the bait, crack down in a way that would be front-page news, the alarm would go out to all fellow writers and assorted lovers of liberty that one of the guild was being abused in his basic human rights guaranteed by our Constitution, by those hyenas in Boston or the Post Office. The wave of publicity was on, and the sales went up. Like too many such precariously balanced schemes, it was wonderful while it lasted, but it carried the seeds of its own decay. Yet those were the days when people really turned out and paraded with flags and placards, provocative songs and slogans, openly inviting arrest and quite often succeeding in being hauled off to the police station in triumph, there to sit in a cell perfectly certain that somebody was going to show up and bail them out before night.

Writers—I was often one of them—did not always confine their aid to freedom of the word, though that was their main concern. They would sometimes find themselves in the oddest company, defending strange causes and weirdly biased viewpoints on the grounds that they most badly wanted defence. But we also championed recklessly the most awful wormy little books we none of us would have given shelf room, and more than once it came over us in mid-parade that this was no downtrodden citizen being deprived of his rights, but a low cynic cashing in on our high-minded application of democratic principles. I suppose for a good many of us, all this must just be chalked up to Experience. After some time, I found myself asking, "Why should I defend a worthless book just because it has a few dirty words in it? Let it disappear of itself and the sooner the better."

No one comes to that state of mind quickly, and it is dangerous ground to come to at all, I suppose, but one comes at last. My change of view began with the first publication in 1928 of *Lady Chatterley's Lover*. He has become, this lover of Lady Chatterley's, as sinister in his effect on the minds of critics as that of Quint himself on the children and the governess in *The Turn of the Screw*. I do not know quite what rôle Lady Chatterley should play to Quint-Mellors. She is not wicked, as Miss Jessel is, she is merely a moral imbecile. She is not intense, imaginative, and dazzled like the governess, she is stupid; and it is useless to go on with the comparison, for she is not the centre of the critics' attention as the Gamekeeper is, she has not that baneful fascination for them that he has. But there is one quality both books have in common and they both succeed in casting the same spell on plain reader and critic alike : the air of evil which shrouds them both, the sense of a situation of foregone and destined failure, to which there can be no outcome except despair. Only, the Lawrence book is sadder, because Lawrence was a badly flawed, lesser artist than James. He did not really know what he was doing, or if he did, pretended to be doing something else; and his blood-chilling anatomy of the activities of the rutting season between two rather dull persons comes with all the more force because the relations are precisely not between the vengeful seeking dead and living beings, but between the living themselves who seem to me deader than any ghost.

Yet for the past several months there has been a steady flood of extremely well-managed publicity in defence of Lawrence's motives and the purity of his novel, into which not only critics, but newspaper and magazine reporters, editorial writers, ministers of various religious beliefs, women's clubs, the police, postal authorities, and educators have been drawn, clamorously. I do not object to censorship being so loudly defeated again for the present. I merely do not approve of the way it was done. Though there were at this time no parades, I believe, we have seen such unanimity and solidarity of opinion among American critics, and many of them of our first order, as I do not remember to have seen before. What are we to think of them, falling in like this with this fraudulent crusade of raising an old tired Cause out of its tomb? For this is no longer just a book, and it never was a work of literature worth all this attention. It is no longer a Cause, if it ever was, but a publicity device and a well-worn one by now, calculated to rouse a salacious itch of curiosity in the prospective customer. This is such standard procedure by now it seems unnecessary to mention it. Yet these hard-headed, experienced literary men were trapped into it once more, and lent a strong hand to it. There is something touching, if misguided, in this fine-spirited show of manly solidarity, this full-throated chorus in defence of Lawrence's vocabulary and the nobility of his intentions. I have never questioned either, I wish only to say that I think from start to finish he was about as wrong as can be on the whole subject of sex, and that he wrote a very laboriously bad book to prove it. The critics who have been carried away by a generous desire to promote freedom of speech, and give a black eye to prudes and nannies, overlook sometimes—and in a work of literature this should not be overlooked, at least not by men whose profession it is to criticize literature—that purity, nobility of intention, and apostolic fervour are good in themselves at times, but at others they depend on context, and in this instance they are simply not enough. Whoever says they are, and tries to persuade the public to accept a book for what it is not, a work of good art, is making a grave mistake, if he means to go on writing criticism.

As for the original uproar, Lawrence began it himself, as he nearly always did, loudly and bitterly on the defensive, throwing out each book in turn as if he were an early Christian throwing himself to the lions. "Anybody who calls my novel a dirty sexual novel is a liar." Further : "It'll infuriate *mean* people; but it will surely soothe decent ones." The *Readers' Subscription* (an American book-club) in its brochure offering the book, carries on the tone boldly: "Now, at long last, a courageous American publisher is making available the unexpurgated version of *Lady Chatterley's Lover*—exactly as the author meant it to be seen by the intelligent, sensitive reader." No, this kind of left-handed flattery won't quite do : it is the obverse of the form of blackmail used by publishers and critics to choke their ambiguous wares down our throats. They say in effect, "If you disapprove of this book, you are proved to be (1) illiterate, (2) insensitive, (3) unintelligent, (4) low-minded, (5) 'mean', (6) a hypocrite, (7) a prude, and other unattractive things." I happen to have known quite a number of decent persons, not too unintelligent or insensitive, with some love and understanding of the arts, who were revolted by the book; and I do not propose to sit down under this kind of bullying.

Archibald MacLeish regards it as "pure" and a work of high literary merit. He has a few reservations as to the whole with which I heartily agree so far as they go; yet even Mr. MacLeish begins trailing his coat, daring us at our own risk to deny that the book is "one of the most important works of the century, or to express an opinion about the literature of our own time or about the spiritual history that literature expresses without making his peace in one way or another with D. H. Lawrence and with this work".

Without in the least making my peace with D. H. Lawrence or with this work, I wish to say why I disagree profoundly with the above judgements, and also with the following:

Harvey Breit: "The language and the incidents or scenes in question are deeply moving and very beautiful—Lawrence was concerned how love, how a relationship between a man and a woman can be most touching and beautiful, but only if it is uninhibited and total." This is wildly romantic and does credit to Mr. Breit's feelings, but there can be no such thing as a total relationship between two human beings—to begin with, what *is* total in such a changing, uncertain, limited state? and if there could be, just how would the persons involved know when they had reached it? Judging from certain things he wrote and said on this subject, I think Lawrence would have been the first to protest at even an attempt to create such a condition. He demanded the right to invade anybody, but he was noticeably queasy when anyone took a similar liberty with him.

Edmund Wilson: "The most inspiring book I have seen in a long time . . . one of his best-written . . . one of his most vigorous and brilliant . . ."

This reminds me that I helped parade with banners in California in defence of Mr. Wilson's *Memoirs of Hecate County*—a misguided act of guild loyalty and personal admiration I cannot really regret, so far as friendship is concerned. But otherwise the whole episode was deplorably unnecessary. My preference has not changed for his magnificent *To the Finland Station* and for almost any of his criticisms and essays on literary and public affairs.

Jacques Barzun: "I have no hesitation in saying that I do not consider Lawrence's novel pornographic." I agree with this admirably prudent statement, and again when Mr. Barzun notes Lawrence's ruling passion for reforming everything and everybody in sight. My quarrel with the book is that it really is not pornographic—the great, wild, free-wheeling Spirit of Pornography has here been hitched to a rumbling little domestic cart and trundled off to chapel, its ears pinned back and its mouth washed out with soap.

Mr. Schorer, who contributes the preface, even brings in Yeats to defend this tiresome book. Yeats, bless his memory, when he talked bawdy, knew what he was saying and why. He enjoyed the flavour of gamey words on his tongue, and never deceived himself for one moment as to the nature of that enjoyment; he never got really interestingly dirty until age had some-what cooled the ardours of his flesh, thus doubling his pleasure in the thoughts of it in the most profane sense. Mr. Schorer reprints part of a letter from Yeats, written years ago, to Mrs. Shakespear: "These two lovers the gamekeeper and his employer's wife each separated from their class by their love and fate are poignant in their loneliness; the coarse language of the one accepted by both becomes a forlorn poetry, uniting their solitudes, something ancient humble and terrible."

This comes as a breath of fresh air upon a fetid topic. Yeats reaches acutely into the muddlement and brings up the simple facts: the real disaster for the lady and the gamekeeper is that they face perpetual exile from their own proper backgrounds and society. Stale, pointless, unhappy as both their lives were before, due to their own deficiencies of character, it would seem, yet now they face, once the sexual furore is past, an utter aimlessness in life shocking to think about. Further, Yeats notes an important point I have not seen mentioned before—only one of the lovers uses the coarse language, the other merely accepts it. The gamekeeper talks his dirt and the lady listens, but never once answers in kind. If she had, the gamekeeper would no doubt have been deeply scandalized.

Yet the language needs those words, they have a definite use and value and they should not be used carelessly or imprecisely. My contention is that obscenity is real, is necessary as expression, a safety valve against the almost intolerable pressures and strains of relationship between men and women, and not only between men and women but between any human being and his unmanageable world. If we distort, warp, abuse this language which is the seamy side of the noble language of religion and love, indeed the necessary defensive expression of insult towards the sexual partner and contempt and even hatred of the insoluble stubborn mystery of sex itself which causes us such fleeting joy and such cureless suffering, what have we left for a way of expressing the luxury of obscenity which, for an enormous majority of men, by their own testimony, is half the pleasure of the sexual act?

I would not object, then, to D. H. Lawrence's obscenity if it were really that. I object to his misuse and perversions of obscenity, his wrong-headed denial of its true nature and meaning. Instead of writing straight, healthy obscenity, he makes it sickly sentimental, embarrassingly so, and I find that obscene sentimentality is as hard to bear as any other kind. I object to this pious attempt to purify and canonize obscenity, to castrate the Roaring Boy, to take the low comedy out of sex. We cannot and should not try to hallow these words because they are not hallowed and were never meant to be. The attempt to make pure, tender, sensitive, washed-in-the-blood-of-the-lamb words out of words whose whole intention, function, place in our language is meant to be exactly the opposite is sentimentality, and of a very low order. Our language is rich and full and I daresay there is a word to express every shade of meaning and feeling a human being is capable of, if we are not too lazy to look for it; or if we do not substitute one word for another, such as calling a nasty word—meant to be nasty, we need it that way—"pure", and a pure word "nasty". This is an unpardonable tampering with definitions, and, in Lawrence, I think it comes of a very deep-grained fear and distrust of sex itself; he was never easy on that subject, could not come to terms with it for anything. Perhaps it was a long hang-over from his childish Chapel piety, a violent revulsion from the inane gibberish of some of the hymns. He wrote once with deep tenderness about his early Chapel memories and said that the word "Galilee" had magic for him, and that his favourite hymn was this:

> *Each gentle dove, and singing bough,*
> *That makes the eve so dear to me,*
> *Has something far diviner now,*
> *That takes me back to Galilee.*
> *Oh Galilee, sweet Galilee,*
> *Where Jesus loved so well to be,*
> *Oh Galilee, sweet Galilee,*
> *Come sing again thy songs to me.*

His first encounter with dirty words, as he knew them to be, must have brought a shocking sense of guilt, especially as they no doubt gave him great secret pleasure; and to the end of his life he was engaged in the hopeless attempt to wash away that sense of guilt by denying the reality of its cause. He never arrived at the sunny truth so fearlessly acknowledged by Yeats, that "Love has pitched his mansion in the place of excrement"; but Yeats had already learned long before in his own experience that love has many mansions and only one of them is pitched there—a very important one that should be lived in very boldly and in hot blood at its own right seasons; but to deny its nature is to vulgarize it indeed. My own belief is this, that anything at all a man and woman wish to do or say in their sexual relations, their love-making, or call it what you please, is exactly their own business and nobody else's. But let them keep it to themselves unless they wish to appear ridiculous at best, at worst debased and even criminal. For sex resembles many other acts which may in themselves be harmless, yet when committed in certain circumstances may be not only a sin, but a crime against human life itself, human feelings, human rights—I do not say against ethics, morality, sense of honour (in a discussion of the motives not of the author perhaps, but of the characters in this novel, such words are nearly meaningless), but a never-ending wrong against those elements in the human imagination which were capable of such concepts in the first place. If they need the violent stimulation of obscene acrobatics, ugly words, pornographic pictures, or even low music—there is a negro jazz trumpeter who blows, it is said, a famous aphrodisiac noise—I can think of no argument against it, unless it might be thought a pity their nervous systems are so benumbed they need to be jolted and shocked into pleasure. Sex shouldn't be that kind of hard work, nor should it, as this book promises, lead to such a dull future. For nowhere in this sad history can you see anything but a long, dull grey, monotonous chain of days, lightened now and then by a sexual bout. I can't hear any music, or poetry, or the voices of friends, or children. There is no wine, no food, no sleep nor refreshment, no laughter, no rest nor quiet—no love. I remember then that this is the fevered day-dream of a dying man sitting under his umbrella pines in Italy indulging his sexual fantasies. For Lawrence is a Romantic turned wrong side out, and like Swift's recently-flayed woman, it does alter his appearance for the worse—and his visions are easy, dream-like, not subject to any real interruptions and interferences—for like children they see the Others as the Enemy—a mixture of morning dew and mingled body-secretions, a boy imagining a female partner who is nothing but one yielding, faceless, voiceless organ of consent.

An organ, and he finally bestows on those quarters his accolade of approval in the language and tone of praise he might give to a specially succulent scrap of glandular meat fresh from the butcher's. "Tha's a tasty bit of tripe, th'art," he says in effect, if not in just those words. And adds (these *are* his words), "Tha'rt real, even a bit of a bitch." Why a bitch is more real than other forms of life he does not explain. Climbing on his lap, she confirms his diagnosis by whispering, "Kiss me!"

Lawrence was a very gifted, distraught man who continually over-reached himself in an effort to combine all the authorities of artist, prophet, messiah, leader, censor, and mentor, by use of an unstable and inappropriate medium, the novel. His poetry and painting aside, he should be considered first as a writer of prose, and as a novelist. If a novelist is going to be so opinionated and obstinate and crazed on so many subjects he will need to be a Tolstoy, not a Lawrence. Only Tolstoy could be so furiously and fiercely wrong. He can nearly persuade you by sheer overwhelming velocity of will to agree with him.

Tolstoy once said—as reported by Gorky in his little memoir of Tolstoy —that in effect (I have the book in the house, but cannot find it now) the truth about women was so hideous he dared not tell it, except when his grave was dug and ready for him. He would run to it—or was it to his coffin—tell the truth about women, and then pull the lid, or was it the clods, over his head . . .

It's a marvellous picture. Tolstoy was merely roaring in the frenzy roused in him in face of his wife's terrible, relentless adoration, her shameless fertility, her unbearable fidelity, the shocking series of jealous revenges she took upon him for his hardness of heart and wickedness to her, the whole mystery of her oppressive femaleness. He did not know the truth about women, not even about that one who was the curse of his life. He did not know the truth about himself. This is not surprising, for no one does know the truth, either about himself or about anyone else, and all recorded human acts and words are open testimony to our endless efforts to know each other, and our failure to do so. I am only saying that it takes Homer or Sophocles or Dante or Chaucer or Shakespeare, or, at rather a distance, Tolstoy, to silence us, to force us to listen and almost to believe in their version of things, lulled or exalted or outraged into a brief acceptance. Lawrence has no grandeur in wrath or arrogance or love; he buzzes and darts like a wasp, irritable and irritating, hovering and bedevilling with a kind of insect-like persistence—he nags, in a word, and that is intolerable from anyone but surely unpardonable in an artist.

This tendency to nag, to disguise poorly as fiction a political, sociological tract, leads Lawrence, especially in this book, into some scenes on the grisly-comic order; they reminded me of certain passages in *The Grapes of Wrath*, and pretty much on the same level, regarded as literature. Yet Steinbeck's genius for bathos never exceeded a certain scene by Lawrence which I have never heard mentioned by anyone, in talk or in print, by any critic however admiring—certainly, I have not heard all the talk or seen all the print on this subject—but I sympathize with this omission for I hardly know where to begin with it. It is the unbelievably grotesque episode of this besotted couple weaving flowers in each other's pubic hair, hanging bouquets and wreaths in other strategic bodily spots, making feeble little dirty jokes, inventing double-meaning nicknames for their sexual organs, and altogether, though God knows it is of an imbecilic harmlessness, and is meant in all solemn God's-earnestness to illustrate true passion at lyric play, I for one feel that I have overheard talk and witnessed acts never meant for me to hear or witness. The act itself I could not regard as shocking or in any way offensive except for its lack of reserve and privacy. Love-making surely must be, for human beings at our present state of development, one of the more private enterprises. Who would want a witness to that entire self-abandonment and helplessness? So it is best in such a case for the intruder to tip-toe away quietly, and say nothing. I hold that this is not prudery nor hypocrisy; I still believe in the validity of simple respect and regard for the dark secret things of life—that they should be inviolable, and guarded by the two who take part, and that no other presence should be invited.

Let us go on with the scene in question. The lovers are in his game-keeper's lodge, it is raining, the impulsive woman takes off to the woods stark naked except for a pair of rubbers, lifting her heavy breasts to the rain (she is constitutionally overweight), and doing eurythmic movements she had learned long ago in Dresden. The gamekeeper is so exalted by this spectacle he takes out after her, faunlike, trips her up, and they splash about together in the rilling rainwater . . . It could, I suppose, be funnier, but I cannot think how. And somewhere in these extended passages the gamekeeper pauses to give his lady a lecture on the working class and its dullness due to the industrial system. He blames everything on the mechanized life "out there", and his complaint recurs with variations: "Though it's a shame, what's been done to people these last hundred years: man turned into nothing but labour-insects, and all their manhood taken away, and all their real life." Hadn't Lawrence got any notion of what had been done to such people the hundred years before the last, and the hundred before that, and so on, back to the beginning?

Yet both the lovers did accept the standards of her world in appearances at least; over and over she observes that her gamekeeper is really quite elegant or self-possessed or looks "like a gentleman", and is pleased to think that she could introduce him anywhere. He observes the same thing of himself from time to time in an oblique way—he is holding his own among them, even now and again putting them down. Here are glimpses of Lady Chatterley sizing up Mellors on their first meeting: "He was a man in dark green velveteen and gaiters . . . the old style, with a red face and red moustache and distant eyes . . . " And later, she noted that "he breathed rather quickly, through parted lips", while pushing his invalid employer's wheel-chair uphill. "He was rather frail, really. Curiously full of vitality, but a little frail and quenched." Earlier she has been described as "a soft, ruddy, country-looking girl, inclined to freckles, with big blue eyes and curling hair, and a soft voice and rather strong, female loins"; in fact, "she was too feminine to be quite smart".

Essentially, these are fairly apt descriptions of Lawrence and Frieda Lawrence, as one would need only to have seen photographs to recognize. This is relevant only because the artist's life is always his material and it seems pointless to look for hidden clues when they are so obviously on the surface. Lawrence the man and Lawrence the artist are more than usually inseparable: he is everywhere, and everywhere the same, in his letters, his criticism, his poetry, his painting, the uneasy, suffering, vociferous man who wanted to be All-in-All in all things, but never discovered what the All is, or if it exists indeed. This will to omniscience is most clearly seen in *Lady Chatterley's Lover*. In the entire series of sexual scenes, growing in heat and intensity quite naturally, with the language not coarsening particularly, it could not be coarser than it began, there is only more of it, with the man showing off his prowess as he perceives his success—all this is exposed from the point of view of the woman. Lawrence constantly describes what the man *did*, but tells us with great authority what the woman *felt*. Of course, he cannot possibly know—it is like a textbook of instructions to a woman as to how she should feel in such a situation. That is not his territory, and he has no business there. This shameless, incessant, nosy kind of poaching on the woman's nature as if determined to leave her no place of her own is what I find peculiarly repellent. The best he can ever do is to gather at second-hand, by hearsay, from women, in these matters; and though he had the benefit no doubt of some quite valid confidences and instruction from women entirely honest with him, it still just looks pretty fraudulent; somehow he shouldn't pretend he is the woman in the affair, too, as well as the man. It shows the obsessional nature of his self-centredness; he gives the nightmarish impression of the bi-sexual snail squeezed into its narrow house making love to itself— my notion of something altogether undesirable even in the lowest possible forms of life. We have seen in his writings his hatred and distrust of women—of the female principle, that is; with some of its exemplars he managed to get along passably—shown in his perpetual exasperated admonition to woman to be what he wants her to be, without any regard to what she possibly may be—to stop having any will or mind or indeed any existence of her own except what he allows her. He will dole out to her the kind of sex he thinks is good for her, and allow her just the amount of satisfaction in it he wishes her to have—not much. Even Lady Chatterley's ration seems more in the head than in the womb.

Yet, where can it end? The gamekeeper, in spite of a certain fragility of appearance, seems to be the fighting-cock sort, wiry and tough enough, and he certainly runs through a very creditable repertory of sexual styles and moods. Yet he is a man of physical limitations like any other. Lady Chatterley is the largish, slow-moving, solid sort, and we know by her deeds and her words she is not worn down by an active mind. Such a woman often wears extremely well, physically. How long will it be before that enterprising man exhausts himself trying to be everything in that affair, both man and woman too, while she has nothing to do but be passive and enjoy whatever he wants her to have in the way he wants her to have it? It seems to me a hopelessly one-sided arrangement, it places all responsibility on him, and he will be the loser. Such a woman could use up half a dozen such men, and it is plain already that she will shortly be looking for another man; I give him two years at the rate he is going, if sex is really all he has to offer her, or all she is able to accept. For if sex alone is what she must have, she will not abide with him.

Jean Cocteau has told somewhere a terrible story of a priest in a hotel, who, hearing the death-rattle of a man in the next room, mistook it for animal noises of a successful intercourse and knocked censoriously on the wall. We should all be very careful not to make the same mistake.

Lawrence, who was prickly as a hedgehog where his own privacies were concerned, cannot in his mischievous curiosity allow to a woman even the privacy of her excremental functions. He has to tell her in so many words just where her private organs are located, what they are good for, and how praiseworthy he finds the whole arrangement. Nothing will do for him but to try to crawl into her skin; finding that impossible, at last he admits unwillingly a fact you would think a sensible person would have been born knowing, or would have learned very early : that we *are* separate, each a unique entity, strangers by birth, that our envelopes are meant as the perfect device for keeping us separate. We are meant to share, not to devour each other; no one can claim the privilege of two lives, his own and another's.

Mr. Schorer in his preface hails the work as "a great hymn to marriage". That, I should say, it is not, above all. No matter what the protagonists think they are up to, this is the story of an "affair", and a thoroughly disreputable one, based on the treachery of a woman to her husband who has been made impotent by wounds received in war; and by the mean trickery of a man of low origins out to prove he is as good as, or better than, the next man. Mr. Schorer also accepts and elucidates for us Lawrence's favourite, most bathetic fallacy. He writes :

The pathos of Lawrence's novel arises from the tragedy of modern society. What is tragic is that we cannot feel our tragedy. We have grown slowly into a confusion of these terms, these two forms of power, and in confusing them we have left almost no room for the free creative functions of the man or woman who, lucky soul, possesses "integrity of self". The force of this novel probably lies in the degree of intensity with which his indictment of the world and the consequent solitude of his lovers suggest such larger meanings.

If Mr. Schorer means to say—he sometimes expresses himself a little cloudily—that the modern industrial world, Lawrence's pet nightmare, has destroyed, among a number of other things, some ancient harmony once existing between the sexes which Lawrence proposes to restore by the uttering of short words during the sexual act, I must merely remind him that all history is against his theory. The world itself, as well as the relationship between men and women, has not "grown into confusion". We have never had anything else, or anything much better; all human life since recorded time has been a terrible struggle from confusion to confusion to more confusion, and Lawrence, aided by his small but vociferous congregation—for there remain in his doctrine and manner the style of the parochial messiah, the chapel preacher's threats and cajolements—has done nothing but add his own peculiar mystifications to the subject.

One trouble with him, always, and it shows more plainly than ever in this book, is that he wanted to play all the rôles, be everywhere and everybody at once. He wishes to be the godhead in his dreary rigmarole of primitive religion, as in *The Plumed Serpent*, but must be the passive female too. Until he tires of it, and comes up with a fresh set of rules for everybody. Mr. Schorer cites a passage from a letter Lawrence wrote to someone when his feelings were changing. "The leader-cum-follower relationship is a bore," he decided, "and the new relationship will be some sort of tenderness, sensitive, between men and men, and between men and women." He gets a good deal of himself into these few words. First, when he is tired of the game he has invented and taught as a religion, everybody must drop it. Second, he seems not to have observed that tenderness is not a new relationship between persons who love one another. Third, he said between men and men, and men and women. He did not say between women and women, for his view of women is utterly baleful, and he has expressed it ferociously over and over. Women must be kept apart, for they contaminate each other. They are to be redeemed one by one through the sexual offices of a man, who seems to have no other function in her life, nor she in his. One of the great enlightenments of Lady Chatterley after her experience of the sentimental obscenities of her gamekeeper is to see other women clearly, women sexually less lucky than she, and to realize that they are all horrible! She can't get away fast enough, and back to the embraces of her fancy man—and yet—and yet——

True marriage? Love, even? Even really good sex-as-such? It seems a very sad, shabby sort of thing to have to settle for, poor woman. I suppose she deserves anything she gets, really, but her just deserts are none of our affair. The pair are so plainly headed, not for tragedy but just a dusty limbo, their fate interests us as a kind of curiosity. It is true that her youth was robbed by her husband's fate in the war. I think he was worse robbed, even, with no way out, yet nobody seems to feel sorry for him. He is shown as having very dull ideas with conversation to match, but he is not more dull than the gamekeeper, who forgets that the lady's aristocratic husband was not born impotent, as Lawrence insists by way of his dubious hero, all upper-class men were. At this point Lawrence's confusion of ideas and feelings, the pull and haul between his characters who go their own dreary way in spite of him, and the ideas he is trying to express through them become pretty nearly complete. It would take another book to thread out and analyse the contradictions and blind alleys into which the reader is led.

Huizinga, on page 199 of his book, *The Waning of the Middle Ages*, tells of the erotic religious visions of a late medieval monk, and adds: "The description of his numerous visions is characterized at the same time by an excess of sexual imagination and by the absence of all genuine emotion." Lawrence used to preach frantically that people must get sex out of their heads and back where it belongs; and never learned that sex lives in all our parts, and must have the freedom of the whole being—to run easily in the blood and nerves and cells, adding its glow of life to everything it touches. The ineptitudes of these awful little love-scenes seem heart-breaking—that a man of such gifts should have lived so long and learned no more about love than that!

FEBRUARY 1960

STUART HAMPSHIRE

"Doctor Zhivago"

AS FROM A LOST CULTURE

THAT *Doctor Zhivago* is one of the great novels of the last fifty years, and the most important work of literature that has appeared since the war, seems to me certain, even when every allowance has been made for the circumstances of its appearance and the effect that this may have upon one's judgement.

The immediate enthusiasm with which it has been received here is not in the least surprising and is no ground for suspicion. This enthusiasm is, I think, quite unconnected with politics in the narrow sense and with Communism, or with any sentimental sympathy with the author's frustrations. The explanation is that, at first reading, a Western European is immediately reminded of all that is best in his own past, of the great tradition of full statement, which he had come to think no contemporary writer could now resume, because the extremes of violence and social change had made any real imaginative reconstruction of the recent past, any whole picture, seem impossible. We have come to take it for granted that the most serious art of our time must be fragmented art and indirect statement. There has for a long time seemed no possibility that anyone should have survived who, in the exercise of his genius, retained all the literary ambitions and philosophical culture of the last century. That it has happened is an extraordinary accident. It is as if in the general devastation one lane of communication with the past has been kept clear and open. Perhaps only a long isolation in a cultural desert could have produced this result, this slow maturing of a work that is independent of any distracting contemporary influences. The fact remains that part of the immediate excitement of the Western reader is a sense of escape and of nostalgia, of a return to the real or imaginary Golden Age when absolute assurance and uncontrived and confident gestures were still possible.

Doctor Zhivago is unlikely to have any great influence on the writing of novels in France, Britain, or America : it is too far away from the main stream and it has been too little affected by the experiments of the last thirty years. It really does seem to come from a lost culture, to be just coeval perhaps with Thomas Mann's *Buddenbrooks*, but certainly not with Faulkner and Sartre. This free, naïve, as opposed to sentimental, writing is probably not something that can be imitated or further developed, because the confidence in a complete philosophy, tested by revolution and violence, of which the naïveté is an expression, is probably everywhere lacking in the West. Pasternak is after all looking back in this novel and leaving his testimony, proved by his experience and final. Since his experience includes the Communist revolution, the looking back is not mere looking back. He has come to terms in his own mind with that way of life which has the most plausible and widely advertised claim to represent the future. In contrast with this, all the writers of the West are in an uncertain, waiting condition, becalmed in a recognized interregnum, not knowing the worst and therefore incapable of any tested, unqualified statement. It is not surprising, therefore, that they turn to satire or sentimental mannerism, to expressions either of despair or of uncertainty. The whole sum of our experience in forty years of violence cannot yet be calculated.

The difficulty that this novel presents, after a first reading, is the difficulty that any carefully composed and long meditated work of art presents. It is naïve art, in Schiller's special sense of the word, but far from naïve, in the ordinary sense, in its composition. The other difficulty is of course the language. The English translation, as English, is certainly better than we are used to in translations from Russian, although the familiar jolts of incongruity do sometimes occur. It allows one to guess that the vocabulary of the original is rich and elaborate, particularly in descriptions of nature and in the dialogues of the poor. But not knowing the original is evidently an enormous loss, which cannot be mitigated. The whole book is informed by an intense feeling for everything that is distinctively Russian, by a characteristic kind of mystical patriotism, which is quite unlike the patriotism of the French or the English; the feeling of Russian landscape and Russian talk are evidently conveyed also in nuances of diction that will have deep associations for any Russian. The endless talk and the endless landscape are as much part of the substance of the novel as the revolution itself, as being the constantly changing background of the central story of love and separation. The vastness of the land, the snow, the episodes of calm and natural beauty after scenes of great violence and misery, are part of the story, which is arranged with a musical sense of fitness in the changes of mood. The whole truth about the experience of these years is to be built up gradually, and, partly for this reason, the first fifty pages of the novel are confused by the lack of a firm narrative. The reader is required to accept a series of impressions, not yet intelligibly related to each other, and a set of unexplained characters who are not clearly identified in his mind until much later. Pasternak does not even attempt the well-known virtues of the storyteller's art. He is writing a philosophical novel, a testimony of thought and experience, and not any kind of novel of character or of the fate of individuals. The villain is an abstract sketch of bourgeois corruption, and the story of his relations with the heroine is mere melodrama.

For this and other reasons any comparison between Pasternak and Tolstoy, either in intention or in effect, appears absurd from the very first page. One thinks of the swift, decisive beginning of *Anna Karenina*, the wonderful clarity and depth of the characters, and the impression left of the whole span of their lives lived in their natural circumstances. Not one of the characters in *Doctor Zhivago*, not even Zhivago himself, is endowed with this rounded naturalness nor are their lives steadily unfolded before the reader. The novel moves forward in short paragraphs and in short episodes, which are all related by strings of coincidence to the central figure; he and the heroine, Lara, together carry the whole weight of the story, as the picture is formed of the old society collapsing and of the new one forming in confusion and terror. If any single literary influence is to be mentioned, it seems to me that the most prominent is Shakespeare. The use of the wild dialogue of the characters of the underplot, the short scenes that somehow, as in *Antony and Cleopatra*, suggest the great events across great distances, and, above all, in the suggestion of signs of the supernatural in the natural order. Pasternak's Russia can contain witches and metaphysical fools alongside images of ideal love escaping from corruption, in which the personalities and idiosyncrasies of the lovers and of the villain play no part. There is something Shakespearian, which I cannot now state clearly, in the sudden blending of the imagery and the philosophical reflections, in the affinities found between thought and natural appearances.

It would be very gross and very dishonest to interpret this novel as primarily a condemnation of Soviet Communism. About the author's intentions no mistake is possible, since, like Proust, he clearly explains his philosophy in all its divisions, of æsthetics, politics, and personal morality, both directly and in words attributed to his characters. The Soviet State is indeed condemned as a degeneration from the revolution, which was the moment of liberty and of the assertion of the forces of life. The revolution itself is represented as one of the few great events of human history, comparable with the overthrow of Roman power as the ancient world ended. The old régime is shown as corrupting personal life as deeply, if less violently, than the Soviet fanaticism that succeeds it. But ultimately political action and organization are incidental to the most serious interests of men and women, which are to be found in the sources of art and of religion. These sources of renewal have been discovered, whenever a man achieves some heightened sense of his own part in the processes of life that makes his own death seem not a final waste. Men arrive at this deliverance and rest, when they have succeeded in communicating perfectly with one other person, giving the testimony of their own experience, either in love or in a work of art. The inconsolable people —Doctor Zhivago's wife and Lara's husband—are those who have never perfectly achieved this. This sense of the overwhelming need to communicate one's own individual experience, to add something distinctive to the always growing sum of the evidences of life, is the most moving theme of the book. The political cruelties, the crimes and errors of the Soviet system, are not made into grounds for final pessimism, and are certainly not the grounds for hopes of counter-revolution or of salvation from the West.

There are several long passages that read like a memory of the early writings of Hegel, particularly two in which Pasternak repeats Hegel's account of the historical rôle of Christianity in creating the modern man, who need no longer be either master or slave. For him Russia, the country in which people "talk as only Russians talk", is plainly the leading nation of this century, and, staying at home and somehow keeping alive the radical tradition of the Russian intelligentsia, he has written a work of universal significance, which offers hope and encouragement. The vindication of the freedom of art, and of private life lived on the appropriate human scale, does not appear in this novel as the conventional and now frigid liberalism of the West. There is no suggestion of nervous fence-building, of the shrill, defensive note of those who live within a stockade, trying not to notice the movements outside, by which they know that their fate is being decided.

Written in proud isolation, *Dr. Zhivago* will, I think, always be read as one of the most profound descriptions of love in the whole range of modern literature.

NOVEMBER 1958

LESLIE A. FIEDLER

The Middle Against Both Ends

I AM SURELY ONE of the few people pretending to intellectual respectability who can boast that he has read more comic books than attacks on comic books. I do not mean that I have consulted or studied the comics— I have read them, often with some pleasure. Nephews and nieces, my own children, and the children of neighbours have brought them to me to share their enjoyment. An old lady on a ferry boat in Puget Sound once dropped two in my lap in wordless sympathy : I was wearing, at the time, a sailor's uniform.

I have somewhat more difficulty in getting through the books that attack them. I am put off, to begin with, by inaccuracies of fact. When Mr. Geoffrey Wagner in his *Parade of Pleasure* calls Superboy "Superman's brother" (he is, of course, Superman himself as a child), I am made suspicious. Actually, Mr. Wagner's book is one of the least painful on the subject; confused, to be sure, but quite lively and not in the least smug; though it propounds the preposterous theory that the whole of "popular literature" is a conspiracy on the part of the "plutos" to corrupt an innocent American people. Such easy melodrama can only satisfy someone prepared to believe, as Mr. Wagner apparently does, that the young girls of Harlem are being led astray by the *double-entendres* of blues records!

Mr. Wagner's notions are at least more varied and subtle than Mr. Gershom Legman's, who cries out in his *Love and Death* that it is simply our sexual frustrations which breed a popular literature dedicated to violence. But Mr. Legman's theory explains too much : not only comic books but Hemingway, war, Luce, Faulkner, the status of women—and, I should suppose, Mr. Legman's own shrill hyperboles. At that, Mr. Legman seems more to the point in his search for some deeply underlying cause than Frederic Wertham, in *Seduction of the Innocent*, with his contention that the pulps and comics in themselves are schools for murder. That the undefined aggressiveness of disturbed children can be given a shape by comic books, I do not doubt; and one could make a good case for the contention that such literature standardizes crime woefully or inhibits imagination in violence, but I find it hard to consider so obvious a symptom a prime cause of anything. Perhaps I am a little sensitive on this score, having heard the charge this week that the recent suicide of one of our college freshmen was caused by his having read (in a course of which I am in charge) Goethe, Dostoevsky, and *Death of a Salesman*. Damn it, he *had* read them, and he *did* kill himself!

In none of the books on comics I have looked into, and in none of the reports of ladies' clubs, protests of legislators, or statements of moral indignation by pastors, have I come on any real attempt to understand comic books : to define the form, midway between icon and story; to distinguish the sub-types : animal, adolescent, crime, western, etc.; or even to sparate out, from the deadpan varieties, tongue-in-cheek sports like *Pogo*, frank satire like *Mad*, or semi-surrealist variations like *Plastic Man*. It would not take someone with the talents of an Aristotle, but merely with his method, to ask the rewarding questions about this kind of literature that he asked once about an equally popular and bloody genre : what are its causes and its natural form?

A cursory examination would show that the super-hero comic (*Superman, Captain Marvel, Wonder Woman*, etc.) is the final form; it is statistically the most popular with the most avid readers, as well as providing the only new legendary material invented along with the form rather than adapted to it.

Next, one would have to abstract the most general pattern of the myth of the super-hero and deduce its significance : the urban setting, the threatened universal catastrophe, the hero who never uses arms, who returns to weakness and obscurity, who must keep his identity secret, who is impotent, etc. Not until then could one ask with any hope of an answer : what end do the comics serve? Why have they gained an immense body of readers precisely in the past fifteen or twenty years? Why must they be disguised as children's literature though read by men and women of all ages? And having answered these, one could pose the most dangerous question of all : why the constant, virulent attacks on the comics, and, indeed, on the whole of popular culture of which they are especially flagrant examples?

Strategically, if not logically, the last question should be asked first. Why the attacks? Such assaults by scientists and laymen are as characteristic of our age as puritanic diatribes against the stage of the Elizabethan Era, and pious protests against novel-reading in the later eighteenth century. I suspect that a study of such conventional reactions reveals at least as much about the nature of a period as an examination of the forms to which they respond. The most fascinating and suspicious aspect of the opposition to popular narrative is its unanimity; everyone from the members of the Montana State Legislature to the ladies of the Parent Teachers' Association of Boston, Massachusetts, from British M.P.s to the wilder post-Freudians of two continents agree on this, though they may agree on nothing else. What they have in common is, I am afraid, the sense that they are all, according to their lights, righteous. And their protests represent only one more example (though an unlikely one) of the notorious failure of righteousness in matters involving art.

Just what is it with which vulgar literature is charged by various guardians of morality or sanity? With everything: encouraging crime, destroying literacy, expressing sexual frustration, unleashing sadism, spreading anti-democratic ideas, and, of course, corrupting youth. To understand the grounds of such charges, their justification and their bias, we must understand something of the nature of the sub-art with which we are dealing.

Perhaps it is most illuminating to begin by saying that it is a peculiarly American phenomenon, an unexpected by-product of an attempt, not only to extend literacy universally, but to delegate taste to majority suffrage. I do not mean, of course, that it is found only in the United States, but that wherever it is found, it comes first from us, and is still to be discovered in fully-developed form only among us. Our experience along these lines is, in this sense, a preview for the rest of the world of what must follow the inevitable dissolution of the older aristocratic cultures.

One has only to examine certain Continental imitations of picture magazines like *Look* or *Life* or Disney-inspired cartoon books to be aware at once of the debt to American examples and of the failure of the imitations. For a true "popular literature" demands a more than ordinary slickness, the sort of high finish possible only to a machine-produced commodity in an economy of maximum prosperity. Contemporary popular culture, which is a function in an industrialized society, is distinguished from older folk art by its refusal to be shabby or second-rate in appearance, by a refusal to know its place. It is a product of the same impulse which has made available the sort of ready-made clothing which aims at destroying the possibility of knowing a lady by her dress.

Yet the articles of popular culture are made, not to be treasured, but to be thrown away; a paper-back book is like a disposable diaper or a paper milk-container. For all its competent finish, it cannot be preserved on dusty shelves like the calf-bound volumes of another day; indeed, its very mode of existence challenges the concept of a library, private or public. The sort of conspicuous waste once reserved for an *élite* is now available to anyone; and this is inconceivable without an absurdly high standard of living, just as it is unimaginable without a degree of mechanical efficiency that permits industry to replace nature, and invents—among other disposable synthetics—one for literature.

Just as the production of popular narrative demands industrial conditions most favourably developed in the United States, its distribution requires the peculiar conditions of our market places: the mass or democratized market. Sub-books and sub-arts are not distributed primarily through the traditional institutions: museums, libraries, and schools, which remain firmly in the hands of those who deplore mass culture. It is in drugstores and supermarkets and airline terminals that this kind of literature mingles without condescension with chocolate bars and soap-flakes. We have reached the end of a long process, begun, let us say, with Samuel Richardson, in which the work of art has approached closer and closer to the status of a commodity. Even the comic book is a last descendant of *Pamela*, the final consequence of letting the tastes (or more precisely, the buying power) of a class unpledged to maintaining the traditional genres determine literary success or failure.

Those who cry out now that the work of a Mickey Spillane or *The Adventures of Superman* travesty the novel, forget that the novel was long accused of travestying literature. What seems to offend us most is not the further downgrading of literary standards so much as the fact that the medium, the very notion and shape of a book, is being parodied by the comics. Jazz or the movies, which are also popular urban arts, depending for their distribution and acceptance on developments in technology (for jazz the gramophone), really upsets us much less.

It is the final, though camouflaged, rejection of literacy implicit in these new forms which is the most legitimate source of distress; but all arts so universally consumed have been for illiterates, even stained glass windows and the plays of Shakespeare. What is new in our present situation, and hence especially upsetting, is that this is the first art for *post*-literates, i.e. for those who have refused the benefit for which they were presumed to have sighed in their long exclusion. Besides, modern popular narrative is disconcertingly not oral; it will not surrender the benefits of the printing press as a machine, however indifferent it may be to that press as the perpetuator of techniques devised first for pen or quill. Everything that the press can provide—except matter to be really read—is demanded: picture, typography, even in many cases the illusion of reading along with the relaxed pleasure of illiteracy. Yet the new popular forms remain somehow prose narrative or pictographic substitutes for the novel; even the cognate form of the movies is notoriously more like a novel than a play in its handling of time, space and narrative progression.

From the folk literature of the past, which ever since the triumph of the

machine we have been trying sentimentally to recapture, popular literature differs in its rejection of the picturesque. Rooted in prose rather than
verse, secular rather than religious in origin, defining itself against the
city rather than the world of outdoor nature, a by-product of the factory
rather than agriculture, present-day popular literature defeats romantic
expectations of peasants in their embroidered blouses chanting or plucking
balalaikas for the approval of their betters. The haters of our own popular
art love to condescend to the folk; and on records or in fashionable night-
clubs in recent years, we have had entertainers who have earned enviable
livings producing commercial imitations of folk songs. But contemporary
vulgar culture is brutal and disturbing: the quasi-spontaneous expression
of the uprooted and culturally dispossessed inhabitants of anonymous
cities, contriving mythologies which reduce to manageable form the threat
of science, the horror of unlimited war, the general spread of corruption
in a world where the social bases of old loyalties and heroisms have long
been destroyed. That such an art is exploited for profit in a commercial
society, mass-produced by nameless collaborators, standardized and debased, is of secondary importance. It is the patented nightmare of us all, a
packaged way of coming to terms with one's environment sold for a dime
to all those who have rejected the unasked-for gift of literacy.

Thought of in this light, the comic books with their legends of the eternally threatened metropolis eternally protected by immaculate and modest
heroes (who shrink back after each exploit into the image of the crippled
newsboy, the impotent and cowardly reporter) are seen as inheritors, for
all their superficial differences, of the *inner* impulses of traditional folk
art. Their gross drawing, their poverty of language cannot disguise their
heritage of aboriginal violence, their exploitation of the ancient conflict
of black magic and white. Beneath their journalistic commentary on A-
bomb and Communism, they touch archetypal material: those shared
figures of our lower minds more like the patterns of dream than fact. In a
world where men threaten to dissolve into their most superficial and
mechanical techniques, to become their borrowed newspaper platitudes,
they remain close to the impulsive, subliminal life. They are our not quite
machine-subdued Grimm, though the Black Forest has become, as it must,
the City; the Wizard, the Scientist; and Simple Hans, Captain Marvel. In
a society which thinks of itself as "scientific"—and of the Marvelous as
childish—such a literature must seem primarily children's literature,
though, of course, it is read by people of all ages.

We are now in a position to begin to answer the question: what do the
righteous really have against comic books? In some parts of the world,
simply the fact that they are American is sufficient, and certain home-

grown self-contemners follow this line even in the United States. But it is really a minor argument, lent a certain temporary importance by passing political exigencies. To declare oneself against "the Americanization of culture" is meaningless unless one is set resolutely against industrialization and mass education.

More to the point is the attack on mass culture for its betrayal of literacy itself. In a very few cases, this charge is made seriously and with full realization of its import; but most often it amounts to nothing but an accusation of "bad grammar" or "slang" on the part of some school marm to whom the spread of "different than" seems to threaten the future of civilized discourse. What should set us on guard in this case is that it is not the fully literate, the intellectuals and serious writers who lead the attack, but the insecure semi-literate. In America, there is something a little absurd about the indignant delegation from the Parent Teachers' Association (themselves clutching the latest issue of *Life*) crying out in defence of literature. Asked for suggestions, such critics are likely to propose *The Readers' Digest* as required reading in high school—or to urge more comic book versions of the "classics": emasculated Melville, expurgated Hawthorne, or a child's version of something "uplifting" like "The Fall of the House of Ussher". In other countries, corresponding counterparts are not hard to find.

As a matter of fact, this charge is scarcely ever urged with much conviction. It is really the portrayal of crime and horror (and less usually sex) that the enlightened censors deplore. It has been charged against vulgar art that it is sadistic, fetishistic, brutal, full of terror; that it pictures women with exaggeratedly full breasts and rumps, portrays death on the printed page, is often covertly homosexual, etc., etc. About these charges, there are two obvious things to say. First, by and large, they are true. Second, they are also true about much of the most serious art of our time, especially that produced in America.

There is no count of sadism and brutality which could not be equally proved against Hemingway or Faulkner or Paul Bowles—or, for that matter, Edgar Allan Poe. There are certain more literate critics who are victims of their own confusion in this regard; and who will condemn a Class B movie for its images of flagellation or bloodshed only to praise in the next breath such an orgy of highminded sadism as *Le Salaire de la Peur*. The politics of the French picture may be preferable, or its photography; but this cannot redeem the scene in which a mud- and oil-soaked truck-driver crawls from a pit of sludge to reveal the protruding white bones of a multiple fracture of the thigh. This is as much horror-pornography as *Scarface* or *Little Caesar*. You cannot condemn *Superman* for the exploitation of violence, and praise the existentialist-homosexual-sadist shockers of Paul Bowles. It is possible to murmur by way of explanation something vague about art of catharsis; but no one is ready to advocate the suppression of anything merely because it is æsthetically bad. In this age of conflicting standards, we would all soon suppress each other.

An occasional Savonarola is, of course, ready to make the total rejection; and secretly or openly, the run-of-the-mill contemner of mass culture does condemn, on precisely the same grounds, most contemporary literature of distinction. Historically, one can make quite a convincing case to prove that our highest and lowest arts come from a common anti-bourgeois source. Edgar Allan Poe, who lived the image of the dandy that has been haunting high art ever since, also, one remembers, invented the popular detective story; and there is a direct line from Hemingway to O'Hara to Dashiell Hammett to Raymond Chandler to Mickey Spillane.

Of both lines of descent from Poe, one can say that they tell a black and distressing truth (we are creatures of dark impulse in a threatened and guilty world), and that they challenge the more genteel versions of "good taste". Behind the opposition to vulgar literature, there is at work the same fear of the archetypal and the unconscious itself that motivated similar attacks on Elizabethan drama and on the eighteenth-century novel. We always judge Gosson a fool in terms of Shakespeare; but this is not the point—he was just as wrong in his attack on the worst written, the most outrageously bloody and bawdy plays of his time. I should hate my argument to be understood as a defence of what is banal and mechanical and dull (there is, of course, a great deal!) in mass culture; it is merely a counter-attack against those who are aiming through that banality and dullness at what moves all literature of worth. Anyone at all sensitive to the life of the imagination would surely prefer the kids to read the coarsest fables of Black and White contending for the City of Man, rather than have them spell out, "Oh, see, Jane. Funny, funny Jane," or read to themselves hygienic accounts of the operation of supermarkets or manureless farms. Yet most schoolboard members are on the side of mental hygiene; and it is they who lead the charge against mass culture.

Anyone old enough to have seen, say, *Rain* is on guard against those who in the guise of wanting to destroy savagery and ignorance wage war on spontaneity and richness. But we are likely to think of such possibilities purely in sexual terms; the new righteous themselves have been touched lightly by Freud and are firm believers in frankness and "sex education". But in the very midst of their self-congratulation at their emancipation, they have become victims of a new and ferocious prudery. One who would be ashamed to lecture his masturbating son on the dangers of insanity, is quite prepared (especially if he has been reading Wertham) to predict the electric chair for the young scoundrel caught with a bootlegged comic. Superman is our Sadie Thompson. We live in an age when the child who is exposed to the "facts of life" is protected from "the facts of death". In the United States, for instance, a certain Doctor Spock has produced an enlightened guide to childcare for modern mothers—a paper-back book which sold, I would guess, millions of copies. Tell the child all about sex, the good doctor advises, but on the subject of death—hush!

By more "advanced" consultants, the taboo is advanced further towards absurdity : no bloodsoaked Grimm, no terrifying Andersen, no childhood verses about cradles that fall—for fear breeds insecurity; insecurity, aggression; aggression, war. There is even a "happy", that is to say, expurgated, Mother Goose in which the three blind mice have become "kind mice"—and the farmer's wife no longer hacks off their tails, but "cuts them some cheese with a carving knife". Everywhere the fear of fear is endemic, the fear of the very names of fear; those who have most ardently desired to end warfare and personal cruelty in the world around them, and are therefore most frustrated by their persistence, conspire to stamp out violence on the nursery bookshelf. This much they can do anyhow. If they can't hold up the weather, at least they can break the bloody glass.

This same fear of the instinctual and the dark, this denial of death and guilt by the enlightened genteel, motivates their distrust of serious literature, too. Faulkner is snubbed and the comic books are banned, not in the interests of the classics or even of Robert Louis Stevenson, as the attackers claim, but in the name of a literature of the middle ground which finds its fictitious vision of a kindly and congenial world attacked from above and below. I speak now not of the few intellectual converts to the cause of censorship, but of the main body of genteel book-banners, whose idol is Lloyd Douglas or even A. J. Cronin. When a critic like Mr. Wagner is led to applaud what he sees as a "trend" towards making doctors, lawyers, etc., the heroes of certain magazine stories, he has fallen into the trap of regarding middling fiction as a transmission belt from the vulgar to the high. There is no question, however, of a slow climb from the level of literature which celebrates newspaper reporters, newsboys, radio commentators (who are also super-heroes in tight-fitting uniforms with insignia), through one which centres around prosperous professionals, to the heights of serious literature, whose protagonists are suicides full of incestuous longings, lady lushes with clipped hair, bootleggers, gangsters, and broken-down pugs. To try to state the progression is to reveal its absurdity.

The conception of such a "trend" is nothing more than the standard attitude of a standard kind of literature, the literature of slick-paper ladies' magazines, which prefers the stereotype to the archetype, loves poetic justice, sentimentality, and gentility, and is peopled by characters who bathe frequently, live in the suburbs, and are professionals. Such literature circles mindlessly inside the trap of its two themes : unconsummated adultery and the consummated pure romance. There can be little doubt about which kind of persons and which sort of fables best typify our plight, which tell the truth—or better : a truth in the language of those to whom they speak.

In the last phrase, there is a rub. The notion that there is more than one language of art, or rather, that there is something not quite art, which performs art's function for most men in our society, is disquieting enough for anyone, and completely unacceptable to the sentimental egalitarian, who had dreamed of universal literacy leading directly to a universal culture. It is here that we begin to see that there is a politics as well as a pathology involved in the bourgeois hostility to popular culture. I do not refer only to the explicit political ideas embodied in the comics or in the literature of the cultural *élite*; but certainly each of these arts has a characteristic attitude : populist-authoritarian on the one hand, and aristocratic-authoritarian on the other.

It is notorious how few of the eminent novelists or poets of our time have shared the political ideals we (most readers of this magazine and I) would agree are the most noble available to us. The flirtations of Yeats and Lawrence with fascism, Pound's weird amalgam of confucianism, Jeffersonianism, and social credit, the modified Dixiecrat principles of Faulkner —all make the point with terrible reiteration. Between the best art and poetry of our age and the critical liberal reader there can be no bond of shared belief; at best we have the ironic confrontation of the sceptical mind and the believing imagination. It is this division which has, I suppose, led us to define more and more narrowly the "æsthetic experience", to attempt to isolate a quality of seeing and saying that has a moral value quite independent of *what* is seen or heard.

> *Time that with this strange excuse*
> *Pardoned Kipling and his views,*
> *And will pardon Paul Claudel,*
> *Pardons him for writing well.*

But the genteel middling mind which turns to art for entertainment and uplift, finds this point of view reprehensible; and cries out in rage against those who give Ezra Pound a prize and who claim that "to permit other considerations than that of poetic achievement to sway the decision would ... deny the validity of that objective perception of value on which any civilized society must rest". We live in the midst of a strange two-front class war : the readers of the slicks battling the subscribers to the "little reviews" and the consumers of pulps; the sentimental-egalitarian conscience against the ironical-aristocratic sensibility on the one hand and the brutal-populist mentality on the other. The joke, of course, is that it is the "democratic" centre which calls here and now for suppression of its rivals; while the *élite* advocate a condescending tolerance, and the vulgar ask only to be let alone.

It is disconcerting to find cultural repression flourishing at the point where middling culture meets a kindly, if not vigorously thought-out, liberalism. The sort of right-thinking citizen who subsidizes trips to America for Japanese girls scarred by the Hiroshima bombing, and deplores McCarthy in the public press, also deplores, and would censor, the comics. In one sense, this is fair enough; for beneath the veneer of slogans that "crime doesn't pay" and the superficial praise of law and order, the comics do reflect that dark populist faith which Senator McCarthy has exploited. There is a kind of "black socialism" of the American masses which underlies formal allegiances to one party or another : the sense that there is always a conspiracy at the centres of political and financial power; the notion that the official defenders of the commonwealth are "bought" more often than not; an impatience with moral scruples and a distrust of intelligence, especially in the expert and scientist; a willingness to identify the enemy, the dark projection of everything most feared in the self, on to some journalistically-defined political opponent of the moment.

This is not quite the "fascism" it is sometimes called. There is, for instance, no European anti-Semitism involved, despite the conventional hooked nose of the scientist-villain. (The inventors and chief producers of comic books have been, as it happens, Jews.) There is also no adulation of a dictator-figure on the model of Hitler or Stalin; though one of the archetypes of the Deliverer in the comics is called Superman, he is quite unlike the Nietzschean figure—it is the image of Cincinnatus which persists in him, an archetype that has possessed the American imagination since the time of Washington : the leader who enlists for the duration and retires unrewarded to obscurity.

It would be absurd to ask the consumer of such art to admire in the place of images that project his own impotence and longing for civil peace some hero of middling culture—say, the good boy of Arthur Miller's *Death of a Salesman*, who, because he has studied hard in school, has become a lawyer who argues cases before the Supreme Court and has friends who own their own tennis courts. As absurd as to ask the general populace to worship Stephen Dedalus or Captain Ahab! But the high-minded petty-bourgeois cannot understand or forgive the rejection of his own dream, which he considers as nothing less than the final dream of humanity. The very existence of a kind of art based on allegiances and values other than his challenges an article of his political faith; and when such an art is "popular", that is, more read, more liked, more bought than his own, he feels his *raison d'être*, his basic life-defence, imperilled. The failure of the petty-bourgeoisie to achieve cultural hegemony threatens their dream of a truly classless society; for they believe, with some justification, that such a society can afford only a single culture. And they see, in the persistence of a high art and a low art on either side of their average own, symptoms of the re-emergence of classes in a quarter where no one had troubled to stand guard.

The problem posed by popular culture is finally, then, a problem of class distinction in a democratic society. What is at stake is the refusal of cultural equality by a large part of the population. It is misleading to think of popular culture as the product of a conspiracy of profiteers against the rest of us. This venerable notion of an eternally oppressed and deprived but innocent people is precisely what the rise of mass culture challenges. Much of what upper-class egalitarians dreamed for him, the ordinary man does not want—especially literacy. The situation is bewildering and complex, for the people have not rejected completely the notion of cultural equality; rather, they desire its symbol but not its fact. At the very moment when half of the population of the United States reads no *hard-covered* book in a year, more than half of all high-school graduates are entering universities and colleges; in twenty-five years almost all Americans will at least begin a higher education. It is clear that what is demanded is a B.A. for everyone, with the stipulation that no one be forced to read to get it. And this the colleges, with "objective tests" and "visual aids", are doing their reluctant best to satisfy.

One of the more exasperating aspects of the cultural defeat of the egalitarians is that it followed a seeming victory. For a while (in the Anglo-Saxon world at least) it appeared as if the spread of literacy, the rise of the bourgeoisie, and the emergence of the novel as a reigning form would succeed in destroying both traditional folk art and an aristocratic literature still pledged to epic, ode, and verse tragedy. But the novel itself (in the hands of Lawrence, Proust, Kafka, etc.) soon passed beyond the comprehension of those for whom it was originally contrived; and the retrograde derivations from it—various steps in a retreat towards wordless narrative: digests, pulp fiction, movies, picture magazines—revealed that middling literature was not in fact the legitimate heir of either folk art or high art, much less the successor of both, but a *tertium quid* of uncertain status and value.

The middlebrow reacts with equal fury to an art that baffles his understanding and to one which refuses to aspire to his level. The first reminds him that he has not yet, after all, *arrived* (and, indeed, may never make it); the second suggests to him a condition to which he might easily relapse, one perhaps that might have made him happier with less effort (and here exacerbated puritanism is joined to baffled egalitarianism)—even suggests what his state may appear like to those a notch above. Since he cannot on his own terms explain to himself why anyone should choose any level but the highest (that is, his own), the failure of the vulgar seems to him the product of mere ignorance and laziness—a crime! And the rejection by the advanced artist of his canons strikes him as a finicking excess, a pointless and unforgivable snobbism. Both, that is, suggest the intolerable notion of a hierarchy of taste, a hierarchy of values, the possibility of cultural classes in a democratic state; and before this, puzzled and enraged, he can only call a cop. The fear of the vulgar is the obverse of the fear of excellence, and both are aspects of the fear of difference: symptoms of a drive for conformity on the level of the timid, sentimental, mindless-bodiless genteel.

AUGUST 1955

Part IV
MEN & IDEAS

HERBERT LUETHY

Montaigne, or the Art of Being Truthful

Reader, here is a truthful book. It warns you, even as you first enter it, that I have set myself only a familiar and private end. I have taken no thought in it either for your needs or my glory. My powers are not equal to such a task. I wish to be seen in it without art or affectation, but simply and naturally: for it is myself I portray. My faults will be found here as they are; also my plain nature, so far as decorum will allow. Had I lived among those people of whom it is said they dwell still under the sweet freedom of nature's first laws, I assure you I would have willingly pictured myself wholly naked. Thus, reader, I myself am the only content of my book; there is no reason for you to employ your leisure on so idle and frivolous a subject. Farewell then! From Montaigne, *the first of March,* 1580.

This was Montaigne's own foreword to the reader when he first set before the public the book, written "for few people and few years", which has since stood fast against the centuries. What remains to be said after this? Montaigne and his book say frankly everything that they have to say about each other : Montaigne about his book and the book about him; and both go to extraordinary lengths to guard against misunderstanding. "Montaigne is neighbour to us all", and the most openhearted, even gossipy neighbour we could wish for. He hides nothing from us, or nothing essential; and if he, who hardly conceals from us a single peculiarity of his diet or his digestion, forgets to speak of other things—completely of his mother, who survived him by nearly ten years, almost completely of his wife, whose existence he mentions once in passing, and of his children, of whom "two or three" died in childhood—then we can conclude only that these were things that touched him little; and that fact, too, rounds out his portrait.

In the same way, what he has to say about God, the world, and his own times is without shadow or mystery : the absolutely straightforward, un-connected, and changeable opinions of a landed nobleman of middle-class temperament and extraction, opinions born more out of his experience and the common judgement of mankind than of any definite *Weltanschauung,* and quite without pretensions to anything higher or more universal. For he is much less concerned to present the results of his thinking, or even to arrive at results at all, than to follow his thought itself in its playful movement, and to carry us with him. We can, indeed, follow him effortlessly, without breathing heavily, for this thought of his never goes very far, it undertakes only little sauntering strolls and always turns back before getting out of sight. Each one of his essays, like the book itself, begins without a purpose; if he sets an object before his mind it is only to put it in motion, as one throws a stone ahead of a dog, not to have him bring it back but to have him run, and is content if he brings back not the stone but an odd piece of wood or a dead mouse.

So it is possible to leaf through the Essays, reading a few pages and turning away at pleasure, as Montaigne himself read, as all his best readers have read him, without fear of losing the thread, for there is none. One learns to know him through his book as one would learn to know one's neighbour in life, through accidental meetings, and the more common the meetings, the more unimportant and unconnected the strokes, the more truthful does the portrait finally become. The best introduction to his book might be simply : Take it and read! or better still : read it and take!—for everyone is free to take what suits him, as Montaigne himself took whatever suited him, in order to make it his own, as, according to his own account, he plucked out of his Plutarch, whenever he picked it up, now a wing and now a leg.

Still, almost everyone who has read Montaigne in this way has mistaken the leg or the wing he brought away for the whole of Montaigne. There have been almost as many different Montaignes as there have been readers of him. For the pious, he was a man of piety, and for the free-thinking, a free-thinker; for the pagan, a pagan, and for Christians, a Christian. For the descendants of the Stoa, he was a Stoic moralist, for Epicureans of the higher or lower variety, he was an Epicurean of their variety; the men of the Enlightenment quoted his judgements on witchcraft and miracles with untiring enthusiasm, their adversaries pointed just as enthusiastically to the long essay called "Apology for Raymond Sebond" and its dethronement of reason. Conservatives found in him a defender of tradition, and the inherited order; the advocates of natural rights saw him as a critic of positive law and of the conventions and veneers of civilization. The list could be extended endlessly, and just as long a list might be drawn up of what his opponents found to reproach him with.

But, in view of all this, how do things stand with his truthfulness? Is it possible to have so many faces without disguising oneself, and so many truths without being a liar?

Montaigne said everything there was to be said about this too, but it has not helped him much. His foreword to the reader is to be taken quite literally—yet that is exactly what almost no one has done. So that if the Essays hardly require an introduction they do perhaps require some advice : not to look in them for what they do not contain—that is, truths about anything or anyone except Michel de Montaigne. His thoughts and opinions may be wrong or right; they are true only insofar as they are *his* thoughts. Their truth does not lie in where they tend, for they tend everywhere, but in the place from which they depart and to which they return. *"Ramener à soi"* is one of the key phrases of the Essays, untranslatable in its full range of meaning; it means to draw back on oneself, to draw to oneself, to take to oneself, but it contains also the logical meaning of a movement of thought from the object to oneself, and the physical gesture of picking up, holding, or embracing. So Montaigne draws to himself what would escape him : his life, his feelings, his thoughts, his book, his very self; and his reproach against the "licentiousness of thought" is nothing else but that it wishes to pass beyond him and his limitations in order to fix itself in the objective, the absolute, and the unlimited. He, Montaigne, wishes to remain with himself.

For this reason his excursions into the more abstruse matters of philosophy remain, even measured by the standards of his time, scanty and negligent, a mere careless gesture of warding off; he does not care about knowledge of things, only about knowledge of himself. Even when he does for once come to grips with the question of how man can know the truth, as in the "Apology for Raymond Sebond", his epistemology remains a kind of shaking of the head : how can man know anything when he cannot even grasp himself? All his philosophic arguments are such arguments *ad hominem,* as unphilosophic as they can be. What has the objective truth of a philosophic proposition to do with the philosopher who propounds it, his indigestion, his passions, and his personal truthfulness?

These are frivolous arguments for anyone who is seeking knowledge of things. But Montaigne has another purpose, for which he wishes never to lose sight of himself, and another frame of reference, which measures truth not by what is said, but by the sayer—which prefers, in other words, subjective truthfulness to objective truth. Every discipline, from physics to theology, can advance step by step from once-given premises to conclusions that pass far beyond the insight and imaginative power of the investigator, and lose all connection with him. Such knowledge, which cuts itself loose from the knower and cleaves to the object, has nothing more to say to him, Michel de Montaigne; it is of no use for self-knowledge. It is for this reason that the disconnectedness, wilfulness, and apparent purposelessness of his essays, the sauntering, tentative, and unpredictable movement of his thought, are not mere wilfulness or incapacity. A thought or a style which submitted itself to any discipline would cease, immediately or wholly, to be his own. He seems always careful to let no structure of thought arise which might stand by itself without his intervention, to let no method intrude between him and his fancies. He prefers, rather, looking on ironically, to let his mind build little houses of cards which he blows down again before they grow too large.

And yet these "mental exercises" reach a greatness, a truth and a profundity, when he follows himself into the twilight borderlands of his consciousness, on the edge of sleep, dreams, distraction, torpor, and death—in those corners where consciousness, Montaigne's consciousness, first becomes fully realized, that is, detached from every connection with the extraneous. These are the places in which he reaches furthest, and we can learn from them not to content ourselves too lightly with Montaigne's seeming superficiality; for much of the dawdling and dallying of the Essays amid the banal and the trivial is, in the same way, a kind of half-sleep of the unconsciousness, in which it permits itself, unknowingly, to be observed. To be sure, many thoughts are brought to light in this way whose interest and even greatness is in themselves; but they are by-products of a thought directed to other ends. For Montaigne, it is not a question of taking the measure of things, but the measure of his eyes. The way in which he sees things, now so, now otherwise, leads to no conclusions about the things, only about himself.

"Montaigne against miracles; Montaigne for miracles," Pascal noted. Montaigne is both at once. He brought together tirelessly and indiscriminately a whole chamber of curiosities, full of all the possible conclusions of his own and all other philosophies, not to play them off against each other, but to display the range and possibility of human thought, and with a little prompting he would accept them all—and the most unusual with the most alacrity. They contradict each other?—yes, but altogether they mark out the borders of human awareness, with all its manifold possibilities. "Truth is the whole." To the Essays, too, Hegel's dictum applies, but altered: Michel de Montaigne's truth is the sum of his contradictions. And this truth of his he demonstrates in his book as Dionysus the Cynic demonstrated motion by walking: there he stands, a whole man, in whom all these contradictions come to harmony.

Truth of another, general, superpersonal kind he does not possess and is not looking for. "I do not see the whole of anything," he says, and adds, smiling: "Nor do those who promise to show it to us." This renunciation troubles him so little that almost every general opinion passes as equally valid with him; rather than worry his head over it, he prefers to hold fast to those opinions customary in his land and his family, certainly as good as any other. He is at pains to set them outside the reach of all human possibility of knowing—this is the whole content of the "Apology for Raymond Sebond"—the better to put them at a distance. They are unattainable, and they do not trouble him. His essays, those little strolls of thought, never set out in search of such truths, but always and only, in search of Montaigne. The whole, which he calls God or Nature, Fate or Order, almost without distinction, gets along very well without him, and he without it : or rather, he is embedded and hidden in it, like the mole or the plant louse, who also knows nothing of how things stand with the universe.

It is this placid, unquestioning taking of things for granted which roused Pascal to indignation. "There are only three types of men : those who serve God, having found Him; those who exert themselves to seek Him, not having found Him; and those who live without seeking Him and without having found Him." It is plain to which of these categories of Pascal's Michel de Montaigne belongs. Whatever he was, a god-seeker he was not. He fulfilled his religious obligations as he fulfilled those of his rank, his marriage, and his public office, and there is no reason to doubt that he fulfilled them honourably and earnestly. But it was not as something of his own, not out of personal conviction, or as an expression of his own essence; it was rather as something expected of him, in the station allotted him by birth and heredity. The separation is astonishingly clear through the Essays, and it requires gross bias not to see it : where Montaigne is speaking in general and about generalities he seldom neglects to weave into his discourse the rhetoric of orthodoxy which was especially advisable in his age of religious persecution; when he speaks of his external behaviour, his morals and habits, he takes pains to note his crossing of himself, his saying of grace, and his attendance at Mass; but when he really turns to himself, when he is no longer speaking of mankind, life and death in general, but of himself, his life and his death, then faith is left behind, as habit and philosophy are left behind, and he is alone with himself.

This then is Montaignean scepticism. But the philosophic label does not really suit him. Certainly, the description of sceptical thought given by Hegel in the *Phenomenology of the Spirit* sounds word for word as if it were meant for Montaigne; it is perfectly true that he "only deals with the particular and wallows in the accidental", that his style of thought is "this senseless drivel alternating from one extreme of undifferentiated self-awareness to the other of chance awareness, confused and confusing", and "it perceives its freedom sometimes as a revolt against all the confusion and accidentalness of being and at other times as a falling back into the unessential and a frolicking about in it". It is, too, "only . . . a musical thinking which never arrives at . . . the objective concept" and "so we see only a personality restricted to, and brooding on, itself and its own little activities, as unfortunate as it is unhappy . . ." How well-aimed this description of the sceptical mind is—and how widely it misses Montaigne! The man who steps before us in the Essays is as little a representative of Hegel's "unhappy consciousness" as he is the damned and despairing figure of Pascal. And just this is perhaps the scandal of Montaigne : to be so aware of that limitation which does not allow him to grasp "the whole", to content himself with the imperfect and the fragmentary, and yet to be so wholly untragic. His scepticism, philosophic as well as religious, is no sorrowful renunciation, because it is not a philosophy, but a form of spiritual hygiene; a device to help hold off the extraneous and give room for what is his own. His truthfulness applies other, but no less stringent, criteria to truth : is it mine? does it fit me? does it remain mine even in sickness, in pain, and in death?

One can only speak of Montaigne in contradictions, and as he himself rambled on from one thing to another, so one can ramble on in speaking of him, for his subject is himself, in which all other subjects are mirrored. He imposed no method on himself, not even a method for self-knowledge, and there is no such method except unconditional honesty with oneself. Those astonishing journeys of exploration he made on the frontiers of the unconscious were only possible because through long acquaintance with himself he had found the right distance to keep, in order—as he says once —to consider himself impartially "like a neighbour, or a tree". One can follow precisely this process through the development of the Essays, the process by which Montaigne wins that distance from himself, that lack of a *parti pris*, which is the hardest part of truthfulness.

The first two books of the Essays, in their earlier form, are full of the general truths of Stoic wisdom; these are the essays of which Montaigne later said that they "smelt a little of the property of others". But then that spiritual hygiene begins to operate, the sceptical questioning of his own wisdom—how do I come to it, I, Michel de Montaigne, landed nobleman of Périgord, fifty years old, a little below average height, afflicted with incipient kidney-stones? What does it mean to *me*? This is the beginning of Montaigne's marvellous truthfulness, this return to self, this limitation of truth to his personal measure; and the Essays have remained unique in the consistency with which they follow the path of honesty—the most personal book in world literature. Unique, perhaps, because they took this path not *a priori* but artlessly and unintentionally at first, then with a growing joy of discovery. For the personal belongs also to things one does not achieve by a purposeful striving after them; the self that, without long detours, at once reaches itself, has in reality gone no distance at all and remains empty. To take the measure of one's eyes it is necessary to seek first the measure of things.

Montaigne reflected very earnestly on things outside himself, on the nature and destiny of man, on the state, on law, virtue, marriage and education, on belief in miracles, on the passions, and, over and over, on the possibility of objective knowledge, always with reference to himself but never with reference only to himself. So this book of self-knowledge is no confession, no autobiography, no self-justification or self-accusation, no *Ecce Homo*. Montaigne does not start from himself, he comes to himself quite simply, as one comes to the point.

In Montaigne all the usual motives for self-description are lacking. He did not write out of a sense of his own uncommonness, his "otherness" or his exemplary quality, either for good or evil; on the contrary, his experiment was all the more valid because of his ordinariness, and one often senses that he is emphasizing this ordinariness, that he is making himself more ordinary than he is. In this way he escaped all the dangers of conscious self-description, the danger of self-enchantment and the perhaps even greater danger of self-abasement, that "sly humility" of confessionals, whose authors tread themselves into the dust in order to demonstrate how high they have raised themselves above themselves. There is no *Weltschmertz*, remorse, rebellion, accusation, inner strife, grief against others or against himself, nothing of all of that which since Rousseau has driven so many failures to spit in the world's face, so many beaten people to write their *De Profundis*, so many sinners to summon the world to a last judgement on themselves. This is the unusual thing: here a rich, healthy, and fairly happy man makes himself known, one who has thoroughly mastered his life and played his part with honour in the public affairs of his city and his countryside. He does not write in order to create a rôle for himself, but to lay one aside, and come to himself.

"Mundus universus exercet histrioniam";—the word "person" itself, is etymologically, "mask". In this comedy where all must act a rôle chosen or imposed, in character-masks which everyone finally accepts as his real visage, with commitments, articles of faith, and dogmas which we "believe we believe" and to which we must adhere out of loyalty to ourselves, without much knowing how we really came to them: in this comedy Montaigne's rôle was thoroughly in order. To set himself at a distance from the mere "making of books", he underlines, rather emphatically on occasion, the man-of-the-world element in himself. He

surrounded his ancestry with an aura of old warrior nobility it was not at all entitled to; he notes with pride that as the mayor of his city he had a marshal to precede him and another to follow him; and, with a vanity full of imperceptible self-irony, he quotes the entire Latin text of his Roman patent of nobility. These traits, too, noted by his Jansenist critics with bitter derision, are essential to him, and they are mirrored in the Essays without dissimulation. He did not renounce the world in order to find himself : he sought to find himself in the world.

But what is left now of the personality he is seeking? Everything that holds it together, ancestry, education, milieu, habit, convention, principles, relations, beliefs, rank, name, and position comes to it from outside, they are allotted, accidental rôles, and yet they make up almost the whole conscious "I". The more closely he considers himself the more his contours blur, the more individuality is dissolved into that many-coloured, unstable, iridescent and fleeting chaos he never, in his contradictoriness, grows tired of describing. Yes, one should play one's rôle fitly, he says—but always as a rôle, without identifying oneself with it or losing oneself in it. And this attitude can be followed on the title pages of the early editions of the Essays; if the first two editions, conforming to the custom of the period, still display the full splendour of the titles possessed by the royal knight, councillor, and mayor, Michel de Montaigne, there is left on the title page of the last edition, supervised by Montaigne himself, only his name.

For the stepping out of his rôle in which the actor betrays himself, a special ear for the undertones of consciousness is needed. All the splendid life of the Essays springs from this keen listening of Montaigne's to his relaxed and outward-turned self. It is true that this kind of thinking goes in circles. But the circle grows smaller and smaller until at last it circles only around the one point at which Montaigne finds himself alone— death. Here all acting ends; "that is a business for one man alone". The thought of death engaged him early, and we can follow the process of his self-discovery in nothing so clearly as in his relation to death. In death he found the ultimate test of truthfulness. To come to terms with it was what Montaigne sought, in the beginning, from philosophy. *Hic Rhodus, hic salta!* "To philosophize is to learn to die", he titled the long chapter on death in the first book, written when he was still full of the wisdom of the ancients about life and death; and all the consolations of Stoicism are here summoned up. Montaigne always understood as philosophy this spiritual elevation of man in the face of his sad, confused, and ephemeral humanity, and that was what he still meant by it when he said later, of himself, "I am no philosopher." He has reached the end of the way when, considering the calm and natural death of the simplest men in the plague year 1585, he rejects Cicero's phrase about the philosophic preparation for death as idle boasting : What is it, to be able to do what every fool and every beast can and must do? to strike a pose in order to endure what everyone must endure anyway? If philosophizing is to learn to die, "well then, let us go to school with stupidity". To learn to live, not die, is wisdom. The essays of his first and last period can be endlessly contrasted, for with the change in his attitude towards death all the perspectives and measuring-rods of life change too.

Yet the last judgements do not cancel the first; nothing is taken back, only added to and deepened. In the beginning it is man, life, and death that occupy him, in the end it is only "my life" and "my death", and he is no longer dealing with a philosophic allegory of death, but experiencing and enduring his own slow dissolution. He, Michel de Montaigne, can no longer push death out of his consciousness, for it is he himself who is dying, together with his consciousness, and no speculation can prevail against this. Here he no longer grants himself the doubt that makes everything else, even miracles, possible; death is the end, and whatever may be on the other side, he, Michel de Montaigne, remains on this side. The consolations of philosophy, like those of religion, he never denies, he leaves them undecided; he accepts extreme unction and the sympathy of friends, but they do not concern him; these are the last actions of a life lived according to custom and usage, since it was not granted him to die unmolested—"quite alone"—journeying and far from home. A man must act his rôle in life to the last instant.

The Stoic, like the Christian, contempt for death is grounded in the contempt for physical life, but the more Montaigne feels himself disappearing the more deeply he feels that this life is all he has, and that it is much and precious. Now he finds in all contempt for life the over-weening pride of the human spirit, the will to lift itself over and beyond itself towards the absolute, a revolt against the unbearable thought of existing today and ceasing to exist tomorrow—against the natural order that embraces both life and death. His last essay, already full of the presence of death and the readiness for it, closes with a hymn to this existence. *"C'est une absolue perfection, et comme divine ..."* In the presence of death Montaigne learned to love life, to "hold it fast with tooth and claw", to savour it to the last drop. Life is earthly, but not therefore void; transitory but not therefore despicable; losable, but not absurd; precious beyond words in its very fragility and unsureness.

In these last dialogues with old age, sickness, and death, there is no more art and no more cleverness, only obedience and assent to the riddling laws of life and death—*amor fati*. But if this is wisdom, then it is wisdom of the humblest and most unassuming kind, the wisdom of all creation, which goes hence unquestioning, without puzzling over the universe in which it lives and dies; the wisdom of the obedient. And if such thankful obedience to the unknowable is piety, then this is piety—but a piety that is wholly of this world. How much of the beauty of the Essays is due to the fact that their movement so truly describes the curve of life through ripeness and to death—the whole of life!

Why did Montaigne write them? He himself posed the question over and over, without finding an answer. Yet we must believe his foreword : he did not write them for us. He wrote them for himself, for his own sake, out of inner necessity; and yet he needed the unknown reader in order to reveal himself to himself. Self-description was the instrument of his self-discovery. For, and this is the last contradiction, there is no self-knowledge which does not make itself known, and no truthfulness without communication. "Whoever does not live a little for others hardly lives for himself." The consciousness of self that remains mute and unexpressed cannot attain self-knowledge. Perhaps there lay, at the source of Montaigne's decision to write down his thoughts, the death of his friend, Etienne de la Boëtie, who shared with him common ideas and ideals. The Essays are the continuation of a broken-off conversation. The whole first period of the Essays is an echo of this intimate association of two humanistic minds, both in love with antique greatness and the wisdom of Stoicism. Now Montaigne was alone, bereft of that "other I" who "alone possessed my true image, and took it with him", and it was "as if I had been cut in half". But this lost image of himself which he tried to reconstruct was hardly the one that emerges in the Essays; the undertaking led him further than he had intended.

We can infer Montaigne's image from the portrait he sketches of La Boëtie; how impersonal, how declamatory in spite of all its real emotion, this essay is! We sense the humanistic enthusiasm for antique greatness "as our century no longer knows it" in which these two come together, the spirit of emulation of the Scipios and Catos which one finds also in La Boëtie's posthumous *Contr'un*. It was only slowly that Montaigne freed himself from the spell of that image of ideal manhood proposed by the Stoa, which was embodied for him in Etienne de la Boëtie. He cannot maintain himself on such heights—in such a rôle—alone, and the great generalities of virtue, truth, and freedom remain empty, for they find no echo. Hesitantly, in a few tentative thrusts, whose keenness for a late-Renaissance mind still filled with the spirit of antiquity we are hardly able to measure any more, he begins to question not mankind itself but these standards for mankind, and to seek the criteria of judgement within himself. And in shaping this new and quite personal image of man he attained his full reality. His book was the triumphant bursting loose of the free man from late-Humanistic epigonism. And through it, Montaigne himself became what he was. Montaigne noted finely the reciprocal process in which he and his book were engaged: "And even if no one were to read me, should I have wasted my time? I no more made my book than it has made *me* . . ." His book has become a true collaborator, and through it the reader becomes one too—"my book", Montaigne says, as he would say "my friend", and, reading his book, we are drawn into this intimacy too. Whence the inexhaustible freshness which speaks to us from this book across more than three and a half centuries, as from no other book of his time, and few of all time.

In the end the richness of this book is the richness of the personality which shared itself with it, wholly and without holding back. It is not the monologue of a crank in his library, brooding over himself. The man who wrote this lived open-eyed among men caught up in the most merciless of civil and religious wars; he stood in his time with both feet, at the end of that colossal century in which the new world was discovered and the world of antiquity rediscovered, which saw the Christian Church tottering on its foundations, and the anthropocentric model of the universe overturned, the century of the conquistadors and the great rebels: Cortez and Copernicus, Luther and Machiavelli, Calvin, Loyola, and Giordano Bruno.

The book, too, is of this time—and what a time! Montaigne began to write his essays in the year of the St. Bartholomew massacre, which gave the signal for slaughter throughout France, and entered history as the ineradicable symbol of betrayal, baseness, and murder in the name of the highest certainties of faith; the night of butchery in Paris, and of the thanksgiving mass with which it was greeted in Rome. All his life Montaigne saw religious war smouldering or blazing all around him, in his city, in his own family, and among his brothers and sisters, three of whom adhered to Calvinism. The twenty years during which he wrote the Essays were twenty years of civil war, hardly interrupted by the worthless peace treaties and edicts of toleration, broken before they came into force. Montaigne's retreat in 1571 "to the lap of the learned Muses, where he will pass in calm and security the days left him to live", was of short duration; the next year he was with the royal army in Poitou sent against rebellious La Rochelle, then bearer of the king's commands to the Parliament of Bordeaux, and in the following year we meet him again and again as agent and mediator between the warring camps. The news of his election as mayor of Bordeaux reached him on his "extended journey" in Italy, and King Henry III wrote to him in Rome to summon him to the immediate and pressing assumption of his office—a difficult one in a city torn by outer and inner quarrels, and become a storm-centre of the Huguenot wars.

But the Michel de Montaigne faithful to church and king was also the confidant and adviser of Henry of Navarre, the chief of the Protestant party, who visited him in his castle and appointed him, already chamberlain to Henry III, to be his own *ex-officio* chamberlain too. An unelevating rôle, and one hard to understand, like the rôle of all those who issue no calls to battle and wage no wars, but seek to make peace instead; suspect, like all moderation; dangerous, like all will to balance in times of fanaticism. So Montaigne also passed, as he once complains, "for Guelf among the Ghibellines and Ghibelline among the Guelfs"—for a Papist among the Calvinists, and a heretic, or, what was almost the same thing, a lukewarm believer, among the Catholic zealots.

He has been called with justice, if also with some exaggeration, the philosopher of Henry IV, who brought peace and order to the French state, and to whom Montaigne, in one of his last essays, dedicated the verses Virgil wrote for Augustus. But if he was the philosopher of Henry IV, it was before the latter's victory, which he did not live to see. Montaigne had party loyalty, but it was not to the party of a dogma. His loyalty was to the old order, embodied in the monarchy which fell to pieces under the blows of both religious parties, the Calvinists as well as the Catholic League. If one wishes to range him with a party then it must be with the "*parti des politiques*", as his contemporaries called that "third force" made up of moderate and tolerant spirits which—hence its designation as "political"—drew a distinction between religious conviction and political practice.

When hereditary succession made the Protestant Bourbon, Henry of Navarre, heir to the throne of the weak and degenerate Valois, the split became open; while the Catholic League sought to deliver the crown of France into the hands of the Spanish Hapsburg, Philip II, or the Lotharingian Duke of Guise, the legitimist party of "the politicals" became simply the patriotic party. But it was only by going over to the religious faith of the majority of his people that Henry IV could finally become the "prince of peace", the "good king" who has entered legend. For those sick alike of the oligarchic city-republics of the Calvinists and the caricature of democracy created in Paris by the League through the long reign of terror enforced by a fanaticized mob, the monarchy appeared as salvation. That the paternal and tolerant régime of Henry IV prepared the way for the absolute monarchy which less than a century later began to destroy his work, is part of the history of another epoch, which had gone on to new problems; for history knows no "solutions" by which everything works out as smoothly as in the arithmetic books and ideological primers, only the triumph of new formulations of a problem over the old ones, the replacement of the religious formulation by the political, and the political by the social—all of them, however, only new forms of the old. What Montaigne says of the political problems of his time is spoken out of that time and his personal experience : it is uncontemporary to us. And yet, in a far deeper sense, it *is* contemporary.

Nowhere is politics the subject of this book. Nowhere does Montaigne draft an ideology or a programme of even the most modest kind; here too it is a question solely of *his* relation to politics and ideology. He was involved in these disorders as a citizen and an official, not as Michel de Montaigne, and the self-contemplation of the Essays is once again the means, in a time of ideological murder and carnage, to gain distance from the struggle, to come to himself, in the full sense of the phrase, to win the inner freedom that the party follower loses. In politics, too, it is a book of spiritual hygiene.

Here again scepticism above all fulfils its cleansing function. In the blackest impasse of the civil war, sharpened to ultimate bitterness by the betrayal of St. Batholomew's Night, while the unity of the kingdom itself was for the first time put in jeopardy, and the "natural right" to rebellion and to execute kings was seized on in turn by Calvinist theoreticians and the zealots of the Catholic League, Montaigne read Sextus Empiricus's "Outline of Pyrrhonism", struck off his philosophical coat-of-arms, showing the arms of a scale poised in wavering equilibrium and the motto *"Que sais-je?"*; and began to set down his "Apology for Raymond Sebond", the only really polemic essay in his work. All certainties are overturned here, with a true lust for destruction and an undiscriminating insatiability, all dogmas reduced to mere opinion, illusion, and conjecture, one as good as the next and each a mere curiosity in the cabinet of human fantasy. Everything is reduced to one level, man and beast, wise man and fool, intellect and instinct, belief and delusion, science, speculation and old wives' tales, and every supposed certainty cancelled by mere confrontation with a dozen contradictory and just as evident certainties. Montaigne notes sarcastically that two hundred and eighty-eight sects arose in antiquity out of the dispute over the highest good alone, and Pascal later copied this remark into his *Pensées*. Religion too is brought into this sphere of mere human supposition, for "it is clear and distinct that we accept our beliefs only in our own fashion and from our own hands, just as other religions have been accepted", according to the accidents of place, birth, and education : "A different latitude, different parents, similar promises and threats, could have produced in the same way a quite contrary belief.

We are Christian in the same sense that we are German or Périgordian . . ."
Curious defence of the good Sebond, who wished "to demonstrate the
truth of our religion by the conclusions of reason!"

No one, probably, will ever succeed entirely in clarifying the strange
labyrinth of this polemical piece, for Montaigne himself has taken pains
to make sure that no one will be able to pin him down to anything—not
even doubt. Perhaps such a mock battle, with reversed weapons, in which
Montaigne undertakes to defend Sebond's proof of religion by reason
while pushing reason (and all human certainties with it) into the void,
was the only way in which a free spirit of that age could create room for
itself to breathe between inexorably hostile dogmas—one thinks of the
quite otherwise motivated, but very similarly constructed, *Defence of
Herodotus* by Henri Estienne, which undertook to prove the credibility
of the wildest fables of the ancient Greeks by assembling a selection of the
even more grotesque miracle stories and fairy tales which the priests of
his time had imposed on a credulous people . . . Yet one need not therefore
impute to Montaigne a case of plain fraud. Here, as everywhere in the
Essays, the occasion and point of departure for the essay, Sebond's "natural
theology", turns quickly into a mere pretext for following Montaigne's
own thoughts down every sideway and bypath. Nor is it a question of
simple enlightened denial or doubt of an article of faith. The possibility of
divine revelation remains open to rare and chosen spirits; but it is clear
that it is not these spirits who are drowning France in fire, murder, and
warfare, while they battle for the mastery of the country. By themselves
the genuinely religious would hardly be numerous enough to form a troop
of militia. The others—and are these others not, in reality, all?—are
possessed, not by the truth, but by blood-frenzy, greed, and hunger for
power. If they weighed truly the fragility of their convictions, the uncertainty of their murderous certainties, if they were in possession of, instead
of beside, themselves, would they not sheath their swords?

He too, Michel de Montaigne, belongs not at all to the graced who
have received the light of holy truth; he too is a Christian like the multitude, as he is a Périgordian, by heredity and habit. It is for just this reason
that he stands fast; precisely because he cannot decide by himself what the
truth is, he holds to that truth which is his by birth—"and since I am in
no position to choose, I follow the choice of others, and remain in the rut
in which God has set me. For otherwise I would roll and roll without
end . . ." With this he contents himself, to this he clings, but modestly;
it is a personal, historically limited faith, which makes no claim to be
binding on those whom God has set in another track. "What sort of truth
is it that ends on this side of the mountains and is a lie for the world

beyond?" It is a rule of behaviour, a "local ordinance", to which Montaigne submits himself in his ignorance; blind, but conscious of his blindness.

So he rejects the Reformation, not as sin and error, but as disorder and a sectarian arrogance of spirit which presumes to pass personal judgement on what is ultimate truth; not because his certainty is better but because he knows the questionableness of all certainties. It would take passionate conviction to change his faith, but it requires only mild conviction to hold to the old one. All the more because Calvin's Genevan papacy was both more demanding and less tolerant than pre-Tridentine Catholicism—and the introduction of the Tridentine creed into France had long been successfully resisted by the Gallican *politiques*—which contented itself with external submission to churchly usage, and gave its approval to the Essays as a tract written in defence of the old faith, until a new wave of fanaticism, two generations later, repudiated as anti-Christian both the Essays and, characteristically, the religious tolerance of the Edict of Nantes. Of course, the zealots were not wrong. Montaigne was indeed, in Sainte-Beuve's pointed phrase, a good Catholic in the exact measure that he was a lukewarm Christian. He, personally, was prepared to let pass every belief and every superstition, "to light one candle to St. Michael and another to the dragon", and with Socrates he held that "the truest opinion of the supernatural is to have no opinion".

Montaigne's loyalty to the old faith does not therefore contradict his scepticism, it is grounded in it. He defended the hereditary church as a conservative, not as a fighter for the true faith; as a *politique*, not as a crusader against heresy. He did not put the light on one side and the darkness on the other, he reserved the freedom to look around him, and to see what became of his convictions in the fists and mouths of their defenders, "who believe they believe because they do not know what belief is", and to recognize the human qualities and virtues of their opponents. He speaks often, in the Essays, with curiosity and astonishment, of the strange phenomenon of party passion, that human loss of self in a "rôle" thanks to which men work themselves up over things which do not in the least concern them. *"Je m'engage difficilement"* is a key sentence of the Essays; he is "not easily inclined to belief nor to disbelief"; and the essay in which he reports how he exercised his mayoral office bears the magnificent title, "On the Management of the Will". His political ethos is the rejection of passion.

He refuses to be passionate even about the tradition he upholds. Every traditional form of order is an inheritance, and nothing else. Church, crown, state, law, family, and marriage are institutions which earn the esteem of a citizen in his rôle as citizen, but only in that rôle; they can claim no compulsion over his way of thinking or his conscience. What exists is neither holy, nor good, nor even reasonable; it has no other virtue but that it exists. Order, the state, law and justice are nothing else but disorder, lawlessness and violence, established and grown venerable by age, and often enough laughable, inhuman, and absurd. "The laws are not law, because they are just, but because they are laws." All human order is non-rational, neither derivable from, nor justifiable by, reason; every schoolboy is able to demonstrate its senselessness, but he had better let it stand : he knows nothing better.

For there is no rational order. Society has grown not out of the test tubes of reason but the disorder of history, not as an abstract logical construction for abstract logical men, but as an empirically discovered form of the living-together of human beings. For the state too, what is truth this side of the Pyrenees is a lie on the other. Like all historical reality it cannot withstand the scrutiny of reason, for it is grounded not on truth but on custom; and yet it is infinitely superior to reason, for it is actual. And the older and more customary it is, the better, for it has survived its violent birth pangs and found its inner equilibrium, it has shown its usefulness and vitality by its survival, and grown to be the normal state of affairs with which everyone is familiar, because he is born to them, and which therefore allow the highest measure of freedom. Whoever assails it risks a relapse into the rule of the fist. Montaigne's whole polemic against the "innovators" is an indictment of the power-pretensions of abstract reason in its attempt to create an order outside historical contingency, and he has only scorn for the ideal states of philosophy, which have no place and no time. Every idea which presents itself as an ideology and claims power over men as a universally valid principle of order, is *hubris* and folly, arrogant transgression.

But even to the existing order he did not concede the right to impair his private freedom : "If the laws I serve threatened me even with their little finger I would go immediately in search of others, wherever they might be . . . I am so greedy for freedom that I would feel hemmed-in if I were denied access to no matter what corner of the Indies." He acquiesced in the external order precisely for the sake of this freedom : freedom, too, he drew to himself as *his* freedom, not as a public postulate; and practical conformity seemed to him a small price to pay in order to defend it. He played the part that was allotted him, in a bad time, as Frenchman, Catholic, Périgordian, citizen, and mayor of Bordeaux, dutifully and without passion, with calm acceptance of his historic "contingency", and thereby preserved the inner freedom to remain Michel de Montaigne, sceptic and citizen of the world. Thus this political attitude flows back into the self-knowledge from which it issued, into the open-eyed acceptance of that contradiction of freedom and obligation, individuality and conformity, in which Montaigne found his own nature—"So I am."

The best fruit of this self-possession is its absolute openness to other things and other men. This deeply liberal spirit was tolerant without that tinge of sufferance, of the magnanimous concession granted by Truth to Error, that so often clings to the word—a word Montaigne does not even know. This enemy of all ideology had an insatiable, unprejudiced curiosity about all ideas, this scorner of all pretensions to special knowledge had an unbounded readiness for learning, this sceptic in regard to every dogma was open to the whole endless variety of spiritual possibilities, the life-forms and life-truths of other men and other peoples, and he treated with respect even those possibilities which were closed to him. Willingly, play-fully, he tests his capacity to assume another opinion and seek its justifica-tion, and it often happens that the game turns to earnest in the process, and he abandons his own to adopt the opinion he began by combating.

To be sure, a great deal also escaped this mind, which grasped so much in the attempt to grasp itself. The soaring lights of inspiration, the mystic vision of the world, the passion for knowledge and perhaps passion itself he sensed only by imaginative intuition, without really experiencing them: the border forms of human existence, the seer, the hero, and the saint, like the radically evil, were foreign to him. The psychic phenomena of trans-port and ecstasy he traced in himself and others again and again, with a mixture of curiosity and aversion; but his whole effort is in the opposite direction : to come to himself, not to allow himself to be transported, to possess himself, not to be possessed. He found this way to himself not by negating, but by affirming what was outside his nature, by the affirmation even of what was to him foreign, mysterious, and incomprehensible.

This rare and precious faculty for setting himself in the place of another being and respecting its inner laws as equal to his own he pushed to its utmost reach : "When I play with my cat who knows if she does not amuse herself more with me than I with her?" All of Montaigne lies in that casual sentence.

Truthfulness is not only a great, it is a difficult, virtue. It demands not merely an open character but a clear head, and that, for a man of Mon-taigne's time, as for our own, was difficult indeed to achieve. Every time of disorder is also a time of disordered minds who know all about God and the world, the cause of things and their background, the meaning of history and the destiny of man—all about everything except themselves. And in such times nothing is more necessary than to come, in the spiritual and even in the clinical sense, to oneself. That is the spiritual hygiene

Montaigne practised as his joyful wisdom, and his only teaching. "With him I would live," Nietzsche wrote, "if the task were set me to make myself at home on earth." It is just this task, perhaps, that we have all been set again.

NOVEMBER 1953

ISAIAH BERLIN

Alexander Herzen

ALEXANDER HERZEN is the most arresting Russian political writer in the nineteenth century. No good biographies of him exist, perhaps because his own autobiography is a great literary masterpiece. It is not widely known in English-speaking countries, and that for no good reason, for it has been translated into English, the first part magnificently by Mr. J. D. Duff, and the whole adequately by Constance Garnett; unlike some works of political and literary genius, it is, even in translation, marvellously readable.

In some respects, it resembles Goethe's *Dichtung und Wahrheit* more than any other book. For it is not a collection of wholly personal memoirs and political reflections. It is an amalgam of personal detail, descriptions of political and social life in various countries, of opinions, personalities, outlooks, accounts of the author's youth and early manhood in Russia, historical essays, notes of journeys in Europe, France, Switzerland, Italy, of Paris and Rome during the revolutions of 1848 and 1849 (these last are incomparable, and the best personal documents about these events that we possess), discussions of political leaders, and of the aims and purposes of various parties. All this is interspersed with a variety of comment, pungent observation, sharp and spontaneous, occasionally malicious, vignettes of individuals, of the character of peoples, analyses of economic and social facts, discussions and epigrams about the future and past of Europe and about the author's own hopes and fears for Russia; and interwoven with this is a detailed and poignant account of Herzen's personal tragedy, perhaps the most extraordinary self-revelation on the part of a sensitive and fastidious man ever written down for the benefit of the general public.

Alexander Ivanovich Herzen was born in Moscow in 1812, not long before the capture of the city by Napoleon, the illegitimate son of Ivan Yakovlev, a rich and well-born Russian gentleman, descended from a cadet branch of the Romanoffs, a morose, difficult, possessive, distinguished and civilized man, who bullied his son, loved him deeply, embittered his life, and had an enormous influence upon him both by attraction and repulsion. His mother, Amalia Haag, was a mild German lady from

Stuttgart in Württemberg, the daughter of a minor official. Ivan Yakovlev had met her while travelling abroad, but never married her. He took her to Moscow, established her as mistress of his household, and called his son Herzen in token, as it were, of the fact that he was the child of his heart, but not legitimately born and therefore not entitled to bear his name.

The fact that Herzen was not born in wedlock probably had a considerable effect on his character, and may have made him more rebellious than he might otherwise have been. He received the regular education of a rich young nobleman, went to the University of Moscow and there early asserted his vivid, original, impulsive character. He was born (in later years he constantly came back to this) into the generation of what in Russia came to be called *Lishniye Lyudi*, "superfluous men", with whom Turgenev's early novels are so largely concerned.

These young men have a place of their own in the history of European culture in the nineteenth century. They belonged to the class of those who are by birth aristocratic, but who themselves go over to some freer and more radical mode of thought and of action. There is something singularly attractive about men who retained, throughout life, the manners, the texture of being, the habits and style of a civilized and refined *milieu*. Such men exercise a peculiar kind of personal freedom which combines spontaneity with distinction. Their minds see large and generous horizons, and, above all, reveal a unique intellectual gaiety of a kind that aristocratic education tends to produce. At the same time, they are intellectually on the side of everything that is new, progressive, rebellious, young, untried, of that which is about to come into being, of the open sea whether or not there is land that lies beyond. To this type belong those intermediate figures, like Mirabeau, Charles James Fox, Franklin Roosevelt, who live near the frontier that divides old from new, between the *douceur de la vie* which is about to pass and the tantalizing future, the dangerous new age that they themselves do much to bring into being.

Herzen belonged to this *milieu*. In his autobiography he has described what it was like to be this kind of man in a suffocating society, where there was no opportunity of putting to use one's natural gifts, what it meant to be excited by novel ideas which came drifting in from all kinds of sources, from classical texts and the old utopias of the West, from French social preachers and German philosophers, from books, journals, casual conversations, only to remember that the *milieu* in which one lived made it absurd even to begin to dream of creating in one's own country those harmless and moderate institutions which had long become forms of life in the civilized West.

This normally led to one of two results: either the young enthusiast simply subsided, and came to terms with reality, and became a wistful, gently frustrated landowner, who lived on his estate, turned the pages of serious periodicals imported from Petersburg or abroad, and occasionally introduced new pieces of agricultural machinery or some other ingenious device which had caught his fancy in England or in France. Such enthusiasts would endlessly discuss the need for this or that change, but always with the melancholy implication that little or nothing could or would be done; or, alternatively, they would give in entirely and fall into a species of gloom or stupor or violent despair, becoming self-devouring neurotics, destructive personalities slowly poisoning both themselves and the life round them.

Herzen was resolved to escape from both these familiar predicaments. He was determined that of him, at any rate, nobody would say that he had done nothing in the world, that he had offered no resistance and collapsed. When he finally emigrated from Russia in 1847 it was to devote himself to a life of activity. His education was that of a dilettante. Like most young men brought up in an aristocratic *milieu*, he had been taught to be too many things to too many men, to reflect too many aspects of life, and situations, to be able to concentrate sufficiently upon any one particular activity, any one fixed design.

Herzen was well aware of this. He talks wistfully about the good fortune of those who enter peacefully some steady, fixed profession, untroubled by the many countless alternatives open to gifted and often idealistic young men who have been taught too much, are too rich, and are offered altogether too wide an opportunity of doing too many things, and who, consequently, begin, and are bored, and go back and start down a new path, and in the end lose their way and drift aimlessly and achieve nothing. This was a very characteristic piece of self-analysis; filled with the idealism of his generation in Russia that both sprang from and fed the growing sense of guilt towards "the people", Herzen was passionately anxious to do something memorable for himself and his country. This anxiety remained with him all his life. Driven by it he became, as everyone knows who has any acquaintance with the modern history of Russia, perhaps the greatest of European publicists of his day, and founded the first free—that is to say, anti-Tsarist—Russian press in Europe, thereby laying the foundation of revolutionary agitation in his country.

In his most celebrated periodical, which he called *The Bell*, he dealt with anything that seemed to be of topical interest. He exposed, he denounced, he derided, he preached, he became a kind of Russian Voltaire of the mid-nineteenth century. He was a journalist of genius, and his articles, written with brilliance, gaiety, and passion, although, of course, officially forbidden, circulated in Russia and were read by radicals and conservatives alike. Indeed it was said that the Emperor himself read them; certainly some among his officials did so; during the heyday of his fame Herzen exercised a genuine influence within Russia itself—an unheard of phenomenon for an *émigré*—by exposing abuses, naming names, but, above all, by appealing to liberal sentiment which had not completely died, even at the very heart of the Tsarist bureaucracy, at any rate during the fifties and sixties.

Unlike many who find themselves only on paper, or on a public platform, Herzen was an entrancing talker. Probably the best description of him is to be found in the book *The Marvellous Decade*, by his friend Annenkov. It was written some twenty years after the events that it records.

I must own [Annenkov wrote] that I was puzzled and overwhelmed, when I first came to know Herzen—by this extraordinary mind which darted from one topic to another with unbelieveable swiftness, with inexhaustible wit and brilliance; which could see in the turn of somebody's talk, in some simple incident, in some abstract idea, that vivid feature which gives expression and life. He had a most astonishing capacity for instantaneous, unexpected juxtaposition of quite dissimilar things, and this gift he had in a very high degree, fed as it was by the powers of the most subtle observation and a very solid fund of encyclopædic knowledge. He had it to such a degree that, in the end, his listeners were sometimes exhausted by the inextinguishable fireworks of his speech, the inexhaustible fantasy and invention, a kind of prodigal opulence of intellect which astonished and delighted his audience.

After the always ardent but remorsely severe Belinsky, the glancing, gleaming, perpetually changing and often paradoxical and irritating, always wonderfully clever, talk of Herzen demanded of those who were with him not only interest, but intense concentration, perpetual alertness, because you had always to be prepared to respond instantly. On the other hand, nothing cheap or tawdry could stand even half an hour of contact with him. All pretentiousness, all pompousness, all pedantic self-importance, simply fled from him or melted like wax before a fire. I knew people, many of them what are called serious and practical men, who could not bear Herzen's presence. On the other hand, there were others who gave him the most blind and passionate adoration.

He had a natural gift for criticism—an unparalleled capacity for exposing and denouncing the dark sides of life. And he showed this trait very early, during the Moscow period of his life of which I am speaking.

Even then Herzen's mind was in the highest degree rebellious and unmanageable, with a kind of innate, organic, detestation of anything which seemed to him to be an accepted opinion sanctified by general silence about some unverified fact. In such cases the deep, predatory, powers of his intellect would rise up in force and come into the open, sharp, cunning, resourceful.

He lived in Moscow, still unknown to the public, but in his own familiar circle he was already known as a witty and a dangerous observer of his friends. What was not then known (though he could not altogether conceal it), was that he kept secret *dossiers*, secret protocols of his own, about his dearest and most intimate friends within the privacy of his own thoughts. People who stood by his side, all innocence and trustfulness, were invariably amazed, and sometimes extremely annoyed, when they suddenly came on one or other side of this activity —the secret activity—of his mind. Strangely enough, Herzen combined with this the tenderest, most loving relations with his chosen intimates, although even they could never escape his pungent analyses. This is explained by another side of his character. As if to restore the equilibrium of his moral organism, nature took care to place in his soul one unshakeable belief, one unconquerable inclination. Herzen believed in the noble instincts of the human heart. His analysis grew silent and reverent before the instinctive impulses of the moral organism as the sole, indubitable truth of existence. He admired anything which he thought to be a noble or passionate impulse, however mistaken; and he never amused himself at its expense.

This ambivalent, as it were, contradictory, play of his nature—suspicion and denial on the one hand and blind faith on the other—often led to perplexity and misunderstandings between him and his friends, and sometimes to quarrels and scenes. But it is precisely in this crucible of argument, in its flames, that up to the very day of his departure for Europe, people's devotion to him used to be tested and strengthened instead of disintegrating. And this is perfectly intelligible. In all that Herzen did and all that Herzen thought at this time there never was the slightest trace of anything false, no malignant feeling nourished in darkness, no calculation, no treachery. On the contrary, the whole of him was always there, in every one of his words and deeds.

And there was another reason which made one sometimes forgive him even insults, a reason which may seem unplausible to people who did not know him. With all this proud, strong, energetic intellect, Herzen had a wholly gentle, amiable, almost feminine character. Beneath the stern outward aspect of the sceptic, the satirist, under the cover of a most unceremonious, and exceedingly unreticent humour.

there dwelt the heart of a child. He had a curious, angular kind of charm, angular kind of delicacy, but it was given particularly to those who were beginning, who were seeking after something, people who were trying out their powers. They found a source of strength and confidence in his advice. He took them into the most intimate communion with himself and with his ideas—which, nevertheless, did not stop him, at times, from using his full destructive, analytic powers, from performing exceedingly painful, psychological experiments on these very same people at the very same time.

This vivid and sympathetic vignette tallies with the descriptions left to us by Turgenev, Belinsky and others of Herzen's friends. It is borne out, above all, by the impression which the reader gains if he reads his own prose, his essays or the autobiographical memoirs collected under the title *My Past and Reflections*. The impression that it leaves is not conveyed even by Annenkov's devoted words.

The chief influence on Herzen as a young man in Moscow University, as upon all the young Russian intellectuals of his time, was of course that of Hegel. But although he was a fairly orthodox Hegelian in his early years, he turned his Hegelianism into something peculiar, personal to himself, very dissimilar from the theoretical conclusions which the more serious-minded and pedantic of his contemporaries deduced from that celebrated doctrine.

The chief effect upon him of Hegelianism seems to have been the belief that no specific theory or single doctrine, no one interpretation of life, above all, no simple, coherent, well-constructed schema—neither the great French mechanistic models of the eighteenth century, nor the romantic German edifices of the nineteenth, nor the visions of the great utopians Saint-Simon, Fourier, Owen, nor the socialist programmes of Cabet or Leroux or Louis Blanc—could conceivably be true solutions to real problems, at least not in the form in which they were preached.

He was sceptical if only because he believed (whether or not he derived this view from Hegel) that there could not in principle be any simple or final answer to any genuine human problem; that if a question was serious and indeed agonizing, the answer could never be clear cut and neat. Above all, it could never consist in some symmetrical set of conclusions, drawn by deductive means from a collection of self-evident axioms.

This disbelief begins in Herzen's early, forgotten essays which he wrote at the beginning of the forties, on what he called dilettantism and Buddhism in science; where he distinguishes two kinds of intellectual personality, against both of which he inveighs. One is that of the casual amateur who never sees the trees for the wood; who is terrified, Herzen tells us, of losing his own precious individuality in too much pedantic preoccupation with actual, detailed facts, and, therefore, always skims over the surface without developing a capacity for real knowledge; who looks at the facts, as it were, through a kind of telescope, with the result that nothing ever gets articulated save enormous, sonorous generalizations floating at random like so many balloons.

The other kind of student—the Buddhist—is the person who escapes from the wood by frantic absorption in the trees; who becomes an intense student of some tiny set of isolated facts, which he views through more and more powerful microscopes. Although such a man might be deeply learned in some particular branch of knowledge, almost invariably—and particularly if he is a German (and almost all Herzen's gibes and insults are always directed against the hated Germans, and that despite the fact that he was half German himself)—he becomes intolerably tedious, pompous and blindly philistine; above all, always repellent as a human being.

Between these poles it is necessary to find some compromise, and Herzen believed that if one studied life in a sober, detached, and objective manner, one might perhaps be able to create some kind of tension, a sort of dialectical compromise, between these opposite ideals; for if neither of them can be realized fully and equally, neither of them should be altogether deserted; only thus could human beings be made capable of understanding life in some profounder fashion than if they committed themselves recklessly to one or the other of the two extremes.

This ideal of detachment, moderation, compromise, dispassionate objectivity which Herzen at this early period of his life was preaching, was something deeply incompatible with his temperament. And indeed, not long after, he bursts forth with a great paean to partiality. "I know," he writes, "that will not be well received. I know that there are certain concepts which simply are not received in good society—rather like people who have been in gaol or have disgraced themselves in some appalling way. I know that partiality is not something which is well thought of. Nevertheless, nobody has ever said anything worth saying unless he was deeply and passionately partial."

There follows a long and typically Russian diatribe against the chilliness, meanness, impossibility and undesirability of remaining objective, of being detached, of not committing oneself, of not plunging into the stream of life. The passionate voice of his friend Belinsky is suddenly audible in Herzen's writings in this phase of his development.

But the fundamental belief which emerges at this time, and is then developed throughout his later life with marvellous poetry and imagination. (I say poetry advisedly; for as Dostaievsky in later years very truly said, whatever else might be said about Herzen, he was certainly a Russian poet; which saved him in the eyes of this jaundiced but, at times, uncannily penetrating critic : Herzen's views or mode of life naturally found little favour in his eyes.)

The thesis which Herzen offered to the world comes to this : that any attempt to explain human conduct in terms of, or to dedicate human beings to the service of, any abstraction, be it never so noble—justice, progress, nationality—even if preached by impeccable altruists like Mazzini or Louis Blanc or Mill, always leads in the end to victimization and human sacrifice. Men are not simple enough, human lies and relationships are too complex for standard formulae and neat solutions, and attempts to adapt individuals and fit them into a rational schema, conceived in terms of a theoretical ideal, be the motives for doing it never so lofty, always lead in the end to a terrible maiming of human beings, to political vivisection on an ever increasing scale. The process culminates in the liberation of some only at the price of enslavement of others, and the replacing of an old tyranny with a new and sometimes far more hideous one—by the imposition of the slavery of universal socialism, for example, as a remedy for the slavery of the universal Roman Church.

There is a typical piece of dialogue between Herzen and Louis Blanc, the French socialist (whom he respected greatly), which Herzen quotes, and which shows the kind of levity with which Herzen sometimes expressed his deepest convictions. The conversation is described as having taken place in London somewhere in the early fifties. One day Louis Blanc observed to Herzen that human life was a great social duty, that man must always sacrifice himself to society.

"Why?" I asked suddenly. "How do you mean, why?" said Louis Blanc. "Surely the whole purpose and the whole mission of man is the well-being of society?" "Oh, but it will never be attained if everybody makes sacrifices and nobody ever enjoys himself." "You are playing with words." "Only the muddle-headedness of a barbarian," I said laughing.

In this gay and apparently casual passage, Herzen embodies his central principle—that the goal of life is life itself, that to sacrifice the present to some vague and unpredictable future is a form of delusion which leads to the destruction of all that alone is valuable in men and societies—to the gratuitous sacrifice of the flesh and blood of live human beings upon the altar of idealized abstractions.

Herzen is revolted by the central substance of what was being preached

334

by some of the best and purest-hearted men of his time, particularly by socialists and utilitarians, namely, that vast suffering in the present must be undergone for the sake of an ineffable felicity in the future, that thousands of innocent men may be forced to die that millions might be happy—battle cries that were common even in those days, and of which a great deal more has been heard since. The notion that there is a splendid future in store for humanity, that it is guaranteed by history, and that it justifies the most appalling cruelties in the present—this familiar piece of political eschatology based on belief in inevitable progress seemed to him a fatal doctrine directed against human life.

The profoundest and most sustained—and the most brilliantly written— of all Herzen's statements on this topic is to be found in the volume of essays which he called *From the Other Shore*, and wrote as a memorial to his disillusionment with the European revolutions of 1848 and 1849. This great polemical masterpiece is Herzen's profession of faith and his political testament. Its tone and content is well conveyed in the characteristic (and celebrated) passage in which he asks:

If progress is the goal, for whom then are we working? Who is this Moloch who, as the toilers approach him, instead of rewarding them, draws back, and as a consolation to the exhausted and doomed multitudes shouting, "We, who are about to die, salute thee!", can only give the mocking answer that after their death all will be beautiful on earth. Do you really wish to condemn human beings alive today to the mere sad rôle of caryatids supporting a floor for others one day to dance upon? Of wretched galley slaves who, up to their knees in mud, drag a barge with the humble words "Future Progress" on its flag? A goal which is infinitely remote is not a goal at all, it is a deception. A goal must be closer—at the very least the labourer's wage or pleasure in work performed. Each epoch, each generation, each life has had, has, its own experience, and *en route* new demands grow, new methods.

He continues:

The end of each generation must be itself. Nature not only never makes one generation the means for the attainment of some future goal; she does not concern herself with the future at all. Like Cleopatra, she is ready to dissolve the pearl in wine for a second's pleasure. If humanity marched straight towards some result, there would be no history, only logic. One has to arrange life as best one can because there is no libretto. If history followed a set libretto, it would lose all interest, it would become unnecessary, boring, ludicrous. Great men would be

335

simply so many heroes strutting on a stage. History is all improvisation, all will, all extemporized. There are no frontiers, there are no time-tables, no itineraries. All that exists is specific conditions, and sacred discontent, the flow of life and its endless challenge to the fighters to try their strength, to go where they will, where there is a road; and when there is no road, there genius will blast a path.

But what if someone were to ask, "Supposing all this is suddenly brought to an end? Supposing a comet strikes us and brings to an end life on earth? Will history not be meaningless? Will all this talk suddenly end in nothing? Will it not be a cruel mockery of all our efforts, all our blood and sweat and tears, if it all ends in some sudden, unexplained brute fashion by some mysterious, totally unexplained event?" Herzen replies that to think in these terms is a great vulgarity, the vulgarity of mere numbers. The death of a single human being is no less absurd and unintelligible than the death of the entire human race; it is a mystery we accept; merely to multiply it enormously and ask, "Supposing millions of human beings die?" does not make it more mysterious or more frightening.

In nature, as in the souls of men, there slumber endless possibilities and forces, and in suitable conditions they develop, they develop furiously. They may fill a world, or they may fall by the roadside. They may take a new direction. They may stop. They may collapse. Nature is perfectly indifferent to what happens. But then, you may ask, What is all this for? The life of people becomes a pointless game. Men build something with pebbles and grass and sand only to see it all collapse again; and human creatures crawl out from underneath the ruins and again start clearing spaces and build huts of moss and planks and broken capitals and, after centuries of endless labour, it all collapses again. Not in vain did Shakespeare say that history was a tale told by an idiot.

To this I reply that you are like those very sensitive people who shed a tear whenever they recollect that man is born but to die. To look at the end and not at the action itself is a cardinal error. Of what use to the flower is its bright magnificent bloom? Or this intoxicating scent, since it will only pass away? None at all. But nature is not so miserly. She does not disdain what is transient, what is only in the present. At every point she achieves all she can achieve. Who will find fault with nature because flowers bloom in the morning and die at night, because she has not given the rose or the lily the hardness of flint? And this miserable pedestrian principle *we* wish to transfer to the world of history. Life has no obligation to realize the fantasies and ideas of civilization.

Life loves novelty. She seldom repeats herself. She uses every accident, simultaneously knocks at a thousand doors, some of which may open —who can tell?

And again:

> Human beings have an instinctive passion to preserve anything they like. Man is born and therefore wishes to live for ever. Man falls in love and wishes to be loved, and loved for ever as in the very first moment of his avowal. But life gives no guarantees. Life does not ensure existence, nor pleasure; she does not answer for their continuance. Every historical moment is full and is beautiful, is self-contained in its own fashion. Every year has its own spring and its own summer, its own winter and autumn, its own storms and fair weather. Every period is new, fresh, filled with its own hopes and carries within itself its own joys and sorrows. The present belongs to it. But human beings are not content with this, they must needs own the future too.
>
> What is the purpose of the song the singer sings? If you look beyond your pleasure in it for something else, for some other goal, the moment will come when the singer stops and then you will only have memories and vain regrets because, instead of listening, you were waiting for something else. You must not be misled by categories that are not fitted to catch the flow of life. What is this goal for which you [he means Mazzini and the liberals and the socialists] are seeking, this permanent goal? A programme? An order? Who conceived it? To whom was the order given? Is it something inevitable? If it is, we are simply puppets. Are we morally free or are we wheels within a machine? I would rather think of life, and therefore of history, as a goal attained, not as a means to something else.

And:

> Is it really the purpose of a child to grow up simply because it does grow up? No. The purpose of a child is to play, to enjoy itself, to be a child; because, if we follow the other line of reasoning, then the purpose of all life is death.

This is Herzen's central political and social thesis, and it enters henceforth into the stream of Russian radical thought as an antidote to the exaggerated utilitarianism of which its adversaries have so often accused it. The purpose of the singer is the song, and the purpose of life is to be lived. Everything passes, but what passes may sometimes reward the pilgrim for all his sufferings. Goethe has told us that there can be no guarantee, no security. Man could be content with the present. But he is not. He rejects beauty, he rejects fulfilment today, because he must own the future also. That is Herzen's answer to all those who, like Mazzini, or the socialists of his time, called for supreme sacrifices and sufferings for the sake of nationality, or human civilization, or socialism, or justice, or humanity—if not in the present, then in the future.

Herzen rejects this violently. The purpose of the struggle for liberty is not liberty tomorrow, it is liberty today, the liberty of living individuals with their own individual ends, the ends for which they move and fight and perhaps die, ends which are sacred to them. To crush their freedom, their pursuits, to ruin their ends for the sake of some vague felicity in the future which cannot be guaranteed, about which we know nothing, which is simply the product of some enormous metaphysical construction that itself rests upon sand, for which there is no logical, or empirical or any other rational guarantee—to do that is in the first place blind, because the future is uncertain; and in the second place vicious because it offends against the only moral values we know; because it tramples on human demands in the name of abstractions—freedom, happiness, justice—fanatical generalizations, mystical sounds, idolized sets of words.

Why is liberty valuable? Because it is an end in itself, because it is what it is. To bring it as a sacrifice to something else is simply to perform an act of human sacrifice.

This is Herzen's ultimate sermon, and from this he develops the corollary that one of the deepest of modern disasters is to be caught up in abstractions instead of realities. And this he maintains not merely against the Western socialists and liberals among whom he lived (let alone the enemy—priests or conservatives) but even more against his own close friend Bakunin who persisted in trying to stir up violent rebellion, involving torture and martyrdom, for the sake of dim, confused and distant goals. For Herzen, one of the greatest of sins that any human being can perpetrate is to seek to transfer moral responsibility from his own shoulders to those of an unpredictable future order, and, in the name of something which may never happen, perpetrate crimes today which no one would deny to be monstrous if they were performed for some egoistic purpose, and do not seem so only because they are sanctified by faith in some remote and intangible Utopia.

For all his hatred of despotism, and in particular of the Russian régime, Herzen was all his life convinced that equally fatal dangers threatened from his own socialist and revolutionary allies. He believed this because there was a time when, with his friend, the critic Belinsky, he too had believed that a simple solution was feasible; that some great system—a world adumbrated by Saint-Simon or by Proudhon—did provide it : that if one regulated social life rationally and put it in order, and created a clear and tidy organization, human problems could be finally resolved. Dostoievsky once said of Belinsky that his socialism was nothing but a simple belief in a marvellous life of "rich and unbelievable splendour, built on new, adamantine foundations". Because Herzen had himself once believed in these foundations (although never with simple and absolute faith) and because this belief came toppling down and was utterly destroyed in the fearful cataclysms of 1848 and 1849 in which almost every one of his idols proved to have feet of clay, he denounces his own past with peculiarly intense indignation :

> We call upon the masses to rise and crush the tyrants. The masses! The masses are indifferent to individual freedom ... They want a government which will rule for them, not against them. But they do not dream of governing themselves ... It is not enough to despise the Crown; one must not be filled with awe before the Phrygian cap either.

He speaks with bitter scorn about monolithic, oppressive communist idylls, about the barbarous "equality of the gallows", about "the slave labour camps" of socialists like Cabet, about barbarians marching to destroy.

> Who will finish us off? The senile barbarism of the sceptre or the wild barbarism of communism; the bloody sabre, or the red flag? ... Communism will sweep across the world in a violent tempest—dreadful, bloody, unjust, swift. Our institutions, as Proudhon so politely put it, will be liquidated. I am very sorry for the death of civilization, but the masses are not sorry; the masses to whom it brings nothing but tears, ignorance, suffering, humiliation.

He is terrified of the oppressors, but he is terrified of the liberators too. He is terrified of them because for him they are the secular heirs of the religious bigots of the ages of faith; because anybody who has a cut-and-dried scheme, a strait-jacket which he wishes to impose on humanity as the sole possible remedy for all human ills, is ultimately bound to create a situation intolerable for free human beings, for men like himself who want to express themselves, who want to have some area in which to develop their own resources, and are prepared to respect the originality, the spontaneity, the natural impulse towards self-expression on the part of other human beings too. He calls this Petrograndism—the methods of Peter the Great. He admires Peter the Great. He admires Peter because he did at least overthrow the feudal rigidity, the dark night, as he thinks of it, of medieval Russia. He admires the Jacobins because the Jacobins dared to do something instead of nothing. Yet he is clearly aware, and became more and more so the longer he lived (he says all this with arresting clarity in his open letter to "An Old Comrade"—Bakunin—written in the late sixties), that Petrograndism, the behaviour of Attila, the behaviour of the Committee of Public Safety in 1792—the use of methods which presuppose the possibility of simple and radical solutions—always in the end lead to oppression, bloodshed, and collapse. He declares that whatever the justification in earlier and more innocent ages of acts inspired by fanatical faith, nobody has any right to act in this fashion who has lived through the nineteenth century and has seen what human beings are really made of— the complex, crooked texture of men and institutions. Progress must adjust itself to the actual peace of historical change, to the actual economic and social needs of society, because to suppress the bourgeoisie by violent revolution—and there was nothing he despised more than the bourgeoisie, and the mean, grasping, philistine financial bourgeoisie of Paris most of all —before its historical rôle has been played out, would merely mean that the bourgeois spirit and bourgeois forms would persist into the new social order. "It is not possible to build houses for free men out of materials designed for prisons." And who shall say that history has proved that Herzen was mistaken?

His loathing of the bourgeoisie is frantic, yet he does not want a violent cataclysm. He thinks that it may be inevitable, that it may come, but he is frightened of it. The bourgeoisie seems to him like a collection of Figaros, but of Figaros grown fat and prosperous. He declares that, in the eighteenth century, Figaro wore a livery, a mark of servitude to be sure, but still something different from, detachable from, his skin; the skin, at least, was that of a palpitating, rebellious human being. But today Figaro has won. Figaro has become a millionaire. He is judge, commander-in-chief, president of the republic. Figaro now dominates the world, and, alas, the livery is no longer a mere livery. It has become part of his skin. It cannot be taken off; it has become part of his living flesh.

Everything that was repellent and degrading in the eighteenth century, against which the noble revolutionaries had protested, has grown into the intrinsic texture of the mean middle class beings who now dominate us. And yet we must wait. Simply to cut off their heads, as Bakunin wanted, can only lead to a new tyranny and a new slavery, to the rule of the revolted minorities over majorities, or worse still, the rule of majorities—monolithic majorities—over minorities, the rule of what John Stuart Mill, in Herzen's view with justice, called conglomerated mediocrity.

Herzen's values are undisguised : he likes only the style of free beings, only what is large, generous, uncalculating. He admires pride, independence, resistance to tyrants; he admires Pushkin because he was defiant; he admires Lermontov because he dared to suffer and to hate; he even approves of the Slavophils, his reactionary opponents, because at least they detested authority, at least they would not let the Germans in. He admires Belinsky because he was incorruptible, and told the truth in the face of the arrayed battalions of German academic or political authority. The dogmata of socialism seem to him no less stifling than those of capitalism or of the Middle Ages or of the early Christians.

What he hated most of all was the despotism of formulæ—the submission of human beings to arrangements arrived at by deduction from some kind of *a priori* principles which had no foundation in actual experience. That is why he feared the new liberators so deeply. "If only people wanted," he says, "instead of liberating humanity, to liberate themselves, they would do a very great deal for human freedom." He knew that his own perpetual plea for more individual freedom contained the seeds of social atomization, that a compromise had to be found between the two great social needs—for organization and for individual freedom—some unstable equilibrium that would preserve a minimal area within which the individual could express himself and not be utterly pulverized, and he utters a great appeal for what he calls the value of egoism. He declares that one of the great dangers to our society is that individuals will be tamed and suppressed disinterestedly by idealists in the name of altruism, in the name of measures designed to make the majority happy. The new liberators may well resemble the inquisitors of the past, who drove herds of innocent Spaniards, Dutchmen, Belgians, Frenchmen, Italians to the *autos-da-fé*, and "then went home peacefully with a quiet conscience, with the feeling that they had done their duty, with the smell of roasting human flesh still in their nostrils", and slept—the sleep of the innocent after a day's work well done.

Let us encourage egoism instead of trying to suppress it, which is anyhow impossible. Egoism is not a vice. Egoism gleams in the eye of an animal. It is wild, self-centred and salutary. Moralists bravely thunder against it, instead of building on it. What moralists try and deny is the great, inner citadel of human dignity. They want to make men tearful, sentimental, feeble, kindly creatures asking to be made slaves. But to tear egoism from a man's heart is to rob him of his living principles, of the yeast and the salt of his whole personality. Fortunately

341

this is impossible. Of course it is sometimes suicidal to try to assert one-self. One cannot try and go up a staircase down which an army is trying to march. That is done by tyrants, conservatives, fools and criminals. Without altruism we are orang-outangs, but without egoism we are nothing but tame monkeys.

Human problems are too complex to demand simple solutions. Even the peasant commune in Russia, in which Herzen believed so deeply as a "lightning conductor", because he believed that peasants in Russia at least had not been infected by the distorting, urban vices of the European pro-letariat and the European bourgeoisie—even the peasant commune did not, after all, as he points out, preserve Russia from slavery. Liberty is not to the taste of the majority—only of the educated. There are no guaranteed methods, no sure paths to social welfare. We must try and do our best; and it is always possible that we shall fail.

The heart of his thought is the notion that the basic problems are perhaps not soluble at all, that all one can do is to try to solve them, but that there is no guarantee, either in socialist nostrums or in any other human con-struction, no guarantee that happiness or a rational life can be attained, in private or in public life. This curious combination of idealism and scepti-cism—not unlike, for all his vehemence, the outlook of Erasmus, Mon-taigne, Montesquieu—runs through all his writings.

Herzen wrote novels, but they have not survived because he was not a born novelist. His stories are greatly inferior to those of his friend, Turgenev, but they have something in common with them. For in Turgenev's novels, too, you will find that human problems are not treated as if they were soluble. Bazarov in *Fathers and Children* suffers and dies; Lavretsky in *A House of Gentlefolk* is left in melancholy uncertainty at the end of the novel, not because something had not been done which could have been done, not because there is a solution round the corner which someone simply had not thought of, or had refused to apply, but because, as Kant once said, "from the crooked timber of humanity no straight thing was ever made". Everything is partly the fault of circum-stance, partly the fault of the individual character, partly in the nature of life itself. This must be faced, it must be stated, and it is a vulgarity and, at times, a crime to believe that permanent solutions are always possible.

Herzen wrote a novel called *Who Is To Blame?* about a typical tragic triangle in which one of the "superfluous men" of whom I spoke earlier falls in love with a lady in a provincial town who is married to a virtuous, idealistic, but dull and naïve husband. It is not a good novel, and its plot is not worth recounting, but the main point, and what is most characteristic of Herzen, is that the situation possesses, in principle, no solution. The lover is left broken-hearted, the wife falls ill and probably dies, the husband contemplates suicide. It sounds like a typically gloomy, morbidly self-centred, caricature of the Russian novel. But it is not. It rests on an exceedingly delicate, precise, and at times profound description of an emotional and psychological situation to which the theories of a Stendhal, the method of a Flaubert, the depth and moral insight of George Eliot are inapplicable because they are seen to be too literary, derived from obsessive ideas, ethical doctrines not fitted to the chaos of life.

At the heart of Herzen's outlook (and of Turgenev's too) is the notion of the complexity and insolubility of the central problems, and, therefore, of the absurdity of trying to solve them by means of political or sociological instruments. But the difference between Herzen and Turgenev is this. Turgenev is, in his innermost being, not indeed heartless but a cool, detached, at times slightly mocking observer who looks upon the tragedies of life from a comparatively remote point of view; oscillating between one vantage point and another, between the claims of society and of the individual, the claims of love and of daily life; between heroic virtue and realistic scepticism, the morality of Hamlet and the morality of Don Quixote, the necessity for efficient political organization and the necessity for individual self-expression; remaining suspended in a state of agreeable indecision, sympathetic melancholy, ironical, free from cynicism and sentimentality, perceptive, scrupulously truthful and uncommitted. Turgenev neither quite believed nor quite disbelieved in a deity, personal or impersonal; religion is for him a normal ingredient of life, like love, or egoism or the sense of pleasure. He enjoyed remaining in an intermediate position, he enjoyed almost too much his lack of will to believe, and because he stood aside, because he contemplated in tranquillity, he was able to produce great literary masterpieces of a finished kind, rounded stories, told in peaceful retrospect, with well-constructed beginnings, middles and ends. He detached his art from himself; he did not, as a human being, deeply care about solutions; he saw life with a peculiar chilliness, which infuriated both Tolstoy and Dostoievsky, and achieved the exquisite perspective of an artist who treats his material from a certain distance. There is a chasm between him and his material, within which alone his particular kind of poetical creation is possible.

Herzen, on the contrary, cared far too violently. He was looking for solutions for himself, for his own personal life. His novels were certainly failures. He obtrudes himself too vehemently into them, himself and his agonized point of view. On the other hand, his autobiographical sketches, when he writes openly about himself and about his friends, when he

343

speaks about his own life in Italy, in France, in Switzerland, in England, have a kind of palpitating directness, a sense of first-handness and reality, which no other writer in the nineteenth century begins to convey. His reminiscences are a work of critical and descriptive genius with the power of absolute self-revelation that only an astonishingly imaginative, impressionable, perpetually reacting personality, with an exceptional sense both of the noble and the ludicrous, and a rare freedom from vanity and doctrine, could have attained. As a writer of memoirs he is unequalled. His sketches of England, or rather of himself in England, are better than Heine's or Taine's. To demonstrate this one need only read his wonderful account of English political trials, of how judges, for example, looked to him when they sat in court trying foreign conspirators for having fought a fatal duel in Windsor Park. He gives a vivid and entertaining description of bombastic French demagogues and gloomy French fanatics, and of the impassable gulf which divides this agitated and slightly grotesque *émigré* society from the dull, frigid, and dignified institutions of mid-Victorian England, typified by the figure of the presiding judge at the Old Bailey, who looks like the wolf in *Red Riding Hood*, in his white wig, his long skirts, with his sharp little wolf-like face, thin lips, sharp teeth, and harsh little words that come with an air of specious benevolence, from the face encased in disarming feminine curls—giving the impression of a sweet, grandmotherly, old lady, belied by the small gleaming eyes and the dry, acrid, malicious judicial humour.

He paints classical portraits of German exiles, whom he detested, of Italian and Polish revolutionaries, whom he admired, and gives little sketches of the differences between the nations, such as the English and the French, each of which regards itself as the greatest nation on earth, and will not yield an inch, and does not begin to understand the other's ideals—the French with their gregariousness, their lucidity, their didacticism, their neat formal gardens, as against the English with their solitudes and dark suppressed romanticism, and the tangled undergrowth of their ancient, illogical, but profoundly civilized and humane institutions. And there are the Germans, who regard themselves, he declares, as an inferior fruit of the tree of which the English are the superior products, and come to England, and after three days "say 'yes' instead of 'ja', and 'well' where it is not required". It is invariably for the Germans that both he and Bakunin reserved their sharpest taunts, not so much from personal dislike, as because the Germans to them seemed to stand for all that was middle-class, cramping, philistine, and boorish, the sordid despotism of grey and small-minded drill sergeants, æsthetically more disgusting than the generous, magnificent tyrannies of great conquerors of history. "With us," said Herzen, "slavery is arithmetical. We are simply too few to resist the

344

huge, overwhelming, crushing force of the Tsarist régime. But German slavery is algebraical. It is part of the very formula of their souls, which nothing can eliminate." This was echoed by Bakunin a decade later: "When an Englishman or an American says 'I am an Englishman', or 'I am an American', he means, 'I am a free man'. When a German says 'I am a German', he means, 'My king is more powerful than all your kings and the soldier who is strangling me now will soon strangle you all'." This kind of sweeping prejudice, these diatribes against entire nations and classes, are characteristic of a good many Russian writers of this period. They are often ill-founded, unjust and violently exaggerated, but they are the authentic expression of an indignant reaction against an oppressive *milieu*, and of a genuine and highly personal moral vision which makes them lively reading even now.

His irreverence and the irony, the disbelief in final solutions, the conviction that human beings are complex and fragile, and that there is value in the very irregularity of their structure which is violated by attempts to force it into patterns or strait-jackets—this and the irrepressible pleasure in exploding all cut-and-dried social and political schemata which serious-minded and pedantic saviours of mankind, both radical and conservative, were perpetually manufacturing, inevitably made Herzen unpopular among the earnest and the devout of all camps. In this respect he resembled his sceptical friend Turgenev, who could not, and had no wish to, resist the desire to tell the truth however "unscientific"—to say something psychologically telling, even though it might not fit in with some generally accepted, enlightened system of ideas. Neither accepted the view that because he was on the side of progress or revolution he was under a sacred obligation to suppress the truth, or to pretend to think that it was simpler than it was, or that certain solutions would work although it seemed patently improbable that they could, simply because to speak otherwise might give aid and comfort to the enemy.

This detachment from party and doctrine, and the tendency to utter independent and sometimes disconcerting judgements, brought violent criticism on both Herzen and Turgenev, and made their position difficult. When Turgenev wrote *Fathers and Children*, he was duly attacked both from the right and from the left, because neither was clear which side he was supporting. This indeterminate quality particularly irritated the "new" young men in Russia, who assailed him bitterly for being too liberal, too civilized, too ironical, too sceptical, for undermining noble idealism by the perpetual oscillation of political feelings, by excessive self-examination, by not engaging himself and declaring war upon the enemy, and perpetrating instead what amounted to a succession of evasions and minor treacheries. Their hostility was directed at all the "men of the forties", and in particular at Herzen who was rightly looked on as their most brilliant and most formidable representative. His answer to the stern, brutal young terrorists of the sixties is exceedingly characteristic. The new revolutionaries had attacked him for nostalgic love of an older style of life, for being a gentleman, for being rich, for living in comfort, for sitting in London and observing the Russian revolutionary struggle from afar, for being a member of a generation which had merely talked in the *salons,* and speculated and philosophized, when all round them was squalor and misery, bitterness and injustice; for not seeking salvation in some serious manual labour—in cutting down a tree, or making a pair of boots or doing something "concrete" and real in order to identify himself with the suffering masses, instead of endless brave talk in the drawing-rooms of wealthy ladies with other well-educated, nobly-born, equally feckless young men—self-indulgence and escapism, deliberate blindness to the horrors and agonies of their world.

Herzen understood his opponents, and declined to compromise. He admits that he cannot help preferring cleanliness to dirt; decency, elegance, beauty, comfort, to violence and austerity, good literature to bad, poetry to prose. Despite his alleged cynicism and "æstheticism", he declines to admit that only scoundrels can achieve things, that in order to achieve a revolution that will liberate mankind and create a new and nobler form of life on earth one must be unkempt, dirty, brutal and violent, and trample with hob-nailed boots on civilization and the rights of men. He does not believe this, and sees no reason why he should believe it.

As for the new generation of revolutionaries, they are not sprung from nothing :

> They are our fault. We begat them, by our idle talk in the forties. These are men who come to avenge the world against us ... the syphilis of our revolutionary passions ... The new generation will say to the old : "You were hypocrites, we are cynics; you spoke like moralists; we shall speak like scoundrels; you were civil to your superiors, rude to your inferiors; we shall be rude to everyone. You bowed and felt no respect, we shall push and jostle and make no apologies."

He says in effect : Organized hooliganism can solve nothing. Unless civilization—the recognition of the difference of good and bad, noble and ignoble, worthy and unworthy—is preserved, unless there are some people who are both fastidious and fearless, and are free to say what they want to say, and do not sacrifice their lives upon some large, nameless altar, and sink themselves into a vast impersonal, grey mass of barbarians marching to destroy, what is the point of the revolution? It may come whether we like it or not. But why should we welcome, still less work for, the victory of the barbarians who will sweep away the wicked old world only to leave ruins and misery on which nothing but a new despotism can be built? The "great case for the prosecution which Russian literature has been drafting against Russian life" does not demand a new philistinism in place of the old. "Sorrow, scepticism, irony, the three strings of the Russian lyre" are closer to reality than the crude and vulgar optimism of the new materialists.

Herzen's most constant goal is the preservation of individual liberty. That is the purpose of the guerrilla war which, as he once wrote to Mazzini, he had fought from his earliest youth. What made him unique in the nineteenth century is the complexity of his vision, the degree to which he understood the causes and nature of conflicting ideals simpler and more fundamental than his own. He understood what made—and what in a measure justified—radicals and revolutionaries : and at the same time he grasped the frightening consequences of their doctrines. He was in full sympathy with, and had a profound psychological understanding of, what it was that gave the Jacobins their severe and noble grandeur, and endowed them with a moral magnificence which raised them above the horizon of that older world which he found so attractive and which they had ruthlessly crushed. He understood only too well the misery, the oppression, the suffocation, the appalling inhumanity, the bitter cries for justice on the part of the crushed elements of the population under the *ancien régime*, and at the same time he knew that the new world which had risen to avenge these wrongs, must, if it was given its head, create its own excesses and drive millions of human beings to useless mutual extermination. Herzen's sense of reality—in particular of the need for, and the price of, revolution, is unique in his own, and perhaps in any age. His sense of the critical moral and political issues of his time is a good deal more specific and concrete than that of the majority of the professional philosophers of the nineteenth century, who tended to try to derive general principles from observation of their society, and to recommend solutions which are deduced by rational methods from premises formulated in terms of the tidy categories in which they sought to arrange opinions, principles and forms of conduct. Herzen was a publicist and an essayist whom his early Hegelian training had not ruined : he had acquired no taste for academic classifications : he had a unique insight into the "inner feel" of social and political predicaments : and with it a remarkable power of analysis and exposition. Consequently he understood and stated the case, both emotional and intellectual, for violent revolution, for saying that a pair of boots were of more value than all the plays of Shakespeare (as the

347

"nihilistic" critic Pisarev once said in a rhetorical moment), for denouncing liberalism and parliamentarism which offered the masses votes and slogans, when what they needed was food, shelter, clothing; and understood no less vividly and clearly the æsthetic and even moral value of civilizations which rest upon slavery, where a minority produces divine masterpieces, and only a small number of persons have the freedom and the self-confidence, the imagination and the gifts to be able to produce forms of life that endure, works which can be shored up against the ruin of our time.

This curious ambivalence, the alternation of indignant championship of revolution and democracy against the smug denunciation of them by liberals and conservatives, with no less passionate attacks upon revolutionaries in the name of free individuals; the defence of the claims of life and art, human decency, equality and dignity, with the advocacy of a society in which human beings shall not exploit or trample on one another even in the name of justice or progress or civilization or democracy or other abstractions—this war on two, and often more, fronts, wherever and whoever the enemies of freedom might turn out to be—makes Herzen the most realistic, sensitive, penetrating, and convincing witness to the social life and the social issues of his own time. His greatest gift is that of untrammelled understanding : he understood the value of the so-called "superfluous" Russian idealists of the forties because they were exceptionally free, and morally attractive, and formed the most imaginative, spontaneous, gifted, civilized and interesting society which he had ever known. At the same time he understands the protest against it of the exasperated, deeply earnest, *révolté* young radicals, repelled by what seemed to them gay and irresponsible chatter among a group of aristocratic *flâneurs*, unaware of the mounting resentment of the sullen mass of the oppressed peasants and lower officials that would one day sweep them and their world away in a tidal wave of violent, blind, but justified hatred which it is the business of true revolutionaries to foment and direct. Herzen understood this conflict, and his autobiography conveys the tension between individuals and classes, personalities and opinions both in Russia and in the West, with marvellous vividness and precision.

The Past and Reflections is dominated by no single clear purpose, it is not committed to a thesis; its author was not enslaved by any formula or any political doctrine, and for this reason, it remains a profound and living masterpiece, and Herzen's greatest title to immortality. He possesses other claims : his political and social views were arrestingly original, if only because he was among the very few thinkers of his time who in principle rejected all general solutions, and grasped, as very few thinkers have ever done, the crucial distinction between words that are about words, and words that are about persons or things in the real world. Nevertheless it is as a writer that he survives. His autobiography is one of the great monuments to Russian literary and psychological genius, worthy to stand beside the great novels of Turgenev and Tolstoy. Like *War and Peace*, like *Fathers and Children*, it is wonderfully readable, and, save in inferior translation, not dated, not Victorian, still astonishingly contemporary in feeling.

One of the elements in political genius is a sensibility to characteristics and processes in society while they are still in embryo and invisible to the naked eye. Herzen possessed this capacity to a high degree, but he viewed the approaching cataclysm neither with the savage exultation of Marx or Bakunin nor with the pessimistic detachment of Burckhardt or Tocqueville. Like Proudhon he believed the destruction of individual freedom to be neither desirable nor inevitable, but, unlike him, as being highly probable, unless it was averted by deliberate human effort. The strong tradition of libertarian humanism in Russian socialism, defeated only in October 1917, derives from his writings. His analysis of the forces at work in his day, of the individuals in whom they were embodied, of the moral presupposition of their creeds and words, and of his own principles, remains to this day one of the most penetrating, moving, and morally formidable indictments of the great evils which have grown to maturity in our own time.

MAY 1956

LIONEL TRILLING

The Smile of Parmenides

ONE DOESN'T HAVE to read very far in Santayana's letters to become aware that it might be very hard to like this man—that, indeed, it might be remarkably easy to dislike him. And there is no point in struggling against the adverse feeling. The right thing to do is to recognize it, to admit it into consciousness, and to establish it beside that other awareness, which should come as early and which should be the stronger of the two— that Santayana was one of the most remarkable men of our time and that his letters are of classic importance.

To say that they are among the best of modern letters is not to say much, is not to say anything. I can think of no modern collections of letters— D. H. Lawrence's and Shaw's excepted—that aren't deeply depressing in their emptiness and lack of energy, in their frightening inability to suggest living spirit. To find an adequate point of comparison for Santayana's letters one has to go back to the nineteenth century. Santayana isn't, of course, equal to Keats as a letter-writer, but that one can even think to say that he isn't, is something. I am led to make the comparison not because the letters of Santayana and of Keats are similar in kind but because they are similar in effect. No recent book has taken possession of my mind as Santayana's has, commanding not assent (or not often) but concurrence—I mean a literal "running along with", the desire to follow where the writer leads. One of the effects of Keats's letters is to suggest that the writer holds in his mind at every moment a clear image of the actual quotidian world and also an image of the universe and of a mode of existence beyond actuality yet intimately related to actuality and, in a sense, controlling it. I don't pretend to understand Santayana's doctrine of essences, not having read the works in which he expounds it; nor, indeed, do I wholly understand Keats's doctrine of essences, although I do perceive that it was central to his thought. I suspect that the two doctrines have much in common and I recommend the exploration of this possibility to a competent philosopher. But quite apart from any connection that may be found between Santayana's thought and Keats's—it was certainly not an influence : Santayana read Keats in the old nineteenth-century way, and was sceptical of the idea that Keats *thought* at all—what one finds in the two men as letter-writers is the force and seduction of their manner of thought, their impulse to think about human life in relation to a comprehensive vision of the nature of the universe.

It is this that accounts for the exhilaration that Santayana's letters induce, a sense of the mind suddenly freed, happily disenchanted, active in a new way. Santayana has several times reminded us how close he was to the men of the English late nineteenth century, how great a part Ruskin and Arnold and Pater played in the formation of this thought. What one becomes aware of from the letters is how close he was to the English Romantics. For the kind of mental sensation he imparts is what the Romantic poets thought of as peculiarly appropriate to the mind, and they often represented it by images of the mind "soaring" or on a mountain peak : it was thus that they proposed the escape from the "bondage" of "earth", the ability to move at will in a sustaining yet unresisting medium, the possibility of looking at life in detachment, from a "height". This is a nearly forgotten possibility of the mind; it is not approved by the hidden, prepotent Censor of modern modes of thought. To look within is permitted; to look around is encouraged; but best not to look down—not realistic, not engaged, not democratic. One experiences the unsanctioned altitude with as much guilt as pleasure.

For this pleasure, or the reminder of pleasure, we are of course grateful to Santayana and drawn to him. Yet at the same time there is the easy possibility of disliking him, or at least of regarding him with ready suspicion. It shouldn't matter. It should, indeed, constitute an added charm. Let us just call it "tension" or "ambiguity" or "irony" or whatever name serves to remind us that there is a special intellectual satisfaction in admiring where we do not love, in qualifying our assent, in keeping our distance.

My own antagonism to Santayana goes back to my college days at Columbia. Irwin Edman, as all his students know, was a great admirer of Santayana and was said actually to be on terms of friendship with the great man. Edman had an amazing gift as a teacher. He could summarize the thought of a philosopher in a way both to do justice to his subject and to make it comprehensible to the meanest intelligence. Or, if the meanest intelligence didn't actually comprehend, it certainly had the sentiment of comprehension. This I can testify to, because, when it came to philosophy, I was the meanest intelligence going. I found it virtually impossible to know what issues were involved; I could scarcely begin to understand the questions, let alone the answers. But when Edman spoke with that wonderful systematic lucidity of his, all things seemed clear.

With, for me, the exception of Santayana. Edman could never make plain to me what Santayana was up to.

If Santayana could now be consulted about why this was so, he would very likely explain that it was because Edman didn't really understand him. He seems to have come to think that no Jew and no Columbia man was likely to understand him. And of course Edman's allegiance to Santayana gradually abated and in the essay which he contributed to Professor Schilpp's *The Philosophy of George Santayana* he maintains that the later developments of the thought of the man who had been his master verged on the irrelevant and, perhaps, the immoral. And in the reply to his critics which Santayana makes in the same volume, he permits himself to speak of Edman's objections as showing a "personal animus".

Yet I have no doubt that Edman's account of Santayana was perfectly just and accurate. What stood in the way of my understanding it was a cherished prejudice. The college group to which I belonged, many of whom were more or less close to Edman, resisted that part of his thought which led him to understand and praise detachment. We were very down on Walter Pater, very hostile to what we called "æstheticism", and we saw Edman's enthusiasm for Santayana as of a piece with his admiration for Pater and as a proof of his mere "æstheticism". I have come to think that Pater is a very remarkable writer, much misrepresented by the critics and literary historians. But at the time we took him to be everything that was *fainéant* and disembodied and precious. Santayana seemed to some of us to be in the line of Pater, brought there if only by his prose, which even now I think is only occasionally really good because all too much of it is "beautiful", as the philosophers never weary of telling us. The famous "perfection of rottenness" which William James said that Santayana's thought represented, was wholly apparent to us, and we did not use the phrase with any touch of the admiration that James really did intend.

In short, what Edman (if I read him aright) eventually came to feel about Santayana after a close study of the later work, I felt out of a prejudice based on hearsay. Against this prejudice not even Edman's lucidity and the sympathy he then had with Santayana's mind could make headway. When an undergraduate entertains a critical prejudice against a literary or philosophical figure, the last person in the world who can change his mind is his teacher.

My case, of course, was not unique. The feeling against Santayana in America is endemic and almost inevitable. It is indeed very difficult for an American, *qua* American—to use the crow-like expression of professional philosophers—to like him or trust him. Of course among the majority of the academic historians of American culture his name is mud. They hustle him off into the limbo they reserve for "aristocratic critics of American democracy". They find it wonderfully convenient to think of him as the "perfection of rottenness"—he is the Gilbert Osmond of their Portrait of a Lady, the Lady being America in the perfection of her democracy and innocence : he is a spoiled American, all too elegant, all too cultivated, all too knowing, all too involved with æsthetic values. Actually they are much mistaken. For one thing, Santayana was very severe in his attitude towards the æsthetic experience—as severe as William James and for rather better reasons. This is one of the remarkable and salutary things about him. He was not in the least taken in by the modern pieties about art; and as he grew older art meant less and less to him, and he thought that it should. As for his rejection of America, it is a good deal more complex, not to say cogent, than historians of American culture usually care to remember. America, it is true, seemed to have affected him adversely in an almost physical way, making him anxious and irritable. But it was to a particular aspect of American life that he directed his antagonism, the aspect of what we, with him, may call its gentility, the aspect of its high culture. And what the academic historian of American culture would do without Santayana's phrase "the genteel tradition" is impossible to imagine. Santayana was ill at ease everywhere in America, but what offended his soul was New England, especially Boston, especially Cambridge. The America of raw energy, the America of material concerns, the America that he could see as young and barbaric and in the line of history he had a tolerance and affection for that were real and not merely condescending. Some years ago the late Bernard De Voto raised a storm of protest and contempt among American intellectuals because he wrote in praise of a certain research on the treatment of third degree burns and insisted that this was a cultural achievement of the first order, that it was an intellectual achievement; he said that it was a fault in American intellectuals that they were not aware of it and did not take pride in it as a characteristic achievement of the American mind. Santayana would have been in agreement with De Voto. In a letter of 1921 to Logan Pearsall Smith, he writes of high American culture as being ineffectual and sophomoric. "But notice :" he goes on, "*all* learning and 'mind' in America is not of this ineffectual Sophomoric sort. There is your Doctor at Baltimore who is a great expert, and *really knows how to do things* : and you will find that, in the service of material life, all the arts and sciences are prosperous in America. But it must be in the service of material life; because it is material life (of course with the hygiene, morality, and international good order that can minister to material life) that America has and wants to have and may perhaps bring to perfection. Think of that! If material life could be made perfect, as (in a very small way) it was perhaps for a moment among the Greeks, would not that of itself be a most admirable achievement, like the creation of a new and superior mammal, who would instinctively suck only the bottle? ... And possibly on that basis of perfected material life, a new art and philosophy would grow unawares, not similar to what we call by those names, but having the same relation to the life beneath which art and philosophy amongst us ought to have had, but never have had actually. You see I am content to let the past bury its dead. It does not seem to me that we can impose on America the task of imitating Europe. The more different it can come to be, the better; and we must let it take its own course, going a long way round, perhaps, before it can shake off the last trammels of alien tradition and learn to express itself simply, not apologetically, after its own heart."

Here, surely, is the perfect dream, the shaping Whitmanesque principle, of the academic historian of American culture. Santayana, it is true, formulates it with a touch of irony and, indeed, on another occasion he avowed his belief that everything good in "the ultimate sense" would come to America from Europe only, and from Latin Europe; and of course he was glad that he would not live to see the new American culture come into being. Yet he had too strong a sense of history, too clear an understanding of cultures, not to be as serious as he was ironic.

No, it is not really Santayana's open rejection of America that troubles us about him. His feelings about America go very deep, go to his first principles. That is why they cannot be related to the shabby canting anti-Americanism of the intellectual middle class of England or of the Continent. A good many things may no doubt be said in dispraise of Santayana, but it cannot be said of him that he had a vulgar mind, that he could possibly think as the *New Statesman* thinks. There was no malice in Santayana's feeling about America, nor does he ever give evidence that he had ever been *offended* by America—he had none of the provincial burgher's hurt vengeful pride which led Dostoievsky to write *A Winter Diary* to get in his kicks at France, or Graham Greene to write *The Quiet American.*

What does alienate Americans from Santayana is the principles upon which his rejection of America is founded. That is, what troubles us is not his negations of America, but the affirmation upon which he based his sense of himself as a European. These disturb us, they put questions to us which we cannot endure.

It isn't possible to speak of Santayana as a representative European. To do so would be to give modern Europe more credit than it deserves. But he was, we might say, the Platonic form or "idea" of a European. To the development of this idea America was necessary. It was not enough for him to have been Santayana of Avila in Castille; there had also to be the Sturgis connection, and Boston, and Harvard. Santayana repelled the belief that as a boy in Boston he had lived an isolated and unhappy life because he was of foreign birth. He was, he writes, the lieutenant-colonel of the Boston Latin School regiment, he acted in the Hasty Pudding plays at Harvard, he was devoted—"(as a spectator)"—to football. Yet he did stand apart; and he was able to look at the culture into which he had been transplanted with a degree of consciousness that was available to no other lieutenant-colonel and to no other leading lady of a Hasty Pudding play. He knew it to be not his culture, and he lived to develop its opposite principle, the idea of a European culture. This was, to be sure, not mono-lithically European; England, France, Spain, Italy, Greece were all separate to him, sharp, clear entities which had different values for him at different stages of his life. But, in contrast to America, they came to-gether as a single idea, they made the idea of Europe.

If we ask what it was that Santayana thought of as separating him from America, as making him characteristically and ideally European (and a philosopher), the answer is that it was his materialism. He seems to have found it very difficult to convince people that he really was a materialist. No doubt in his more technical works there are grounds for the resistance to his claim that his materialism was basic to all his thought; of these I have no knowledge. But one reason for the resistance is that people don't expect materialists to compose in highly wrought prose, exquisite and sometimes all too exquisite; we don't expect subtlety and vivacity, supposing, no doubt, that materialists must partake of the dull density of "matter"; we don't expect them to give a very high value to poetry and all fictions, especially the fictions of religions. In 1951 Santayana finds it necessary to write, "Naturalism . . . is something to which I am so thoroughly wedded that I like to call it materialism, so as to prevent all confusion with the *romantic* naturalism, like Goethe's, for instance, or that of Bergson. Mine is the hard, non-humanistic naturalism of the Ionian philosophers, of Democritus, Lucretius, and Spinoza." And he goes on : "Those professors at Columbia who tell you that in my *Idea of Christ in the Cospels* I incline to theism have not read that book sympathetically. They forget that my naturalism is fundamental and includes man, his mind, and all his works, products of the generative order of nature."

From Santayana's materialism comes his detachment. Maybe, of course, if we want to look at it psychologically, it is the other way around—the materialism rationalizes the detachment which was temperamental. But certainly the two things go together in Santayana, just as they did in Spinoza, who was perhaps Santayana's greatest hero of thought. The world is matter, and follows the laws of matter. The world is even, he is willing to say, a machine, and follows the laws of its devising. The world is not spirit, following the laws of spirit, made to accommodate spirit, available to full comprehension by spirit. It permits spirit to exist but this is by chance and chancily : no intention is avowed. And the world, we might go on to say, is Boston to the boy from Avila; the world is the Sturgis family to the young Santayana—not hostile, yet not his own, not continuous with him. It is, as he says, his host, and he must have reflected that the word implies not only a guest but a parasite!

When Bouvard and Pécuchet gave themselves to the study of Spinoza, Flaubert's favourite philosopher, they felt as if they were in "a balloon at night, in glacial coldness, carried on an endless journey towards a bottomless abyss and with nothing near but the unseizable, the motionless, the eternal". We do not feel *quite* this as we read Santayana's letters. They are far too full of intended grace, of conscious charm, too full of the things of this world. But the abyss is there, and his dreadful knowledge of it is what Americans fear in Santayana, just as it is the American avoidance of the knowledge of the abyss that made Santayana fear America and flee it. The knowledge of the abyss, the awareness of the discontinuity between man and the world, this is the forming perception of Santayana's thought as it comes to us in the letters. It is already in force at the age of twenty-three—it makes itself manifest in the perfectly amazing self-awareness and self-possession of the letters he writes from his first trip abroad just after his graduation from Harvard. The philosophical detachment is wholly explicit; and we see at once that it is matched by a personal detachment no less rigorous. For Santayana friendship was always of high special importance. He could be a loyal and devoted friend, as witness his constancy to the unfortunate and erratic Frank Russell, Bertrand Russell's elder brother, his predecessor in the earldom; he could be finely sympathetic, as witness his letter to Iris Origo on the death of her only son. But friendship had for him a status in his life like that of art. Art, however lovely, however useful, was not reality; at best it was an element of reality; and sometimes, he said, it interfered with the apprehension of reality. So too he never deceived himself about friendship; its limits were clear to him very early and he never permitted himself to be deceived into thinking that a friend was himself. Nothing could be more striking than Santayana's equal devotion and remoteness to his youthful letters to his friends. He put all his intelligence and all his sympathy at their service, but never himself. It is, in its own way, very fine; but no American reader, I think, can help being made uncomfortable by this stern and graceful self-possession, this rigorous objectivity, this strict limitation, in so very young a man.

And our American discomfort is the more intense, I believe, because we cannot but perceive that Santayana's brilliant youthful reserve is his response to his youthful consciousness of what I have called the abyss. His friend Henry Ward Abbot writes to him out of one of those states of cosmological despair which were common enough among young men even as late as 1887, asking Santayana to consider the problem of life from "the point of view of the grave"; Santayana replies in this fashion : "What you call the point of view of the grave is what I should call the point of view of the easy chair. [That is, the point of view of detached philosophic contemplation.] From that the universal joke is indeed very funny. But a man in his grave is not only apathetic, but also invulnerable. That is what you forget. Your dead man is not merely amused, he is also brave, and if his having nothing to gain makes him impartial, his having nothing to lose makes him free. 'Is it worth while after all?' you ask. What a simple-hearted question. Of course it isn't worth while. Do you suppose when God made up his mind to create this world after his own image, he thought it was worth while? I wouldn't make such an imputation on his intelligence. Do you suppose he existed there in his uncaused loneliness because it was worth while? Did Nothing ask God before God existed, whether he thought it would be worth while to try life for a while? or did Nothing have to decide the question? Do you suppose the slow, painful, nasty, bloody process, by which things in this world grow, is worth having for the sake of the perfection of a moment? Did you come into the world because you thought it worth while? No more do you stay in it because you do. The idea of demanding that things should be worth doing is a human impertinence."

But then, when Abbot continues the question in a later letter, Santayana says, "The world may have little in it that is good : granted. But that little is really and inalienably good. Its value cannot be destroyed because of the surrounding evil."

It is a startling thing for a youth to say, as startling as his exposition of the point of view of the grave, and these two utterances may surely be thought of as definitive of Santayana's later thought. Whatever his materialism leads Santayana to, it does not lead him to a radical relativism pointing to an ultimate nihilism. It does not lead him to a devaluation of life, to the devaluation of anything that might be valued. On the contrary —it is the basis of his intense valuation. Here indeed, we might almost say, is one *intention* of his materialism, that it should lead to a high valuation of what may be valued at all. If we are in a balloon over an abyss, let us at least value the balloon. If night is all around, then what light we have is precious. If there is no life to be seen in the great emptiness, our companions are to be cherished; so are we ourselves. And this, I think, is the essence of the European view of life as it differs from the American. Willa Cather is not in my opinion a very intelligent or subtle mind, but she did show in her novels an understanding of the European attachment to *things* and how it differed from the American attachment. The elaborate fuss that she made about cuisine, about wine, and salads, and bread, and copper pots was an expression of her sense of the unfeeling universe; cookery was a ritual in which the material world, some tiny part of it, could be made to serve human ends, could be made human; and insofar as she represents cookery as a ritual, it is the paradigm of religious belief, and goes along with her growing sympathy for Catholicism, of which the chief attraction seemed to be not any doctrinal appeal it had but rather its being *so very European*. That is, what hope the Catholic religion offered her took its sanction from the European confrontation of the abyss—the despair that arises from the knowledge of the material nature of the world validates all rituals and all fictions that make life endurable in the alien universe.

If I apprehend Santayana aright, what Miss Cather felt in a very simple way, he felt in a very elaborate way. That is why he was so acutely uncomfortable in America. Santayana knew that America was not materialistic, not in the philosophic sense and not really in the moral sense. What he says about America's concern with the practical life and with "material well-being" does not contradict this. If anything, it substantiates it.

For if the Americans were truly materialistic, they would recognize the necessity of dualism, they would have contrived a life of the spirit apart from and in opposition to the life of material concern. But for the American consciousness the world is the natural field of the spirit, laid out to be just that, as a baseball diamond or a tennis court is laid out for a particular kind of activity; and what the American wins is not enjoyed as a possession but, rather, cherished as a trophy. The European sees the world as hard and resistant to spirit; whatever can be won is to be valued, protected, used, and enjoyed. But the high valuation of the material life makes, as it were, the necessity for its negation in an intense respect for the life of spirit.

What exasperated Santayana was the American refusal to confront the hard world that materialism proposes, the American preference for seeing the world as continuous with spirit. His animus against Emerson's transcendentalism was extreme, and what he felt about Emerson he felt about all of American philosophic thought, as we see from the brilliant *Character and Opinion in the United States*. The inclusion of the word "character" in that title is significant. One of the things that must especially involve our interest in the letters is what we perceive to be a chief preoccupation of the writer—the concern for character, for self-definition, for self-preservation. This concern is intimately related to Santayana's materialism. Santayana defined himself in the universe by detachment from it. And what is true of him in the largest possible connection is also true of him in smaller connections. Thus, he had no sooner received his first Harvard appointment than he began to think of the moment when he could retire from Harvard, which he did at the first possible opportunity. It was not merely that he was a foreigner, or that he saw himself as of a different breed from the American academic, or that he could not support what, in an early letter, he calls the "damnable worldliness and snobbishness prevalent at Harvard". It was rather that he needed to define himself by withdrawal.

And how very precise his self-definition is. We see it in the cool self-possession of his dealings with William James. In his early relation with Santayana, James as a teacher is in a very different rôle from that in which we find him in that all too famous anecdote of Gertrude Stein at Radcliffe, when, to Gertrude Stein's having written nothing in her examination book except the statement that the afternoon was too fine for examinations, James replied with agreement and an A for the course. I have never admired James for this—it seems to me that he gave an unfortunate impetus to all the contemporary student cant about how teachers ought to behave, that, for example, they should be *human*. I like much better James's coming down on Santayana for not having done the conventional thing with his travelling fellowship; I like it in part because it gave Santayana the opportunity to stand up to his superior and to affirm himself and to hold himself ready to take the consequences. And this he does in a way that no American youth could have equalled, with a sincere regard for James, with a perfect if not wholly ingenuous courtesy, with the full sanction of his view of the world, an entire readiness to wipe out his academic career before it should have begun. It isn't exactly endearing; it makes the beginning of our sense that we shall not like Santayana at all. But it is very impressive, it is often very fortifying.

That sense of himself which Santayana shows in his letters to James was what he saw lacking in American life. His novel, *The Last Puritan*, is, as he says, about a man who, with all the personal and material gifts, "peters out", and the tragedy of this he felt to be so terrible that he "actually cried over the writing of it". He speaks of the petering out of most of the young American poets who do not escape to hibernate in Europe. And petering out was, it seems, the fate of most of his Harvard friends—it was not that they were worn out by American life, nor that they were hampered by economic circumstances, or perverted by bad ideals; it was that they did not know how to define themselves, they did not know how to grasp and possess; we might say that they did not know how to break their hearts on the idea of the hardness of the world, to admit the defeat which is requisite for any victory, to begin their effective life in the world by taking the point of view of the grave. Perhaps the whole difference between Santayana and America is summed up in an exchange between him and William Lyons Phelps. No two men could have been more worlds apart than Phelps and Santayana, but Santayana liked Phelps —he was American academic life, and American kindliness, he was all the massive excitement of the Yale-Harvard game, which Santayana relished, making it a point always to stay with the Phelpses whenever the game was in New Haven. When *The Last Puritan* appeared Phelps was distressed by the book and Santayana had to deal with his objection that he did not "love life" and also with the objection that there were no "good people" in the book. To which Santayana replied, "I don't think you like *good* people, really, only sweet people—like Annabel [Mrs. Phelps] and you!" The sentence seems to me momentous in its definition of American life. In that life sweetness is an academic trait, and very lovely and valuable it is. But we find it very hard to imagine that definition of character which is necessary for the strain of what Santayana calls goodness.

As for Santayana himself, his effort of self-definition had, in some ways, an amazing success. He was manifestly not a sweet man, although there are some engagingly kind letters to people whose defences he knew to be weak, students, young philosophers, old friends who suddenly called themselves to mind after half a century. That he was a good man has been questioned and the question seems to me a very reasonable one—there is certainly something deeply disquieting about his temperament. But there can be no doubt of the firmness of his self-definition; there can be no doubt that he did not peter out. The surrender of hope that he made at an early age, the admission of defeat that many interpret as an essential cynicism or even as a kind of malevolence may not be life-giving to most of his readers; but it was a regimen that preserved him in life in a way that must astound us. He lived to be nearly ninety, and up to the end there is no intellectual event that he does not respond to with full alertness and full power and full involvement. His comments on Edna St. Vincent Millay make a definitive estimate of her; a few years later he is no less precise about Faulkner. He absorbed Freud far better than most intellectuals and his essay on *Beyond the Pleasure Principle* deals in a remarkable way with Freud's materialistic assumptions that would make Santayana sympathetic to him. He is much interested in the poetry of Robert Lowell, and also in the stories of Somerset Maugham, the point of his interest in the latter being his "wonder at anybody wishing to write such stories". In general he is responsive to the modern element in literature—he was fascinated by Joyce and captivated by Proust; but he says he has no enthusiasm for D. H. Lawrence, Dostoievsky, and Nietzsche : he has had from Aristotle all they can give him. The vivacity and cogency of his mind never abate.

In the letter to Abbot which I quoted earlier he had written that "the point of view of the grave is not to be attained by you or me every time we happen to want anything in particular. It is not gained except by renunciation. Pleasure must first cease to attract and pain to repel, and this, you will confess, is no easy matter. But meantime, I beg of you, let us remember that the joke of things is one at our expense. It is very funny, but it is exceedingly unpleasant". The ironic smile at the universal joke never left the face of his writing, but neither, I think, did the sense of how unpleasant the joke was. The smile drove philosophers to distraction and led some of them to say that he wasn't a philosopher at all—maybe a poet. "If you took [my lucubrations] more lightly perhaps you would find them less aggravating," he wrote to Professor Lamprecht. He himself thought a smile might say much—in a letter to Father Munson he speaks of the importance in his philosophic life of a passage of Plato's *Parmenides* "about 'ideas' of filth, rubbish, etc., which the moralistic young Socrates recoils from as not beautiful, making old Parmenides smile. That smile of Parmenides made me think". Of Santayana's smile we feel it does no less.

DECEMBER 1956

ANTHONY WEST

H. G. Wells

I FIND IT DIFFICULT to write dispassionately of H. G. Wells. One of my earliest memories of him, too early for me to date, is of the occasion on which I first discovered the physical aspect of death. It was at a time when I had a treasure box, a small cigarette tin I believe, with a hinged lid. In it I kept some of the old-fashioned glass marbles, a button with a coat-of-arms upon it, and a few things of that kind which had taken my fancy. To these I one day added a few heads of snapdragon. I hoped that I would find them there in their bright prettiness whenever I wanted to look at them. But when I opened the box again after several days had gone by it held corruption and green moulds, and I screamed with dismay. I do not remember all the details of what followed, but I remember taking refuge from H. G.'s incomprehension under a gate-legged table, and I remember his lifting the edge of the table-cloth to peer in at me where I crouched, still screaming in grief and fear, and muttering "I just don't understand you".

It was a phrase he repeated, and with the same bewilderment, to me during his last illness. He was sitting with a light rug over his knees on a chair which had been placed where he could catch the sun on the glassed-in balcony at the back of his house in Hanover Terrace. We were sharing silences rather than talking. He was already extremely weak, and he husbanded his energies through long drowsy periods in which he seemed almost comatose, surfacing, so to speak, only occasionally when he wished to give his full attention to something or somebody. I would go to see him, in the hope of catching his interest and drawing him up to the surface. I wanted to drive out of his mind an impression—I do not care, even now, to think how he had been given it—that I had been "got hold of" by a pro-Nazi conspiracy somehow entrenched in the British Broadcasting Corporation which was then employing me in its News division. These conspirators were, he had been told, blackmailing me in some way and forcing me into some mysteriously discreditable line of conduct for an arcane ulterior purpose, the nature of which I have never been able to discover. This nightmare cobweb of misunderstanding had fallen between myself and my father in the first stages of the V-1 attack on London; it remained upon our faces through all the time the attack lasted, through the stranger time of V-2, until the war receded into the Pacific and left London in shocked and stunned silence. At first my father seemed too ill to be bothered with the necessary explanations. Then he made a partial recovery and I was able to hope. I sat with him often, when I was not on duty in the newsroom at the BBC, longing for the moment when he would open his mind to me. But the occasion never came, and at last I became aware that it never would. Sitting beside him one day, at once in the closest proximity to him and utterly remote from him, and, thinking him asleep, I fell into a passion of misery and buried my face in my hands. How long this spasm of pain lasted I don't know, but when its intensity slackened I suddenly became conscious that I was being watched. I looked up to find his eyes fixed upon me with all the clarity of his fully-conscious mind behind them. We stared at each other for an instant before he said, once again, "I just don't understand you." Then the light left his face. He had, as it were, turned himself off, and had relapsed into his dozing state on the frontier between sleep and death. The last chance of communication had gone, and there was never to be another. Rather more than a year later I chartered a boat named the Deirdre owned by a Captain Miller of Poole in Dorset, my half-brother came down from London bringing with him H. G.'s ashes, and we went out to scatter them on the sea at a point on a line between Alum Bay on the Isle of Wight and St. Alban's Head on the mainland. As we returned I found myself surprised at the extent of my bitterness. That I should have preferred my father to realize that I had been going through a sufficiently banal marital crisis, rather than to believe that I was falling into the hands of blackmailers who had been using me as a tool for treasonable purposes, was easy enough to understand. But that I should feel so violently about the matter when he was no longer in a position to believe anything at all shocked me, as it still does.

It will be realized why in those circumstances a self-protective device told me that Wells's mind was clouded by illness at a much earlier stage than it probably was to any significant extent. For some years after his death I reacted angrily to the criticisms of the quality of his thought which made so much of the extreme pessimism of his last writings and utterances. These were, and still are, being represented as an abandonment of a superficial optimism in the face of those realities of which his coming death was a part. The suggestion is made that they were some kind of final admission that he had been wrong about the nature of things for the greater part of his life. I felt at one time that this was a wilful exploitation of the auto-intoxication of a very sick man who no longer enjoyed full command of himself. But since sifting my recollections of his talk, and doing a great deal of preparatory work on his biography, I incline to another view. I cannot now agree that his final phase of scolding and complaining at human folly represented any essential change in his views at all. What happened as his powers declined from 1940 onwards was that he reverted to his original profoundly-felt beliefs about the realities of the human situation. He was by nature a pessimist, and he was doing violence to his intuitions and his rational perceptions alike when he asserted in his middle period that mankind could make a better world for itself by an effort of will.

This contention may seem grotesque to those who have a picture of him firmly entrenched in their minds as a kindly, avuncular figure promising men a birthday with lavish presents every week if the scientists were only given control of society. Last year Dr. Bronowski took time off from his duties as Director of the Coal Research Establishment to tell Section L of the British Association: "H. G. Wells used to write stories in which tall, elegant engineers administered with perfect justice a society in which other people had nothing to do but be happy: the Houyhnhnms administering the Yahoos. Wells used to think this a very fine world; but it was only 1984 . . ." This represents the received view. Mr. St. John Ervine in his life of Shaw asserts that Wells believed that infinite social progress was inevitable unless there were some global catastrophe; and George Orwell attributed his final despair to a belated realization that science was just as effective on the side of evil as on the side of good. And only the other day Mr. Geoffrey Barraclough, Professor Arnold Toynbee's successor in the Stevenson Research Chair of International History in London, was telling us that the evolutionary conception of society found its supreme expression in Wells's *Outline of History*. According to him this postulates that "the development of intelligence is the work of 'natural selection', and that inexorable laws of natural selection will result in the replacement of the present imperfect society by one in which a finer humanity will inhabit a more perfect world."

The diffuseness and looseness of much of Wells's writing, and the tone of a great deal of his occasional journalism, lends itself to this distortion of his basic ideas. But the fact remains that the body of work which bears his name contradicts these assumptions about his views, and the reader who undertakes to examine all of his writing scrupulously is in for a number of surprises. Wells received a scientific education and he never fell into the fallacy of confusing the Darwinian conception of evolution with the idea of progress. The idea of progress depends fundamentally on a picture of the universe in which mind is increasingly valuable, and which is also increasingly orderly. Wells's first serious piece of writing was a paper called "The Rediscovery of the Unique" of which he remained proud throughout his career. Though it does not reach a standard which would be acceptable to professional philosophers and logicians, it restates with clarity and force the idea which Hobbes put forward in *Leviathan* (I, iv) when he says that there is "nothing in the World Universal but Names, for the things named are every one of them Individual and Singular". This is the foundation stone of the mechanistic view according to which the whole world is "nothing but a mere heap of dust, fortuitously agitated" and the universe a similar aggregation. It is impossible to believe in progress if you believe in a universe in which mind figures as a local accident, and which by its nature cannot support any permanent moral order or indeed any permanent thing.

That Wells was deeply committed to this view is evident from his first novel, *The Time Machine*, which has its climatic scene at a point some thirty million years in the future. The planet has ceased to revolve. It no longer supports human life, and it is evident that the time is rapidly approaching when it will no longer support life at all. A cosmic catastrophe is impending which will finally obliterate the material context in which such concepts as mind, consciousness, and value can possess any meaning. The possibility of such a situation is irreconcilable with the idea of progress, and Wells states his disbelief in it in this book without ambiguity. The questions which the Time Traveller asks himself on the first phase of his journey into the future are interesting, and revealing :

"What might not have happened to men? What if cruelty had grown to be a common passion? What if in this interval the race had lost its manliness, and had developed into something inhuman, unsympathetic, and overwhelmingly powerful? I might seem some old-world savage animal, only the more dreadful and disgusting for our common likeness—a foul creature to be incontinently slain."

What is implicit in these questions is the idea that an evolutionary trend that would make man a more intellectual animal might also make him a much less humane one. This not only questions the idea of progress, but also suggests that virtue is not innate in the intellect as Victorian moralists were inclined to believe. I stress this point because it seems to me to be an important one if one wants to understand Wells's thinking. The conventional picture then was, and still to a considerable extent is, of a conflict between mind and man's animal nature, with the virtues seated in the intellect and the defects in the instincts and the animal behaviour patterns. Wells suggests that morals and ethics have their basis in man's behaviour as a social animal. That is to say that disinterested behaviour develops from a hunting animal's practice of bringing food back to its lair for its mate and its young; and that humanitarianism, and the sympathies that make life endurable, develop from the animal habit of snuggling in a hugger-mugger, as puppies or kittens do, for warmth. The intellect on the other hand is amoral and ultimately recognizes the single value of efficiency, so that a continuation of the line of development that had made man a reasoning animal might ultimately make him more callous, indifferent, and cruel, and not more moral. This nagging fear of the liberated intellect as something inhumane was to play an important part in Wells's later work, but he raised it in *The Time Machine* only to drop it in favour of an explicit statement about natural selection. The premise is that the nineteenth-century layered class society constituted an artificial environment to which man was adapting himself. The donnée for the purpose of *The Time Machine* was that it was going to endure; so the Time Traveller finds, in the year A.D. 802,701 that adaptation has divided the human race into two distinct subspecies. The descendants of the old ruling and propertied classes live above ground and fear the dark, those of the workers and managers subterraneously in fear of the light. Both are hopelessly degenerate, and neither considers the Time Traveller to be an old-world savage, because neither group is capable of sufficient sustained thought to frame so elaborate a concept. It is with something of a shock that one finds that what has brought about their debasement is precisely the complete success of mankind in establishing a technological society and world order of the kind to which Wells is supposed to have given his unqualified endorsement. At some point during the eight hundred thousand year interval men completely mastered their environment and solved all the social problems. When they were comfortable they stopped thinking, and then degenerated along the lines of their own inherent weaknesses.

One of the difficulties of writing about Wells is that his mind was undisciplined, and that on any given point he can be found either to contradict himself, or to appear to do so. *The Time Machine* was immediately followed by *The Island of Dr. Moreau*, which Wells discussed much later, in the twenties, as if he had accepted a dualistic picture of human nature while he was writing it: "Humanity is but animal rough-hewn to a reasonable shape and in perpetual internal conflict between instinct and injunction." This would give innate virtue a refuge in the intellect, and would allow for optimism as a possibility. But what happens in *The Island of Dr. Moreau* is a disaster, the liberated intellect in the person of a Darwinian humanitarian arrives on the island and disintegrates its theocratic moral order by making an appeal to reason which assumes that Dr. Moreau's victims are moral creatures with better natures. When they are set free from the Hobbesian régime of terror under which they have been living it is revealed that they are, beneath Dr. Moreau's scar tissue, brutes interested only in the satisfaction of their appetites. So far as a conflict between instinct and injunction goes, it is no contest; order and law are imposed on the brutish inhabitants of the island by an exterior force, and as soon as that is removed the system collapses. What the book in fact expresses is a profound mistrust of human nature, and a doubt about the intellect's ability to contain it. There is even a doubt about the intellect as a possible containing force, since its rôle in the story is a purely destructive one.

The Island of Dr. Moreau relates closely to two other stories, a short novel and a short story, which deal with the same theme of the liberated intellect as a destructive element. *The Invisible Man* is a parable about the amoral aspects of the scientific outlook, and invisibility figures in it as a symbol of intellectual isolation. *The Country of the Blind* is a much more mature version of the same parable, in which the symbolic situation of the sighted man in the community of the blind is even more harrowing. In both stories men are cut off from normal human feeling and corrupted by the sense that their special knowledge gives them a right to power over the unenlightened. They both end by running amok in the same lonely terror which overtakes the visitor to Dr. Moreau's Island. The theme is carried further in *The War of the Worlds* and in *The First Men in the Moon*. The Martians, like the ruling class on the moon, are brain cases with the merest of vestigial bodies, symbols of the intellect triumphant over the animal. The point that technological mastery has given the Martians a sense that they are free from moral responsibility is obscured by the surface action in *The War of the Worlds*. Most readers do not see beyond the fact that the Martians arrive, and treat Europeans as Europeans had been treating native populations and animals in the hey-day of colonialism, to the deeper argument. But there is no possibility of misunderstanding the description of lunar society which appears towards the end of *The First Men in the Moon*. The unfettered intellect rules, and respect for efficiency stands in the place of morality. What has come into being is the worst kind of slave state. It has reduced most of its members to simple automata. Many of them are actually deformed physically to fit them more precisely for specific social functions. When the labourers of various types are not required they are laid aside in induced coma until they are needed. Wells's scientist, Cavor, reports on this society with naïve approval, so that there can be no doubt about what he is getting at. The clear implication is that a further extension of human intellectual powers in the post-renaissance direction of abstract rational thinking will lead to the growth of cruel and inhuman planned societies which will be utterly indifferent to human values and individual happiness. Human sympathies will be stifled, and endless cruelties perpetrated in the name of an abstract common good, because logical analysis finds that human sympathies have no basis in the sort of reality that it can recognize. The scientific apparatus for examining reality is hostile to values in so far as it shows that any system of values is purely arbitrary. In the end, what Wells is saying in *The First Men in the Moon*, is that the basis of operations which Huxley recommended in his famous Romanes lecture, and which he had himself adopted and stated in the concluding paragraphs of *The Time Machine*, is not viable. Because if a mechanistic view of the universe is constructed by the right hand the left will inevitably loose its grip on any ethical system it may have decided to grasp.

It may seem that this is reading something into *The First Men in the Moon* which is not there, but Wells went out of his way to state it in a mundane context in *When the Sleeper Wakes*. Many people recall this novel of 1899 as a description of the triumph of gadgetry with its descriptions of flying machines, television, public address systems, and air-conditioned roofed-in cities. It stands as the optimistic and naïvely uncritical forerunner of Aldous Huxley's *Brave New World*, and Orwell's *1984*. In fact Wells's society of 3002 includes many of the worst features of both these later constructions. It "features" a deliberately debased and systematically misinformed proletariat, constant surveillance and thought control, and an amoral brutality; and these things are described as evils. The difference between Wells's horrors and those described by Huxley and Orwell resides mainly in points of detail. Wells was writing before the two great wars and the dictatorships had made the state as dangerous an engine as it now seems. For Wells the enemy was monopoly capitalism as it presented itself in the form of the great corporations. But his business state is just as monstrous as the police state of Orwell's imagination, and is perhaps worse in that it does not bother to persecute individuals as individuals, but simply treats people in terms of social categories and utility. Wells's equivalent of Big Brother, Ostrog, the head of the super-corporation's governing body says: *"I can imagine how this great world of ours seems to a Victorian Englishman. You regret all the old forms of representative government . . . the voting councils and parliaments and all that eighteenth-century tomfoolery. You feel moved against our pleasure cities. I might have thought of that—had I not been busy. But you will learn better . . . the pleasure cities are the excretory organs of the State, attractive places that year after year draw together all that is weak and vicious, all that is lascivious and lazy, all the easy roguery of the world, to a graceful destruction. They go there, they have their time, they die childless, and mankind is the better . . . And you would emancipate the silly brainless workers that we have enslaved, and try to make their lives easy and pleasant again. Just as they have sunk to what they are fit for ... I know these ideas; in my boyhood I read your Shelley and dreamt of liberty. There is no liberty save wisdom and self-control. Liberty is within, not without ... suppose that these swarming yelping fools in blue [the proles wear blue uniforms] got the upper hand of us, what then? They will only fall to other masters. So long as there are sheep Nature will insist on beasts of prey. It would mean but a few hundred years' delay. The coming of the aristocrat is fatal and assured. The end will be the Overman —for all the mad protests of humanity. Let them revolt, let them win and kill me and my like. Others will arise—other masters. The end will be the same."*

From his viewpoint in 1899 Wells was able to see that the growth of a technological society would throw up régimes much worse than those of such simple-minded tyrants as Napoleon III. Ostrog is more like Hitler than anything which had then been seen, he was probably conceived as a criticism of Carlyle's hero worship, while the society he presides over is a criticism of the structural aspects of Plato's Republic.

I have dwelt on these early books of Wells's because they seem to me to show how foreign to his thought the ideas that either evolution or technical development would inevitably produce a moral order, or even a better order, were. I think, too, that the view of human nature taken in these early books accounts for the flaw in the later ones which now makes them seem ill-considered and confused. These are forced in so far as they say things which Wells wishes to believe, and in which he, ultimately, does not believe. What he ultimately does not believe in is the ability of the human animal to live up to its ideals. *The Time Machine, The Island of Dr. Moreau,* and *When the Sleeper Wakes,* all state this idea quite bluntly. In mid-career Wells stopped saying this and adopted the progressive line, stating a body of ideas which can be called Wellsian.

These can be summarized roughly as follows. Education and the liberal tradition have produced a disinterested group of men of goodwill capable of taking hold of the drift of modern life and of giving it coherent direction. Cheap paper and mechanized printing together with the prosperity and leisure produced by industrialization have made universal education a practical possibility. An educated community (as distinct from a merely literate one) would be able to establish rational relationships with other communities. Improved communications would bring these educated communities into increasingly close contact with each other and a world community would develop. A sense of kinship would grow up among all men, and instead of squandering their creative potential in pointless and destructive wars they would learn to settle their differences by negotiation and agreement. A world order would take shape in which racial, regional, and national frictions would have no place. Men would work happily together to bring each other a fair share of the world's abundant wealth. There are no logical objections to this as a plausible future course of development for human society if the romantic view of human nature is once accepted, and man is taken to be a creature of infinite possibility. If man is such a creature, it is then just a matter of adopting this rational aim and making a great collective effort to secure it. Wells wished to proceed, and to persuade other people to proceed, on this basis. But he knew that in the long run all human effort was futile and that man was base. The world was Dr. Moreau's Island and the men of goodwill were building on sand with obdurate material which by its essence excluded any possibility of success. Wells's "progressive" writing represents an attempt to straddle irreconcilable positions, and it involved a perpetual conflict of a wasteful character. In all too much of his work he is engaged in shouting down his own better judgement.

The change of front from an explicit pessimism to an apparent optimism dates roughly from 1901 and the publication of *Anticipations*. It coincides with Wells's entry into the sphere of influence of the Fabian Society in political matters and of that of William James in philosophy. James's name shows up in a list of men recognized as great by the business state described in *When the Sleeper Wakes*. This may suggest that Wells may have had some doubts about his ideas at first but the reference is misleading. Wells admired James greatly and gave Pragmatism his very emphatically expressed approval. It is easy enough to see why, since James's main positions are designed to plug the holes in Huxley's Romanes lecture. Huxley's straddle involved mental compartmentation. One part of the mind accepted the mechanistic view of the universe and one kind of truth, the other accepted the idea of a moral order and another kind of truth to which the first was hostile and destructive. James invented the idea of operative truth which is supposed to cover the difficulty :

"... *ideas* (*which themselves are but parts of our experience*) *become true just in so far as they help us to get into satisfactory relations with other parts of our experience.*"

"*True ideas are those we can assimilate, validate, corroborate, and verify. False ideas are those we cannot.*"

"*The true, to put it very briefly, is only the expedient in the way of our thinking, just as 'the right' is only the expedient in the way of our behaving.*"

The two first of these propositions dispose of the mechanistic view of the universe much as a lazy housemaid disposes of dust by sweeping it under the rug. The truth about the universe which it states neither helps us to get into satisfactory relations with other parts of our experience nor is subject to verification. (It is possible to postulate conditions in which mind, consciousness, and experience would have no meaning, but not to verify or experience them.) The basis for pessimism therefore loses its status as truth. The last proposition deals with any realistic appreciation of human nature : it is inexpedient to consider man base, at any rate when one is trying to construct a better world, so that the idea may be dismissed as untrue.

However much these propositions may have appealed to Wells's humanitarian feelings, they grated on his æsthetic sense and his intelligence fought with them, so that it became an increasing effort to pretend that they "worked". The doubts emerge as early as 1904, in *The Food of The Gods*. This is a progressive parable about the way in which human undertakings have outgrown petty national states and their parochial administrative units. It had its genesis in a talk on Areas of Administration given at the Students' Union in the Grosvenor Road in March 1903—with Beatrice Webb in the chair. It is rounded out with a pep-talk for the new order. But, and the but is a large one, the scientists who produce the food of the Gods have no idea of what they have done. The Skinners, who put it into use in the world, are monstrous parodies of the average man, and the food produces super-rats as well as super-men and super-chickens as a result of their sloppiness and carelessness. The book is very convincing as long as it is describing how things go wrong and hardly convincing at all when it attempts to say how they will go right. What it effectively describes is the frustration and destruction of a great possibility by inferior human material. The optimism of the conclusion rests on a trick. The food of the Gods has produced a new, larger, nobler breed of human being adequate to the technological possibilities open to it, and the future rests with them. The device is transparent, and it is hard not to feel that the evasion of the real problem, of what can be done with human nature as it is, is a conscious one. It is the first of a series of such calculated evasions. They are less apparent in the books about people than elsewhere, but they emerge from these too : *Kipps, Tono-Bungay, Ann Veronica, The History of Mr. Polly, The New Machiavelli, Marriage, The Passionate Friends*, and *The Wife of Sir Isaac Harman*, all superficially suggest that Wells is asking the question "what shall we do with our lives" as if the answer could be "whatever we wish". But the line of development followed in the books shows an underlying doubt about this answer. They show a steadily diminishing confidence in the possibility of individual solutions. What emerges at the end of the chain is the idea of the Mind of the Race, a group intellect which will be freed from individual weaknesses, and which will save humanity from its instincts. This group intellect is to be served

371

by semi-religious orders or devotees, the Samurai, who are to surrender their lives to it. But at the back of this conception is an awareness that it is not consistent with human nature that such a surrender should in fact take place. This recognition led to Wells writing a series of catastrophe books, stories in which he imagines that human nature undergoes some fundamental change that will permit the construction of a Utopian society. The ideas of Hobbes play a large part in these fantasies. Fear, generated by a cosmic disaster as *In the Days of the Comet*, or by atomic war in *The World Set Free* (1914), leads men to submit to some kind of central world government modelled on the Common Power described in *Leviathan*. But the idea of a change in human nature itself is the *sine qua non* of his utopias, and in the end Wells conceded that such a change was not within the realm of possibility. His much-parodied *Men Like Gods* is the point of concession, and it is odd that those who have criticized the book as representing the unpracticality and unreality of his idealism in its extreme form have not noticed the fact. The ideal beings which inhabit its Utopia exist in a free zone which is not within the realm of human reality. They are special creations like the giant children in *The Food of The Gods* and like them they are designed to evade the truth about human nature. They live in another universe outside the earth's spatial scheme altogether, which is part of a very elaborate construction indeed :

"Wonder took possession of Mr. Barnstaple's mind. That dear world of honesty and health was beyond the utmost boundaries of our space, utterly inaccessible to him now for evermore; and yet, as he had been told, it was but one of countless universes that move together in time, that lie against one another, endlessly like the leaves of a book. And all of them are as nothing in the endless multitudes of systems and dimensions that surround them. 'Could I but rotate my arm out of the limits set to it,' one of the Utopians had said to him, 'I could thrust it into a thousand universes.'"

This is optimism at the last ditch, an allowance of the cold comfort of an eternal moral order somewhere in a system of plural universes wholly inaccessible to human experience. And beyond that, the construction has the effect of making the book not a debate between man-as-he-might-be and man-as-he-is, but an essentially sterile clash between reality and an unattainable ideal. At best it is a cry of distress, a plea for things to be other than they are. *Men Like Gods* is in reality an altogether pessimistic book. Read in conjunction with *The Undying Fire*, which prepared the way for it, and which is a violently expressed hymn of loathing of things as they are, it leaves no doubt that in his last writings Wells was only giving a new form to beliefs which he had held all along. *The Undying Fire* is particularly moving, to those who have any sympathy with Wells at all. It shows the pendulum of his mind swinging away from its natural despairing bent over to the side of determination to construct something better out of human opportunities and back, again and again. Men are good enough to do something better than this, he says, gesticulating at the mess of the horrible world of 1919; and something better would be worth building however briefly it were to endure—and then he swings back: *"I talk ... I talk ... and then a desolating sense of reality blows like a destroying gust through my mind, and my little lamp of hope blows out ..."* These words were written when he was fifty-one, and they cannot be attributed to the loss of powers which are held to account for the tone of his writing from 1942 onwards. The difference between the two phases is that in 1919 his physical buoyancy and vitality supported his will to reject what he knew in his bones. In 1919, in *The Undying Fire*, he wrote:

"I can see nothing to redeem the waste and destruction of the last four years and the still greater waste and spiritless disorder and poverty and disease ahead of us. You will tell me that the world has learnt a lesson it could learn no other way, that we shall set up a League of Nations now and put an end to war. But on what will you set up your world League of Nations? What common foundations have you made in the last four years but ruins? Is there any common idea, any common understanding yet in the minds of men?"

The utterance is a despairing one. But Wells reacted to it by setting himself the task of attempting to fabricate the necessary common idea. *The Outline of History* was designed to provide a universal history which would serve as the basis for a patriotism of humanity, as national histories serve as a basis for national patriotism. What the book states is, not that progress is inevitable, but that mankind has a common historical background, not a racial or a regional one. It goes on to say that given the will mankind might, by a tremendous concerted effort, establish a world order in which all its energy could be consumed in constructive and creative enterprises, physical, æsthetic, and intellectual. The pendulum swung from one extreme to the other between 1919 and 1920; with the publication of *Men Like Gods* in 1923 it had swung right back.

If I appear to be saying that Wells was inconsistent, it cannot be helped, inconsistency is the natural consequence of an unresolved conflict in a writer's work or thought. Wells's inconsistencies could be quite dazzling at times. I remember receiving a kind of marriage sermon from him when I was first married in which he made a great point of monogamy and fidelity as being an essential to true happiness. Later on I received a number of tongue-lashings on the subject of divorce: when I told him that I had always thought of him as a man who had saved himself much unhappiness by divorce, he objected that this had no bearing on the fundamental principle. Later on we had some violent arguments on the question of pacifism. I had read a substantial part of *The Autocracy of Mr. Parham* in the light of a case for pacifism, and I still find it very hard not to do so. But in 1939 I was surprised to find that Wells took the line that once the country was at war it was the citizen's job to do what he was told to do without argument. We had many heated discussions about this which generally became a great deal more heated whenever I began to defend myself with the phrase "but you said, in Mr. Parham, that..." "*That* has nothing to do with it, nothing at all..." During the extremely bitter internal dispute among the Fabians in the early nineteen-hundreds Shaw attacked Wells on these grounds, attributing his lack of intellectual discipline to the fact that he had such tremendous facility and rapidity of mind that he had never had really to face any practical or intellectual difficulty, he had always been able to dodge. This may be so. But I am inclined to trace the trouble to the central dilemma, and to think that inconsistency and evasion became a habit of mind because he could never bring himself to deal with it. He comes out with it in *Boon* :

"'And that is where I want to take you up,' said Wilkins. 'I want to suggest that the mind of the race may be just a gleam of conscious realization that passes from darkness to darkness...'

'No,' said Boon.

'Why not?'

'Because I will not have it so,' said Boon."

Wells was Wilkins and Boon at once, and also Hallery, the intensely serious exponent of moral values who introduces an almost Calvinist note into the book. It was, of course, *Boon* with its parody of Henry James, and its harsh criticism of æsthetic values, which finally established his reputation as a Philistine. From *Boon* onwards he made increasingly strident attacks on literary values which are, in my view, only partially explicable by his sense that in the state in which the world found itself æsthetics were a luxury for which there was not enough time. It is my view that these attacks, which went along with his reiterated statements that his own work had no literary value, that it was merely journalism, attached to contemporary issues, which would become meaningless inside a couple of decades, reflected a troubled inner sense that there was something profoundly wrong about his own course of development. In the end I believe, on the strength of conversations which I had with him on the particular subject of what he meant by Dr. Moreau, and on some related topics, that he came to feel that a realization of the truth of the human situation, in all its ultimate hopelessness, was much more likely to stir men to present effort to make life more tolerable than any pretence. He felt, or so I think, that he had made a mistake in not quashing *Boon*'s easy sentimentality. He knew in his bones that the æsthetes were right, and that the writer's sole duty is to state the truth which he knows. At the close of his life, from *The Croquet Player* onwards, he was trying to recapture the spirit in which he had written *The Island of Dr. Moreau*, and what haunted him, and made him exceedingly unhappy, was a tragic sense that he had returned to the real source of what could have been his strength too late.

All this is, of course, about the inward centre of his work. Few people have brought so much buoyant vitality to the business of living, or have exercised so stimulating an effect on their friends. He spread a spirit of pleasure about him, and he made every kind of mental activity seem to be the best of sport. Although he made a number of enemies through impatience and lack of tact he made many more friends whose friendship endured through episodes which would not have been forgiven in a lesser man, and who when all was said and done rejoiced in having known him. Beyond that close circle of people who knew him there was the larger army whose hearts were warmed by the abundant spirit and courage which emanate from his writing and which make it easy to miss the intensity of his internal struggle with his demon.

FEBRUARY 1957

375

ERICH HELLER

Ludwig Wittgenstein*

The hell-fire of life consumes only the select among men.
The rest stand in front of it, warming their hands.

Friedrich Hebbel

WHAT MANNER OF MAN was Ludwig Wittgenstein? One answer, which is easy to come by, vague, large, and true, is : a man of rarest genius. Of all words that defy definition—which may be, simply, all words—genius is the most defiant. But how else describe a man who was a logician of the first order; a writer of German prose abundant in intellectual passion and disciplined clarity (perhaps only talent is needed for writing such prose in any other language, but certainly genius for writing it in German); an engineer of great promise and some achievement; the architect of a modern mansion; a gifted sculptor; a musician who very probably would have

---

* The occasion of these notes is the recent appearance of Ludwig Wittgenstein's *The Blue And Brown Books* (Basil Blackwell, 1958), and Norman Malcolm's *Ludwig Wittgenstein—A Memoir*, with a Biographical Sketch by Georg Henrik von Wright (Oxford University Press, 1958). *The Blue And Brown Books*, illuminatingly prefaced by Mr. Rush Rhees, were dictated by Wittgenstein to some of his pupils at various times between 1933 and 1935. They are indispensable for any study of the intellectual history that led, within the lifetime of the mature generation of Anglo-Saxon philosophers, to a fundamental change in philosophical opinion—a break outwardly less dramatic but probably more significant than that which occurred when Bertrand Russell and G. E. Moore banished the very much "post"-Hegelian metaphysics of F. H. Bradley and Bernard Bosanquet from the academic scene.

It is the most strange characteristic of the new "revolution" that it was the same man, Ludwig Wittgenstein, who both perfected the "old system" (in the *Tractatus Logico-Philosophicus*, finished by 1918, first published in 1921) and initiated its destruction (with *Philosophical Investigations*, complete by 1949, posthumously published in 1593). Mr. Malcom's *Memoir*, greatly assisted by Professor von Wright's informative sketch, is a noble biographical document, the more moving by virtue of its simplicity and affectionate restraint. It is from this book that the biographical references of my notes are taken.

E.H.

become, had he chosen this career, a remarkable conductor; a hermit capable of enduring for long periods the utmost rigours of mind and loneliness; a rich man who chose poverty; a Cambridge professor who thought and taught but neither lectured nor dined?

He was also an Austrian who conquered British philosophy; but this, as befits Austrian conquests, was due to a misunderstanding. At least he himself believed that it was so. When the pages of the journal *Mind* were filled with variations of his philosophical themes, he praised a certain American detective-story magazine, and wondered how, with the offer of such reading matter, "anyone can read *Mind* with all its impotence and bankruptcy". When his influence at Oxford was at its height, he referred to it as "a philosophical desert" and as "the influenza area." These are ironical exaggerations, but undoubtedly serious as expressions of Wittgenstein's discontent.

Why should he have been so displeased with the rôle his thought played in contemporary philosophical circles? What was the source of his suspicion that a misunderstanding was viciously at work in the proliferation of his views and methods throughout the departments of philosophy? And if it was a misunderstanding, was it avoidable? These questions raise a bigger one: what is the nature of philosophical opinion?

There are philosophies which, however difficult they may be, it is in principle easy to teach and to learn. Of course, not everyone can teach or learn philosophy—as little as higher mathematics; but the philosophies of certain philosophers have this in common with higher mathematics that they present the simple alternative of being either understood or not understood. It is, in a final analysis, impossible to *mis*understand them. This is true of Aristotle, or St. Thomas Aquinas, or Descartes, or Locke, or Kant. Such philosophies are like mountains: you can climb to their tops or you can give up; or like weights: you can lift them or they defeat you; and in either case you will know what has happened and "where you are". But this is not so with the thought of Plato, or St. Augustine, or Pascal, or Kierkegaard, or Nietzsche. Their philosophies are like human faces on the features of which are inscribed, disquietingly, the destinies of souls; or like cities rich in history. "Do you understand Kant?" is a question like "Have you been to the summit of Mont Blanc?" The answer is *yes* or *no*. "Do you understand Nietzsche?" is like asking "Do you know Rome?" The answer is simple only if you have never been there. The trouble with Wittgenstein's thinking is that it sometimes looks more like Descartes': you believe you can learn it as you learn logic or mathematics. But it almost always is more like Pascal's: you may be quite sure you cannot. For to understand it on its own level is as much a matter of imagination and character as it is one of "thinking". Its temperature is of its essence, in its passion lies its seriousness, the rhythm of its sentences are as telling as is that which they tell, and sometimes it is a semi-colon which marks the frontier between a thought and a triviality. How is this? Are we speaking of an artist or a philosopher? We are speaking of Ludwig Wittgenstein. *"Der Philosoph behandelt eine Frage; wie eine Krankheit."* It is a profound semi-colon, and not even Miss Anscombe's competent work as a translator could save the profundity : "The philosopher's treatment of a question is like the treatment of an illness" is, by comparison, a flat *aperçu*.

Philosophy, for Wittgenstein, was not a profession. It was a consuming passion; and not just "a" passion, but the only possible form of his existence. The thought of losing his gift for philosophy made him feel suicidal. He could not but have contempt for philosophers who "did" philosophy and, having done it, thought of other things : of money, publication lists, academic advancements, university intrigues, love-affairs, or the Athenaeum—and thought of these things in a manner which showed even more clearly than the products of their thought that they had philosophized with much less than their whole person. Wittgenstein had no difficulty in detecting in their style of thinking, debating, or writing, the corruption of the divided life, the painless jugglery with words and meanings, the shallow flirtation with depth, and the ear deaf to the command of authenticity. Thinking for him was as much a moral as an intellectual concern. In this lay his affinity with Otto Weininger, for whom he had great respect. The spectacle of the detachability of a thought from a man filled him with loathing and with an anger very much like that with which Rilke in the fourth of the *Duino Elegies* denounced, through the image of the dancer, the cursed non-identity between performer and performance:

> *...How gracefully he moves!*
> *And yet he is disguised, a dressed-up philistine,*
> *Who will come home soon, entering through the*
> *   kitchen.*
> *I cannot bear these masks, half-filled with life.*

Had Wittgenstein ever cared to write about himself, this apparently most "intellectual" of philosophers might have said :

> I have at all times thought with my whole body and my whole life. I do not know what purely intellectual problems are ... You know these things by way of thinking, yet your thought is not your experience but the reverberation of the experience of others; as your room trembles

when a carriage passes. I am sitting in that carriage and often am the carriage itself.

This, however, was written by Nietzsche. And it was Nietzsche whom he resembled in many other ways : in his homelessness, his restless wanderings, his perpetual search for the exactly right conditions in which to work, his loneliness, his asceticism, his need for affection and his shyness in giving it, his intellectual extremism which drove thought to the border of insanity, the elasticity of his style and (as we shall see) in one philosophically most important respect. Like Nietzsche then, he knew that philosophical opinion was not merely a matter of logically demonstrable rights or wrongs. This most rigorous logician was convinced that it was above all a matter of authenticity—and thus, in a sense, not at all of negotiable opinions. What assumed with him so often the semblance of intolerable intellectual pride, was the demand, which he made upon himself still more than upon others, for the absolutely authentic utterance. The question was not only "Is this opinion right or wrong?" but also "Is this or that person *entitled* to this or that opinion?" This lent to his manner of debating the tone, at times, of an Old Testament prophetic harshness : he would suddenly be seized by an uncontrollable desire to mete out intellectual punishment. He reacted to errors of judgement as if they were sins of the heart, and violently denied opinions, which in themselves—if this distinction were possible—might have been harmless enough or even "correct"; and denied them because they were untrue in the self that uttered them : they lacked the sanction of the moral and intellectual pain suffered on behalf of truth.

Wittgenstein, as Mr. Malcolm remembers, once said, using a comparison with swimming, that "just as one's body has a natural tendency towards the surface and one has to make an exertion to get to the bottom—so it is with thinking". And in talking about the stature of a philosopher, he remarked "that the measure of a man's greatness would be in terms of what his work *cost* him". It is Kantian ethics applied to the realm of thought: true moral goodness was for Kant a victory over natural inclination, the costlier the better. Nietzsche too was, by character and insight, such a Kantian moralist of the intellectual life; yet he, who was never more ingenious than in producing the devastating argument against himself, could also say this :

The labour involved in climbing a mountain is no measure of its height. But where knowledge is concerned, it is to be different; at least this is what we are told by some who consider themselves initiates : the effort which a truth costs is to decide its value! This crazy morality is founded upon the idea that "truths" are like the installations in a Swedish gymnasium, designed to tire one out—a morality of the mind's athletics and gymnastic displays.

Perhaps it is a pity that Wittgenstein was not the man *also* to say things of this kind. It might have lightened the burden of earnest irritability carried by many a contemporary philosophical debate.

II

The appreciation of Wittgenstein as a person and thinker (and how misleading is this "and"!) is bedevilled by a persistent optical delusion. The high moral pathos of his life (in which his "legend" has already taken firm roots) *seems* at first glance to be unconnected with the drift and trend, the content and method of his philosophical thought. Every page of Pascal or Kierkegaard or Nietzsche at once conveys, however impersonal may be the subject-matter, a sense of urgent personal involvement. But it is possible for anyone but the most sensitively predisposed to read many pages of Wittgenstein's without suspecting that the ruthless precision and often apparently eccentric virtuosity of this thinking, which has neither models nor parallels in the history of philosophy, is anything but the result of the utmost intellectual detachment. Its first emotional effect upon the reader may well be one of exasperated melancholia—the effect which Robert Musil (not for nothing an Austrian contemporary of Wittgenstein's) ascribes in *The Man Without Qualities* to a certain thinker:

> He had drawn the curtains and worked in the subdued light of his room like an acrobat who, in an only half-illuminated circus tent and before the public is admitted, shows to a select audience of experts his latest break-neck leaps . . .

Yet Wittgenstein's work is none the less suffused with authentic pathos, and will one day be seen as an integral part in the tragically self-destructive design of European thought.

If by some miracle both European history and thought continue, then the future historians of thought will be not a little puzzled by Wittgenstein. For nothing could be less predictable than that a work which more deeply than any other affected contemporary Anglo-Saxon philosophy, Wittgenstein's *Philosophical Investigations*, should have as its motto a sentence from the classical comic playwright of Austria, Nestroy. Or that its philosophical author should have experienced a kind of religious awakening thanks to a performance of *Die Kreuzelschreiber* by Anzengruber, a considerably lesser Austrian dramatist. However, these will be minor surprises, less important, certainly, than Professor von Wright's perspicacious discovery of the affinities between Wittgenstein's manner of thinking and writing and that of the great eighteenth-century German aphorist Lichtenberg. But of greater weight still would be the realization that the name of Wittgenstein marks the historical point at which, most unexpectedly, the cool, analytical intellect of British philosophy meets with those passions of mind and imagination which we associate first with Nietzsche and then, in manifold crystallizations, with such Austrians as Otto Weininger, Adolf Loos, Karl Kraus, Franz Kafka, and Robert Musil.

Like Otto Weininger, Wittgenstein believed in the surpassing ethical significance of thinking, and in thought as both a deeply personal and almost religiously supra-personal dedication. With Adolf Loos he shared the radical rejection of all ornamental comforts and decorative relaxations of the mind, and the concentration on the purest lines of the intellectual architecture; with Karl Kraus, the conviction of an inescapable bond between the forms of living, thinking, feeling, and the forms of language (Wittgenstein's dictum, "Ethics and æsthetics are one," may serve as a perfect characterization of Karl Kraus' artistic *credo*). As far as Kafka and Musil are concerned, a comparison between their styles of writing (and therefore modes of perception) and Wittgenstein's would certainly be as fruitful as that between his and Lichtenberg's; and the more revealing because there can be no question of influence beyond the anonymous and peculiarly Austrian dispensations of the *Zeitgeist*, which even suggests that there is a family resemblance between the logical structures, the motives and intentions, of Wittgenstein's *Tractatus* and those of Schönberg's musical theory—for Schönberg too is guided by the conviction that the "language" of his medium, music, has to be raised to that level of logical necessity which would eliminate all subjective accidents. It is in such a constellation of minds that Wittgenstein is perhaps truly at home, whereas in the history of British philosophy he may merely "hold an important position". This at least is one way of accounting for the discomforts he suffered from the British philosophical climate and on a philosophical scene which so deceptively appeared to be largely of his own making.

What are the motives and intentions of Wittgenstein's philosophy? What is, beyond and above its own philosophical declarations, the historical meaning of that "revolution" which changed the face of Anglo-Saxon philosophy in the course of Wittgenstein's gradual modification and final abandonment of some of the principles laid down in his *Tractatus Logico-*

Philosophicus? Has it analogies with the revolutionary effects of other philosophies?

In his book, *My Philosophical Development*, Bertrand Russell engages in a bitter attack on the author of *Philosophical Investigations*, a broadside which, if it is not damaging, is yet illuminating.* The man who was one of the first to recognize Wittgenstein's *Tractatus* as a work of philosophical genius (even if he interpreted it too exclusively as the culmination of his own doctrine of "Logical Atomism") says now of the *Philosophical Investigations* that he has not found in it "anything interesting".—"I cannot understand why a whole school finds important wisdom in its pages." He abhors the suggestion, which he believes to be implied in Wittgenstein's later work, "that the world of language can be quite divorced from the world of fact", and suspects that such a view must render philosophical activity trivial ("at best, a slight help to lexicographers, and at worst, an idle tea-table amusement") by insidiously giving to "language an untrammelled freedom which it has never hitherto enjoyed". He disagrees with the disciples of Wittgenstein most radically when they tend to regard "as an outdated folly the desire to understand the world"—as distinct, it would seem, from their own desire to understand the workings of language. If incomprehension can ever be significant, then this can be said of Lord Russell's estimate of *Philosophical Investigations*. For he certainly knew what he attacked when once upon a time he victoriously fought the domineering influence of Bradley's idealism, and also knew what he welcomed when Wittgenstein first sent him the *Tractatus*. But the later Wittgenstein is to him, on his own confession, "completely unintelligible". This might clearly show which of the two recent changes in philosophical outlook—Russell's dislodging of Bradley, or Wittgenstein's superseding of Wittgenstein—is the more profound.

Bertrand Russell was at intellectual ease with Bradley as well as with the Wittgenstein of the *Tractatus* because both were, like he himself, philosophers thinking *within* the metaphysical tradition of European philosophy. This goes without saying in the case of Bradley. In the case of the *Tractatus* it may sound alarming. But it is true to say that in its own way—and an exceedingly subtle way it is!—the *Tractatus* participates in a pre-Kantian metaphysical faith: that there is, in however small an area of human understanding, a pre-established correspondence between the cognitive faculties of man and the nature of the world. In other words: what man thinks and feels—and therefore *says*—about the world, has a chance of being *metaphysically* true. At a time when philosophers were still on intimate terms with God, this metaphysical faith found its luminously comprehensive dogma: God is no deceiver; He has created the world and

* See "Russell and Wittgenstein", in *Encounter* 1959, January, pp. 8, 9.

planted in man the desire to understand it; He has also endowed him with perception and rationality, which man cannot help taking for the servants of this desire. Could it have been God's intention to frustrate it from the outset by giving man nothing but the *illusion* of understanding? Is the creature made in his own image to be the eternal dupe of the universe? The simple faith that this cannot be lies at the heart of even the most complex philosophical systems which ever since the seventeenth century have profoundly affected European thought. This faith is discernible behind the scholastic apparatus of Leibniz's Pre-established Harmony and Descartes' *Cogito ergo sum*, those grandiose attempts logically to demonstrate the integral accord between human thought and the true nature of Being. And it is the same faith in reason's power, to "comprehend the wondrous architecture of the world", which inspires the great cosmic discoveries of that age. "Thanks be unto you, my Lord, our Creator, for granting me insight into the beauty of your creation." Thus speaks Kepler in concluding *The Harmony of the Cosmos*.

It is a far cry from Descartes to Wittgenstein's *Tractatus*. Yet there is an angle of vision from which the *Tractatus* looks like a last victory of the traditional metaphysical faith : a Pyrrhic victory.

Compared to the vast dominions that metaphysical thought had claimed in the past for its settlements of truth, there is now hardly more than a little province of "significant" speech in a vast area of silence. But within this catastrophically narrowed space man can still confidently assert some truths about the world, utter words the meaning of which is not imprisoned within themselves, and speak sentences the significance of which is not wholly embedded within the flux of linguistic commerce and convention. No, there are still words and sentences which are true in an absolute sense, reflect "that which is the case", and *picture Reality*. Of course, this ideal correspondence between picture and model, thought and world, language and reality, is not easily attained. Its condition is the observance of the strictest logical rules. Thus it will hardly ever occur in the actuality of human speech. Yet it is realized, nevertheless, in the *essence* of language : indeed, it is its *real meaning*. True, in order to speak "essentially" and "significantly", we must leave much unsaid. But once we respond to the "atomic facts" (the bricks of the intelligible world) with "atomic propositions" or their "truth-functional compounds" (concepts which Wittgenstein, considerably modifying and refining them, took over from Russell), our speech, and therefore our thought, is perfectly attuned to Reality : for "Logic is not a theory but a mirror-reflection of the world". And although Wittgenstein courageously insisted that in proposing this relationship between language and fact he himself broke the law governing meaningful propositions, his *Tractatus* is yet built upon a site salvaged from the meta-physical estate of the Pre-established Harmony. The ground, however, was soon to give; and as it gave, Bertrand Russell (for one) saw nothing but collapse. And it is true that from the *Blue Books* onwards Wittgenstein immersed himself in a philosophical enterprise which, if set up against the traditional hopes of philosophers, looks desperate indeed.

For its intention is to cure philosophers of a sickness the name of which may well be—philosophy. His aphorism of the philosopher's treating ques-tions as if they were patients has more than epigrammatic relevance.

III

The break between *Tractatus* and *Philosophical Investigations* is of the same kind as that between Nietzsche's *The Birth of Tragedy* (1871) and his *Human, All-too-Human* (1879). In both cases it was brought about by the abnegation of metaphysics, the loss of faith in any pre-established correspon-dence between, on the one hand, the logic of our thought and language, and, on the other, the "logic" of Reality. In the course of those eight years stretching from *The Birth of Tragedy* to *Human, All-too-Human*, Nietzsche came to believe that he had freed himself of this "philosophical prejudice"—which he diagnosed as the prejudice vitiating the whole history of thought—by turning (to use Wittgenstein's obviously autobio-graphical words from *Investigations*) his "whole examination round. (One might say : the axis of reference of our examination must be rotated, but about the fixed point of our real need.)" Nietzsche could have written this. Indeed, it might serve as an exact description of what he claimed as his great achievement : to have turned through 180° our whole horizon around the point of our "real need" which "needed" another vision, a need radically different from that

> which had been at work in forming the . . . [traditional] categories of thought; namely, the need not to "recognize" but to subsume, to schematize, and, for the sake of communication and calculation, to manipulate and fabricate similarities and samenesses . . . No, this was not the work of a pre-existent "idea"; it happened under the persuasion of usefulness : it was profitable to coarsen and level down things; for only then were they calculable and comfortable . . . Our categories are "truths" only in so far as they make life possible for us : Euclidean space is also such a purposeful "truth" . . . The inner compulsion not to con-tradict these "truths", the instinct to reach our kind of useful conclu-sions is inbred in us, we almost *are* this instinct. But how naïve to take this as proof of a "truth *per se*". Our inability to contradict proves im-potence and not "truth".

It was Nietzsche's declared intention not to follow any longer this "instinct" and thus to cure the philosophical sickness of centuries, just as it was Wittgenstein's to "solve the philosophical problems" by recognizing their source in "the functioning of our language"—"*in spite* of an instinct to misunderstand it". For Nietzsche the truth about man was that he must live without Truth. This was the "real need". The creature that would satisfy it Nietzsche called Superman—and never mind the offensive word, poetically begotten in a great mind by a Darwinian age. In his letters he often used less grandiose, if not less ambitious, words in speaking of his philosophical goal, words to the effect that

> he felt as though he were writing for people who would think in a quite different way, breathe a different air of life from that of present-day men : for people of a different culture . . .

But this is reported by Professor von Wright as a saying of Wittgenstein's.

It would, of course, be absurd to represent Wittgenstein as a latter-day Nietzsche, and the comparison is certainly not meant to "manipulate and fabricate similarities and samenesses". The two philosophers could hardly be more different in scope and object, approach and humour, key and tempo of their thought. Yet they have in common something which is of the greatest significance : the creative distrust of *all* those categorical certainties that, as if they were an inherited anatomy, have been allowed to determine the body of traditional thought. Nietzsche and Wittgenstein share the genius for directing doubt into the most unsuspected hiding-places of error and fallacy : namely where, as Wittgenstein puts it, "everything lies open to inspection", where everything is simple and familiar, where, day in day out, man takes things for granted—until suddenly one day just this fact strikes him as the "most striking and most powerful". This may happen on the day when suspicion reaches the notion of "meaning", that is, the idea, held however vaguely, that through some kind of cosmic arrangement, made by God or logic or the spirit of language, a definite meaning had become attached to the world, to life, to facts, or to words. When Nietzsche discovered the "death of God" the universe of meanings collapsed—everything, that is, that was founded upon the transcendent faith, or was leaning against it, or was intertwined with it : in fact, *everything*, as Nietzsche believed; and henceforward everything was in need of revaluation.

With Wittgenstein the decisive change of vision, which occurred between *Tractatus* and *Investigations*, seemed centred upon a more modest event : the vanquishing of the belief in a categorical logic of language, and hence in a categorically harmonious relationship between words and world. But the event behind the event was of the same magnitude. It entailed the same crisis of metaphysical confidence that, with some metaphysically more fanatical Germans and Frenchmen, leads to the great perversion of metaphysics: the lost belief in any rationally reliable dealings with Reality was replaced by the notion that (on the contrary) it was a Pre-established Absurdity which determined the relationship between the intellectual constitution of man and the true constitution of the world. Nietzsche was the first to conceive of such a possibility. After him European art and literature excelled in showing man and world labouring under the tragic or melancholy or grotesque or hilarious compulsion to make nonsense of each other. And there is a historical sense in which the two extremes of contemporary philosophizing—Heidegger's tortuous metaphysical probings into language and Wittgenstein's absorption in language-games (and some of the examples he chooses reveal an almost Thurber-like talent for absurd and grotesque inventions)—can be seen as two aspects of the same intention: to track down to their source in language and there to correct the absurdities of the human endeavour to speak the truth. It is an intention which was by no means alien to Nietzsche. Certainly, his universal suspicion did not spare language, and some of his utterances on the subject are almost literally indistinguishable from Wittgenstein's.

Very early in his philosophical life, Nietzsche knew that he "who finds language interesting in itself has a mind different from him who only regards it as a medium of thought", and he left no doubt which of the two he regarded as the more *philosophical* mind: "Language is something all-too-familiar to us; therefore it needs a philosopher to be struck by it." This is Nietzsche's way of saying the same as Wittgenstein when he discovered that "the most important aspects of things are hidden from us by virtue of their simplicity and familiarity". Or when some time later Nietzsche found that "the philosopher is caught in the net of *Language*", he meant much the same as Wittgenstein who, referring to his own *Tractatus*, said: "A *picture* held us captive. And we could not get outside it, for it lay in our language and language seemed to repeat it to us inexorably." Indeed, Nietzsche sounds as if he had in mind the metaphysics of the *Tractatus* when he speaks of the conclusion of a primitive metaphysical peace which once upon a time fixed "what henceforward is to be called truth": "A universally valid and compelling notation of facts is invented and the legislation of language issues into the principal rules for truth"—in the manner, precisely, of Wittgenstein's *Tractatus*: "To give the essence of proposition means to give the essence of all description, therefore the essence of the world." *But* Nietzsche asks: "Is language the adequate expression for all realities?" And soon he was to be still surer that it was not. On the contrary, the grammatical and syntactical order of language, its subjects, predicates, objects, casual and conditional connections, were "the petrified fallacies of reason" which continued to exercise their "seductive spell" upon our intelligence.

> Philosophy is a battle against the bewitchment of our intelligence by means of language.

This last aphorism is by Wittgenstein; but it would be impossible to guess where Nietzsche ends and Wittgenstein begins.

IV

One of Wittgenstein's aphorisms (unfortunately mistranslated by Miss Anscombe—a rare flaw in her work) runs as follows:

> Philosophy results in the discovery of one or another piece of simple nonsense, and in bruises which the understanding has suffered by bumping its head against the limits of language. They, the bruises, make us see the value of that discovery.*

And in one of the jottings of his late years Nietzsche wrote under the heading FUNDAMENTAL SOLUTION:

> Language is founded upon the most naïve prejudices... We read contradictions and problems into everything because we *think only* within the forms of language... *We have to cease to think if we refuse to do it in the prison-house of language*; for we cannot reach further than the doubt which asks whether the limit we see is really a limit... *All rational thought is interpretation in accordance with a scheme which we cannot throw off.*

Yet neither Nietzsche nor Wittgenstein "ceased to think". In Nietzsche's thought, the persistent misgiving that the established conventions of philosophical language did not cater for our "real" intellectual needs was only one facet of his central thesis: with the death of God, with the silencing of that Word which was at the beginning, *all* certainties of faith, belief, metaphysics, morality, and knowledge had come to an end, and henceforward man was under the terrible compulsion of absolute freedom. His choice

---

* And this is one of Karl Kraus' aphorisms on language: "If I cannot get further, this is because I have banged my head against the wall of language. Then, with my head bleeding, I withdraw. And want to go on."

was that of either creating, with the surpassing creativity of the Creator, his own world, or of spiritually perishing. For the world *as it is* has neither meaning nor value. Meaning and value must be *given* to it : by God or by man himself. If God is dead and man fails, then nothing in this world has any value and our own language deceives us with all its ancient intimations of higher meanings.

> In the world everything is as it is and happens as it does happen. *In* it there is no value—and if there were, it would be of no value.

These sentences from Wittgenstein's *Tractatus* might have been invented by Nietzsche—and many like these were in fact invented by him—when in *The Will to Power*, like an inspired actor, like an initiate, he spoke the mind of European Nihilism which he so urgently desired to overcome.

Wittgenstein's *Investigations* would be as trivial as Bertrand Russell thinks they are, were their infinite intellectual patience not informed with a sense of urgency not altogether unlike that which inspired Nietzsche's prophetic impetuosity. To bring some light into "the darkness of this time"—this was the hesitant hope of the author of *Philosophical Investigations*. This hope, like all true hope, was founded upon the paradox of faith : the faith despite doubt. It was, with Wittgenstein, the faith in language; and language retained for him its all-importance even after it had ceased to be the mirror of Reality. For when all the dangers of language are exposed, when the captivity is shown in which our minds are held by its metaphors, when the witchcraft is denounced with which it assails our intelligence, there still remains the ineradicable trust in its ultimate wisdom and its power to heal our disease.

Nothing in Wittgenstein's work is more vulnerable to further questioning than this trust; indeed, its very intellectual vulnerability establishes it as his faith. Often he speaks of language with utmost vagueness :

> When philosophers use a word—"knowledge", "being", "object", "I", "proposition", "name"—and try to grasp the *essence* of the thing, one must always ask oneself : is the word ever actually used in this way in the language in which it has its home?*

One may well ask, who, with language speaking in a hundred tongues through our literatures, dialects, social classes, journals, and newspapers, establishes this "actual use"? Shakespeare? Donne? James Joyce? the

* Was it the vagueness of this which induced the translator to use "language-game" where the German is simply *"Sprache"*?

Oxford Dictionary? the College Porter? the local M.P.? the habitual reader of the *News of the World*? And when Wittgenstein says: "What *we* do is to bring words back from their metaphysical to their everyday usage," or "When I talk about language . . . I must speak the language of every day," one cannot help being struck by the homely imprecision of this programme. One wonders why he should not rather wish to bring language back to Lichtenberg's or Gottfried Keller's usage, or to the speech of Karl Kraus, which was in fact much closer to Wittgenstein's own than that of a Vienna or London "everyday". Or again, he says:

> Philosophy may in no way interfere with the actual use of language; it can in the end only describe it . . . It leaves everything as it is.

or

> We must do away with all *explanation*, and description alone must take its place.

But might we not be "held captive" by a picture "actually used" in language, and can we be sure that "actual usage" will never "bewitch our intelligence"? And if it does, how are we to loosen its grip without "explaining" its nature? (And I am using "explain" here as it is "actually used".)

Or is Schopenhauer, who so indignantly "interfered" with the "actual use" made of language by those who corruptly spoke and printed it every day, guilty of errors of judgement *because* he wrote a prose modelled on the example of a classical literary tradition as remote as can be from the everyday traffic in words?

And what is the "everything" that philosophy "leaves as it is"? Not, surely, the manner of thinking and uttering thoughts. Many philosophers, like all great poets, have deeply affected perception, and therefore language, and therefore have changed our world: Plato, for instance, or Descartes, or Rousseau, or Kant, or Nietzsche, or indeed Wittgenstein.

When Wittgenstein speaks of the language of every day, he does not mean what "actual usage" would suggest he means. In fact, he means Language—something that is of supreme importance as the repository of human community, understanding, knowledge, and wisdom. What he calls "actual usage" and "the language of every day" is hardly more than the uneasy concession made by an absolute faith to the demand for an empirical criterion, or else his manner of disdainfully denouncing the violations of language of which many a philosophizer has been guilty in his pursuit of spurious heights and depths. With two aphorisms of

Investigations above all, Wittgenstein can be observed in the very act of avoiding, in the manner of an empiricist fighting shy of metaphysics, the open declaration of his all-but-metaphysical belief in language:

> The problems arising through a misinterpretation of our forms of language have the character of *depth*. They are deep disquietudes; their roots are as deep in us as the forms of our language, and their significance is as great as the importance of our language.

How true; and yet how disquieting is the word "misinterpretation"! What does it mean? It seems to suggest that there is, or can be, an absolutely reliable rule for deciding, philosophically or philologically, what is a correct and what is a false interpretation of every particular "form of language". But no such standard can apply to a medium like language, which has no little share in the allusiveness of dance and gesture, the elusiveness of music, the ungrammatical extravagancies of life itself. For no sooner have we left the field of logic, grammar, and syntax, than we have entered the sphere of æsthetics where we no longer wonder whether a writer has "interpreted" words correctly, but rather whether he has used them well or badly; and this will be a matter not of any power to interpret but of something more adequately described as the feeling for language, a feeling which has its ground in sensibility or genius, and has been formed by tradition—that is, by the particular "form of life" within which alone, according to Wittgenstein, language has its meaning.

"To imagine a language," he says, "means to imagine a form of life."

That this is so, is one of Wittgenstein's most striking realizations; and indeed it not only renders the "rules of language", as he well knew, logically unmanageable but also makes their "description", which he hoped for, a task that could not be fulfilled by even a legion of Prousts and Wittgensteins. For what is *the* "form of life" which, in one language, is shared by Goethe and Hitler, or, in another, by Keats and the *Daily Mirror*?

The word "misinterpretation" in the quoted aphorism conveys yet another suggestion which is even more erroneous; namely, that depth is a by-product of error. But if words like depth and truth and error are to have any meaning at all, then truth is deeper than falsehood. Indeed the suggestion is withdrawn by the aphorism's very form and rhythm which unmistakably intimate that language itself, not merely its misinterpretation, has the character of depth, and that the disquietudes which arise from it are as deep as is the peace which sometimes it may bring: through a great writer and even, rarely, through a philosopher whose thought is deeply rooted in the mystery of words—or, to use the terms of that other aphorism of Wittgenstein: in the ground of language. For this second aphorism comes close to revealing his metaphysical secret.

"What is it that gives to our investigation its importance," he asks there with the voice of an imaginary interlocutor, "since it seems only to destroy everything interesting? (As it were all the buildings, leaving behind only bits of stone and rubble.)" And he replies. "What we are destroying is nothing but houses of cards and we are clearing up the ground of language on which they stand."

The ground of language—it is a transparent metaphor. And what shines through it is a mystical light, even if there is nothing left for it to illumine but a philosophical landscape most thoughtfully cleared of all the fragile and disfiguring edifices built throughout the ages by the victims of linguistic delusion, such as Plato, St. Thomas Aquinas, Spinoza, or Immanuel Kant.

It is an ending a little like that of Goethe's *Tasso* where a man, a poet, with all his certainties shattered, grasps hold of his last possession: language. It has remained an open question of literary interpretation whether that ending spells an ultimately happy consummation or a tragedy. But so far as philosophy is concerned, this enters with Wittgenstein the stage which has been reached in this epoch by many another creative activity of the human mind—by poetry, for instance, or by painting: the stage where every act of creation is inseparable from the critique of its medium, and every work, intensely reflecting upon itself, looks like the embodied doubt of its own possibility. It is a predicament which Nietzsche has uncannily anticipated in a sketch entitled "A Fragment from the History of Posterity". Its subject is "The Last Philosopher". Having lost faith in a communicable world, he is imprisoned within his own self-consciousness. Nothing speaks to him any more—except his own speech; and, deprived of any authority from a divinely ordered universe, it is only about his speech that his speech can speak with a measure of philosophical assurance.

Wittgenstein says in *Philosophical Investigations*: "What is your aim in philosophy?—To show the fly the way out of the fly-bottle." But who asks? Who answers? And who is the fly? It is an unholy trinity; the three are one. This way lies no way out. This way lie only fly-bottles, and more and more fly-bottles.

SEPTEMBER 1959

IRVING KRISTOL

"... And People Opening Veins in Baths"

WHAT MARKS THE TRUE greatness of a writer is, first, the peremptory
and sovereign way he imposes himself on successive generations of readers;
and second, the mystery that attends his ultimate "meaning", his inex-
haustibility before the commentator. One is almost tempted to say that his
mystery is his meaning: his words impress us as fragments torn from a
greater silence, where the whole truth is to be found, though not by us.
There are not many such writers altogether. Most of them are poets and
dramatists. Some are novelists and philosophers. Very few are historians.
Thucydides perhaps belongs among them; Tacitus certainly.

Tacitus is the historian of the extreme situation, without hope and without despair, almost without humanity. Yet, paradoxically, just as the *deus
absconditus* of the theologians could be known through his absence, so it
is this seeming want of humanity that quickens our own sense of its existence. Thus:

> *The general rage against* [the fallen favourite] *Sejanus was subsiding,
> calmed by the executions already carried out, yet retribution was now
> decreed against his remaining children. Therefore, they were taken to
> prison, the boy understanding what lay ahead, the girl suspecting it so
> little that many times she asked what wrong she had done, what place
> she was being taken to, saying that she would not do it again, and that
> she should be punished as children are. Contemporary writers report that,
> the execution of a virgin being unheard of, the hangman violated her
> beside the noose. Then both were strangled and their bodies thrown on
> the Gemonian steps.*

The girl's name we do not know, nor anything else about her. In the blood-
spattered pages of the *Annals*, her fate can hardly be called exceptional.
Tacitus gives no sign of pity; and whatever it is that the reader feels, pity
is not quite the word for it. The effect of this passage may best be compared to an experience most of us probably do not have more than once in
our lives; when we dream of our own death, not with any sentimental

pathos, but with a cold, clinical detachment, simply seeing it happen, an event among an infinity of events, in an infinity of time and space—and then we awake, feeling in a way we never did before what it means to be a human being in a universe where human beings need not exist.

In his *Agricola*, Tacitus refers to those who were spared by Domitian's terror, and says that they "had outlived both others and themselves". He was one of those who survived himself. Despising Imperial Rome, he served it well, and was in turn well rewarded with high posts and privileges. The whole import of his chronicle is that this is a time when nothing can be done : the zero point of the human condition. He condemned those who opposed the régime, for he saw no alternative to it and they only worsened matters; and those who supported it, for it was base. He censured Seneca for betraying his Stoic-republican principles by toadying to Nero; he censured Thrasea Pætus for being loyal to these same principles and offering resistance to Nero; and he praised both for dying well. Monarchy, aristocracy, and democracy were all unstable forms of government, leading to tyranny. The only good one was a "mixed constitution" as described by Polybius and Cicero—but it was beyond the capacity of men to establish such a state. It was permissible to think about "primeval man, untouched as yet by evil impulse", and his *Germania* is just such a fantasy. But his own age was fatally marked, the people corrupt and beyond redeeming, the barbarians rebellious and menacing. The sole honourable behaviour was to avoid contention and die bravely. Nor was there anything to hope for from the gods, "who care nothing for the happiness of men, only for their punishment". All tokens of divine intervention were fraudulent :

Many prodigies occurred. A woman gave birth to a snake. Another woman was killed in her husband's arms by a thunderbolt. The sun suddenly went dark...But these portents meant nothing. So little were they due to the gods that Nero continued his reign and his crimes for years to come.

The full Tacitean quality does not come through in Professor Michael Grant's new "plain English" translation.* On the other hand, its simplicity and readability will presumably attract many readers who might otherwise fight shy of so baroque an historian; and the introduction and appendices are models of erudite popularization. Like Shakespeare, Tacitus will endure almost any loving translation, and Professor Grant's is indisputably that. For, again like Shakespeare, he is complaisant to all human intentions.

And how complaisant! There is a still unwritten chapter in the history of

* *Tacitus on Imperial Rome.* Translated by Michael Grant. The Penguin Classics. 5s.

393

Western political thought that would deal with the varying uses made of Tacitus (and of Machiavelli too, with whom he has such an odd affinity). The classical revival of the Renaissance propelled him into a new and highly ambiguous career—no longer a Roman chronicler, but a political guide to "real" politics as opposed to the "imaginary" politics of the medieval mind. Somehow, by a transvaluation of values we do not even now fully understand, the medieval ideas of a good society, of the moral obligations of ruler and ruled, of a transcendent standard by which political actions were to be measured—all these were suddenly felt to be pretentiously hollow, while the unalloyed hellishness of the *Annals* (especially of Books I-VI, dealing with Tiberius) came to be regarded as a revelation of the "realities" of political life.

It was Guicciardini, one of the founders of *Realpolitik* and friend of Machiavelli, whi first enunciated this new approach to Tacitus : "Cornelius Tacitus teaches very well those who live under a tyranny how to conduct themselves prudently; as he also teaches tyrants how to found a tyranny." Here was a school for dictators that was also a school for tyrannicides : one chose one's banner and enlisted. Gentle Montaigne saw in Tacitus "a nursery of ethical and political instruction for the aid and ornament of those who have something to do with managing the affairs of the world". And Nicolas Perrot, translating the *Annals* for Richelieu, advised him that "it is in his [Tacitus] learned writings that one is taught the art of ruling". The new secular monarchies studied the cunning, the hypocrisy, the ruthlessness of Tiberius; courtiers quoted Tacitus and Machiavelli (often confusing the two); this was the essence of royal wisdom. At the same time, however, there were those who found in Tacitus precisely the strength to withstand the new secular tyrannies : Justus Lipsius, the founder of international law, and editor of the first modern edition of Tacitus's works; and Chénier, the French republican dramatist and poet, who declaimed : *"Son nom prononcé fait pâlir les tyrans."*

The French Revolution even saw the emergence of what one modern historian has called "Red Tacitism"—Tacitus as a sans-culotte; but by that time the idea of politics as being entirely profane and "realistic" was so taken for granted that interest was declining in Tacitus as a political mentor. Instead of being admired as a political sage, he began to be condemned as a nasty-minded and inaccurate historian. Politics was now safely profane; the need was to make it respectable. Tyrants were to be neither imitated nor opposed : the very idea of tyranny was to be abolished, along with the superstitions of those dark centuries that had never been able to elevate themselves sufficiently to see History and Humanity, but merely men and their deeds. It was Voltaire who sounded the cry, by charging Tacitus with "degrading humanity"; and Napoleon, naturally preferring the glory of tyranny to its gore, registered an indignant protest that in the *Annals* one found "nothing save accusations and men accused, persecutions and the persecuted, and people opening veins in baths". The historians of the nineteenth century followed suit and quickly engaged in a co-ordinated effort to convict Tacitus of historical error, in order to rehabilitate such Tacitean monsters as Tiberius, Nero, and Domitian. It was one of the greatest missionary enterprises in the history of scholarship, and one of the most successful. It is now as difficult to find a historian to speak ill of these men as it once was to find anyone to speak well of them (for even the new absolute monarchs never dared go so far). There is unanimity behind Mommsen's judgement that Tiberius was "the most capable emperor Rome ever had". And his latest biographer, Dr. Gregorio Marañon,* a physician-turned-historian, is as eager to "explain" Tiberius as any social worker is to "explain" a juvenile delinquent: he had suffered a childhood trauma when his mother divorced his father to marry Augustus, though sexually feeble he was married to a nymphomaniac, etc. etc. It all makes a plausible and, in a morbid way, fascinating case-book. It has the further advantage that we see the ulcerous and suppurating face of the man, rather than the smooth marble bust of the emperor that the professional historians seem to prefer. But in the end it comes to the same conclusion, that the portrait of Tiberius that Tacitus gives is little less than a slander.

What is striking about this revision of Tacitus is that it is necessarily based on Tacitus himself, since he is our only significant source for the history of the period: and it is Tacitus himself, too, who makes the work so relatively easy. Though he asserted that he wrote *sine ira et studio*, he certainly did not mean by this anything akin to the academic ideal of "objectivity". Evil he might be helpless before, but he could not fail to recognize it, and he assumed that those who did evil were themselves wicked. It is rare that he made a statement of fact about Tiberius without also making a more or less gross insinuation. Thus, we read: "About the same time a serious illness of Julia Augustus made it necessary for the Emperor [Tiberius] to hasten his return to the capital, the harmony between mother and son being still genuine, or their hatred concealed." Usually he was more subtle than this and there are many occasions when we have to read him very closely indeed to perceive that he has in fact denied what one thought he had said. But it is not at all difficult for a diligent scholar, by snipping off the "facts" from the "value judgements", to compose a new mosaic which is very different from the Tacitean original.

* *Tiberius: A Study in Resentment.* By Gregorio Marañon. Hollis and Carter. 25s.

To be sure, there remain the corpses, the murdered and mutilated and self-destroyed. These the scholar may dispose of, first, by counting them to demonstrate that their sum was less than astronomical, then by allowing for exaggeration, and finally by turning his attention to the Pax Romana, the efficient imperial administration, and all those other glorious things that make up History.

Now Tacitus had no idea that Tiberius and Nero were making a contribution to History. His problem was: how did they, and all of Rome with them, come to such depravity? His general answer was: under tyrannies men are unmanned: "The ties of our common humanity had been dissolved by the force of terror; and before each advance of cruelty, compassion receded." As for the tyrant, he is simply the most wicked of men—else why should he have become a tyrant in the first place? In this he was but repeating a commonplace of classical political philosophy, which took it for granted that men aspired to tyranny out of an evil impulse. That is why he felt no compunction in ascribing the worst motives to the tyrant's most innocent-looking actions.

We have lost the habit of judging tyrants so harshly, for we are more attentive to their historical rôles, their "objective" tasks, than to their human meanings. It is the supreme virtue of Tacitus that, as we read him, the mists of History fade away, and we see only "Persecutions and the persecuted, and people opening veins in baths".

MAY 1956

Part V
STORIES

EDMUND WILSON

The Messiah at the Seder

A MIDDLE-AGED GROUP of old friends had gathered for the Passover Seder. The host was the son of a rabbi and had studied for ordination in his youth at the Jewish Theological Seminary, but he now worked on the staff of a Jewish magazine. The men guests were a professor of Hebrew; a Viennese psychoanalyst; and a formerly active Marxist, who had fallen back on editing an encyclopædia. The scholar and the Marxist were accompanied by their wives, but the analyst was at present estranged from his, and the hostess's sister made the fourth woman : a handsome vivacious girl, somewhat younger than the others and unmarried. The Seder is designed to be a family affair, but it happened, on this occasion, that no children took part in the ceremony. Those of the host and hostess were under ten and had been put to bed; the Marxist and his wife were childless; the Hebraist's sons were married and living in other cities; and the adolescent son of the analyst had been carried off by his mother. Though parts of the Seder service are especially intended for children and cannot have their full effect without them, it was perhaps on this occasion, in view of what happened, just as well that there were no children present.

None of the company in their ordinary lives conformed with the observances of Orthodox Judaism. Only the professor and his wife practised a kosher cuisine, and the dinner tonight was not kosher. But most had had some schooling in Hebrew, and all had been brought up in the old way. All enjoyed celebrating this festival, which strengthened the family unit, re-enforced the ties among friends, affirmed the solidarity of the Jewish people. In all this it differed much from any feast-day or holy service of their neighbours, either Catholic or Protestant—for it combined a family party like Christmas dinner with a ritual of resurrection that resembled an Easter Mass. The men, although mostly beardless—the professor was the only exception—all wore, for the special occasion, the close-fitting round black caps that made them at home in the Jewish world, and all read aloud from the Haggadah, the traditional Hebrew text, of which each had a copy before him. Two of the wives, who knew no Hebrew, abstained, but the hostess and her sister participated, since they, also, were the children of a rabbi. This text, in its lyrical eloquence, its variety and its flexibility—for it ranges from rhymes for the children to exalted psalms in praise of God—its invocation of sanctions that dignify the meagrest meal, its exultant reawakening of the Jewish sense of consecration, which springs to life among the human actualities of the homeliest Jewish family, was felt by them all as a spell that involved the long dinner-table, white-naperied, gleaming with wine-glasses and studded with the red and yellow bottles that contained the ceremonial wine; and connected them—there in a modern apartment of uptown West-Side New York—with the legendary past of their people, or rather, with something that was scarcely for them either legendary or even past, since it still lived among them there, and that was not what had happened but what they were living. For, dealing with events that—in terms of our time—must have occurred four thousand years before, composed now in Biblical Hebrew, now in Aramaic of the Exile, now in the dialect of the Talmud, now borrowed from the hymns of the Middle Ages, blending Provence with Babylon, the Haggadah is timeless: excreted, as it is, by the anonymous process of centuries, it concentrates in one vibrant poem the despairs and the hopes of millennia.

The celebrants at a Seder are supposed to recline in the manner of a Roman banquet, but today this is only approximated by a cushion or two behind the host. The ritual this evening, to be sure, was a little cavalierly treated, but it is one of the charms of the Seder that it combines the petition and the pæan to God with a comfortable informality, and they had not had tonight any intimation that something of importance was due to occur. The Hebrew had been fluent, the singing quite good. Almost all knew the music from childhood, and they could pick up the ancient cadences as readily as the words of a prayer. The sister-in-law of the host had a fresh and silvery voice that caressed and enlivened the spirit. The host had blessed the banquet, and the first cup of wine had been drunk. The host had rinsed his hands in a fingerbowl, and the Karpas had been passed around: sprigs of parsley dipped in salt water that represented the bunches of hyssop, dipped in the blood of the Paschal lamb, which, on the eve of the Exodus from Egypt, were used to mark the doorways of the Israelites, so that the Angel of Death would pass by them. He had broken the middle Mazzah, a brittle unleavened biscuit, and had stuck away a piece of it in the cushions behind him, and, with the aid of his neighbours on either side, he had held up before him the tray on which lay the egg and the shankbone of lamb: "This is the bread of affliction that our fathers ate in the land of Egypt. All who are hungered—let them come to eat; all who are needy—let them come and celebrate the Passover. Now we are here, but next year may we be in the land of Israel! Now we are slaves, but next year may we be free men!"

The four questions were now asked—failing a child, by the youngest person present, who was the sister-in-law of the host: "How is this night different from other nights?" in respect to the four points of the ritual of dining—which leads to the announcement of the coming-forth from Egypt, with its pleasant little digression, the story of the five rabbis who sat up so late at night telling of this event that their pupils, the next morning, had found them still talking and had to summon them to morning prayer. Then the episode of the four sons: the clever one, the rude one, the simple one, and the one who is too young to know how to ask—to each of whom, in suitable terms, the meaning of the ritual must be explained. The goblets had been raised and put down, the Mazzoth covered and uncovered: the promise made to Abraham, the bondage in Egypt, the outcry to God, who remembers—"And God saw the children of Israel, and God knew"; the enumeration of the plagues of Israel, with a drop of wine spilled for each, and the summing-up of these by the strange mnemonic device—"the scorpion stung the uncle"—invented by the Rabbi Judah.

Then, the hymn of Thanksgiving to God, with its trumpet-like refrain "Dayéynu!" which raises the note of rejoicing at His benefits beyond hoping to Israel. They had eaten of the Mazzah, in remembrance of the bread, baked in haste without leaven, that their fathers had brought with them out of Egypt; of the Bitter Herb—a dish of horse radish— in memory of the bitterness of their misery in bondage, but sweetened by the Haroseth, a relish of chopped apples, raisins, and almonds—which stands for the mortar that the Israelite captives were forced to mix for their masters, and which has several other meanings as well. They had drunk the second glass of wine. They had rinsed their fingers in bowls and had listened to the benediction.

The hostess and her sister now brought on the dinner, for which each of the families present had provided one of the dishes. It began with the customary hard-boiled egg served in a bowl of salt water—at once a tongue-whetting *hors d'œuvre* and a reminder, again, of affliction, and went on to a main course of chicken, a permissible substitute for the Paschal lamb. They drank freely now, during dinner, in a non-ritualistic way, and the talk became very lively. They mingled discussion of current events with some effort to keep up the tradition of interpreting and analysing the service. They criticized the Jewish press, condemning it in all its departments, and not sparing the magazine of which their host was an editor. The analyst had some new jokes about Israel. The professor spoke with sharp severity of an eminent Jewish scholar, to whom he referred as "a *yeshiva bochar*". The sister-in-law, next to the analyst, allowed herself to play up to him with dark sidelong glances, and even to propound to him one of her dreams, of which he gave her a frivolous interpretation: "Right off the bat, I'd say that the big black dog was McCarthy, for whom you feel an unconfessed admiration." The wife of the Marxist at one point inquired the origin of the word *Afikoman*, applied to the section of Mazzah that the host hides behind his cushion, and it was explained to her that, according to the Mishnah, this was derived from one or the other of two Greek words meaning, respectively, a festal song and an after-dinner dessert. This piece of unleavened biscuit is eaten at the end of the banquet, and figures as a symbolic substitute for any further form of entertainment. It is forbidden, when the Seder is over, to go on to any other affair.

Now the ritual had been resumed with the comedy of this Afikoman. The fragment of Mazzah is supposed to have been stolen by the youngest child present from the cushions where the father has hidden it, and to be ransomed, at this point in the ceremony, for the minimum price of a quarter. But this evening the part had been played by the handsome sister-in-law, who took an audacious line. When the host had reached for the Afikoman, and had exclaimed that it must have been stolen, and when the sister-in-law had produced it and had been asked what she would take to give it back, she had answered that he could give her in return for it that map of the Middle East, with the names all printed in Hebrew, that he had been showing them before dinner. He managed not to commit himself clearly to this, but she handed him back the Afikoman, which was now broken into bits and handed around the table. Everybody ate a piece. To eat a large amount of the Afikoman is said to prolong life, but though some remembered this, no one did more than nibble. Now the invocation of blessings began again, and the third ritual cup was drunk. "Pour out Thy wrath," they chanted, "upon the heathen that have not known Thee, and upon the kingdoms that have not called upon Thy name : for they have devoured Jacob and have laid waste his dwelling-place. Pour out upon them Thine indignation and let Thy fierce anger overtake them. Pursue them in wrath and destroy them from under the heavens of the Lord."

At this point, the host left the table, went into the hall of the apartment, and opened the door into the outer hall. This was done for the Prophet Elijah, who circulates among his people and is present on certain occasions. A chair is set out for Elijah at the ceremony of circumcision, and is left there for three days, till the child is over the worst. At Passover, however, he had never yet come; he was expected—when the hour should arrive—to announce the Messiah's advent. When the fourth cup of wine was poured, a special silver goblet was also filled and set apart on the table for the prophet. This was called the Cup of the Redemption, because it was prepared for the moment when Israel should be redeemed and led back by the Messiah to its home in Jerusalem.

The host had regained his place, and they were proceeding with the chanting of the Haggadah when the professor of Hebrew, who was opposite the door, became aware that someone had entered, and, looking up, beheld a tall old man whom he took at first for an Arab. This visitor was dressed in a kind of white cloak that had long sleeves and came to his knees, and a headdress that was a large folded napkin with the ends crossed under his chin and tied on with a heavy cord. He wore sandals, and his bare legs were sinewy, sunburnt, and hairy. His face was as dark as dark leather, and his coarse hair and beard were untrimmed. The professor stopped reading, and everybody looked up. The old man stopped just inside the door and, throwing back his head, began to declaim in a voice somewhat high and nasal and with heavily marked rhythms that gave almost the effect of singing. It seemed to them that they recognized the language as Hebrew, but they could not make out what he was saying. The guttural sounds suggested to some that the language he was speaking was Arabic. It was only the concluding sentence that they definitely understood, for it contained two of the most familiar Hebrew nouns : "Peace will now come over the whole earth!"

"What a hideous travesty," the Hebraist thought, "of the ancient pronunciation!" He had read that among the Caucasian Jews it was a custom for some young man of the family to appear as a pilgrim come back from Jerusalem to tell them that the Redemption would not now be long, and he was not able to make up his mind whether one ought to resent a prank and say to the visitor, "That isn't funny!" or accept it as a possible feature of the Seder. In any case, it was up to their host. He remembered that the host's parents came from Southern Russia. He might perhaps himself have arranged this.

But now a second visitor presented himself, putting his hand on the old man's shoulder and making him stand aside. This was a lean but strong-shouldered little man, wearing the black Jewish skull cap and dressed in a blue double-breasted suit, who had high cheek-bones, a vehement chin and a fine, sharply beak-like nose. His pale complexion was flushed, and a look of obsessive intensity was sparked from his myopic green eyes, but when he spoke, it seemed plain that he was forcing himself to avoid an exalted tone.

"I don't know whether you got what he said," he began. "This is the Prophet Elijah. He's just announced my coming."

"And who are you?" demanded the scholar.

"The Messiah, believe it or not—You're sceptical. I think that we can soon convince you."

"I should question that," the Hebraist retorted, with a disagreeable smile. "Don't you know that the Messiah does not arrive till three days after Elijah's announcement?"

"If you really want to convince us," said the head of the house, smiling with more amiability, "you'll have to give us the Seven Miracles."

"Talmudic folk-lore!" said the visitor. "We don't need to bother with that. The more we speed things up the better. But you're worrying about credentials. Well, first of all, I'll give you my story." It was evident that he had it on tap. "There was nothing at all out of the ordinary about my early boyhood. I was a run-of-the-mill child prodigy. My father made middle-class furniture in Brooklyn. He was successful but he hadn't had an education, and he wanted to make up for it through me. I had mastered the calculus at eight—I played the cello and composed at ten. I graduated from college at thirteen and did advanced work in nuclear physics. But the day I became Bar Mitzvah—the night after I'd been at the synagogue—I was lying in bed—awake—and I heard a voice that called me: 'Shemuel! Shemuel!'—my name is Samuel—and I answered, 'Hineyni.' The Lord first spoke to me then. He told me I was to lead my people back to the land of Israel. Then, on May 14th, 1947—just seven years later, and forty-seven, notice—I heard the Voice speak to me again. It told me that a year from that day the big in-gathering would have begun and Israel would be proclaimed a free and independent state. I was just twenty-one at the time, and I was working on Long Island on the atom bomb. The Lord, blessed be He, told me again that I was to lead back my people to Jerusalem—that the nations were to be governed from Zion and peace was to come to the world—just what Elijah was telling you. I threw up my job then and fasted, and then—when I was weak with hunger—I was constantly in touch with the Lord. He told me to work for an organization that was raising money for Israel. That went on for seven years. Then came the final call—last year—the Eve of Passover and the day when Maimonides was born: Nisan 14—May 14, Nisan 14, and both double seven—it bridges the gap between the calendars—and that gave me conclusive proof that it wasn't an hallucination. Note also that, according to our calendar, it was the year 5714—seven and double seven. I was told that a year from that Passover the time would have come to save Israel and for Israel to save the world. I've been working on the project all year. In a sense, we worked it out together. But it's only the upshot that interests you, and that is that the Redemption is at hand—you must get transportation for Israel at the earliest possible moment. The arrangements haven't all been made yet, but there'll be extra planes and boats put on—about that I can be quite positive. Well, there you have the story, and if you don't accept me now, you will a little later on, when the Power behind me begins to work. In the meantime, just to look at our friend here"—and he put his hand on Elijah's shoulder—"ought to say something to you."

The old man, while the Messiah was talking, had been looking around the room with his dark and transfixing eyes, trained like guns from beneath shaggy eyebrows and flanking a magistral Hebraic nose. The young man quickly slipped aside and took down from the dining-room wall a Picasso and a Modigliani, which he set on the floor behind him, with their faces against the wall.

"I didn't want him to be smashing them," he said. "He might think they were Baal or something."

The host's handsome sister-in-law began to feel rather self-conscious. She was wearing large dangling earrings and a bright-red damask gown. Personal adornments, of course, were permitted by the Talmud if properly made, and she remembered that there were earrings in the Bible, but Elijah did look terribly austere. Even if he were not Elijah, but just some insane fanatic, one would hate to be blasted by him! She dropped her eyes to the table: had she really been thinking, she wondered, about having an affair with the analyst?

"Won't you please sit down," said the host. He brought in chairs from another room, and his wife made places for the visitors. He was by no means persuaded of their authenticity but—well versed in rabbinical lore —it came back to him, as the old prophet took his seat and sat erect with one hand on his knee and the other in a kind of pocket that was formed at his breast by a fold of his cloak, that the pious Rabbi Judah of Regensburg had once, at a certain circumcision, been able to perceive that Elijah was absent from his appointed chair, which had augured—it proved, truly —that the child would abandon the Jewish faith. He could not, in any case, but be glad that the visitors had found them at their correct observances. His wife was a little embarrassed at having chicken instead of lamb, and she had hesitated about offering them the non-kosher dinner, but the host now invited them to eat.

"Not for me," said the young man, "but the Prophet might like a snack. This is the first time he's come to a Seder, and I think he'd enjoy eating something." A brief question in Hebrew brought a nod from the old man. The hostess went to heat up something, and in the meantime the formidable visitor, casting his eye about, identified the goblet set out for him and drained it at a single draught. This a little astonished the host, for the time had not yet come in the ceremony when the fourth cup of wine is drunk; but he remembered from Second Kings 23:22 that between the days of the Judges and the very late reign of Josiah no Passover had ever been celebrated—so that Elijah would not know the ceremony—although wasn't the ritual itself even much later than that?—the four cups of wine, he thought, had been mentioned first in the Mishnah.

But such questions were blurring in his mind. Had he drunk too many glasses at dinner, besides the ceremonial three? Or was he actually feeling the Power of which the young man had spoken, the Power behind him and Elijah? Did they not both have a radiance about them?—did they not, together, create a field in which was intensified and rarefied the yellow electric light? From the moment they sat down at the table, it was impossible not to treat them with deference. They brought silence, imposed themselves. It seemed most difficult to ask them questions. Yet the thought had dawned in every mind that the self-presented Messiah was one of those forced infant prodigies who break down from precocious effort. Had not the nocturnal call of the Lord been suggested by his name, Samuel? The analyst had been watching him shrewdly, had noted that he had left off the glasses without which he was nearly blind in order to make a better impression, that he had had some experience in public speaking and, physically so unprepossessing, had acquired certain tricks of tone to propitiate and win an audience. Yet the gaze now laid bare by the discarding of his lenses had about it something fervent and gentle that first touched one, then evoked respect; his passion, so determinedly repressed, as he told about his call from God, seemed to burn away a commonness of accent.

The analyst itched to examine him, to lay bare the links of suggestion, the mechanism of instinct and impasse which had braced him to the strength of his delusion. He himself had been very careful not to push his own son too much; but then his wife, once a patient of his, had messed the relationship up, and might, he feared, make the boy another neurotic. The childless wife of the scholar was wondering whether her husband, a despotic and pitiless pedant, would have tried to turn their boy into a prodigy, and, having sometimes indulged herself in the dream of an ambitious son who would become a big business executive, was just as glad she had not had to risk it. The hostess, bringing on the hot plate, had asked the young man again whether he was sure he would not have a snack —she could see he was starving himself. "There's no fasting on Passover," she smiled. But he dismissed it with a negative nod. She thought of her own fat-cheeked children : she would never, she told herself, allow them to go rocketing out of her orbit; but maybe his parents were dead!

A constraint fell upon the whole company. The Marxist was the first to break through it. "Let us ask you a practical question"—he put it to the Messiah as man to man : "Do you expect all the Jews in the world—all the Jews that aren't in Israel already—to emigrate with you there?"

"In the long run, we certainly expect it, but we're not giving everyone the call tonight."

"May I ask what your principle of selection is?"

"Only those that are holding Seders. We figure that we at least have a chance with *them*. They include, of course, a number of non-believers, or people who *think* that they are, but the fact that they celebrate Passover would indicate that their ties with Judaism are not completely severed."

"Will you have the time to call on every Seder—tonight or tomorrow night?"

"I visit many Seders simultaneously. Between 7 a.m. today and 7 tomorrow morning, I am visiting every Seder from Oslo to Valparaiso."

This stopped the questioner for only a second. "How do you manage that?"

"How do Milt Berle and Monsignor Sheen manage to appear at the same time on every TV screen in New York?"

"That's only a projected photograph, but you're present with us here in this room, and you say that you're also present at a number of other Seders."

"That's correct. You can see me here; you can hear me; I can handle those pictures; but all the time my real basic self is at my headquarters on Ninety-Second Street directing the whole thing."

"I see," said the Marxist.

The analyst took it up: "Can you tell us how this is accomplished?"

"You wouldn't be able to grasp it. It hasn't been worked out by man, so the steps would be unintelligible. I don't understand it myself. It's only the Lord, blessed be He, who makes it possible for me to do all this."

Another queer but apposite reference came back into the mind of the host. The learned Lipmann-Mülhausen, in his *Sepher ha-Nizzahon*, had dealt with precisely the problem of the appearance of the Prophet Elijah simultaneously in different places, and had disposed of practical objections in terms of the pervasion of sunlight and the ubiquity of the Angel of Death.

"But supposing," pursued the Marxist, "that your call is successful tonight. There surely isn't room in Israel for all the dispersed Jews holding Seders."

"We won't be confined to the present area."

"How so?"

"Well, just give a thought to those plagues you've been reading about in the Haggadah. You're going to pick up the paper tomorrow and see that all the Arabs are dropping dead."

The Marxist could not help smiling; the Hebrew scholar sneered. The analyst asked a question in his professional matter-of-fact way: "And how will *that* be accomplished? Bacteriological warfare?"

"You're a long distance behind us again. It's done by a simple vibration —but not, in the crude sense, electrical. Don't worry about the humanitarian angle: death is instantaneous."

"You'll have a disposal problem," suggested the Marxist.

"The bodies crumble to dust. They blow away and mix with the sand."

"Will the other countries," the Marxist inquired, "accept Jewish hegemony? If I understand you, that's what you aim at."

"They will see we have the Lord behind us, and our prestige will rapidly increase."

"You're not afraid," the Marxist pressed him, "that pulverizing all the Arabs will create a bad impression?"

"It'll be the most conspicuous miracle since the crossing of the Red Sea. Who cares about Pharaoh's army?"

"I'm interested"—the host changed the subject—"in the theological aspect. Is there to be a Day of the Lord?"

"There is."

"Would you care to develop that subject? Maimonides tells us that the dead are to rise."

"We can't do anything with that at the present time. We've already got enough mixed elements. And even with the formerly Arab areas, we're not able to accommodate everybody—the dead as well as the living."

"What about reward and punishment?" the hostess's sister asked. She had already had two serious love affairs, one with a married man.

"Yes," said the host: "we read in Saadia that everyone will be steeped in a divine fire, and that this fire will shine for the redeemed without burning them, but eternally burn the unredeemed without shining on them."

"Saadia is not the last word. Maimonides is not the last word," the Messiah replied with assurance.

"But there *will* be reward and punishment?"

"Correct. There will be what I have termed an Assize of Exclusion— exclusion on rigorous principles."

"What will happen to the people excluded?"

"Will they be pulverized?" inquired the analyst.

"Only Arabs will be pulverized," the Messiah replied. "Jews who are unredeemed will not be permitted to live in Israel."

"And you," said the analyst quietly, "are to be the judge of Redemption?"

"With the help of the Lord, yes."

"I am wondering," said the host, "how these things are to be decided. If it is a question of observance of the Law, there is nobody in this room who would qualify."

"So far as observances go, we have of course adapted ourselves to the

modern developments of Judaism. A good many of the observances, as the
Name well knows, have long ago outlived their usefulness; some are unscientific. There's no question of discrimination against members of Conservative or Reformed congregations—or even against good Jews who
don't go to the Temple at all. But a minimum of observance we do demand
—that's why we begin at the Seder. The Commandments, however, are a
different matter. That's where we go along with Maimonides. Grave in-
fractions will be hard to outweigh."

"But of course you will have other criteria?" the Marxist asked a little
aggressively.

"Of course : our decisions will be made in accordance with a code of
morality which has been formulated by strict definitions."

"It hardly seems fair," said the host, "that we shouldn't have been told
about this." His wife, the rabbi's daughter, firmly backed him up : "If
we've never been told this code, how could we know that we were violating
it?" "And they're asking us to go back," thought her sister, still uneasy
on the score of the Seventh Commandment, "with the risk of being thrown
out!"

"It's based on the Ten Commandments, and it conforms to the best
tradition of Judaism. It's an extension of the Commandments themselves.
We interpret them in such a way as to take into account the new conditions that have come to prevail since they were first handed down. That's
all I can tell you now."

"Couldn't you give us an idea," asked the analyst, "of the way in which
this system of interpretation would work in a specific instance?"

"It's useless to discuss it," the Messiah declared. "You'll be able to learn
something about it when you see it applied in practice. But actually you'll
never be able fully to comprehend it. The wisdom of the Lord, as you know,
passes understanding. Even the greatest prophets could not compass all
His aims and methods, and even I, who am admitted to His confidence,
must fall short of the full revelation. I've helped Him to organize the
Judgement in an orderly and practical way, but for difficult decisions I
must go to Him."

This seemed to arouse the Marxist, who, brusquely, took a bolder line.
"You've spoken," he said, "of your training in the mathematical sciences,
and also, to some extent, in music. Are we to take it for granted that you're
equally at home in all the arts and professions?"

"Potentially, yes; but that's irrelevant. Our judgement in any given case
is strictly a moral matter : it doesn't involve the specific skill in which
the individual may be proficient."

"I ask because I don't understand how it is possible to judge an individual working in any field without thoroughgoing training in that field, life-long experience of it. Morality that is correct implies correct doctrine. Admittedly, as you were saying, the Torah and the Talmud—including the Commandments—are codes that belong to the earlier phases of social-economic development. They are useless to guide us today among the con-tradictions of modern society, the mazes of modern politics. And how can social theory, how can political procedure, be judged by a professional physicist? I assume that you are not a Marxist. For a Marxist it would have been quite impossible to work even a day, even an hour, in a labora-tory making the bomb!"

"Marx is one of our prophets——"

"Exactly: the greatest of our prophets. But one has to study Marxist theory, to become adept at Marxist practice, in order to know how to dis-criminate between the true and the false. The false is sometimes subtly disguised: to detect it is not so easy. It is obvious, for example, that Stalinists—Stalinists of whatever complexion, and along with them, the heirs of Stalin—are summarily to be condemned. I should myself be glad to see them destroyed. But we are not to conclude from this that all the adherents of Trotsky are necessarily to be admitted: there are few of them —very few—who could make out a case for themselves as candidates for Redemption——"

"How about the Weinburgites, Harry?" the host interrupted with a mischievous look. "Have we got to let them all in?"

"I am raising a serious question," the Marxist, put out, replied. He had passed, without taking account of it, from an attitude of sophisticated scepticism to an acceptance of the crisis as real.

"I'm in fundamental agreement with Harry," the analyst intervened, "except that I'm an orthodox Freudian instead of belonging to a splinter sect."

"Weinburgism is normative Marxism . . ."

"All right: well, in just the same way, Freudianism for me is norma-tave Freudianism—correct psychoanalytic theory. Sigmund Freud is another of our prophets—You would agree to that, wouldn't you?" He turned to the Messiah.

"In a sense, yes: I grant you——"

"In the deepest sense. And Freud has been as badly betrayed by those who professed to follow him as Marx or Moses has. I should not care to see any of these betrayers redeemed any more than Harry would the Stalinists." His debonair manner was ebbing and allowing to break through its surface the rock of fundamental conviction. "These loose and sloppy impostors, who disregard the discipline of the Freudian method, who cannot see the inevitability of the fundamental Freudian conceptions—who indulge and ruin their patients, who trifle with them and take their money, who leave them in the moral abasement of their unresolved complications, because they cannot face the problems themselves—these problems that require effort, self-mastery, objective thinking—because they cannot face these problems, which involve unpleasant realities and difficult readjustments, any better than the patients can—such quacks should be treated as criminals! I should be glad to see them all pulverized, beginning with Jung! And here I agree in principle with what my friend has just said. It is impossible to judge of such matters unless one has been a practising analyst."

"You forget," the Messiah retorted, rising to the challenge to combat, "that I have behind me One who has spoken to Marx and Freud, and who can judge the deviations of their followers better than you can do."

"You forget," said the Marxist, "that every good Jew has that One behind him."

"When we get around to the dead"—the Messiah took higher ground —"Freud and Marx will themselves be judged."

"And the Prophets?" cried the Hebraist. "Are *they* to be judged?"

Though the scholar had for a long time been silent, no one of the company present was more resistant than he. He had been scrutinizing Elijah as the old man ate, and the suspicion of his authenticity had seemed to him conclusively confirmed. There is a Biblical word for knife—*m'akhelet*— which is evidently derived from the verb *to eat*, and this has been taken as evidence that the instrument was used at meals. Jealous of the credit of the ancient Jews as pioneers of civilization, the professor was strongly of this opinion, and when he had seen the ninth-century Elijah tearing the chicken apart with his fingers, he had with difficulty repressed his indignation. As the argument grew more heated, this burst. "But this alleged prophet here," he followed up, "it is certainly permitted to judge. I will give you my own judgement. No such Hebrew jargon as his was ever spoken in ninth-century Israel, nor anywhere else then or since. This we know with complete certainty!" He turned to Elijah and addressed him in Yiddish: "Haven't I seen you on the stage at the Yiddish theatre?"

Elijah looked up from his plate, then glanced at the Messiah for explanation.

"You mustn't say such things to him," the young man warned the professor. "He's never learned any Yiddish—in spite of all the circumcisions he's been to—but he might think you're not being respectful."

The little professor, however, was unable to contain himself. "Tell me" —he renewed the charge, this time speaking in Hebrew pronounced in accordance with his own system—"did you learn that language from the ravens?"

"Look out!" said the Messiah. "Don't do it!"

"Ravens?" the Prophet repeated, lifting his eyebrows in a piercing smile and stretching out both hands towards the viands. "I have no need of ravens here!"

"He thinks you're being hospitable," the young man said. "Now, let it go at that. Have the sense to let him alone."

"I simply want to put it on record," said the Hebraist, speaking to the company in English, "that I do not accept their pretensions. I regard them as bare-faced frauds—contemptible blasphemous frauds!"

"Listen!" the Messiah protested. "He still stands high with the Name. Remember what happened to those heathen cultists, when their god let them down on Mount Carmel!"

"Yes: lay off, Lou," intervened the host.

"Well," said the Messiah, rising, "there's no need for us to stay any longer. I'll be seeing you all before long. Any doubts you may still have tonight will, I think, be dispelled tomorrow."

Elijah arose and blessed them. He and the Messiah—in the general silence—left the apartment together, the young man closing the hall door behind them.

"Let's not argue now," said the host. "Let's finish the Seder first."

They took up the Haggadah where they had left it off; went through the thanksgiving hymns punctiliously and rather subduedly. The final words, "To next year in Jerusalem"—familiar though they were—frightened some, put an unexpected question to all. Out of bravado, the Marxist and the analyst—assisted by the vivacious sister-in-law—struck up the children's rhyme, the *Had Gadya*, that parallels *The House that Jack Built*, but this was allowed to peter out.

No one wanted to speak of what had happened. "Well," said the host at last—putting a half-humorous matter-of-fact face on it—"we'll be able to check in the morning whether the Arabs are dropping dead."

But though by this time it was well past midnight, nobody dared to suggest going out to buy a morning paper, and all the guests very soon left.

The Messiah came to himself in his room on East Ninety-Second Street. It was at first an agony of reintegration, of recalling, and concentrating in his own single person, the projected multiple selves that had visited the thousands of Seders. Fatigue, incoherence, unbearable strain : gasping from the efforts of self-dispersal, the pangs of organic self-reconstitution, he felt at moments that he could not survive, that he was losing his hold on the world. Then at last he became aware, in the grey early-morning light, of the familiar equipment of his room. He was lying on the wooden bed—close to the floor, with no headboard or footboard—that he had had a local carpenter knock together for him; and, opposite, against the wall, stood a desk, bought at second-hand, stuffed and piled with his folders and papers. There were also a small bookcase and some second-hand filing-cabinets. On the wall were hung a photograph of Zion and, spread out, the embroidered prayer-shawl he had worn at his confirmation. On a chair beside the bed lay a paper bag, a pasteboard container for coffee, and the glazed-paper wrapper of a chopped-egg sandwich with which he had fortified himself just before taking off for his visits. The foody smell of these was repellent. On a shelf he caught sight of the alarm clock which he had set for seven the night before, in case he should be still in his trance. He could not make out the time. Had it just gone off without his having heard it? Was it still to go off? He shuddered. How it would crash like a rocket-bomb on his already tortured nerves. Yet he did not reach for his glasses.

At this moment, the alarm exploded. He made himself rise to his feet, snatched the clock from the shelf and turned it off. He sat a moment on the side of the bed, then he lay down again. Ignorant of the ravages of dissipation, he had known the abysmal depletions that follow intellectual excess. But the recovery from these had been hastened by the sense of accomplishment, triumph; the tissues of the mind soon mended. This morning there was a lesion that did not heal; a horror of failure, of bafflement, lay at the back of his aching brain. He shrank from assembling his experiences, reliving them, extracting their meaning. He tried to curb his natural quickness of mind, to lapse into stupor, to dull his wits. But inertia, self-obfuscation were repugnant to him, impossible for him. Spasmodically, with dim fits of fainting, the powers of his mind revived. More and more swiftly and deftly, like one who sifts the contents of an auction-room or sorts out a stacked correspondence, he examined, correlated, analysed his visits of the night before. But below the rapid movements of his mind the conviction of his mission lay stunned.

Then a deathly collapse engulfed him: "Rejected!" he exclaimed to himself. "Rejected! I ought to have expected it! They resisted me, repulsed me, mocked me. It's I who am the Suffering Servant of Isaiah, despised and rejected of men!"

But he pulled himself together, sat up, and summoning, affirming the formulas of prayer, he appealed to the Lord aloud.

"I have failed, my Lord," he said. "Your servant is sick in spirit."

Silence: a terrible fear made the young man sit tense on the edge of the bed, hardly daring to breathe.

Then came the expected Voice, filling, including the room: "You will be made whole again."

"But it hasn't worked out as we thought it would."

Silence: his desperate dread compelled the poor boy to go on, to revert to the self-confident tone with which he had talked to the Deity when he had first unfolded his plans: "Let me give you the picture as I see it. Undoubtedly you can throw more light on it—I beg Thee," he quickly added, lest he seem to qualify Omnipotence, "that Thou wilt aid me to understand Thy will."

"To begin with the Orthodox end: they would give one look at me and throw me out—on account of no earlocks and beard. Well, we more or less anticipated that. I thought—and I believe you approved—that, on the whole, it was more important to make the modernized ones feel at ease, and anyway that was the note we wanted to strike. I was counting on Elijah—though I'd never seen him then—to put it over with the Orthodox, but the trouble is that, being so first-millennial, so rugged, so much the product of a primitive outdoor life, he doesn't look much more like their idea of a Jew than I do. They thought he was crazy and I was a fake. In fact, that's what most of them thought. But the worst of it is that none of them—or almost without exception—is willing to accept my authority. They will accept their rabbi's authority, but—much as they pretend to adore you—they won't recognize the Over-all Power. That's the trouble with a church with no hierarchy. The Catholics could swing it, but we've got no machine. Those fanatical old-timers in Mea Shearim won't accept the Chief Rabbi of Jerusalem. They set their own rabbi up against him, and they couldn't think of imagining a Day of the Lord in which anyone but themselves would come out on top. Of course, they're the lunatic fringe, but it's the same with all the Orthodox as against the Reformed. If we got the emigration started, they'd organize resistance against it; they'd work up a counter-propaganda and denounce me as another Sabbatai Zevi. And even those who have no worship are carrying the same narrow spirit into whatever their department is. The Marxists and the analysts and the scholars of every kind all seem to have their element of Mea Shearim. Every field has its own sects, its own rabbis, and the followers of any rabbi can't face the possibility that the disciples of another rabbi may be counted among the righteous. Why, there's even a music expert—a disciple of the Rabbi Schoenberg—who wants to exclude from Redemption all the modern composers who don't practise the pure twelve-tone system. He told me he would refuse absolutely to recognize the competence of our Final Assize unless I could give him the assurance that neither Bloch nor Milhaud would be passed. There's even a literary critic—a rabbi himself, with his own disciples—who says that he can't run the danger of finding himself assigned to a category which might include certain critics who don't subscribe to his doctrine. The core of that doctrine is that—evaluating in moral terms—there are only five novelists in English whose work can be taken seriously.

"And I'm speaking now only of the people that we thought we could more or less count on! You know how the rest of them are. They don't want to go to Israel at all, except maybe for a tourist trip. These city lawyers and doctors and men who have built up businesses—half the time they don't care anything about Judaism. They're making good money somewhere or they're good at their work or both, and beyond that they don't want to be bothered. The only group, so far as I can see, that shows any real interest in the project are the unsuccessful small business and professional men who still go to the synagogue and who hope to better themselves. They think that, when the Day of the Lord comes, their piety may get them further than their abilities ever have. They and a few very young people who go to Hebrew-speaking summer camps and are passionately patriotic about Israel. But nobody else is with us. There's nothing like the response we hoped for."

The Voice replied—the young man listened, in spite of his jaunty tone, with anxious and taut attention. "You must not say 'we'," the Voice chided. "I was never so hopeful as you. I am no longer quite omniscient, as I used to be. Mankind sometimes gets away from me, as I never allowed it to do in the days of Eden and Babel. I have had my forebodings and doubts."

His confidence in his Deity not fortified, the Messiah fell to blaming his people. "The Jews," he came out with it, "could never agree, and why should we—why should *one* ever expect them to lay off their disputation even in the shadow of the Judgement Day? But the Exile, the Diaspora have aggravated this weakness. I am sure you are fully aware of the harm that has been done them by Protestantism. Living in Protestant countries, they have taken over the Protestant habits of thought: the idea of deciding for oneself, following one's own conscience, setting oneself up as a judge. Even among those who trust in Thee, blessed be Thy Name, each of them wants to feel that he's got his own private line to you. They're getting to be just like the Protestants—they believe in themselves, not you. Yet they got it out of our Bible—in a way it's there—and if it's there, you—Thou didst put it there. After all, Thou spokest to all kinds of people—Amos the shepherd or anybody could turn out to be a prophet. You must—Thou needst must have known what would eventually happen."

The Voice did not speak for some time. The young man dropped his face and covered his eyes, assuming a reverent attitude but leaving the point he had made.

Then it answered: "Did it ever occur to you that you yourself are lacking in faith, that you have become disrespectful in addressing Me, that you've taken a good deal into your own hands, and that, now that the result does not satisfy you, you are showing a reprehensible impertinence in attempting to take Me to task?"

It was the turn of the Messiah to be silent.

"I am an unworthy servant, Lord!" he cried. "Forgive me for forgetting that, weak though I am, Thy hand will be strong to uphold me. We'll see how they all feel tomorrow when they read about what's happened to the Arabs."

"The Arabs will be spared," said the Voice.

"They'll be spared? But I've promised they would be destroyed. You can hardly go back on that!"

"That would do no good now. If My people do not believe, this sign would not bring them to Zion. They will simply be convinced that the Middle East is a dangerous place to live."

"But if all the Jews are spared?"

"I have some reputation for justice—though I believe you were implying a moment ago that I had not dealt justly with you. The Arabs, at the hands of My people, have already suffered some injustice, and many of My people know it. Why wipe them all out for no end?"

"Wouldn't the world be better without them?"

"They, too, have learned from My Word—they worship Me, too, in their fashion."

The Messiah curbed himself from retorting: "You're getting entirely too broad-minded!"

"But what a garbling it is of Thy Word!" was what he exclaimed aloud.

"You pity your own disappointment," answered God, partly quoting Himself, "and shall I not pity Ishmael, that great people of more than twenty million persons, who hardly know their right hand from their left, and also many camels?"

In the irritation caused by dismay, the young man had the impulse to sneer: "Do you have to give me those old gags?" But what he asked was, "There's not to be a Judgement Day?"

"Not at once."

"Am I still the Messiah?"

"You must live like any other man."

"But I've built my whole life up to this—ever since you first called me, ever since I became Bar Mitzvah!" He had to rein himself in again not to cry out, "You can't do this to me! I might have succeeded in the Gentile world. I could have been a big commercial physicist. I was working on the bomb when you took me away—I was one of the coming men. Now I can never go back : after tonight, I'll be listed as a screwball. You wouldn't let me make good with the goys, and now I can't lead my people back to Israel. What do you expect me to do?" But what he said was, "My Lord, be blessed to eternity. Thy servant has failed Thee : forgive him, I beg, and direct him to the path of righteousness. Where shall I turn next?"

"Go back to your old work," said the Voice. "Go on raising money for Israel. Maybe some good will come of it."

OCTOBER 1956

417

NADINE GORDIMER

A Thing of the Past

THE HOUSE IN MAADI was as quiet as it had been in the days when they were all out of it, going about their business and their pleasure; yet they were all there. Madame Achilet played patience behind the bougainvillaea on the veranda and did not lift her eyes if someone walked past. Irene was writing in the big studio on the roof. Her husband Max was in the darkened library. Even when the children were home from school the great empty garden took their voices like depthless green waters swallowing a handful of coins.

Who was dead? No one—the old man, Achilet Pasha, whose wealth had made the wonderful garden, had died years ago. But the house was dead; the sort of life that had fed it was gone. Irene's husband Max, who had nothing to do all day, sometimes had the fantasy that he was the last white man left in Africa. He sat among the dim shapes behind the shutters and felt himself alone, not only in Egypt, but in the whole continent.

It was not true, of course, that the Achilet family were alone even in Cairo. There were a few others who had missed the exodus of the foreign community that had begun when the King was banished and reached its peak after the Suez Canal was nationalized; but these others were merely stragglers, and they were leaving one by one, month by month. The Alexandria Achilets had gone, and Irene's brothers and their families; the aunts had gone, and the old Pasha's brother. Of all the big and powerful family, with its French, Greek and Jewish antecedents, only Irene and her small family remained. "I'm a hostage," Irene would explain to infrequent visitors, with her pealing, fidgety laugh that ended or interrupted everything she said. She was a soft woman of thirty-eight, with the special liveliness of an inherited emotional temperament that had been nurtured in an atmosphere of indulgence and privilege. Like many people who have had it too good, she had courage. It took the form, in her, of the show of a refusal to change. She pulled a face at each fresh notice of sequestration; she shrugged her shoulders and laughed over her own efforts to help her children do their homework in the new medium of instruction, Arabic, that they had had to accustom themselves to since the French school was closed; she wore about the silent house the gay pants and clinging shirts that, other years, she had worn on the Riviera. She was no longer young, and the lines of her pretty, sallow face, with the big black, amusing eyes, had softened and sagged, like the small, voluptuous lines of her body. "Irene feels she can't go while she can do something for the others by hanging on," her husband would explain. Irene hadn't lost *all* her property; there was the house in Maadi among other things. She still had some influence, and some connections, too, and as long as she stayed in Egypt she had the chance of getting a trickle of compensation out to her brothers and those other members of the family who had been completely dispossessed. The moment she packed up and left, of course, she would have to leave everything behind her.

It often seemed to Max, her husband (alone in the shuttered library), that, apart from the money, there would be nothing left to leave behind, soon. The old lady, Madame Achilet, had built herself a house of cards to shelter a shadow; the spirit of the children was camping out, without a home—and he, himself, and Irene? It was difficult to judge, with Irene. She was the third generation of her family to be born in Egypt. Even though she did not belong to Egypt—was part of that expendable, exotic life of the cities—she seemed to have been conditioned, by the lives of the people, of whom she had never been in the least aware, to something of their acceptance of the passing of kings and palaces and the successive waves of conquering hordes. There could be no other explanation for her wry and yet almost cheerful, unnoticing submission to the silent house. She was writing a play, she said; she had always been writing a play, she had taken it up and put it down like a piece of embroidery, between entertaining, spending the summer in Europe and the winter in Switzerland or Luxor. It was hard to imagine that the play would ever be finished, or could hope to fill the long days. For himself, her husband was an architect, and as a foreigner, no longer allowed to practise his profession. He went on working at home, for a time; he drew plans for all those buildings that no client had ever wanted. And then this sense of freedom went out, no star but a child's rocket. He went to play golf every morning with someone else who was hanging on; a woman as idle as he was, who tried to attract him into the pastime of an affair. Then he began to follow the routine that looked as if it would last. Every morning after breakfast he walked once or twice round Achilet Pasha's tropical garden, and then he shut himself in the library and pulled the shutters against the heat. Rolls of plans glowed redly, like tunnels in the dimness; they grew brittle as time went by, and the edges were ragged where the servant's duster brushed them. His own hands sometimes touched against them, too. He sat at the desk and smoked. Sometimes he read a little from the middle of any book taken out of the shelf behind him. He dozed. Idleness was a dungeon into which he had been flung.

"Perhaps we'll hang on long enough for things to be all right again, and everyone will be able to come back," said Irene gaily, with one of her eloquent shrugs. "Who knows?"

Her husband looked as if he hadn't heard, but behind his quiet, bored face he was experiencing a moment of passionate horror. They had floated like oil on the thin, poor life of the country—Irene, himself, all of them. Lately he had begun to struggle with a guilt like nausea, at the surfeit of the life that he had lived. He turned away his head and swallowed, as if someone had thrust a piece of corpse-meat at his mouth.

Irene came over and picked up his hand. She laughed and her breasts lolled apart under her cotton sweater. "Come on, now," she said cheerfully, "things just as unlikely have happened here before now, darling. It's not at all impossible, eh?"

Max Leonard was a South African and it was through the war that he had come to marry Irene Achilet. It sounded a pretty brazen sort of story, but it was a common one in all countries that the war touched, and at the time it had happened very simply, without much thinking and perhaps without any real volition on anyone's part. Irene had been married before, very young, to a young Frenchman. He was an archæologist, and when he arrived in Egypt he had come to Achilet Pasha's house on an introduction from someone in Paris. Irene was eighteen, just back from school in France herself, and in that state of innocent excitability that is often the first and sometimes the strongest state of sexual attractiveness in a girl. She and Jules Sidon walked straight into a trance of delight in each other; he could not possibly have been expected to resist her and the trap she did not even know she had set was waiting to take him. It was impossible for them not to finger each other (she had to pinch the lobe of his clean ear, he had to feel out the bend of her elbow) in a kind of birds' dance of courtship, and old Achilet saw that it was hopeless to oppose the youthful marriage. They were married and Irene trailed off into the desert behind Sidon to love him at night in his tent. He had thought the world consisted of digging and studying what was dug up, before he was confronted with Irene, and now thought that it consisted of digging, studying, and Irene. All day she wandered about the digging site in a pair of Sidon's old khaki trousers, with her hair tied up in a rag of a scarf and her face oiled against the winter sun. She did not worry Sidon but sometimes he explained some shard or carved fragment to her as if he were training some new male assistant sent out from the Institute in Paris. In summer they lived in the house in Maadi that Irene's father had built for them, and often Sidon would put aside his cataloguing and writing and drive out with her to sleep the night in the desert. Sidon knew no human beings other than the ancient Egyptians and Irene Achilet; and then the war came, and all the others crowded in.

Sidon was called back to France and he went into the army. Irene stayed at home in Cairo. She went to meet him once, in Beirut, when they managed to spend two weeks together. And then for nearly three years, while France fell, while he fought now in this country, now in that, they did not see each other. The house in Maadi was lent to the British Army as a convalescent home, and Irene moved into a flat overlooking the Nile. She wrote letters to Sidon, she drew up a reading plan for herself, to study archæology, and she took her part in the elaborate social life of the foreign community to which she belonged, and which had received fresh impetus in the entertainment of the men the war had brought to Egypt. She was very young still, and soon Sidon had been away for a longer time than she had lived with him. She was terrified that he would die, but then the years went by and he didn't die, and her terror subsided. There were thousands of people living as she lived; it seemed to be the natural order of things that men should dine and talk and drink not with their own women, but with the women of other men, who, in their turn, were in the company of yet other women, on another side of the world.

She met the South African captain, Max Leonard, in the house of her uncle in Alexandria, and later, when he was in Cairo on leave, he came to see her. She invited him to dinner with other friends, they went out dancing together. The next time he came to Cairo on leave, it was suddenly quite different, he called and sat stiffly on the terrace, and she did not know what to say. The old tension—the silent whirlpool drawing them to its centre—that had existed so uniquely, so extraordinarily between Sidon and her : she felt it again, quite simply, with this man who wasn't Sidon. He wasn't at all like Sidon, she didn't feel any of the other things that she had felt about Sidon, the things that very young girls feel—but she felt this. She went away with Max Leonard for a week-end, somewhere un-likely—Port Said, of all places—and she felt contented, gay, and lazy. There were many other affairs like it at the time; they were interludes of peace and happiness in the displacement of feelings that distresses people in war. They were sexual and innocent; and sometimes the partners became friends, as well. Whenever he could get away from the desert, Max lived at the flat with her. Sometimes Max indulged in fantasies about a future life with her, but they were not painful. "If I could take you to South Africa with me, I'd show you some things that'd have you gasping," he said, with affectionate reference to her quick enthusiasms, "I'd take you up the Drakensberg with the pack ponies right over into Basutoland. I'd take you to the Congo. I'd drive you all round the Cape Peninsula, we'd get a cottage in a fishing village——" She laughed and wrinkled her nose. "I'd rather take you skiing in Switzerland. Right up to one of the small villages. I bet you'd learn quickly. I'd rather have the snow."

When Irene's husband Sidon came back at last, Max was in the Western Desert, not a day's drive from Cairo. Irene and her family met Sidon and went back to the old Achilets' house for a celebration lunch. After lunch Irene and Sidon went into the garden to stroll and talk; it was the first time that they were alone together. Sidon, with his curly fair hair and his glasses that seemed to concentrate his gaze on her, as if she were some beautiful limestone head suddenly freed from the sand of the past, said to her, "Irene, I couldn't write and tell you. For the last eight months I've been having an affair with a woman in England. I must tell you now."

"Oh Jules," she said, "I know! I know!"

"Irene, what's the matter?" Sidon was stiff and pale.

"I've been having—I had something like that myself. I couldn't write, either."

Sidon was silent. He looked up quickly, aware, at the palm trees, as a man does when he has taken an unfamiliar turning and lost himself.

"I can't explain it. I longed for you, Irene."

"I know," she said.

"Was he in Cairo?" said Sidon.

"He's a South African, in the Western Desert. Not far," said Irene. When he did not speak she said, "He's there now."

He still did not speak.

She leaned towards him, urgently, and smiled. "Jules, don't let's take it as a tragedy. We're grown up now. It couldn't be helped, could it? We were such infants when we married. Jules, please; please, Jules, don't be sad; just smile at me, just once . . ."

He managed it, though perhaps it broke his heart; really broke that young heart from which the moment of freedom—essential to attain—is so painful. From that moment on he began to live like a grown man, with the conditional instead of the absolute.

They talked for a few minutes, like old friends in mourning. They were calm, almost confident. Then Jules said, "About the flat——" "I'll give up the flat," said Irene. "We'll get another one, and perhaps we'll get the house in Maadi back, soon."

"Perhaps I shouldn't move into the flat," he said, "for a few days, until you move out of it—don't you think?"

She felt forlorn. "You don't have to see the flat, if you'd rather not," she said, shyly.

Suddenly they felt sure there would be no divorce; they would begin together again, start right at the beginning with a new courtship, even.
"Oh no, it's not as bad as that," he smiled. "I don't mind seeing it."

Unfortunately he came one morning when Max was there. Sidon was staying in the flat of a trusted friend (neither Irene nor Sidon wanted the Achilets to know that he was not sharing the flat with her) and he popped in about eight in the morning to pick up some of his old civilian clothes. The South African, in pyjamas, came to open the front door.

The three of them sat on the terrace, drank coffee, and talked sensibly. Below, the smooth Nile bellied a little with the first of the flood water, like a great sail. Then Max left and Irene and Sidon talked some more. Irene told Sidon the truth, which was that she had sent for Max to explain her feelings to him, and he had slept the night, quite decorously, in the living-room. Sidon knew that Irene could not lie to him, and he nodded his acceptance. Suddenly he said to her in French, which the South African could not speak—"But Irene, do you love him?" He watched for her answer kindly, keenly, short-sightedly, as he used to watch to see if she had grasped some deceptively simple archæological point.

"I loved you," she answered in French, in the tone of something she was sure of. "I thought that was all."

And then he said, speaking English again, "Yes, as you said, it was all so different then. We were children." They agreed that Irene was confused and that they would not rush into a divorce.

But they were drifting to one already—unaware, really; helpless, it seemed—and in due time it happened. After the divorce Irene lived with Max until 1945, when he went home to South Africa to be demobilized, and then he returned to Cairo and they were married. It was a very good marriage; Irene was perhaps happier in it than Max, probably because she was by nature of a happier temperament than his—he found life suspect, though he had not yet found it out, and was watchful of it. There was a lot of building going on after the war, and the good conections of the Achilet family brought him scope and success as an architect. Their three children were born to them in the house in Maadi that Achilet Pasha had built for Irene, and they lived the rich and comfortable cosmopolitan life that Irene had been born to. Max was able to go to Brazil, Europe, and America to keep in touch with the work of his great contemporaries, and his natural inclinations, given international opportunity, led him to become a man of culture outside the special interests of his work. He went back to South Africa only once, in the early fifties. His brother said to him, "You're not like us at all, any more"; but he himself felt he did not know *them*, for they were preoccupied with a problem that he, with his coin collection, his Turkish glass collection, and his passion for early Japanese woodcuts, did not think of outside the daily glance at newspaper columns—they were conscious of the fact that they were white men, few, guilty, and unloved, in a continent of black. The small, warm, fusty context of home to which he had returned was discovered to be an exposed place. It did not trouble him much at the time; he simply did not go back to South Africa again; there was the whole of Europe, after all.

As frequently happens in a sophisticated community, Irene's first brief marriage had become so much—to use her own slangy phrase—"ancient history" that the former partners quite often met in the ordinary course of social life, entirely without embarrassment. Also, as frequently happens when a romantic marriage has dissolved, the two who it had seemed would do only for each other had quickly found others who would do just as well. Sidon had not left Egypt; he had stayed on and married a nice girl, some connection of the Italian ambassador; they had two children who attended the same school as the Achilet-Leonard children—that was, until the French school closed down. Max and Irene would exchange any tid-bit about Sidon quite unselfconsciously along with the other gossip of the town; when Sidon wrote an archæological treatise that won him some French academic honour, Irene telephoned Lila Sidon to give the Sidons Max's and her congratulations. Irene always referred to her ex-husband by his surname, as if he were some public personality whom she had once met; she remarked to Max, "Who would have thought it?—they say he'll get a decoration from France one of these days. My poor father, how cross he'd be if he knew"—she laughed and pulled a droll face—"he was quite sure Sidon would come to nothing." Two years after Suez, the Sidons were among the few who were still in Egypt; like the Achilets in the house in Maadi, they too, were hanging on, it was said because Sidon had just begun an important piece of excavation when the ban on foreign archæological expeditions was enforced, and he was determined to wait for it to be lifted. Irene and Sidon's wife quite often bumped into each other at Groppi's garden, and one would pause at the other's table to talk for a few minutes about a concert, the children's progress at school, or other commonplaces.

Two years after Suez, Irene looked at her husband anxiously when he came out of the darkened library at the sound of the lunch-bell every day. "What sort of a morning did you have?"

His face was stiff with loneliness, hours without the sound or sight of anything but his own thoughts. He cleared his throat and smiled. "All right." A moment later he remembered, and said, "And you?" She was off at once, with relief, in chatter, pouring herself a glass of sherry, stretching her short legs, yawning cheerfully; she had written four letters, she had telephoned so-and-so, she had read this or that.

One day she said to him, "How are you getting on with the plans for the villa? Can't I see them yet?"

He drew breath guiltily, let it go again.

Animation and interest, self-forgetfulness dropped from her pretty face; she waited for him to contradict her understanding of the truth, to hide it from her.

"I haven't got far enough yet."

"But three—six months. More." She waited, without hope.

"We won't ever get to Italy," he said gently.

She sat bolt upright. She was suddenly excited, in her way. "Why do you say that? Don't you *want* to go? Don't you want us to have a house out of this place, in a country we've loved all our lives? Good God, you've always said that the one place you want to build yourself a house is on the hills above Nemi . . . Why do you say that?"

"We're still here," he said.

"Why do you say that?" she insisted, ignoring him, her eyes challenging with fear. "Why do you say we won't get there? Don't you *want* to get out of this?"

He did not know how to answer her, for he knew he could not tell her that it was not just *this*—the life in which they were without privilege and were allowed to exist only under sufferance—that he wanted to escape; he feared the possibility, however remote, of a return to the life they had lost. The year when he had gone home to South Africa, his brother had said, "You are not one of us at all, any more"; he had come, at last, to understand what those men themselves felt, few, guilty, and unloved, in the black men's continent, belonging not there nor yet anywhere.

Directly after lunch she raced upstairs to her studio like a schoolgirl. She did not appear until it was growing dark. "I've been going through everything again," she said, "all the papers. I'll go and see Delbanco again tomorrow. If we could only get some sort of security for my brother's property, and wangle to get Mama's account released, I'd let the rest go."

She was a capable girl, all right, and a good trier. But it was no good. The money could not be got out; the property was in jeopardy. They stayed where they were, and Max actually did draw up the plans for the Italian villa, to comfort her.

And then one afternoon he was sitting reading in a cool, gloomy arbour of the old pasha's garden when he saw her flash down one of the paths separated from him by shrubs and the sword-leaves of some rare lily plants. It always touched him to see her run, as if she were still a young girl, unaware of her thickened, slackened, woman's body. He thought that she was probably looking for one of the children and he went on reading, but in a moment he heard her calling his name—"Max! Ma-ax?"—and he stood up and called back, "Here! By the pond." She had been out for lunch, quite an event for those days, and he had not seen her all day. "Nobody in the house knew where you were," she said, sitting down with her hands closely linked between her knees; she had changed out of her town clothes into her usual trousers and espadrilles. "I couldn't have got very far," he said, with a smile. "How was the day?" She did not answer and gave him one of her deep, secret, intriguing smiles, two lines that had once been dimples indenting her cheeks. "Max," she said, "let's go. That's all. Let's leave everything and go. What does it matter? You'll find work. It needn't necessarily be Italy. Brazil, anywhere. We'll live on what you can earn and look after Mama ourselves."

His heart began to thump very slow and hard. "D'you mean it?"

"Yes," she said. "Yes. I've made up my mind. Let's go, Max. We've had enough."

Excitement, release, swept into him like power. Go, and never come back, never come back? he wanted to shout splendidly; but he remembered that this was her home she was leaving, this city, this house, this artificial tropical wilderness kept going by an intricate pumping system from the Nile, this pool covered, as if with a dust-sheet, by a wrinkled green scum of disuse. Instead, he said, "Oh God, Irene, I'm sure it's the right thing. I haven't wanted to persuade you, but I've always thought so. It's best for your mother, the children, all of us."

She had the pleased, quavering-faced look of someone who is trying to be modest about something big that he has done. "You've been so good, darling Max," she said emotionally. "You've been rotting away in that library."

The next day he went into town for the first time for months. He made to himself the excuse of something he wanted to buy, but the truth was that he simply wanted to feel himself in the world, among people again. About half-past one he went into small Groppi's and ordered a vermouth and waited with a sense of pleasure for someone he knew to come in, so that he could tell him, "We're leaving you know." He greeted an acquaintance across the room, but it was not until his drink was finished that an old friend, Mario Peretti (it was his wife with whom Max had had to curtail his golf games), came over and sat down in the empty chair at the little table.

"So?" said Mario, eyebrows lifting above the line of his thick glasses, "what brings you here? What an occasion!"

"Have a vermouth, Mario," said Max, grinning.

"O.K. And why not? Certainly I'll have a vermouth with you. It isn't many times that I get a chance for you to buy me a drink."

"And what about at my house?"

"Oh, that's not the same," said Peretti. "From the cellar it's not the same. It's not cash."

"Well, I suppose you've heard our big news," said Max, when their drinks had come.

"What's that?" said Mario, wiping the rim of his perfectly clean glass with a handkerchief.

"I'm sure Irene's been on the phone to Greta this morning?"

Peretti shrugged. "Greta was with Irene in town yesterday, but she didn't say anything to me. I haven't heard a word. What's it all about?"

"We decided last night. Mario, we're leaving. Packing up and walking out, at last," said Max.

Peretti drew in towards him across the table in admiring intimacy, smiling. "Is that so? So you're going? Well, good luck to you! That's the second lot I've heard about in two days. Did you hear that Jules Sidon is clearing out?"

"Sidon?"

"But Lila Sidon met Greta and Irene yesterday, and told them then. Came up to their table and announced it. Sidon's been given some big job —the South Seas, I think. He's going to lead an American expedition. They're leaving Cairo for good, too. She must have some property; they won't see that again. Shall we eat here? Are you going to have lunch with me?"

Max finished his drink in one long draw and stood up as he put the glass back in its saucer. "Mario, no, I can't. I must get back to Maadi, you know."

"But what for? It's lunch-time."

Max smiled. "Yes. That's it. I must get back for lunch."

It was true that he felt he must get back to Maadi. He must get back there at once. He drove as if it were certain that there would be something waiting for him there in the house, something that would—what? He did not know, but he was sure that he would recognize it instantly for whatever it was, when he got there. The slam of the car door was muffled by the heavy silence that hung about the house. A sprinkler was making shining runnels on the dusty leaves of the bougainvillaea; old Madame Achilet must have been resting upstairs and was not at her card-table. He closed the front door behind him and entered the big living-room where only the two abstract paintings seemed to keep their swirling, changing forms in the fuzzy light that came through the shutters. He went softly and heavily over the carpets, and as he was passing out of the room he realized that there was something—someone was sitting in one of the deep chairs. He turned and went to her. She sat with her legs drawn up tightly under her, like someone in pain. "Max?" she said, as if he were asleep and she did not want to wake him. "I've found out about the formalities, we'll get away without any difficulty. The house may give a bit of bother, but that can easily——" He did not speak, but he made a movement to hush her. She turned her head and the light that sifted into the room round the outline of the window near her lifted her face out of the dusk. He looked at her, fully, for a few seconds, but she could not see his face clearly and did not know that he could see hers.

When he had seen her, he sat down on the arm of her chair, and put out his hand; it touched her hair once, and then withdrew, and instead he began to stroke her hand. There was a strange silence about him, as if it were a struggle for him to do this. She was anxious to explain, asking, perhaps, for an explanation—"I was born here, everything's happened to me here. My whole life. This house—it's the house my father built for me——"

"Yes," he said, "of course."

"It's all over," she said, and tried to laugh.

"Yes, of course," he said. He sat on, silently stroking her hand. He could feel the set of his face in the dimness. "Yes, of course."

SEPTEMBER 1959

CYRIL CONNOLLY

Shade Those Laurels*

As if divining my disappointment: "Read that last sentence again, Kemble," he interrupted. *"And more, perhaps, than any man living,"* I continued, *"Sir Mortimer appreciates and has taught others to appreciate the things which we can touch or see—this visible world."* "Yes, it's good," went on my Editor—"so much better than the one we're using. A thousand pities you're not a celebrity: it's names we like on this paper, especially when a famous author, whom most of our readers have never heard of— ha!—gets a knighthood on his birthday. Tell you what: I'll change a letter here and there and we can turn it into something. *'More perhaps than any man now living, Sir Mortimer appreciated the things which he could touch or see!'* I never like to scrap a good bloke or a good sentence. Take care of this and we'll run you off a proof when you come back— meanwhile don't let him grab it. He mightn't think it funny." "But really, I can't let you do this—why I'm——" "It'll pay for your journey. Fair enough?"

And so that very evening I found myself going down to stay with our newest knight, Sir Mortimer Gussage, K.B.E., with a draft of his own obituary in my breast-pocket.

Tallboys was a place I had long been determined to visit: the house has given its name to the *de luxe* edition of his collected works where it is figured on the title page beyond its lime avenue in an almost impertinent perfection. I was under no illusion about the purpose of my invitation, nor for a moment did I suppose that Sir Mortimer would have asked me if I had not been able to mention at a party that I was doing a piece on him for his birthday. By lifting a finger Sir Mortimer could have met anyone in the kingdom. As an unimportant novel reviewer, my privilege had to be earned. And so it happened that, four days later, I found myself sliding into Salisbury station, descending with the misty October twilight, to be

* This is the first section, quite complete in itself, of a novel in progress. Of the events here related, Mr. Connolly writes: All the characters are imaginary. The "I" is not "me"—yet.

429

met among the churns on the long, cold platform by the great man's most finished masterpiece.

Laurian Gussage stepped forward and shook my hand. "You *are* Stephen Kemble? You *must* be! Daddy will be so pleased you have come." Her voice was low and crisp, her great eyes wide apart—a brownish green— her face rather round, above the grey Paris scarf, were it not for a high forehead from which the dark hair was swept back. She wore broad-waled blue corduroy trousers under a three-quarter-length camel coat and tried to seize my bag. We made our way through groups of clanking soldiers to a small closed Sunbeam Talbot and soon were driving over the river, past the Cathedral and out along the Blandford road.

"I wonder what you'll make of Tallboys. Isn't it your first visit?" "Who's going to be there?" I countered. "Oh, it's just a family party for Daddy's birthday tomorrow. There's Daddy and Cressida, that's my stepmother— and Jane Sotheran—'Sacharissa', you know." "Gracious!" "Don't let them both tear you to pieces." "Are they so carnivorous?" "Oh no! Not destructive. They just like young men. And then there's 'Ginger' Bartlett —he's Daddy's publisher—and Hugh Curry Rivel, his oldest friend; he's a writer too. And Julian Frere, who's a young Cambridge disciple and sup- posed to be terribly clever, and that's the lot, except for Norman and Mona." "Who are they?" "Norman and Mona Farran; they have the mill nearby but they're always over at the house. Norman's another very old friend of Daddy's and Mona does his letters and typing." "Are they writers too?" "Good heavens, no; Norman has a fruit farm." "And you?" "I'm trying to be a painter; I feel I've had enough of the written word and *'la vie littéraire'*." "You think it's a bad life? I'm a would-be novelist, don't forget." She looked at me reflectively. "I don't think it's life at all."

We had been twisting in the dark along roads which had narrowed stealthily to lanes until at last we crossed a little bridge and shot up a leafy drive while the headlights illuminated a square brick house with a shell- shaped wooden porch. As we drew up with a crunch of gravel and bruising of rosemary, the front door swung open on to a bright pine-panelled hall. While a foreign-looking manservant in a wrinkled white jacket with a button missing was taking my bag and coat away, Laurian pushed me into a large living-room, where the whole alarming party stood assembled round an open log fire. "I've brought you the new admirer, Daddy," and for the second time in my life I found myself shaking hands with the man whose work had changed it. A "humanist" is perhaps a discredited word, let us say rather—an illuminator, a life-enhancer, a priest-king or a poet in the original sense of "maker"; one who has tried to distil from his imagination an imperishable elixir for the unborn, the discriminating, and the lost. With his pointed bronze beard, his noble brow and piratical blue eyes, his vigorous nose and full rich mouth, by his whole buoyant air of ironical expectation, he suggested the High Renaissance, the man of action who was yet dedicated to poetry and learning, like Sir Fulke Greville of whom he had so understandingly written, Kenelm Digby, or Killigrew, made the subject of his only play. He gave me a warm hand-clasp and a smile of appreciation. "Good of you to come," he boomed. "I don't think you've met my wife." "Mr. Kemble, your servant, sir." Cressida made me a little curtsey, her two brown arms gripping the pleats of her quilted skirt in a ballet dancer's gesture, and then she lifted her small nineteen-twentyish face up to mine. "Of course, I know all about you." Her voice was a tiny silver bell and every syllable blown out of her mouth like a smoke ring. She took my arm just above the elbow in a light yet somehow clinging and over-intimate grip, and led me up to the haughty Sacharissa. "How do you do!" Miss Sotheran's voice was deep and resonant and her greeting went down the scale like a dropped guitar. She, too, smiled and there was something I didn't quite like about that either, for she put out a hand from which all life had been withdrawn so that I appeared to be holding it up with a fearful familiarity. "And now our merry gentlemen, God rest them," enunciated Cressida. "Mr. Bartlett, our publisher, let nothing him dismay." I greeted an erect and shambling figure in a blue city suit with a large open porous face and flabby paw. "And Mr. Curry Rivel." A self-consciously "interesting" head with a swelling Egyptian back to it, posed on the neck like an early photo of Rupert Brooke but shrivelled by the secret processes of middle age; dry lips, pale unfriendly eyes, sandy hair brushed back and whitening at the sides like wind-blown wheat, and a flying hand I seemed hardly to touch, while a high-pitched voice disposed of me by rising on the last syllable. "How do you DO!" "Oh yes, Mr. Kemble, and I was nearly forgetting, here's someone of your own age to play with. This is Mr. Frere —Julian, behold another acolyte to swing the censer with you for the Knight of the Split Caesura." A man in his early thirties, and so actually considerably older than me as was obvious to both of us, put down his evening paper. He was tall and almost good-looking; his face dark and intelligent but somehow slightly battered, like an "export reject" of a rather good design. He reminded me of a less suave and rather more *louche* counterpart of Senator McCarthy. "How do you do, Mr. Kemble. Of course I read your novel reviews." "Yes?" There was charm in his careless tone. "Or do my level best to: for like all young critics you seem to have forgotten Dr. Johnson—'a horse that can count up to ten is a remarkable horse, not a remarkable mathematician.'" He stuck out a long, grimy, close-bitten finger and pushed my cambric handkerchief further down the breast-pocket.

431

"I'll thank you not——" I began, but Sir Mortimer clapped his hands, standing erect with one leg slightly advanced like a bronze Æginetan warrior. "Cocktails at last." As they were being passed round by the dishevelled servant (I nearly said "house-boy"), the Norman Farrans arrived, and amid general greetings I was introduced to them. The one man present who was so original as not to write had a quiet face with fine, sad eyes and a mild, doggy look that went well with his old tweeds, while his wife, Mona Farran, was distinctly shabby; she wore coral earrings and there were lumps of grey in her short black hair; her green skirt was too high to my way of thinking and revealed woollen stockings twisted round the knee. Sir Mortimer offered me a martini. "And how was London? Deliciously noisy, I expect, with Charles Morgan away. You'll find us abominably quiet here, I'm afraid. The recreation of North Wiltshire is the bottle, of South Wiltshire, dressing up. Here on the borderline between them, we seldom dress—not even *lederhosen*—and we don't drink—or at any rate not nearly as much as we should like to. And now, let us go in— Cressida!" He barked her name out in quite a different tone, like a command, and she made a little face at Mr. Curry Rivel as we began to shuffle towards the door, like sand in an hour-glass, all seeming to hold back yet one by one contriving to pass through.

The dining-room was large, high, and like the hall panelled in some pale wood; it looked unexpectedly formal for such an easy-going house— or was it so easy-going? For I noticed that the men were all in dark suits; even Norman Farran's tweed was a peaty black-brown Donegal, while the women, except for his wife, were in low dresses. Laurian too had changed into something white and was beside me again, glowing like a camellia. A glittering crystal chandelier was suspended above the oval Sheraton table where two branching cut-glass candlesticks sent out their wavering sprays. In the centre was a plain rose bowl from which a diminuendo of goblets radiated star-wise in the direction of each guest; we all had an old print with a glass top as a table-mat and even a written place-card. I dared to hope the heavy capitals were Laurian's, for I found myself put between her and Sir Mortimer. "Most of us have to share a lady tonight," he said, "so I have given you the best of the bunch and penalized you with myself as your neighbour." His voice had a curious resonance; an irresistible voice in which something profoundly masculine seemed to struggle with an imperishable gaiety and charm; whatever he was saying, his tone made of it a treat, an enlightenment, a special occasion, while his laugh—a single deep, infectious "Ha"—was like the lifting of the cover from a silver entrée dish on a cold morning. I did not know how to reply and mumbled my embarrassment while I looked carefully around me.

I am interested in table arrangement, it belongs to a mummified world which I am too young to remember. I decided that these people must all be where they were for a particular reason. "Sacharissa" was famous enough to be on Sir Peregrine's right—and Cressida? She had given herself an important dud in "Ginger" Bartlett and a consolation prize—clever Mr. Julian Frere. The two dim Farrans would presumably be fitted in last and so the one who seemed badly placed was Mr. Curry Rivel. Unless he was keen on "Sacharissa"? He did not look it. They were both middle-aged— she in the florid purple phases of the malady, he in the grip of alopecia, his main crop of hair receding at the temples, while eyebrows, ears, and nostrils sent out a few last despairing shoots. I have always found it pay to regard any collection of people as enemies until they have been proved friendly, but I have learnt to conceal my suspicion. Say little; cast a cold eye; let them speak first and appear to take them at their own valuation —smile like a selective weed-killer—and in a few minutes most of the people one meets for the first time will have irretrievably betrayed themselves. First impressions are best because they arise before we have allowed people to impose on us. Sacharissa—a mauve blancmange, I noted; Cressida —a marmoset with a chic suggestion of Saint Anthony's pig. Curry Rivel— a dried joss-stick; Bartlett—a randy major in the Pioneer Corps; Frere— a Third Programme barrow-boy; Laurian and Sir Mortimer—my only allies. Good—we were three against five—seven if one threw in the colourless Farrans. I thought of my favourite gangster, "Baby-Face" Floyd, snapped a smile on my face as one cocks a revolver, and waited the attack.

"I'm sure you don't know what is the hardest thing in the world to do," exclaimed Sir Mortimer, "especially if one is that despised thing, a perfectionist." "To write a flawless page," I hazarded. "To keep one's figure," boomed Sacharissa. "To ripen, by natural means and in the open, a Doyenné de Comice pear." Hugh Curry Rivel's reedy civil servant's voice was precise, well-bred, Peacockian. "Taking your dictation, Sir Mortimer," rogued Mona Farran. Laurian made no contribution and when I caught her eye she only giggled. "A flawless page," went on Sir Mortimer, "I said the hardest thing in the world to do—I did not propose the impossible." "Oh, what about *David and the Sybil*, you old hypocrite?—a modest Merlin at his Table Round!" "No Sacharissa, I can tell you it's nothing to do with our art, though the Round Table comes into it. No, nothing so literary as that. It's just to give the perfect diner—one in which everything comes off; the food, the wine, the china, the glass, the silver, the service, the guests—good talk, good fare, good people, good digestions. 'Dinner's everything,' as Hofmann wrote, *'C'est le but des actions humaines.'* They say food is a substitute for love. Well, it's certainly a bloody good one. Every night I think—well, perhaps this time tomorrow we shall have done it—and every time some little thing goes wrong." "And tomorrow's your birthday!" "Yes, this is the dress rehearsal for that supreme occasion, and who knows—it may turn out to have surpassed the feast!" "Well, let's see first what we have in our nose-bag." Hugh Curry Rivel stretched out for the menu beside him in its white jade holder and handed it to Sacharissa, who intoned reverently :

CLEAR TURTLE SOUP

SOLE COLBERT

ROAST PARTRIDGE

HARICOTS VERTS   GAME CHIPS

CHEESE SOUFFLÉ

COX'S ORANGE   PITMASTON PINEAPPLE   IRISH PEACH

DOYENNÉ DE COMICE   KENTISH COBS

"Well, Fate has accepted your challenge, Hugh, the elusive pear is there!" "Not Fate," cried Mona, "but my husband. We haven't a fruit farm for nothing—and you're right, they are difficult things to ripen. If Sir Mortimer didn't happen to be so fond of them, we'd never bother." "I expect you find it a very dull menu," insisted my host, "but it has three advantages; it's easy to procure, it's foolproof to cook, and—this is a big and —it's the kind of unassuming sauce-free food that goes well with our wines. And in this house wine takes precedence. Let's see what we're drinking : with the turtle, an old Solera that was of age when Rimbaud and Verlaine played boy in Howland Street—a Montrachet, discreet as Docteur Blanche, to keep a flinty eye on the fish—a Romanée Saint Vivant as old as Prufrock that should hold your attention, Mr. Kemble—and when the birds are stomached and while the cheese soufflé exhales its brief 'Coronemus', the last—or almost the last—of my Yquem '21. *Reverentia!* And with the dessert we shall listen to the deplorable confessions of a magnum of dear Hugh Walpole's pink champagne."

"And you say this is only the dress rehearsal," I glamoured. "And so therefore a most important occasion, a *répétition générale*. For tomorrow night I may still keep a few surprises. You will notice, for instance, that both hock and claret are absent from this evening's menu—and so are lobster and pheasant and foie gras and muscats and nectarines ... If I weren't a writer, Mr. Kemble, I'd express myself through my collections, and if I didn't collect, I'd say it with claret, and if I couldn't get any claret, I'd long ago have toddled off to a better world. I thought also of perhaps trying to reproduce a typical menu from the Goncourt journals; you remember that turbot with the marvellous cream sauce which Flaubert served to them at Croisset the Easter before his apoplexy." "Apoplexy!" whistled Curry Rivel. "I always understood it was a syphilitic seizure, not unconnected with his stomatitis." "Surely we can leave it at epilepsy, a visitation of *le grand mal*, as the indiscreet Du Camp maintained," cried Sacharissa. "Epilepsy—who falls for that? What about the purple mark Maupassant saw round his neck?" "Proof positive," snapped Frere, "as Lenormant implies, that he had hanged himself in his bath. The niece and nephew had only just time to get the huge body into the bedroom. The whole thing was hushed up." "I have a letter from Dumesnil," replied Sir Mortimer, "who spoke to the doctor who found him. He said it was undoubtedly what we should call a stroke." "But since then Jean Pommier has discovered the letter to his brother in which he inquired about treatment for syphilis." "Rustchuk Hanem? *De la littérature!*" "Syphilis"— "Epilepsy"—"Suicide"—"Over-eating!'"—"Gentlemen—*mes enfants*— Sacharissa, desist I beg you—this is meant to be Morty's perfect dinner and you're turning it into a 'Crowner's Quest'." "Cressida—your pardon." "Naughty boy—and you're fifty-five tomorrow." "Flaubert, Baudelaire, Baudelaire's brother, Maupassant, Maupassant's brother, Daudet—the badge of genius—they all had it." Rivel was still muttering.

I turned to the soup, aromatic with basil and calipee, which we had all allowed to get cold, and to the formidable Solera standing beside it. We were waited on by a trim parlourmaid and by the same manservant in his shrunken white jacket. And now it was delightful to concentrate on the little leathery soles involved in their lumps of parsley butter and on the gunmetal white burgundy which went round with them. It was only then I had time to notice how unusual were all the accessories: spoons and forks were thinner in the waist than any I had seen and were marked on the stem with deep lions and whiskered leopards; everything glittered and tapered extravagantly; all around were china shells and pink and green baskets of china strawberries or bundles of asparagus and brown ducks whose backs were lids, and there was even a crackled china melon. The candlelight broke violet from the hanging lustres and was reflected in the glass chains which were looped across the double table candlesticks; our glasses were warm yet fragile, with thin stems and a pliant waxen transparency, in the centre the silver bowl was by contrast extremely severe and held some huge pink flowers that I had never seen before. Behind us on the sideboard were the fruit dishes; some of glass like moon-stained ice and others a part of some lustred shell service whose dishes were piled with apples and cobnuts, while in a kind of nautilus were three or four enormous pears. "Where's the Pitmaston pineapple?" I said to Laurian. "Oh, it's not a real pineapple. It's the name of an apple, a little honey-musk russet—so is the Irish peach—we're great apple connoisseurs here." The visible world, I thought, with a vengeance! She laughed. "Yes, we're connoisseurs of everything—'nutty, compact and fertile,' that's me,

'Aromatic, blushes pink, and a good cropper'—all things bright and beautiful, as long as no one else has got them—all creatures great and small, provided they're edible." "I think you're perfectly right." "Oh yes, so many do—not a shrimp is peeled without a dissertation, not a sparrow falls to the ground without a post-mortem, not a gooseberry is taken without a permit." "But in a way that's as it should be. To a great artist everything in life must be of equal importance—doesn't your father say somewhere that just as a straight line is really a number of infinitesimal points which we can't see, so a good life is a number of infinitesimal moments, but all equal in value, and each implying an act of choice. 'The theory of perpetual discrimination' he has called it. It's only the weak who think one moment or one point is more important than another." Hugh Curry Rivel, I noticed, was listening intently. Sir Mortimer was still talking Goncourt to Sacharissa: "Then you would have been my George Sand," he was telling her. Laurian grew more thoughtful. "But it's not exactly like that— for one thing some points on the line *must* be more important than others —the first and probably the last—and so it is with a human life—the two moments which start something and which end something are called birth and death, and all the connoisseurship and discrimination and 'hard gem-like flame-throwing' that goes on here seems to hush up and imprison a more real kind of living. We don't mention birth because it's so far behind or death because it's too close—and all this 'expertise' seems to me a diversion to retard the passage of time. I expect Canute became a terrific connoisseur of waves as he called on them one after another. Anyhow, it makes me glad not to live by a possession-clock, to have only a few sticks in my studio, a plastic teacup and an ironstone jug and basin." *"Mademoiselle se croît trop artiste pour aimer les belles choses?"* It was said with venomous distinctness. I glared across at Hugh Curry Rivel, who had sent over this unexpected volley, but couldn't concoct an answer. He held up his glass of burgundy to his nose, took a sip, rotated the glass with the base gripped between thumb and forefinger, and then swallowed a large mouthful. The wine was clear and bright as the red juice which oozed from my tender partridge's well-pronged flank. I took a swig myself and pressed my leg close to Laurian's to demonstrate my sympathy. I felt her long, hard thigh respond to mine, the knee-joints touching, and then my calf brushed against hers, as if our legs had suddenly been locked into position—even our ankles met. I was strangely disturbed and frightened.

We now appeared to have exhausted our amiability at this end of the table and so we turned to listen to the others like a jazz band making way for the rumba orchestra. "Well, Cressida, it's all fixed," said Sir Mortimer, "my birthday treat tomorrow is to include both drinking and dressing up. A *soirée chez Magny*—a dinner from the Goncourt journal! Sacharissa insists that I myself impersonate Flaubert but I refuse unless she plays the maternal rôle of George Sand. Hugh, here, will be our liverish Edmond de Goncourt, and Julian, my disciple, the young Maupassant—Guy *le chauve'* —our 'green man' Norman can be Alphonse Daudet (even he will have heard of 'Tartarin'), and our new guest, Mr. Kemble here, shall be young Zola. Cressida, you will have to play *'La Muse'*, Louise Colet, and you, Ginger, our faithful publisher, Carpentier. Laurian and Mona can be the two ladies of my household." "In fact your niece and mother." "Thank you, Hugh." "I'd rather be *La Présidente* than that odious Louise Colet," cried Cressida ,"she had more chaps for one thing." Lady Gussage gave a low laugh : I would almost have said a coarse chuckle, quite different from her usual silvery detonation. "Well, we shall all have to drink a toast to *'Notre grand Flau'*," said Curry Rivel, "in Goncourt's favourite *'cramant nature'*. I wonder, by the way, what the Hermit of Croisset would have thought of your knighthood. *'Les honneurs déshonorent, les titres dégra-dent,'* wasn't it?" "He must have been a bit of a bourgeois," interrupted Julian, "or you couldn't call him *'notre grand Flau'*, or even 'the Hermit of Croisset'. Imagine calling Baudelaire *'notre cher Bau——'* " "Or Maupas-sant *'notre brave Mau'*," said Hugh, "or Daudet 'Dau' or Zola 'Zo——' " *"Ma basta,"* piped Cressida, "let's enjoy tonight for once without Le Petit Larousse. And can't we have the dinner in a period when women were invited for their looks?" "What about a Roman dinner?" said Julian. "The women only came in afterwards." "All Roman dinners end up at Trimalchios," replied Sir Mortimer, "and I don't want to retire constantly to the Vomitorium or to have my coffin brought on by Angelo here (he waved to the servant) or to eat a quantity of stuffed livestock with liberated pigeons flying about the room, each with an *hors d'œuvre* inside him like Japanese boxes. I always thought that meal lasted much too long." "I know I should hate Roman cooking," said Sacharissa. "That horrible garum—what did Carême call it? *'Foncièrement lourde et sans finesse.'* " "Why not try one of their more specialized menus?" the sneering tone of Mr. Julian Frere took up. "Like the dinner *'en deuil'* Domitian gave his senators. You remember, Mortimer? The floor, the walls, and the ceiling of the room were black, so were the chairs, and the guests were introduced one by one during the night. Each found that a little column had been put in front of him, like those they set on tombs, on which his name was engraved, with a lamp like those they hung in sepulchres; then naked young slaves with blackened bodies stole like ghosts into the hall and danced ceremoniously round the guests before placing themselves at their feet; then they brought on the dingy little titbits which were offered to the dead, served on black plate. The senators were all expecting to have their throats cut and maintained complete silence while Domitian meandered on about the latest murders and assassinations, until he sent them rumbling home with unfamiliar escorts, frozen with fear in their closed litters." "I seem to remember he went on dispatching callers to them all through the small hours," said Curry Rivel, "who brought with a loud knocking first their silver columns, then their black plate, and then the slave who had waited on them, now washed and whitened, while each imperial present petrified them with further terror." "Certainly." "Well, I invite you all to dinner tomorrow, but I'm no Domitian," said Sir Mortimer. " '*Ego nolo Cæsar esse*.' But what a writer old Suetonius was— that arid grammarian's style which always just avoids melodrama or bathos." "Dion Cassius," muttered Frere. "And what kind of Roman dinner could I tempt you with, Norman—a fruitarian orgy?" The local green finger turned his sad spaniel eyes on his wife's employer. "Not just fruit—perhaps a few mushrooms—like Claudius." "One mushroom wasn't it?" said Curry Rivel. "One very big mushroom," answered Julian, " '*delectabile boletum*.' " "What, you've read Suetonius too, Norman, in between chemical sprays!" laughed Sir Mortimer. "In the Loeb was it— or Bohn or Kelly?" "Not Suetonius—only Robert Graves, in a Penguin." He spoke quietly, as if unaware that he was being made a butt. "I don't believe we girls will have any more fun with these Roman celebrations than in your stuffy old Goncourt," tinkled Cressida. "Can't we just have a delicious unassuming modern birthday party with some slap and tickle and leave it at that? Sacharissa?" "*D'accord!*" "Laurian?" "*Double d'acc.*" "Mona?" "Most certainly!" "Unless clever pretty Mr. Kemble has any original notions?" "Who? Me? Oh no, at least I don't think so." "Well, let's leave the decision to our strong, silent publisher. Ginger, what do you say?" It was indeed the first time I had heard the sombre fellow open his mouth. "The only dinner I ever attended which came completely up to scratch," he said thickly, his false teeth clicking briskly over the labials, "was one evening at the old Algonquin." He began a rambling apologetic disquisition in which, like a smothered fog-signal, one caught the names of departed dollar-earners, literary wags, and pickled punsters—all the glossy affluent nobodies who had flourished while Sir Mortimer had slaved in obscurity at his *David and the Sybil* or pondered those small works of art wherein the formal pellucid brilliance of the twenties was irradiated by an underlying unrest and dawning anxiety like the prelude to the *Rheingold*. I remembered the prophetic ending of his strange poem "Time to go in":

> "*All the prawns in the sea choking in a glass jar,*
> *And summer strangled in a ruin of elms.*"

By contrast, the celebrities of Mr. Bartlett's story seemed only to exist, like the publisher himself, when seeing off the Fitzgeralds at Grand Central or playing poker with the Bromfields a day out from Nantucket. "Another remarkable occasion at the Savoy Grill, our English Algonquin," he went on, "where I saw the disastrous results of Rebecca's clam-chowder wager —gastronomically disastrous I mean, for as Heywood Broun cracked back to Bennett: 'It's not your liver, Arnold, I'm worried about, it's your circulation'—Ha! Ha!" *"La table élégante est le dernier rayon de soleil qui caresse les vieillards,"* whispered Sacharissa. "Grimod?" said Curry Rivel. "No, le Marquis de Cussy whom Baudelaire admired—or was that Custine?" "I don't know—it's like Marmontel and Carmentelle." "Pugin or Puget." They were off. "Sénac de Meilhan and Maine de Biran." "Orrery and Ossory." "Condillac and Condorcet." "Mahaffey and Cavaffy."

Laurian turned suddenly to me. "You told me you knew Sacharissa's books as well as Hugh's—were you being funny?" "Not intentionally." "I mean—have you ever read any?" "Why, yes." "And what do you think of them?" "Curry Rivel seems to me precious, pedantic, sterile; Sacharissa sensible, flowing, earthy, dramatic, but somehow boring and vulgar. He's like the little-finger nail rasping on a guitar, she's the flat palm twanging the bass—your father is—well—Segovia." "You mean he combines them?" "I mean that a book like *David and the Sybil* (I know one should not go on as if it were the only one he has written), somehow unites the astringent erudition of Curry Rivel with the warmth and power of Sacharissa, and there's something else too, a kind of macabre insolence, like Julian Frere's conversation, only much more exquisite and graceful." "Yes, I understand —and thank you. It's all there and even a touch of Norman's green finger. Autumnal sugar, country common sense."

"I suppose that's what we mean by genius, all the various little talents of an age amalgamating into something greater, a composite whole, a unique aroma." "I heard the words 'unique aroma' from my young neighbour. Very appositely, for here we have precisely that." And Sir Mortimer shattered my word-picture as he filled the deepest and narrowest of the goblets with an amber ichor whose bouquet (how am I doing?) exhaled the sunshine of Southern Septembers strained through the faun's blown grape-skin. Sir Mortimer raised his hand and blandly surveyed his guests. "Well—here it is. 1921. A good year, and a great summer; the first time one could go abroad after the last war but one, the beginning of the twenties: experiment, freedom, extravagance, hope. *'Teste David cum Sybilla,'* as I was quoting then, and before *'solvet sæclum cum favilla'* had become the writing on the wall. 'See fulfilled the prophet's warning/

Heaven and earth in ashes burning.' And now of all that excess and promise, of all that liberty and laughter, of Capri and the Kurfürsten-damm, Toulon and Montparnasse, Aldous's *Crome Yellow*; Firbank at the Tour Eiffel; Lytton's *Queen Victoria*; Valéry and Proust—we have only the gold from this bottle—and Tom Eliot of course—to still our gathering fear and the doubts which haunt us. Never mind! There are some young people here whose vintage is not yet gathered; may theirs be the outstanding one! Hugh! Norman! Mona! Sacharissa! Ginger! Let us drink to those whose festival, as Leopardi said, is still before them. To my Cressida, who has yet to find her Troilus, to Laurian, to Julian who hasn't yet apostasized on his old friend, and to young Mr. Kemble here with his keen eye and virginal palate. Remember, young man, all I can I tell you about life : beneath the comedy burns the tragedy; beneath the tragedy lies the ecstasy. The gaiety is in the gravity. You have only to dig."
"With a Hey, Nonny Nonny," whispered the ill-mannered Curry Rivel. They raised their glasses and drank with pompous cordiality like the Guardians in *The Cocktail Party*. Five of them now to four of us, for Sacharissa, evidently sore about her age group, didn't seem anxious to collaborate. Norman Farran grew suddenly vocal, "Reply, reply." "Yes, Julian, you answer," from Hugh. "Cressida, Cressida," from Ginger Bartlett. "Laurian," from Norman. "Mr. Kemble," chirped Mona, fiddl-ing with a grey kiss-curl that had got into her glass. The four young people nervously attacked the wobbling slabs of brown cheese soufflé which Angelo had set in front of them. There were purple wine-stains on his white sleeve—evidently another humanist. "Reply, reply," chorused our elders. "Give us a toast—a rule of life—a gnomic maxim," Sir Mortimer chided. "My mind is a complete blank," fluted Cressida. "Oh, Sacharissa, why aren't you with us." "When in doubt I try out all the last words of Roman Emperors," said Hugh. "One always fits." "Don't give them so much help, they're spoiled already," interrupted Sir Mortimer. "Mine are Claudius's then,' from Julian Frere, " '*Ut puto, concacavi me*,' which I might translate : 'Goodness gracious, I've bogged in my bags.' " "A toast, a toast." Laurian lifted a golden glass in her pale, firm hand. "Down the hatch!" I was tongue-tied and Julian seemed to have said my say. The Roman emperors had deserted me. Cressida stood up with all the artificial poise she invariably commanded. "Camera! Lights! Silence! I happen to think this is a serious moment; for the first time I drink as the wife of a knight as well as of a genius. As some of you may know, most of my youth has been passed in small repertory theatres, and to us a knight—except he of the Burning Pestle, which never came my way—was either Elizabethan —like Falstaff or Aguecheek—or Restoration, where I'm more at home. A sorry, shambling, sexy crew—Sir Lucius Bedwell, Sir Timothy Dildo,

Sir Peregrine Pego—you all know the form. Even—dare I whisper it?—
Lady Gussage sounds like a comic rôle to me, very different from fair
Cressid. So I'm not sure if I'm as utterly thrilled by my elevation as I
should like to be, though I'm woman enough to prefer it to being the wife
of a C.H., an O.M., a P.C., and all those empty initials. So I'm not
going to drink to the knighthood—and I'm not going to drink to the
birthday, because that's for tomorrow night, and I'm not going to drink to
Morty the Man—'ancient person of my heart'—because I've other ways of
showing what I think of him." "With a Hey, Nonny, Nonny!" "Sh—
silence." "So I drink to his books, to all his books, The Tallboys edition,
and of course as well to Hugh and *his* books and Sacharissa and *hers* and
to dear old 'Gingah' who publishes us all and so never can afford the
newest Bentley, and to Mona who types him and Norman who supplies
him with Vitamin C, but above all I drink to his new book, the work in
progress—may we soon be allowed to read it, and when it comes out of the
wind tunnel, may it belong specially to Julian and Laurian and Mr. Kemble
and me as *David and the Sybil* and the rest belonged to Ginger, Sacharissa,
Mona, and Hugh. Compañeros! 'The new book!'" We all applauded
and thumped and raised our glasses, now bubbling with Sir Hugh's old
and faintly corky champagne. I gazed round the table. Sir Morty had never
appeared so handsome, his face was full of colour, he resembled a dapper
Pelasgic deity, a spruce, bearded Zeus, or the smiling, satisfied husband on
an Etruscan tomb. Julian was looking a bit green. There were beads of
sweat on his forehead, now covered by a limp black lock. Mona was
giggling. Bartlett seemed rather blank, like a man who's walked into the
wrong club, while Hugh was frowning over his glass. I looked at Laurian
who winked her Botticelli eye at Sacharissa, who was gazing at Norman,
even as Norman seemed to be far away, staring over my shoulder. I turned
round and saw behind me on the wall a portrait of Laurian by Duncan
Grant or Henry Lamb or some such period piece. I looked again, it was of
a woman a few years older. I guessed at once. Her mother. It was a less
happy, more sophisticated face, with the hair worn low upon the brow as
in the twenties, the eyes lustrous and enigmatic, the lips slightly parted; a
loose brown jumper and a huge pearl necklace merging with a brown
county landscape; there were no pearls round Laurian's throbbing white
neck—only moonstones. "The book, the book," I shouted. "Title please,"
said Cressida. "Can't you give us the gen, sir," simpered Julian with mock
humility. "Pour it on, pour it on," cried Laurian, and Hugh murmured
stupidly, "With a Hey, Nonny, Nonny!" "I can't tell you much at this
stage," went on Sir Mortimer, "but it's very good of all of you to take
such an interest. I'm trying to do something rather complicated. An autobiography that's not written quite as one—more in the nature of La

441

Bruyère's Characters—a few pages about all the people, all the situations, all the types, all the tangibles that have always so fascinated me throughout my life; the agents and reagents of my electuary. A home-made tarot pack as it were, of my influences; perhaps you could call it a bread-and-butter letter to the twentieth century. I've got only a working title so far, from one of the Roman Emperors again—'Eyes, look your last'—and I hope soon to find a better. I'm really trying to pass in review all the people and things to whom one day I shall most dread saying goodbye and to put them into focus, making each the subject of a prose poem—an Enigma Variation—round their attributes, like the Epistles of Horace set to the music of Pelléas and Mélisande; ancient gourmets like Ausonius and Archestratus; favourite philosophers like Democritus, Pythagoras, Aristippus, Lucretius, Berkeley, and Hume (*le bon David*); playwrights like Congreve, dandies like Selwyn; beaux like Brummell; centenarians like Fontenelle and Xenophilus and Chevreuil; or people who lived at the right time like Rogers, Peacock, Luttrell, and Lorenzo da Ponte or the photographer Nadar; painters like Altdorfer and Mabuse and Bosch and Patinir, Watteau, Fragonard, Liotard, and La Tour; elegiac poets of all time from Theognis and Mimnermus, Tibullus, and Propertius to Baudelaire and Toulet; story-tellers from Apuleius to Villiers de L'Isle-Adam; travellers from Herodotus to Beckford; letter-writers from Cicero to Barbey D'Aurévilly, novelists from Petronius to Svevo; essayists from Horace and Montaigne to Landor and Hazlitt; and my favourite talkers and the beautiful women I have loved in literature, and their animals, Madame de Pompadour's 'Fidelité', Madame du Deffand's 'Tonton', Leonardo's lady with a ferret (which is really a pine-marten); and the places, the plants, the fruit, the china and furniture, the things one can never have enough of, like Carione and Scarlatti, the stray faces, the girl on the links at Carmel and the one on the Blue train—everything, all my rich thievery 'bundled up into a loose adieu'. I've always felt that no one—not even Montaigne or Boswell or Gide—has carried egotism to the complete and final expression when, by sheer concentration, it is turned inside out and becomes its opposite. Ego into All. Even Huysmans failed; he gave his arch egotist such bad health that he couldn't reach the final. I, on the other hand, may say I have never felt better. Yet I am carrying my egotism to the point at which I'm about to pass the sense barrier, which must be as dangerous as the speed of sound, in order to come out on the other side with an affirmation of the universal self in precipitate which will enable the young and, I hope, the unborn to behold themselves, their real destiny, their true personality, in a kind of magic mirror, as I see you all in the crystal ball of this chandelier. So I hope to come down to you, one day :

'Like that self-begotten bird
In the Arabian woods embost
That no second knows or third
And lays e'erwhile a holocaust . . .'"

His voice was spell-binding as Casals's 'cello. We sat on in silence, watching the sixteen candles gutter. "After all, what a criminal thing it is that my Yquem can produce such an effect when my prose cannot: yet one should be able to put the very bouquet of all the summers one has enjoyed into language, the *'pourriture noble'* of the grapes, the October glory of the mottled leaves, the weaving supplication of the tendrils, the patch of brown spreading on the golden quince. And that reminds me—I don't quite get all my vitamin C from Norman here—we still attempt a few freaks in the conservatory. Laurian, will you bring them in?" She disappeared and quickly returned with a cut-glass dish of what looked like cheap cocktail sausages. "Here you are, Daddy—and, on top, my own special treat that I was keeping till tomorrow—a solitary passion fruit from the pride of the plant-house." I remarked a wrinkled purplish object like a decayed ping-pong ball. "Splendid. I'd never even noticed it! I shall wait till I'm truly five and fifty and take it up to bed at midnight. Meanwhile, who will try an *Actinidia*? Norman, I'm sure you'd like a change from your régime of Cox and Worcester! You may have a green finger. Try one of my little brown thumbs!" Norman seized the nasty furry creature and proceeded to skin it, revealing a blackish slime. "Are you sure they're ripe?" "Ripe as we'll ever get them." "What exactly are they?" I ventured. "My pet plant—*Actinidia sinensis*, the Chinese gooseberry, as pretty a climber as you could wish and excellent in a cold house, where *Passiflora edulis* is such a bad starter. 'Male and female created he them.' We've just a pair. Who's never had one?" "I ate some last year," said Julian. "Me too," said Cressida, "we'll share one this time!" They started pulling at it like a cracker and Julian got the biggest half which he managed to swallow. Cressida only nibbled hers and made a face. By now we were all sharing them, and pulling at them with our neighbour, Ginger with Norman, Mona with Hugh, Morty with Sacharissa, and Laurian with me. She won the larger half: I tasted mine, it was quite pleasant and, indeed, very like an insipid gooseberry, but better packed. Laurian was licking hers, as if it were an ice-cream cone, and her tongue came out like a pointed lizard flickering scarlet over the broken fruit. Something seemed to turn over inside me and I looked panic-stricken into her steady eyes, which matched the brown-green berry. "That leaves one over for me to take to bed," laughed Sir Mortimer, as he placed it with his passion fruit and his Pitmaston russet. "A liberal *'en tout cas'* for birthday night-starvation. I've

443

often thought with affection of the great fruit-eaters. Louis XIV always had a tableful beside him. You can see one in the big portrait in the Wallace Collection. And that Pope who died of eating too many of those little yellow figs—and poor Mussolini. Do you remember, Hugh, when Lina Waterfield went to interview him and he showed her his latest photos and asked her what she thought. Then he held one up and chuckled, '*Sempre più terribile* and how do I do it?' " ("Always more awe-inspiring," he translated for Mona.) "Then the Duce pointed to a basket and bellowed : 'Frutta, frutta, frutta!' " "Well, he wouldn't have marched to Rome on one of these," said Cressida, "he'd have fallen before you could say *'Dov'è la ritirata?'* " She rose and held her skirt wide as in a Velasquez, while all the women followed. Julian kept the door open, Sacharissa tacked out majestically under full canvas, Mona doggedly behind her, Laurian in her white satin sauntered off under protest, still munching an apple; and then the men closed round the decanter, which was parked in front of Hugh Curry Rivel. I now sat between him and Ginger Bartlett, Morty on his other side, then came Julian Frere and the fruit farmer. Hugh should by rights have passed me the port, instead he glared at me with distaste and turned away. "Morty," he drawled, "do you mind if I give you a back-hander," and he slid the decanter over to him. I was livid. "Yes," he continued, "you can't beat a red hock, I always say, at the turn of the year." Julian spilt the port as he helped himself, after Morty, who then sent the decanter back in the proper direction, and I poured out a glass with a concentration which was not lost on my neighbour. Ginger looked uncomfortable, but filled up his, and Norman took a very little, seeming sadder than ever, while only Hugh appeared master of the situation. I began to miss Laurian. All the glow and warmth and promise had faded from the scene. It was a city of the dead. The candles had grown long black "thieves" which were dripping wax on to the polished table; I was sitting in front of Cressida's array of half-emptied glasses, which were all savaged with lipstick. Sacharissa, I noticed, had put a cheap cigarette out in her finger-bowl and another was stubbed into the remains of the *Actinidia*. Mona had spilt the mustard with her cheese soufflé and left a pile of blackened bread pellets, while someone else had buckled their silver-gilt dessert fork on a home-grown pear. I felt suddenly drowning, as if sinking desperately into an abyss of lost identity after Curry Rivel's rudeness and Julian Frere's hostile stare. "Who are you?" I asked myself. "And who the hell cares? Laurian, help, rescue, *au secours*!" Then I looked up. She was there, smiling from her mother's portrait, the round, dark, melting, Sir Peter Lely face, the eyes veiled in compassionate intelligence. My lost self found its way home. "Tell me, Mr. Curry Rivel," I lobbed back, "used you to find a red hock any help as an aphrodisiac?"

"My dear young man," he threatened, "don't you know your 'Paneros'? The answer is there ain't no sich animal." "What about yohimbine? Even Douglas admitted that." "Certainly, Julian, but it is a dangerous drug which can only be administered under medical supervision." "I once read an ancient art of love," Sir Mortimer mediated, "which recommended only two cures—satyrion, whatever that is, and skirret, a herb which once flourished in our cottage gardens." "Satyrion, my dear Morty, is an orchid," said Norman, "whose bulbs have always suggested testicles and hence potency to the old and foolish, and skirret, a Chinese plant which spread to Germany where it was much fancied by the ancient Romans. Skirret has long white roots, rather like parsnip, sweetish to the taste and faintly phallic. *Sias siarum*. You can probably get it from Bunyards." "Geese are very fond of it." "Ha! Geese! My book said that even to hold it in the hand reassembled the vital juices." "Like an electric eel," said Julian. "I've heard dear old Arnold Bennett say you can't beat oysters and champagne," volunteered Ginger Bartlett. "You can't beat *Anno Domini* either," said Sir Mortimer. "One consolation," went on Hugh, "is that we can only be stimulated at our age by what properly belongs to our libido. No more false starts, no barking up the wrong tree or ringing a stale doorbell." "Ringing the wrong doorbell can sometimes be rather amusing," wheezed the publisher. "But I know what you mean. We can still keep a gel, but we can't expect her to be faithful." "Suppose, Hugh, you are married, though," said Sir Mortimer. "Then I'm sorry for you. For if at our age we will stand to attention only for our secret desires, then they are irregular verbs which are seldom to be conjugated in the marriage bed. Still, most wives have now so much on in side bets that they don't make such a fuss as they used. They hardly notice whether their husband is there or not. How would you like to have to make a public demonstration of your bedmanship, Sir Mortimer, with Cressida as your opponent in the centre court? That's what might have happened to you in your beloved seventeeth century, and I don't suppose a second helping of *Sias siarum* or satyrion would have been of much help." We all stared at Curry Rivel and then at Sir Mortimer, who was spellbound. He gazed at Hugh with large wondering eyes that bulged slightly, so that one could see their profile sideways, like his daughter's; his mouth was slightly open and the tip of his tongue protruded. "Go on," he whispered, "what would have happened?" Rivel stuck out a long, minatory forefinger. I noticed the tuft of reddish hair on the phalanx. "I will tell you." We all gulped some port. "But I can't tell you very much. It was called '*Le Congrès*' and though it had been abolished by Justinian as unchristian the women seem to have got it put back in France about the middle of the sixteenth century. You remember that a marriage could be dissolved if the husband was shown through

445

some defect in his equipment to be unfit for copulation and generation. Such as caused the divorce between the Emperor Lothair and his queen, Teutoberga. The smallness of the member, I believe, was in that case generally accepted as the obstacle. However, such malformations are infrequent and the object of the public congress was to present a husband accused by his wife of impotence with a chance to prove himself a man in front of some independent witness, usually the Bishop's steward and his ecclesiastical court. It met with considerable opposition and was described as simply a pretext for divorce thought up by lecherous ladies who had put the idea into the judges' heads, for only one man in a thousand can satisfy so sceptical an audience, and he would be an exhibitionist rather than a marvel of fecundity. During the hundred years while the congress was reintroduced into France there was a great increase in the number of marriages thus dissolved, and so in 1677 the Parliament of Paris abolished it. The repeal arose from the case of René de Cordouan, Marquis de Langey, in 1659. He had been summoned by his first wife to prove his potency in public congress and had failed. By his next wife, Diane de Navailles, he had had seven children. Another Frenchman who failed in his congress before the episcopal court of Le Mans in 1655 was able afterwards to force his wife to produce their legitimate son and so obtained his acquittal. But I hope Cressida is not threatening you with such an ordeal," he went on, "for I don't believe it would cut any ice with a modern jury. If, however, you should fancy the experiment for its own sake, Morty, you couldn't do better than begin with a selected audience from around this table. You would feel among friends. I'm sure dear Cressida would accord you this concession, and even if we detected no deformity and you yet failed signally and publicly to perform your married obligations, you might still claim to have been bewitched, that some enemy had knotted a piece of wolf's tendon or cat skin with coloured thread while the priest was proclaiming 'ego vos jungo' at your wedding; they had 'noué l'aiguillette', as it was called, and the only cure for that would be for you to urinate through your lady's wedding ring—which at our time of life, my dear Morty, is not as easy as it looks."

I found his monologue quite as repellent as much else that had shocked me since my arrival, but I also thought it of considerable interest although no way to address a great man, and I was all the more surprised therefore when Julian Frere suddenly rose to his feet, clapped his hand over his wide clown's mouth and began to zigzag, snipe-like towards the door. "My God!" yelled Sir Mortimer—for Julian, his free hand thrust forward like a sleep-walker's, was working his way up to a china cabinet. "The Sèvres, the Sèvres," squeaked Mortimer. I a flash Ginger Bartlett had grabbed him; he spun him round like a blindfolded figure and sent him off on a straight course to the door. "That's the last of your tame Boswell, Morty. I'm afraid we shall have lost him for the rest of the evening. Mr. Kemble will have to deputize." "You might at least apologize to Julian, Mr. Rivel," I put in, "you've shocked him to the core!" "I think when you are more used to the ways of this house you will realize that it is the Tuke Holdsworth '20 to which he should have apologized for his *non sum dignus*'." "Thank you, Ginger," said Sir Mortimer. "As usual, we talk and you act—I haven't forgotten the evening when the Waterford punch bowl went. He has the most extraordinary cunning in this condition," said Sir Mortimer to me; "he can break the back of a rosewood chair simply by the angle he sits in it. An unconscious knowledge of tensile stresses. We have no punch bowl now, but a silver centre-piece—Cromwellian too, a real 'Ironside'— it can look after itself." "What are the flowers in it?" "I'm glad you asked; another little surprise for our local green-fingers. You behold the fabulous Egyptian lotus, or *Nelumbia negundo,* the sacred bean. For the perfect dinner party I need such flowers with no scent. Otherwise they might confuse the wine. They must also be large and firm yet not too tall and hold up well so that we can hear general conversation round my table, if so we choose, yet not see each other too easily. I'd rather look at them. And— why not? They should be unique. 'Human beans', as Pythagoras said. You grow them too?" He turned to Norman. "No, I haven't the heat unfortunately." "It's not just the heating. I don't believe they would stand commercial exploitation and a series of scalding inoculations and monthly sprayings from large chemical contraptions so that they might increase, enlarge, defy the blights and viruses and wasps, red spider and fungi, lose all quality and delicacy and bring in a sound three per cent in alternate years." There was a distant noise of breaking glass and flushing toilets, a crash from the hall and women's voices. Sir Mortimer rose. "I think we should follow my young admirer's example and try to join the ladies, for I expect they are all in pieces."

As we left, Norman drew his host back into the dining-room. Hugh and Ginger crossed the hall into the drawing-room and I found time to slip off to the lavatory in the hall which Julian had vacated. When I came back I passed the dining-room door and overheard Sir Mortimer in his old tone of authority. "Impossible, quite impossible." "That is final?" "Absolutely, my dear chap." I hurried away as the door opened. I think it is wrong to eavesdrop, though it's different, of course, just to listen for a moment, in case it concerns oneself.

No sooner was I in the drawing-room than I made a bee-line for Laurian who was looking at a photograph album, but I had first to pass a narrow Regency sofa. "Ah, Mr. Kemble—now you can tell us." I found myself squeezed down between Cressida and Sacharissa. "Tell you what?" "Why, all about yourself. How many questions will you answer?" As she spoke Sacharissa managed to make her words vibrate like the silence after Big Ben. Her expression held a contemptuous impertinence which seemed to strip me of all defences. She had only to say the word "Mr." to make me feel completely ridiculous. Cressida took it up. "Will you promise—cross my heart and swear—to answer six questions—three from each—absolutely truthfully?" "What's my reward?" "You shall claim your reward when we know how you've answered. It might be a surprise." "All right," I agreed weakly. I always answer all questions truthfully if only they'd known. "But first, some coffee," said Cressida, "or I shall have failed in my knightly duties. Black?" "Thank you." "One lump?" "Two." "Brandy or Crème de Menthe?" "Neither, thank you." "Cigarettes?" "I'd rather have a chocolate." She took one also and drew back her lips to bite it slowly and neatly in two with her small white teeth. It meant, I thought, "This is how I eat things. This is how I could eat you. I am a dangerous animal"—except that, like everything she did, it might have come out of some play. "Well, here we go. Question one—how old are you?" "Twenty-six." Then from Sacharissa, "Two—are you married?" "No." "Have you got a mistress?" "No." "Are you a virgin?" I looked at this large blooming woman with her mocking expression. What should I say? I gazed into her dark eyes. "Fortunately—yes." She turned to Cressida. "Your witness." "Are you queer?" "Fortunately, no." "Are you in love with Laurian?" I felt like jelly. For a long moment I could not answer. Then I looked straight at her. "For a half an hour—until I met you——" "And since you've met me?" "Oh, Lady Gussage, that's the seventh question! I claim my reward." "Quite right, *jeune homme*," said Sacharissa. "What shall it be?" "I'll sleep on it and let you know." "All right—but answer one more question. What's your Christian name?" "Stephen." "Stephen—it would be!" I felt like a child whom the wrong person has tickled.

Sir Mortimer appeared and offered me a thin cigar which I refused. I don't smoke myself and I find it a horrifying spectacle to watch normally civilized people turning into repressed maniacs as they cough and choke or clutch their pockets, interrupt each other's stories, pinch each other's matches, fill their own cases when no one is looking, and drop ash into cups and cushions or, worst of all, between the pages of books. But I prefer cigars. There are fewer of them. They smell nicer (non-smokers have a very keen sense of smell) and people are more careful where they deposit the ash. But not the stub, and I know of few filthier odours the next morning than an old cigar end soaked in coffee or brandy lying in a waste-paper basket by the bed. My mother was always singing a song about "a cigarette with lipstick's traces", which seemed to me a catalogue of everything I disliked. How would Laurian pass the test? I went off to investigate. To my horror she was sitting with Mr. Frere, playing Halma. "Feeling better?" I ventured. He looked up, held his finger to his lips, tapped his head, hunched his shoulders over the board where the ridiculous little men were copulating with each other in intricate coloured tentacles, and waved me away. Sir Mortimer patted me on the shoulder. "We're going off to have a rubber of bridge in my study—there'll be some drinks in a moment." He opened a door at the far end of the room and disappeared with Bartlett, Curry Rivel, and Sacharissa. I didn't feel like another *tête-à-tête* with either Cressida or the Farrans and so I tried the door at the opposite side. It opened into the conservatory. I switched on the light. It was a delightful place, a Regency addition to the house with one of those swinging bamboo sofas in the middle, some painted, palm-shaped, wrought-iron columns, and a variety of plants and creepers round the walls. I lay down on the sofa, rocked gently, and let the cool air soothe my brow, which was fuming with jealousy and Tuke Holdsworth. I knew my short life had reached a turning-point. In London my paper awaited me, the clean packet of crisp, fresh, bad novels, with the best plums already picked out, which was my weekly fare, the nosebag I had to eat through; the ever-present chance of some extra bit of work, an art exhibition, a trip to Paris or Bordeaux or Bâle or Aberdeen which was paid for by some cultural association or a group of wine merchants, anybody with a vested interest in claret or Burns or Bernoulli or Mérimée, perhaps even a *"rencontre intellectuelle"* at Geneva, a session of the European parliament at Strasbourg or, most prized of all, the Biennale at Venice. A chance of something to do, somewhere to go, when the married experts were too broke to take their wives. Then home to my rather superior boarding-house in Chelsea with the Italian cooking and the young men with a Foreign Office manner, my old school friend John Rainer on the floor below, my leafy attic looking over to Wren's hospital, my own novel to try to finish, the single Paul Klee drawing over the gas fire, the Tallboys Edition, complete, by my bed. This was the known world, safe, if I chose, for another ten years, while beyond this door where I sat were the dragons, the *terra incognita*, the lovely inscrutable female animal at the Halma table. Should I press forward or withdraw? I thought of her mother's glance of reassurance from the portrait and of the wild leg which I had nearly tamed. Then I thought of wives and of women in general. Tears and screams and bad temper, girdles with empty stockings attached lying on chairs, lipstick, hair combings, tiny safety razors going dryly over legs and arm-pits, false laughs into telephones, my mother's thin and angry face and my father's sneering tones. "My idea of hell, Isabel, would be to have to come to you for money." "And mine, *dear*, to depend on *you* for sex." Nymphonaggers! So that way Halma leads . . . There was a footstep on the gravel; the outer door of the conservatory opened and Sir Mortimer strode in. He looked tired, white, and harassed, and I hurried to explain that I myself had just stepped by to cool off. "How's the bridge?" I ended. "I suppose you are dummy." "Bridge—ha!—dummy," he repeated. "Yes, that is exactly what I am—you know something of gardening?" "Nothing at all, I am afraid. What are all these?" "Creepers and climbers mostly—I'm rather keen on them; so feeble and so aimless yet they get exactly where they want; they rise by doodling : oh the cruel strength of the weak! They're not as alive as a good book, but they're certainly more alive than the average human 'bean'—this one in the tub here is a scented rhododendron, Lady Alice Fitzwilliam. The tub, by the way, is copied from those in the Orangerie at Versailles. This is delicate *Mandevilla suaveolens*, this is delicious *Hoya carnosa*, the wax plant with its brown boot-laces, and here is *Passiflora edulis*, the Brazilian passion flower that's suddenly laid an egg. Mustn't lose it by the way." He patted his pocket. "This is *Semele androgyne* from Tenerife—a rum beggar; this lot are some of the more particular clematis and jasmine, straight as a corkscrew, ruthless as a little woman. This is a *Lardizabala*—hasn't earned its keep yet—but I hope to eat that one day too. Here's a humdrum vine, Madresfield Court, a black muscat —nice plant and no mildew—here's a yellow wattle—mimosa to you— which Cressida's very fond of; and here, in this tank, the wonderful Sacred Lotus. Of course it's not really quite a cold-house, as when the drawing-room door's left open we can warm it up. We cheat, I'm afraid. But I like to tease poor Norman with his utilitarian outlook and his limited intelligence; all his fruit have such dreadful names, like 'Belle de Boskoop' and 'American Mother'. This one's a queer chap by the way. He must have come in as a seed with my 'cup-and-saucer' creeper here, *Cobæa scandens*. I thought he was a weed at first, but he soon got round me with those jolly red leaves. Nice habit too, and this year, after some scented white flowers last spring, he's sprouting berries." It didn't look up to much to me. "Perhaps it's a castor-oil plant." "Oh no, nothing so ordinary as that or we'd be using it for ordeals. There's a good subject for you by the way— ordeals of all nations—fire, water, the Calabar bean, the tanghin tree of Madagascar, the manchineel of the Caribs, the deadly upas under which condemned criminals were allowed to sleep. So simple—the innocent vomit, the guilty digest and die. There must be something to it. And here's my first and last love, *Daphne odora*—she's not much to look at now, but in February when there's so little else, she comes out in a tightly packed cluster of pale flowers with the most intense of all the jasmine, orange-blossom, viburnum type of scents. It's not an odour of spring, but one that defies winter and 'the sullen edicts of her mutinous season', and the more you smell it the deeper it recedes, layer within layer. Of course it's tender, but it's August that kills them, not February. You don't smoke, I've noticed. No writer should. You'll keep a nose for these things. My young Boswell now," he tapped his cigar ash over the *Daphne*, "he believes that 'the road of excess leads to the palace of wisdom'. We used to call him 'the Dancing Don' until he danced his way out of a fellowship. And now something tells me I too shan't be able to rely on his services much longer. Perhaps some God has sent you to me in his place. You live by the will, I think, and you're too young to have been dominated by psychoanalysis. It's ruined poor Julian, ruined his health, his judgement, and his self-respect— and of course his vocabulary; he knows the answer before we can think of the question, he can't even dance now; it's become 'a compensatory play therapy'." "But he still admires you, sir, I can see that. When Mr. Curry Rivel went too far in there, he was sick." "Innocence upchucked! Well, I suppose you could put it like that—but never trust him. All admirers are alike. They want to get inside your skin and to have it they'll flay you alive." "Oh, Sir Mortimer—I'm an admirer too." "I suspect you want something else of mine." "Yes, your style." "Are you sure that's all? Well, I bequeath it to you. It's quite easy—a little oil in the vinegar, a little vinegar in the oil, and a clove of garlic rubbed round the bowl. It's not my style of course—Chateaubriand, Flaubert, Baudelaire, Huysmans—they all knew the secret. You must try to feel unpleasant things so truthfully that they become pleasant, and vice-versa. Laugh at the funeral, weep at the wedding. Remember we all carry in ourselves an inexhaustible source of vitality which is pure spirit. Art is the only vehicle which can hold and subjugate its burning activity. Life is unworthy of such fire; except at rare moments life drags us down. But art, alas, is for the few, for the lucky, for the lonely. Art is always round the corner. For the majority there is nothing but sex and money, money and sex, *'at nos vino scortisque demerso?'* And how they all hate art! especially literature; and none of course hate it more than the literary—so remember : creation is its own reward. Creation— not the processing and packaging of what we have created—and it is our only pleasure and our only reward. After all, what's literature? An arrangement of vowels and consonants—that's poetry. And prose then?—an arrangement of consonants and vowels. There's nothing in the world so beautiful as one's next book or so bad as the last one. I divide people up into those who produce life and beauty and those who consume them, and when I have to make up my mind about someone, I always apply my test. Producers and Consumers—it sounds so simple. And I prefer producers who can't produce to consumers who are disguised as producers, the better to consume us. There are some of each here tonight; I wonder if you can

451

tell them apart—you should learn to recognize the consumers by their vocabulary—it's more pretentious—they are nearly always rich or homo-sexual or both—the rich used to be patrons of art, now they are the artist's most jealous rivals. Three maladies I have lived to see destroy my world— or are they the same one? The increasing meanness of the rich, the ubiqui-tous infiltration of homosexuality, and everybody a snob about everything. And now I must get back to my rubber." He went out by the garden door and made off towards the study, which probably had a french window. I contemplated the "productive" vine in its October livery, rank and barnacled, mottled with mauve and crimson, still carrying one or two desiccated bunches of black grapes which drooped pathetically among the carefree exuberance of the "consuming" evergreens. I picked up a fallen leaf of the unknown plant and put it in my wallet. Then I felt cold again and opened the inner door to return to the fire.

Laurian made room for me beside her on the sofa. She smiled and then I understood that there can be moments at the beginning of a relationship when by a visual intuition the eyes pierce right through to the essential magic of another person, which is indeed the vitality of pure spirit. My jealousy had been groundless. I even tried to pass a little of my happiness on to poor Mona, who was by my other side. "Do you have to get up very early to fruit-farm?" I said. "No, not very. But don't worry, we're leaving all the same." "Oh, I didn't mean that." Then Cressida drew me in to her conversation with the other two men. "I'm just describing the perfect dish for the perfectionist's birthday," she trilled, "do listen— Stephen—Julian—Mona—Norman! Well, you take a large olive and stuff it with capers and anchovy, then soak it in pure olive oil and tuck it inside a beccafico—that's a little fig bunting—after cutting off its head and claws —the bird's I mean. Then you put the beccafico inside a nice fat ortolan, and after taking most of its bones out, as well as cutting off its claws and its head, you stuff the ortolan inside a nice fat juicy quail, straight off the vines, and you wrap a vine leaf round it—we can certainly manage that— and stuff it in a small plover. Put the plover, with a slice of very thin bacon round it, inside a fine young partridge—if you can—and the partridge inside a lovely tender woodcock, well hung. And the woodcock, with a few croûtons of bread, inside a teal, and the teal, wrapped in bacon of course, inside a young guinea-fowl—they're too tough after the first year when they get their 'jugglers'. And the guinea-fowl inside a fine white Surrey chicken, and the chicken inside a capercailzie, very well hung indeed—that's always the hardest part—and the capercailzie inside a nice green goose—make sure its feet are still soft and its beak is flexible. And the goose inside a splendid Christmas turkey—and finally a real gourmet stuffs the turkey inside an enormous bustard—one used to see them in Hungary—and then you fill in all the gaps with Lyon chestnuts, sausage meat, and stuffing. Next you put the whole thing in a large pot with onions pricked with cloves, ham chopped up very small, celery, mignonette (why mignonette? wait!), a *'bouquet garni'*, plenty of bacon, salt, pepper, spices, coriander, and a couple of cloves of garlic. Seal it up hermetically with pastry so that it's quite airtight. Then cook it very slowly for twenty-four hours on a gentle fire so that it gets the heat equally, preferably in the oven. Now, listen carefully—we're getting to the holy of holies of cooking! We have here the quintessence of forest, marsh, plain and farmyard, all these juices and emanations are being stealthily volatilized and united and blended into the most exquisite whole, a unique gastronomic experience—but meanwhile this quintessence has penetrated to the very heart of the whole matter, that is to the olive. So you carve open the bustard very carefully and throw it out of the window or give it to the dogs if you have any; same treatment for the turkey, the goose, the capercailzie, the chicken, the guinea-fowl, the teal, the woodcock, the partridge, the plover, the quail, the fieldfare, the ortolan, the poor little beccafico, until finally in a spirit of true gratitude and admiration we serve dear old Morty up the olive. He will have to hold it for a long time in his mouth. I'm told it's *'vâchement succu . . .'* "

We all laughed, some louder than others, according to our sense of *'déjà lu'*. I felt as if I had listened to a recital of the whole of Cressida's love-life, and she was still preening herself on her cleverness when the Farrans rose to bid us good night. "Do come over to tea with us tomorrow," said Mona, "it's quite close, just the other side of the village, the old mill, you can't miss it. Now I must find my outer shoes." Norman shook my hand with gentle persistence. "Yes, do come, if you can tear yourself away from all this magnificence. And bring Laurian." They had just left when the bridge four appeared and pressed us all to whisky. I wanted to ask Curry Rivel a question. "Tell me," I said, "I've been thinking about what you told us. Did you ever *'nouer l'aiguillette'* yourself?" "Good heavens, no— well, not exactly, but when I lived in the Tarn I do remember a strange affair. There was a young chap whom I considered had been impertinent. He was just getting married to a maid of mine. As he left the villa I called out, 'That settles it, *je te nouerai l'aiguillette.'* I thought no more about it. But he did—and he believed it—and for a month he couldn't go to bed with his wife, and the harder he tried the worse it became, she grew more and more unco-operative; when he got into her bed his stomach would swell like a pumpkin and he could only obtain relief by keeping altogether out of her way. She, of course, began to loathe the sight of him.

Naturally, I tried to make everything all right when she told me, but they wouldn't listen and made out to everyone I had bewitched them. In the end it was only cleared up by the priest by whom they had been married. Cock's testicles on broad beans broken under the bed are a cure (the ancient food of the dead incidentally), so be careful not to cross my path, young fellow!" Suddenly everyone remembered the time and began to wish Sir Mortimer a happy birthday. Cressida made us all sing the doleful jingle. The great writer stood in the doorway as he accepted our congratulations, bidding us good night and looking slowly round at the china birds and the flowers and the bright fire, the Watteau and Tiepolo drawings and a pair of elongated figure-paintings by Marcellus Laroon. I thought I had never seen anyone so handsome, so compelling, with his Mediterranean figure, his warm and luminous personality dominating the room. He had a large red notebook under one arm and his plate of fruit in the other. He raised it above his head when he saw me and handed me the book to hold while he waved his other hand to the company. "Ah, good night, my young disciple. Remember my advice and steer clear of consumers. They'll gobble you up like they've gobbled me. Julian, you will show Mr. Kemble to his room, which is opposite yours, and you will treat him with the deference due to your successor, for your apprenticeship, I fear, is ending. I am afraid there is nothing more I can teach you. Go forth and prosper! But you— Stephen Kemble :

> *'But you, whom ev'ry Muse and Grace adorn*
> *Whom I foresee to better fortune born*
> *Be kind to my remains; and, oh, defend*
> *Against your judgement your departed friend!*
> *Let not th'insulting Foe my fame pursue*
> *But shade those laurels which descend to you.'* "

It was spoken with such mellow and piercing sweetness that we all applauded. For a moment he still remained smiling in the doorway, a glowing bearded Wotan, his spear unshattered, while he performed a vague gesture of benediction over Laurian and Cressida with the raised fruit, and then he bowed to Sacharissa with his inscrutable expectant smile, seized his red notebook from me, and disappeared upstairs, his stooping, rather heavy back bunched in to his wine-dark smoking jacket, a bald patch showing from behind like a pink celluloid duck's bottom clamped on his head, his chestnut hair a shade too long over his velvet collar. One could see nature had generally intended him to face his audience. A moment afterwards Hugh solemnly offered his arm to Sacharissa, who also said good night to me. " 'Whom every Muse and every Grace adorn'—we shall see, we shall see." I noticed that she was taking a large whisky with her. No sooner were they out of the room than Julian returned to life. "You heard that, Cressida—I've got the sack. The same old formula—nothing more we can teach you, we fear. You should find a wider scope for your activities outside the curriculum. Too old at thirty-three! Humanism is a club with an entrance fee of £2,000 a year." He clapped his hands and a skew-eyed smile froze his wide mouth, his long legs shot out sideways like Valentin le Desossé's, as with his white face glazed like a Rouault clown's, he trucked up to Cressida, firing his hand like a Sten-gun, then tap-danced a little, "broke" professionally, and whirled her off round the room. She, too, danced like a Degas ballerina, with her nubbly little legs, on their points, and her supple fingers cracking. They carried on an isolated dialogue between their personalities, she twirling, and pirouetting and interpolating fragments of bolero, he beginning the Miller's Dance from *The Three Cornered Hat* and then bopping it up into a kind of expressionistic stomp, his dead-pan face with its lock of black hair sagging in front of him in a stylized rictus. Effective, I had to admit, though vulgar. I too, would have liked to ask Laurian to dance, but I felt handicapped as there was no music. Julian came to a stop with one of those fading cadenzas that we perform in our dreams, picked up Cressida, threw her over his shoulder, and carried her out of the room with one little leg outstretched, the other bent, and her arm held out with finger crooked, like a mechanical toy. Laurian said, "I'd better show you to your room; I don't suppose anyone else will." The house was very simply arranged, the pattern of hall with living-room leading into study on one side and dining-room leading into kitchen on the other was carried out on two floors; Cressida and Sir Mortimer were on either side of the stairhead, each with a bathroom, while Sacharissa and Hugh Curry Rivel, with a bathroom between them, looked out over the back. On the floor above were Laurian and her bathroom and Julian, and on the other Ginger Bartlett, another bathroom, myself. The Italian couple were in a built-on flat off the kitchen and were helped by two girls from the village during the day. The bathrooms had been made out of dressing-rooms and powder closets and in no way altered the architecture of the house. A light came from under Sir Mortimer's door as we passed and another from my neighbour the publisher. I noticed with relief a fitted basin in my bedroom; I didn't want to wash in the bathroom between us until he was out of the way, for of all the visitors he was the one with whom I had established least contact, though some day he might prove the most useful. "I hope you have everything," said Laurian. I looked round at the pleasant white room with an electric fire burning, a pair of bird pictures by Simon Bussy, a caricature of Roger Fry, and a scribbled Lear landscape, at the single four-poster in plain mahogany with my white Egyptian cotton pyjamas neatly laid out, at the water carafe and biscuits by my bed and the little row of books, three or four volumes of Turgenev, a dozen old copies of *Life and Letters* and *Horizon*, *Wylder's Hand*, *Modern Love*, *Gryll Grange*, *Jacob's Room*, Francis Birrell's anthology of famous last words; I noticed the pale Samarkand rug, the heavy red curtains drawn across the mild October night, the glowing bedside-lamp, and I knew that I had everything that I could possibly want. The room epitomized the enlightened pre-war comfort of which I realized I could never breathe enough; the security which now was out of nearly every reach, which once the addiction had taken root, one would almost commit murder to preserve. Indeed many people had killed Germans, Italians, Austrians, Hungarians, Japanese, just in order to keep it going, for to fight for one's country is to fight for one's standard of living, and if these things in themselves were not enough, there was Laurian standing beside me. "You need a *calm* mother" as my father once said. "A rock to jump off." It came over me that I hadn't felt quite so strongly about her since dinner. Something had broken the spell. It was another spell—her father's voice and perhaps more than a little bit of Cressida's. I was no longer obedient only to her low tones and direct gaze, but made restless by her father's words; his interest in me was breathlessly exciting, but when I tried to think of that fine head which reflected the extraordinary Renaissance wholeness of his personality, I couldn't see him plainly either—only Cressida's body being carried out on Julian's shoulder, the rigid thigh, the bent brown arm. "Thank you very much, for absolutely everything. Where are you?" She led me across the passage and opened the door into an even warmer-looking room where I glimpsed a row of little silver gymkhana cups and a smaller sketch or painting of her mother. "Good night. Breakfast downstairs from nine onwards—dressing-gowns permitted," she said abruptly, and closed the door.

I have stayed too little in other people's houses not to find the nights very strange. When the guests are put away in their boxes till the morning and the theatre closed, there must be a simultaneous lifting of masks all over the house, a confrontation in the mirror of wrinkle and roll as memories and medicine bottles are brought out and the bray of one's own voice dies away. I wondered if I was going to have one of my own "blackouts" among these unfamiliar surroundings when one is conscious only of consciousness and absolutely of nothing else for an interminable second while the heart seems to stop. Then as I got into my bed I thought of all the other single visitors who had used it, their hopes and desires, their cumulative flatulence and indigestion, the worries they had tried to shut out between Saturday and Monday and to which they had inevitably to return.

Tomorrow I must have a look at the visitors' book. These always fascinate me; I like to watch the self-assured signatures that turn up week after week suddenly falter and disappear as they get too old or ill or poor to be asked again, as the sociability is squeezed out of them, or as the genial host dies and the philistine heir takes his place. I like also to see the grand beginnings of a reign peter out into a string of poor relations and punctual toadies until the page begins to die a natural death and the guests' names are pencilled in afterwards because they can't be bothered to sign them, and the book itself starts on its downhill journey to the junk shop or the loft. All the windy pretensions of a generation of noisy nobodies who turn up to stuff themselves every Christmas and suddenly conk out like the turkeys that were fattened for them or the bad champagne on their sour stomachs! Consumers, consumers disguised as producers—you should know them by their vocabulary: *"Couldn't* have enjoyed myself more— *couldn't* have been more agreeable—bless you, you *dear* people, thanks for a *wonderful* time." Then it came over me that in these houses they have a habit of taking one's clothes away to be brushed in the early morning so that when I get up I never can find the comb which I always carry. I jumped out of bed to turn out my pockets. There was my wallet, with the ten-shilling note I was going to leave as tip—consumer's conscience money —my return ticket, another pound and some silver, the leaf I had picked up; there was my nylon comb in its little case. And yet an absence was postulating itself. My God—where was the obituary? I went through all my pockets and three times over the breast-pocket where I seemed to remember having stuffed it. It might still be in my overcoat or it might have fallen out somewhere downstairs. I knew I should get no sleep till I found it. Supposing the servants swept it up tomorrow morning! I put on my brown dressing-gown and red slippers and tiptoed out. All was quiet in the passage and there was a little light on the landing from a window above the stairs. When I came to the next floor, I listened. Silence. I crept on down, crossed the hall, went into the dining-room and turned on the light. There was a smell of apples, port, and stale cigar smoke. Some preliminary clearing-up had been done and there was no sign of any strip of paper beside my place. I went into the sitting-room, switched on a lamp, and looked in the sofa where I had been sitting. Not a trace. I was approaching the conservatory and my hand was on the door when I heard a laugh, a low sensual chuckle. Cressida! "Go on—admit it—he's a cross between a rabbit and a ferret." That was Julian's sleazy voice. The answer was another low laugh followed by a slap: the hollow dry detonation of a man's hand on a woman's naked buttock—and then no sound but the rhythmic metal creaking of the swinging garden sofa, groaning and sighing like rigging at night. I turned and ran. Back in the hall I halted and went

457

through my overcoat pockets with no success, and I was tiptoeing up the stairs again when I heard a door open. I shrank back against the wall. Sacharissa stood in the arch of her room, against the light; she was in a flowered and flowing nightgown, one hand was pressed against her chest. She looked absolutely ghastly. She had not just taken her make-up off, she had removed her mask as well. I saw a face haggard with calamity; lines round her neck, lines down from the ends of her mouth, lines on her brow, eyes staring out into some appalling vision with the grey opacity of dead oysters—a drawing of Lady Macbeth by Fuseli, a Regency Clytemnestra. She looked up and down the passage for a moment, then silently closed her door. I continued my ascent and reached my room without incident, only breathing safely again when I was back in bed. Then the words hit me. "A cross between a rabbit and a ferret." Could he mean—would he dare? Again I jumped out of bed, turned on the light, and looked in the glass. My usual round face with the features which passports call "regular" —the blue eyes, curly hair, which has been untruthfully described as albino since my eyebrows and eyelashes are perfectly visible, and the small, tidy mouth—stared back at me. A face *"égal à soi-même"*. No—he must be jealous of me to devise such an insult, and jealous because I had made a strong enough impression on her to give him cause. But the ignominious disloyalty of their relationship!—and under Sir Mortimer's own roof. Should I have opened the door? Should I tell him in the morning? Should I leave? He had relied on me—was it not my duty? I thought again of that bestial laugh, the expanding thigh and the soft creaking like a rowlock, and I was seized in a tumult of horror and fascination. If him, why not me? Then I remembered the liberty he had taken when he pushed my handkerchief down. Could he have pulled the typescript out at the same time? Would I have put it in my breast-pocket? I began once more to mull over the proceedings at the office until I could no longer clearly remember anything. I tried to read, but even Turgenev seemed insipid. I ate my biscuits, drank my water, got out and looked for more books. I discovered a few old novels and then two of Sacharissa's wartime efforts. One was a horrible short-lived best-seller, *Diggory Dock, Smallholder*, in which a city clerk, when rejected for the Army, takes to the land, cultivates a few chalky acres with barley and brussels sprouts, captures a German parachutist, and marries a fascinating *"femme de lettres"* who is the widowed lady of the manor. I think the Ministry of Information must have distributed it. There were only thirty pages but they worked like pentathol.

I was woken by Laurian, fully dressed and very pale. "It is ten o'clock," she said. "I have come to tell you that Daddy had a stroke some time during the night and never recovered consciousness. He died about half-an-hour ago. The doctor is with him and wants to see you." She went out without looking at me and spoke from the door, "You had better wait in the dining-room. Angelo will pack for you." In a few minutes I had dressed and shaved and was rushing downstairs. The dining-room was empty, but I detected a small reproachful spirit flame which still kept vigil over coffee and hot milk and also a poached egg and sausage in a covered dish, prepared before the blow had fallen. Since I seemed to be in some kind of disgrace I relapsed into the greedy, obstinate silence which I had found the best weapon against my parents and afterwards so useful at school and during my glimpse of the Army. It was a fresh country egg, the sausage was brown and crisp, the coffee delicious. I went on to a piece of toast and some bitter Oxford marmalade. Laurian came in just as I had finished. "This is Doctor Hislop," she said. The doctor was thin and sunburnt and looked more like Harley Street than Wiltshire, the type of coming man whose name is last on bulletins of royal illness. "This is a very bad business, Mr. Kemble. I will keep you no longer than is necessary. You knew Sir Mortimer well?" "I only met him once before yesterday, at a cocktail party." "He took a great fancy to you, I understand." "I am very glad to hear it." "He seemed to you in good health and spirits last night?" "Perfectly. I thought he looked very well. Almost too well." "What do you mean by that?" "I mean he had a very high colour." "When was that?" "After dinner—and when he went to bed he was pale." "You didn't see him afterwards?" "Not at all." "I see. Well, as you know, Sir Mortimer had a cerebral hæmorrhage during the night. He was of course a hyper-tensive type, but such things are usually brought on at his age by a shock of some kind. Sometimes by over-exertion, sometimes by bad news, sometimes just by bad temper. This was found on his pillow. Do you recognize it?" "Yes." "You wrote it?" "Yes." *"More than anyone now living Sir Mortimer appreciated the things which he could touch or see*—what on earth do you mean by that?" "I should have thought it was perfectly clear." "Clear that you knew he was going to die when you wrote it?" "No. I mean it is an obituary such as every big newspaper keeps in its files for celebrities." "Then why did you bring it with you?" "I had originally written it as a tribute for his birthday. 'Sir Mortimer Gussage. An appreciation.' My editor did not require this and so he had altered the tenses. The changes in the typescript are his. He will corroborate me if you will get in touch with him." "Then what induced you to show it to Sir Mortimer?" "I never did anything of the kind. The paper disappeared during the evening and I myself think it was stolen and deliberately put in Sir Mortimer's possession by someone who was jealous of me." "Who do you mean?" "Mr. Julian Frere." "That's nonsense." "No, I don't think it is," said

Laurian. "Daddy said in front of all of us that he accepted Mr. Kemble as a new disciple instead of Julian." "Well, I am afraid I shall have to keep this. I don't think at present an inquest is necessary. Sir Mortimer's rages were proverbial and I had been fearing something like this for the last year or so. With a blood pressure of 200 one can't afford the larger emotions. But in case the authorities should want to look at it, I shall seal it in this envelope here—and may I have your address? I am afraid, Mr. Kemble, that a most malicious error of taste and judgement must lie heavy on your conscience for some years to come." Angelo put his head in. "Signor's taxi here." "You have taken advantage of the hospitality of a great and generous man to play an odious and dangerous practical joke on him, and even if it were through an accident that he came into the possession of this paper, I cannot absolve you from the discourtesy of bringing it into the house with such fatal consequences. You will understand that Lady Gussage is too upset to see you and that her other guests are not minded to. As her medical adviser as well as Sir Mortimer's, I must request you to go." "Certainly. After the way I have been treated I have no wish to stay. I only ask you to show the same alacrity in getting rid of Mr. Frere, who has played this revolting trick on Sir Mortimer and myself. I shall of course consult my solicitors." I found myself replying in exactly the language derived from stormy scenes in Victorian novels, which he had already used to me and I felt a little better, for Laurian had been impressed. Then I remembered Angelo and put my hand in my pocket. I'd left all my money upstairs. "With your permission, I'm going up to fetch my wallet," I said. "I must have left it in the drawer by my bed. Don't wait, please. Goodbye, Laurian. Dr. Hislop, my compliments." I raced on tiptoe up the stairs while they both remained just inside the dining-room. The money was where I'd left it and I was coming back through the silent house when I was seized with an inscrutable impulse. Why not? I had as much right, surely, as anyone. On the first-floor landing I paused, then quietly opened Sir Mortimer's door. There was no one in the room. I walked quickly over and raised the sheet. He lay in perfect repose with the strange emptiness of the dead. The eyes were closed, his pointed beard, sharp nose, and waxen brow were like some painted Elizabethan effigy on a Cotswold tomb, while everything else in the room but his body seemed to pulsate with his indignant and infinitely lonely presence. His expression was withdrawn as if brooding on some unattainable epithet. Only the colour, a high suffused purple round the throat which contrasted with the pallor of the brow, reminded me of the description of Flaubert as viewed by Maupassant. I looked down at the noble head which had for so long spun the words that had created my own valid beliefs and on the one person in the house who didn't believe that I had tried to kill him, the first corpse

I had ever seen—my "cold feary father"—then I dropped the sheet. I noticed the big red notebook by his bed and lifted the cover. "EYES, LOOK YOUR LAST," was printed on the fly-leaf in huge capitals. "A valediction" by Mortimer Gussage, and underneath he had written a quotation from Peacock, "Nothing in this world is perfect but the music of Mozart." I turned over the tawny hand-woven pages. They were all blank.

As I was leaving I glanced at the waste-paper basket. A familiar object reposed among the crumpled circulars, the empty husk of the solitary passion fruit, Laurian's birthday gift to her father. An appropriate souvenir! I picked it up and put it in my overcoat pocket. When I got back to the hall (my whole journey had taken only two or three minutes) she was waiting by the door. I noticed the visitors' book on the hall table and felt a wild desire to force it open and perpetuate my abbreviated visit: "Stephen Kemble. Saturday, Oct. 16th–Sunday, Oct. 17th. 'The Sunday Recorder', Fleet St."—but no further delay was permissible. Laurian spoke: "I waited to tell you that I believe you. I can't say any more. Goodbye. Thank you for coming." "Please answer me one question. Who found him?" "Cressida. She went in to see why he hadn't rung for breakfast; that was at half-past nine. He was unconscious, but still breathing then; but he died before Dr. Hislop could get here. He is a Harley Street man who spends week-ends in the village." "And my article?" "She found it on the pillow." "Could she have put it there?" "She would never do such a thing. She adored Daddy." "Had he eaten anything in the night?" "Half a pear and the Pitmaston pippin; the remains were on his plate with his Chinese gooseberry, which he hadn't touched. He usually ate some fruit as soon as he got into bed. I suppose that was about one o'clock this morning." I said nothing. I believed that even as I had apprehended her true self from a glance she had seen into mine. I went up close to her and put my hands on her shoulder. She raised her long, white face. We closed our eyes and let our two bowed foreheads touch, for a second or two, holding our hands together, fingers upward, palm against palm. I felt her sorrow, her solitude, her courage, her devotion to her father flowing into my heart. "Fairest Cordelia, that are most rich, being poor/most choice forsaken and most loved despised." I tried to put everything I had felt for father and daughter into the bone in my forehead. "I love you. I will wait for you. When I can help you, send for me," I telepathized through my head. I felt the faint pressure of her nipples firm on my chest as she leant against me. We opened our eyes and were standing again on the wide stone steps by the blue tangle of rosemary. I gave Angelo his ten shillings. "Is Cressida taking it very badly?" I asked. "She has been wonderful. So efficient. Sacharissa is more upset. There's so little for her to do, really—and she had a presentiment." I got into the cab. "You know where to find me?" "Yes." We drove round the gravel sweep in front of the house and then headed down the lime avenue which only a few hours ago I had seen for the first time. Laurian remained in the door with her arm raised in an antique farewell, and from all the concave unrestored panes in the Georgian windows I had the impression of staring eyes. I shrank back into my corner as the driver accelerated through the stone gates and turned down into the valley, swerving to avoid the two Farrans who were walking up to the house. She was red-eyed, holding a large handkerchief and dressed in black, he wore a black tie, this time with green tweeds, and looked straight ahead with an expression not so much of grief as of sheer and utter panic. "The few—the lucky and the lonely," as Sir Mortimer had called us—did not seem to include Mr. Diggory Dock.

MARCH 1956

DAN JACOBSON

Fresh Fields

WHEN I WAS AT THE university in Johannesburg there was one living South African writer whom I, like most of my friends with literary inclinations or ambitions, greatly admired. That writer was Frederick Traill, poet, essayist, and novelist. To us it seemed that Traill, almost alone in the twentieth century, had shown that it was possible for a man to make poetry out of the forlorn, undramatic landscapes of our country, out of its ragged *dorps*; out of its brash little cities that pushed their buildings towards a sky too high above them; out of its multitudes of people who shared with one another no prides and no hopes. And because Traill had done it, we felt that with luck, with devotion, we might manage to do the same. Like Traill, we might be able to give a voice to what had previously been dumb, dignity to what had previously been without association or depth; in our less elevated moods we could hope simply that like Traill we would be able to have our books published in London, and have them discussed in the literary reviews.

Traill was for us, therefore, not only a poet, he was a portent or a promise. It was taken for granted among us that Traill should live in England, whence all our books came; his exile, indeed, was part of the exhortatory significance of his career. In England Traill had remained aloof from the political and artistic furores of his time. He had issued no polemics; he had not voiced his opinions of Britain's foreign policies; he had lived in obscurity throughout the war. The little that we knew of him in South Africa was that he had made his home in the country, well away from London, that he had always shunned publicity, and that he was known to few people.

All of this, I found out when I first came to England a few years after the war, was true. Everybody had heard of him; nobody knew where he lived; many people thought he was dead, for it was a very long time since he had published his last volume of verse. For me the revelation of that first visit to England can be described most simply by saying that in coming to England I saw, wherever I looked, the word made flesh—made brick, too; made colour; made light; made trunk and leaf. But in the midst of this

463

sudden solidification or enfleshment of almost everything I had ever read, Traill remained no more than a name to me. All around me was the country that others had described and celebrated; the one man who had uttered the words for my own distant country remained unknown. I picked up what gossip I could about him; but there was very little of it. I heard that he was married; that he was childless; that his wife was ailing. And that was about all. Eventually, when I met a director of the firm which had published Traill's books—Parkman was the man's name—Arnold Parkman—I blurted out to him the admiration I felt for Traill, and my sense of frustration that there seemed no chance of meeting him. Calmly, the publisher replied, "You should write to him. I'm sure he'll be pleased to hear from you." He must have seen that I was taken aback by the simplicity of the suggestion, because he added, "Frederick's really a very friendly man, you know. I wish he wrote more, that's all."

"So do I," I said.

But I made no promise to write to Traill. Like many people of my generation (I suspect) I wished to lead some kind of "literary life" without in any way appearing to do so: the thought of writing, as an aspirant author, to a great name—and Traill's name was a great one to me—made me feel embarrassed, pushful, and, worst of all, unfashionable. That kind of thing, I felt, might have been all very well twenty or thirty years before; but in post-war, comfort-clutching, cigarette-grabbing, shabby, soiled Britain—no, it just wouldn't do. Not for me. All the same, when the publisher told me that Traill lived in South Devon, and gave me the name of the village in which he lived, I made a careful note of it. I felt I had a proprietary interest in South Devon; my girl-friend's parents lived there, and I had visited them, and had travelled about a little in the area.

I didn't remember seeing the name of the village, Colne, on any map or signboard; but when I next visited my future in-laws, I took out a large-scale map and found the village on it without any difficulty. And one fine day (the day was really fine: in mid-summer, cloudless and hot) I set out on a cross-country bus-trip to Colne. The trip promised to be a long one, involving two or three changes, and I did not know what I would do when I got there; I did not even know the name of the house in which Traill lived. But I set out on the journey as though it was something I had always intended to do, and without any doubt that I should succeed in seeing him.

Colne was pleasant without being picturesque. It had a stubby little church with a tower, hidden behind trees, it had a village store and a whitewashed pub with a bench and table in front of it, it had a police station, a village hall, and a war memorial. The road did not run straight through the village, but turned, spread itself between the pub and the store, and then swung upwards again, towards Dartmoor. For miles the road had been climbing, and from Colne one looked back and saw fields and hedges and woodlands tilted against one another, or sweeping smoothly over the curves of hills, or lying in sunken valleys. And above them all, on the far side of Colne, was the bald, high brow of the moor, its nakedness made more emphatic by the rich, close signs of cultivation evident everywhere else. Below Colne, the land had been measured and measured again, parcelled into little lots, divided a hundredfold by the hedges which met at corners, ran away at angles, lost themselves in the woodlands, emerged at angles beyond. And, but for the moor, there was greenness everywhere—so many shades of green, from the palest yellow-green of the stubble where the first fields had been cut, to the darkness of the hedges, which you would have thought to be black, had they not been green also.

Most of the houses in Colne seemed to advertise Devonshire Cream Teas, but I went to the pub where I was offered a plate of biscuits with some cheese. I took the food and a lager, and went outside to eat my meal in the sun. The little open space in front of the pub was almost at the edge of the village, not its centre, and I looked out directly on a hedge, the road, a field, an open barn. There were few people about. I saw the village store being closed for the lunch-hour; some workmen who had been bending over a tractor in the barn nearby went into the public bar; a moustached old man with a military bearing and a hard red skin went into the saloon bar. Several car-loads of tourists passed along the main road, on their way to the moor; several other cars came in the other direction, from the moor, with bunches of heather stuck into their radiator grilles. Three packed coaches went up in a convoy : I had heard the complaint of their engines, in the quiet of the afternoon, from miles away.

And then I saw Frederick Traill walking towards me. Though he had rarely been photographed I knew it was him immediately. He was tall; he was bent, bald, and old. I felt a pang to see how old he was; the photographs, my own image of him, had prepared me to meet a younger man. He walked by me, with a glance down at the table, through his small steel-rimmed glasses. I was sure that I was betraying some kind of confusion; I was embarrassed by the crumbs on the table. But he walked on without a second glance, and I turned to see him go into the pub, bending his head at the door. His tweed jacket was peaked over the back of his neck; it hung loosely, wide over his hips.

I finished my food in a hurry; I did not want to be caught with it still in my hands when he came out. But I need not have worried, or hurried. The minutes passed; the workmen came out and went back to their tractor; a car carrying two men and two women stopped a few yards from me, and they all went noisily into the bar. I could have followed them, but I sat where I was : I felt that I would rather approach Traill where no curious or affable barman could overhear us, no stranger could stare. As I sat there I rehearsed how I was going to introduce myself to him; what I was going to say to him. Vainly, foolishly, I even permitted myself the fantasy that he might have heard of me, might have read something I had written, though I had so far published only a couple of stories in the most obscure and ill-printed of little magazines.

In fact, when I approached him as he came out of the pub, he shook his head almost as soon as I opened my mouth. "Mr. Traill?" I had said, and he stood there, shaking his head, looking at me and over me, his glasses low on his small nose.

"You aren't Frederick Traill?" I felt foolish, and small—literally small, because he was much taller than I, and had the advantage of the step as well.

Still he shook his head. But he said, "Yes, I am Frederick Traill."

I was relieved to hear him speak, and not only because he had acknow-ledged his identity. He kept his mouth half-closed as he spoke, but his accent was unmistakable : it was my own. "I thought you must be," I said. "I recognized you from your photographs."

He looked suspiciously at me; then moved forward, as if to come down the step. I took a pace back. "I hoped I might see you," I said. "I heard from Arnold Parkman that you lived in Colne. I'm staying near High Coombe for a few weeks. I'm from South Africa originally."

I caught a glance from his small, pale blue eyes. "You are? What part of South Africa?"

"Lyndhurst."

For the first time he smiled faintly. "I know Lyndhurst. I used to visit an uncle of mine there when I was a boy."

"You wrote *Open Mine* about it."

"Yes, I did," he said, without much apparent interest in what he was saying; without surprise that I should have known the poem. He stepped down and began walking away; I hung behind, at a loss. I might have let him go, without another word, if I hadn't thought to myself, *That man there is Frederick Traill*. I saw his bald head, and beyond it the Devon countryside; and I felt that if I let him go the encounter would seem no more than a childish dream of my own.

How I was to wish later that I had let him go! But I did not. I called out, "Mr. Traill."

He stopped and turned to me. "Yes."

"I wanted to talk to you," I said. "Your work meant so much to me, when I was in South Africa. And—and to lots of people I knew. I'd be so glad if you could—if you would let me——"

466

"I don't give interviews," he said bluntly.

The oddity of the remark did not strike me at the time: how many people could there have been who had made the pilgrimage to Colne in order to interview him for the press? "I don't belong to any newspaper," I replied.

"No?"

"No, it's just that I've read your work."

He seemed to consider for a moment what I had said, and then said hesitatingly, "What did you want to ask me about?"

"Everything."

Again he smiled faintly, as if from a distance. "Well, as long as you don't expect me to answer everything . . ." The gesture of his shoulders was an invitation to me to join him, which I eagerly did. Together, we walked up through the village; then we turned from the main road and went up a stony little lane. There were a couple of small houses on the lane, but we passed these, and came to a wooden gate, set at the right angle between a brick wall on one side and a stone wall on the other. The stone wall ran on with the lane, until trees hid it from sight. "This is the back-entrance to the house," Traill explained, as he led me through the gate, and closed it behind us. "The lane goes right round to the front." Then he said, "My vegetable garden; I spend a lot of time on it." The vegetable garden was big and obviously kept up with great care. The house itself was an old rambling double-storey cottage with a slate roof and walls half-clad with slate. The house leaned, it bulged, it opened out unexpectedly at doors and little windows; it straightened itself at a chimney that ran all the way down one wall. We walked around the house, past a walled flower garden; in front of the house there was a meadow, as green and sunken as any pond, with a gravelled drive running to one side of it. The entrance to the drive was hidden behind a bank of trees. Beyond those trees, at a distance of many miles, the single pale curve of a hill filled the horizon.

It was a lovely, ripe, worked-over place. We sat down in deck-chairs on a little lawn in front of the house, and talked casually, for a while, about the weather and the view. But eventually the conversation turned to Traill's work. I told him of the admiration I felt for it; I told him something of what I and my friends had felt his career to be for us; I said how sorry I was that he had not written anything for so long. And while I talked, I kept looking at him, taking in, for memory's sake, his long, slack figure, with his legs crossed at the ankles and his hands clasped behind his head; his bespectacled, small-featured face, with its clusters of wrinkles at the sides of his mouth and eyes. His head was almost entirely bald, and his scalp was faintly freckled. I could see that he was pleased by what I was saying, but I felt that he was saddened by it too, and eventually I fell silent, though there was much which I hadn't yet said to him and though I was disappointed that I had not drawn him out to speak more.

But he said nothing about his work; instead he asked me about mine. He asked me what I had done, where I had published; he questioned me about themes and settings. He had read nothing of my work, but his questions were all kindly, and he spoke to me as I had hardly dared to hope he would: as a professional speaking to an apprentice to the same trade or craft. His voice was deep; his manner of speech was lazy; still he spoke through a half-closed mouth. I was all the more surprised, therefore, when, without changing his position or opening his mouth wider, yet speaking with great vehemence, he said suddenly, "Go home!"

For a moment I thought he was simply dismissing me, and I got up, confused and taken aback. Again he said, "Go home!" and added a moment later, with one hand waving me back into my chair. "Don't do what I did! Go home!"

I sat down and stared at him. "Can't you understand what I mean?" he said, in response to that stare. "You'll do nothing if you stay here. It's your only chance, I tell you. Go home. Get out of this place."

He leaned forward and said bitterly, "I don't want to tell you how many years it is since I've published anything. And that's why I tell you to go back to South Africa. I know, I know," he said, waving off an interruption with one hand, though I had not spoken, "I know you'll tell me that South Africa's provincial, and dull—except for the politics, and who wants that kind of excitement?—and there's nobody to talk to. And here there's everything—books, and people, and everything you've ever read about. Elm trees," he said sardonically, and pointed to the trees at the bottom of the meadow—"and meadows," he added, "and villages like Colne. It's wonderful, you can't imagine anything better. You can't imagine ever tearing yourself away from it. But can't you see that as you live in it, year after year, all the time your own country is getting further and further away from you? And then what do you do?" He slumped back in his chair and put his hands behind his head again. "I can tell you," he said. "You sit here, looking at the elm trees and the meadow. You work in the garden; you go for a drink at lunch-time; you go to the market-town once a week, and sit in the cinema there. They've got three, you know, in Mardle, three cinemas! And you try to work; and there's nothing for you to work on, because you've left it all behind."

We were both silent, though I could see that he had not yet finished what he had to say. "I tell you," he went on, "when I came here I had my store with me, and I began unpacking it, and the more I unpacked the more there seemed to be. I felt free and happy, ready to work for a lifetime. And all around me was this—all this—just what I had hankered for, out there in the veld. Until one day I found that there was no more work for me to do, the store was finished. And then what was I to do? Where was I? What did I have left? Nothing—nothing that I felt was really my own. So now I'm dumb. Dumb, that's all."

And this time he had finished, and still there was nothing I could say. At last, not so much because I was curious and wished to draw him out, but simply because I felt sorry for him, I asked, "Why didn't you go home? You could have, all these years."

He looked at me oddly. Then he said, "My wife isn't well. She hasn't been well for many years. I suppose you could call her bed-ridden, though it's a word she hates to hear."

"I am sorry."

He said nothing to this; and shortly afterwards I got up from my chair. I had to be going back to the village, to catch my bus.

"You must be off?" Traill asked.

"Yes, I'm afraid so. It really has been a privilege meeting you, Mr. Traill. And I do appreciate the way you've given your time to me."

"Oh—time! I've got lots of time."

He saw me off as far as the back gate; right at the end, when we said good-bye and shook hands, he seemed reluctant to let me go. "All this, you understand," he said, "is my wife's." He did not gesture, but I knew him to be referring to the house and the grounds. He stood with his eyes half-closed, and the sunlight glinted off the top of his head. "She loves this place. So do I really. It was quite impossible for me to leave. How could I?" Then he grasped my hand again, and said firmly, "Go home, while you can. Don't make the mistake I made. Go home!"

He turned and went through the gate; I stood for a moment in the shadowed lane, with the sunlight streaming above me and falling in bright patches on the leaves of the bank on the other side. There was no sound but that of his footsteps, beyond the stone wall. I did not like to think of what he was going back to; of what he lived with. Yet the place was beautiful.

The place was beautiful, England was beautiful : rich, various, ancient, crowded, smoking with industry. But I was much dispirited, as I rode away from Colne in the bus that evening. The warnings and the advice Traill had given to me echoed all the fears I had felt about coming to England, even before Traill had spoken to me of his life. And that life, and the work it had produced, we had conceived to be our models! Give up England, or give up writing, Traill had seemed to say to me; and I wanted to do neither.

I was much surprised, and flattered, when I received a letter from Frederick Traill a few weeks later. It had been addressed to me at one of the magazines which I had mentioned to Traill as having published a story of mine. In the letter Traill asked me to send on to him, if I would, something of my work, published or unpublished, as he would really be most interested to see it. The day on which I received the letter I made up a parcel of carbon copies of stories and other pieces, most of which had been going from magazine to magazine for months, and posted the parcel to him, with a letter in which I thanked him for the interest he was showing in my work, and for his kindness to me when we had met.

I began waiting for a reply almost immediately. One week passed, a second, a third. Two months after I had sent the manuscripts away I was still waiting for a reply. Four months later, when I thought about it at all, my impatience had given way to a sense of injury which I tried to convince myself was unwarranted. Six months later I was horrified to read a long narrative poem by Traill which was unmistakably a re-working of one of the unpublished stories I had sent him.

Traill's poem was published in one of the leading literary monthlies. Delighted to see Traill's name on the cover, I had bought a copy of the magazine at a tube-station. I read the poem sitting on one of the benches on the platform. The train for which I was waiting came in and went out, and still I sat there—hotly, shamefully embarrassed, as though I had been the one who had committed the offence. I had no doubt that the offence was gross; but I did not in the least know what I could do about it. How could I write to him, the man whom I had so much admired, and had wanted to emulate, accusing him of having stolen my plot, my character, my setting? And there was no doubt that he had done so, none at all; there could be no question here of "unconscious reminiscence". As I sat on that station bench I cursed myself for my curiosity in going to see Traill; I damned myself for ever wanting to have anything to do with writers or writing. And within the general flush of shame I felt fierce resentment and anger too. The crook! The phoney! With his cottage in the country and his bald head and his sick wife and his advice. His advice! I went home and drafted twenty letters to Traill, but I tore them all up. Shame was stronger than anger. I just couldn't say to him what he had done, let alone tell him what I felt about it.

And not only could I not write to Traill; I could not tell anyone else about it either. The sense of shame I felt held me back; and so too did my feeling that no one would believe me. It enraged me to think that Traill had relied on the strength of his position as against mine, and on the very shamefulness of what he had done, to secure my silence. I could not smile at what had happened (after all, it had happened to *me*!) nor, though I tried, could I assure myself loftily that it was better to be cribbed from than to crib. I should add that the poem itself attracted a great deal of attention, and was welcomed on all sides as the return to form of a writer who had been silent for too long.

When in the "Forthcoming Features" panel in the same magazine I saw shortly afterwards an announcement of another long poem by Frederick Traill, I went back to my pile of manuscripts and chose one among them as the most likely for Traill to have stolen from this time. I was not wrong. The poem appeared—a long poem in dialogue. Again, it had my characters, my setting, even a scrap or two of my dialogue. I felt strangely proud, when I read the poem, of having made the correct guess; and then I knew that it hadn't been a guess at all : I had chosen correctly because I knew Traill's work so intimately.

Mockingly, winkingly, the idea suddenly presented itself to me of writing a story with the deliberate intention of suiting it to Traill's purposes, and of sending it on to him, challenging him to make the same use of it as he had made of the others. The idea came as if it were no more than a joke; but that night, all night, I was working on the joke. And the next evening I had finished the story. Like the others, it was based on a reminiscence of childhood; like them, it was set in my home-town, Lyndhurst. I typed the story out the day after, and before I could get cold feet I put it in an envelope and posted it off to Traill, together with a note saying that I was pleased to see that my stories had stimulated him into writing once again, and that I hoped he would find the story I was sending him equally profitable. It was a sly little note, really, all innuendo, like the submission to him of the story itself, but I didn't feel ashamed of it. To tell the truth, now that I had approached Traill, even in this way, I felt a lessening of shame about the whole series of events; for the first time I began to think of them as being comical, looked at in a certain aspect.

Then I prepared to wait for Traill's response, which I fully expected to read, in due course, in the pages of one of the literary magazines. What I did not expect was that I should answer a ring on the door one afternoon, shortly after I had come back from the school at which I was then teaching, and find Traill waiting shyly for me on the porch. He was wearing a fawn raincoat and a hat with its brim turned down at the front and the back; he looked ill-at-ease and more rustic, in Swiss Cottage, than I had remembered him as being in Devon. "I hoped I'd find you in," he said awkwardly. "How are you?"

I stared at him. In my imagination he had become a monster of hypocrisy and unscrupulousness; but he stood before me simply as a rather slow and soft-spoken old man, with a small tired face. "Won't you come in?" I asked; and then, while he hesitated, I remembered what my room looked like. "Actually," I said, "I was just on my way down to have a cup of tea somewhere. Won't you join me?"

"With pleasure."

We went to a tea-room which has since disappeared; it is now a bamboo-decorated coffee-bar. But then it was still in all its sombre, Edwardian, mahogany-coloured glory. The panelled walls and the massive chairs and tables were all agleam with polish; the waitresses wore long black multi-buttoned dresses and little green caps on their heads; an open fire burned in a grate. The food, inevitably, was execrable. Traill was hungry, as it turned out, and had to eat a meat-pie which was a little paler outside, and a little darker inside, than the sauce in which it lay. I just had tea. While he ate Traill told me that he very rarely came up to London; it was difficult to leave his wife, as they had to get a woman to live in the house while he was away; in any case he did not much care for London. But he had had to come up to attend to various business matters, and he had thought it would be a good opportunity to look me up.

Was he going to make his confession now? As I waited, I was wondering how I was going to respond to it? Coldly? Angrily? Or pityingly? But Traill gave me no opportunity to adopt any predetermined attitude. He said in a firm, guiltless voice. "Those stories of yours, they're pretty derivative stuff, aren't they? The last one you sent me is by no means the worst, in that way. And you do know," he went on, "who they're derived from, don't you?"

His blue eyes were severe in expression, and they stared directly at me. "It gave me a strange feeling, at first, to meet my own ghosts like that," he said. "It was very disturbing; I didn't like it. When I read the stories I felt . . . how can I describe it to you? . . . that was where I'd been, yes; there was where I had come from. But none of it was clear, none of it was right, those ghosts had never really lived. And then the more I read the clearer it became to me what the ghosts were trying to say. I understood them. I knew them," he said, "even if you didn't."

"So you took them——" I interrupted. .

"Yes," he admitted calmly. "And surely you can see that I made a better job of it than you did. My poems are better poems than your stories are stories, if you see what I mean."

"But even if that's true——!"

"You mean, I still had no right to take your ideas? I thought that's what you'd say. And I sympathize with you, believe me. I'd sympathize even more if you hadn't told me what you did about my work, and what it meant to you. And if I hadn't been able to see it for myself, in the work.

Your ideas? Your ideas?" he repeated with scorn; and then, as if collecting himself, "All the same, I'm most grateful to you. Those manuscripts of yours have stimulated me, in all sorts of ways, they've set me going again. I'm tremendously grateful."

He fell silent abruptly,. leaving me struggling for breath, for relief, for release. When I finally managed to bring out my reply it surprised me almost as much as it did Traill. "Then you can have the lot," I said. "And you're welcome to them. I don't want any of them. I don't want to be like you. I don't want to go home." Suddenly I discarded a burden I had been carrying for too long, and all sorts of scruples, hesitations, and anxieties fell away with it. "I'll take my chance right here, where I am. It's my only hope. If I don't strike out now, I'm sunk. And if I am to be sunk," I said, "I'd rather it happened now, than when I'm at your age. You can have what you've already got, and you can have all the stuff that's still in my room. It's all yours, if you want it. Take it, take the lot."

"I will," Traill said simply, after a long silence.

So we parted amicably enough, outside the house in which I boarded, Traill with his arms full of the files I had thrust enthusiastically upon him. "Good luck," I said; I had difficulty in restraining myself from clapping him on the back. There went my youth, I thought, looking at the bundle in Traill's clasp; but I felt younger and more hopeful than I had for many months, than I had since coming to England.

I still feel that I did the right thing. The only trouble is that Traill has just published a new and very successful volume of poems; whereas I still live on hope, just on hope.

OCTOBER 1961

473

JAMES AGEE

A Mother's Tale

THE CALF RAN UP THE little hill as fast as he could and stopped sharp.
"Mama!" he cried, all out of breath. "What *is* it! What are they *doing*!
Where are they *going*!"

Other spring calves came galloping too.

They were all looking up at her and awaiting her explanation, but she
looked out over their excited eyes. As she watched the mysterious and
majestic thing they had never seen before, her own eyes became even more
than ordinarily still, and during the considerable moment before she
answered, she scarcely heard their urgent questioning.

Far out along the autumn plain, beneath the sloping light, an immense
drove of cattle moved eastward. They went at a walk, not very fast, but
faster than they could imaginably enjoy. Those in front were compelled by
those behind; those at the rear, with few exceptions, did their best to keep
up; those who were locked within the herd could no more help moving
than the particles inside a falling rock. Men on horses rode ahead, and
alongside, and behind, or spurred their horses intensely back and forth,
keeping the pace steady, and the herd in shape; and from man to man, a dog
sped back and forth incessantly as a shuttle, barking, incessantly, in a
hysterical voice. Now and then one of the men shouted fiercely, and this like
the shrieking of the dog was tinily audible above a low and awesome sound
which seemed to come not from the multitude of hooves but from the centre
of the world, and above the sporadic bawlings and bellowings of the herd.

From the hillside this tumult was so distant that it only made more delicate the prodigious silence in which the earth and sky were held; and, from
the hill, the sight was as modest as its sound. The herd was virtually hidden
in the dust it raised, and could be known, in general, only by the horns
which pricked this flat sunlit dust like little briars. In one place a twist of
the air revealed the trembling fabric of many backs; but it was only along
the near edge of the mass that individual animals were discernible, small in
a driven frieze, walking fast, stumbling and recovering, tossing their armed
heads, or opening their skulls heavenward in one of those cries which
reached the hillside long after the jaws were shut.

474

From where she watched, the mother could not be sure whether there were any she recognized. She knew that among them there must be a son of hers; she had not seen him since some previous spring, and she would not be seeing him again. Then the cries of the young ones impinged on her bemusement: "Where are they going?"

She looked into their ignorant eyes.

"Away," she said.

"Where?" they cried. "Where? Where?" her own son cried again.

She wondered what to say.

"On a long journey."

"But where *to*?" they shouted. "Yes, where *to*?" her son exclaimed, and she could see that he was losing his patience with her, as he always did when he felt she was evasive.

"I'm not sure," she said.

Their silence was so cold that she was unable to avoid their eyes for long.

"Well, not *really* sure. Because, you see," she said in her most reasonable tone, "I've never seen it with my own eyes, and that's the only way to *be* sure; *isn't* it?"

They just kept looking at her. She could see no way out.

"But I've *heard* about it," she said with shallow cheerfulness, "from those who *have* seen it, and I don't suppose there's any good reason to doubt them."

She looked away over them again, and for all their interest in what she was about to tell them, her eyes so changed that they turned and looked, too.

The herd, which had been moving broadside to them, was being turned away, so slowly that like the turning of stars it could not quite be seen from one moment to the next; yet soon it was moving directly away from them, and even during the little while she spoke and they all watched after it, it steadily and very noticeably diminished, and the sounds of it as well.

"It happens always about this time of year," she said quietly while they watched. "Nearly all the men and horses leave, and go into the North and West."

Out on the range, her son said, and by his voice she knew what enchantment the idea already held for him.

"Yes," she said, "out on the range." And trying, impossibly, to imagine the range, they were touched by the breath of grandeur.

"And then before long," she continued, "everyone has been found, and brought into one place; and then . . . what you see, happens. All of them."

"Sometimes when the wind is right," she said more quietly, "you can hear them coming long before you can see them. It isn't even like a sound, at first. It's more as if something were moving far under the ground. It makes you uneasy. You wonder, why, what in the world can *that* be! Then you remember what it is and then you can really hear it. And then, finally, there they all are."

She could see this did not interest them at all.

"But where are they *going?*" one asked, a little impatiently.

"I'm coming to that," she said; and she let them wait. Then she spoke slowly but casually.

"They are on their way to a railroad."

There, she thought; that's for that look you all gave me when I said I wasn't sure. She waited for them to ask; they waited for her to explain.

"A railroad," she told them, "is great hard bars of metal lying side by side, or so they tell me, and they go on and on over the ground as far as the eye can see. And great wagons run on the metal bars on wheels, like wagon wheels but smaller, and these wheels are made of solid metal too. The wagons are much bigger than any wagon you've ever seen, as big as, big as sheds, they say, and they are pulled along on the iron bars by a terrible huge dark machine, with a loud scream."

"Big as *sheds?*" one of the calves said sceptically.

"Big *enough*, anyway," the mother said. "I told you I've never seen it myself. But those wagons are so big that several of us can get inside at once. And that's exactly what happens."

Suddenly she became very quiet, for she felt that somehow, she could not imagine just how, she had said altogether too much.

"Well, *what* happens," her son wanted to know. "What do you mean, *happens?*"

She always tried hard to be a reasonably modern mother. It was probably better, she felt, to go on, than to leave them all full of imaginings and mystification. Besides, there was really nothing at all awful about what happened . . . if only one could know *why*.

"Well," she said, "it's nothing much, really. They just—why, when they all finally *get* there, why, there are all the great cars waiting in a long line, and the big dark machine is up ahead . . . smoke comes out of it, they say . . . and . . . well, then, they just put us into the wagons, just as many as will fit in each wagon, and when everybody is in, why . . . " She hesitated, for again, though she couldn't be sure why, she was uneasy.

"Why then," her son said, "the train takes them away."

Hearing that word, she felt a flinching of the heart. Where had he picked it up, she wondered, and she gave him a shy and curious glance. Oh dear, she thought. I should never have even *begun* to explain. "Yes," she said, "when everybody is safely in they slide the doors shut."

They were all silent for a little while. Then one of them asked thoughtfully,

"Are they taking them somewhere they don't want to go?"

"Oh, I don't think so," the mother said. "I imagine it's very nice."

"*I* want to go," she heard her son say with ardour. "I want to go right now," he cried. "Can I, Mama? Can I? *Please?*" And looking into his eyes, she was overwhelmed by sadness.

"Silly thing," she said, there'll be time enough for that when you're grown up. But what I very much hope," she went on, "is that instead of being chosen to go out on the range and to make the long journey, you will grow up to be very strong and bright so they will decide that you may stay here at home with Mother. And you, too," she added, speaking to the other little males; but she could not honestly wish this for any but her own, least of all for the eldest, strongest, and most proud, for she knew how few are chosen.

She could see that what she had said was not received with enthusiasm.

"But I want to go," her son said.

"Why?" she asked. "I don't think any of you realize that it's a great *honour* to be chosen to stay. A great privilege. Why, it's just the most ordinary ones are taken out on to the range. But only the very pick are chosen to stay here at home. If you want to go out on the range," she said in hurried and happy inspiration, "all you have to do is to be ordinary and careless and silly. If you want to have even a chance to be chosen to stay, you have to try to be stronger and bigger and braver and brighter than anyone else, and that takes *hard work*. Every day. Do you see?" And she looked happily and hopefully from one to another. "Besides," she added, aware that they were not won over, "I'm told it's a very rough life out there, and the men are unkind.

"Don't you see?" she said again : and she pretended to speak to all of them, but it was only to her son.

But he only looked at her. "Why do you want me to stay home?" he asked flatly : in their silence she knew the others were asking the same question.

"Because it's safe here," she said before she knew better; and realized she had put it in the most unfortunate way possible. "Not safe, not just that," she fumbled. "I mean . . . because here we *know* what happens, and what's going to happen, and there's never any doubt about it, never any reason to wonder, to worry. Don't you see? It's just *Home*," and she put a smile on the word, "where we all know each other and are happy and well."

They were so merely quiet, looking back at her, that she felt they were neither won over nor alienated. Then she knew of her son that he, anyhow,

477

was most certainly not persuaded, for he asked the question she most dreaded: "Where do they go on the train?" And hearing him, she knew that she would stop at nothing to bring that curiosity and eagerness, and that tendency towards scepticism, within safe bounds.

"Nobody knows," she said, and she added, in just the tone she knew would most sharply engage them, "Not for sure, anyway."

"What do you mean, *not for sure*," her son cried. And the oldest, biggest calf repeated the question, his voice cracking.

The mother deliberately kept silence as she gazed out over the plain, and while she was silent they all heard the last they would ever hear of all those who were going away: the last great cry, as faint almost as a breath; the infinitesimal jabbing vituperation of the dog: the solemn muttering of the earth.

"Well," she said, after even this sound was entirely lost, "there was one who came back." Their instant, trustful eyes were too much for her. She added, "Or so they say."

They gathered a little more closely around her, for now she spoke very quietly.

"It was my great-grandmother who told me," she said. "She was told it by *her* great-grandmother, who claimed she saw it with her own eyes, though of course I can't vouch for that. Because of course I wasn't even dreamed of then; and Great-grandmother was so very, very old, you see, that you couldn't always be sure she knew quite *what* she was saying."

Now that she began to remember it more clearly, she was sorry she had committed herself to telling it.

"Yes," she said, "the story is, there was one, *just* one, who ever came back, and he told what happened on the train, and where the train went and what happened after. He told it all in a rush, they say, the last things first and every which way, but as it was finally sorted out and gotten into order by those who heard it and those they told it to, this is more or less what happened:

"He said that after the men had gotten just as many of us as they could into the car he was in, so that their sides pressed tightly together and nobody could lie down, they slid the door shut with a startling rattle and a bang, and then there was a sudden jerk, so strong they might have fallen except that they were packed so closely together, and the car began to move. But after it had moved only a little way, it stopped as suddenly as it had started, so that they all nearly fell down again. You see, they were just moving up the next car that was joined on behind, to put more of us into it. He could see it all between the boards of the car, because the boards were built a little apart from each other, to let in air."

478

Car, her son said again to himself. Now he would never forget the word.

"He said that then, for the first time in his life, he became very badly frightened, he didn't know why. But he was sure, at that moment, that there was something dreadfully to be afraid of. The others felt this same great fear. They called out loudly to those who were being put into the car behind, and the others called back, but it was no use; those who were getting aboard were between narrow white fences and then were walking up a narrow slope and the men kept jabbing them as they do when they are in an unkind humour, and there was no way to go but on into the car. There was no way to get out of the car, either : he tried, with all his might, and he was the one nearest the door.

"After the next car behind was full, and the door was shut, the train jerked forward again, and stopped again, and they put more of us into still another car, and so on, and so on, until all the starting and stopping no longer frightened anybody; it was just something uncomfortable that was never going to stop, and they began instead to realize how hungry and thirsty they were. But there was no food and no water, so they just had to put up with this; and about the time they became resigned to going without their suppers (for by now it was almost dark), they heard a sudden and terrible scream which frightened them even more deeply than anything had frightened them before, and the train began to move again, and they braced their legs once more for the jolt when it would stop, but this time, instead of stopping, it began to go fast, and then even faster, so fast that the ground nearby slid past like a flooded creek and the whole country, he claimed, began to move too, turning slowly around a far mountain as if it were all one great wheel. And then there was a strange kind of disturbance inside the car, he said, or even inside his very bones. He felt as if everything in him was *falling*, as if he had been filled full of a heavy liquid that all wanted to flow one way, and all the others were leaning as he was leaning, away from this queer heaviness that was trying to pull them over, and then just as suddenly this leaning heaviness was gone and they nearly fell again before they could stop leaning against it. He could never understand what this was, but it too happened so many times that they all got used to it, just as they got used to seeing the country turn like a slow wheel, and just as they got used to the long cruel screams of the engine, and the steady iron noise beneath them which made the cold darkness so fearsome, and the hunger and the thirst and the continual standing up, and the moving on and on and on as if they would never stop."

"*Didn't* they ever stop?" one asked.

"Once in a great while," she replied. "Each time they did," she said, "he thought, 'Oh, now *at last*! *At last* we can get out and stretch our tired legs and lie down! *At last* we'll be given food and water!' But they never let

479

them out. And they never gave them food or water. They never even cleaned up under them. They had to stand in their manure and in the water they made."

"Why did the train stop?" her son asked; and with sombre gratification she saw that he was taking all this very much to heart.

"He could never understand why," she said. "Sometimes men would walk up and down alongside the cars, and the more nervous and the more trustful of us would call out; but they were only looking around, they never seemed to do anything. Sometimes he could see many houses and bigger buildings together where people lived. Sometimes it was far out in the country and after they had stood still for a long time they would hear a little noise which quickly became louder, and then became suddenly a noise so loud it stopped their breathing, and during this noise something black would go by, very close, and so fast it couldn't be seen. And then it was gone as suddenly as it had appeared, and the noise became small, and then in the silence their train would start up again.

"Once, he tells us, something very strange happened. They were standing still, and cars of a very different kind began to move slowly past. These cars were not red, but black, with many glass windows like those in a house; and he says they were as full of human beings as the car he was in was full of our kind. And one of these people looked into his eyes and smiled, as if he liked him, or as if he knew only too well how hard the journey was.

"So by his account it happens to them, too," she said, with a certain pleased vindictiveness. "Only they were sitting down at their ease, not standing. And the one who smiled was eating."

She was still, trying to think of something; she couldn't quite grasp the thought.

"But didn't they *ever* let them out?" her son asked.

The oldest calf jeered. "Of *course* they did. He came back, didn't he? How would he ever come back if he didn't get out?"

"They didn't let them out," she said, "for a long, long time."

"How long?"

"So long, and he was so tired, he could never quite be sure. But he said that it turned from night to day and from day to night and back again several times over, with the train moving nearly all of this time, and that when it finally stopped, early one morning, they were all so tired and so discouraged that they hardly even noticed any longer, let alone felt any hope that anything would change for them, ever again; and then all of a sudden men came up and put up a wide walk and unbarred the door and slid it open, and it was the most wonderful and happy moment of his life when he saw the door open, and walked into the open air with all his joints trembling, and drank the water and ate the delicious food they had ready for him; it was worth the whole terrible journey."

Now that these scenes came clear before her, there was a faraway shining in her eyes, and her voice, too, had something in it of the faraway.

"When they had eaten and drunk all they could hold they lifted up their heads and looked around, and everything they saw made them happy. Even the trains made them cheerful now, for now they were no longer afraid of them. And though these trains were forever breaking to pieces and joining again with other broken pieces, with shufflings and clashings and rude cries, they hardly paid them attention any more, they were so pleased to be in their new home, and so surprised and delighted to find they were among thousands upon thousands of strangers of their own kind, all lifting up their voices in peacefulness and thanksgiving, and they were so wonder-struck by all they could see, it was so beautiful and so grand.

"For he has told us that now they lived among fences as white as bone, so many, and so spiderishly complicated, and shining so pure, that there's no use trying even to hint at the beauty and the splendour of it to anyone who knows only the pitiful little outfittings of a ranch. Beyond these mazy fences, through the dark and bright smoke which continually turned along the sunlight, dark buildings stood shoulder to shoulder in a wall as huge and proud as mountains. All through the air, all the time, there was an iron humming like the humming of the iron bar after it has been struck to tell the men it is time to eat, and in all the air, all the time, there was that same strange kind of iron strength which makes the silence before lightning so different from all other silence.

"Once for a little while the wind shifted and blew over them straight from the great buildings, and it brought a strange and very powerful smell which confused and disturbed them. He could never quite describe this smell, but he has told us it was unlike anything he had ever known before. It smelled like old fire, he said, and old blood and fear and darkness and sorrow and most terrible and brutal force and something else, something in it that made him want to run away. This sudden uneasiness and this wish to run away swept through every one of them, he tells us, so that they were all moved at once as restlessly as so many leaves in a wind, and there was great worry in their voices. But soon the leaders among them con-cluded that it was simply the way men must smell when there are a great many of them living together. Those dark buildings must be crowded very full of men, they decided, probably as many thousands of them, in-doors, as there were of us, outdoors; so it was no wonder their smell was so strong and, to our kind, so unpleasant. Besides, it was so clear now in every other way that men were not as we had always supposed, but were

481

doing everything they knew how to make us comfortable and happy, that we ought to just put up with their smell, which after all they couldn't help, any more than we could help our own. Very likely men didn't like the way we smelled, any more than we liked theirs. They passed along these ideas to the others, and soon everyone felt more calm, and then the wind changed again, and the fierce smell no longer came to them, and the smell of their own kind was back again, very strong, of course, in such a crowd, but ever so homey and comforting, and everyone felt easy again.

"They were fed and watered so generously, and treated so well, and the majesty and the loveliness of this place where they had all come to rest was so far beyond anything they had ever known or dreamed of, that many of the simple and ignorant, whose memories were short, began to wonder whether that whole difficult journey, or even their whole lives up to now, had ever really been. Hadn't it all been just shadows, they murmured, just a bad dream?

"Even the sharp ones, who knew very well it had all really happened, began to figure that everything up to now had been made so full of pain only so that all they had come to now might seem all the sweeter and the more glorious. Some of the oldest and deepest were even of a mind that all the puzzle and tribulation of the journey had been sent us as a kind of harsh trying or proving of our worthiness; and that it was entirely fitting and proper that we could earn our way through to such rewards as these, only through suffering, and through being patient under pain which was beyond our understanding; and that now at the last, to those who had borne all things well, all things were made known : for the mystery of suffering stood revealed in joy. And now as they looked back over all that was past, all their sorrows and bewilderments seemed so little and so fleeting that, from the simplest among them even to the most wise, they could feel only the kind of amused pity we feel towards the very young when, with the first thing that hurts them or they are forbidden, they are sure there is nothing kind or fair in all creation, and carry on accordingly, raving and grieving as if their hearts would break."

She glanced among them with an indulgent smile, hoping the little lesson would sink home. They seemed interested but somewhat dazed. I'm talking way over their heads, she realized. But by now she herself was too deeply absorbed in her story to modify it much. *Let* it be, she thought, a little impatient; it's over *my* head, for that matter.

"They had hardly before this even wondered that they were alive," she went on, "and now all of a sudden they felt they understood *why* they were. This made them very happy, but they were still only beginning to enjoy this new wisdom when quite a new and different kind of restiveness ran among them. Before they quite knew it they were all moving once again, and now they realized that they were being moved, once more, by men, towards still some other place and purpose they could not know. But during these last hours they had been so well that now they felt no uneasiness, but all moved forward calm and sure towards better things still to come; he has told us that he no longer felt as if he were being driven, even as it became clear that they were going towards the shade of those great buildings, but guided.

"He was guided between fences which stood ever more and more narrowly near each other, among companions who were pressed ever more and more closely against one another; and now as he felt their warmth against him it was not uncomfortable, and his pleasure in it was not through any need to be close among others through anxiousness, but was a new kind of strong and gentle delight, at being so very close, so deeply of his own kind, that it seemed as if the very breath and heartbeat of each one were being exchanged through all that multitude, and each was another, and others were each, and each was a multitude, and the multitude was one. And quieted and made mild within this melting, they now entered the cold shadow cast by the buildings, and now with every step the smell of the buildings grew stronger, and in the darkening air the glittering of the fences was ever more queer.

"And now as they were pressed ever more intimately together he could see ahead of him a narrow gate, and he was strongly pressed upon from either side and from behind, and went in eagerly, and now he was between two fences so narrowly set that he brushed either fence with either flank, and walked alone, seeing just one other ahead of him, and knowing of just one other behind him, and for a moment the strange thought came to him, that the one ahead was his father, and that the one behind was the son he had never begotten.

"And now the light was so changed that he knew he must have come inside one of the gloomy and enormous buildings, and the smell was so much stronger that it seemed almost to burn his nostrils, and the smell and the sombre new light blended together and became some other thing again, beyond his describing to us except to say that the whole air beat with it like one immense heart and it was as if the beating of his heart were pure violence infinitely manifolded upon violence: so that the uneasy feeling stirred in him again that it would be wise to turn around and run out of this place just as fast and as far as ever he could go. This he heard, as if he were telling it to himself at the top of his voice, but it came from somewhere so deep and so dark inside him that he could only hear the shouting of it as less than a whisper, as just a hot and chilling breath, and he scarcely heeded it, there was so much else to attend to.

"For as he walked along in this sudden and complete loneliness, he tells us, this wonderful knowledge of being one with all his race meant less and less to him, and in its place came something still more wonderful : he knew what it was to be himself alone, a creature separate and different from any other, who had never been before, and would never be again. He could feel this in his whole weight as he walked, and in each foot as he put it down and gave his weight to it and moved above it, and in every muscle as he moved, and it was a pride which lifted him up and made him feel large, and a pleasure which pierced him through. And as he began with such wondering delight to be aware of his own exact singleness in this world, he also began to understand (or so he thought) just why these fences were set so very narrow, and just why he was walking all by himself. It stole over him, he tells us, like the feeling of a slow cool wind, that he was being guided towards some still more wonderful reward or revealing, up ahead, which he could not of course imagine, but he was sure it was being held in store for him alone.

"Just then the one ahead of him fell down with a great sigh, and was so quickly taken out of the way that he did not even have to shift the order of his hooves as he walked on. The sudden fall and the sound of that sigh dismayed him, though, and something within him told him that it would be wise to look up : and there he saw Him.

"A little bridge ran crosswise above the fences. He stood on this bridge with His feet as wide apart as He could set them. He wore spattered trousers but from the belt up He was naked and as wet as rain. Both arms were raised high above His head and in both hands He held an enormous Hammer. With a grunt which was hardly like the voice of a human being, and with all His strength, He brought this Hammer down into the forehead of our friend : who, in a blinding blazing, heard from his own mouth the beginning of a gasping sigh; then there was only darkness."

O, this is *enough*! it's *enough*! she cried out within herself, seeing their terrible young eyes. How *could* she have been so foolish as to tell so much!

"What happened then?" she heard, in the voice of the oldest calf, and she was horrified. This shining in their eyes : was it only excitement? no pity? no fear?

"What happened?" two others asked.

Very well, she said to herself. I've gone so far; now I'll go the rest of the way. She decided not to soften it, either. She'd teach them a lesson they wouldn't forget in a hurry.

"Very well," she was surprised to hear herself say aloud.

"How long he lay in this darkness he couldn't know, but when he began to come out of it, all he knew was the most unspeakably dreadful pain. He

484

was upside down and very slowly swinging and turning, for he was hanging by the tendons of his heels from great frightful hooks, and he has told
us that the feeling was as if his hide were being torn from him inch by
inch, in one piece. And then as he became more clearly aware he found
that this was exactly what was happening. Knives would sliver and slice
along both flanks, between the hide and the living flesh; then there was a
moment of most precious relief; then red hands seized his hide and there
was a jerking of the hide and a tearing of tissue which it was almost as
terrible to hear as to feel, turning his whole body and the poor head at
the bottom of it; and then the knives again.

"It was so far beyond anything he had ever known unnatural and
amazing that he hung there through several more such slicings and jerk-
ings and tearings before he was fully able to take it all in : then, with a
scream, and a supreme straining of all his strength, he tore himself from
the hooks and collapsed sprawling to the floor and, scrambling right to his
feet, charged the men with the knives. For just a moment they were so
astonished and so terrified they could not move. Then they moved faster
than he had ever known men could—and so did all the other men who
chanced to be in his way. He ran down a glowing floor of blood and down
endless corridors which were hung with the bleeding carcasses of our kind
and with bleeding fragments of carcasses, among blood-clothed men who
carried bleeding weapons, and out of that vast room into the open, and
over and through one fence after another, shoving aside many an astounded
stranger and shouting out warnings as he ran, and away up the railroad
towards the West.

"How he ever managed to get away, and how he ever found his way
home, we can only try to guess. It's told that he scarcely knew, himself,
by the time he came to this part of his story. He was impatient with those
who interrupted him to ask about that, he had so much more important
things to tell them, and by then he was so exhausted and so far gone that
he could say nothing very clear about the little he did know. But we can
realize that he must have had really tremendous strength, otherwise he
couldn't have outlived the Hammer; and that strength such as his—which
we simply don't see these days, it's of the olden time—is capable of things
our own strongest and bravest would sicken to dream of. But there was
something even stronger than his strength. There was his righteous fury,
which nothing could stand up against, which brought him out of that fearful place. And there was his high and burning and heroic purpose, to keep
him safe along the way, and to guide him home, and to keep the breath of
life in him until he could warn us. He did manage to tell us that he just
followed the railroad, but how he chose one among the many which
branched out of that place, he couldn't say. He told us, too, that from time

485

to time he recognized shapes of mountains and other landmarks, from his journey by train, all reappearing backward and with a changed look and hard to see, too (for he was shrewd enough to travel mostly at night), but still recognizable. But that isn't enough to account for it. For he has told us, too, that he simply *knew* the way; that he didn't hesitate one moment in choosing the right line of railroad, or even think of it as choosing; and that the landmarks didn't really guide him, but just made him the more sure of what he was already sure of; and that whenever he *did* encounter human beings—and during the later stages of his journey, when he began to doubt he would live to tell us, he travelled day and night—they never so much as moved to make him trouble, but stopped dead in their tracks, and their jaws fell open.

"And surely we can't wonder that their jaws fell open. I'm sure yours would, if you had seen him as he arrived, and I'm very glad I wasn't there to see it, either, even though it is said to be the greatest and most momentous day of all the days that ever were or shall be. For we have the testimony of eye-witnesses, how he looked, and it is only too vivid, even to hear of. He came up out of the East as much staggering as galloping (for by now he was so worn out by pain and exertion and loss of blood that he could hardly stay upright), and his heels were so piteously torn by the hooks that his hooves doubled under more often than not, and in his broken forehead the mark of the Hammer was like the socket for a third eye.

"He came to the meadow where the great trees made shade over the water. 'Bring them all together!' he cried out, as soon as he could find breath. 'All!' Then he drank; and then he began to speak to those who were already there : for as soon as he saw himself in the water it was as clear to him as it was to those who watched him that there was no time left to send for the others. His hide was all gone from his head and his neck and his forelegs and his chest and most of one side and a part of the other side. It was flung backward from his naked muscles by the wind of his running and now it lay around him in the dust like a ragged garment. They say there is no imagining how terrible and in some way how grand the eyeball is when the skin has been taken entirely from around it : his eyes, which were bare in this way, also burned with pain, and with the final energies of his life, and with his desperate concern to warn us while he could : and he rolled his eyes wildly while he talked, or looked piercingly from one to another of the listeners, interrupting himself to cry out, '*Believe* me! Oh, *believe* me!' For it had evidently never occurred to him that he might not be believed, and must make this last great effort, in addition to all he had gone through for us, to *make* himself believed; so that he groaned with sorrow and with rage and railed at them without tact or mercy for their slowness to believe. He had scarcely what you could call a voice left, but with this relic of a voice he shouted and bellowed and bullied us and insulted us, in the agony of his concern. While he talked he bled from the mouth, and the mingled blood and saliva hung from his chin like the beard of a goat.

"Some say that with his naked face, and his savage eyes, and that beard and the hide lying off his bare shoulders like shabby clothing, he looked almost human. But others feel this is an irreverence even to think; and others, that it is a poor compliment to pay the one who told us, at such cost to himself, the true ultimate purpose of Man. Some did not believe he had ever come from our ranch in the first place, and of course he was so different from us in appearance and even in his voice, and so changed from what he might ever have looked or sounded like before, that nobody could recognize him for sure, though some were sure they did. Others suspected that he had been sent among us with his story for some mischievous and cruel purpose, and the fact that they could not imagine what this purpose might be, made them, naturally, all the more suspicious. Some believed he was actually a man, trying—and none too successfully, they said—to disguise himself as one of us; and again the fact that they could not imagine why a man would do this, made them all the more uneasy. There were quite a few who doubted that anyone who could get into such bad condition as he was in, was fit even to give reliable information, let alone advice, to those in good health. And some whispered, even while he spoke, that he had turned lunatic; and many came to believe this. It wasn't only that his story was so fantastic; there was good reason to wonder, many felt, whether anybody in his right mind would go to such trouble for others. But even those who did not believe him listened intently, out of curiosity to hear so wild a tale, and out of the respect it is only proper to show any creature who is in the last agony.

"What he told, was what I have just told you. But his purpose was away beyond just the telling. When they asked questions, no matter how curious or suspicious or idle or foolish, he learned, towards the last, to answer them with all the patience he could and in all the detail he could remember. He even invited them to examine his wounded heels and the pulsing wound in his head as closely as they pleased. He even begged them to, for he knew that before everything else, he must be believed. For unless we could believe him, wherever could we find any reason, or enough courage, to do the hard and dreadful things he told us we must do!

"It was only these things he cared about. Only for these he came back."

Now clearly remembering what these things were, she felt her whole being quail. She looked at the young ones quickly and as quickly looked away.

"While he talked," she went on, "and our ancestors listened, men came quietly among us; one of them shot him. Whether he was shot in kindness or to silence him is an endlessly disputed question which will probably never be settled. Whether, even, he died of the shot, or through his own great pain and weariness (for his eyes, they say, were glazing for some time before the men came), we will never be sure. Some suppose even that he may have died of his sorrow and his concern for us. Others feel that he had quite enough to die of, without that. All these things are tangled and lost in the disputes of those who love to theorize and to argue. There is no arguing about his dying words, though; they were very clearly remembered:

" *'Tell them! Believe!'* "

After a while her son asked, "What did he tell them to do?"

She avoided his eyes. "There's a great deal of disagreement about that, too," she said after a moment. "You see, he was so very tired."

They were silent.

"So tired," she said, "some think that towards the end, he really *must* have been out of his mind."

"Why?" asked her son.

"Because he was so tired out and so badly hurt."

They looked at her mistrustfully.

"And because of what he told us to do."

"What did he tell us to do?" her son asked again.

Her throat felt dry. "Just . . . things you can hardly bear even to think of. That's all."

They waited. "Well, *what?*" her son asked in a cold, accusing voice.

" *'Each one is himself,'* " she said shyly. " *'Not of the herd. Himself alone.'* That's one."

"What else?"

" *'Obey nobody. Depend on none.'* "

"What else?"

She found that she was moved. " *'Break down the fences,'* " she said less shyly. " *'Tell everybody, everywhere.'* "

"Where?"

"Everywhere. You see, he thought there must be ever so many more of us than we had ever known."

They were silent. "What else?" her son asked.

" *'For if even a few do not hear me, or disbelieve me, we are all betrayed.'* "

"Betrayed?"

"He meant, doing as men want us to. Not for ourselves, or the good of each other."

They were puzzled.

"Because, you see, he felt there was no other way." Again her voice altered : " *'All who are put on the range are put on to trains. All who are put on to trains meet the Man With The Hammer. All who stay home are kept there to breed others to go on to the range, and so betray themselves and their kind and their children for ever.*

" *'We are brought into this life only to be victims; and there is no other way for us unless we save ourselves.'*

"Do you understand?"

Still they were puzzled, she saw; and no wonder, poor things. But now the ancient lines rang in her memory, terrible and brave. They made her somehow proud. She began actually to want to say them.

" *'Never be taken,'* " she said. " *'Never be driven. Let those who can, kill Man. Let those who cannot, avoid him.'* "

She looked around at them.

"What else?" her son asked, and in his voice there was a rising valour.

She looked straight into his eyes. " *'Kill the yearlings,'* " she said very gently. " *'Kill the calves.'* "

She saw the valour leave his eyes.

"Kill us?"

She nodded. " *'So long as Man holds dominion over us,'* " she said. And in dread and amazement she heard herself add, " *'Bear no young.'* "

With this they all looked at her at once in such a way that she loved her child, and all these others, as never before; and there dilated within her such a sorrowful and marvelling grandeur that for a moment she saw nothing, and heard nothing except her own inward whisper. "Why, *I* am one alone. And of the herd, too. Both at once. All one."

Her son's voice brought her back : "Did they do what he told them to?"

The oldest one scoffed, "Would we be here, if they had?"

"They say some did," the mother replied. "Some tried. Not all."

"What did the men do to them?" another asked.

"I don't know," she said. "It was such a very long time ago."

"Do you believe it?" asked the oldest calf.

"There are some who believe it," she said.

"Do *you?*"

"I'm told that far back in the wildest corners of the range there are some of us, mostly very, very old ones, who have never been taken. It's said that they meet, every so often, to talk and just to think together about the heroism and the terror of two sublime Beings, The One Who Came Back, and The Man With The Hammer. Even here at home, some of the old ones, and some of us who are just old-fashioned, believe it, or parts of it anyway. I know there are some who say that a hollow at the centre of the

489

forehead—a sort of shadow of the Hammer's blow—is a sign of very special ability. And I remember how Great-grandmother used to sing an old, pious song, let's see now, yes, 'Be not like dumb-driven cattle, be a hero in the strife.' But there aren't many. Not any more."

"Do *you* believe it?" the oldest calf insisted; and now she was touched to realize that every one of them, from the oldest to the youngest, needed very badly to be sure about that.

"Of course not, silly," she said; and all at once she was overcome by a most curious shyness, for it occurred to her that in the course of time, this young thing might be bred to her. "It's just an old, old legend." With a tender little laugh she added, lightly, "We use it to frighten children with."

By now the light was long on the plain and the herd was only a fume of gold near the horizon. Behind it, dung steamed, and dust sank gently to the shattered ground. She looked far away for a moment, wondering. Something—it was like a forgotten word on the tip of the tongue. She felt the sudden chill of the late afternoon and she wondered what she had been wondering about. "Come, children," she said briskly, "it's high time for supper." And she turned away; they followed.

The trouble was, her son was thinking, you could never trust her. If she said a thing was so, she was probably just trying to get her way with you. If she said a thing wasn't so, it probably was so. But you never could be sure. Not without seeing for yourself. I'm going to go, he told himself; I don't care *what* she wants. And if it isn't so, why then I'll live on the range and make the great journey and find out what *is* so. And if what she told was true, why then I'll know ahead of time and the one *I* will charge is The Man With The Hammer. I'll put Him and His Hammer out of the way for ever, and that will make me an even better hero than The One Who Came Back.

So, when his mother glanced at him in concern, not quite daring to ask her question, he gave her his most docile smile, and snuggled his head against her, and she was comforted.

The littlest and youngest of them was doing double skips in his efforts to keep up with her. Now that he wouldn't be interrupting her, and none of the big ones would hear and make fun of him, he shyly whispered his question, so warmly moistly ticklish that she felt as if he were licking her ear.

"What is it, darling?" she asked, bending down.

"What's a train?"

APRIL 1958

NIGEL DENNIS

The Pukey

MR. TROY'S REFUSAL to have a pukey in the house had caused enormous trouble in the family. "Pukeys are nasty, degenerate things," he said : "they make filthy messes all over the floor, they corrupt the young, they interrupt homework and sap the nation, and we have nowhere to put one." His wife would answer : "Well, well, we are getting distinguished, aren't we? It seems we're the Duke of Devonshire. Let me tell you that Blanche and Mabel both have pukeys in their drawing-rooms, and far from being corrupted, they are happier." Young Miss Troy appealed to her father's sense of status, saying : "Everywhere I go, Father, it's always : 'What did your pukey do last night?' I have to admit we haven't got one." "Oh, all right," said Mr. Troy, after a couple of years, "I'll let the pukey-man come and give a demonstration."

A few days later, the man arrived with the pukey and put its box against the wall opposite the fireplace. When Mrs. Troy asked : "Won't it catch the draught there?" the pukey-man only laughed and said : "The point about a pukey, madam, is that it's bred to be insensible." "But it is *alive*, isn't it?" asked Mrs. Troy quickly, "because we'd never pay for something dead. And if it's alive, won't the dog resent it?" "Both dog and budgie will be unconscious of it, madam," said the pukey-man, "a pukey speaks only to a human brain." "Well, cut the brainy cackle and open the box," said Mr. Troy roughly.

Let us admit at once that the first impression the pukey made on Mr. Troy was a good one. Even lying stupefied on the carpet, its eyes had a wondering gaze that fell hardly short of sweetness. "It's not just going to flop down like that all the time, is it?" asked Mr. Troy, to hide the fact that he liked it so far. "Give it a minute, my dear sir!" begged the pukey-man, "it's hardly got its bearings." "Pay him no attention!" exclaimed Mrs. Troy, "he's been picking on pukeys for years." "Oh, what shall we *call* it?" cried Miss Troy.

She had hardly spoken when the pukey shuddered from snout to stern and let its muzzle fall right open, showing six rows of vivid pink gums

491

and bubbles of sparkling saliva : "No teeth; that's curious!" muttered Mr. Troy. Then, with no warning, it vomited all over the carpet—a perfectly-filthy, greenish-yellow mess—causing Mrs. Troy to cry spontaneously: "Oh, the filthy little beast!" and Miss Troy to say: "Oh, Mum, don't *fuss*!" and Mr. Troy to say: "I told you it would foul everything up. Take the little brute away!" "An ounce of patience, if you please," asked the pukey-man, "or how can it grow on you?" "I'm sure that's true—and I don't mean I don't like it," said Mrs. Troy, rallying. "Isn't it actually *good* for the carpet?" Miss Troy asked the pukey-man, "I know the Vicar said, reasonably used, it was." "That is perfectly correct, Miss Troy," said the pukey-man, "it's not the vomit but the abuse of it." "Now, there's a remark I always like to hear," said Mr. Troy.

At that moment the pukey, which had been staring at its own emission in a rather vague, contented way, changed its expression entirely. A sort of pathetic anguish came over its whole face : it held its snout sideways and looked at Miss Troy in a pleading, tender way. "Oh, *look!*" cried Mrs. Troy, "it's trying to say it didn't mean bad." They were all wrenched by the pukey's fawning expression, and when it slobbered and grovelled and brownish tears dripped from the corners of its eyes, Mrs. Troy could have hugged it. "Damned sentimental, hypocritical brute!" said Mr. Troy, "I still reserve my judgement." But he was the first to jump in his seat when the pukey, suddenly throwing-up on to the carpet a clot of gritty mucus, followed this up with a string of shrieks and groans. Everyone was deafened except Miss Troy, who sensed at once that the pukey was illustrating the dilemma of girls of her own age in search of happiness. "Why, bless my soul!" said Mrs. Troy soon, "it's trying to have *sex*, that's what it is"—and sure enough, the pukey was now twisting its hind-parts in the most indecent way and rubbing its flanks in its own vomit. "I'll not have that in *my* house," said Mrs. Troy, pursing her lips, "it's just plain filth, and showing-off." "My dear madam, it never actually *gets* there," said the pukey-man : "nothing ever really *happens*." "Oh, Mother, you and Father make everything seem obscene!" said Miss Troy, "even love." "Well, as long as it only suggests but can't actually do it, I don't mind," said Mrs. Troy, watching the pukey with a new curiosity. "My mind is still unmade up," said Mr. Troy.

Worn out, it seemed, by sexual frustration, the pukey lay still for a moment. Then, suddenly fixing its eye on Mrs. Troy, it gave her such a glare of horrible malignancy that she reached for her husband's arm. Next minute, there was a dreadful spectacle : throwing itself into a spasm of rage, the pukey began tearing and biting at its own body, like a thing bent on suicide. "Stop it! Stop it! Put the lid on!" screamed Mrs. Troy, "it's cruel, and drawing blood." "Frankly, you'll have to adjust to that madam," said the pukey-man, "because it fights more than anything else." "Oh, then, that's decisive for me," said Mr. Troy, "because I love to see a good scrap." "It *is* the men who like that best," agreed the pukey-man, as the pukey went through the motions of winding its entrails round the throat of an enemy and jumping on his face. "I don't *mind* its fighting," Mrs. Troy said grudgingly, "but I'll put its lid on if it overdoes it. I like *beautiful* things best." The words, alas, were hardly out of her mouth when the pukey, sighting backwards over its spine like a mounted cow-boy firing at his pursuers, shot her full in the face with an outrageous report. "Now, no grumbling, Mother!" screamed poor Miss Troy, know-ing her mother's readiness to take affront. "But it's *not* nice!" protested Mrs. Troy, fanning herself with an evening paper. "Oh, Mother, can't you see it *means* nothing?" cried Miss Troy, "it's not like *us*, with our stan-dards." "Standards or no," said Mrs. Troy, "I never saw Mabel's pukey do that to *her*." "Ah, but this is an improved model, madam," said the pukey man.

"Am I correct in supposing," asked Mr. Troy, "that nothing substantial ever comes out of its rear end anyway?" "That is correct, sir," answered the pukey-man, "all secretion and excretion are purely visual and oral. The vent is hot air at most : hence, no sand-box." "Yet it has a belly on it," said Mr. Troy, "I know because I can see one." "You can see a belly, sir," answered the pukey-man, "but you can't see any guts, can you?" They all laughed at this, because it was so true.

After throwing-up another couple of times ("Mercy, what a messy little perisher it is!" said kind Mrs. Troy), the pukey became inordinately grave and a whole rash of wettish pimples spread over its face. "Well, you are in luck!" said the pukey-man, jumping up as if genuinely interested, "it never does this more than once a week at most. Can you guess what it is?" They all racked their brains, guessing everything from sewage farming to guitar-playing, and still couldn't imagine; until Miss Troy, who was the quickest of the family, screamed : "*I* know! It's *thinking*!" "*Mes com-pliments*, young lady," said the pukey-man, bowing.

They all watched the pukey thinking because it was so unexpected; but none of them really liked it. "When it vomits, it only makes me laugh," said Mr. Troy, "but when it thinks, *I* feel like vomiting." "I just feel nervous and embarrassed, like it was something you'd seen and shouldn't," said Mrs. Troy, and even Miss Troy for once agreed with her mother, saying, "You feel it's only doing it as a change from being sick, but it's the same really." "Don't judge it too hardly," said the pukey-man, "surely the wonder is that with no brains it can think at all." "Has it really no brains?" asked Mr. Troy, curious. "No, sir," said the pukey-man : "that's *why* its thinking makes you sick." "Funny sort of animal, I must say," said Mr. Troy, "thinks without brains, bites without teeth, throws-up with no guts, and screws without sex." "Oh, *please* stop it thinking!" begged Mrs. Troy. "I had an experience once that smelt like that." At which words, the pukey's pimples disappeared completely and, lying prone with its paws out, it gave Mrs. Troy a smug, complacent look, showing all its gums in a pleading whimpering. "Oh, the little angel! It wants to be congratulated for having thought!" cried Mrs. Troy : "then we *will*—yes! we *will*, you smelly little darling—you little, stinking, clever, mother's thing!" "I find that touching, too," said Mr. Troy, "no wonder there's so much nicker in pukeys." "It's for love and culture, too, Dad," Miss Troy reminded. "Thank you, Miss Troy," said the pukey-man, "we breeders tell ourselves that too."

During the next hour the pukey did all manner of things—such as marching like the Coldstream Guards, dancing and balancing on one paw like Pavlova, folding its arms like a Member of Parliament, singing the national anthem, plucking away at its parts mysteriously, fighting like mad, and making such vulgar explosive noises at both ends that the Troys were all left speechless with wonder. What charmed them as much as anything was feeling that the pukey made no distinction about what it did : whether it was fawning or screeching, or thinking or puking, it made it all like the same, because it loved each thing equally and looked at you always so proudly for it. "I can only say you breeders must be jolly highly-skilled," summed-up Mr. Troy, "to root out all the natural organs and still poison the air." "It's more a sixth sense than a skill," said the pukey-man modestly, "and one which your wife, I may say, seems to have instinctively." This was the first compliment Mrs. Troy had had since she gave birth to Miss Troy, and to cover her natural embarrassment she said sharply, "Well, put its lid on again now and take it away. We'll come and fill out the Never-never forms tomorrow."

With the pukey gone, it wasn't like the same home. The walls seemed to have been sprayed with a dribble the colour of maple-syrup, and dead flies kept dropping from the ceiling. The state of the carpet was beyond description, although the last thing the pukey had done before the lid closed was puff a sort of scented detergent powder over the stinking mess it had made. But the Troys were much too impressed to worry about the room : they could only think of buying the pukey and doing this every night. "It baffles me," said Mr. Troy, as they went to bed: "it's not human, it's not mechanical, it's not like any animal I've ever known." "What it leaves on the carpet is human through-and-through," said Mrs. Troy, and they all laughed at this because it was so true.

JULY 1960

Part VI
POEMS

W. H. AUDEN

Streams
(For Elizabeth Drew)

DEAR WATER, clear water, playful in all your streams,
As you dash or loiter through life who does not love
    To sit beside you, to hear you and see you,
   Pure being, perfect in music and movement?

Air is boastful at times, earth slovenly, fire rude,
But you in your bearing are always immaculate,
    The most well-spoken of all the older
   Servants in the household of Mrs. Nature.

No one suspects you of mocking him, for you still
Use the same vocables you were using the day
    Before that unexpected row which
   Downed every hod on half-finished Babel,

And still talk to yourself: nowhere are you disliked;
Arching your torso, you dive from a basalt sill,
    Canter across white chalk, slog forward
   Through red marls, the aboriginal pilgrim,

At home in all sections, but for whom we should be
Idolaters of a single rock, kept apart
    By our landscapes, excluding as alien
   The tales and diets of all other strata.

How could we love the absent one if you did not keep
Coming from a distance, or quite directly assist,
    As when past Iseult's tower you floated
   The willow pash-notes of wanted Tristram?

And Homo Ludens, surely, is your child, who make
Fun of our feuds by opposing identical banks,
    Transferring the loam from Huppim
  To Muppim and back each time you crankle.

Growth cannot add to your song: as unchristened brooks
Already you whisper to ants what, as Brahma's son,
    Descending his titanic staircase
  Into Assam, to Himalayan bears you thunder.

And not even man can spoil you: his company
Coarsens roses and dogs but, should he herd you through a sluice
    To toil at a turbine, or keep you
  Leaping in gardens for his amusement,

Innocent still is your outcry, water, and there
Even, to his soiled heart raging at what it is,
    Tells of a sort of world, quite other,
  Altogether different from this one

With its envies and passports, a polis like that
To which, in the name of scholars everywhere,
    Gaston Paris pledged his allegiance
  As Bismarck's siege-guns came within earshot.

Lately, in that dale of all Yorkshire's the loveliest,
Where, off its fell-side helter-skelter, Kisdon Beck
    Jumps into Swale with a boyish shouting,
  Sprawled out on grass, I dozed for a second,

And found myself following a croquet tournament
In a calm enclosure, with thrushes popular:
    Of all the players in that cool valley
  The best with the mallet was my darling.

While, on the wolds that begirdled it, wild old men
Hunted with spades and hammers, monomaniac each,
    For a megalith or a fossil,
  And bird-watchers stalked the mossy beech-woods.

Suddenly, over the lawn we started to run
For, lo, through the trees in a cream and gold coach
    Drawn by two baby locomotives,
  The god of mortal doting approached us,

Flanked by his bodyguard, those hairy armigers in green
Who laugh at thunderstorms and weep at a blue sky :
    He thanked us for our cheers of homage,
    And promised X and Y a passion undying.

With a wave of his torch he commanded a dance;
So round in a ring we flew, my dear on my right,
    When I awoke. But fortunate seemed that
    Day because of my dream and enlightened,

And dearer, water, than ever your voice, as if
Glad—though goodness knows why—to run with the human race,
    Wishing, I thought, the least of men their
    Figures of splendour, their holy places.

JUNE 1954

Vespers

IF THE hill overlooking our city has always been known as Adam's Grave, only at dusk can you see the recumbent giant, his head turned to the west, his right arm resting for ever on Eve's haunch,

can you learn, from the way he looks up at the scandalous pair, what a citizen really thinks of his citizenship,

just as now you can hear in a drunkard's caterwaul his rebel sorrows crying for a parental discipline, in lustful eyes perceive a disconsolate soul,

scanning in desperation all passing limbs for some vestige of her faceless angel who in that long ago when wishing was a help mounted her once and vanished :

For Sun and Moon supply conforming masks, but in this hour of civil twilight all must wear their own faces.

501

It is now that our two paths cross.

Both simultaneously recognize his Anti-type: that I am an Arcadian, that he is a Utopian.

He notes, with contempt, my Aquarian belly: I note, with alarm, his Scorpion's mouth.

He would like to see me cleaning latrines: I would like to see him removed to some other planet.

Neither speaks. What experience could we possibly share?

Glancing at a lampshade in a store window, I observe it is too hideous for anyone in their senses to buy: He observes it is too expensive for a peasant to buy.

Passing a slum child with rickets, I look the other way: He looks the other way if he passes a chubby one .

I hope our senators will behave like saints, provided they don't reform me: He hopes they will behave like *baritoni cattivi* and, when lights burn late in the Citadel,

I (who have never seen the inside of a police station) am shocked and think: "Were the city as free as they say, after sundown all her bureaus would be huge black stones":

He (who has been beaten up several times) is not shocked at all but thinks: "One fine night our boys will be working up there."

You can see, then, why, between my Eden and his New Jerusalem, no treaty is negotiable.

In my Eden a person who dislikes Bellini has the good manners not to get born: In his New Jerusalem a person who dislikes work will be very sorry he was born.

In my Eden we have a few beam-engines, saddle-tank loco-motives, overshot waterwheels and other beautiful pieces of obsolete machinery to play with : In his New Jerusalem even chefs will be cucumber-cool machine minders.

502

In my Eden our only source of political news is gossip: In his New Jerusalem there will be a special daily in simplified spelling for non-verbal types.

In my Eden each observes his compulsive rituals and superstitious taboos but we have no morals : in his New Jerusalem the temples will be empty but all will practise the rational virtues.

One reason for his contempt is that I have only to close my eyes, cross the iron footbridge to the tow-path, take the barge through the short brick tunnel and

there I stand in Eden again, welcomed back by the krumhorns, doppions, sordumes of jolly miners and a bob major from the Cathedral (romanesque) of St. Sophie (*Die Kalte*) :

One reason for my alarm is that, when he closes his eyes, he arrives, not in New Jerusalem, but on some august day of outrage when hellikins cavort through ruined drawing-rooms and fish-wives intervene in the Chamber, or

some autumn night of delations and noyades when the unrepentant thieves (including me) are sequestered and those he hates shall hate themselves instead.

So, with a passing glance we take the other's posture : Already our steps recede, heading, incorrigible each, towards his kind of meal and evening.

Was it (as it must look to any god of cross-roads) simply a fortuitous intersection of life-paths, loyal to different fibs,

or also a rendezvous between accomplices who, in spite of themselves, cannot resist meeting

to remind the other (do both, at bottom, desire truth?) of that half of their secret which he would most like to forget,

forcing us both, for a fraction of a second, to remember our victim (but for him I could forget the blood, but for me he could forget the innocence) on whose immolation (call him Abel, Remus, whom you will, it is one Sin Offering) Arcadias, Utopias, our dear old bag of a democracy, are alike founded :

For without a cement of blood (it must be human, it must be innocent) no secular wall will safely stand.

FEBRUARY 1955

ROBERT LOWELL

Ford Madox Ford
1873–1939

THE LOBBED boll plops, then dribbles to the cup.
A birdie, Fordie! But it nearly killed
The ministers. Lloyd George is holding up
The flag. He gabbles, "Hop-toad, hop-toad, hop-toad!
Hueffer has used a mashie on the green!
It's filthy art, Sir, filthy art!"
You answered, "What is art to me and thee?
Will a blacksmith teach a midwife how to bear?"
Bulldog of the King's English, what is art?
New thresholds, new anatomies? Or was
It war, the sport of kings, that your *Good Soldier,*
The first French novel in the language, taught
Those Georgian Whig magnificoes at Oxford,
At Oxford decimated on the Somme?
Ford, mustard gassed and buried seven miles
Behind the lines at Nancy of Belleau Wood,
And five times blackballed for promotion, you
Emerged, a Jonah—O divorced, divorced
From the whale-fat of post-war London. Boomed,
Cut, plucked and booted! You had learned your art.
Sandman! Your face, a childish *O.* The sun
Is pernod-yellow, and it gilds the heirs
Of all the ages there on Washington
And Stuyvesant, your Lilliputian squares—
Here writing turned your pockets inside out.
But Master, mammoth mumbler, tell me why
The bales of your left-over novels buy
Less than a bandage for your gouty foot.
Wheel-horse, O unforgetting elephant,
I hear you huffing at your old Brevoort,

Timon and Falstaff, while you heap the board
For publishers. Fiction! I'm selling short
Your lies that made the great your equals. Ford,
You were a kind man, and you died in want.

APRIL 1954

THEODORE ROETHKE

Words for The Wind

I

Love, love, a lily's my care,
She's sweeter than a tree.
Loving, I use the air
Most lovingly : I breathe;
Mad in the wind I wear
Myself as I should be.
All's even with the odd,
My brother the vine is glad.

Are flower and seed the same?
What do the great dead say?
Sweet Phoebe, she's my theme :
She sways whenever I sway.
"O love me while I am,
You green thing in my way!"
I cried, and the birds came down
And made my song their own.

Motion can keep me still :
She kissed me out of thought
As a lovely substance will;
She wandered; I did not :
I stayed, and light fell
Across her pulsing throat;
I stared, and a garden stone
Slowly became the moon.

The shallow stream runs slack;
The wind creaks slowly by;
Out of a nestling's beak
Comes a tremulous cry

I cannot answer back;
A shape from deep in the eye,
That woman I saw in a stone,
Keeps pace when I walk alone.

II

The sun declares the earth;
The stones leap in the stream;
On a wide plain, beyond
The far stretch of a dream,
A field breaks like the sea;
The wind's white with her name,
And I walk with the wind.

The dove's my will today.
She sways, half in the sun:
Rose, easy on a stem,
One with the sighing vine,
One to be merry with,
And pleased to meet the moon.
She likes wherever I am.

Passion's enough to give
Shape to a random joy:
I cry delight: I know
The root, the core of a cry.
Swan-heart, arbutus-calm,
She moves when time is shy:
Love has a thing to do.

The loam gleams like wet coal;
The green, the springing green
Makes an intenser day
Under the rising moon;
I smile, no mineral man;
I bear, but not alone,
The burden of this joy.

III

Under a southern wind,
The birds and fishes move

North, in a single stream;
The sharp stars swing around;
I get a step beyond
The wind, and there I am;
I'm odd and full of love.
Wisdom, where is it found?—
Those who embrace, believe.
Whatever was, still is,
Says a song tied to a tree.
Below, on the ferny ground,
In rivery air, at ease,
I walk with my true love.

What time's my hear? I care.
I cherish what I have
Had of the temporal :
I am no longer young
But the winds and waters are;
What falls away will fall;
All things bring me to love.

IV

The breath of a long root,
The shy perimeter
Of the unfolding rose,
The green, the altered leaf,
The oyster's weeping foot,
And the incipient star,—
Are part of what she is.
She wakes the ends of life.

Being myself, I sing
The soul's immediate joy.
Light, light, where's my repose?
A wind wreathes round a tree.
A thing is done : a thing
Body and spirit know
When I do what she does :
Creaturely creature, she! —

I kiss her moving mouth,
Her swart hilarious skin;
She breaks my breath in half;
She frolicks like a beast;
And I dance round and round,
A fond and foolish man,
And see and suffer myself
In another being, at last.

MARCH 1954

R. S. THOMAS

Lament for Prytherch

WHEN I WAS young! When I was young!
Were you ever young, Prytherch; a rich farmer,
Cows in the byre, sheep in the pen,
A brown egg under each hen,
The barns oozing corn like honey?
You are old now. Time's geometry
Upon your face by which we tell
Your sum of years has with sharp care
Conspired and crossed your brow with grief.
Your heart, that is dry as a dead leaf
Undone by frost's cruel chemistry,
Clings in vain to the bare bough
Where once in April a bird sang.

JULY 1954

DAVID WRIGHT

Monologue of a Deaf Man

'Et lui comprit trop bien, n'ayant pas entendu'—Tristan Corbière

It is a good plan, and began with childhood
As my fortune discovered, only to hear
How much it is necessary to have said.
Oh silence, independent of a stopped ear,
You observe birds, flying, sing with wings instead.

Then do you console yourself? You are consoled
If you are, as all are. So easy a youth
Still unconcerned with the concern of a world
Where, masked and legible, a moment of truth
Manifests what, gagged, a verb should have told,

In observer of vanity and courage
And of these mirror as well; that is something
More than a sound of violin to assuage
What the human being most dies of: boredom
Which makes hedgebirds clamour in their blackthorn cage.

But did the brushless fox die of eloquence?
No, but talked himself, it seems, into a tale.
The injury, dominated, as an asset;
It is there for domination, that is all.
Else what must faith do deserted by mountains?

Talk to me then, you who have so much to say,
Spectator of the human conversation,
Reader of tongues, examiner of the eye,
And detective of clues in every action;
What could a voice, if you heard it, signify?

The tone speaks less than a twitch and a grimace.
People make to depart, do not say 'Goodbye'.
Decision, indecision, drawn on every face
As if they spoke. But what do they really say?
You are not spared, either, the banalities.

In whatever condition, whole, blind, dumb,
One-legged or leprous, the human being is,
I affirm the human condition is the same :
The heart half broken in ashes and in lies,
But sustained by the immensity of the divine.

Thus I too must praise out of a quiet ear
The great creation to which I owe I am
My grief and my love. O hear me if I cry
Among the din of birds deaf to their acclaim
Involved like them in the not unhearing air.

NOVEMBER 1954

W. S. GRAHAM

Blind Tide Emblazoning

BLIND TIDE emblazoning
My death for ever on
The sheldrake dark, unperish
Me here this night. Unperish
Me burning in these words
Murmured and roared through
The listening brain of silence
To where she listening lies.

Are you awake listening?
Or are you sound? The tide
Slowly turns and slowly
The nets of night swing
Round to face the west.
We drift at the nets under
Continual cries wheeling.
What winging shapes of silence
Are for us? The herring
Have had their run for the night.
Our money is in the net
Or out. And now we'll haul
And run for home. Are you
Awake or sound and deep
In the bolster-buried ear
Adrift? Slip by sleep's gates.
Slip by sleep's gates and out
From your lost shire and over
The shore's long curlewing
Move through the shallows out.
Never the like of bright
Steerers overhead
Started as now. Wended,

So many lie within
Your musing ear. Orion
Is brightly barbed. Again
The glint inlays the gunwale.
The wind is rising. I would
From the fires of this sea
Waylay the headlong dead.
Come nearer to hear. See,
There they arm themselves
With Love and wave the fray
Nearer us as they rise
Through every word. Through you
This branching sea burns
Me away. What blinded tons
Of water the world contains.

And yet now out of all
Its bellowing deep and shoals
Let me be fond. Love,
Let me be fond a while.

Bear these words in mind
As they bear me soundly
Beyond my reach. Through you
They love. But they in time
Do murder in that name.

Yet quick forget. It's all
Only a tale. Slowly
The great dialogues darken
Upon me and all voices
Between us move towards
Their end in this. Silence
Shapes before I draw breath.
Stay still. Listen so still.
There! Did you hear? Some ear
Speaks me by stealth to death.
Call through that time where once
You fondly strayed and all
The flooer o' Galloway
Wad doon an dee. So soon
She fell under a thorn

515

And me. So it arose
A lapwing wandered us.
The song is shed and now
I'm minded of Calum, a man
Out of Kintyre or out
Of my tongue spoken and straight
The thirst chimes me back,
And words are a thirsty lot.
I have a hake in my throat.
You'll barely know his voice
Now for his millstoned life
Speaks through the branks of grief.
The unkind iron casts
His meaning out. The mute
Harp hangs with aconite.
Yet not mistake. Let him
Begin in time. Calum,
Come out from that black drouth.
We'll man the bottled barque
In Mooney's. Remember there
You first rendered the sash
Of foam your father wore.
May she be musing there
Tonight. For her I have
The length and breadth of love
That it shall lusty keep
Her mind and body good.
Her bent is mine. Calum
My tongue is Opening Time
And my ear is in its prime.
Ahoy Mooney. Draw back
The ancient bacchus bolts.
Stand clear of the gates.
And clear we are. So now
Calum, what will you have?
I'll call the rounds. Remember,
When we fished out of Kilmore
They made their own at the farm.
We drank it dripping hot
Out of an antique worm.
Now, Calum, here's to the keel.
Lift up your drinking arm.

I've waited so long for this,
To meet you in the eye
And in the ear. And now
All time's within our reach.
Drink and these words unperish
Us under the golden drench.

Welcome my dear as heir
To yes again the long
Song of the thorough keel
Moving us through the pitch
Of night in a half gale.
Here at the gunwale farewell
Gives us away this homeward
Night keeled into the final
Breathless element.
Always surely your bent
Is mine. Always surely
My thoroughfare is you.
And that is you by both
The high helmet of light
And by the beast rearing
To sire in the dark kiln.
Watch as you go. Hold
The mizzen there as the sea's
Branches burn and emblazon
Our death under every eye
And burn us into the brain
Of silence in these words.
The lit cardinals swing
Round as we swither off
Our course in a following sea.
Yet the bow climbs back
Shearing the amorous foam
And flourishes in this word
The angel-handed sword.
My love, soon to be held
Still in the last word,
Under out of the spray
Is best. But first, see!
By whose ambition shined
Do the signs arm themselves

So bright tonight to stride
At large for Love? Now where
You once lay lie. We all
Must die and we must all
Lie down in the beast cause.

Language becomes us. The ram
At large moves through this huge
Utterance in which we lie
Homelessly face to face.
Farewell then as your skill's
Worth, you wandering keel.
Make your best wake. Drive
Headlong through the salt
Thicket and thoroughfare
That offers her for ever.

My love my love anywhere
Drifted away, listen.
From the dark rush under
Us comes our end. Endure
Each word as it breaks at last
To become our home here.
Who hears us now? Suddenly
In a stark flash the nerves
Of language broke. The sea
Cried out loud under the keel.
Listen. Now as I fall.

Listen. And silence even
Has turned away. Listen.

FEBRUARY 1955

ELIZABETH JENNINGS

Mirrors

WAS IT a mirror then across a room,
A crowded room of parties where the smoke
Rose to the ceiling with the talk? The glass
Stared back at me a half-familiar face
Yet something hoped for. When at last you came
It was as if the distant mirror spoke.

That loving ended as all self-love ends
And teaches us that only fairgrounds have
The right to show us halls of mirrors where
In every place we look we see our stare
Taunting our own identities. But love
Perceives without a mirror in the hands.

APRIL 1955

THOM GUNN

On the Move

"Man, you gotta Go."

THE BLUE jay scuffling in the bushes follows
Some hidden purpose, and the gust of birds
That spurts across the field, the wheeling swallows,
Have nested in the trees and undergrowth.
Seeking their instinct, or their poise, or both,
One moves with an uncertain violence
Under the dust thrown by a baffled sense
Or the dull thunder of approximate words.

On motor-cycles, up the road, they come:
Small, black, as flies hanging in heat, the Boys,
Until the distance throws them forth, their hum
Bulges to thunder held by calf and thigh.
In goggles, donned impersonality,
In gleaming jackets trophied with the dust,
They strap in doubt—by hiding it, robust—
And almost hear a meaning in their noise.

Exact conclusion of their hardiness
Has no shape yet, but from known whereabouts
They ride, direction where the tires press.
They scare a flight of birds across a field:
Much that is natural, to the will must yield.
Men manufacture both machines and soul,
And use what they imperfectly control
To dare a future from the taken routes.

It is a part solution, after all.
One is not necessarily discord
On earth; or damned because, half animal,

One lacks direct instinct, because one wakes
Afloat on movement that divides and breaks.
One joins the movement in a valueless world,
Choosing it, till, both hurler and the hurled,
One moves as well, always toward, toward.

A minute holds them, who have come to go :
The self-defined, astride the created will
They burst away; the towns they travel through
Are home for neither bird nor holiness,
For birds and saints complete their purposes.
At worst, one is in motion; and at best,
Reaching no absolute, in which to rest,
One is always nearer by not keeping still.

DECEMBER 1955

W. S. MERWIN

The Mountain

ONLY ON the rarest occasions, when the blue air,
Though clear, is not too binding (as, say,
For a particular moment just at dusk in autumn)
Or if the clouds should part suddenly
Between freshets in spring, can one trace the rising
Slopes high enough to call them contours; and even
More rarely see above the treeline. Then
It is with almost a shock that one recognizes
What supposedly one had known always :
That it is, in fact, a mountain; not merely
This restrictive sense of nothing level, of never
Being able to go anywhere
But up or down, until it seems probable
Sometimes that the slope, to be so elusive
And yet so inescapable, must be nothing
But ourselves : that we have grown with one
Foot shorter than the other, and would deform
The levellest habitat to our misshapen
Condition, as is said of certain hill creatures.

Standing between two other peaks, but not
As they : or so we have seen in a picture
Whose naïve audacity, founded as far as can be
Determined, on nothing but the needs
Of its own composition, presents all three
As shaped oddly, of different colours, rising
From a plan whose flatness appears incredible
To such as we. Of course to each of us
Privately, its chief difference from its peers
Rests not even in its centrality, but its
Strangeness composed of our own intimacy
With a part of it, our necessary

Ignorance of its limits, and diurnal pretence
That what we see of it is all. Learned opinions differ
As to whether it was ever actively
Volcanic. It is believed that if one could see it
Whole, its shape might make this clearer, but that
Is impossible, for at the distance at which in theory
One could see it all, it would be out of sight.

Of course in all the sense in which any
Place or thing can be said not to exist
Until someone, at least, is known to have been there,
It would help immeasurably if anyone
Should ever manage to climb it. No one,
From whatever distance, has ever so much as seen
The summit, or even anywhere near it; not, that is,
As far as we know. At one time the attempt
Was a kind of holy maelstrom, Mecca
For fanatics and madmen, and a mode of ritual
And profane suicide (since among us there is nowhere
From which one could throw oneself down). But there have been
Expeditions even quite recently, and with the benefit
Of the most expensive equipment. Very few
Who set out at all seriously have
Come back. At a relatively slight distance
Above us, apparently the whole aspect and condition
Of the mountain changes completely; there is ceaseless wind
With a noise like thunder and the beating of wings.

Indeed, if one considers the proximity
Of the point at which so much violence
Is known to begin, it is not our failure
That strikes one as surprising, but our impunity :
The summer camps on near gradients, ski-lifts in winter,
And even our presence where we are. For of those
Who attained any distance and returned, most
Were deafened, some permanently; some were blind,
And these also often incurably; all
Without exception were dazzled, as by a great light. And those
Who perhaps went furthest and came back, seemed
To have completely lost the use of our language,
Or if they spoke, babbled incoherently
Of silence bursting beyond that clamour, of time

Passed there not passing here, which we could not understand,
Of time no time at all. These characteristic
Effects of the upper slopes—especially the derangement
Of time-sense, and the dazzling—seem from earliest
Antiquity to have excited speculation.

One legend has it that a remote king-priest figure
Once gained the summit, spent some—to him non-sequent
But to them significant—time there, and returned
"Shining", bearing ciphers of the arcane (which,
Translated into the common parlance, proved
To be a list of tribal taboos) like clastic
Specimens, and behaved with a glacial violence
Later construed as wisdom. This, though
Charming, does not, in the light of current endeavour
Seem possible, even though so long ago. Yet
To corroborate this story, in the torrent
Gold has been found which even at this
Late date appears to have been powdered by hand,
And (further to confuse inquiry) several
Pediments besides, each with four sockets shaped
As though to receive the hoof of a giant statue
Of some two-toed ungulate. Legend being
What it is, there are those who still insist
He will come down again some day from the mountain.

As there are those who say it will fall on us. It
Will fall. And those who say it has already
Fallen. It has already fallen. Have we not
Seen it fall in shadow, evening after evening,
Across everything we can touch; do we not build
Our houses out of the great hard monoliths
That have crashed down from far above us? Shadows
Are not without substance, remind and predict;
And we know we live between greater commotions
Than any we can describe. But, most important:
Since this, though we know so little of it, is
All we know, is it not whatever it makes us
Believe of it—even the old woman
Who laughs, pointing, and says that the clouds across
Its face are wings of seraphim? Even the young

Man who, standing on it, declares it is not
There at all. He stands with one leg habitually
Bent, to keep from falling, as though he had grown
That way, as is said of certain hill creatures.

SEPTEMBER 1955

RICHARD SELIG

Boyhood of Theseus

He came as if from tunnels. The green field
First stabbed, stunned, then calmed his sight:
He was home. The dark worm whose guts he filled
With longing, he left happily for light.

He did not then perceive that sky, too, was skin
He could not penetrate nor long abide;
That each emergence brought him deep within
Himself, himself more visibly inside.

Over the rippled road, past the green outhouse,
The stuttering windmill, the grey silo,
Where all alone the bull, tethered, bellows
Roaring the roofs of the grass down; where roots lie low

He stands at a distance to gaze, a small boy
Admiring the black flanks and rich unquietness
Of that voice full of seed and storm and joy.
Great in that city of muscle and bone, his smallness

Withered, sired by this beast, he suddenly grows
Strong in his tower of coming manhood, leaps the shore
Of short breath and little time to what he knows:
His spirit shall destroy the Minotaur.

JULY 1955

CYRIL CONNOLLY

A Thought from Propertius

II. XVI. 47–54

GOOD NEWS we bring the expectant generation
  Our banquet broke no bones : be this our due!
So kiss me, love; enjoy our mortal station
  When all that you can give are still too few.

As leaves that wither from a blackened ceiling
  And on the wine-bowl's midnight ocean fume
Are we who put our trust in this deep feeling
  Regardless of the hour which seals our doom.

translated by Cyril Connolly

Haec certe merito poterunt laudare mindres
  Laeserunt nullos pocula nostra Deos.
Tu modo, dum licet, hunc fructum ne desere vitae;
  omnia si dederis oscula, pauca datis.
Ac veluti folia arentes liquere corollas
  Quae passim calathis strata natare vides:
Sic nobis, qui nunc magnum speramus amantes
  Forsitan includet crastina fata dies.

FEBRUARY 1956

527

DYLAN THOMAS

Elegy

Too PROUD to die, broken and blind he died
The darkest way, and did not turn away,
A cold kind man brave in his narrow pride

On that darkest day. Oh, forever may
He lie lightly, at last, on the last, crossed
Hill, under the grass, in love, and there grow

Young among the long flocks, and never lie lost
Or still all the numberless days of his death, though
Above all he longed for his mother's breast

Which was rest and dust, and in the kind ground
The darkest justice of death, blind and unblessed.
Let him find no rest but be fathered and found,

I prayed in the crouching room, by his blind bed,
In the muted house, one minute before
Noon, and night, and light. The rivers of the dead

Veined his poor hand I held, and I saw
Through his unseeing eyes to the roots of the sea
(An old tormented man three-quarters blind,

I am not too proud to cry that He and he
Will never never go out of my mind.
All his bones crying, and poor in all but pain,

Being innocent, he dreaded that he died
Hating his God, but what he was was plain :
An old kind man brave in his burning pride.

The sticks of the house were his; his books he owned.
Even as a baby he had never cried;
Nor did he now, save to his secret wound.

Out of his eyes I saw the last light glide.
Here among the light of the lording sky
An old blind man is with me where I go

Walking in the meadows of his son's eye
On whom a world of ills came down like snow.
He cried as he died, fearing at last the spheres'

Last sound, the world going out without a breath:
Too proud to cry, too frail to check the tears,
And caught between two nights, blindness and death.

O deepest wound of all that he should die
On that darkest day. Oh, he could hide
The tears out of his eyes, too proud to cry.

Until I die he will not leave my side.)

＊

This unfinished Elegy of Dylan Thomas was given the title
"Elegy" in the latest version of the poem after the provisional
titles "The Darkest Way" or "Too Proud to Die" or "True
Death" had been used in preparatory drafts. Among his papers
he left sixty pages of manuscript work towards the poem,
including this note:

(1) *Although he was too proud to die, he did die, blind,
in the most agonizing way but he did not flinch
from death & was brave in his pride.*

(2) *In his innocence, & thinking he was God-hating, he
never knew that what he was: was an old kind man
in his burning pride.*

(3) *Now he will not leave my side, though he is dead.*

(4) *His mother said that as a baby he never cried; nor did
he, as an old man; he just cried to his secret wound
& his blindness, never aloud.*

The rest of the manuscript work consists of phrases, lines, couplets, and line-endings, and transcripts of the poem in various degrees of completeness. The two most complete versions, which are clearly the latest, are both written in quatrains. One, with no title, has no division into verses, and the second, with the title "Elegy", is divided into verses of three lines. This, to me, seems to be the latest version of all, and seems to hold the final form the poem was to take. The poem extends to the seventeenth line, ending "to the roots of the sea", after which there is a line which is deleted.

The extension of the poem has been built up from the manuscript notes. The lines are all found there, except that two or three have been adjusted to fit the rhyming scheme. "Breath" was an isolated marginal word which I have used in line thirty-four; and "plain", which ends line twenty-three, has been added to "was" without justification from the manuscript. In the third line I have chosen "narrow pride" as against "burning pride" although "burning" occurs more often than "narrow" in the transcripts; but it was "narrow" in that line that he quoted to me from memory when I last saw him.

Of the added lines sixteen are exactly as Dylan Thomas wrote them, and the remainder are only altered to the extent of an inversion or one or two words. Their order might well have been different. The poem might also have been made much longer. It recalls the earlier poem, also written for his father : "Do not go gentle into that good night"; but it is clear that in this last poem Dylan Thomas was attempting something even more immediate and more difficult.

VERNON WATKINS

FEBRUARY 1956

ROY FULLER

The Final Period

I WATCH across the desk the slight
Shape of my daughter on the lawn.
With youth's desire my fingers write
And then contain an old man's yawn.

At first my only verb was "give",
In middle age sought out a god:
Ugly and impotent I live
The myth of a final period.

I see within the tetrastich
A jealousy as gross, intense,
As ulcered that real love of which
Art's tragedies alone make sense.

He pulses still the man of force—
The armoured chest, the boar-thick yards;
And here the woman-nature, coarse
Beneath the dainty silks and fards.

Appalling that should still arise
All that is dead and was untrue,
That my imagination flies
Where now my flesh may not pursue.

Life goes on offering alarms
To be imprisoned in the cage
Of art. I must invent more charms
To still the girl's erotic rage:

Frozen in their betrothal kiss,
The innocent boy will never move
To loose the codpiece, and his miss
Stay spellbound in her father's love—

And yet the actual girl will sigh
And cross the garden with her flowers;
And I will leave the desk, and try
To live with ordinary powers.

Bermuda or Byzantium—
To some Utopia of forgiving
And of acceptance I have come,
But still rebellious, still living.

The first absurd haphazard meeting
With one loved unrequitedly,
The insurrection caused by fleeting
Words of my own, while I stood by—

Those fatal and recorded times
Return like heartburn, and I see
Behind heroic plangent rhymes
Unutterable deficiency.

Even this noon of greens and blues;
June's badges, roses of human red;
Birds in the cavern of the yews;
A lark's quaver figure in my head;

The car in the lane that circumvents
The archipelagos of dung—
These trivial concomitants
Of feeling, these, too, must be sung.

And in the song all will be whole,
Immortal, though the author pass—
Ended his little speaking rôle—
On to the doomed and venal mass.

She comes whom I would marble through
Her painful and tumultuous years,
So she would wake at last in true
Epochs, to music of the spheres.

JULY 1956

VERNON WATKINS

Angel and Man

Angel: Day breaks. All sighs are ended.
       The sleep of earth, the long night sleep, is over.

Man: Faint incarnation in the mists of dawn,
      Why do you rouse desires I have laid down
      On this sad field where the world tends her wounded
      And shrouds their limbs whose eyes are shut for ever?
      You are not of this life, but of the days
      Of immaturity when, with upturned eyes,
      I lay awake, a child, expecting miracles.
      I think I waited for a star to fall.
      Now it is different, and those early oracles
      Have lost that power I in those nights would feel.
      Yes, once I thought my dreams had been fulfilled.
      I thought I saw, quite early in a field,
      The annunciation of the morning star,
      And that the world had ended with that light.

Angel: That early moment is come true, though late.
      That moment was a prophecy of this.
      To me alone was given night's darkest wisdom,
      I am the first to learn what is for all.

Man: Do not so look at me, for I am ill.
      I would believe you, but I cannot.
      Too much is hidden.
      I hear your speech, but when your speech has faded
      It is the earth that counts, where these men lived.
      All these the eyelid buried,
      These the rough earth hides,
      Where are they, then?

Angel: They are gone to the root of the tree.
       Just as the red sun went behind the hill,
       They pierced the shadows of imagined rest.

Man: If sighs are ended they should wake now, too.

Angel: They do wake, though your ears are not attuned
       To those sunk voices which the ground transfigures.
       They are like lightning, or the time in sleep
       Circling the earth from which the slow leaf breaks.
       They do wake, in the murmur of the leaves.

Man: The leaves made that same sound when they were living
       But it was not their voices when they lived,
       Nor is it now. Let others be deceived.
       I know this for a place where footsteps halted
       And where each footstep knocked upon the ground,
       Seeking true consolation. Think of this.
       Spirits were laid here to whom some were dear,
       Who left them, sorrowful. Garments touched the leaves,
       And where they passed I understood a language
       Breathed in the robe and heard by the dumb ground.
       I accept this for my portion. Grief was theirs,
       And grief, their lot, is likely to be mine.
       Yet in the last, most solitary dark
       There lives an equilibrium in the soul
       Depending on forgiveness. Grant me this,
       And I shall hold truth fast without remorse
       Under the turning stars.

JULY 1956

RICHARD EBERHART

The Return

STILL marvelling at the light,
Impersonal, on the mountain peaks, a halcyon
Glow; it strains to me,
To the last intimacy.

Then, quick to seize on intuition,
I thought I knew; now I know
I do not know. Time has refracted
Ineluctable meanings.

Now, the sight is more satisfactory.
Decades make us mountainous.
Life did not know what time could do.
My long light streams out to you.

APRIL 1957

535

WILLIAM PLOMER

Ludwig the Second

*"Remind me to look happier tomorrow."—Ludwig II in a
note to a servant at Hohenschwangau, April 24th, 1886.*

In this High Country of the Swan
I reign, and I am sometimes pleased
With what I plan and look upon:
So life's complexity is eased.

But not for long! Anxiety returns.
This hateful century is to blame.
Bring me some ice! My forehead burns!
Frock-coated vultures watch my name.

Bring in the lamps! I want to be alone
Yet not alone. Nobody knows how great
My loneliness and kingliness have grown.
Is it that I was born too late?

Build me a cliff-top Schloss, a ruby throne,
A resonant Wagner-Hall of Song:
I'll hear the music-myths alone.
I need a palace one mile long.

I want a million nobody will lend
To build my Chinese palace, Falkenstein.
More than pagodas I require a friend
To obey—and then command—this heart of mine.

Guilt vitiates love: they never told me that.
Each act of pleasure desecrates my dream.
Remorse runs in, quick as a rat,
A bare-tailed rat, to gnaw my self-esteem.

Gudden is not a man I care for, therefore
What is he here for? Doktor Gudden lies!
What do those other people stare for?
They're all in Bismarck's pay, all spies!

Order the sleigh! Send Hornig to the hut!
Is there a moon? I'm nearly ready now.
The plates are cold! See that the doors are shut!
Borrow two million! Make a lower bow!

Hold up the glass! I wish to trace
The growing sabotage of guilt and sorrow.
It is not regal, such a ravaged face:
Remind me to look happier tomorrow.

A warning oboe! Forest glades exhale
The smell of moss, a sense of loss. I'll turn and take
My downward path. Muffle the drums! I shall not fail
To fight for silence in my swan-lit lake.

APRIL 1957

ROBERT GRAVES

The Second-Fated

MY STUTTER, my cough, my unfinished sentences,
Denote an inveterate physical reluctance
To use the metaphysical idiom.
Forgive me : what I am saying is, perhaps this :

Your accepted universe, by Jove's naked hand
Or Esmun's, or Odomankoma's, or Marduk's—
Choose which name jibes—formed scientifically
From whatever there was before Time was,
And begging the question of perfect consequence,
May satisfy the general run of men
(If "run" be an apt term for patent paralytics)
That blueprints destine all they suffer here,
But does not satisfy certain few else.

Fortune enrolled me among the second-fated
Who have read their own obituaries in *The Times*,
Have heard "Where, death, thy sting? Where, grave, thy victory?'
Intoned with unction over all their still clay,
Have seen two parallel red-ink lines drawn
Under their manic-depressive bank accounts,
And are therefore strictly forbidden to walk in grave-yards
Lest they scandalize the sexton and his bride.

We, to be plain with you, taking advantage
Of a brief demise, visited first the Pit,
A library of shades, completed characters;
And next the silver-bright Hyperborean Queendom,
Basking under the sceptre of Guess Whom?
Where pure souls matrilineally foregather.
We were then shot through by merciful lunar shafts
Until hearts tingled, heads sang, and praises flowed;

And learned to scorn your factitious universe
Ruled by the death which we had flouted;
Acknowledging only that from the Dove's egg hatched
Before aught was, but wind—unpredictable
As our second birth would be, or our second love :
A moon-warmed world of discontinuance.

NOVEMBER 1957

TED HUGHES

Thrushes

TERRIFYING ARE the attent sleek thrushes on the lawn,
More coiled steel than living—a poised
Dark deadly eye, those delicate legs
Triggered to stirrings beyond sense—with a start a bounce a stab
Overtake the instant and drag out some writhing thing.
No indolent procrastinations and no yawning stares,
No sighs or head-scratchings. Nothing but bounce and stab
And a ravening second.

Is it their single-mind-sized skulls, or a trained
Body, or genius, or a nestful of brats
Gives their days this bullet and automatic
Purpose? Mozart's brain had it, and the shark's mouth
That hungers down the blood-smell even to a leak of its own
Side and devouring of itself : efficiency which
Strikes too streamlined for any doubt to pluck at it
Or obstruction deflect.

With a man it is otherwise. Heroisms on horseback,
Outstripping his desk-diary at a broad desk,
Paring at a tiny ivory ornament
For years : his act worships itself—while for him,
Though he bends to be blent in the prayer, how loud and above what
Furious spaces of fire do the distracting devils
Orgy and hosannah, under what wilderness
Of black silent waters weep.

MARCH 1958

540

STEPHEN SPENDER

Subject: Object: Sentence

A SUBJECT thought, because he had a verb
With several objects, that he ruled a sentence.
Had not Grammar willed to him substantives
Which he came into, as his just inheritance?

His objects were *wine, women, wealth,*
A whole subordinate clause—*all life can give.*
He grew so fond of having these that, finally,
He found himself becoming too subjective.

Subject, the dictionary warned, means *being ruled by
Person or thing.* Was he not passion's slave?
To achieve detachment, he must be objective
Which meant to free himself from the verb *have.*

Seeking detachment, he studied the context
Around his sentence, to place it in perspective:
Then parsed it, made a critical analysis,
And then re-read it, feeling more objective.

Then, with a shock, he realized that *sentence*
Like *subject-object* is treacherously double.
A *sentence* is condemned to stay as written—
As in *life-* or *death- sentence,* for example.

APRIL 1958

OLIVER BERNARD

Trees

THE TREES follow me into spring unwilling,
Lagging behind they hold out arms which end
In cold small hands. They try, staying where they are,
To think themselves some raiment. In the dark
I leave them standing in gardens between the houses,
Fish out a key for mine and go upstairs.
Morning is waiting patiently and knows
I and the trees and everything will be
Punctual where we meet in her good time.

JULY 1956

PHILIP LARKIN

The Whitsun Weddings

THAT WHITSUN, I was late getting away:
　　Not till about
One-twenty on the sunlit Saturday
Did my three-quarters-empty train pull out,
All windows down, all cushions hot, all sense
Of being in a hurry gone. We ran
Behind the backs of houses, crossed a street
Of blinding windscreens, smelt the fishdock; thence
The river's level drifting breadth began,
Where sky and Lincolnshire and water meet.

All afternoon, through the tall heat that slept
　　For miles inland,
A slow and stopping curve southwards we kept.
Wide farms went by, short-shadowed cattle, and
Canals with floatings of industrial froth;
A hothouse flashed, uniquely; hedges dipped
And rose; and now and then a smell of grass
Displaced the reek of buttoned carriage-cloth
Until the next town, new and nondescript,
Approached with acres of dismantled cars.

At first, I didn't notice what a noise
　　The weddings made
Each station that we stopped at: sun destroys
The interest of what's happening in the shade,
And down the long cool platforms whoops and skirls
I took for porters larking with the mails
And went on reading. Once we started, though,
We passed them, grinning and pomaded, girls
In parodies of fashion, heels and veils,
All posed irresolutely, watching us go,

As if out on the end of an event
   Waving goodbye
To something that survived it. Struck, I leant
More promptly out next time, more curiously,
And saw it all again in different terms:
The fathers with broad belts under their suits
And seamy foreheads; mothers loud and fat;
An uncle shouting smut; and then the perms,
The nylon gloves and jewellery-substitutes,
The lemons, mauves, and olive-ochres that

Marked off the girls unreally from the rest.
   Yes, from cafés
And banquet-halls up yards, and bunting-dressed
Coach-party annexes, the wedding-days
Were coming to an end. All down the line
Fresh couples climbed aboard; the rest stood round;
The last confetti and advice were thrown,
And, as we moved, each face seemed to define
Just what it saw departing: children frowned
At something dull; fathers had never known

Success so huge and wholly farcical;
   The women shared
The secret like a happy funeral;
While girls, gripping their handbags tighter, stared
At a religious wounding. Free at last,
And loaded with the sum of all they saw,
We hurried towards London, shuffling gouts of steam.
Now fields were building-plots, and poplars cast
Long shadows over major roads, and for
Some fifty minutes, that in time would seem

Just long enough to settle hats and say
   I nearly died
A dozen marriages got under way.
They watched the landscape, sitting side by side
—An Odeon went past, a cooling tower,
And someone running up to bowl—and none
Thought of the others they would never meet
Or how their lives would contain this hour.
I thought of London spread out in the sun,
Its postal districts packed like squares of wheat:

There we were aimed. And as we raced across
   Bright knots of rail
Past standing Pullmans, walls of blackened moss
Came close, and it was nearly done, this frail
Travelling coincidence; and what it held
Stood ready to be loosed with all the power
That being changed can give. We slowed again,
And as the tightened brakes took hold, there swelled
A sense of falling, like an arrow-shower
Sent out of sight, somewhere becoming rain.

JUNE 1959

EDWIN MUIR

The Day Before the Last Day

IF IT COULD come to pass, and all kill all
And in a day or a week we could destroy
Ourselves, that is the beginning only
Of the destruction, for so we murder all
That ever has been, all species and forms,
Man and woman and child, beast and bird,
Tree, flower and herb, and that by which they were known,
Sight and hearing and touch, feeling and thought,
And memory of our friends among the dead.
If there were only a single ear that listening heard
A footstep coming nearer, it would bring
Annunciation of the world's resurrection.
A sound! We would not know even the silence
Where all was now as if it had never been.

Mechanical parody of the Judgement Day
That does not judge but only deals damnation.
Let us essay a hypothetical picture.

"All these and all alone in death's last day.
Before them stretches the indifferent ocean
Where no wave lifts its head and stagnant water
Lies spent against the shore. Yet as they wait
A wan light from the east falls on their faces
And they cannot bear the light, and hide in the ground,
Yet have no comfort there, for all are alone.
And there awaken the dark ancestral dreams.
They dream that the grave and the sea give up their dead
In wonder at the news of the death of death,
Hearing that death itself is balked by death.
And those who were drowned a year or a thousand years
Come out with staring eyes, foam on their faces,

And quaint sea-creatures fixed like jewelled worms
Upon their salt-white crowns, sea-tangle breasts,
That they, the once dead, might know the second death.
And then a stir and rumour break their dream,
As men and women at the point of death
Rise from their beds and clasp the ground in hope
Imploring sanctuary from grass and root
That never failed them yet and seemed immortal.
And women faint with child-birth lay their babes
Beside them on the earth and turn away
And lovers two by two estranged for ever
Lie each in place without a parting look.
And the dying awakened know
That the generous do not try to help their neighbours,
Nor the feeble and greedy ask for succour,
Nor the fastidious complain of their company
Nor the ambitious dream of a great chance lost
Nor the preacher try to save one soul. For all
Think only of themselves and curse the faithless earth.
The sun rises above the sea, and they look and think :
'We shall not watch its setting'. And all get up
And stare at the sun. But they hear no great voice crying :
'There shall be no more time, nor death, nor change,
Nor fear, nor hope, nor longing, nor offence,
Nor need, nor shame'. But all are silent, thinking :
'Choose! Choose again, you who have chosen this!
Too late! Too late!'
And then : 'Where and by whom shall we be remembered?' "

Imaginary picture of a stationary fear.

JUNE 1959

547

ALAN ROSS

Rock Paintings, Drakensberg Mts.

THESE mountains of up-pointed spears
Hold eland, oribi and rhebok
Capering over yellow rock
In sandstone caves that form a barrier

Eastward mauve and vertical,
Westward greenly gradual.
Sweet grasses swish below like silk
Torn at dark by prowling buck.

Baboons on red and scrabbling paths
Scatter dust in layers of talc,
Imitating as they stalk
Human gestures, defiant oaths

—A form of sympathetic magic
More goodnatured now than tragic,
Though practised by the bushman hunter,
Re-creating as a painter

Animals he hoped to capture,
Art was not a surplus rapture,
But a means of softening up
Hartebeeste and antelope.

Here walls of cave and sky converge,
Illustrating primal urges
Bush-pigs scuttle from cracked rocks,
Bush-girls thrust their weighted buttocks

Squatting as they chant in line
Round pots of boiling porcupine.
The painted bushman aims his bow,
The real sunset starts to flow

ROCK PAINTINGS, DRAKENSBERG MTS.

Across this sweeping mountain range
And still, despite ten centuries' change,
Art remains a kind of hunt
Eliminating fear and cant,

A means of pinning down
An object, by the sheer act
Of drawing animal or loved one,
Making absence into fact.

SEPTEMBER 1959

LOUIS MacNEICE

Solitary Travel

BREAKFASTING alone in Karachi, Delhi, Calcutta,
Dacca, Singapore, Kuala Lumpur, Colombo, Cape Town,
But always under water or glass, I find
Such a beginning makes the day seem blind.

The hotels are all the same, it might be pawpaw
Instead of grapefruit, different flowers on the tables,
But the waiters, coffee-coloured or yellow or black,
All smile but, should you smile, give nothing back.

And taking coffee alone in the indistinguishable airports,
Though the land outside be empty or man-crammed, oven or icebox,
I feel the futility of moving on
To what, though not a conclusion, is foregone.

But the Customs clamour, the stamp is raised, the passport
Like a chess game played by mail records the latest
Move of just one square. Which is surely seen
By the black bishop and the unsleeping queen.

And so to the next hotel to the selfsame breakfast,
Same faces of manager, waiter, fellow-traveller,
Same lounge or bar whose test tube walls enfold
The self-indulgent disenchanted old.

Time and the will are frozen. If I could only
Escape into icebox or oven, escape among people
Before tomorrow from this neutral zone
Where all tomorrows must be faced alone . . .

JUNE 1960

JAMES DICKEY

Facing Africa

THESE are stone jetties,
And, in the close part of the night,
Connected to my feet by long
Warm, dangling shadows
On the buttressed water,
Boats are at rest.

Beyond, the harbour mouth opens
Much as you might believe
A human mouth would open
To say that all things are a darkness.
I sit believing this
As the boats beneath me dissolve

And shake with a haunted effort
To come into being again,
And my son nods at my side,
Looking out also
Into dark, through the painted
Living shadows of dead-still hulls

Toward where we imagine Africa
To bloom late at night
Like a lamp of sand held up,
A top-heavy hourglass, perhaps,
With its heaped, eternal grains
Falling, falling

In the lower, green part
Which gives off quick, leafy flashes
Like glimpses of lightning.
We strain to encounter that image
Halfway from its shore to ours :
To understand

The undermined glowing of sand
Lifted at midnight
Somewhere far out above water,
The effortless flicker of trees
Where a rumour of beasts moves slowly
Like wave upon wave.

What life have we entered by this?
Here, where our bodies are,
With a green and gold light on his face,
My staring child's hand is in mine,
And in the stone
Fear like a dancing of peoples.

APRIL 1960

KINGSLEY AMIS

The Huge Artifice

An Interim Assessment

ENOUGH OF this great work has now appeared
For sightings to be taken, the ground cleared,
Through the main purpose—*what it's all about*
In the thematic sense—remains in doubt,
And it seems certain, even at this stage,
That seriousness adequate to engage
Our deepest critical concern is not
To be found here. First : what there is of plot
Is thin, repetitive, leaning far too much
On casual meetings, parties, fights and such,
With that excessive use of coincidence
Which marks authorial inexperience.
We note, together with many signs of haste,
A great deal in most questionable taste :
Too many sex-scenes, far too many coarse
Jokes, most of which have long lost all their force.

It might be thought that, after a slow start,
Abundant incident made amends for art,
But the work's "greatness" is no more than size,
While the shaping mind, and all that that implies,
Is on a trivial scale, as can be guessed
From the brash nature of the views expressed
By a figure in an early episode, who
Was clearly introduced in order to
Act as some kind of author-surrogate,
Then hastily killed off; an unfortunate
Bid to redress a grave strategic lapse.

553

More damaging than any of this, the gaps
In sensitivity betrayed are vast.
Concepts that have not often been surpassed
For affectation, downright nastiness
And ignorance—that poverty is less
Fatal than self-love, that corruption runs
Like pox through families, that the lucky ones
Will stay lucky—such are not only forced
Anywhere into dialogue, but endorsed
By the scheme of action, manifesting there
An inhumanity beyond despair.

One final point remains. It has been urged
That a few characters are not quite submerged
In all this rubbish, that they can display
Reason, justice and forethought on their day,
And that this partly exculpates the mind
Which was their author. Not at all. We find
Many such in the history of art
(So this reviewer feels) who stand apart,
Who by no purpose but their own begin
To struggle free from a crude origin.

MAY 1960

Sight Unseen

As I was waiting for the bus
  A girl came up the street,
Detectable as double-plus
  At seven hundred feet.

Her head was high, her step was free,
  Her face a lyric blur,
Her waist was narrow, I could see,
  But not the rest of her.

554

At fifty feet I watched her stop,
  Bite at a glove, then veer
Aside into some pointless shop,
  Never to reappear.

This happens every bloody day:
  They about-turn, they duck
Into their car and belt away,
  They hide behind a truck.

Look, if they knew me—understood,
  There might be cause to run;
Or if they saw me, well and good;
  And yet they don't, not one.

Love at first sight: by this we mean
  A stellar entrant thrown
Clear on the psyche's radar-screen,
  Recognized before known.

All right—things work the opposite
  Way with the poles reversed;
It's galling, though, when girls omit
  To switch the set on first.

MAY 1960

NOTES ON AUTHORS

LAURIE LEE, born in 1914, worked with British film units from 1939-43. Among his books are *A Rose for Winter* and *Cider With Rosie*.

GORONWY REES, born in Aberystwyth in 1909, was Principal of the University College of Wales from 1953-57. His books include *The Multi-Millionaires* and *A Bundle of Sensations*.

MARY McCARTHY, the eminent American critic and novelist, was born in 1912. She has published, among other books, *The Groves of Academe, Venice Observed, Memories of a Catholic Girlhood* and *On the Contrary*.

KENNETH TYNAN is the theatre critic of *The Observer* and the author of *Curtains*. He was recently appointed Literary Manager of London's new National Theatre.

MELVYN J. LASKY, born in New York City, founded the well-known German monthly *Der Monat* in Berlin in 1948. In 1958 he moved to London as co-editor of *Encounter*. He is the author of *The Hungarian Revolution* and *Africa for Beginners*.

ROBERT GRAVES, born 1895 in London, now lives in Majorca. He has published historical novels, critical essays and studies in mythology, as well as numerous volumes of poetry. In 1961 he was elected Professor of Poetry in the University of Oxford.

WAYLAND YOUNG, born 1923, lives in London and is the author of *The Montesi Scandal, Strategy for Survival,* and *Disarmament*. As Lord Kennet, he sits in the House of Lords.

H. R. TREVOR-ROPER, born 1914, is Regius Professor of Modern History in the University of Oxford. Among his books are *The Last Days of Hitler, The Gentry,* and *Historical Essays*.

GEOFFREY GORER was born in London in 1905. His books include *The Americans* and *The Life and Ideas of the Marquis de Sade*.

NANCY MITFORD, born in 1904, lives in Paris. Her books include *The Pursuit of Love, Love in a Cold Climate, Voltaire in Love* and *Don't Tell Alfred*.

EVELYN WAUGH, born 1903, has published among many other well-known novels *Decline and Fall, Brideshead Revisited, The Ordeal of Gilbert Pinfold,* and *Unconditional Surrender.*

EDWARD SHILS is Professor of Sociology at the University of Chicago and Senior Fellow of King's College, Cambridge. Among his books are *Torment of Secrecy, Political Development in the New States,* and *The Intellectual Between Tradition and Modernity.*

DANIEL BELL is Professor of Sociology at Columbia University and has published a collection of his papers under the title *The End of Ideology.*

ARTHUR KOESTLER, born in Budapest in 1905, lives in London. Among his books are *Darkness at Noon, The Sleepwalkers, The Lotus and the Robot,* and *The Act of Creation.*

C. P. SNOW, born 1905, has been professional scientist, Civil Service Commissioner, and novelist. He sparked off the famous "Two Cultures" controversy with his Rede Lecture and is the author, among other books, of the *Strangers and Brothers* novel-sequence.

ROBERT WARSHOW, who was born in 1917 and died in 1955, was an editor of *Commentary* magazine. His book of essays, *The Immediate Experience: Movies, Comics, Theatre, and Other Aspects of Popular Culture* was published posthumously.

STEPHEN SPENDER, born 1909, is co-editor of *Encounter,* and previously co-edited *Horizon* with Cyril Connolly. Among his books are *World Within World, Collected Poems,* and *The Struggle of the Modern.*

W. H. AUDEN, born in England in 1907, lives in New York City and Kirchstetten, Austria, and is now an American citizen. He was Professor of Poetry at Oxford from 1956–61. Among other volumes of poetry and criticism, he is the author of *New Year Letter, Look, Stranger, Nones, Homage to Clio,* and *The Dyer's Hand.*

KATHERINE ANNE PORTER was born in Texas in 1894. She has published several volumes of short stories and critical essays; *Ship of Fools,* a novel, is her most recent work.

STUART HAMPSHIRE, born 1914, Fellow of All Souls College, Oxford, and Professor of Philosophy in the University of London since 1960, is now Professor of Philosophy at Princeton. Among his books are *Spinoza* and *Thought and Action*.

LESLIE A. FIEDLER is Professor of English at Montana State University and the author of *Love and Death in the American Novel, No! In Thunder*, and *Pull Down Vanity*.

HERBERT LUETHY is a well-known Swiss historian and journalist, and the author of *The State of France*.

ISAIAH BERLIN, born 1909, is Chichele Professor of Social and Political Theory in the University of Oxford. Among his books are *The Hedgehog and the Fox, The Inevitability of History, The Age of Enlightenment*, and *Two Concepts of Liberty*.

LIONEL TRILLING, born 1905, is Professor of English at Columbia University, and author of *The Liberal Imagination, The Opposing Self, Freud and the Crisis of our Culture*, and *A Gathering of Fugitives*.

ANTHONY WEST, born in Norfolk in 1914, now lives in the United States. Among his books are *D. H. Lawrence, Another Kind, Heritage, Principles and Persuasions*, and *River's End*.

ERICH HELLER was previously Professor of German Literature at University College, Swansea, and is now at Northwestern University, Illinois. His books include *The Disinherited Mind* and *The Ironic German*.

IRVING KRISTOL was assistant editor of *Commentary*, and then co-editor of *Encounter* from 1953–58. He is now one of the directors of the publishing house, Basic Books, in New York.

EDMUND WILSON, born 1895, was for several years editor of the *New Republic*. Among his books are *Axel's Castle, To the Finland Station, Memoirs of Hecate County, Apologies to the Iroquois*, and *Patriotic Gore*.

NADINE GORDIMER, born in South Africa in 1923, lives in Johannesburg. Her books include *Friday's Footprint* and *An Occasion for Loving*.

CYRIL CONNOLLY, born 1903, was the founder and editor of *Horizon*. He is now the literary critic of the *Sunday Times*. Among his books are *The Rock Pool, Enemies of Promise, The Unquiet Grave, The Condemned Playground,* and *The Missing Diplomats.*

DAN JACOBSON, born 1929 in South Africa, now lives in London. He is the author of *The Evidence of Love, A Long Way from London, A Dance in the Sea,* and *Time of Arrival.*

JAMES AGEE, born in Tennessee in 1909, died 1955, worked on *Fortune* and then on *Time* where he reviewed books and films. Among his books are *A Death in the Family, Let Us Now Praise Famous Men,* and two volumes of *Agee on Film.* He also wrote the scripts for *The Quiet One* and *The African Queen.*

NIGEL DENNIS, novelist, playwright, and theatre critic of *Encounter*, has written *The Making of Moo, Cards of Identity* and *August for the People.*

ROBERT LOWELL, born 1917 in Massachusetts, lives in New York. He has lectured in English at various American universities and is the author of *The Mills of the Kavanaughs, Life Studies,* and *Imitations.* He was awarded the Pulitzer Prize for poetry in 1947.

THEODORE ROETHKE, born 1908, lives in Seattle where he is Professor of English at the University of Washington. Among his volumes of poetry are *The Lost Son, Words for the Wind, I Am! Says the Lamb,* and *The Waking,* which was awarded the Pulitzer Prize for poetry in 1954.

R. S. THOMAS is Vicar of St. Michael's, Eglwysfach, Wales. His books include *Song at the Year's Turning, Poetry for Supper,* and *Stones of the Field.*

DAVID WRIGHT, born 1920 in Johannesburg, lives in London. He has edited anthologies and literary magazines, and published *Poems,* two volumes of *Moral Stories,* and *Monologue of a Deaf Man.*

W. S. GRAHAM, born 1921 in Liverpool, is the author of *Second Poems, The White Threshold,* and *The Night Fishing.*

ELIZABETH JENNINGS, born 1926, lives in Oxford. She won the Somerset Maugham Award in 1956 with *A Way of Looking* and later published *A Sense of the World, Every Changing Shape,* and *Song for a Birth or a Death.*

THOM GUNN, born 1929 in England, lives in San Francisco where he is Assistant Professor in English at the University of California. He has published, among other books, *Fighting Terms, The Sense of Movement* and *My Sad Captains,* and is a winner of the Somerset Maugham Award.

W. S. MERWIN, born 1927 in Pennsylvania, is the author of *A Mask for Janus, The Dancing Bears, Green with Beasts,* and *The Drunk in the Furnace.*

RICHARD SELIG died in New York in 1957 at the age of 26. His collected poems have recently been published.

DYLAN THOMAS, born 1914 in Swansea, died in New York in 1953, was the author of *The Map of Love, Deaths and Entrances* and *Under Milk Wood,* among other books.

ROY FULLER, born 1912, lives in London and has published *A Lost Season, Brutus's Orchard, The Ruined Boys,* and *The Father's Comedy.*

VERNON WATKINS, born 1906 in Wales, is the author of several volumes of poems, of which the most recent are *Cypress and Acacia* and *Affinities.*

RICHARD EBERHART, born 1904, is Professor of English at Dartmouth College. His books include *Reading the Spirit, Undercliff, Great Praises* and *Collected Verse Plays.*

WILLIAM PLOMER, born 1903 in the Northern Transvaal, lives in Sussex. His books include *Paper Houses, Sado, A Shot in the Park, At Home,* and *Collected Poems.*

TED HUGHES, born 1930 in Yorkshire, won the Somerset Maugham Award in 1960 and the Hawthornden Prize in 1961, and has published *The Hawk in the Rain, Lupercal,* and *Meet My Folks!,* a volume of children's verse.

OLIVER BERNARD, born in 1925, is the author of *Country Matters,* and translator and editor of the Penguin edition of Rimbaud's poems.

PHILIP LARKIN, born 1922, lives in Hull where he is Librarian of the University. He has published two novels, *A Girl in Winter* and *Jill*, as well as his volumes of poetry, *The North Ship* and *The Less Deceived*.

EDWIN MUIR was born in Orkney in 1887 and died at Cambridge in 1959. *The Day Before the Last Day* was one of the last poems he wrote. His books include *Collected Poems, An Autobiography, The Structure of the Novel,* and *The Estate of Poetry*.

ALAN ROSS, born 1922, is editor of the *London Magazine*. His books include *Something of the Sea, To Whom It May Concern, Danger on Glass Island,* and *African Negatives*.

LOUIS MACNIECE, born 1907 in Belfast, is a programme director for the B.B.C. He has published many books, of which the most recent are *Autumn Sequel, Visitations, Eighty-Five Poems, Solstices,* and a radio play, *The Administrator*.

JAMES DICKEY was born in 1923 in Atlanta, Georgia, and served in the U.S. Air Force during World War II and the Korean War. He has published *Into the Stone and Other Poems, Drowning With Others,* and *Springer Mountain*.

KINGSLEY AMIS, born 1922 in London, is a Fellow of Peterhouse, Cambridge, and lectured in English at the University College of Swansea from 1949–61. His books include *A Frame of Mind, Lucky Jim, A Case of Samples, Take a Girl Like You,* and *New Maps of Hell*.